WILL'S BEST

www.stmartins.com

All of the puzzles that appear in this work were originally published
in *The New York Times* from November 22, 1993 to March 10, 2012.
Copyright © 1993, 1994, 1995, 1996, 1997, 1998, 1999, 2000, 2001, 2002, 2003, 2004,
2005, 2006, 2007, 2008, 2009, 2010, 2011, 2012 by The New York Times Company.
All rights reserved. Reprinted by permission.

ISBN 978-1-250-02531-9

First Edition: March 2013

10 9 8 7 6 5 4 3 2 1

WILL'S BEST

CELEBRATING THE 20th ANNIVERSARY OF THE NEW YORK TIMES PUZZLEMASTER

Edited by Will Shortz

ST. MARTIN'S GRIFFIN 🜨 NEW YORK

INTRODUCTION

Twenty years is a long time.

It's how long Rip Van Winkle slept in "The Legend of Sleepy Hollow."

It's how long William the Conqueror ruled England.

"Gunsmoke" and "Law & Order" were each on the air for 20 years (not counting endless reruns).

It's how long Kareem Abdul-Jabbar played in the N.B.A., and how long chessmaster Garry Kasparov was ranked #1 in the world.

The Yankees have had 20 consecutive years of winning seasons (and counting).

And as of 2013, it's how long I've been the crossword editor of *The New York Times*. (Wow!)

When I was interviewed for the job in 1993, I was asked what I might do differently than my predecessors. The first thing I said was what I didn't want to change—the intellectual timbre of the puzzle, its level of difficulty, and the other features that make it stand out from other crosswords.

Desired changes:

- First and foremost, add bylines to the daily crosswords, so the constructors would be recognized for their work. The daily constructors had worked anonymously up to then. I knew that bylines would spur creativity and quality, and the contributors deserved recognition besides.

- Encourage a broader range of constructors—keeping the older ones, who'd been the mainstay of the *Times* up to then, but adding younger ones to the mix.

- Feature more innovation in themes, lessen the amount of obscurity and crosswordese in the constructions, have more modern cultural references in the clues, and overall be more playful.

I think the *Times* crossword has improved a lot over the past 20 years, as the contributors have become more skilled and sophisticated. Frankly, some of the puzzles I accepted and ran in the early days wouldn't pass muster today. Even some from just two or three years ago might not quite make the grade now. That's how quickly the bar is raised.

On the following pages is a big, fat collection of 400 daily *Times* crosswords from the past 20 years. You can see the changes through the years for yourself.

Some of the constructors in this book weren't even born when I started in 1993!

I hope I'm still around, and shepherding the *Times* crossword, another 20 years from now.

—Will Shortz

DIFFICULTY KEY

Easy: ⭐

Medium: ⭐ ⭐

Hard: ⭐ ⭐ ⭐

ACROSS

1 Understood
4 Some tracks
9 ___ Rizzo ('69 Hoffman role)
14 Santa ___ winds
15 Actress Anouk
16 Significant person?
17 Kauai keepsake
18 Small person
20 Legit
22 Caroline Schlossberg, to Ted Kennedy
23 Type style: Abbr.
24 Big Mama
25 Church part
29 Rummy variety
32 The mark on the C in Čapek
33 Calendar period, to Kirk
37 Caustic substance
38 Traditional tune
40 Pub quaff
42 Logical newsman?
43 Long-lasting curls
45 Depicts
49 Health-food store staple
50 Jerry Herman composition
53 Dash
54 Michelangelo masterpiece
56 Journalist Greeley
58 Used booster cables
62 Tina's ex
63 Correspond, grammatically
64 Regarded favorably
65 Pince-___
66 Former Justice Byron
67 Air-show maneuvers
68 Palindrome center

DOWN

1 French
2 ___ time (singly)
3 Taipei's land
4 Honolulu locale
5 Fat fiddle
6 Fuse word
7 First name in hotels
8 Big rigs
9 Campus mil. grp.
10 Daughter of Zeus
11 Calendar abbr.
12 Theology sch.
13 Eye
19 ___-man (flunky)
21 Hooch container
24 Magna ___
26 Rights grp.
27 "Oy ___ !"
28 ___ out (supplement)
30 Hoosegows
31 Footrace terminus
32 Stage actress Hayes
34 MS follower?
35 Love, Italian style
36 Newcastle-upon-___, England
38 Esne
39 Judge's exhortation
40 Prone
41 Name of 13 popes
44 Oscar the Grouch, for one
46 Julia Louis-Dreyfus on "Seinfeld"
47 Pool-ball gatherer
48 Common cause for blessing
50 Strawberry, once
51 "Any Time ___" (Beatles tune)
52 Auto-racer Andretti
55 Words of comprehension
56 "David Copperfield" character
57 Ten to one, e.g.
58 Gossip
59 "That's disgusting!"
60 High-tech med. diagnostics
61 Foreman stat

by Fred Piscop

ACROSS

1. Mississippi Senator Cochran
5. Nutty
9. Gangbusters at the box office
14. River to the Rhine
15. Lena of recent films
16. Like the skies in "Ulalume"
17. Sorts
18. Carty of baseball
19. Oh, so many moons
20. Go astray
23. Stack-blowing feeling
24. Countdown start
25. Tak's opposite
26. Alphabetical run
27. As a whole
31. Bit
33. Mezzo-soprano Marilyn
34. Santa Fe Trail town
35. Pickle
38. Red of firefighting fame
39. Words of wonderment
40. With respect to
41. "Whip It" rock group
42. Drawing card
43. The Divine Miss M.
44. Play the siren
46. Smelt, e.g.
47. Aquarium oddity
49. Cry of delight
50. It has its point
51. Harvest goddess
52. Not yet in full bloom
58. Tubby the Tuba creator Paul
60. Reed of note
61. Light-footed
62. Hint
63. Order in the court
64. W.W. I German admiral
65. Pond covering
66. Silent O.K.'s
67. With defects and all

DOWN

1. Shadow
2. Christmas play prop
3. Synagogue cabinets
4. Not dose
5. World's third-largest island
6. '79 sci-fi thriller
7. Muscle spasms
8. Bird that summers in the Arctic
9. Agree
10. Sugary suffix
11. Many skiers use these when they [see diagonal]
12. Writers Jean and Walter
13. Assault
21. Mink's relative
22. Pretension
27. '64 musical "___ a Ball"
28. Leaf's starting point
29. Getting across
30. Stew ingredient
31. Skier Phil
32. Original Jed Clampett
34. Score for Barry Sanders
36. Observe
37. Great Scott of 1857
40. Sound as ___
42. Animal that sleeps with its eyes open
45. Noodle topper
46. Candy
47. Must, slangily
48. Part of an Argentine autumn
50. Steer clear of
53. River of Spain
54. Greek peak
55. Third addendum to a letter
56. ". . . ___ saw Elba"
57. Shoemakers' bottles
59. Trevino's org.

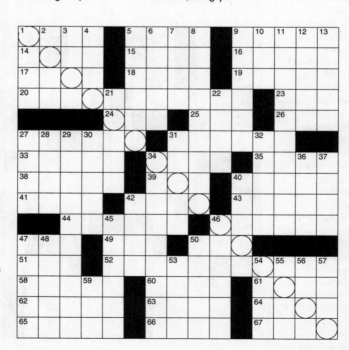

by Lois Sidway

ACROSS

1 Caspar or Balthazar, e.g.
6 Rope material
10 Chorale part
14 Florida city
15 Jai ___
16 La Scala presentation
17 NO UNTIDY CLOTHES
20 Walking on air
21 Macadam ingredient
22 ___ Cruces, N.M.
23 Prepared
24 Harem
26 Claus Subordinate
29 Apocalypse
31 Gene material
32 Seldom seen
34 "QB VII" author
36 Lump of jelly, e.g.
39 GOVERN, CLEVER LAD
43 "You said it!"
44 Writer Shere
45 Approve
46 W.W. II grp.
48 Agrippina's son
50 German pronoun
51 Answer to "What's keeping you?"
55 Mount near ancient Troy
57 Item in a lock
58 "I" affliction
59 1990 Bette Midler film
62 BLATHER SENT ON YE
66 Neighborhood
67 Le Mans, e.g.
68 Conductor Georg
69 Back-to-school time: Abbr.
70 Bouquet
71 Friend of Henry and June

DOWN

1 Word on the Oise
2 Long (for)
3 Food critic Greene
4 Arm bones
5 Fried lightly
6 Actor Charles of "Hill Street Blues"
7 Overhead trains
8 Not shiny
9 A captain of the Enterprise
10 Dance, in France
11 On ___ (doing well)
12 1979 treaty peninsula
13 Authority
18 Alternate road
19 Los Angeles suburb
24 Obviously pleased
25 Big name in viniculture
26 Physics unit
27 Zhivago's love
28 "It Came ___ Outer Space"
30 Mezz. alternative
33 "It's true," in Torino
35 French resort town
37 Forest florae
38 ___ B'rith
40 Fingernail polish
41 Realism
42 Salon selection
47 Rossini character
49 Potemkin mutiny site
51 Jots
52 Skiing's Phil or Steve
53 Tiptoe
54 Air Force arm: Abbr.
56 Illinois city
59 Cassandra
60 Falana or Montez
61 Opposing
63 Dracula, sometimes
64 Sgt., e.g.
65 Frozen Wasser

by Stephanie Spadaccini

ACROSS

1 New Woman rival
5 One-liners
9 Soccer legend
13 Egg-shaped
14 TV oldie "Green ___"
16 Vientiane's land
17 Building code requirement
19 Prod
20 Pilgrim John
21 Most pleasant
23 Madam's mate
25 July 4, 1776, e.g.
26 Opposite of vert.
29 W. Hemisphere org.
32 Mr. Arnaz
34 The lowdown on dancing?
36 Kind of car or sandwich
38 Use a crayon
41 Ratted (on)
42 Armbone
43 By oneself
44 Writer Hunter
45 Hauls
46 Stimulate, as curiosity
47 Measure out
48 Provence city
50 Stalin ruled it
52 "The Bridge of San Luis ___"
53 Stephen of "The Crying Game"
54 Late tennis V.I.P.
57 Dawn goddess
59 Lustrous fabric
61 "Faust," for one
65 [Shock!]
67 Summer treat
70 Matures
71 Go 1-1 in a doubleheader
72 Letterman's "Top Ten," e.g.
73 Model's position
74 "Auld Lang ___"
75 Not so much

DOWN

1 Divan
2 "Hear no ___ . . ."
3 Cooking fat
4 Hightails it
5 Oil alternative
6 U.N.C. and U.Va. grp.
7 In a lofty style
8 Artist's brown
9 +
10 Bulldozer
11 Captain's record
12 Language suffix
15 Church offshoot
18 Arthurian lady
22 Slippery one
24 Sum up
27 Not quite spherical
28 Los Angeles motorist King
29 Of the eyes
30 Magnetism
31 Shades
33 By oneself: Prefix
35 News entry
37 Home port
39 Burden
40 Hall-of-Famer Pee Wee
49 Was in session
51 Motel vacancy
55 Does needlework
56 Mounds
58 "How do you ___ relief?"
60 Church nook
62 Writer Wiesel
63 Flagmaker Betsy
64 Picnic pests
65 Cumberland, e.g.
66 In the past
68 One for Wilhelm
69 Numbered rd.

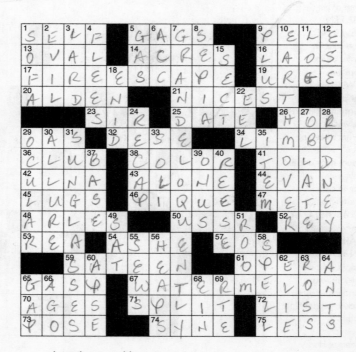

by Sidney L. Robbins

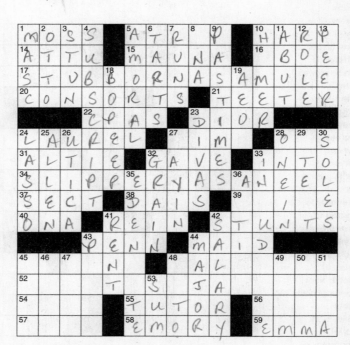

ACROSS

1 Rolling stone's deficiency
5 Anchor position
10 Complain
14 Aleutian island
15 ___ Loa
16 Literally "high wood"
17 Obstinate
20 Royal spouses
21 Be on the brink
22 Professional bean counters
23 Designer Christian
24 Hardy's pal
27 Describe
28 Org. founded in 1948
31 Bandleader Shaw
32 Imparted
33 Sondheim's "___ the Woods"
34 Elusive
37 Branch Davidians, e.g.
38 Speaker's platform
39 Worker's wish
40 Off ___ tangent
41 Curb, with "in"
42 Daredevil acts
43 Actor Sean
44 Lady in an apron
45 "Yessir," e.g.
48 Moon of Jupiter
52 In the altogether
54 Final notice
55 Teach one-on-one
56 Lion's den
57 Like 52-Across
58 Atlanta university
59 Thompson of "Howards End"

DOWN

1 Opposite of fem.
2 Mr. Preminger
3 Daze
4 Like the 2 in B$_2$
5 Not knowing right from wrong
6 Small pies
7 Hosiery snags
8 Actress Claire
9 Diversions
10 Future star
11 Border on
12 Actor's part
13 Look with squinty eyes
18 Sheepish lass
19 A long time
23 Prima donnas
24 Rope a dogie
25 Former Senator Specter
26 City east of Syracuse
27 Store up
28 ___ a million
29 Alamogordo event, 7/16/45
30 Shoe bottoms
32 Rye or corn
33 Silent, or almost so
35 Toothless
36 With pretentiousness
41 Tear
42 $200,000, for Clinton
43 Pro golfer Calvin
44 TV's "___ Dad"
45 Presently
46 "Elephant Boy" star, 1937
47 Have brake problems
48 Roman statesman and censor
49 Thailand, once
50 Adjust the sails
51 Polish border river
53 Add

by Joel Davajan

ACROSS

1 Artistic skill
6 Card game also called sevens
12 Holed out in two under par
14 Warned
16 English essayist Richard
17 Burglar
18 Cools, as coffee
19 Pumpkin eater of rhyme
21 Summer drink
22 Employee health plan, for short
23 Horse trainer's equipment
25 Black cuckoos
26 Long, long time
28 Like some schools
29 Sweetens the kitty
30 Smart alecks
32 Traffic circle
33 Charlie Brown's "Darn!"
34 Ex-Mrs. Burt Reynolds
35 Charge with gas
38 Adorned
42 Vineyard fruit
43 Kismet
44 Snick's partner
45 Detest
46 Alternative to eggdrop
48 A Gershwin
49 Drunk ___ skunk
50 Analyze a sentence
51 Actor John of TV's "Addams Family"
53 Locale
55 Money-back deal
57 Boot camp denizen
58 Noted family in china manufacture
59 Arabs
60 Cancel the launch

DOWN

1 "L'état ___": Louis XIV
2 Army grub
3 Ripening agent
4 Butler's "The Way of All ___"
5 ___ Aviv
6 Observed Lent
7 Change the hemline
8 ___-do-well
9 "La-la" preceder
10 Home of the '96 Olympics
11 Poorer
13 Arranges strategically
15 Smart
18 Sullivan's "really big" one
20 Summers, in Haiti
24 Sharp
25 Clowning achievements?
27 Mexican shawl
29 Top-flight
31 Arena receipts
32 Drive in Beverly Hills
34 Epistles
35 Shocked
36 Pencil ends
37 Knocking sound
38 Forbids
39 Bootee maker
40 Most Halloweenlike
41 Doyen
43 Smithies
46 Dwindled
47 High-muck-a-muck
50 Fir
52 Prefix with masochism
54 Item of office attire
56 Fuel efficiency rater: Abbr.

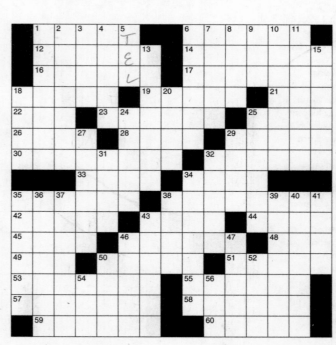

by William P. Baxley

ACROSS

1 Like Ike
5 Vassar student
9 One 39-Across
13 "I cannot tell ___"
14 Heraldic band
15 Sandbags maybe
16 Holds up
17 Café additive
18 Chemically nonreactive
19 Chiffonier
21 One 39-Across ✓
23 One 39-Across ✓
25 Verboten: Var.
26 Cantankerous
32 Rep.'s rival
35 "___ be a cold day in Hell . . ."
38 Ancient region of Asia Minor
39 Each of eight in this puzzle
43 Like measles
44 Elliptical
45 Compass dir.
46 Home to Denali National Park
48 Teases
51 One 39-Across ✓
56 One 39-Across ✓
60 Stay informed
62 Island group near Fiji
63 Periodical of haute couture
65 Small dog breed, for short
66 One 39-Across ✓
67 Plaintiff
68 Get ready
69 Fusses
70 Grounded planes
71 Lighten up

DOWN

1 Fishhook part
2 One way to read
3 Sign of autumn's beginning
4 Go AWOL
5 One 39-Across ✓
6 ___ pro nobis
7 Statesman Root
8 Coup ___
9 Former Transportation Secretary Federico ___
10 Penultimate fairy tale word
11 Wonk, maybe
12 Pocket
15 Actress Ullmann
20 One-time link
22 Symbol for density
24 Expenditure
27 Singer Ocasek of the Cars
28 Classic drama of Japan
29 Seth's son
30 Ocho ___, Jamaica
31 One 39-Across ✓
32 1982 movie thriller
33 Iniquitous
34 Pianist Hess
36 Broadway comedy of 1964
37 Live's partner
40 ___ Palmas (Canary Islands seaport)
41 Benevolent guy
42 Macs
47 King Kong, e.g.
49 Quilt-making gathering
50 Treeless plain
52 Like the Boston-accented pronunciation of many words
53 Card catalogue abbr.
54 Where the fat lady sings
55 Zaps
56 Ask to produce proof of age
57 Melville novel
58 Participates in a regatta, perhaps
59 One of the Bobbsey twins
61 ___ Le Pew
62 Loan-granting Fed. agcy.
64 Fill a flat?

Handwritten note at right:
Columbia
Yale
Harvard
Dartmouth
U Penn
Cornell
Princeton
Brown

by Peter Gordon

Completed grid (handwritten):

1 A	2 D	3 D		5 C	6 O	7 E	8 D		9 P	10 E	11 N	12 N
13 A	L	I	E		14 O	E	T		15 L	E	V	E	E
16 R	O	B	S		17 L	I	T		18 I	N	E	R	T
19 U		E	U	20		21 H	A	22 R	V	A	R	D
		23 D	A	R	24 T	M	O	U	T	H		
		25 T		B	U		26 O	R	27 N	28 E	29 R	30 Y	31
32 D	33 E	34 M		35 I	T	36 L	L		38	N	I	A
39 I	V	Y	40 L	41 E	A	G	U	E	42 S	C	H	O	O	L
43 V	I	R	A	L		44 O	V	A	L		45 S	S	E
46 A	L	A	S	K	47 A		48 R	I	49 B	50 S		
			51 P	52 R	I	53 N	C	E	T	O	54 N	55
56 C	57 O	58 R	59 N	E	L	L		60 K	E	E	P	U	61 P
62 S	A	M	O		63 E	L	64 L	E		65 P	E	K	E
66 B	R	O	W	N		67 S	U	E	R		68 P	R	E	Y
69 A	D	O	S		70 S	S	T	S		71 E	A	S	E

ACROSS

1 Colorful salad ingredient
10 Plant pest
15 Throw some light on
16 El ___ (Spanish painter)
17 Acting ambassador
19 Mooring rope
20 The sky, maybe
21 Perry's creator
22 Pop's Carly or Paul
25 It's a drag
27 Country rtes.
28 It has its ups and downs
30 Turner of Hollywood
31 "Duke Bluebeard's Castle" composer
32 Super-soaked
33 Literature as art
36 Urger's words
37 Aloha State
38 Ooze
39 Bombast
40 70's sitcom "___ Sharkey"
43 Watered-down ideas
44 Subsequently
45 Teri of "Tootsie"
46 "___ Andronicus"
48 Samantha's "Bewitched" husband
50 Facetious advice in a mystery
54 Indoor design
55 Carouse
56 Birthplace of 16-Across
57 By and large

DOWN

1 ". . . for ___ for poorer"
2 Founder of est
3 Talks Dixie-style
4 Diagram a sentence
5 Competitive advantage
6 Boat's departure site
7 Rocket's departure site
8 It's after zeta
9 Foul caller
10 One more time
11 Schoolmarmish
12 Birthright
13 Bar accessory
14 ___ Passos
18 Go with the ___
22 Layup alternative
23 Quarantine
24 Be militaristic
26 Manner
28 It can sting
29 Before, in palindromes
30 Actress ___ Singer
31 Radar screen image
32 Rouse to action
33 Brief break
34 It's worth looking into
35 Clavell's "___-Pan"
36 Recipe abbr.
39 Mess-hall meal
40 Clint Eastwood's city
41 Kind of scream
42 Obstinate
44 Pelf
45 Miss Garbo
47 Jog
48 Hamlet, for one
49 Nowhere near
50 Fed. medical detectives
51 Sunny-side-up item
52 Lawyer Baird
53 Cambodia's ___ Nol

by Eric Albert

ACROSS

1 Actress Winger
6 Park, in Monopoly
11 "Honest" fellow
14 Where Gauguin visited van Gogh
15 Funnyman O'Brien
16 Bloodshot
17 "Cheers!" in Cherbourg?
19 Chang's Siamese twin
20 Brand of lemon-flavored drink
21 Daydream
23 Koch and Wynn
24 Pampering, for short
26 It's heard in a herd
27 Garibaldi in Genoa?
33 Pickle
36 Subject for a supermarket tab
37 Avaricious one
38 October gem
40 Beam fastener
42 1963 Oscar winner
43 Arose
45 Danger
47 Hang in the breeze
48 Madrid's equivalent of a Texas university?
50 Performance
51 Had lunch
52 Montana and Moon, in brief
55 Gladstone rival
60 Real
62 "Poppycock!"
63 Pre-photo pronouncement in Geneva?
65 Some
66 Skirmish
67 "Dallas" Miss
68 Simonize
69 Classic theater name
70 4-Down again

DOWN

1 Peri opera
2 Made a boner
3 Post-sneeze word
4 Take money for a spare room
5 Loner
6 Agt.'s share
7 Creator of Lorelei Lee
8 Med. subj.
9 Winter melon
10 Competitor
11 Vicinity
12 Early German carmaker
13 Barely beat, with "out"
18 Woman's top
22 Cartoonist Wilson
25 Islamic leader
28 Crowbar
29 Portugal and its neighbor
30 Barely managed, with "out"
31 Raise
32 Alternative to Charles de Gaulle
33 Clinton's runs
34 Each
35 First name in spying
39 Moon-based
41 Alternative to Certs
44 "Desmoiselles d'Avignon" artist
46 Bloodletting practitioner
49 Potted
52 Put down
53 Count in music
54 Winter weather
55 Extract
56 New Rochelle college
57 Charon's domain
58 Kind of beer
59 Relationship words
61 Prefix with play or scope
64 Favorite relative in politics?

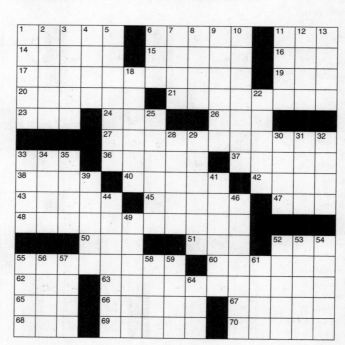

by Mark Danna

ACROSS

1 Canyon sound
5 Cross-legged exercises
9 August forecast
14 Bumbler
15 50–50
16 Mohawk Valley city
17 Kitchen fat
18 Shea Stadium nine
19 Pressed one's luck
20 Big-eared animal
21 Vacation locale
23 In ___ (ready for release)
25 Sign of summer
26 Cordage
29 It's printed in the back
34 Gerald Ford's birthplace
36 Banned apple spray
38 By way of
39 Vacation locale
42 Declare
43 Congressman Gingrich
44 Solemn procedures
45 "___ forget"
47 1959 Fiestas song
49 Comic Charlotte
51 Outcome
54 Vacation locale
60 Have a tab
61 Like gold
62 On-the-cob treat
63 Ilsa of "Casablanca"
64 Wrist movement
65 Tale starter
66 Pre-owned
67 Army vehicles (You're welcome!)
68 Blue-green
69 Jolly, to the British

DOWN

1 Brilliance
2 Sharply disagree
3 Monmouth Park events
4 ___ man out
5 Sana native
6 "Back to you"
7 Fetches
8 Photographer Adams
9 Rock of Hollywood
10 Jazz locale
11 Muralist Joan
12 Cake decorator
13 Janet Reno's home county
21 Lacquer
22 Pine
24 Associate
27 Put the finger on
28 Is brilliant
30 Painter's mishaps
31 Russian parliament building
32 Sea swooper
33 "Broom Hilda" creator Myers
34 Whitish gem
35 Military command?
37 "Wheels"
40 Late-late show hour
41 Vacation events
46 Violent downfalls
48 Tornado part
50 Orlando attraction
52 Shareholder
53 Sleepwear item
54 ___-Hartley Act
55 Hip-shaking in Kauai
56 Actress Moran
57 Rube
58 TV knob
59 Whale of a movie
63 Broadway hit of 1964–65

by Thomas W. Schier

ACROSS

1 Christiania today
5 Noggin tops
10 Hind's mate
14 Hullabaloo
15 Open-eyed
16 "Damn Yankees" vamp
17 Ike was one
20 Track officials
21 Testify
22 "Rule, Britannia" composer
23 Early Briton
24 Social groups
27 Garlic relative
28 Asian holiday
31 Culture mores
32 Coxswain's crew
33 ___ Marquette
34 G.I. newspaper
37 Cures leather
38 "That's interesting"
39 Opt
40 Two-by-two vessel
41 Reared
42 Worth
43 Shed
44 Escape
45 Roman villa locale
48 Apollyon adherent
52 Biblical beacon
54 Seller's caveat
55 Backcomb hair
56 Mechanical memorization
57 Smoker's sound
58 Mead research site
59 Animal team

DOWN

1 Switch settings
2 Eye opening
3 Kind of flow
4 Bell workers
5 Thin metal disks
6 Cognizant
7 Salts
8 Dr.'s graph
9 Most rundown
10 Nodded
11 Pamplona runner
12 Hale of "Gilligan's Island"
13 10 on the Beaufort scale
18 Pressure
19 Spoon
23 Intrinsically
24 Jai alai basket
25 It makes scents
26 Part of the evening
27 Put on cargo
28 Dakota digs
29 Upright
30 Blood and acid, e.g.
32 Beginning
33 Bohemian beers
35 Berlin events of 1948
36 Recap
41 Machetelike knife
42 Wimbledon champ Gibson
43 Code name
44 1980 DeLuise flick
45 Royal Russian
46 "___ girl!"
47 Ski spot
48 Coal stratum
49 Hotcakes acronym
50 Bristle
51 Revenuers, for short
53 "___ sport"

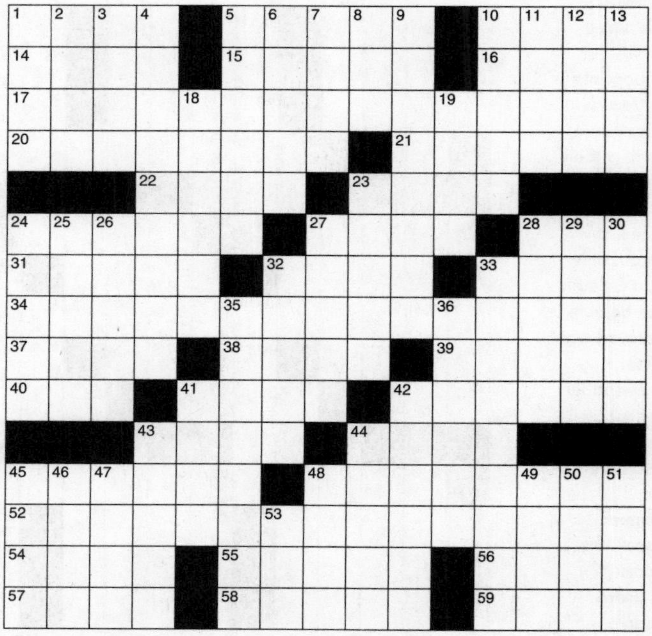

by Joel Davajan

ACROSS

1 One who reunes
5 Bic or Parker products
9 Lox's partner
14 Computer offering
15 Face shape
16 Shade of white
17 No ifs, ___ or buts
18 Soho so-long
19 Lounges lazily
20 Start of a quip
23 Consumed
24 Israeli airport
25 ___ chango (magician's command)
29 "That was close!"
31 Horror film frightener
34 Oscar de la ___
35 Mimi Sheraton subject
36 Obstinate one
37 Middle of the quip
40 Hor.'s opposite
41 ___ of March
42 French avenue
43 It's north of Calif.
44 Chance ___ (meet accidentally)
45 Not present
46 Columbus univ.
47 One, in Orléans
48 End of the quip
55 His beloved was Beatrice
56 Old newspaper section
57 Hide
59 Rags-to-riches writer
60 Roughneck
61 Bombeck, the columnist
62 Hops brews
63 Sea eagle
64 Cooper's was high

DOWN

1 Internists' org.
2 Give temporarily
3 Remove, as a knot
4 Daydream
5 Spud
6 Dodge
7 European defense grp.
8 Dross
9 Swell, as a cloud
10 Have nothing to do with
11 Course game
12 A Gardner
13 Fleur-de-___
21 Old Nick
22 Coasters
25 Utah city
26 Allude (to)
27 ___ nous
28 Editor's mark
29 Part of NOW
30 Breaks up clods
31 Company B awakener
32 ". . . in tears amid the ___ corn": Keats
33 Ism
35 Rover's playmate
36 Tormé and Gibson
38 Raise the end of
39 Cacophonous tower
44 Does a groomsman's job
45 Whosoever
46 Bewhiskered animal
47 Author Sinclair
48 Fabric texture
49 "Come Back Little Sheba" playwright
50 Prod
51 Rating a D
52 Aboveboard
53 Florida's Beach
54 Pollster Roper
55 A tiny bit
58 Ecru

by Betty Jorgensen

ACROSS

1 "Shane" star
5 Late actor Phoenix
10 "Dark Lady" singer, 1974
14 "___ in a manger . . ."
15 Author Zola
16 "___, from New York . . ."
17 Haircuts?
19 Kathleen Battle offering
20 "___ we having fun yet?"
21 Glowing
22 Kuwaiti structure
24 Opening word
26 Broadway show based on a comic strip
27 Dubuque native
29 Imperturbable
33 Become frayed
36 Former spouses
38 Conceited smile
39 Hawkeye portrayer
40 Recording auditions
42 Garfield's canine pal
43 Pilots let them down
45 Cushy
46 Catches some Z's
47 It fugits
49 Gullible
51 Sufficient
53 Knucklehead
57 Horoscope heading
60 Police blotter abbr.
61 Prospector's find
62 World rotator?
63 Fake embroidery?
66 Augury
67 "This way in" sign
68 ___ carotene
69 Emcee Parks
70 Nursery packets
71 Flowery verses

DOWN

1 Actor Lorenzo
2 Conscious
3 Odense residents
4 Recolor
5 Critiqued
6 ". . . ___ a man with seven wives"
7 ___ ordinaire
8 "Candle in the Wind" singer ___ John
9 Copal and others
10 Vandalized art work?
11 Put on staff
12 Heinous
13 Kind of estate
18 Movie Tarzan ___ Lincoln
23 Whoppers
25 Smog?
26 Showy flower
28 Lumber camp implements
30 Verdi heroine
31 Stumble
32 Makes do, with "out"
33 Float
34 Madame's pronoun
35 Eden resident
37 Divan
41 Scoundrels
44 Its usefulness goes to waste
48 Cumin and cardamom
50 Test tube
52 Actor Greene
54 Courted
55 Livid
56 Ann Richards's bailiwick
57 Poor fellow
58 "Be our guest!"
59 Concluded
60 Thunderstruck
64 Part of a year in Provence
65 Cable add-on

by Norma Steinberg

13

14 ⭐

ACROSS

1 Dog star
5 Gull's cousin
9 Eyeball bender
14 Ground grain
15 Mini revelation
16 Red-eyed bird
17 Haitian despot
20 Cordwood measure
21 Jewish dance
22 Out's opposite
23 Vidal's Breckinridge
25 Actor Young of TV's 67-Across
27 Is grief-stricken
30 Book subtitled "His Songs and His Sayings"
35 Supped
36 Relative of a Bap. or Presb.
37 Balkan capital
38 Gabor sister
40 Thimbleful
42 Dryden work
43 Help get situated
45 Plugs of a sort
47 Saturn's wife
48 1956 Rosalind Russell role
50 "For ___ us a child is born"
51 Headlight?
52 Survey chart
54 Seaweed product
57 ___ fixe
59 Reached the total of
63 Popular psychologist
66 Paul Anka hit
67 See 25-Across
68 Deep blue
69 Throat malady
70 Achy
71 James Mason sci-fi role of 1954

DOWN

1 Rock band equipment
2 Usher
3 Mend, in a way
4 Alternatives to The Club
5 Round stopper
6 Delights
7 Change the décor
8 Kind of network
9 Roman breakfast?
10 Light beers
11 "Jewel Song," e.g.
12 Mariner's peril
13 Raced
18 She played Grace Van Owen on "L.A. Law"
19 Passepartout, to Phileas Fogg
24 Strongly scented plant
26 Stellar Ram
27 Fiji neighbor
28 City in northern Japan
29 Set in motion
31 Dinnerware
32 Building contractor
33 Not suitable
34 Final authority
36 Madness
39 Oust
41 Nurse, maybe
44 Directed toward a goal
46 Hair fixative
49 Office connections?
50 Donny Osmond, e.g.
53 Record-holding N.F.L. receiver ___ Monk
54 Postfixes
55 Sandpaper surface
56 Opened a crack
58 Catalonian river
60 Hawaiian hen
61 In shape
62 Kon-Tiki Museum site
64 Shrill bark
65 Lyric poem

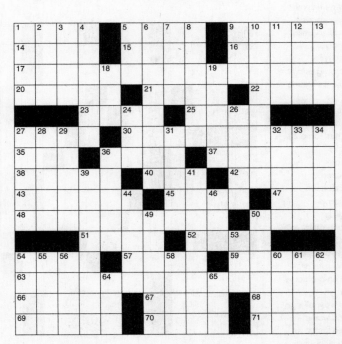

by Janie Lyons

ACROSS

1 Zubin with a baton
6 Old streetlight
13 Daley and others
14 Gravel-voiced actress
15 Iron shortage
16 Commit
17 Just the highlights
18 Slammin' Sam
19 Trendy
20 Getting better, as wine: Var.
22 Up to now
24 Size up
26 Paints amateurishly
28 Almost shut
32 Kind of symbol
33 One whom Jesus healed
34 Rodeo rope
35 Dashboard reading, for short
36 Leave the pier
38 Acquire
39 Ask on one's knees
41 Had
42 Lunch order
43 Belgrade dweller
44 In abeyance
45 Sciences' partner
46 Tooth
48 Comfort
50 Probe
53 Some pads
55 Accident mementos
58 Serves a sentence
60 Byrnes of "77 Sunset Strip"
61 Brown paint, e.g.
62 Six-footer?
63 Resort locale
64 Newspaper section

DOWN

1 Lion's pride?
2 It's hard to miss
3 Respect
4 Nonsense
5 Simile center
6 Comic Kaplan
7 Assuages
8 Picture with its own frame
9 Wheel bolt holder
10 King of comedy
11 Part of a pair
12 Sound of relief
13 Scuff up
14 It's hard to say
18 Fastens with a pop
21 "I have no ___!"
23 ___ chi ch'uan
24 Tail ends
25 Temptation for Atalanta
27 1991 American Conference champs
29 It's hard
30 Listing
31 Sounds off
33 Digital-watch readout: Abbr.
34 Postal letters
37 Have a hunch
40 1970 Jackson 5 hit
44 Looking while lusting
45 Waylay
47 Time and again
49 In unison
50 Tots up
51 Afternoon TV fare
52 Lifetime achievement Oscar winner Deborah
54 Mingo portrayer
56 Puerto ___
57 Play place
59 Take part in a biathlon
60 Kipling novel

by Harvey Estes

ACROSS

1. Atop
5. Clubbed
10. Motes
14. New York Cosmos star
15. Chou ___
16. Oklahoma tribesman
17. Lord Nelson site
20. Part of an electrical switch
21. Zeroes
22. Hectored
23. Sans verve
24. Medicament
27. Winter woe
28. Ottoman official
31. The Donald's ex
32. Fly like Lindbergh
33. Aits in Arles
34. Prepare for an Indian attack
37. Raison d' ___
38. 30's actress Grey and others
39. Nighttime noise
40. Beam
41. Sponsorship
42. Feeds a furnace
43. Belgian river
44. Baseball union boss Donald
45. Like llamas
48. Sends quickly
52. Ships' drop-off location?
54. Sea flyer
55. Gnawed away
56. Composition closure
57. Crazy bird?
58. Monopoly payments
59. Formerly

DOWN

1. Goes (for)
2. ___ Beach, Fla.
3. Airline to Jerusalem
4. Testimonial
5. It's hummed
6. 1973 hit by the Rolling Stones
7. Covered
8. The "E" in E.N.T
9. Prohibit
10. Wampum
11. I-70's western terminus
12. Ilk
13. Golf course 18
18. Of some electrodes
19. Printer's spacer
23. Tree trunks
24. Potato preparer
25. "Requiem for ___" (Broadway song)
26. Take the plunge
27. Lawyer Roy M. and others
28. "Take ___ at this!"
29. Type
30. Bridge of ___ (Euclid proposition)
32. Way up?
33. Blissful state?
35. Produce
36. Wheezing cause
41. Birthright seller
42. TV listing
43. Modern-day Sheba
44. Tops
45. Ex-steelworkers chief
46. Fiery fiddler
47. 1962 Bond villain
48. Solar disk
49. Mr. Stravinsky
50. Lawyers' degrees
51. Install in office
53. "___ you sure?"

by Joel Davajan

ACROSS

1 They're plucked
6 Busy as ___
10 Lake formed by Hoover Dam
14 Bye
15 Druid, e.g.
16 Presque ___, Me.
17 Close behind
20 Chair plan
21 Setter or retriever
22 "Fables in Slang" author
24 Part of a bridal bio
25 Words after "The last time I saw Paris"
34 Buck follower
35 Muddies the water
36 "The Company"
37 Bara and Negri
39 Years in Paris
40 Mole
42 Native: Suffix
43 Comedienne Fields
45 Hebrides language
46 Completely unperturbed
50 Olympian: Abbr.
51 Knock-knock joke, e.g.
52 Sounds the hour
56 1967–70 war site
61 Discourage
63 Japanese aboriginal
64 Assassinate
65 Put up
66 Cuff
67 Cod relative
68 Drinks with straws

DOWN

1 It's a laugh
2 1985 film "My Life as ___"
3 ___ of passage
4 Drudge
5 Dairy bar order
6 Otto's "oh!"
7 English channel, with "the"
8 Like many textbook publishers
9 Adjective for Rome
10 Cellar growth
11 Old gas brand
12 Sleep like ___
13 Excellent, in slang
18 Cry of achievement
19 Ancient capital of Macedonian kings
23 Corrigenda
25 June in Hollywood
26 Sister of Thalla
27 Alfa ___
28 Sock ___
29 Quinine water
30 Smarten
31 Lip-puckering
32 Hair-coloring solution
33 ___ et Magistra (1961 encyclical)
38 It causes sparks
41 Lapidarist's object of study
44 City on Lake Winnebago
47 Tar
48 Actor Gooding, Jr.
49 Glues
52 Earth
53 Bluefin
54 Scat cat
55 It's north of Neb.
57 Flying: Prefix
58 TV exec Friendly
59 Capa ___ (westernmost point in continental Europe)
60 Colonists
61 ___ de deux
62 Fork

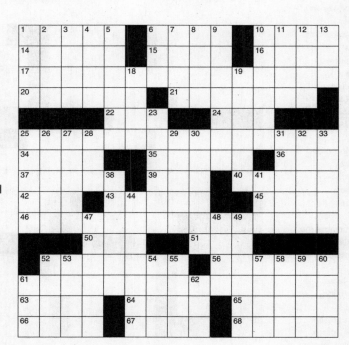

by Ronald C. Hirschfeld

ACROSS

1 Gore's "___ in the Balance"
6 One who's "agin" it
10 Train unit
13 "___ Without Windows" ('64 song)
14 Supermarket meat label
15 Territory
16 Major Bowes updated?
18 Fat
19 Home on the range
20 Kind of signal
21 Part of SEATO
22 Mail HQ
23 Breakfast order
25 Lift up
29 Woodworker's choice
32 Belgian airline
34 Bests
38 Hemingway opus
41 Dub again
42 Took ten
43 Ingenious
45 Shows remorse
46 Up
50 Marinaro and others
52 Slough
53 Reckon
56 Bosom companions
60 "Remember the neediest," e.g.
61 Olympia Dukakis film
63 Fast time
64 Capri, for one
65 Misrepresent
66 Pupil's place
67 African lake
68 Volvo worker

DOWN

1 Bridge seat
2 Comic Johnson
3 Imitation morocco
4 Civil wrong
5 ___ Pinafore
6 Cottonwoods
7 Grammy-winning pianist
8 Yacht heading
9 Person of will
10 1929 event
11 High nest
12 "M*A*S*H" character
15 "Too bad!"
17 Parapsychology study
22 Authentic
24 Singing sisters
25 D.C. zone
26 Comic Bert
27 Have ___ in one's bonnet
28 Probe
30 Flat sign?
31 Vienna is its cap.
33 In opposition to one another
35 River to the Seine
36 Town near Padua
37 Osmose
39 Melmackian of TV
40 60's org.
44 Craved
46 With room to spare
47 "Little Orphant Annie" poet
48 Goodnight girl
49 Pants part
51 ___ Plaines
54 Deluxe
55 Southeast Kansas town
56 Witch's ___
57 Golden, e.g.
58 Tart
59 ___ Ball (arcade game)
62 Kitchen meas.

by Sidney L. Robbins

ACROSS

1 Rumble
6 Not fancy?
10 Difficult obligation
14 "___ of do or die"
15 Bing Crosby best seller
16 Guthrie the younger
17 Hearty entree
20 Kibbutzniks dance
21 Reverse
22 Must
23 Place to crash
25 Kipling novel
26 Tasty side dish
35 Mortgage matter
36 Words before "in the arm" or "in the dark"
37 Detective's cry
38 Them in "Them!"
39 Common key signature
40 Composer ___ Carlo Menotti
41 Cpl., for one
42 Feed a fete
43 Stood for
44 Yummy dessert
47 Cherbourg chum
48 Latin I?
49 Lamb Chop's "spokesperson"
52 Oceania republic
55 Windmill segment
59 Eventual bonus?
62 Cream-filled sandwich
63 Debouchment
64 Internet patrons
65 Blubber
66 Yeltsin veto
67 Koch's predecessor

DOWN

1 Calculator work
2 Radar blip
3 Thieves' hideout
4 They're loose
5 "Yikes!"
6 "The Afternoon of a ___"
7 In the thick of
8 First name in perfumery
9 Venture
10 Japanese mats
11 Olympic hawk
12 Bed-frame crosspiece
13 "Mikado" executioner
18 Sport whose name means "soft way"
19 Polo, e.g.
24 Circulars
25 Carpenter's woe
26 French bread?

27 High-priced spread?
28 ". . . and eat ___"
29 Subj. of a Clinton victory, 11/17/93
30 Key
31 Midway alternative
32 River nymph
33 The Gold Coast, today
34 "À votre ___!"
39 Java neighbor
40 Columbus, by birth
42 "Nancy" or "Cathy"
43 Puss
45 Server on skates
46 Dos + cuatro
49 Take third
50 Take on
51 "___ on Film" (1983 book set)
52 Conniving
53 Coach Nastase
54 Rock's Joan

56 Sphere
57 "Cheers" habitué
58 Alternatively
60 Lady lobster
61 Ungainly craft

by David A. Rosen

20

ACROSS

1 Like Job
8 Bob or beehive
14 Leisurely musical pieces
15 Decrees
17 Pentagon advocate?
19 Parlor piece
20 Ex-Knick coach Jackson
21 Author of "Life in London"
22 Heart of France
24 Part
25 Visit Robert Reich?
31 Medical apprentice
32 Ease
37 Blue "Yellow Submarine" characters
38 Revised
40 Ancient beginning
41 Off course
42 Foggy Bottom boat?
46 Narc's collar
50 "Since ___ Have You"
51 Not for
52 Juan's uncle
53 Pescadores neighbor
59 Reno's piano practice?
62 Tympanic membrane
63 Guides, in a way
64 Brews tea
65 Menu listings

DOWN

1 Falsifies accounts
2 Chick ender
3 White House heavyweight
4 Beach Boys' "___ Around"
5 "___ kleine Nachtmusik"
6 Titan tip
7 Poetic monogram
8 Spa installation
9 Maestro Toscanini
10 Words often exchanged
11 Twice as unlikely
12 Down Under dog
13 "Love Story" star
16 January 1 song ending
18 Riding the waves
23 Bullfight cries
25 Walk with difficulty
26 Unwanted classification, once
27 Printing style: Abbr.
28 Hawaiian state bird
29 Kingston and others
30 Fee schedule
33 Friend of Ernie
34 Sills solo
35 Caterpillar construction
36 Advantage
38 Calling company
39 Intersection maneuver
43 Asks for a loan
44 They trip up foreigners
45 Magician's sound effect
46 First or home, e.g.
47 Last of the Mohicans
48 Genesis
49 Spanish squiggle
54 ___ were (so to speak)
55 Ovid's way
56 Oenologist's interest
57 Entr'___
58 Costner character
60 Prior, to Prior
61 G.I. ___

by Randolph Ross

ACROSS

1 John Denver's "Christmas in ___"
6 "Tuna-Fishing" painter
10 Among
14 "___ Eyes" (1969 song)
15 Actor Richard
16 Bounty rival
17 Refinement
18 Witticisms
19 Vigor
20 1950 Sinatra hit
23 West Bank org.
24 "Just a ___"
25 Three strokes, perhaps
28 Actress Sommer
31 Shares
36 Feared test
38 Troubles
40 Weaken
41 1955 Sinatra hit
44 Improve
45 Rig
46 Shut off
47 Beachwear
49 Relax
51 Audit conductor, for short
52 Guy's date
54 Eternity
56 1961 Sinatra hit
64 "Warm"
65 Minnow eater
66 Driving hazard
68 Petruchio's mate
69 Shillelagh land
70 10th-day-of-Christmas gift
71 Swerve
72 Henna and others
73 Follow

DOWN

1 Blue-chip symbol
2 Lively dance
3 Chihuahua change
4 Bar, in law
5 Compass part
6 Half begun?
7 Excited
8 Stucco backing
9 Foot part
10 Swear
11 Ryun's run
12 Basil's successor
13 Niels Bohr, e.g.
21 The Man Without a Country
22 More aloof
25 Propels a gondola
26 Bouquet
27 Bird "perched upon a bust of Pallas"
29 Toddlers
30 Dramatist Rice
32 Goddess of discord
33 Raccoon kin
34 Lawn tool
35 Is apparent
37 Impart
39 Ditto
42 Saw
43 Elevated
48 Stood up
50 Kind of switch
53 Distrustful
55 Run site
56 Prepares the presses
57 Plumber's concern
58 Behind
59 Ale
60 Pennsylvania port
61 Roadhouses
62 They go into locks
63 Relative of Hindustani
67 Volte-face WNW

by Albert J. Klaus

ACROSS

1 Hearth debris
6 Atmosphere
10 Columnist Bombeck
14 Room to ___
15 Skater Heiden
16 High time?
17 Critical juncture
20 Parade
21 Some oranges
22 Roasting items
25 Sometimes they get the hang of it
26 Woolly one
30 Carnegie Hall event
32 Where Marco Polo traveled
33 Tomb tenant
34 All fired up?
37 Future brass
41 Modeled, maybe
42 Mountain ridge
43 Peruvian of yore
44 Neptune's fork
46 Physicist Niels
47 Work, work, work
49 Its password was "Mickey Mouse"
51 Trotsky rival
52 Straight shooters?
57 Stops rambling
61 Algerian seaport
62 Broadway groom of 1922
63 Sister of Thalia
64 Bridge seat
65 Bank holding
66 Prepare to shave

DOWN

1 Cleo's snakes
2 Flyspeck
3 "Let the Sunshine In" musical
4 Sea bird
5 Bristles
6 W.W. I grp.
7 Mausoleum item
8 "Road to ___"
9 Beginnings of poetry?
10 Involve
11 Beauty aid
12 Folkways
13 Writer Beattie and others
18 Poet translated by FitzGerald
19 Toledo locale
23 Depended
24 Perfumed
26 Senate output
27 On the briny
28 "Gorillas in the ___"
29 Hit a fly, perhaps
31 Mean
34 Host Jay
35 Yen
36 Ivan, for one
38 Church front area
39 Expensive rug
40 Fish in a way
44 Aptitude
45 Weight allowance
47 Pack away
48 "Falcon Crest" star
50 "Egad!"
51 Barge
53 McHenry, e.g.
54 Münchhausen, for one
55 Within: Prefix
56 Common sign
58 Sash
59 Cause for overtime
60 Clucker

by Sidney L. Robbins

ACROSS

1 Crocus bulb
5 "Son of the Sun"
9 Set-to
14 Pastiche
15 Score in pinochle
16 "A house is not ___"
17 Restaurant request
18 Vessel for Jill
19 "Anticipation" singer
20 Song by 11-Down
23 Vinegary
24 Scottish hillside
25 Westernmost Aleutian
27 A clef
32 Unsettle?
35 Scruff
38 "Aeneid" locale
39 Musical or song by 11-Down
42 Nobelist Wiesel
43 Rows before P
44 Gorky's "The ___ Depths"
45 Had a hunch
47 Carol
49 Daffy Duck talk
52 Bedtime annoyances
56 Song by 11-Down
61 Mercutio's friend
62 Cigar's end
63 Prefix with China
64 An acid
65 Alert
66 Ending with gang or mob
67 Guided a raft
68 Kane's Rosebud
69 Libel, e.g.

DOWN

1 Pause sign
2 Relating to $C_{18}H_{34}O_2$
3 Dyeing instruction
4 Some handlebars
5 Collision
6 Circa
7 Mountaineer
8 Psychiatrist Alfred
9 Tennessee Senator Jim
10 I.O.U.
11 Late, great composer
12 Mine: Fr.
13 "State of Grace" star
21 Thurber's Walter
22 Informal goodbye
26 Word on a coin
28 Student of animal behavior
29 Make coffee
30 Knowledge
31 Spectator
32 Farm mothers
33 Base
34 "The doctor ___"
36 Barley beard
37 Exploited worker
40 It may be golden
41 Actress Verdugo
46 Friend of Harvey the rabbit
48 Belgian port
50 Mergansers' kin
51 Perfumery bit
53 Showed allegiance, in a way
54 Downy bird
55 Stable sound
56 Envelop
57 Our genus
58 Biographer Ludwig
59 Hawaiian honker
60 To be, to Henri

by Joy L. Wouk

ACROSS

1 Child's getaway
5 Nurse's stick
9 Malpractice target
14 Margarine
15 Part of a cash register
16 Sam or Tom, e.g.
17 Businessperson's oxymoron
20 Crowbar
21 Runner Devers
22 Sums
23 "Get ___!"
25 Cut up
27 Vipers
30 Indignant person's oxymoron
35 Actor Erwin
36 Breezy
37 Refer (to)
38 Dinner bird
40 Command to Fido
42 Jewish dinner
43 Mideast language
45 Flood survivor
47 W.W. II grp.
48 Oxymoron for a homely person
50 Cheek
51 Riches' opposite
52 Took a powder
54 Jacob's brother
57 Bare
59 Speechify
63 Coffee drinker's oxymoron
66 Passé
67 Within: Prefix
68 Model married to David Bowie
69 Steeple
70 Slumber
71 Library item

DOWN

1 Monk's hood
2 Lotion ingredient
3 Former talk-show host
4 Fireplace equipment
5 Penn, e.g.: Abbr.
6 Belly dancers
7 Edison's middle name
8 Mathematician Pascal
9 Sine ___ non
10 Straighten out
11 Sarcasm
12 Dolt
13 Barbies' mates
18 Enrage
19 Bow of silents
24 Black bird
26 Three-time Super Bowl-winning coach
27 Tin Pan Alley org.
28 One of the Beatles
29 Chrysalises
31 In competition
32 Lindley of "The Ropers"
33 Creativity
34 Indoor balls
36 Writer Loos
39 Busybody
41 Stashes
44 Caesar's swans
46 Certain vote
49 Shylock
50 Magellan, e.g.
53 Lee to Grant
54 Concludes
55 It's seen in bars
56 Against
58 Unit of force
60 BB's
61 Word after "go!"
62 Sea eagle
64 Humorist George
65 "Oh, darn!"

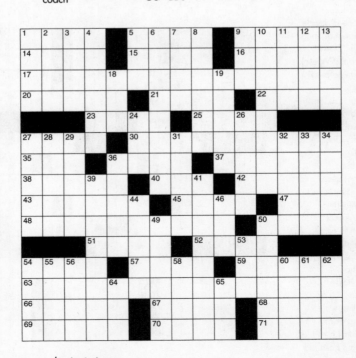

by Janie Lyons

ACROSS

1 College digs
5 Haggadah-reading time
10 Coarse hominy
14 Piedmont city
15 Cuisine type
16 The Magi, e.g.
17 Railbird's passion
20 Certain wind
21 Check
22 Opposite of "yippee!"
23 Buyer caveat
24 Bottoms
27 Darlings
28 Railroad abbr.
31 Old toy company
32 Trim
33 It's not a dime a dozen
34 Bettor's bible
37 Grocery buy
38 Sword of sport
39 Archaic "prior"
40 Political abbr.
41 Cutting reminder?
42 Didn't quite rain
43 Broadcasts
44 Baptism, e.g.
45 Corner piece?
48 Some legal documents
52 Across-the-board bet
54 Mont. neighbor
55 Mercantilism
56 Mrs. Chaplin
57 Curaçao ingredient
58 Downy duck
59 Snoopy

DOWN

1 Desert dessert
2 Agcy. founded in 1970
3 Hwys.
4 Results of some errors
5 Summer wear
6 Some House of Lords members
7 Word before free or calls
8 Ike's command, for short
9 Double-check the seat belts
10 Muddles
11 "Judith" composer
12 Cold-war fighters
13 Starting gate
18 Like some gates
19 A Kringle
23 Penthouse home?
24 Pheasant broods
25 Words to live by
26 Stoop
27 Race-track runner
28 Snob
29 Notre planète
30 1947 Horse of the Year
32 "___ Got a Brand New Bag"
33 Track hiatus time
35 Have fun
36 Like trotters, e.g.
41 Dust collector?
42 Actor Martin
43 Dismay
44 "The Cloister and the Hearth" author
45 Switch
46 Roofing item
47 Chip in
48 Interpret
49 "Git!"
50 Geologists' times
51 Waffle
53 Dernier ___

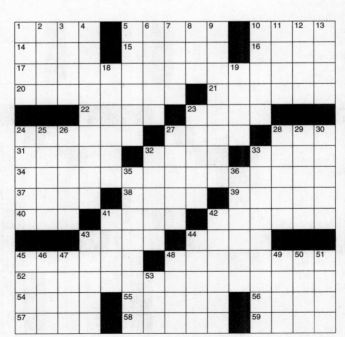

by Joel Davajan

ACROSS

1. Wrongs
5. Stockyard group
9. Sail supports
14. Govt. agents
15. War of 1812 battle site
16. Member of a crowd scene
17. Give stars to
18. Basketball's Chamberlain
19. 1993 Formula One winner Prost
20. Old "House Party" host
23. Knocks down
24. Reserved
25. 1975 Stephanie Mills musical, with "The"
28. Hot time in Paris
29. Take turns
33. Kind of package
34. More albinolike
35. Phobic
37. P.G.A.'s 1992 leading money winner
39. Rickey Henderson stat
41. Hunter of myth
42. Well ventilated
43. Least exciting
45. Rotary disk
48. Sign of summer
49. Mathematician's letters
50. Throw
52. N.F.L. receiver for 18 seasons
57. Booby
59. Not in use
60. Crips or Bloods
61. Uris's "___ Pass"
62. Baylor mascot
63. Skirt
64. Check writer
65. Slumped
66. Actress Charlotte et al.

DOWN

1. Attack by plane
2. Turkish hostelry
3. Stinging plant
4. Fish-line attachment
5. Axed
6. Dancer Bruhn
7. Small brook
8. Loathe
9. Substantial
10. Wheel shaft
11. Noted film trilogy
12. Angle starter
13. ___ Jose
21. Hebrew for "contender with God"
22. Eponymous poet of Greek drama
26. Temper
27. British alphabet ender

30. Elderly one
31. Gumshoe
32. "___ With a View"
33. Columnist Herb
34. Supplicate
36. Thread of life spinner, in myth
37. Savageness
38. Late actress Mary
39. NaCl, to a pharmacist
40. Truss
44. Deviates from the script
45. Party to Nafta
46. Exact retribution
47. Enters a freeway
49. Persian Gulf land
51. Trevanian's "The ___ Sanction"
53. Green target
54. Madison Avenue product

55. Ardor
56. Boor
57. Cutup
58. Noche's opposite

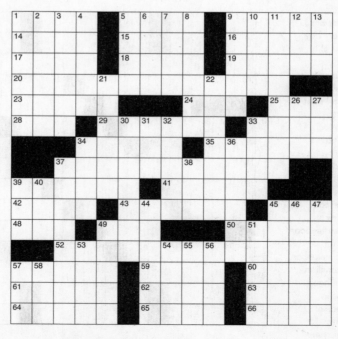

by Janet R. Bender

ACROSS

1 Rig
5 Big dos
10 At a distance
14 Ur locale
15 New York's ___ Tully Hall
16 Berg opera
17 M
20 Kicker's aid
21 Names in a Saudi phone book
22 Bury
23 Cut and run
24 Yearn
26 Talk radio guest
29 Playwright O'Casey
30 Army rank, for short
33 African lily
34 Brazzaville's river
35 Through
36 H
40 Fabergé objet
41 Collection
42 Candied items
43 1969 Three Dog Night hit
44 Pup's complaints
45 Talent for cocktail talk
47 Some heirs
48 Time founder
49 "Orlando" author
52 Forum fashion
53 Quarry
56 Y
60 Organ setting
61 Type style
62 Eros
63 Ruptured
64 Tell's target
65 Currycomb target

DOWN

1 Investigate, in a way
2 Tribe whose name means "cat people"
3 Old gray animal?
4 Some ratings
5 Newgate guard
6 1966 Caine role
7 Wagons-___
8 German cry
9 Bishop's domain
10 Solo
11 Candid cameraman
12 Der ___ (Adenauer)
13 Krupp family home
18 Tall writing?
19 Tiny swimmer
23 Took off
24 Director Marshall
25 "Othello" plotter

26 Item in a locket
27 Collimate
28 Moose, e.g.
29 Divans
30 Opera prop
31 Pioneer atom splitter
32 Kingfisher's coif
34 ___ de ballet
37 Opposite of hire
38 St. Patrick's home
39 Publicity
45 Conductor Ormandy
46 Analyze verse
47 Skier's site
48 Dietary
49 ___ Point
50 "___ victory!"
51 Stink
52 Substitute
53 Cougar

54 Caddie's offering
55 Home of Jezebel
57 ___ la-la
58 School dance
59 Scottish cap

by Robert Zimmerman

ACROSS

1 Wealthy person
5 Takes advantage of
9 "The Forsyte ___"
13 Likeness
15 Kind of stick
16 Sheriff Tupper of "Murder, She Wrote"
17 Social hangout
19 Sea swallow
20 Home turnover
21 Knock out of kilter
23 Illuminated
24 Terminator
25 Bear up there
29 Steep slope
33 Crier of Greek myth
35 Wakens
39 Bettor's challenge
43 Show fright
44 Weird
45 Followed orders
48 N.Y. Police ___
49 Exodus priest
53 Mauna ___
55 Responded unintelligibly
58 "Last stop! ___!"
62 Abner's pal and namesakes
63 Diamond coup
66 Relative of the flute
67 Auction actions
68 Indian boat
69 Part of Halloween makeup
70 Church nook
71 Endure

DOWN

1 Informal greetings
2 Eastern V.I.P.
3 Wind instrument?
4 They'll be hunted in April
5 Big sports news
6 Loudly weep
7 "Holy moly!"
8 Kind of loser
9 Beelzebub
10 Change
11 Watkins Glen, e.g.
12 "Lou Grant" star
14 Lod airport airline
18 Nobelist Wiesel
22 Esteem
25 German link
26 Kind of squad
27 Lemonlike
28 Singer Lane
30 Cuomo's predecessor
31 Son of Prince Valiant
32 Australian hopper
34 Long Island town
36 Tool storage area
37 Limerick site
38 Barber's cut
40 Wane
41 Bullring shout
42 Receive
46 Pass
47 Cabbage Patch item
49 Visibly happy
50 Caribbean getaway
51 "___ has it . . ."
52 Start
54 Actor Guinness
56 Old lab burner
57 Trapdoor
59 Milky gem
60 Arm bone
61 Pueblo town
64 Employee card and others
65 Still and all

by Sidney L. Robbins

ACROSS

1 Spirogyra or frog spit
5 Impression
9 Diamond protector
13 Burpee bit
14 Conclude, as negotiations
16 See 31-Across
17 Lefty celebrity relative
20 Turkish title
21 Customary practice
22 Strengthens, with "up"
23 Tugs
25 "Babes in Toyland" star, 1960
28 Head of the costume department?
30 Leonard and Charles
31 With 16-Across, former Phillies manager
34 "Queen ___ Day" (old game show)
35 Corporate abbr.
36 Have a hunch
37 Lefty artist
41 Shows one's humanity
42 Bud
43 ___ Fein
44 Voted
45 Great
46 Overwhelms with humor
48 Catch in a net
50 Pipe type
52 Highest point in Sicily
55 Course for a newcomer to the U.S.: Abbr.
57 Lament
58 Lefty actor
62 French 101 word
63 Copy of a sort
64 Noted rap artist
65 Gloomy
66 Overdecorated
67 Danson et al.

DOWN

1 Composers' org.
2 Three miles, roughly
3 Lefty President
4 Foofaraw
5 Horus's mother
6 Star in Cygnus
7 Baa maid?
8 Razor-billed bird
9 Kind of sax
10 Publican's offerings
11 Ridicule persistently
12 Is worthwhile
15 Lefty actress
18 Five-year periods
19 Refusals
24 Pontiac Silverdome team
26 Camden Yards team
27 Polaroid inventor
29 Lefty comedian
31 Lefty comedian
32 Continental trading group
33 Lawyer in both "Civil Wars" and "L.A. Law"
36 Student's worry
37 Roman law
38 Before, to Byron
39 Jutlander, e.g.
40 In a despicable way
45 Writer Quindlen
47 Blotto
48 $C_4H_{10}O$
49 Subs
51 Bridge seats
52 Horse that made sense?
53 One of the Jackson 5
54 Tannish color
56 Hot
59 Chaperoned girl
60 Actress Joanne
61 Paroxysm

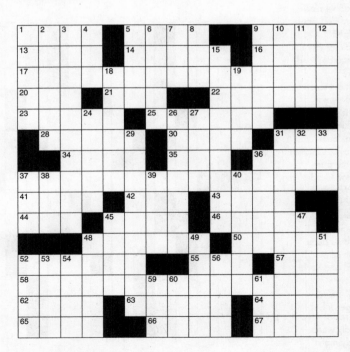

by Peter (Lefty) Gordon

30

ACROSS

1 More exuberant, as a laugh
5 Snatch
9 "Cold hands, ___"
14 Mast-steadying rope
15 Hitchcock's "___ Window"
16 Of a region
17 Now's partner
18 Eggshell
19 Rubberneck
20 Altar in the sky
21 Sault ___ Marie
22 Yarmulke
24 Capts.' subordinates
25 Campaign donor grp.
26 Some bikes
28 "___ the season . . ."
29 Upper regions of space
31 Scrabble piece
32 Mare's offspring
33 Judged
35 Place for E.M.K.
36 Concordes land there
37 Without reservation
40 Little demon
43 Corn site
44 Prolonged attacks
48 Steak order
49 Vesuvius's Sicilian counterpart
51 Boston Garden, e.g.
52 Gametes
53 Theater aide
55 White House defense grp.
56 Barbie's beau
57 Sixth sense
58 Joad and Kettle
59 Wilder's "___ Town"
60 Singer John
62 Gibbons
64 Desiccated
65 Means of connection
66 Gambler's "bones"
67 Like some cars
68 Pulse indication
69 Collectors' goals
70 February 14 symbol

DOWN

1 Like some candy boxes
2 Repeat
3 Otalgia
4 Place for ham and Swiss
5 Miss Garbo
6 Modern
7 Swiss river
8 Movie star with a kick?
9 Ethnic group portrayed in A. R. Gurney's plays
10 ___ Deco
11 Person who can move buildings
12 Kind of arts or law
13 With cruelty
21 ___ throat
23 Alters
27 Discourages
30 Overact
32 Where to go between acts
34 Restrains
38 Reporters' needs
39 Tale tellers
40 Jilted lover's woe
41 Entangler
42 Sanchez Vicario of tennis
45 Columbus, by birth
46 Guaranteed
47 University in Fairfield, Conn.
50 Mien
53 Slow on the uptake
54 Mitigates
61 Bouncer's demand
63 Pizza
64 California's Big ___

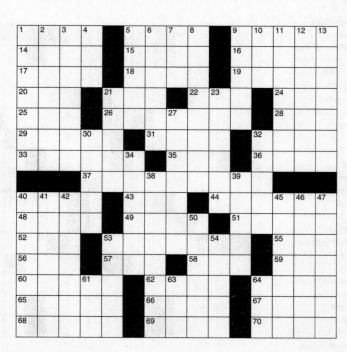

by Nancy Joline

ACROSS

1 Scroogian comments
5 Grandson of Adam
9 Biblical possessive
12 Sheltered, at sea
13 Spot for Spartacus
14 Carnival ride cry
15 "Ho, ho, ho" fellow
18 Seems
19 Hockey's Bobby et al.
20 Blue Eagle initials
21 Feasted
23 "My salad days when I was ___": Shakespeare
30 Favorite dog name
31 Closes in on
32 The East
33 Word in a price
35 Volcano spew
36 Deli cry
37 Cause for liniment
38 Not-so-prized fur
40 River inlet
41 Bucky Dent slew it at Fenway Park in 1978
45 Zorba portrayer
46 Tennis call
47 Sulk angrily
48 Many Dickens stories, originally
52 Civil War currency
56 Merit
57 Nintendo hero
58 One of the Simpsons
59 Sot's problem
60 Jot
61 Prepares the dinner table

DOWN

1 Mexican peninsula
2 Crooked
3 Maids
4 Moon goddess
5 Misreckons
6 Born
7 Indivisible
8 ___ Marcos, Tex.
9 Arid region of India
10 Chick watchers
11 Thus far
13 Take with ___ of salt
14 Utility employee
16 It comes in balls
17 Bad news at a talent show
21 "Bull ___" (Costner film)
22 Psyche parts
23 Word in a monarch's name
24 Extent
25 National treasuries
26 Tidy up
27 Teen heartthrob Priestley
28 Undeliverable letter, in post-office talk
29 13th-century invader
34 Monastery head
38 D.C. legislator
39 El Greco's "View of ___"
42 Nothing: Fr.
43 Pianist Peter
44 Part of rock's C.S.N. & Y.
47 Brotherhood
48 Comic bit
49 "I cannot tell ___"
50 Ultimate
51 Madrid Mmes.
52 Dropout's degree: Abbr.
53 Status letters, perhaps
54 "Say ___"
55 Dernier ___

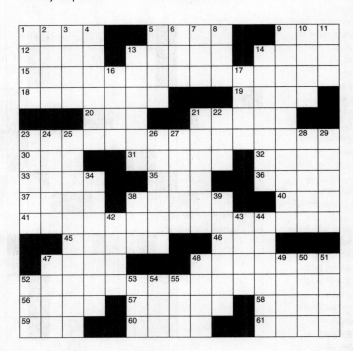

by Jonathan Schmalzbach

ACROSS

1 Buddy
5 Balance sheet listing
10 Helper: Abbr.
14 New Rochelle college
15 They fly in formation
16 Wife of ___ (Chaucer pilgrim)
17 Ordnance
18 Fill with glee
19 Out of the weather
20 Battle in which Lee defeated Pope
23 Sunday talk: Abbr.
24 Activity
25 Fountain treat, for short
26 Battle in which Bragg defeated Rosecrans
31 Singer Coolidge et al.
32 Corner
33 11th-century date
36 Heaven on earth
37 Change
39 Earth sci.
40 Marry
41 Fine poker holdings
42 Hawks
43 Battle in which Grant defeated Bragg
46 John Wilkes Booth, e.g.
50 Tempe sch.
51 Items on a "must" list
52 Battle in which Lee defeated Burnside
57 Retread, e.g.
58 Go along (with)
59 Wrangler's pal
61 Overlook
62 Some are heroic
63 Mideast land
64 Promontory
65 Kilmer opus
66 Niño's nothing

DOWN

1 Spy grp.
2 Baseball, informally
3 Not deserved
4 Not fem.
5 Work to do
6 Infrequently
7 Petticoat junction
8 "Cómo ___ usted?"
9 Chelsea Clinton, e.g.
10 Embarrass
11 Nacho topping
12 Rib-eye
13 One's nearby
21 Dumbarton ___ (1944 meeting site)
22 P.D.Q.
23 Item in a hardware bin
27 Fire
28 Nuclear experiment
29 Coffee server
30 Start for fly or about
33 Three-hanky film
34 City once named for Stalin
35 Rick's beloved et al.
37 Herr's "Oh!"
38 "Cry ___ River"
39 General Motors make
41 Parcel of land
42 High-hat
44 Words before "I'm yours"
45 Tax
46 "Sweet" river of song
47 Record blot
48 Actress Garr et al.
49 Playwright Clifford
53 Engrossed
54 Mr. Stravinsky
55 Saskatchewan tribe
56 Atop
60 Kind of testing

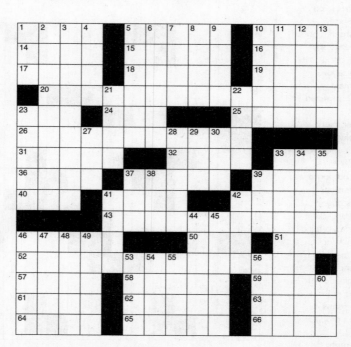

by Jonathan Schmalzbach

ACROSS

1 "West Side Story" song
6 200 milligrams
11 Low island
14 1968 song "All ___ the Watchtower"
15 River to the Missouri
16 Fuss
17 Seaver's nickname
19 Robert Morse Tony-winning role
20 House cleaner, in England
21 "Absolutely"
22 Legal profession
24 Queen Victoria's house
26 Freight charge
27 Half-wit
28 Better than a bargain
29 Polynesian carvings
33 "Hail, Caesar!"
34 Netman Nastase
37 Sheepish
38 Cup's edge
39 Battery part
40 Anti-prohibitionists
41 Disfigure
42 Get extra life from
43 Portaged
45 Patriotic uncle
47 Rocket's cargo
49 Crib-sheet contents
54 Earthy colors
55 Veneration
56 Hand-cream ingredient
57 "Harper Valley ___"
58 Decorative tree
61 Sock in the jaw
62 Address grandly
63 Coeur d' ___, Idaho
64 Flood relief?
65 Pave over
66 Coiffed like Leo

DOWN

1 "Concentration" objective
2 Hello or goodbye
3 Type type
4 Opening
5 Stone, for one
6 Kitchen gadgets
7 Garage-sale words
8 Spitfire fliers, for short
9 Work up
10 Electronics whiz
11 Western spoof of 1965
12 "What ___" ("I'm bored")
13 "___ Sixteen" (Ringo Starr hit)
18 Package-store wares
23 Skater Zayak
25 Place for posies
26 Call back
29 Wrecker
30 "___ had it!"
31 News locale of 12/17/03
32 Shoe part
33 Auto option, informally
35 Wallet contents, for short
36 Shoebox letters
38 Alan or Cheryl
39 Kind of buildup
41 Gauge
44 Inertia
45 Finn's pal
46 Once again
47 "Where's ___?" (1970 flick)
48 Part owner?
50 Half of a Western city name
51 Pulitzer-winning novelist Glasgow
52 TV exec Arledge
53 Basted
55 Cinema canine
59 ___ out (missed)
60 Descartes's conclusion

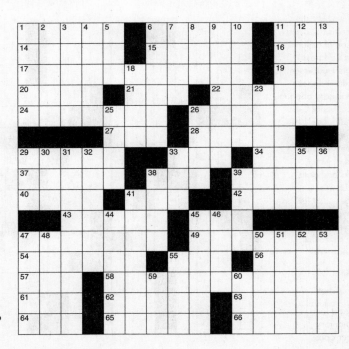

by Fred Piscop

ACROSS

1 Tot's talk, perhaps
5 Encourages
9 First-grade instruction
13 Stinks
15 "Thanks ___!"
16 Swing around
17 Like factory workers
19 U, for one
20 Elsie's bull
21 "Mommie ___" (Christina Crawford book)
23 "What's ___ for me?"
25 Take a potshot
26 Teller of white lies
29 Stage whisper
30 Give the eye
31 Quick bites
33 Advances
36 Baseball's Gehrig
37 Trunk
39 Runner Sebastian
40 Remains
43 Person of action
44 King's address
45 Illegal inducement
47 Mexican dishes
49 Speak-easy offering
50 Saxophonist Getz
51 Candid
53 Waiter's jotting
56 Actress Archer
57 Kind of jury
61 Bucks and does
62 Otherwise
63 Singer ___ Neville
64 Lawyer: Abbr.
65 Tackle-box item
66 City inside the Servian Wall

DOWN

1 Tennis shot
2 Run in neutral
3 Body's partner
4 Logician's start
5 Sidekick
6 Sum total

7 Wart giver, in old wives' tales
8 Emphasis
9 On a horse
10 Edit
11 No blessing, this!
12 Shipped
14 Fragrance
18 Marco Polo area
22 Dye color appropriate to this puzzle
24 Vacuum tube
26 Go belly up
27 Borodin's prince
28 Texas' state flower
29 Balance-sheet pluses
32 Golf club V.I.P.
34 Illustrator Gustave
35 Comprehends
38 Patrick Henry, e.g.
41 Bodega
42 Clothing specification

44 Boating hazard
46 Saharan tribesman
48 Newswoman Shriver
49 Intelligence-testing name
51 Actress Thompson
52 Glamour rival
54 River of Spain
55 Leeway
58 "It's no ___!"
59 Slippery one
60 Opposite SSW

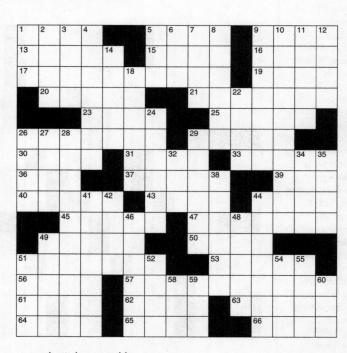

by Sidney L. Robbins

ACROSS

1 Break down grammatically
6 Items in a still life
11 Braincase
13 "___ Fables"
15 Considers bond values again
16 Reduce to ashes
18 Fred's sister
19 ___ Speedwagon
20 Not give ___
21 Mediocre
22 Argued
24 Loudonville, N.Y., campus
25 Classical name in medicine
27 Sprinted
28 "___ Believer" (Monkees hit)
31 Barn topper
32 Football squad
36 Court ruling
37 Hint to solving the eight italicized clues
39 ___ Jima
40 Ignite
42 Plane or dynamic preceder
43 Actress Ryan
44 Deteriorate
45 Curses
47 Sprockets linker
50 Reps.' counterparts
51 Riding whip
55 Natural gait
56 Emily, to Charlotte
57 Madrid attraction
58 Kind of lot
60 Zebralike
62 March laboriously
63 Paired nuclides
64 Catch suddenly
65 Harvests

DOWN

1 Trims
2 Kind of recording
3 Passage ceremony
4 Cash's "A Boy Named ___"
5 Printers' widths
6 Set the standard for
7 Architect Saarinen
8 Chemical suffix
9 Lettuce variety
10 Bowling save
11 Tomorrow: Lat.
12 Try again
14 Laurel or Musial
17 Wetlands watchdog
19 Deserters
22 Venus, for one
23 River to the Laptev Sea
24 Game fish
26 50's singer Frankie
27 Supplies with better weapons
28 Kind
29 ___ tai (cocktail)
30 Cereal bristle
33 Robust energy
34 Pronoun in a cote?
35 Norfolk ale
38 20+ quires
41 Evaporated
46 Act niggardly
47 Actor Gulager
48 Emcee
49 Copycats
50 More extreme
52 Mustard plants
53 Baltic Sea feeder
54 Pea places
56 Long account
57 Swift sailing boat
59 B-F connection
60 Salutation for Edmund Hillary
61 Half a fly

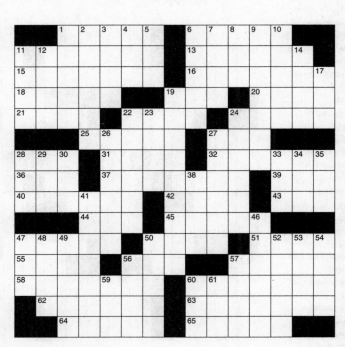

by D. J. Listort

ACROSS

1 Dumbfounded
5 Acquire, as expenses
10 Singer Campbell
14 Colombian city
15 Hughes's plane Spruce __
16 1890's Vice President __ P. Morton
17 1959 Rodgers and Hammerstein hit
20 "You can __ horse to . . ."
21 Bridal path
22 Predicament
24 Obote's successor
26 1956 Comden-Green-Styne collaboration
33 On __ (counting calories)
34 Man with a title
35 Soviet space vehicle
36 Pride and envy, e.g.
37 Old hat
38 "Aurora" painter
39 Kind of cap or cream
40 Radio host of note
41 First U.S.-born saint
42 1930 Gershwin musical
46 Sigmatism
47 Achy
48 Whiz kid
51 Blotto
54 1983 Herman-Fierstein musical
60 "Metamorphoses" poet
61 Wish granters
62 TV's Oscar
63 Hitches
64 Mill material
65 Murder

DOWN

1 Part of a play
2 Star of TV's "Wiseguy"
3 "Waiting for the Robert __"
4 Puts out of commission
5 Desert critter
6 Persona __ grata
7 How some packages are sent
8 R. & R. org.
9 Ring leader?
10 Sticking together
11 Decreasingly
12 Demonic
13 Garibaldi's birthplace
18 Keats or Shelley
19 Popular street name
23 Invent
24 Snaps handcuffs on
25 Gentle, as breezes
26 Grounds
27 Kingly decree
28 Passenger ship
29 Gobble
30 "__ man with seven . . ."
31 Curtain material
32 Nine-to-five routine
37 Conks out
38 Mutinied
41 __-comic (play type)
43 Long narratives
44 Alan, Larry or Stephen
45 Tap-dance
48 Crushing news
49 Four-star review
50 __ rain
52 Admiral Zumwalt
53 Actress Moore
55 Chicken's counterpart
56 Atmosphere: Prefix
57 Prefix with lateral
58 Omicrons' predecessors
59 Thesaurus listing: Abbr.

by Alex K. Justin

ACROSS

1 Trounce
8 "My gal" of song
11 Castleberry of "Alice"
14 Have coming
15 Soldier's fare
17 Traveled militarily
18 Catch-22 situation
19 Black and white, e.g.
21 U.S.N. rank
22 Ireland
23 Cosmo and People, e.g.
26 I, to Claudius
27 "___ Lisa"
31 Shower mo.
32 Scruggs of bluegrass
34 Epithet for a tyrant
36 Not a warm welcome
39 Flower child
40 A big blow
41 De Maupassant's "___ Vie"
42 Some of Wordsworth's words
43 Legendary Hollywood monogram
44 Ed of "Daniel Boone"
45 Roller coaster cry
47 "Society's Child" singer Janis ___
49 Sang-froid
56 In progress
57 Vegetarian's no-no
59 Alley of "Look Who's Talking"
60 Rodeo ropes
61 Ship's heading
62 Always, poetically
63 Majority's choice

DOWN

1 S. & L. offerings
2 Lover's
3 Christiania, today
4 Scarlett and others
5 Bear Piccolo
6 Civil rights leader Medgar
7 Change the décor
8 Punic War general
9 Knight's attire
10 Slip-up
11 Fight sight
12 Mislay
13 Washington bills
16 Mai ___
20 Like Captain Ahab
23 Like a he-man
24 Sap sucker
25 Bellyache
26 Be off the mark
27 Denver summer time: Abbr.
28 Disgrace
29 Nary a person
30 Saint whose feast day is January 21
32 Biblical judge
33 Word of support
34 Bugs's voice
35 Hairy ancestor
37 Obsolescent disks
38 Engine part
43 Like slim pickings
44 Lacking iron, maybe
45 Essayist E. B.
46 Three-time skating gold medalist
47 Model
48 Novelist Malraux
49 Furnace fuel
50 Getting ___ years
51 Bogeyman
52 Pop music's ___ Lobos
53 Gardner of mysteries
54 Backside
55 Overindulge
58 Chairman's heart?

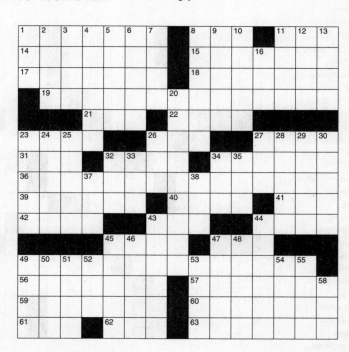

by Harvey Estes

ACROSS

1 Play opening
5 Ran
9 Shawl or afghan
14 Forsaken
15 Yellow brick, e.g.
16 Moonshine
17 Unencumbered
19 Composed
20 Follower of 21-Across?
21 Follower of 20-Across?
22 Small: Suffix
23 Ripped
24 Dems. opposition
27 Proverbial distancer
32 Sleepy Hollow schoolmaster
34 Ampersand
35 Firpo of the ring
36 Folk tales
37 Ship's officers
39 ___ time (never)
40 Upshots
41 Morning hrs.
42 Waffle topping
43 Kind of disease, facetiously
47 Hook shape
48 Alphabet quartet
49 Unmixed, as a drink
51 Character actor George
54 Starts
58 In the thick of
59 Be afraid to offend
60 Hope of Hollywood
61 Manhattan campus
62 Gamblers' game
63 Boorish
64 Some combos
65 Sharp put-down

DOWN

1 ___ Romeo (automobile)
2 Hip
3 De ___ (too much)
4 Words before "red" or "running"
5 Literary sister
6 Give some slack
7 Maneuver slowly
8 White House monogram
9 Block
10 Fun and games
11 Kind of beer
12 Eight, in combinations
13 A question of time
18 Singer Lenya
21 Merchandise
23 Manner of speaking
24 Staff leader
25 University of Maine site
26 TV announcer Don
28 1980 DeLuise movie
29 Bizarre
30 "Peanuts" character
31 Stock plans providing worker ownership: Abbr.
33 Young 'uns
37 Horace and Thomas
38 BB's
42 Disreputable
44 Some are spitting
45 World cultural agcy.
46 Flirts
50 Stylish Brits
51 Baby powder
52 Poet Khayyám
53 ___ fide
54 Where humuhu-munuku-nukuapuaa might be served
55 Filly or colt
56 Roman marketplaces
57 Quit
59 Abbr. in a mail-order ad

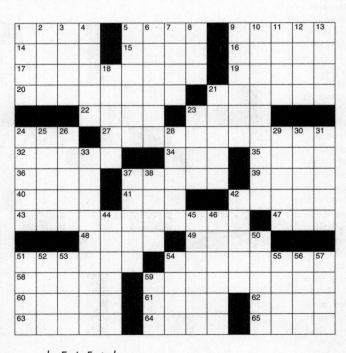

by Ernie Furtado

ACROSS

1 Colo. acad.
5 Start fishing
9 "Dancing Queen" pop group
13 Mata ___
14 Tear to shreds
16 Tactic
17 Singer Antoine from New Orleans
19 Intense anger
20 Carty of baseball
21 ___ and kin
23 "The Company"
24 Mister twister
28 San Francisco area
29 Antitoxins
30 Laughed, in a way
32 Transfer, as a legal proceeding
36 "Tie a Yellow Ribbon" tree
37 Native land
39 Inform (on)
40 Fantasized
44 Durante's "Mrs."
48 Cosmonaut Gagarin
50 1956 Oscar-winning actress
51 Birthday-suit activity
55 One of L.B.J.'s dogs
56 Munich's river
57 Max or Buddy
59 Till compartment
61 Film hit of 1934
65 Dermatologist's diagnosis
66 Underwater acronym
67 Tevye portrayer on stage
68 Feminist Millett
69 Mikulski and Murkowski: Abbr.
70 Once more

DOWN

1 TV initials
2 Region of heavy W.W. II fighting
3 Heart of the grocery?
4 Champion named 9/1/72
5 ___ Magnon
6 Goal
7 Acerbic
8 Acropolis attire
9 Bank loan abbr.
10 Longtime Supreme Court name
11 Humphrey, to Bacall
12 TV's "___ in the Life"
15 Commotion
18 Act like the Apostle Thomas
22 "___ goes!"
25 ___ Harbour, Fla.
26 Playoff breathers
27 Machine part
28 "___ she blows!"
30 Food fish
31 A dwarf
33 Syracuse players
34 Floral container
35 Biblical suffix
38 Moist
41 Novelist Rand
42 City bond, for short
43 Secret lovefests
45 Appearance at a sit-down?
46 Suspect's "out"
47 Top-rated TV show of the 60's
49 Baking potatoes
51 Kind of therapy
52 Mol's country
53 "___ my case"
54 "Goodnight" ___
58 Steak order
60 Marie, e.g.: Abbr.
62 Aruba product
63 Nolte's "48 ___"
64 Right away

by David J. Kahn

ACROSS

1 Bakery byproduct
6 Went by plane
10 Copied
14 Arizona features
15 Scottish isle
16 Lemon's partner
17 With 36-Across and 55-Across, a sales pitch disclaimer
20 Baden-Baden and others
21 Shea team
22 Eastern V.I.P.
23 Mr. Caesar
24 Ship to ___
25 "Swan Lake," e.g.
29 Tiny bit
31 Not native
32 Printer's employee
33 Printer's measures
36 See 17-Across
39 His wife took a turn for the worse
40 Obsolescent piano key material
41 Bellini opera
42 Hoarder's cry
43 Telescopist's sighting
44 Strength
47 Opponent
48 Xerox competitor
49 "When I was ___ . . ."
51 In ___ of
55 See 17-Across
58 Person 'twixt 12 and 20
59 "The King and I" setting
60 Singer Cara
61 Misses the mark
62 Paddles
63 Waco locale

DOWN

1 Concert hall equipment
2 Harvest
3 Greek mountain
4 Wrestlers' needs
5 Type of cobra
6 Shot
7 Artist's pad?
8 Son of Seth
9 Revolutionary, e.g.
10 "Remember the ___"
11 Heartbroken swain
12 Leno, for one
13 Bucks and does
18 Give forth
19 Indian noblewoman
23 Feeling
24 Suffix with tip or dump
25 Get-out-of-jail money
26 In addition
27 Bit of fluff
28 Mr. Durocher
29 Harden
30 "Sure, why not?"
32 Borodin's "Prince ___"
33 To be, in Paree
34 Secretarial work
35 Burn
37 Confess
38 "___ on your life!"
43 Fashion
44 "60 Minutes" regular
45 Reason out
46 Sentence subjects
47 Country homes
48 Pigeon coop
49 ___ da capo
50 Noted James Earl Jones stage role
51 Entice
52 The holm oak
53 Erupter of 1669
54 Applications
56 G.I. entertainers
57 Command to Fido

by Sidney L. Robbins

ACROSS

1 Israeli port
6 "Of ___ I Sing"
10 Flattened circle
14 Fall flower
15 Is under the weather
16 Accumulation
17 It's lined with bars
19 Palindromic pop quartet
20 Irritate
21 Snoozing
23 "Just a ___"
26 Failures
27 Leadership group
32 Rigorous exams
34 Bay window
35 1985 film "___ Williams"
36 Mexican coin
40 Carte blanche
43 Fly alone
44 Identical
45 Identically
46 Rancher's cattle
47 Lawn pests
48 Ravel work
52 Lair
54 Polar covering
55 Makes watertight
61 When doubled, a Samoan port
62 1959 Doris Day film
66 Airline to Jerusalem
67 ___ Lackawanna Railway
68 Hawaiian island
69 Cowgirl Evans
70 Actor Alan
71 Won't

DOWN

1 Door holder
2 Late tennis V.I.P.
3 Followers: Suffix
4 Yard sections
5 Comic Johnson
6 Shape of St. Anthony's cross
7 That guy's
8 Yale Bulldog
9 Bake in sauce
10 October stones
11 Feelings, in slang
12 Playwright Edward
13 Bounds
18 "The A-Team" star
22 Stranded sailor's call
24 Central arteries
25 Indulged in reveries
27 Corny throwaways
28 Folkie Guthrie
29 Watch's face
30 Nevada city
31 Moose
33 Electrical unit
36 Game with sticks
37 Sinful
38 "For heaven's ___!"
39 Bullring cries
41 Impediment, at law
42 Computer capacity, for short
46 Mrs. in Madrid
48 Two-legged
49 Florida city
50 Over 21, liquorwise
51 Pierre's school
53 Sgt. or cpl.
56 Shoemaker's tools
57 Beehive state
58 Actress Turner
59 Part of K.K.K.
60 Comical playlet
63 Mr. Gershwin
64 Cover
65 Conducted

by Sidney L. Robbins

ACROSS

1 Vacuum tube filler
6 Wanders
11 Underwear initials
14 March composer
15 Key above G
16 Majors or Myles
17 Happenchance
19 Once ___ while
20 Barber of baseball
21 Sprite
22 Made
24 City near Utah Lake
26 "Desire Under the ___"
29 Head of a familia
30 Peeved
33 When Operation Overlord took place
34 Bygone coif
36 Mmes., across the Pyrenees
38 Dined
39 Jodie Foster's directorial debut, 1991
43 Douglas or alpine, e.g.
44 Choir members
45 Pub quaffs
46 Seventh day activity
48 Improves
51 Monkeyshine
53 Carriage, in the country
54 Cousin of the English horn
58 Bushy-tailed animal
60 Princess's sleep disturber
62 Dishcloth
63 Greek vowel
64 Child's means of propulsion
68 Soak flax
69 More cheerful
70 Takes to the trails
71 Opposite NNW
72 Brainstorms
73 Apply

DOWN

1 Houston player
2 Oarsman
3 Tour leader
4 W.W. II Intelligence org.
5 N.B.A.'s Archibald
6 Club fund-raiser
7 Light switch position
8 Miss. neighbor
9 Chess finale
10 Robert Fulton's power
11 Notoriously risky social event
12 Respects
13 Sharpshooter
18 Fashion's Cassini
23 "Far out"
25 Shopping place
27 1939 James Stewart title role
28 Que follower, in song
31 ___ bene
32 Mr. Quayle
34 Drives away
35 A-number-1
37 Christmas tree topper
40 Atty.'s degree
41 Parisian summers
42 What's more
43 Constitution creators
47 Actor Matheson
49 Narrows
50 Watchful one
52 Welsh dog
55 Accelerator's counterpart
56 Western
57 Cast out
59 Little hopper
61 North Carolina county
65 Drain cleaner
66 Pasture
67 General Mills cereal

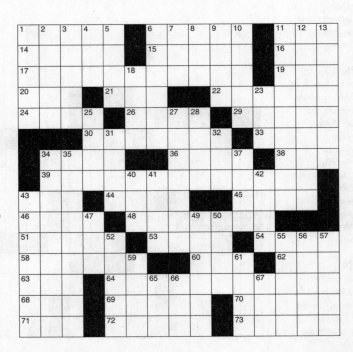

by Rich Norris

ACROSS

1 Movie spin-off TV series
5 "Arms and the Man" playwright
9 Little Goody Two ___
14 Director Preminger
15 Video
16 Blood vessel
17 With 37-Across and 59-Across, a familiar finale
19 With 58-Across, where to read 17-Across, etc.
20 Whooped
21 Combines
22 Appear
23 Sailor
24 Kind of ball
28 Naughty child's Christmas gift
32 Baden Baden, e.g.
35 English scarf
36 Israeli native
37 See 17-Across
40 Boxing site
41 "___ say more?"
42 Morse code message
43 Marsh growth
44 Much more expensive
45 Had been
46 Impressed deeply
50 Did a con job on
54 Mollified
58 See 19-Across
59 See 17-Across
60 Askew
61 French statesman Coty
62 Ripped
63 Rain gear
64 Bohemian
65 Raced

DOWN

1 Hole maker
2 One of the Three Musketeers
3 Inscribed pillar
4 According to ___
5 Agitate
6 "___ a nice day!"
7 Copied
8 Tie the knot
9 More secure
10 Kind of frost
11 Not secondhand: Abbr.
12 To be, in Paris
13 Pronounces
18 Logician's propositions
21 Hopping ___
23 Utmost extent
25 Fire residue
26 Play parts
27 Where Inchon is
28 Toy gun "ammo"
29 Sashes
30 Mr. Guthrie
31 Emulates hens
32 Twinkler
33 Skin opening
34 Author James
36 Meadowsweet
38 Pass receiver
39 Summer drink
44 "Dear old ___"
45 Bridge seats
47 Gentle breezes
48 Legally prevent
49 Moline, Ill., company
50 Penetrate
51 Pact since 1949
52 Mishmash
53 Whipping reminder
54 Insist
55 Confined, with "up"
56 Birds of ___
57 ___ Scott Decision, 1857
59 Pitcher's stat

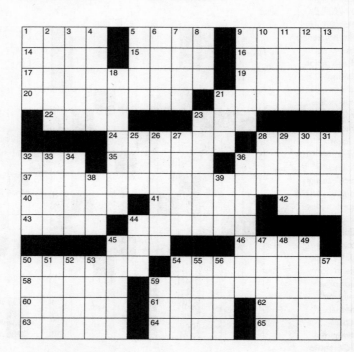

by Sidney L. Robbins

44

ACROSS
1 Wasn't colorfast
4 "Le ___ de Monte Cristo"
9 Napoleon's force
14 Gardner of "Mogambo"
15 1935 Triple Crown winner
16 Closes in on
17 Coastal area
19 Birdlike
20 Unyielding
21 Driver's need
23 Old town official
25 Gets the soap out
26 Investigated with "about"
29 No-caffeine drink
31 Drives
33 Freight weight
34 Part of Q.E.D.
37 ___ capita
38 Had a hankering
41 Anger
42 Barber's action
44 Stars and Bars inits
45 Commandment breaker
47 Batman, to the Joker
50 Astronomer Carl
51 "___ and rejoice": Psalms
53 Under, in verse
55 Largest newspaper in Calif.
57 Became less clear
61 Chilean port
62 Major pipe
64 Family car
65 "Hard ___ I" (nautical command)
66 Mr. Gershwin
67 Idyllic spots

68 Legal wrongs
69 "___ Miz"

DOWN
1 Pro ___
2 Eager
3 Zilch, to Zapata
4 Like Lahr's lion
5 Mideasterner
6 Dull finishes
7 Word before more and merrier
8 Jazzman Hines
9 Tylenol alternative
10 Income
11 Watch's center
12 Clear the slate
13 Workers of puzzledom
18 Host

22 Worth and Castle
24 Give new job skills
26 Small drinks
27 Augury
28 Full moon occurrence
30 "___ Ryan's Express"
32 Leave the union
35 Space
36 Slender-billed sea bird
39 Palm Sunday mount
40 Warps
43 Big-billed sea bird
46 Biblical prophet
48 Marseille moms
49 Pie slice, in geometry
51 World-weary
52 Like many seals

54 On the qui vive
56 The Sultan of ___
58 Dublin legislature
59 Dublin's country
60 Genetic materials
63 G.I.'s address

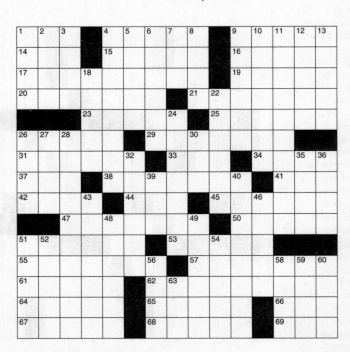

by Christopher Page

ACROSS

1 Pizarro victim
5 ___ and dangerous
10 Rights org. estab. 1960
14 One who's socially challenged
15 With 4-Down, M.L.K. declaration of 8/28/63
16 Pentateuch: Var.
17 Gen. Bradley
18 Invoice word
19 "Love ___ leave it"
20 M.L.K. honor, 1964
23 In the past
24 Blaster's need
25 Passing mark
26 Cabinet department
31 Tosspot's spot
33 Chinese tea
34 Saint of Avila
36 Rights org. estab. 1942
38 Mr. Onassis
39 Rights org. led by M.L.K.
43 M.L.K. and others
47 Writer Rosten
48 ___ rasa
51 Inferential
54 Pizarro's theft from 1-Across
55 Up to, briefly
57 Luau dish
58 Song sung by M.L.K. and others
65 See 71-Across
66 Nonswimmer, maybe
67 Drawn tight
68 Hanging loosely
69 Surrounded by
70 Lawyer: Abbr.
71 With 65-Across, former French president
72 Play areas
73 Sci. class

DOWN

1 Aware of
2 Verne's captain
3 Cancer zodiacally
4 See 15-Across
5 Heathrow, e.g.
6 Onetime Korean president
7 Doll's cry
8 Force out
9 Peace policy
10 Swizzle
11 Handbill heading
12 M.L.K.'s alma mater, 1951
13 Drive recklessly
21 T-shirt size: Abbr.
22 Sch. orgs.
26 New Deal grp.
27 Cry of surprise
28 Bang up
29 Tête-à-tête
30 Ghostlike
32 ___ deferens
35 Marmalade ingredient
37 Outback bird
40 CIX + XLI
41 Potok's "My Name is Asher ___"
42 Miler Sebastian
44 Lady Bird's middle name
45 One that keeps track?
46 Certain skiing events, slangily
48 Wrecker
49 Interstice
50 ___ University (where M.L.K. earned his doctorate)
52 Intersection: Abbr.
53 Candy mint
56 Andean animal
59 Ballyhoo
60 Scent
61 Sell
62 "Drat!" is a mild one
63 Silent
64 Word origin: Abbr.

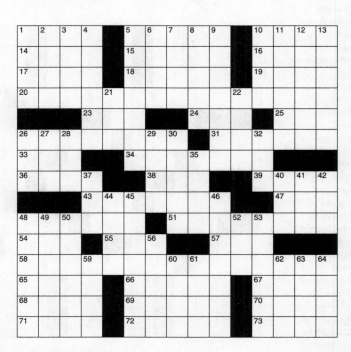

by Walter Covell

ACROSS

1 Snitch
6 1986 World Series champs
10 "You said it!"
14 More washed out
15 Over
16 Pop singer Laura
17 Former Senator Specter
18 Pro ___
19 Bushy hairstyle
20 1970 George Harrison hit
23 Astronaut's "fine"
24 Catch sight of
25 Tropical animals
27 Bill Haley's band
30 Tackle box gizmo
32 Jazz's Kid
33 Stendhal hero Julien
35 Wedding guest
38 Take à la magicians
40 Sinatra standard
42 Wise
43 February forecast
45 Katmandu's land
47 Narcs' grp.
48 "So Big" author
50 Robert Shapiro, e.g.
52 Singer West
54 Pocket bread
55 Shoemaker's helper, in story
56 60's sitcom
62 Composer Janacek
64 Nabisco brand
65 Walkie-talkie
66 Landlocked Asian country
67 Void's partner
68 In ___ (stuck)
69 Scurriers
70 Strike out, as copy
71 Post offices have them

DOWN

1 W.W. II meat
2 On one's guard
3 Woes
4 Shortstop Reese
5 Hemingway and others
6 "Back to the Future" role
7 List shortener
8 Baum dog
9 "In the Heat of the Night" locale
10 Literary olio
11 Lerner-Loewe musical
12 Inaccuracy
13 Crannies
21 British college
22 "Tuna-Fishing" painter
26 Bic products
27 Flatfoots
28 Ph.D. exam
29 1989 Daniel Day-Lewis film
30 Underground way
31 Applaud
34 Sandberg of the Cubs
36 "The African Queen" screenwriter
37 Abrade
39 Track contest
41 Ivy Leaguer
44 Barbershop request
46 Football fling
49 ___ question (certainly)
51 Japanese mustard
52 Perry's secretary
53 City SSE of Buffalo
54 Capitalist tool
57 Quiz choice
58 Terrible rigor
59 Norse chief
60 Supreme Court complement
61 Lays down the lawn
63 Draft letters

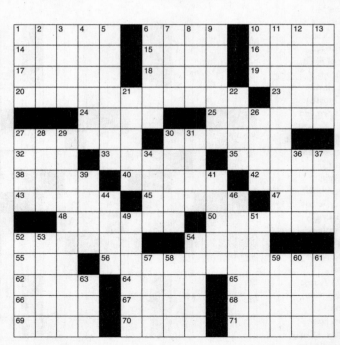

by Gregory E. Paul

ACROSS

1 This might be a lot
5 Paradigm
10 Sprite
13 Word after long or dog
14 Fragrance
15 Compete
16 Sydney of "The Maltese Falcon"
18 Lady of Eden
19 Added too many pounds
20 Displayed contempt
22 Snick's partner
23 Burglarize
26 Bummer
27 Lost Ark seekers?
30 Snatch
33 Where to hang one's hat
36 "Carmen" or "Aida"
37 Moline manufacturer
38 Alluring woman
40 Despondent
41 Upright
42 Goodnight lass
43 Steps over a fence
45 Hush-hush govt. org.
46 Gardener's item
47 ___ Palace
49 Cape Canaveral org.
51 Hardly bold
52 Sandy's barks
56 Interviewer Barbara
59 Restaurant
61 Levin who wrote "Deathtrap"
62 "Of Thee I Sing" role
65 Kind of horn
66 It's enough to bring a tear to the eye
67 Swiftness
68 Owned
69 Neck parts
70 Steps on the evolutionary ladder

DOWN

1 Baseball's Hank
2 Minotaur's home
3 Short jacket
4 Poet Millay
5 Welcome giver?
6 Bruin Bobby
7 Accomplishes
8 Corrects
9 Afterward
10 Landscaping item
11 As we speak
12 Oats, e.g.
13 Urges, with "on"
17 Undress
21 Anxious
24 Texas city
25 Scolds
28 Top-notch
29 Red vegetable
31 Firecracker paths
32 Obsolescent VCR format
33 Letters before omegas
34 Cork's site
35 It was colonized circa A.D. 986
37 Fawn or doe
39 "This foolishness must ___ once!"
44 Kind of cake
47 Canopus's constellation
48 Minor despot
50 Affix, as a button
53 Della of pop
54 Stews
55 "Auld Lang ___"
56 Accompanying
57 Coloratura's piece
58 Cut
60 Turkish honcho
63 Shoe part
64 Printers' measures

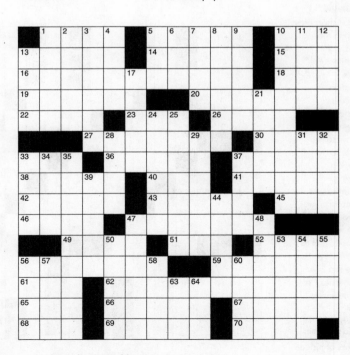

by Sidney L. Robbins

ACROSS

1 Blvd. crossers
4 #2, informally
8 Defeater of Hannibal at Zama
14 Pasture
15 Shakespearean villain
16 Chaucer's ___ Inn
17 Civil war, e.g.
19 List ender
20 Mr. Rathbone
21 Dour
23 Chicago-to-Atlanta dir.
24 Slept "soundly"
26 "Hud" Oscar winner Patricia
28 Snap, crackle and pop, e.g.
34 Criminal charge
37 City on the Mosel
38 Razor sharpener
39 Help in the getaway
41 Architectural piers
43 Location
44 Catcalls
46 Moffo and Magnani
48 In low spirits
49 Fe, fi, fo, fum, e.g.
52 Willing
53 Swimwear manufacturer
57 Perform
60 Pole figure
63 Be unfaithful to
64 "Calm down!"
66 "Life is a bowl of cherries," e.g.
68 White winter coat
69 Primary
70 More than none
71 Clears of hidden problems

72 Rival rival
73 Born

DOWN

1 Neatniks' opposites
2 Ross Perot, e.g.
3 Final authority
4 Cataclysmic
5 Attention
6 Sometimes they're super
7 ___ l'Évêque (French cheese)
8 Not monaural
9 Dozes
10 Olympic basketball coach Hank
11 Buddies
12 Rainbow goddess
13 Garfield's foil
18 Spanish Surrealist

22 One in the running
25 "Dumb ___" (old comic)
27 Plenty
29 Mosque feature
30 Big name in insurance
31 Goddess of discord
32 Least bit
33 Mimicked
34 Indian prince
35 Victim of sibling rivalry
36 Sir Robert of London's bobbies
40 Advanced math
42 "Je ne ___ quoi"
45 Averring
47 Elsa in "Lohengrin"
50 Overacts

51 ___ tide
54 Wharton's Frome
55 Lorna of an 1869 romance
56 Deli phrase
57 Scored a hole-in-one
58 Inner workings
59 Grave
61 Poet Lazarus
62 More than a snack
65 N.Y. school
67 Waitress's bit

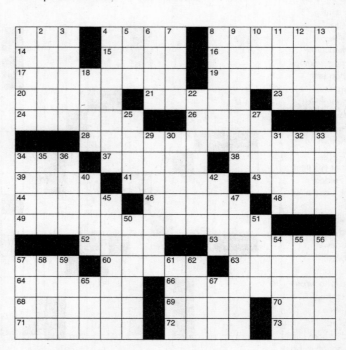

by Richard Hughes

ACROSS

1 Person with a beat
4 Mafia kingpin
8 Keeps one's fingers crossed
13 Voiced
15 Prime draft status
16 Maine college town
17 Deal with quickly
20 Isolate, in a way
21 I.O.U.
22 Phila. clock setting
23 N.F.L. linemen: Abbr.
24 Prince Valiant's firstborn
26 ___ Moines
28 Save steps
35 Point one's finger at
37 Panorama
38 Too
39 Prefix with type
40 Actress Thompson et al.
41 Traveling type
42 Mideast chief
43 "Gypsys, Tramps & Thieves" singer
44 Politico Jackson
45 Is easily riled
48 China's Chou En-___
49 Yang's partner
50 Ancient text "___ Te Ching"
53 They give you a shot in the arm
56 Pre-1917 honcho
59 Guitar feature
61 Be cheated
64 Speechify
65 "Pretty Woman" star
66 "Alas"
67 Morocco's capital
68 Medical suffix
69 Elephant's weight, maybe

DOWN

1 Promising rookie
2 Long-armed ape, informally
3 Islamabad denizens
4 Hold fast
5 Enero to diciembre
6 Fringe benefit, for short: Var.
7 ___ of office
8 Owl
9 Hockey's Bobby
10 Jab
11 Country Slaughter
12 Squeezable
14 "___ Misérables"
18 Allay, as thirst
19 Word before peak or walk
25 Indian rug
27 Wells Fargo vehicles
29 Unconcerned with right and wrong
30 East ___ (Manhattan resident)
31 Substantial, as a meal
32 Seal
33 Exploits
34 Ripped
35 Insipid
36 Peru's capital
40 Unstable person, slangily
44 Coup d'état group
46 Perfumed bag
47 Angles
51 Prefix with meter
52 Versifier Nash
53 Mr. Sikorsky
54 Actress Miles
55 Knife
57 Golden Fleece ship
58 Atlas lines: Abbr.
60 Genetic stuff
62 Amtrak term.
63 Dernier ___

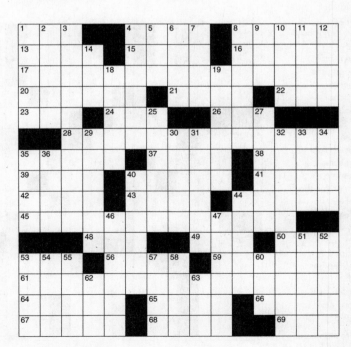

by Ernie Furtado

ACROSS

1 Scenic view
6 Hombres' homes
11 E.T.S. offering
14 Back way
15 "Yup"
16 Four-in-hand
17 John ___
19 Military inits.
20 Kind of diet
21 Tango requirement
22 Cob or drake, e.g.
23 Well-groomed
25 Red wine
27 ___ Mahal
30 Wineglass part
32 Right: Prefix
33 Sharif and Bradley
35 Mr. Fixit
39 Backgammon equipment
40 Attribute
41 River of northern France
42 Sure thing?
44 Mooring site
45 Exposed
46 Campus building
48 ___ Palmas, Spain
49 Guiding light
51 Logs some z's
53 Log some z's
54 Auditor, for short
57 Arabian coffees
61 Skill
62 John ___
64 Half of a 1955 merger
65 Serf
66 Garden bulb
67 At any time, poetically
68 British ___
69 Musial and Laurel

DOWN

1 Like fireplace logs
2 Advertising award
3 "___ right with the world"
4 Relative of the weasel
5 Huxley's "___ in Gaza"
6 Wrigley Field player
7 "Cat on ___ . . ."
8 Third place
9 Overlord
10 "Listen!"
11 John ___
12 Bride's path
13 Bit of dogma
18 Immediately, in the operating room
22 Diacritical mark
24 ___ firma
26 Garland
27 One of Taylor's exes
28 Friend of François
29 John ___
31 1971 hit "___ Bobby McGee"
34 Edit
36 Mountaineer's spike
37 Voyaging
38 Seines
40 Infantry lines
43 Spanish treasure
44 Customs duties
47 Incline
49 Drill grip
50 Halloweenlike
52 Advance person
55 Medicinal tablet
56 Medicinal plant
58 Hawaiian dance
59 "Z ___ zebra"
60 Weakens
62 Upsilon's successor
63 "___ De-Lovely"

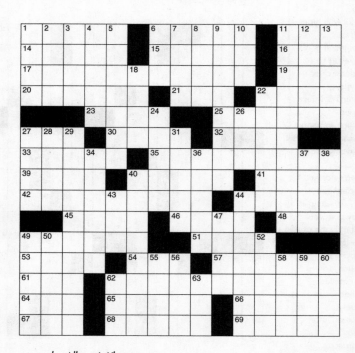

by Albert J. Klaus

ACROSS

1 Office note
5 Buss
10 Fiddler, for one
14 Gung-ho
15 It's grasping
16 Catcher's base
17 Margaret Rutherford film portrayal
19 Skin cream ingredient
20 Peculiar
21 Goddess of discord
22 Apprehend
24 Part of R.O.T.C.
26 1963 Pulitzer biographer Leon
27 Gettysburg general
28 1984 Tom Selleck film
32 Author ___ Chandler Harris
35 Tartan wearer
37 Succinctly worded
38 Worrier's woe, they say
40 Weed digger
41 Vista
42 Tiny: Prefix
43 Poet Sexton
45 Canine command
46 Utah banned in 1882
48 Doctors' org.
50 Wisecrack
51 Lobbed explosive
55 Polemist
58 Humanities
59 Checkers side
60 Auto racer Yarborough
61 Mickey Spillane film portrayal
64 Quiz choice

65 "The Tempest" sprite
66 "Earth in the Balance" author
67 Detected
68 Mary Poppins, e.g.
69 Hoarse horse?

DOWN

1 Thatcher's successor
2 Dodge
3 In one's ___ eye
4 Pindar product
5 Goes on a crash diet
6 One of the Osmonds
7 Heidi's home
8 Newspaper feature: Abbr.
9 Prepares dough
10 Warner Oland film portrayal
11 Part to play
12 Andy's pal on old radio
13 Sugar source
18 Only
23 Takes five
25 Ralph Bellamy film portrayal
26 Chowed down
28 Bonkers
29 Nest site
30 Anglo-Saxon worker
31 Lively dance
32 Start, as a dead battery
33 Mishmash
34 Book after Proverbs: Abbr.
36 ___ at the bit
39 Scalawag

44 Temporal
47 Eddie Rickenbacker, e.g.
49 Arizona city
51 Environmentally-minded
52 Knight's suit
53 Plow man
54 King Edmund's successor
55 "Hamlet" has five of them
56 Pink, as steak
57 Borden product
58 Analogous
62 Kin of a Keogh plan: Abbr.
63 Selznick studio

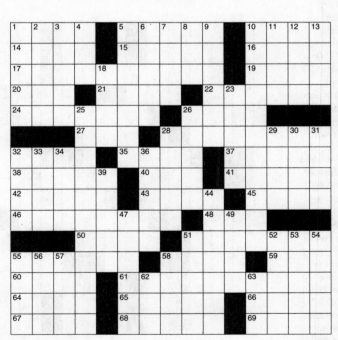

by Gregory E. Paul

ACROSS

1 Kind of acid
6 ___ de Triomphe
9 Doesn't read carefully
14 Another kind of acid
15 Mousse alternative
16 Apportion
17 Santa Clara Co. address
19 Lose one's amateur status
20 Affront
21 ___ Speedwagon
23 Finsteraarhorn is one
24 Property restriction
25 Bowling alley buttons
28 Bobby here
29 Draft org.
30 Obsess
31 Flimflam
32 Carnation spot
33 Less 32-Down
34 Author of 2005's "Juiced"
37 Political pamphlet
39 Skylark maker
40 City near Sparks
41 Tutu event
43 Summit
46 Summer drink
47 "Rabbit Run" and "Rabbit Redux," e.g.
48 "___ Lisa"
49 Colorado Indian
50 Be in the red
51 Bullet type
53 "A Year in Provence" author Peter
55 "Forget it!"
58 Shower time
59 In high spirits
60 Cicero's was Tullius

61 Oozes
62 Make a palindromic living?
63 Upright

DOWN

1 Two Byzantine emperors
2 Some Mideasterners
3 Gets the soap out
4 ___ Joe, of "Tom Sawyer"
5 Refrigerate
6 Census info
7 Room type
8 Bordeaux, e.g.
9 Nigeria's former capital
10 Jeff Lynne rock band

11 "The Godfather" actor
12 "A Chorus Line" song "What I Did ___"
13 Cork in a bottle
18 Zebra feature
22 Summer on the Seine
26 Bigwig
27 Having a market, as goods
30 Speedy
31 Part of a royal flush
32 Batty
33 Splinter group
34 Brontë heroine
35 Void's partner
36 Bedtime for Alonzo
37 Psychological injuries

38 Bureaucracy
41 Theatrical finale
42 Settle a score
43 Still ahead
44 "Hold on"
45 Company with a subsidiary
47 Christmas songs
48 Word before league or domo
52 Sandberg of baseball
54 Back talk
56 Maryland's state tree
57 Three-way circuit

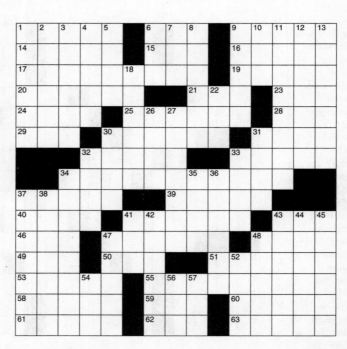

by Matt Gaffney

ACROSS

1 ___ Park, N.Y.
5 Cider season
9 Layer of paint
13 Kind of collar
14 Together, musically
15 1982 Stallone action role
16 Florsheim product
17 With 62-Across, words of caution
19 Sen. Kennedy
20 Mr. Lugosi
21 Athletes' negotiators
22 Spartacus, e.g.
24 Wing: Prefix
26 Intelligent sea creature
28 Early American statesman ___ King
33 Vituperate
35 How some packages are sent
37 Small rail bird
38 Ones who don't enunciate
40 Lashes down
42 City near Monaco
43 Restaurant bill
45 Tropical eels
46 Scouts do good ones
48 Diet
50 Australian marsupial
52 Muse of poetry
55 Catered event
59 Lawyers' degrees
61 Auto part
62 See 17-Across
64 "___ boy!"
65 Sea eagles
66 Actor James ___ Jones

67 "Portnoy's Complaint" author
68 6-3, 4-6, 6-1, e.g.
69 "___ bien!" (French accolade)
70 Carpet layer's calculation

DOWN

1 Pauses
2 Singer Waters
3 With 30-Down, what 17- and 62-Across are
4 A quarter of four
5 Lose color
6 Newspaper publisher Ochs
7 Asylum resident
8 Permit
9 Neanderthals' home
10 Harbinger

11 Adjoin
12 Take these out for a spin
15 Harshness
18 Civil War vets' org.
20 ___ of the ball
23 Canceled
25 Biblical son
27 Sprightly
29 Underworld money lender
30 See 3-Down
31 Chemistry Nobelist Harold
32 Lip
33 Sunder
34 Writer Wiesel
36 Moore of "Indecent Proposal"
39 F.D.R.'s mother, ___ Delano
41 Arrives

44 Protective glass cover
47 On the ___ (declining)
49 In abundance
51 ___ pro nobis
53 Sip
54 D-Day beach
55 Thumbs-up votes
56 Golfer's shout
57 Allen of "Candid Camera"
58 War deity
60 Oil quantities: Abbr.
63 Still and all
64 Mr. Gershwin

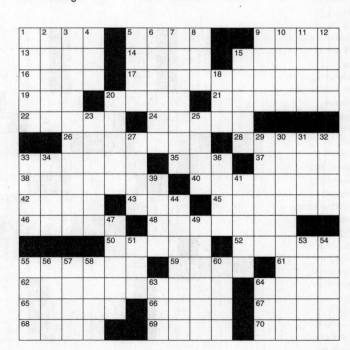

by Sidney L. Robbins

ACROSS

1 Keep ___ (persevere)
5 Sitcom diner
9 Most of Iberia
14 Dial sound
15 In ___ (mired)
16 Glue
17 Goldwyn discovery Anna ___
18 Houston university
19 Get the lead out
20 Geology, e.g.
23 Gibson of tennis
24 Three, in Thuringen
25 Sheepcote comment
28 Baseball's Maglie
29 ___ rod (Biblical item)
31 Airborne particulates
34 Where Lois and Clark work
38 Hook's henchman
40 River, in 9-Across
41 "American Gigolo" actor
42 Athlete's ambition
47 Pitch
48 Post-W.W. II Prime Minister
49 Golfer Woosnam
51 ___ Perce Indians
52 Imitated
55 High points
59 Shakespearean showplace
61 Cousteau concern
64 Pivot
65 Follow
66 Slick vehicle?
67 Seasons on the Somme
68 Gen. Robt. ___
69 Annual tournaments
70 Tweed Ring lampooner
71 Monster's loch

DOWN

1 On the briny
2 Utter
3 Like argon
4 Nine ___ of the law
5 Sicilian port
6 Idle of "Monty Python"
7 Clear
8 Guide
9 Regular programming pre-emptor
10 Peel
11 Naked ___ jaybird
12 1986 hit "___ Only Love"
13 Born
21 Kind of waiter or water
22 Tide type
25 Noted Seine landscapist
26 End of ___
27 Late bloomer
30 Old barroom tune
31 City on the Nile
32 Slew
33 Airport booth leaser
35 Anger
36 Permit: Abbr.
37 "___ hoo!"
39 Pipe connection
43 From whom buyers buy
44 Cult film "___ Man"
45 Superlatively wealthy
46 The brave do it
50 Tidy up
53 Buddy of TV
54 Actress Burke
56 Out-of-date
57 Hears, as a case
58 Graf rival
59 Secluded valley
60 Calendar abbr.
61 Court
62 Start of a cheer
63 Pub brew

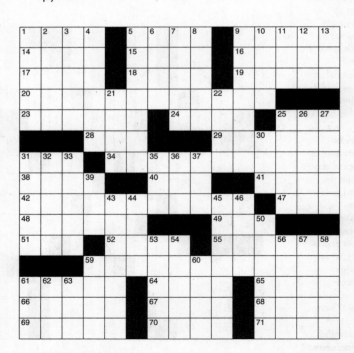

by Randy Sowell

ACROSS

1 March instrument
5 Succeed in life
10 Brigham Young's home
14 Desertlike
15 Sky blue
16 Jesus' attire
17 Date tree
18 Sight at sunup
20 "___ Need Is the Girl" ("Gypsy" song)
21 Nav. rank
22 Hosts' counterparts
23 Nullify
25 Has ___ with
26 Undamaged
28 Hemmed
32 Move like a crab
33 Membership on Wall Street
34 Days of the dinosaurs
35 Card game
36 Salesmen sometimes leave them
39 Neighbor of Md.
40 Touch
42 N.B.A. star Thurmond
43 Escorted
45 Capital of Baja California Norte
47 Early invaders of England
48 Gallup product
49 Father, to Li'l Abner
50 International org.
53 Untold centuries
54 Butterfingers's cry
57 Stamp on some mail
59 Tallow source
60 Baldie's head
61 Individual items

62 Narrowly defeat
63 Jim-dandy
64 Discharge
65 Destine for trouble

DOWN

1 Tidbit in Toledo
2 Caspian feeder
3 Love letter
4 Halsey, for one
5 Most willing
6 Layer in the atmosphere
7 Minks and sables
8 Prince Valiant's firstborn
9 Flare up again
10 Imperativeness
11 Bushy clumps
12 Help in the holdup

13 Chops
19 Night in Nimes
24 Court coups
25 Start of a Dickens title
26 Farrakhan's belief
27 Weeper of myth
28 Seven: Prefix
29 "Hello"
30 Watergate Senator Sam
31 College heads
33 Minute
37 Similar item
38 Light punishment
41 Race track figure
44 Told all about
46 Caesar's partner in 50's TV
47 Most reasonable
49 Displays petulance

50 Sweeping hairstyle
51 Lunchtime
52 Salinger girl
53 Actress Adams
55 "___ My Heart" (1913 hit)
56 Stalk
58 Chang's Siamese twin

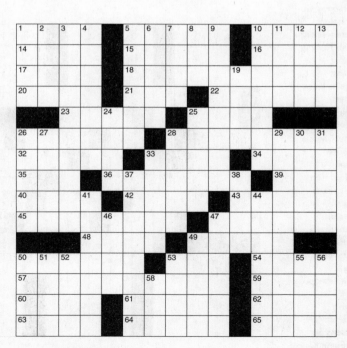

by Bernice Gordon

ACROSS

1 "Lights out" tune
5 U.S. terr. until 1912
9 Dieter's lunch
14 Opposite of sans
15 ___ Raton
16 Noted violinmaker
17 Chaucer's Wife of ___
18 Radar screen image
19 Kayak
20 Pre-Utah team
23 Breakfast-in-bed item
24 Comic Johnson
25 Put on years
26 Hushed
28 Priest's robe
30 Clairvoyance
33 Alcohol awareness org.
35 Writer Fleming
37 Slender
39 Pre-Los Angeles team
42 Elicited
43 Anglo-Saxon letter
44 "Typee" sequel
45 Like Gen. Powell
46 Dadaist Hans
48 Ukr. or Russ., once
50 Some dash widths
51 Eurasia's ___ Mountains
53 King ___
55 Pre-Indianapolis team
61 Furnish
62 Artful
63 Manhandle
65 American Kennel Club rejects
66 Sister and wife of Osiris
67 New York canal
68 Mississippi tributary
69 Mammilla
70 Cell: Prefix

DOWN

1 Bill
2 Trendsetting, perhaps
3 Waned
4 ə
5 This ans., e.g.
6 Kind of bed
7 Colder
8 Revolutionary Emiliano
9 Pouches
10 Key of Mozart's Symph. No. 29
11 Actress Turner
12 The gamut
13 Number after nueve
21 Olive that's very thin
22 TV family, 1952–66
25 Jurassic Park compound
27 Crude container
29 Brief letters?
30 Basic
31 Forte
32 Mexican moola
34 Happy associate
36 Opposite SSE
38 I, to Claudius
40 Mauna ___
41 Reading problem?
47 Loss's partner
49 Orson Welles studio
52 Stood up
54 Early Mexican
55 The Ronettes' "___ Baby"
56 Shade of blue
57 Jump for Oksana Baiul
58 One of the Jackson 5
59 ___ facto
60 Skin abnormality
64 Pope who excommunicated Martin Luther

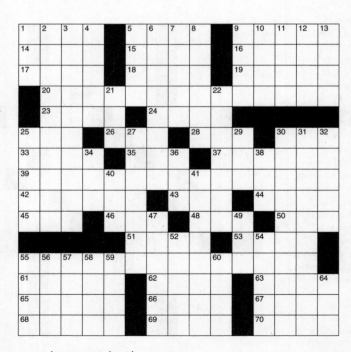

by Martin Schneider

ACROSS

1 Mosquito marks
6 It might be arched
10 Talks gangsta-style
14 "The Tempest" spirit
15 Country path
16 Dutch cheese
17 Pirates' flag
19 Medical researcher's goal
20 Aardvark snacks
21 More than big
22 Onetime hostess Maxwell
23 ___ Alamos
24 Spendthrift
26 Goods cast overboard
30 Halts
32 Kind of label
33 Con artist's aide
34 Baden-Baden, e.g.
37 Popular sort
40 Take advantage of
41 Unaccompanied
42 Clamor
43 Babble
44 In the open, as beliefs
45 High-spirited horses
48 Etch A Sketch, e.g.
49 Mil. defense systems
50 Escargot
53 Book after Job
57 Swag
58 All-for-one feeling
60 It's just for openers
61 Russia's Mountains
62 Make amends
63 Antler wearer
64 Red-ink amount
65 Stared open-mouthed

DOWN

1 ___ California
2 Collar straightener
3 Pinball no-no
4 Slippery fish
5 On the ___ (furtively)
6 Lumps
7 Fury
8 Change for a five
9 "___ of London" (1935 film)
10 Playtime
11 Grown-up
12 Analyze grammatically
13 Libel
18 Kitchen, e.g.
23 Rigging rope
25 In generous amounts
26 Amulet
27 Son of Seth
28 Bathroom feature
29 The sun
30 Glowed
31 Cause of beach erosion
33 Lampblack
34 Use a letter opener
35 Sit
36 Overwhelmed
38 Generous drink serving
39 Mauna ___
43 Ask, ask, ask
44 Like Lindbergh's flight
45 Meal starter
46 Hearty steak
47 Overact
48 Money drawers
51 Roman "fiddler"
52 "Oh, woe!"
53 Movie pooch
54 Mince
55 Fork prong
56 Hightailed it
59 Joker

by Sidney L. Robbins

ACROSS

1 Naïve ones
6 Crosswise to a ship's middle
11 ___ Malaprop (Sheridan character)
14 Massey of "Love Happy"
15 Yankee Yogi
16 Hour on a grandfather clock
17 Twiggy broom
18 End-all's companion
19 One-liner
20 "Unfinished"
23 "Glitter and Be ___" ("Candide" song)
24 Coop denizen
25 State of France
26 Relieved sound
29 "Foucault's Pendulum" author
31 "Ich bin ___ Berliner"
33 Lennon's lady
34 Crack the case
36 More pleasant
40 "Classical"
43 Reddish dye
44 ". . . and ___ grow on"
45 Ingested
46 Approves
48 ___ Lanka
49 Home of Iowa State
50 Severe disappointment
53 Overhead rails
55 Hokum
57 "Kaddish"
63 Great many
64 Coordination loss: Var.
65 Pavarotti, for one
66 Prefix with sex or cycle
67 Beau
68 Mother's-side relative
69 Aerialist's safeguard
70 Clockmaker Thomas et al.
71 M.P.A.A. approved

DOWN

1 Lobster eaters' needs
2 British P.M. Douglas-Home
3 Hokum
4 Ample
5 Dance in Rio
6 A.M. or P.M., e.g.
7 "Pastoral"
8 Remove chalk
9 Francis of "What's My Line"
10 Neighbor of Senegal
11 Strength
12 Cowboy's rope
13 Tourist attraction
21 Ken Follett's "___ the Needle"
22 Bottled spirits
26 Undergrad
27 Apropos of
28 Thug
30 Sister of Euterpe
32 Dope
34 Good, long bath
35 Always
37 Study for finals
38 Villa-building family
39 Hwy. numbers
41 Understood
42 Swizzles
47 Certain sofa
49 Parthenon goddess
50 Kid's shooter
51 Sierra ___
52 Trip that's out of this world?
54 Slightest
56 Aquatic mammal
58 Loses rigidity
59 Actress Carrie et al.
60 ___ the kill
61 Learning method
62 1857's ___ Scott Decision

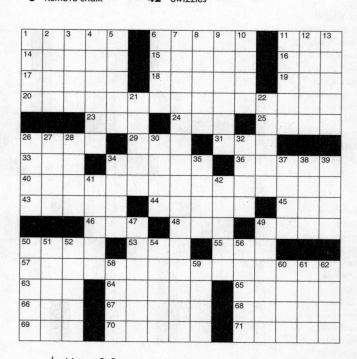

by Nancy S. Ross

ACROSS

1 City near Kyoto
6 Saturate
10 Gallows reprieve
14 Threesome
15 "So long"
16 Cro-Magnon's home
17 Jungle dweller
20 Poet and tentmaker's son
21 It's unique
22 Buckeye State
25 Burn
27 Christopher of "Superman"
31 Campaigned
32 Sunday songs
34 Anticrime boss
35 Zest
38 Synthetic rubber
40 17-Across's formal title
43 Ailments
44 Skirt movement
46 Elderly
47 Descendant
50 Opposite WNW
51 Bowling lane button
53 Playwright David
54 Like target pigeons
55 Pout
57 Mrs. Peel from "The Avengers"
59 Phrase from 17-Across
66 Declare
67 Legal memo starter
68 Kind of eclipse
69 Sneaky look
70 Constellation component
71 Stage direction

DOWN

1 Giant slugger
2 Mexican Mrs.
3 Inner-tube innards
4 Hummer's instrument
5 Edenite
6 Building floor, in London
7 Lummox
8 Johnnie Cochran, e.g.
9 Actress Madeline
10 Ray Bolger film role
11 Astaire specialty
12 "Hail, Caesar!"
13 "___, ma'am"
18 Partner of Crosby and Stills
19 Always, to a poet
22 Assn.
23 Trucker's business
24 Shoe pads
26 More than forgetfulness
28 Old Testament prophet
29 Singer Williams
30 Before
33 Message from the Titanic
36 NBC's peacock, e.g.
37 Uneven
39 Two of these make a qt.
41 Platoon members, for short
42 Coward
43 Deface
45 Relative of "pssst!"
48 Complier
49 Jules Verne captain
52 Craggy peak
54 Kind of cooking
56 Terrorists' weapons
58 Wagon train puller
59 Glove compartment item
60 Mate of 5-down
61 Golf ball's perch
62 Gun lobby grp.
63 Colony pest
64 Scot's denial
65 Flub

by Randall J. Hartman

ACROSS

1 Witches
5 "The Metamorphosis" author
10 Office honcho
14 Skin soother
15 Violas' neighbors in an orchestra
16 It's west of Ark.
17 "Love ___ leave it"
18 "Hungry Like the Wolf" singers
20 Vegetarian's no-no
22 Twixt 12 and 20
23 Actor Dick of "Bewitched"
24 Defense acronym
25 ___ cum laude
27 Freight weight
28 Poet laureate Cecil Day ___
32 Juárez ones
33 Remove vital parts from
34 Scold
35 6 on a phone
36 Bullfighter
38 Actor Cariou
39 San Diego nine
41 Panhandle
42 Fakir's income
43 More cagey
44 "Kidnapped" monogram
45 Eliminate
46 See eye to eye
48 Defect
49 They're far out
52 Candy from a machine
55 1969 hit by the Archies
57 Mr. Nastase
58 Counterfeiters' foes
59 Muslim prince
60 Hawkeye Pierce's portrayer
61 Dian Fossey subjects
62 British tube
63 "A bit of talcum/is always walcum" writer

DOWN

1 Tresses
2 Der ___ (Adenauer)
3 Self-righteous
4 O'Hara's "___ and Soda Water"
5 Minolta rival
6 Adjoin
7 Part of F.Y.I.
8 1977 Oscar actress
9 Six-time Emmy winner Ed
10 Rascal
11 Green pods
12 Dross
13 Mentally sound
19 Casino employee
21 Victorian, for one
24 Distinguished
25 Parotitis
26 Historical record
27 Howard Carter's 1922 discovery
29 Whitman College site
30 Paraphernalia
31 Taste or touch
33 Oil alternative
34 Swamp
36 Wall Street news
37 TV host O'Connor
40 Former White House family
42 Kind of coffee
44 Job hunter's need
45 Slippery ___
47 Calibrate anew
48 Like winter animals
49 Hammett hound
50 Low-cut shoe
51 Double curve
52 Food critic Greene
53 Pots' tops
54 Wife of Jacob
56 Toothpaste type

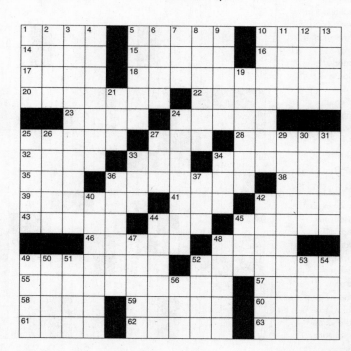

by Gregory E. Paul

ACROSS

1 Friendly
5 Pro ___ (perfunctory)
10 Vegas calculation
14 Lip balm ingredient
15 Ryan or Tatum
16 Urban unrest
17 National monument dedicated 10/28/1886
20 Show respect for
21 Dress
22 Fairy tale villain
25 Spies' org.
26 PC key
29 47-Across poet
35 Farce
37 "___ Like It Hot"
38 Clear the blackboard
39 Ambulance wail
41 Coffee alternative
42 Catnapper
43 First month of the ano
44 Bed-and-breakfasts
46 Kids' indoor ball material
47 Poem inscribed on 17-Across, with "The"
50 Draft org.
51 Place for thieves
52 Send out
54 Lawrence of Arabia portrayer
58 Cry of delight
62 President who dedicated 17-Across
67 Take it easy
68 Adhesive resin
69 Huron, for one
70 Watcher
71 "The Divine Comedy" poet
72 Examine closely

DOWN

1 Do the dishes
2 Palo ___, Calif.
3 Horse with a gray-sprinkled coat
4 "Ditto"
5 Enemy
6 Songstress Yoko
7 N.B.A. official
8 ___ de mer (seasickness)
9 Silverstone of "Clueless"
10 Lunch box treat
11 Grime
12 Biblical verb
13 Eye inflammation
18 Prod
19 Burned brightly
23 Apt. divisions
24 Strong feeling
25 Make pure
26 German city north of Cologne
27 "Rise and ___!"
28 Seven-time A.L. batting champ Rod
30 Prayer responses
31 Elvis ___ Presley
32 Utterly destroys
33 Computer operators
34 Feudal workers
36 First planet: Abbr.
40 Piece of pasta
45 Total
48 Gave a longing look
49 Small, medium or large
53 Turnpike tabs
54 Give a longing look
55 Waiter's load
56 Seep out
57 Finished
59 W.W. II females' service grp.
60 Durante's "___ Dinka Doo"
61 Idyllic place
63 Tax return preparer, for short
64 Actor Chaney
65 Abbr. after a telephone number
66 Eustacia of "The Return of the Native"

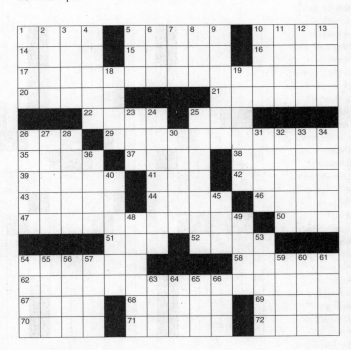

by R. Norris

62

ACROSS

1 Pequod skipper
5 Mizzen and jigger, e.g.
10 Engine disks
14 Lascivious look
15 Abbr. on a record label
16 Skin cream ingredient
17 Song a k a "Somewhere, My Love"
19 Noon, in Nantes
20 Potbelly, e.g.
21 Society page word
22 Black, in poetry
23 1982 Meryl Streep film
27 Gangsta ___
29 Gymnast's goal
30 Word before rod or staff, in Psalms
31 Brother of Jacob
33 Gallery display
35 Prom couples
40 Popular mail order company
44 Look of contempt
45 Bit of paronomasia
46 Floor square
47 Patty Hearst's kidnap grp.
50 Foot in the forest
52 Nile viper
53 Saul Bellow's Pulitzer-winning novel
59 Out of port
60 Hubbub
61 Cowardly Lion portrayer and family
64 Thanksgiving dishes
65 "Anything that can go wrong will"
68 Freudian topics
69 "Green ___"
70 Singer Tennille
71 Lucy's partner

72 "Now you ___, now . . ."
73 Pique

DOWN

1 "___ Well That Ends Well"
2 Miami five
3 Lockheed Martin field
4 Acclaim for Pavarotti
5 Pin location
6 Volcanic fallout
7 Vista
8 Most docile
9 Cry at an awards ceremony
10 Minor role
11 Excuse
12 Oregon Indian
13 English Channel feeder
18 Be Kind to Editors and Writers Month: Abbr.
24 "___ me out"
25 Crucifix letters
26 Jekyll's counterpart
27 Races, as a motor
28 Z ___ zebra
32 Salt Lake City athlete
34 Spigot
36 Dramatize, with "out"
37 Iron man event
38 Wriggly fish
39 Escalator part
41 Approximately
42 Has dinner
43 Hidden catch
48 Alpaca cousins
49 Bring forward as evidence
51 Scheming

53 Did fieldwork?
54 Grammarian's concern
55 Office notes
56 Deep voices
57 Baseball manager Joe
58 Prison protests
62 Punjabi princess
63 Hot Lips Houlihan player
66 Canton-born architect
67 Former White House inits.

by R. J. Hartman

ACROSS

1 Blue-ribbon position
6 Tiny aquatic plant
10 Radar screen dot
14 Thespian
15 "Crazy" bird
16 Moreno of "West Side Story"
17 School essay
18 Pepper's partner
19 "Oh, woe!"
20 Start of a comment by critic George Jean Nathan
23 Like hen's teeth
26 "I surrender!"
27 Part 2 of the comment
32 Washington Mayor Marion
33 Sharpens
34 Puppy's bite
37 Opera singer Pinza
38 Virile
39 Zola courtesan
40 Kind of whisky
41 Ill-fated ship Andrea ___
42 Olympian's prize
43 Part 3 of the comment
45 Atlantic fish
48 Fish-eating hawk
49 End of the comment
54 Helps
55 Natural balm
56 Prefix with -pedic
60 Prefix with logical
61 Not the front or back
62 Arctic, for one
63 Sign gas
64 "___ Dreams" (1994 documentary film)
65 Nairobi's land

DOWN

1 More than hefty
2 "___ bin ein Berliner"
3 Expy., e.g.
4 Hat for a siesta
5 Excessively sweet
6 As well
7 Goof off
8 Game on a green
9 Not pro
10 Intellectually gifted
11 State flower of New Hampshire
12 "Darn ___!"
13 Old hat
21 Joey ___ & the Starliters (60's group)
22 Chicago team
23 Cavalry sword
24 Nutso
25 Eagle's nest
28 Swiss ___ (vegetable)
29 Gin's partner
30 China's Zhou ___
31 Actress Susan
34 Ralph who wrote "Unsafe at Any Speed"
35 Silly
36 Very friendly
38 Dairy farm sound
39 Chief Joseph's tribe
41 Dumbbell
42 Identified wrongly
43 Special boy
44 Overly
45 Beau
46 Rebuke
47 Bucking bronco event
50 "Candy / Is dandy . . ." humorist
51 Mishmash
52 Kind of list
53 Mondale or Quayle, e.g.
57 Countdown start
58 Cow chow
59 Go ___ diet

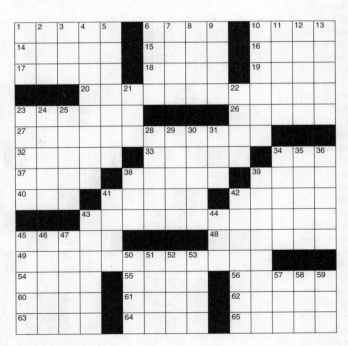

by P. Wilson

64

ACROSS

1 "___ your name" (Mamas and Papas lyric)
6 Fell behind slightly
15 Euripides tragedy
16 Free
17 Forecast
19 Be bedridden
20 Journalist Stewart
21 Rosetta ___
22 1960's espionage series
24 ___ Perignon
25 Quilting party
26 "Drying out" program
28 Umpire's call
30 Tease
34 Tease
36 Standard
38 "The Tell-Tale Heart" writer
39 Lead story in tomorrow's newspaper (!), with 43-Across
43 See 39-Across
45 Gold: Prefix
46 ___ Lee cakes
48 Bobble the ball
49 Spanish aunts
51 Obi
53 Bravery
57 Small island
59 Daddies
61 Theda of 1917's "Cleopatra"
62 Employee motivator
65 Otherworldly
67 Treasure hunter's aid
68 Title for 39-Across next year
71 Exclusion from social events
72 Fab Four name
73 They may get tied up in knots
74 Begin, as a maze

DOWN

1 Disable
2 Cherry-colored
3 Newspaperman Ochs
4 Easel part
5 Actress Turner
6 Ropes, as dogies
7 Place to put your feet up
8 Underskirt
9 First of three-in-a-row
10 Lower in public estimation
11 Onetime bowling alley employee
12 Threesome
13 English prince's school
14 60's TV talk-show host Joe
18 Superannuated
23 Sewing shop purchase
25 TV's Uncle Miltie
27 Short writings
29 Opponent
31 Likely
32 Actress Caldwell
33 End of the English alphabet
35 Trumpet
37 Ex-host Griffin
39 Black Halloween animal
40 French 101 word
41 Provider of support, for short
42 Much-debated political inits.
44 Sourpuss
47 Malign
50 "La Nausee" novelist
52 Sheiks' cliques
54 Bemoan
55 Popsicle color
56 Bird of prey
58 10 on a scale of 1 to 10
60 Family girl
62 Famous ___
63 Something to make on one's birthday
64 Regarding
65 Quite a story
66 Dublin's land
69 ___ Victor
70 Hullabaloo

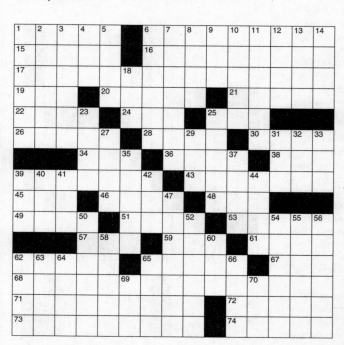

by J. Farrell

ACROSS

1 Garbage boat
5 Ingrid's "Casablanca" role
9 I.O.U.'s
14 Singer Guthrie
15 "Get a ___ of that!"
16 Nouveau ___
17 Nightgown-clad nursery-rhyme character
20 Reverse image, for short
21 ___ the lily
22 Be present at
23 Grow dim
24 Jackie's second husband
25 Heavens
26 Saying of Caesar
31 Banishment
32 Put on
33 No, to Nikita
37 Towering
38 Item
40 Snapshot, Mad. Ave.-style
41 Captain Hook's assistant
42 Tic-tac-toe win
43 Nearsighted Mr.
44 1960 Terry-Thomas film farce
48 Tie the knot
51 Fleur-de-___
52 Bloody
53 Twenty questions category
55 Concerning
56 Alternative to a subway
59 Shakespearean comedy (original spelling)
62 Smooth and glossy
63 Persian sprite
64 Brainstorm
65 "___ la vista, baby!"
66 Former spouses
67 Bruce or Laura of Hollywood

DOWN

1 Cut, as a log
2 Prairie Indian
3 Designer Cassini
4 "Unbelievable!"
5 Fighting ___ (Big Ten team)
6 Lounged around
7 Port ___, Egypt
8 Summer cooler
9 Rex Reed, e.g.
10 Help for the puzzled
11 Clinton staffer Harold
12 Use your brain
13 Squalid
18 "___ at the office"
19 Bandleader Fred
23 Actor Dafoe
24 Door-to-door cosmetics company
26 Docs for dachshunds
27 Quiz
28 Cairo's river
29 Dialect
30 Odious reputation
34 Berra or Bear
35 Prince William's school
36 Grabbed
38 "___ a Mockingbird"
39 Works in the garden
43 French mothers
45 Where Nome is home
46 Pay no heed to
47 Action star Chuck
48 Former 49ers coach Bill
49 W.W. II's ___ Gay
50 Jackknife and others
54 Encounter
55 Wild goat
56 Presage
57 Exploiter
58 Getz or Kenton
60 Imitate
61 Pot top

by S. Spadaccini

ACROSS

1 State firmly
5 Born's partner
9 Famous rib donor
13 Heart
14 Stead
15 Teacake
16 Like Hawthorne's "Tales"
18 Peer
19 "My Fair Lady" scene
20 Second-stringer
22 Five-to-one, e.g.
26 St. Teresa of ___
28 Some stock buys
30 Galley type appropriate for this puzzle?
32 Speaker's place
33 "Darn!"
35 Pretend
36 Addl. telephone off a main line
37 Hamlet
39 Rita Hayworth spouse ___ Khan
40 Page of music
42 Speak to the hard-of-hearing?
43 Dog biter
44 Has contempt for
46 Alternative to Nikes
48 Valued violin
49 Publish lies about
50 Queen ___ lace
52 Short trip
56 Compel
58 Extra-base hit
62 Contract signer
63 Official language of Pakistan
64 Vogue rival
65 Head honcho
66 Tournament passes
67 Fine pajama material

DOWN

1 Official proceedings
2 Wedding exchange
3 The Red
4 45's and 78's
5 Sandwich order
6 ___ Bravo
7 Slippery one
8 Garb
9 Get
10 Gobbledygook
11 Santa ___ (Pacific wind)
12 Sportscaster Allen
15 Sycophantic
17 And more
21 It'll take you for a ride
23 Spelling of "Beverly Hills 90210"
24 "Paradise of exiles": Shelley
25 Workers in stables
27 Soap plants
28 Mexican state
29 " "
31 One-named Irish singer
32 Assts.
34 Oregon's capital
37 Ernest or Julio Gallo
38 Elation
41 Hypnotic states
43 Searches for provisions
45 "Sprechen ___ Deutsch?"
47 Lower California, familiarly
51 Ticket remainder
53 Good fruit with a bad name?
54 Dickens girl
55 Quite a trip
56 Stretch the truth
57 Warbler Yoko
59 Kind of humor
60 Lyric poem
61 School transportation

by E. Lexau

ACROSS

1 One of the Three Bears
5 Dog restraint
10 "___ It Romantic?"
14 Misfortunes
15 Dramatist Edward
16 Swirl with a spoon
17 School cutup
19 Moon goddess
20 Basic belief
21 "You said it!"
22 Garden of Eden man
23 Slept noisily
25 Muscular
27 Pony's gait
29 Like some committees
32 Young 'uns
35 Between-meals eater
39 Hubbub
40 Drink cooler
41 Art student's subject
42 On, as a lamp
43 Pie ___ mode
44 Longtime PBS series
45 Artist Paul
46 Kind of sentence
48 ". . . one ___ two!" (Welk intro)
50 Gobbles (up)
54 Wreck, as a train
58 1970 Kinks hit
60 Poker players' markers
62 Catch cowboy-style
63 "We try harder" company
64 Head of P.E. class
66 ___-majeste
67 "Stand and Deliver" star Edward James ___
68 Mister, in Munich
69 Pretentiously cultured
70 Harvests
71 "That's clear"

DOWN

1 Early Brits
2 Revolutionary hero Ethan
3 City in north Texas
4 Declares
5 Fond du ___, Wis.
6 Scat queen Fitzgerald
7 Manhattan Project project
8 Underground passage
9 Redhead's dye
10 Cuba, e.g.
11 Quiet schoolroom
12 Ship of 1492
13 Coal car
18 Suffix with trick or prank
24 Fashion's Karan
26 Cautious
28 Perfectly
30 "Garfield" dog
31 Pigeon's home
32 Fibber
33 Rights defender, for short
34 Honor for the A-team?
36 Alphabet trio
37 Dance at a Jewish wedding
38 Improve
41 Model ___ Nicole Smith
45 Pakistani port
47 Playwright Sean
49 Oscar ___ Renta
51 Hardship
52 Christopher Morley's "Kitty ___"
53 Highest, in honors
55 Grave matter?
56 River to the Rhone
57 Actor Peter
58 Bit of a song refrain
59 Partner of "done with"
61 "Knock it off!"
65 Road curve

by F. & L. Sabin

68 ☆

ACROSS

1 Help in a heist
5 Neighbor of St. Pete
10 ___ podrida
14 Etna output
15 "Our Town" role
16 Close
17 Cereal "for kids"
18 Pitcher Ryan
19 Restrain
20 John Stuart Mill treatise
22 Senator Hatch
23 Airport sched. abbr.
24 "Erotica" singer
26 Part of a place setting
30 Angola's capital
32 Stinging wasp
34 Amtrak stop: Abbr.
35 Colorless
39 Party to a defense treaty
40 Old-time anesthetic
42 Cunning trick
43 Fluctuate repeatedly
44 West of Hollywood
45 Sadistic sort
47 Diamond arbiter
50 Small fry
51 Spat
54 Early Beatle Sutcliffe
56 Single entities
57 In a precarious situation
63 "Make ___" (captain's directive)
64 Astronomer Tycho
65 Just
66 Scrabble piece
67 Russo and Magritte
68 Christmas tree topper
69 Bullring cheers
70 Idolize
71 Bill Clinton's birthplace

DOWN

1 Like Charlie Parker's sax
2 Farm building
3 Wicked
4 It's hailed by city dwellers
5 Principle
6 Lacking principles
7 Jazz bassist Hinton
8 Schoolyard friend
9 Novelist Rand
10 1963 Drifters song
11 Live's partner
12 What Mr. Chips taught
13 Gladiator's place
21 Nota ___
22 Peculiar
25 Cost ___ and a leg
26 Open carriage
27 Sport shirt
28 Paris airport
29 Rodgers and Hart musical
31 Theater employee
33 Site of Super Bowl XXX
36 Milieu for Lemieux
37 "I cannot tell ___"
38 Hive dwellers
41 Fitted
46 Sundries case
48 "___ Doubtfire"
49 Book before Job
51 Capital just south of the equator
52 "Wait ___ Dark"
53 Supermarket section
55 "___ Eyes" (1969 song)
58 Prefix meaning "one-billionth"
59 Snack
60 Passionately studying
61 Thunder sound
62 Bronte heroine
64 Maidenform product

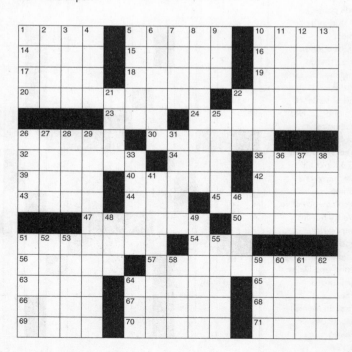

by G. E. Paul

ACROSS

1 Dish of leftovers
5 Ink problem
9 Ill-tempered woman
14 Turkish official
15 Money to buy a car, maybe
16 Kind of fairy
17 1981 Treat Williams film
20 Followers of Xerxes
21 Socks cover them
22 Nevertheless
23 Weep
24 Groups entering Noah's ark
25 Yield, as a dividend
26 Actress Arthur and others
27 Taxi
30 Knight's horse
33 Jai ___
34 Middling
35 1945 Mel Torme song
38 Thin
39 Start of a counting-out rhyme
40 Like an old bucket of song
41 Memorable period
42 E-mail, e.g.
43 "It's freezing!"
44 Fountain order
45 Butt
46 ___ Vegas
49 Mail-related
52 Spy for the U.S.
54 1996 Hillary Clinton best seller
56 Purloined
57 More than ajar
58 ___ of Man
59 Crossed one's fingers
60 Ice block
61 Toot

DOWN

1 One of the Seven Dwarfs
2 Go along (with)
3 Polo or tee
4 Storied boy with silver skates
5 Not sharp, as eyesight
6 Off one's rocker
7 Clods
8 Explosive
9 Ones copying from Dictaphones
10 Pawns
11 Disturb
12 Suffix with kitchen
13 Philosophers' questions
18 Loud insect
19 Michener best seller
24 Moist-eyed
25 Job benefit
26 Mixture
27 Boil or broil
28 "___ forgive our debtors"
29 Former German capital
30 Enticing store sign
31 Ivan or Nicholas
32 Sicilian mount
33 Rocket stage
34 Lead player
36 Compass part
37 Everyday
42 Wet through and through
43 Sheep noise
44 Unfresh
45 Missouri or Delaware
46 Renter's paper
47 Polygon's corner
48 At quite an incline
49 "Nonsense!"
50 Palindromic emperor
51 Halt
52 Superman attire
53 Silver-tongued
55 Weep

by M. Huret

ACROSS

1 Half a school yr.
4 Part of CD
8 Brings home
13 "American Gigolo" actor
14 Capri, e.g.
15 German sub
16 Halo
17 "Coming of Age in Samoa" author
18 Tycoon J. Paul ___
19 60's singer who "walks like a man"-servant?
22 Chinese gambling game
23 Sprinted
24 "Yuck!"
27 Airport abbr.
28 Ancient Brit
31 Actress Reynolds
33 Talks up, so to speak
35 Depend (on)
36 Life-style expert who's a perfect housekeeper?
40 Bargain seeker's event
41 Radio woe
42 Sign of acne
45 Basics
46 ___ Lanka
49 Critic ___ Louise Huxtable
50 Paris's ___ de la Cite
52 Miss Prynne of "The Scarlet Letter"
54 PBS host who's good in the kitchen?
57 Nichelle Nichols's role on "Star Trek"
60 ___ Fein
61 Lariat
62 Folk or rap, e.g.
63 Awestruck
64 Ripened
65 Environs
66 Hankerings
67 Fenced-in area

DOWN

1 "Sunday in the Park With George" painter
2 Gofer's chore
3 Intended
4 Reduce in size
5 "You're clear"
6 Eastern European
7 Lebanese tree
8 Conductor Ormandy
9 Assist in crime
10 Degenerate badly
11 Revolutionist Turner
12 Pigpen
13 Faux pas
20 Fini
21 Young chap
24 Above, in Berlin
25 Decorate expensively
26 "Watch it!"
29 Cartoonist Addams
30 Head, in Italy
32 Bric-a-___
33 Get ready, for short
34 Pierce
36 One of "the help"
37 ___ mater
38 Some prints
39 Older but ___
40 Health resort
43 Walt Whitman bloomers
44 Actor Wallach
46 Moe, for one
47 Begin again, as a debate
48 Annoyed
51 Russell Baker specialty
53 Leftover piece
54 Operatic solo
55 Buster Brown's dog
56 Any day now
57 She played June in "Henry & June"
58 "Ben-___"
59 Exploit

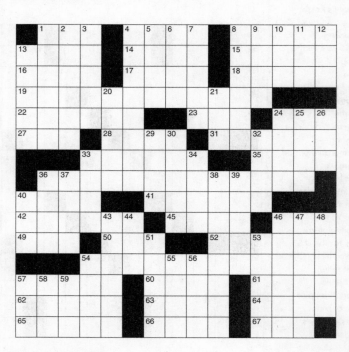

by S. Spadaccini

ACROSS

1 Came apart at the seams
5 Ann ___, Mich.
10 Without
14 Mimics
15 Actress Rigg
16 Show appreciation at a concert
17 Complimentary close
19 ___ mater
20 Smeltery input
21 Old-fashioned poems
22 More sedate
24 Muffin ingredient
26 Shrewd
27 German spa
28 Deli side order
31 Spanish houses
34 Singer Crystal
35 Flamenco exclamation
36 Desertlike
37 Brooklyn's ___ Island
38 Czar before Feodor I
39 Ballpoint, e.g.
40 University of Florida footballer
41 ___ Litovsk (1918 treaty site)
42 Quit for the day
44 Pod occupant
45 Ice skating figure
46 With 43-Down, a complimentary close
50 Old Iran
52 ___ Lee cakes
53 Madhouse, so to speak
54 Guinness and others
55 Complimentary close
58 Madden
59 Formal goodbye
60 Kind of hygiene
61 Lock openers

62 "You've got the wrong guy!"
63 Nota ___

DOWN

1 Forbidden
2 Soap ___
3 Change, as a clock
4 Superlative suffix
5 Sneaker brand
6 Out of bed
7 "A Christmas Carol" cries
8 Singleton
9 Mischievous
10 Musical ladders
11 Complimentary close
12 Dub
13 Box, but not seriously
18 Ordinary bait
23 James who wrote "A Death in the Family"
25 Necklace ornament

26 More coquettish
28 Church law
29 Despondent comment
30 Traveled
31 Andy of the funnies
32 Region
33 Complimentary close
34 "I have the answer!"
37 Native of old China
38 Seniors' nest eggs, for short
40 1958 movie musical
41 Sired, in biblical times
43 See 46-Across
44 Chase
46 Sheik's bevy
47 Sky-blue
48 Fastballer Ryan
49 Holmes's creator
50 Place the car

51 "Night" author Wiesel
52 Diamonds or spades
56 Prefix with meter
57 ___ blind

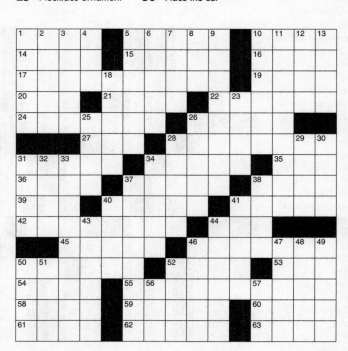

by D. L. Wilk

ACROSS

1 Proficient
6 Greek promenades
11 Vestment for the clergy
14 Rival of Paris
15 Tin Woodman's quest
16 Animal house
17 "Cheyenne" star
19 Prom wear
20 Cause of strain pain
21 Musical Horne
22 Wind dir.
23 Hoosier pro
26 Fr. holy woman
29 Tourmaline, e.g.
30 Jacuzzi
31 Tones
33 "Red Roses for a Blue Lady" singer
36 Swashbuckler Flynn
40 Not a blood relative
42 Sal of song
43 "Lorna ___"
44 Turkish title of old
45 Freudian interests
47 Semiquaver, e.g.
48 "___ alive!"
50 Cone bearer
52 Voting aye
53 Meadowlark Lemon, once
59 Calif. airport
60 Fishing item
61 Military command
65 Friend of Francois
66 1982 Harrison Ford film
68 Last letter in London
69 Charlton Heston epic
70 Certain rocket engine
71 Before, to poets
72 Takes out
73 Hives

DOWN

1 St. Louis landmark
2 Welfare, with "the"
3 Arabian bigwig
4 Helsinki coin
5 Hauling around
6 ___ Na Na
7 "I cannot ___ lie!"
8 Like some buckets
9 Madison Square Garden and others
10 Out of cash
11 Tenochtitlan resident
12 No-goodnik
13 Kind of shorts
18 Got wet up to the ankles
24 Screen presentation
25 Hitter of 755 home runs
26 Side-wheeler, for one
27 Sushi staple
28 Congers
32 Master, in Calcutta
34 Pester
35 Up in the sky
37 Part of the mouth
38 Aware of
39 Lascivious look
41 It may rock you to sleep
46 Ravi Shankar's instrument
49 Cry in "A Streetcar Named Desire"
51 Half of a round trip
53 Shiny coating
54 More hobbled
55 Fe_2O_3, e.g.
56 Don't just stand there
57 "Golden" song
58 1966 hit "Walk Away ___"
62 Pantry pests
63 Spanish muralist
64 Son of Aphrodite
67 Sullivan and Asner

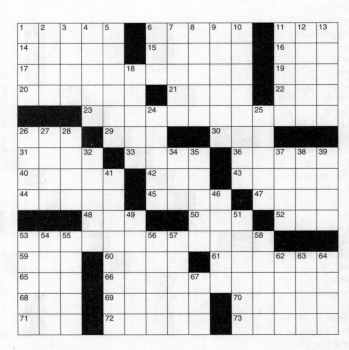

by R. Hartman

ACROSS

1 Shortly
5 NaCl
9 Kind of cheese
14 Letterman rival
15 Wash's partner
16 Noodles
17 Traveling ice-cream seller
20 Acapulco gold
21 Active person
22 Assistants
23 Overcast
25 Denver of "The Dukes of Hazzard"
26 Fire residue
27 Gorbachev policy
31 List components
34 Press, as clothes
35 Prevaricate
36 1976 film about a Little League team
40 Oliver North's rank: Abbr.
41 Syncopated songs
42 Vast chasm
43 Getting a move on
46 Lobster eater's accessory
47 Possess
48 Outstanding athlete
52 On land
55 Not in use
56 "Honest" President
57 1958 best seller set in Southeast Asia
60 Oslo's land, on stamps
61 Scored 100 on
62 Henri's head
63 Brilliantly colored fish
64 Unites
65 Rabbit dish

DOWN

1 Choir members
2 India's first P.M.
3 Tie ___ (get smashed)
4 Yuletide beverage
5 Rushing sound
6 Yellow fever mosquito
7 Lion player of 1939
8 Capote, familiarly
9 Turns bad
10 Head of a pen
11 "Woe ___!"
12 Walk of Fame symbol
13 ___-serif (type style)
18 Ukraine port
19 Central American pyramid builders
24 Mary's pet
25 Snow-cleaning vehicles
27 One of the Allman Brothers
28 Oil of ___
29 Sexist letter start
30 Dick Tracy's love
31 Seven-year phenomenon
32 10 C-notes
33 Wriggly fish
34 Foolish
37 Utter nonsense
38 One who dips out water
39 Subsides, as the tide
44 However
45 Some T-shirts
46 Has an open wound
48 Carrying guns
49 Be silent, in music
50 Diminish in intensity
51 Ask for more Time?
52 "___ added expense"
53 Boutique
54 Wife of Zeus
55 Confront
58 Go off course
59 Part of T.G.I.F.

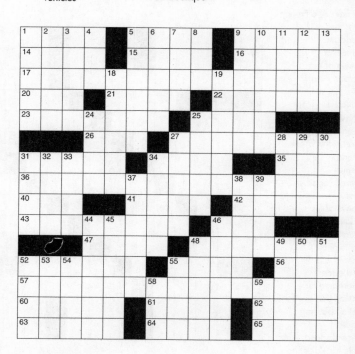

by F. Piscop

ACROSS

1 Charlie Chan portrayer Warner
6 Letters after a proof
9 1908 Peace Nobelist Fredrik
14 Auger or drill
15 ___ Today
16 A McCoy, to a Hatfield
17 747 and DC-10
19 "___ which will live in infamy": F.D.R.
20 Greek earth goddess
21 British submachine gun
22 Temporary stay
26 Literally, face to face
29 Accents in "resume"
30 Precooking solution
31 18-wheelers
32 Founder of a French dynasty
33 Meadow
34 Ninnies
35 Seeker of the Golden Fleece
36 Take ___ at (criticize)
37 Singer Kamoze
38 Spanish gent
39 "Zorba the Greek" setting
40 Genius
42 Attired for a frat party
43 Convertibles
44 Additional helpings
45 Moonshine containers
46 Phnom ___
47 Old adders
49 Nickname for DiMaggio
54 Italian bowling game
55 Record speed: Abbr.
56 Role for Valentino
57 Some sharks
58 Caribbean, e.g.
59 Circumvent

DOWN

1 Goal: Abbr.
2 Singer Rawls or Reed
3 Pitcher's pride
4 Lincoln's state: Abbr.
5 Small parachutes
6 Wicked "Snow White" figure
7 "Como ___ usted?"
8 Prosecutors, for short
9 Skedaddles
10 Like the Incas
11 "Les Miserables" protagonist
12 C.P.R. administrant
13 Deli bread
18 See 30-Down
21 Theda Bara, e.g.
22 With more attitude
23 Pacific islands, collectively
24 Single calisthenic
25 Big name in elevators
26 Gaseous mist
27 Conceptualized
28 Where oysters sleep?
30 With 18-Down, home canning items
32 ___ Major (southern constellation)
35 Army vehicles
36 35-Across's vessel
38 Cheap cigars
39 Apache chief
41 Plaster finish
42 Camp sight
44 Alabama city
46 Pontiff
47 Defense syst.
48 Feathered stole
49 Some namesakes, for short
50 Gretzky's grp.
51 Game, in France
52 Ending with human or planet
53 Supplement, with "out"

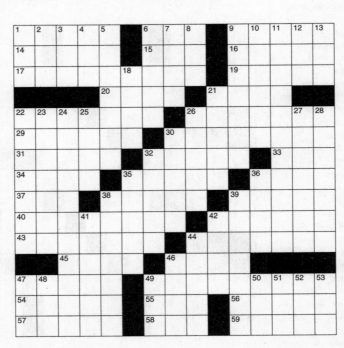

by D. Niles

ACROSS

1 One-named supermodel
5 Ready and willing's partner
9 One praised in Mecca
14 Attorney General Janet
15 Paris's Rue de la ___
16 French valley
17 Tiny tunnelers
18 Ingrid's "Casablanca" role
19 Not evenly padded, as a mattress
20 Like an animal . . .
23 Historical period
24 Use a crowbar
25 Cream puff, for one
29 Miles per hour, e.g.
31 At the present
34 In the future
35 O. Henry's "The Gift of the ___"
36 ___ Gigio (frequent Ed Sullivan guest)
37 . . . vegetable . . .
40 Pulled to pieces
41 Ontario tribe
42 Blabs
43 Muddy home
44 The former Mrs. Bono
45 Better than better
46 Texas patriot Houston
47 Buddy
48 . . . or mineral
55 Assign, as a portion
57 Polly, to Tom Sawyer
58 "The Andy Griffith Show" role
59 River by the Louvre
60 Manuscript encl.
61 What a cowboy calls a lady

62 Flute player
63 New World abbr.
64 Alka-Seltzer sound

DOWN

1 Mideast hot spot
2 Bill of fare
3 The "A" of ABM
4 Pinocchio's giveaway
5 Bee colony
6 Light wood
7 One of "The Simpsons"
8 Test
9 Magnetism
10 Stinky
11 7-Up ingredient
12 Dadaist Hans
13 "Yo!"
21 ___ cotta
22 Of the eye
25 Treaties

26 "The game is ___": Holmes
27 Tale
28 Prefix with photo or phone
29 Indy entrant
30 Tropical fever
31 Lofty
32 Foreign-made General Motors cars
33 Deserving the booby prize
35 Stallion's mate
36 Federal agents, informally
38 Noodlehead
39 New York city
44 Reagan's predecessor
45 Speed demon's cry
46 Precious ___
47 Parson's home
48 Accident on ice

49 "The Right Stuff" org.
50 U.S. Pacific territory
51 Frolic
52 October gem
53 "See you," in Sorrento
54 1996 running mate
55 Nile viper
56 Maui garland

by S. Spadaccini

ACROSS

1 Bushy coif
5 Belle or Bart
10 "Dancing Queen" pop group
14 It goes with runners
15 Army Corps of Engineers construction
16 Burrow
17 In direct competition
19 Mid 12th-century date
20 Long fish
21 Rich Little, e.g.
22 Drew out
24 Three-sided sword
25 Savage
26 One of the Greats
29 Half step, in music
32 Partner of ways
33 Shack
34 Corn crib
35 Early Andean
36 More rational
37 Diplomat's skill
38 Fr. holy woman
39 Burger King, to McDonald's
40 Where the loot gets left
41 Autumn drink
43 Crave, with "for"
44 "You Must Remember This" author
45 Kennel cry
46 Browning automatics
48 Effrontery
49 Menlo Park initials
52 Shut noisily
53 Kind of combat
56 Gambling, e.g.
57 ___ orange
58 Mitch Miller's instrument
59 Squint
60 Firefighting need
61 Old TV detective Peter

DOWN

1 Connors defeater, 1975
2 Hightail it
3 Not imagined
4 Roulette bet
5 Inclined
6 Snicker
7 Say it's so
8 New Deal proj.
9 Jesus Christ, with "the"
10 Virtually
11 One after the other
12 Ill temper
13 Saharan
18 Uses a camcorder
23 Resort near Copper Mountain
24 Soprano Berger
25 Angle on a gem
26 Plain People
27 Slowly, in music
28 In-person, as an interview
29 Sub detector
30 Recess
31 Computer command
33 Wealthy ones
36 Two-headed lady exhibit, e.g.
37 Part of L.S.T.
39 Liturgy
40 Film producer Ponti
42 More tranquil
43 Horse restraint
45 Sheriff's star, e.g.
46 Invitation letters
47 Tennis's Nastase
48 Pesky insect
49 No-no: Var.
50 Erelong
51 First place
54 Simile center
55 Not a sharer

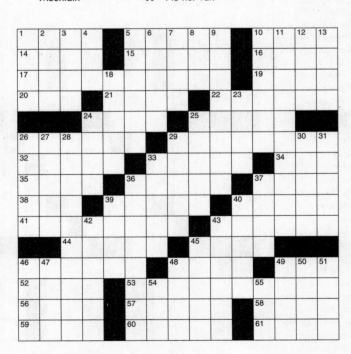

by G. E. Paul

ACROSS

1 Spring
5 Upper-story room
10 Ali who said "Open sesame!"
14 Latin journey
15 Material for uniforms
16 Arab prince
17 Plot size
18 "Greetings!"
19 Suffix with million
20 Chickens that lay brown eggs
23 Toward shelter
24 Old French coin
25 Mad ___ (Wonderland character)
28 Pedaler's place
33 Kitchen garment
34 Interstate hauler
35 Actress Myrna
36 Attraction for winter vacationers in the South
40 ___ Aviv
41 Followers: Suffix
42 ___ the Barbarian
43 Soup crackers
46 ___ Anderson of TV's "Baywatch"
47 Half of dos
48 Play part
49 Easy-gaited saddle horse
57 Pitcher Nolan
58 Bridal walkway
59 Not for
60 "Rule Britannia" composer
61 Like certain dentures
62 Tide type
63 Ground grain
64 Snoozes
65 Remove, in editing

DOWN

1 Pinocchio, at times
2 Make art on glass
3 Pertaining to aircraft
4 Lion or coyote
5 Sorer
6 "One of ___ days, Alice . . ."
7 Money drawer
8 1985 movie "To Live and Die ___"
9 Kind of cap
10 Face hardship bravely
11 She's a sweetie in Tahiti
12 Wren or hen
13 Greek Mars
21 1985 Nicholas Gage best seller
22 Buck's mate
25 Sword handles
26 Cop ___ (negotiate for a lighter sentence)
27 Folklore dwarf
28 Defeats
29 Radio host Don
30 Skirt type
31 Having a key, in music
32 "Laughing" animal
34 Encl. for a reply
37 Jurassic Park revival
38 La ___ opera house
39 One's birthplace
44 Burrow
45 Ending with nectar or saturn
46 ___ that be
48 Rent again
49 Mine vehicle
50 Jane who loved Mr. Rochester
51 Zola novel
52 Ex-Cleveland QB Brian
53 Intuitive feelings
54 Where the patella is
55 And others: Abbr.
56 Properly aged

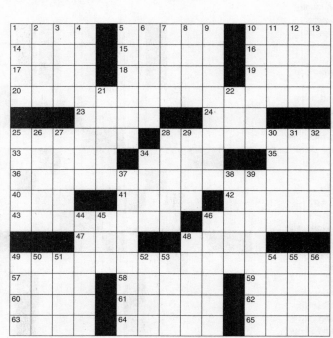

by S. J. Walther

ACROSS

1 ___ blocker
5 Cabbie
9 Desert flora
14 Latin 101 word
15 Cousin of a Tony
16 Autumn color
17 Singer McEntire
18 Give the slip to
19 Squirrel away
20 Alien art form, some say
23 Magnum and others, for short
24 Give it ___ (try)
25 "Now, about . . ."
26 Getaways
28 Hilton Head Island, for one
30 Prohibitionists would like to prohibit it
33 Caught but good
36 Danish money
37 Agreement
40 Interrupt, as a dancer
42 Parroted
43 Fitzgerald and others
45 Bee and snake products
47 Boo-boos
49 Turkey moistener
53 Cartoon skunk ___ Le Pew
54 TV ad
56 "Norma ___"
57 SASE, e.g.
59 Fruit pastry
62 Ravel work, with "La"
64 Legal scholar Guinier
65 Villa d' ___
66 "Give peace ___ time, O Lord": Morning Prayer
67 Prime time hour
68 Mets stadium
69 Gently gallops

70 Pub round
71 Like a Granny Smith apple

DOWN

1 Where train commuters drink
2 Come to the fore
3 No-nos
4 Pronto!
5 Kind of medicine
6 Call off a takeoff
7 50's western "The ___ Kid"
8 Ship's central beam
9 Russian horseman
10 Take steps
11 Auto disassembly site
12 Actress Hatcher
13 Gets one's goat
21 Singer Irene
22 Building wing
27 Quagmire

29 Recorded
30 Point after deuce
31 Single
32 Conducted
34 Disposable diaper brand
35 Bordeaux summer
37 Foot: Lat.
38 The works
39 Carriage horse sound
41 People who don't count
44 Evening meals
46 ___ Hari
48 Each
50 Country singer Yearwood
51 Resurrection Mass day
52 Warm up again
54 Escargot
55 Tubular pasta

57 Stephen King topic
58 Prefix with second
60 Arm bone
61 Hornets' home
63 Take to court

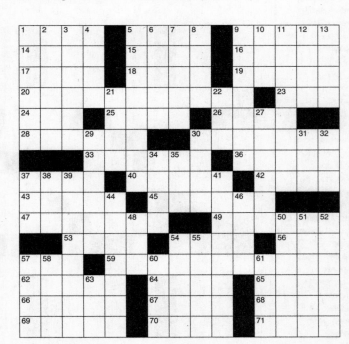

by E. C. Gorski

ACROSS

1 Wood-turning tool
6 Welcome smell
11 Undergrad degrees
14 Disney mermaid
15 Site of golfing's Ryder Open
16 Genetic trait carrier
17 Make an error
19 Consume
20 Part to play
21 Teacher in a turban
23 Conciliate
27 Gotten back, as land in battle
29 Villain
30 Capital of Tasmania
31 Welles of "Citizen Kane"
32 Golden Horde member
33 Premium cable channel
36 Diana of the Supremes
37 Munchhausen's title
38 Lima, e.g.
39 Suffix with superintend
40 Rubbernecker
41 Fanny ___ of the Ziegfeld Follies
42 Area of Manhattan
44 Lighthouse light
45 Artist's studio
47 Make manhattans and such
48 Ear parts
49 Is up
50 Zoo bird
51 Be outrageous
58 ___ room
59 Deceive
60 Charge
61 "For shame!"
62 Mystery writer's award
63 Nairobi's land

DOWN

1 Terhune's "___: a Dog"
2 Opposite of "Dep." on a flight board
3 Tijuana uncle
4 With it, 40's-style
5 It loops the Loop
6 Dancer Astaire
7 Caftan
8 ". . . man ___ mouse?"
9 ___ de mer
10 Selected athlete
11 Get a party going
12 "What's in ___?"
13 Luxurious sheet material
18 Hydrant hookup
22 Card game for two
23 Dean Martin song subject
24 Juan of Argentina
25 Not take responsibility
26 1961 space chimp
27 Copter part
28 Israeli statesman Abba
30 Quarters in a sultan's palace
32 Grow narrower
34 Breakfast sizzler
35 Upturned, as a box
37 Cotton bundle
38 Baby sitter's nightmare
40 Chewy part of meat
41 Bananas
43 Hearty drink
44 Alternative to a shower
45 With ears pricked
46 Weighty books
47 Ulan ___, Mongolia
49 ___ carotene
52 Help
53 Beer barrel
54 Feed lines to
55 Massachusetts cape
56 Braggart knight of the Round Table
57 H, to Greeks

by C. F. Murray

ACROSS

1 Slam-dunks
5 Stiller and ___
10 Prefix with business
14 Like Nash's lama
15 Waters of song
16 Amorphous mass
17 1935 Cole Porter song
20 Pundit
21 Olio
22 Disney's "___ and the Detectives"
25 Vietnam's Ngo ___ Diem
26 No longer hold up
29 F. Scott Fitzgerald had one: Abbr.
31 New York's ___ Island
35 Swellhead's problem
36 Number of mousquetaires
38 Invited
39 Unofficial Australian "anthem"
43 Anon's partner
44 ___ objection (go along)
45 Nurse's bag
46 Lax
49 Garden tool
50 Molly Bloom's last word in "Ulysses"
51 Pot builder
53 Torture chamber item
55 Well-to-do
59 Gut-wrenching feeling
63 1939 Andrews Sisters hit
66 ___ ideal (perfect model)
67 "Camelot" tunesmith
68 Mariner Ericson
69 Memo abbr.
70 Winter hazard
71 Advanced

DOWN

1 Steven of Apple computers
2 Once more
3 Prefix with phone
4 Ooze
5 Encountered
6 Biblical verb ending
7 "Beg your pardon"
8 Bridge action
9 One of the Carringtons, on "Dynasty"
10 Largest of the United Arab Emirates
11 Fluent
12 Author Jaffe
13 "___ to differ!"
18 Pacific Fleet admiral of W.W. II
19 Lady's partner
23 Letters from Calvary
24 Den fathers
26 Drain
27 Century plant
28 Automaton
30 Go-getter
32 Loquacious
33 Jockey Arcaro
34 ___-foot oil
37 Daub
40 Demonstration test
41 Singer Paul
42 Cobbler's tip
47 Slight
48 Base runner's stat
52 Register
54 Small hill
55 "Dancing Queen" pop group
56 Podiatrists' concerns
57 Potential Guinness Book entry
58 Shade giver
60 Open delight
61 Scrape, as the knee
62 Electee of 1908
64 Female with a wool coat
65 Tennis call

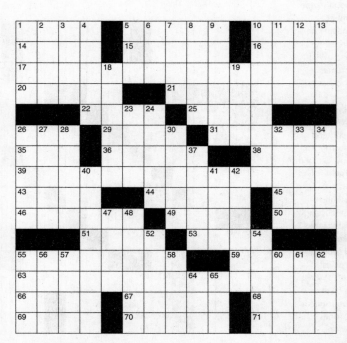

by A. S. Verdesca

ACROSS

1 Courtyards
6 ___ d'etat
10 Part of a gateway
14 Middays
15 Facilitate
16 Denver's home: Abbr.
17 Disoriented
20 Dancers Fred and Adele
21 ___-Japanese War
22 Actor Sparks
23 ___ end (very last part)
25 Prime-time hour
26 Soviet labor camp
30 Party to a defense pact
31 Spirited horse
32 Prophet who anointed Saul
34 Mimic
37 Disoriented
40 Jet to Heathrow
41 Vigorous
42 Actress Spelling
43 Operatic prince
44 Dead, as an engine
45 Had been
48 Guinness Book suffix
49 One of the Gershwins
51 Once more
53 Captain Picard series
58 Disoriented
61 State south of Ky.
62 Kind of smasher
63 Sharp as ___
64 Chair
65 They hold hymnals
66 Where Seoul is

DOWN

1 Paul who sang "Having My Baby"
2 Shipping units
3 Cheer (for)
4 Andean of old
5 Inquiring
6 Relinquished
7 Schmoes
8 G.I. entertainers
9 Each
10 Rights protection grp.
11 Chicken house
12 In the ball park
13 Board, as a trolley
18 "Able was I ___ . . ."
19 Historic county of Scotland
23 Botches
24 Native Alaskan
26 Wanders (about)
27 "Exodus" author
28 Endure
29 Roseanne's network
30 Love, in Lourdes
32 Urban woes
33 Monastery V.I.P.
34 Over
35 Where the Amazon originates
36 Make a change for the verse?
38 China and environs, with "the"
39 One ___ time
44 Noted site of Egyptian ruins
45 Floats gently
46 Be of one mind
47 Finnish bath
49 News paragraphs
50 "Far out"
52 "Money ___ everything!"
53 Pack
54 Dog in Oz
55 Bring up
56 Suffix with exist
57 America's first commercial radio station
59 Seance sound
60 Dined

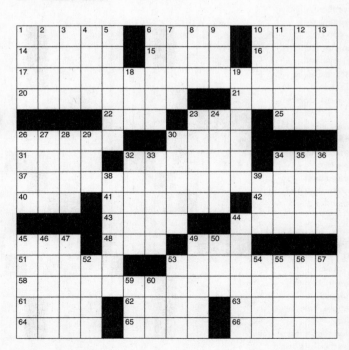

by S. L. Robbins

ACROSS

1 Rushes (along)
5 Amassed
10 They cover Highland heads
14 Neglect
15 Mes numero uno
16 "In a cowslip's bell ___": "The Tempest"
17 One nourished by daydreams?
19 Rotten to the ___
20 One of "Them!" things
21 Author O'Brien
22 Ready for framing
24 Genealogical chart
25 New Rochelle college
26 One who counts calories?
32 Perspiration perforations
33 Alternative to a watering can
34 Khan married to Rita Hayworth
35 Detective Charlie
36 Dress style
38 Classic art subject
39 Elephant's weight, maybe
40 Israeli Abba
41 "For ___ sake!"
42 One with a high-iron diet?
46 Hollywood giants?
47 Jemima, for one
48 Farm trough
51 ___ .45
52 Dallas school, for short
55 Strip of wood
56 One fond of dining on tongue?
59 Florence's river
60 Destroy
61 Motion supporters
62 High schooler's test, briefly
63 Went out with
64 Key letter

DOWN

1 "J'accuse" author
2 Springsteen's "___ Fire"
3 English P.M. called "The Great Commoner"
4 Alphabet trio
5 Carolina river
6 More ridiculous
7 "I ___ Song Go Out of My Heart"
8 Before, to a poet
9 Member of Alice's tea party
10 Popular breath mint
11 Loads
12 Slough
13 Burpee's bit
18 Some Bosnians
23 ___ Morrow Lindbergh
24 Feds
25 Clothes presser
26 Not at all
27 Heavens: Prefix
28 Tableware
29 ___ cuisine
30 Presbyter
31 Deli loaves
32 Election numbers: Abbr.
36 Sucked up
37 Statutes
38 Its eye is needed in a "Macbeth" recipe
40 Slight advantage
41 Sophia's Carlo
43 Boiling mad
44 "Tao Te Ching" author
45 Quieted
48 Part of an envelope
49 Auricles
50 Lab burner
51 Layer
52 Hebrides island
53 Make the acquaintance of
54 Twinkling bear
57 Man-mouse link
58 Taxi

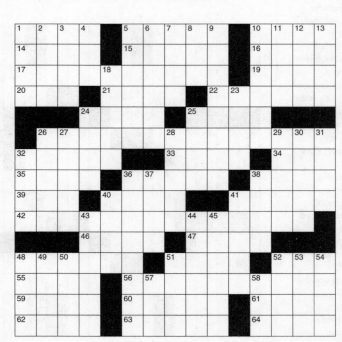

by J. Schmalzbach

ACROSS

1 Poverty
5 Mutual of ___
10 Track tipster
14 Neighborhood
15 Artist Bonheur and others
16 Like Solomon
17 Watch face
18 Whitney's partner in airplanes
19 Pizazz
20 1970's New York Knick's nickname
23 Western alliance: Abbr.
24 Sidestep
28 Grotto
32 20- and 51-Across, e.g.
35 States firmly
36 To ___ (precisely)
37 "___ the season to be jolly"
38 Hank Ketcham comic strip
42 Purpose
43 Harrow's rival
44 Dog: Fr.
45 When American elections are held
48 Rio ___ (border river)
49 Take care of, as duties
50 Nearly worthless coin
51 1960-66 N.B.A. scoring leader, informally
59 Jellystone Park bear
62 "I don't give ___!"
63 Scent
64 G.I. addresses
65 Jazz singer Vaughan
66 Burn soother
67 Didn't part with
68 Pickpocketed
69 Physics unit

DOWN

1 Walk in the baby pool
2 La Scala solo
3 Not distant
4 Six-foot or more
5 Annie, e.g., in the comics
6 Folkways
7 "Rush!"
8 Abhor
9 30's movie dog
10 Midnight
11 Source of Rockfeller money
12 Red, white and blue initials
13 Hamilton's bill
21 Trunks
22 Seminary subj.
25 Reach
26 Cleared, as a winter windshield
27 Ancient Palestinian
28 West Pointers
29 Boulevard
30 Buyer
31 Suffix with east or west
32 One of the Three Musketeers
33 MTV's target viewer
34 Haw's partner
36 Bar member: Abbr.
39 Poseidon's realm
40 Pale colors
41 Shelter grp.
46 Double curve, as in yarn
47 "How ___ love thee? Let me . . ."
48 "Faust" dramatist
50 Sand bar
52 Sweetheart
53 "Anything but ___!"
54 Bullfight bull
55 "The Wind in the Willows" character
56 Without thought
57 Diving bird
58 Chestnut or walnut
59 Talk, talk, talk
60 Unlock, in poetry
61 Republicans, collectively

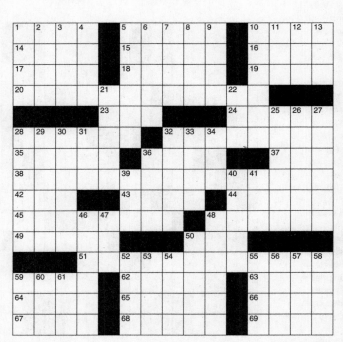

by G. E. Paul

ACROSS

1 Pitchers
6 Take to the dump
11 Say "pretty please"
14 Republican politico Alexander
15 Skip the big wedding
16 Genetic letters
17 1978 Faye Dunaway film
20 I.B.M. or 3M, e.g.: Abbr.
21 In this place
22 Taboos
23 ___ of war
24 Luxuriate, as in the sun
25 Tone down
26 Incredible bargain
28 Boeing product
29 The "I" in T.G.I.F.
30 George Bush's home now
34 Peer Gynt's mother
35 1932 Will Rogers film
37 Tofu source
38 Late singer named for a Dickens character
39 Midmorning
40 Douglas ___
41 Adagio and allegro
45 Pennsylvania, for one
47 Food inspection inits.
50 Suffix with convention
51 Kind of closet
52 Italian princely family name
53 Mata ___
54 1948 Ava Gardner film
57 N.Y.C. subway operator

58 Olympic judge
59 Come up
60 Prodigy competitor, for short
61 Used colorful language
62 40- and 51-Across, e.g.

DOWN

1 Puts into office
2 Exit
3 Come out
4 Bronchitis symptom
5 Full house sign
6 Tennis's Monica
7 Co-worker of Lois and Jimmy
8 Libertine
9 30-day mo.
10 Subject for George Washington Carver
11 Wave, as a weapon

12 Along the way
13 Helium and neon, e.g.
18 Mortgage agcy.
19 Teeming group
24 Hard punch
25 French assembly
27 On-board greeting
28 Bishop of old TV
31 Loosen, as laces
32 Recipe directive
33 "Long" or "short" amount
34 "Don't look ___ like that!"
35 Fait accompli
36 Singer Coolidge
37 53 minutes past the hour
39 Puget Sound city
40 Frenzies
42 Villain
43 Look over

44 Record-setting van Gogh canvas
46 ___ King Cole
47 Fallen house of literature
48 Squirrel away
49 Rock's ___ Leppard
52 Outside: Prefix
53 Munchen Mr.
55 Detroit labor grp.
56 Grape masher's work site

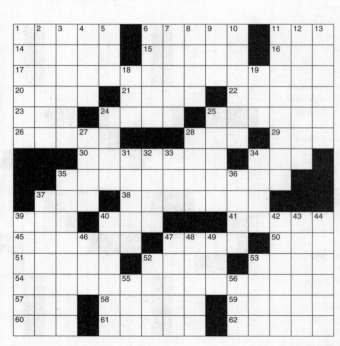

by E. C. Gorski

ACROSS

1 Garb for Superman
5 Ice cream dessert
10 Work detail, for short
14 Singer Guthrie
15 Ness of "The Untouchables"
16 ___ Strauss (jeans maker)
17 What a ghost may give you
19 Coup d'___
20 Boundary
21 Meat cuts
22 Stockholmer
23 Wise one
24 Pay no attention
26 Georgia city where Little Richard was born
29 Western hero
31 Keeps away from
33 "Whose Life ___ Anyway?" (1981 movie)
34 Suffix with cash
37 Factory on a stream
38 Department at an auto shop
40 Fairy tale starter
41 Tally (up)
42 Bundled cotton
43 "Well said!"
45 Honkers
48 A Musketeer
49 Pass ___ (make the grade)
50 Poll amts.
52 Bar for a bird
53 California lake resort
55 Notwithstanding, briefly
58 Actress Chase
59 With feet pointing in
61 Above, in Berlin
62 Not moving
63 Singer Fitzgerald
64 Articulates
65 Go along (with)
66 Enemy's opposite

DOWN

1 Hamster's home
2 "East of Eden" brother
3 Slog (through)
4 Dawn goddess
5 Obscure
6 Hardy and North
7 Bearing
8 Most domineering
9 Numerical ending
10 Quite a few, after "a"
11 "Network" co-star
12 Dodge, as a question
13 Commend
18 African antelope
22 Perturbed state
23 Loam
25 Grain for grinding
26 Baby doll's cry
27 Enthusiastic
28 One way to quit
30 Personnel person
32 Outpouring
35 Reverberate
36 "Cheers" actor Roger
39 Emulating Paul Revere
40 Inning parts
42 This and that
44 Granola-like
46 Katharine Hepburn has four
47 Globe
49 Opera star Nellie
51 "Veddy" British actor Robert
52 Papal name
54 Finish for teen or golden
55 Auto commuter's bane
56 "War is ___"
57 Singer Anita
59 Actress Zadora
60 Wonderland drink

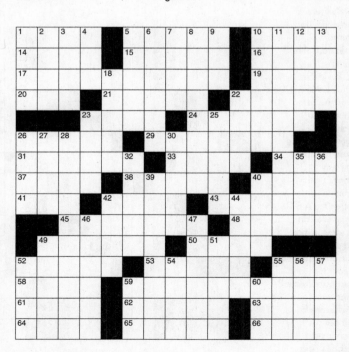

by S. Spadaccini

ACROSS

1 Poland's Walesa
5 Fine violin
10 With 39-Across, featured boxing match
14 "As Long ___ Needs Me" ("Oliver!" song)
15 Two-door
16 Capital on a fjord
17 Gallows reprieve
18 Quite healthy
20 Eternally, to poets
21 Downwind
22 "We ___ the World"
23 Not firsthand
25 Biting
29 Patisserie employee
30 Application information
31 Downhill runner
33 Amusement park features
35 Uncles and others
36 Around
38 "___ Ruled the World" (1965 hit)
39 See 10-Across
41 Rope-a-dope exponent
42 Angers
45 Angers
46 Rural way
48 Comes to the rescue
50 Teaches the A B C's
51 Self-defense art
54 Like some humor
55 Kind of chop
56 Kovic of "Born on the Fourth of July"
57 "Designing Women" co-star
61 Pinochle combo
62 Food bar
63 An archangel
64 Baseball's Rose
65 Talon
66 Litigants
67 Hullabaloo

DOWN

1 Light in a light show
2 Lauder of cosmetics
3 "The Most Beautiful Girl" singer
4 "Yo!"
5 Tackle box gizmos
6 "And so ___"
7 Hold sway over
8 Imitate
9 Spectacular failure
10 Part of MOMA
11 "Unaccustomed ___ am . . ."
12 Spot in the mer
13 Visual O.K.
19 To avoid the alternative
21 Parliamentary stand
24 Current status
25 Tax filer's dread
26 1978 Gerry Rafferty hit
27 Ammonia-derived compound
28 Parts of dollars
30 Played a flute in a march
31 Temporary protectors
32 New Hampshire's state flower
34 Actress Bonet and others
37 Colorado city
40 "I saw," Caesar-style
43 Oedipus' foster father
44 Marine fishes
47 Servilely defer (to)
49 H-L connectors
51 Wild card
52 Conductor Georg
53 Secondary to
55 ___-dieu (pew part)
57 Medic
58 Angled annex
59 Pasture
60 It neighbors Braz.
61 AWOL hunters

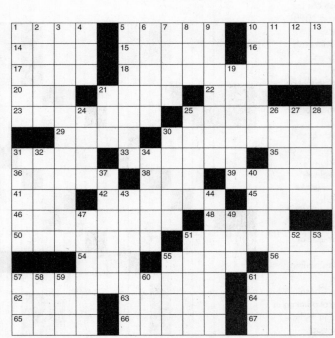

by T. W. Schier

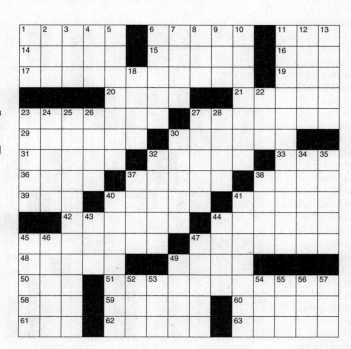

ACROSS

1 Desert plants
6 Swap
11 Stomach muscles, for short
14 Extraterrestrial
15 King or queen
16 Do some soft-shoe
17 Big name in video rentals
19 Kimono accessory
20 Musical partner of Crosby and Stills
21 Madison Avenue worker
23 Big monkeys
27 French artist Henri
29 Adjusts to fit
30 Extreme cruelty
31 Religious factions
32 Top floor
33 Rainbow shape
36 Lodge members
37 Air raid alert
38 Words of comprehension
39 Tiny bit, as of cream
40 Asia's ___ Peninsula
41 Bus station posting: Abbr.
42 Mickey of "National Velvet"
44 Word said to a photographer
45 Split with a hatchet
47 Scorched
48 Contract with a car dealer
49 Limerick, e.g.
50 Bic filler
51 Yegg
58 "We're number ___!"
59 Eskimo boat
60 Lariat's end
61 Neighbor of Isr.

62 Little finger
63 Soaked

DOWN

1 Quick way around town
2 The whole shooting match
3 A.F.L.'s partner
4 Gumshoe
5 Tied up
6 Supporting beam
7 "High priority!"
8 Supermodel Carol
9 Ruby or Sandra
10 Unpredictable
11 Cyclotron
12 Rum cakes
13 Vertebra locale
18 Prohibits
22 Malign, in slang
23 Established

24 Writer ___ Rogers St. Johns
25 Exhausting task
26 Chooses
27 Chum, to a Brit
28 Tennis score
30 Homeless animal
32 Felt crummy
34 Pee Wee of Ebbets Field
35 Yielded
37 Having one's marbles
38 Cake finisher
40 Advances
41 Tribal healers
43 Western treaty grp.
44 Sonny's ex
45 Advertising awards
46 Comedian Bruce
47 Overly self-confident
49 Mountain

52 "___ Blue?" (1929 #1 hit)
53 Five smackeroos
54 Dove sound
55 Keystone character
56 Sixth sense, for short
57 Juan Carlos, e.g.

by F. Piscop

ACROSS

1 Anesthetize, in a way
4 Some chain clothing stores
8 Video game hub
14 Play the part
15 Zone
16 Stops the tape temporarily
17 "Little" extraterrestrials
19 Passe
20 Had a bug
21 Inspirationalist Norman Vincent ___
23 Before, in verse
24 Home on the Black Sea
26 Smart-alecky
28 Pop duo with the album "Swamp Ophelia"
34 Reply to a masher
38 Satellite ___
39 Bunk
40 Actress Anderson
41 Newton or Stern
43 Actress Thurman and others
44 Small choir
46 Outfielder's cry
47 Oct. precursor
48 Drinks with gin, Cointreau and lemon juice
51 Greeting at sea
52 Undignified landing
56 Hardly Mr. Right
59 Facilitates
62 Unpaid factory worker
64 "All ___!"
66 Some Gainsborough forgeries
68 Ice cream parlor order
69 Two-wheeler
70 Sometime theater funder: Abbr.
71 Be at
72 French holy women: Abbr.
73 Blow it

DOWN

1 Crazy (over)
2 Pungent
3 Inscribed column
4 Leader called Mahatma
5 Tattoo place
6 Coop sound
7 Psychologically all there
8 Noted Harlem hot spot, with "The"
9 Durham's twin city
10 Bossy's chew
11 Connors opponent
12 ___ John
13 Isabella d'___ (Titian subject)
18 Continental trading org.
22 Khyber Pass traveler
25 1941 Glenn Miller chart topper "You ___"
27 Reverent
29 Lets down
30 "Let me repeat . . ."
31 Where the Vatican is
32 Giant hop
33 Method: Abbr.
34 Leisurely
35 Ness, for one
36 One doing a con job?
37 Michelangelo masterpiece
42 So-so grades
45 Iran's capital
49 Stinking rich
50 Shopping binges
53 Defensive tennis shot
54 Have ___ to pick
55 One who's not playing seriously
56 Home for la familia
57 Go up against
58 Word of warning
60 Drops off
61 Cut
63 Pre-1917 ruler
65 Fruit juice
67 Hawaiian music maker

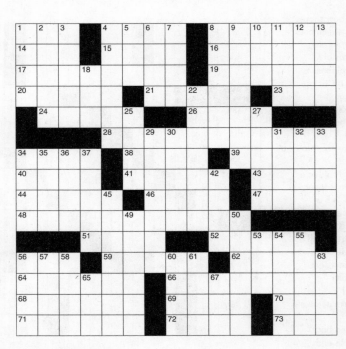

by E. C. Gorski

ACROSS

1 Ravioli base
6 Numbered hwys.
10 Nicholas was one
14 Sour
15 The Emerald Isle
16 "What's ___ you?"
17 18-wheelers
18 Communication means for computer-phobes
20 Grotesque imitation
22 Eat like a rabbit
23 Trees with cones
24 Tries again
25 Cornell's home
27 Passover event
28 Spanish gold
29 Moral principle
31 Convened again
35 Eggheady sort
37 "Cheers!" in Cherbourg
39 Dumb ___ (scatterbrain)
40 Length of yarn
42 Spud
44 Q-U link
45 Agrees (with)
47 Bang and buzz, e.g.
49 Graphed
52 "Lorna ___" (1869 romance)
53 Reddish brown
54 Comes to light
57 Communication means at the office
59 Eat away
60 Once, once
61 Blue-pencil
62 "The Thinker" creator
63 Henna and others
64 Old newspaper section
65 Sugary

DOWN

1 Auld lang syne, with "the"
2 Perfect server
3 Communication means at sea
4 "Jeopardy!" staple
5 "___ makes the heart . . ."
6 Takes five
7 Minuscule
8 Period of history
9 Trawled
10 Having trees
11 Knifes
12 Like Pisa's tower
13 Parts
19 Pepsi bottle size
21 Train reservations
24 Split the cards again
25 Charged particles
26 "Star ___"
27 "___ Marner"
30 More than disliked
32 Communication means for emergencies
33 Language spoken in Dingwall
34 Does lacework
36 Upsets
38 Jose Carreras, for one
41 British fertilizer
43 Ones at the top of their business?
46 Stapleton Airport site
48 Lined up
49 Pent up
50 "Faster!"
51 Belittle
52 Because of
54 Tizzy
55 Actress McClurg
56 Faxed
58 Bachelor's last words

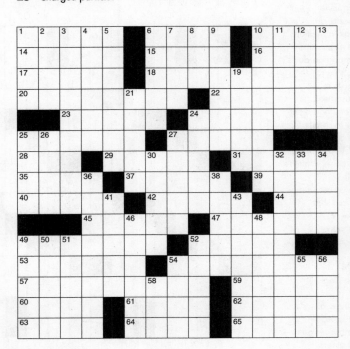

by M. E. Brindamour

ACROSS

1 Pickle container
4 Motionless
9 Fashion
14 Matriarch of all matriarchs
15 Actor Romero
16 Boiling
17 Weighed in
20 Light lunches
21 To any extent
22 List-ending abbr.
23 Moo juice container
25 Grp. overseeing toxic cleanups
28 Perfect rating
29 Most prudent
31 Become raveled
32 Painful spots
33 Carroll adventuress
34 Caused disharmony
38 Napping spots
39 Magazine exhortation
40 Break in relations
41 Out of business
43 Compaq products
46 ___ Miss
47 Engulfs in amusement
48 Cream ingredient
49 Tear to shreds
51 Part of MOMA
53 Blabbed
57 ___ pedis (athlete's foot)
58 Take to the stump
59 Certain shirt
60 Anxiety
61 Wanderer
62 Japanese honorific

DOWN

1 High-fliers
2 Fly
3 Change tactics
4 Like an eclair
5 Composer Rorem and others
6 Superlative ending
7 Short cheer
8 Firestone features
9 Clergyman
10 Kind of surgery
11 Indoor court
12 Indian with a bear dance
13 Some M.I.T. grads
18 Chum
19 Leave be
23 Wielded
24 Partner of search
26 Warsaw ___
27 Word of assent
29 Canton cookware
30 Land west of Eng.
31 Current
32 Sing "shooby-doo"
33 Out for the night
34 Aggravate
35 Part of a church service
36 Piano-playing Dame
37 Ariz.-to-Kan. dir.
38 Sign of stage success
41 Professor Plum's game
42 Pomeranian, for one
43 Stitched folds
44 Window of an eye
45 Breath mint brand
47 Sloppy-landing sound
48 Suffix with stock
50 France's ___ de Glenans
51 Queens team
52 Follow the code
53 ___ Puf fabric softener
54 Wrestler's goal
55 Have a go at
56 Gen. Arnold of W.W. II fame

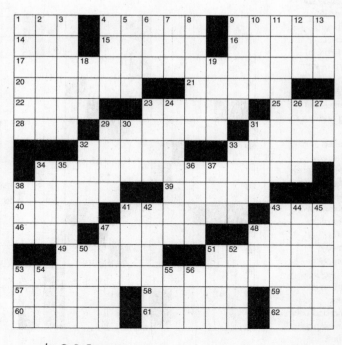

by G. R. Ferguson

ACROSS

1 Not fiction
5 Prefix with legal or chute
9 Fire starter
14 Hand lotion ingredient
15 At any time
16 Macho dude
17 Author Fleming and others
18 Extinct bird not known for its intelligence
19 Sky-blue
20 Louisa May Alcott classic
23 Envision
24 Deli loaves
25 Participants in a debate
27 World's fastest sport, with 2-Down
29 Footfall
32 Sounds of satisfaction
33 Thomas ___ Edison
35 "Woe is me!"
37 Walkway
41 Nightgown wearer of children's rhyme
44 Four-door
45 It has a keystone
46 Lass
47 "Now ___ seen everything!"
49 Store, as a ship's cargo
51 Aye's opposite
52 Woven cloth or fabric
56 Not able to hear
58 "___ Believer" (Monkees hit)
59 Don Ho standard
64 Sprite
66 Destroy
67 ___ one's time
68 It's a piece of cake
69 Atlanta arena, with "the"
70 "What's ___ for me?"
71 Affirmatives
72 Endure
73 Kett of the comics

DOWN

1 Flunk
2 See 27-Across
3 Artificial
4 Irritable and impatient
5 Place for a statue or a hero
6 Affirm
7 Give a makeover
8 Fragrance
9 Major Chinese seaport
10 Candy that comes in a dispenser
11 Tickle the funny bone
12 Harder to find
13 Strike zone's lower boundary
21 "___ Miserables"
22 Memorable time
26 Taking advantage of
27 Shark tale
28 Sheltered from the wind
30 First name in scat
31 Couples
34 Watch for
36 Religious splinter group
38 Miser
39 Trevi Fountain coin
40 Slippery
42 People asked to parties
43 Murder mystery
48 Yale grad
50 World Wide ___
52 A bit blotto
53 Writer Zola
54 The line y = 0, in math
55 Register, as a student
57 60's protest leader Hoffman
60 City in Arizona
61 Storage containers
62 Do magazine work
63 ___ high standard
65 Skating surface

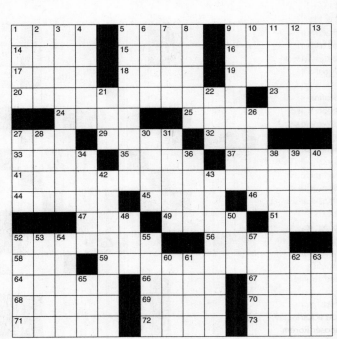

by S. Burns

ACROSS

1 Some sports cars, for short
5 Foundation
10 Yield
14 Grimm villain
15 Novelist Jong
16 Jump at the Ice Capades
17 British heavy metal group
19 Canned meat brand
20 Disney's Dwarfs, e.g.
21 Printings
23 Support for Tiger Woods?
24 Pop singer Peeples
26 Prepares leather
27 Do a few odd jobs
32 ___ Ababa
35 Cape Cod resort town
36 Acuff of the Country Music Hall of Fame
37 Androcles' friend
38 Headgear for Hardy
39 Celebration
40 Worshiper's seat
41 Bruce Wayne's home, for one
42 Valentine's Day gift
43 Inexpert motorist
46 Klondike strike
47 Org. that advises the N.S.C.
48 Computer key abbr.
51 One who works for a spell?
55 Sauteed shrimp dish
57 Not this
58 Huck Finn portrayer, 1993
60 Bring to ruin
61 As a companion

62 To be, in Tours
63 Afrikaner
64 London length
65 Fortuneteller

DOWN

1 Ceiling supporter
2 Conform (with)
3 Search blindly
4 E-mailed
5 "Hit the bricks!"
6 Jackie's second
7 Pro or con
8 Chilled the Chablis
9 Hygienic
10 Dealer's employer
11 Film box datum
12 Cain of "Lois & Clark"
13 Stately shaders
18 Luncheonette lists
22 Tropical root
25 Look after, with "to"

27 Wrestler's goal
28 Diamond flaw?
29 Decorative heading
30 Bit of marginalia
31 Changes color, in a way
32 European chain
33 The Almighty, in Alsace
34 Reduce in rank
38 Class distraction
39 On behalf of
41 Having a Y chromosome
42 Boxer's stat
44 Alter deceptively
45 Countenance
48 Overplay onstage
49 Fern fruit
50 Autumn beverage
51 Hit, as the toe
52 "You gotta be kidding!"

53 Model Macpherson
54 Very funny fellow
56 Makes one's jaw drop
59 Dad's namesake: Abbr.

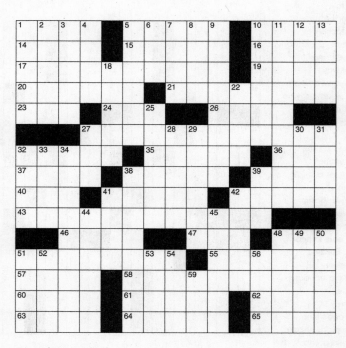

by P. Jordan

ACROSS

1 Sandwich shop
5 Fitzgerald and others
10 "We're looking for ___ good men"
14 North Carolina college
15 Gettysburg victor
16 Pepsi, for one
17 41339
20 Sweet liqueur
21 Gallic girlfriends
22 Ascot
23 ___-Coburg-Gotha (British royal house)
25 62060
33 Affixed with heat, as a patch
34 ___ number on (mess up)
35 Campground letters
36 20's gangster Bugs ___
37 Each of the numbers in this puzzle's theme
38 Being a copycat
40 They: Fr.
41 ___ Tse-tung
42 Tone deafness
43 49236
47 "Horrors!"
48 Hawaiian wreath
49 Companionless
52 They're handy by phones
57 97352
60 I in "The King and I"
61 Heathen
62 Glow
63 Cheer (for)
64 Lodge member
65 Reading light

DOWN

1 "It was ___ vu all over again"
2 Enthusiasm
3 Graph points
4 Signs, as a contract
5 Sentiment
6 Of the pre-Easter season
7 TV's Ricki
8 Summer refresher
9 Thurmond, e.g.: Abbr.
10 Shrewdness
11 Points of convergence
12 Actress Sommer
13 Streets and avenues
18 Places atop
19 Metered vehicle
23 Ladled-out food
24 Pie ___ mode
25 Copycat
26 On ___ (proceeding successfully)
27 Back: Prefix
28 Pig ___ poke
29 Dialect
30 Approving
31 Ancient Aegean land
32 Late astronomer Carl
37 Like the Marx Brothers
38 More pale
39 Taro dish
41 "Hi ___!" (fan's message)
42 Common solvent
44 Like many diet products
45 Quaker pronoun
46 Actress Massey et al.
49 Slightly open
50 Late-night host
51 ___ consequence (insignificant)
52 Canceled
53 Bells' sound
54 Water, to Joaquin
55 College student's home
56 Rice Krispies sound
58 Engine speed, for short
59 ___ Paulo, Brazil

by R. Hughes

ACROSS

1 Pre-entree dish
6 Sit in the sun
10 Cozy home
14 Reflection
15 Opposing
16 Go ___ (exceed)
17 The "N" of U.S.N.A.
18 "Forever"
19 "Get going!"
20 Go
23 Withdraw from the Union
26 Those going 80, say
27 Med. cost-saving plan
28 And so on
30 Historical period
31 Teen woe
33 It makes an auto go
35 ___ latte
40 Go
44 Intuit
45 Hankering
46 Castle's protection
47 Chef's measure: Abbr.
50 Something to go to a bakery for
52 Wash. neighbor
53 Delivered a sermon
58 Comments to the audience
60 Go
62 Milky-white gem
63 Sacred Egyptian bird
64 War story, Greek-style
68 Chant at a fraternity party
69 Swiss painter Paul
70 The brainy bunch
71 George Washington bills
72 Arid
73 Cousin of a Golden Globe

DOWN

1 Transgression
2 Doc's org.
3 Restroom, informally
4 Wide-open
5 Deceive
6 False god
7 Black cattle breed
8 Treeless plain
9 Mouth, to Ralph Kramden
10 One always on the go
11 Call forth
12 Cut off
13 Lock of hair
21 "Take your hands off me!"
22 Instruct
23 Pre-Ayatollah rulers
24 Host
25 Sir Arthur ___ Doyle
29 Saturn, for one
32 Mag workers
34 Pigpen
36 Order between ready and fire
37 Result of a bank failure?
38 Distress signal
39 ___ Park, Colo.
41 "Go get it, Fido!"
42 Jitterbug's "cool"
43 First digital computer
48 Arab leaders
49 Little rock
51 Inuit
53 Kind of ID
54 Wisconsin college
55 Story, in France
56 Ayn Rand's "___ Shrugged"
57 Less moist
59 South Sea getaways
61 Words of comprehension
65 Business abbr.
66 Simile's middle
67 ___ es Salaam

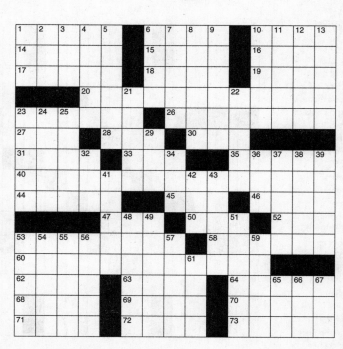

by Stephanie Spadaccini

ACROSS

1 Org. that guarantees bank holdings
5 Poets
10 Egyptian snakes
14 Moon goddess
15 German sub
16 Patricia who co-starred in "The Fountainhead"
17 Late newsman Sevareid
18 Waken
19 The Supremes, e.g.
20 1989 Spike Lee film
23 French school
24 Weights
25 Letter before beth
28 Kapow!
30 Top 3 hit of 1963 and 1977
34 Mont Blanc is one
37 "Play it ___ lays"
38 Studio sign
39 Light bulb, in cartoons
40 Happened upon
41 Moonshine
43 Camp beds
44 Suns
45 ___-Kettering Institute
48 Chilled meat garnish
51 Unwelcome sight in the mail
57 In the past
58 Finger-pointer
59 Cake finisher
60 Backside
61 States
62 Jasmine or morning glory
63 Commits a sin
64 Present, for example, in English class
65 Mini-whirlpool

DOWN

1 Vamoosed
2 Five-peseta coin
3 Any part of J.F.K.: Abbr.
4 Ornamental container in a flower shop
5 Grand Canyon transport
6 Irate
7 Cheek cosmetic
8 Elan
9 Proofer's mark
10 "La Marseillaise," e.g.
11 Printing flourish
12 Benjamin Moore product
13 Trudges (through)
21 Classical nymph who spoke only by repetition
22 Holier-___-thou
25 Economist Smith
26 Emit coherent light
27 Perform copy desk work
28 Formal order
29 Wedding dance
31 Eradicate, with "out"
32 Burden
33 One of the Bobbsey twins
34 Appends
35 Onion relative
36 Bears' hands
39 Like Mount St. Helens, now
41 "___ Lisa"
42 Wading bird
43 Supplies the food for
45 Plant reproductive part
46 Unsocial sort
47 Award for "Braveheart"
48 Saatchi & Saatchi employees
49 Litigators
50 Intrinsically
52 Tiny pest
53 Roof overhang
54 Battery fluid
55 Repair
56 Wolves, for wolfhounds

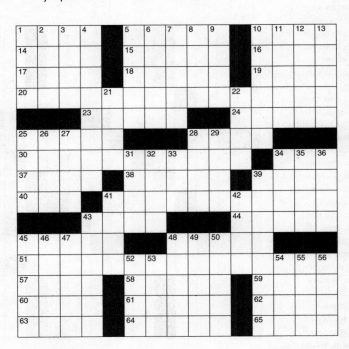

by Derek Allen

ACROSS

1 Cobblers
5 City near Phoenix
10 "Half-Breed" singer
14 Med. sch. course
15 All possible
16 Part of A.P.R.
17 Nimble
18 Dancer Jeanmaire
19 Persia, today
20 The Boy King
21 Sculpture in the Louvre
23 Madalyn O'Hair, e.g.
25 "Norma ___"
26 Deborah's role in "The King and I"
27 Reason for a small craft advisory
32 Paris newspaper, with "Le"
34 Blow one's top
35 Circle segment
36 Baker's dozen
37 Sign of spring
38 Headliner
39 What Dorian Gray didn't do
40 "___ Irish Rose"
41 Computer device
42 Dogpatch dweller
44 Author John Dickson ___
45 Bill's partner
46 Costa Rican export
49 Former Ford offering
54 Org. that sticks to its guns
55 Bread spread
56 Memorable ship
57 Count calories
58 Gen. Bradley
59 Modify
60 ___ Domini
61 Precious metal
62 Lascivious looks
63 He was a "Giant" star

DOWN

1 Naples noodles
2 Enter, as data
3 1955 hit for the Crew-Cuts
4 Pig's digs
5 Mother ___
6 The Super Bowl, e.g.
7 Diner's card
8 Nov. electee
9 Tears?
10 "___ and Misdemeanors"
11 Mata ___
12 Useful Latin abbr.
13 Gambler's mecca
21 Ivy plant
22 It may be Far or Near
24 Brings to a close
27 Town ___ (early newsman)
28 Regrets
29 Apollo mission
30 Intervals of history
31 Farm measure
32 Repast
33 Today, in Turin
34 Southernmost Great Lake
37 Irregular
38 Carolina rail
40 "___ Ben Adhem" (Leigh Hunt poem)
41 Tailless cat
43 International agreement
44 Wickerworkers
46 Sketch comic John
47 Sports center
48 Squelched
49 Synthesizer man
50 "Tickle Me" doll
51 Genuine
52 Where Bill met Hillary
53 Lo-fat
57 Father figure

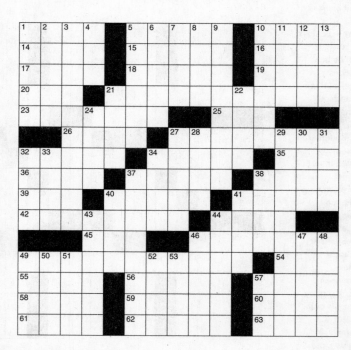

by Gregory E. Paul

ACROSS

1 Poet Sandburg
5 Sand bar
10 Jemima, e.g.
14 Guy with an Irish Rose
15 "College Bowl" host Robert
16 Chew (on)
17 Off-color
19 New York theater award
20 Escalator alternative
21 Boat propellers
23 "___ Maria"
24 Tear-jerker in the kitchen
26 "Bald" baby bird
28 Big toe woe
30 Patsy's pal on TV's "Absolutely Fabulous"
31 Dapper fellow
32 Foe
34 Numbskull
37 Catch sight of
39 Saccharine
41 Garbage boat
42 Chartres chapeau
44 "Deutschland uber ___"
46 High season, on the Riviera
47 Before the due date
49 African antelopes
51 Actress Loren
53 Four-time Gold Glove winner Garvey
54 Chicken ___ king
55 ___ platter (Polynesian menu choice)
57 Bug's antenna
61 What not to yell in a crowded theater
63 Off-key
65 Tied, as a score
66 Revolutionary patriot Allen
67 Lo-cal
68 Funnyman Foxx
69 Horned zoo beast
70 Son of Seth

DOWN

1 Elliot of the Mamas and the Papas
2 Be next to
3 Latvia's capital
4 French Foreign ___
5 Rap or jam periods
6 Stetson, e.g.
7 Betelgeuse's constellation
8 Thomas Edison's middle name
9 Looked lecherously
10 In the past
11 Off-center
12 Innocent
13 Sound from an aviary
18 Sgt. Bilko
22 Stated
25 Street sign with an arrow
27 Wildebeests
28 Pedestal
29 Off-guard
30 Embroidered hole
31 Cotillion V.I.P.
33 Director Brooks
35 Bunkhouse beds
36 Female sheep
38 "You bet!"
40 It's used for a call in Madrid
43 Excursion
45 Lifeguard, sometimes
48 Giver of compliments
50 Thread's partner
51 Morley of "60 Minutes"
52 Martini garnish
53 Japanese dish
56 ___ helmet (safari wear)
58 Reclined
59 Inner: Prefix
60 1 and 66, e.g.: Abbr.
62 Finis
64 Campbell's container

by Stephanie Spadaccini

ACROSS

1 "Let's go!"
5 Miss Cinders of old comics
9 Stravinsky's "Le ___ du printemps"
14 It's pulled on a pulley
15 Music for two
16 Farm units
17 Once more
18 Schooner part
19 Signified
20 Hit NBC comedy
23 Passing grade
24 Director Howard
25 X's in bowling
27 It's behind home plate
32 Sugar source
33 "___ American Cousin" (1859 comedy)
34 Results of big hits?
36 "Gandhi" setting
39 Shiite, e.g.
41 1997 has two
43 Brothers and sisters
44 Flattens
46 Plains home
48 Tam-o'-shanter
49 Yin's counterpart
51 Not the subs
53 Liberace wore them
56 A.F.L.'s partner
57 Tempe sch.
58 Novelty timepiece
64 Cinnamon unit
66 ___-Seltzer
67 First name in supermodeldom
68 Actress Berry
69 Alice doesn't work here anymore
70 Campus authority
71 Buzzing
72 Organic fuel
73 Klutz's utterance

DOWN

1 Pack in
2 "___ Lisa"
3 Like a William Safire piece
4 Alternative to J.F.K. and La Guardia
5 Oilers' home
6 Molokai meal
7 For fear that
8 Esqs.
9 Belushi character on "S.N.L."
10 Expert
11 Bartender's supply
12 "Walk Away ___" (1966 hit)
13 ___ Park, Colo.
21 Pear type
22 Like some stocks, for short
26 Lodges

27 Part of an old English Christmas feast
28 Atmosphere
29 Hodgepodge
30 Cross out
31 Glazier's items
35 Back-to-school time: Abbr.
37 Building support
38 Egyptian threats
40 Romeo
42 Maine's is rocky
45 Tee-hee
47 Psychiatrist Berne
50 Bearded creature
52 "Holy ___!"
53 Russian-born violinist Schneider, informally
54 These, in Madrid
55 Rascal
59 "Twittering Machine" artist

60 Neighbor of Kan.
61 Nondairy spread
62 Bit of thunder
63 Dolls since 1961
65 Cato's 151

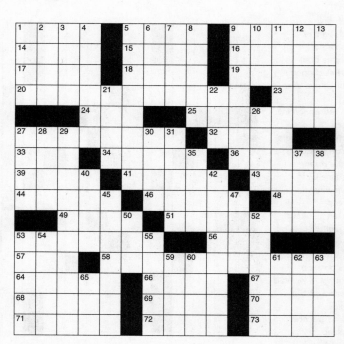

by Elizabeth C. Gorski

ACROSS

1 "Too bad!"
5 Sen. Lott
10 Hardly colorful
14 Parks who wouldn't take discrimination sitting down
15 12-inch stick
16 Superb
17 Water conduit
18 China's Zhou ___
19 Do, re or mi, e.g.
20 "Little Orphan Annie" character
23 "There ___ young . . ." (common limerick start)
24 WNW's reverse
25 Plant dripping
28 ___ Kippur
31 Newsman Pyle
35 Puts up
37 Spigot
39 Switch positions
40 Santa Claus
44 Noted business conglomerate
45 Great Lakes cargo
46 C_2H_6
47 Sweetie
50 1040 grp.
52 Last name in cosmetics
53 Photo ___ (media events)
55 Supreme Court Justice Black
57 Nobel author, informally
63 Pack (down)
64 To no ___ (worthless)
65 Snake eyes
67 Lemon go-with
68 Menu at Chez Jacques
69 One of the corners at Four Corners Monument
70 Blockhead

71 Gouged sneakily
72 Akron product

DOWN

1 It may be slung in a sling
2 Dumptruckful
3 Where China is
4 B.L.T., e.g.
5 Deuce toppers
6 Takeoff site
7 Actress Raines
8 Not distant
9 Cree or Crow
10 Martha Graham, e.g.
11 Castle, in chess
12 Orkin targets
13 Quilting party
21 "The Divine Comedy" poet
22 Take advantage of
25 Install to new specifications

26 Poet's Muse
27 Brawl
29 Partner for this and that, with "the"
30 Spoil
32 Wanderer
33 Absurd
34 Ruhr Valley city
36 Box-office letters
38 Bit of Trivial Pursuit equipment
41 Dernier ___
42 Coach Amos Alonzo ___
43 Discard
48 Went one better than
49 Place for a little R and R
51 Devout Iranian
54 Rough cabin
56 Proceeding independently

57 Item for Jack and Jill
58 Bullets and such
59 Writer Hunter
60 Stallion's mate
61 The "A" in ABM
62 Vintage
63 Special attention, for short
66 "___ Drives Me Crazy" (1989 #1 hit)

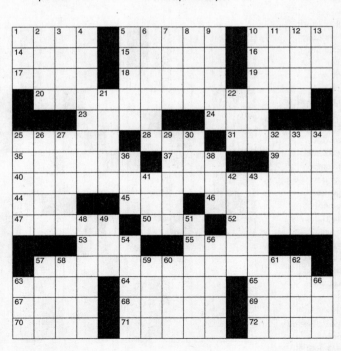

by Gregory E. Paul

ACROSS

1. Certain drapes
6. Atlantic food fish
10. Gator's kin
14. Cop ___ (confess for a lighter sentence)
15. White-tailed flier
16. Deli offering
17. Colt 45, e.g.
19. List member
20. "That's a lie!"
21. Household
23. 70's-80's robotic rock group
25. The United States, metaphorically
27. Uris hero
28. Dance, in Dijon
29. Member of the 500 HR club
30. Rock impresario Brian
31. Surgical fabric
33. Ant, in dialect
35. "Texaco Star Theater" host
39. Cut down
40. Brilliance
43. High dudgeon
46. Mai ___
47. Go on to say
49. "Bravo!"
50. It once settled near Pompeii
53. Part of a whole
54. Kangaroo movements
55. Hayfield activity
57. Prefix with China
58. Kind of cereal
62. Shade of red
63. Conception
64. Bizarre
65. Bronte heroine
66. Pre-1821 Missouri, e.g.: Abbr.
67. He had Scarlett fever

DOWN

1. Uncle of note
2. New Deal prog.
3. Stream deposit
4. "I can't ___" (Stones refrain)
5. Morton product
6. "Rocky II," e.g.
7. Diabolical
8. Due halved
9. Words of assistance
10. "I ___" (ancient Chinese text)
11. Record again
12. Where to find Eugene
13. Awaken
18. Early Shirley role
22. Signed up for
23. U.N.'s Hammarskjold
24. Former polit. cause
26. ___ of the Unknowns
28. Like some greeting cards
32. Nine-digit number, maybe
33. Ultimate point
34. R.N.'s offering
36. Send
37. Trompe l'___
38. Stretch
41. He KO'd Quarry, 10/26/70
42. Asian holiday
43. Tipple
44. "Didja ever wonder . . . ?" humorist
45. Successful escapee
47. Incarnation
48. Spanish Surrealist
51. Certain investment, informally
52. More competent
53. Jesse who lost to Ronald Reagan in 1970
56. Composer Stravinsky
59. Ending with quiet
60. N.Y.C. subway
61. Modern information source, with "the"

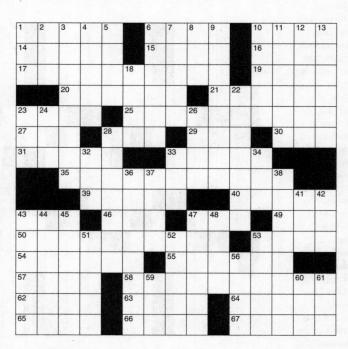

by Alan Arbesfeld

ACROSS

1 Birthplace of Columbus
6 Doesn't exist
10 Dog-paddle, say
14 Baking chambers
15 Headline
16 "___ you don't!"
17 What the jury does after deliberating
20 Poker starter
21 Small and weak
22 Swearing to tell the truth, and others
23 The highest degree
24 Perjured oneself
25 Facility
26 Sleuth, informally
27 Not real
29 Michael Douglas, to Kirk
32 Heavenly hunter
35 Passes easily
36 Knight's wife, in olden times
37 Legal reach, metaphorically
40 Actress Lanchester
41 "___ Misbehavin'"
42 Siskel's partner
43 Wreak vengeance on
44 Chicken style
45 Big blast maker
46 Biblical garden
48 Cash substitutes
50 Test-___ treaty
53 A Beatle
55 It's clicked on a computer
56 Vigor
57 Judge's cry
60 Thirteen popes
61 Toward shelter, nautically
62 Word with ear or peace
63 Dict. items
64 Antidrinking org.
65 + end

DOWN

1 Tennis star Ivanisevic
2 News basis
3 Under, in poetry
4 A single time
5 Baseball bat wood
6 Philately offering
7 Awaits sentencing
8 Dark blue
9 Number of coins in an Italian fountain
10 Ice cream drinks
11 January store happening
12 Distance between belt notches, maybe
13 Witty sayings
18 Like the "Iliad" and "Odyssey"
19 Wander
24 Songstress Horne
25 Sunrise direction
26 Ceremonial gown
28 Bulk
30 "Rubáiyát" poet
31 Salamander
32 Designer Cassini
33 Part to play
34 Rather than
35 Gallic girlfriend
36 Money owed
38 Reason for postponement
39 Egg producers
44 Critic Walter
45 Composer's output
47 Chemise
49 Marveled aloud
50 Shoe designer Magli
51 Broadcast
52 ___ Dame
53 Auctioned off
54 Shade giver
55 "To Live and Die ___" ('85 film)
56 West German capital
58 "___ shocked!"
59 Spy org.

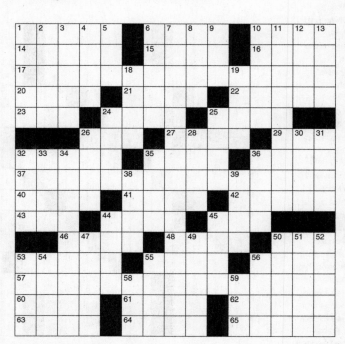

by Mark Moldowsky

ACROSS

1 "Chapter Two" star James
5 Provide for, as a party
10 Sacred bird of the Pharaohs
14 Tough-guy actor Ray
15 Skylit courts
16 Fisherman's offering?
17 "The Twilight Zone" host
19 Lily Pons specialty
20 Small bill
21 Dec. holiday
22 New Haven Line stop
24 Scolds
26 Newswoman Shriver
27 Sing Sing inhabitant
28 Machine part fastener
31 Where to pin a pin
34 "Olympia" painter
35 Sis's sib
36 Una década has 10
37 More rational
38 ___ slaw
39 Docs
40 Ellington and Wellington
41 Parts of apples
42 Venomous snake
44 Swab
45 Backpacker
46 Defensive wall
50 Wall Street type
52 Gang's area
53 Pierre's friend
54 Stockings
55 Armed robber
58 "It's ___ you!"
59 The "p" of 6p
60 ___ in a poke
61 Turns right
62 P.L.O.'s Arafat
63 Cowboy Roy's better half

DOWN

1 Chocolate substitute
2 "___ at last!"
3 Cousin of 42-Across
4 Refusals
5 Bizet heroine
6 Hammond product
7 Hall-of-Famer Speaker
8 Strauss's "___ Heldenleben"
9 High-quality writing medium
10 Slanted type
11 Maine resort
12 Hipbones
13 Baseball feature
18 Laud
23 Once, once
25 Tops
26 Flowing tresses
28 Porch chair craftsman
29 ___ Stanley Gardner
30 Troubles
31 Aladdin's treasure
32 "The King ___"
33 Quickly
34 Manufacturer
37 James Bond, e.g.
38 Nightclub of song
40 Place for a finger?
41 Where Prince Philip was born
43 MTV fare
44 Promissory note in a casino
46 Designer Emilio
47 Argentine expanse
48 Cybermessages
49 Bit of color
50 55-Across, maybe
51 1948 Hitchcock thriller
52 Cans
56 Sri Lanka export
57 Expand unnecessarily

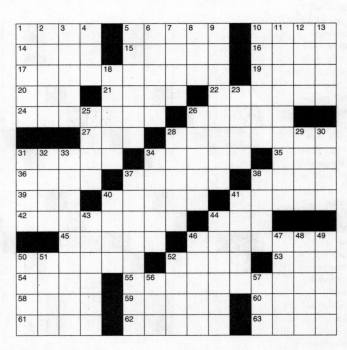

by Ed Early

ACROSS

1 Electrical overload protector
5 Surrealist Salvador
9 Fodder holder
13 Where to see "E.R." or "Ellen"
14 Archeological site
15 "Star Wars" director George
16 Oklahoma Indian
17 ___'acte (intermission)
18 Portly plus
19 Like dentists?
22 Org. overseeing quadrennial games
23 Neighbor of Syr.
24 Like trampolinists?
30 Bleats
34 Friendly Islands, formally
35 Mandolin's ancestor
36 551, in Latium
37 Bind, as a chicken for roasting
38 Gilbert and Sullivan princess
39 Pre-entree course
41 Martians and Venusians, for short
42 Esposito of hockey
43 Irish county north of Limerick
44 Film unit
46 Like tree surgeons?
48 Advice-giving Landers
50 German spa
51 Like fencers?
59 "It was the ___ I could do"
60 Lifeless
61 "Whoops!"
62 Otherworldly
63 Money drawer
64 It's nothing to Agassi
65 Bikini, e.g.
66 Exclusive
67 Bridge

DOWN

1 Eat it
2 "___ us a son is given"
3 Put in an overhead bin, say
4 Prime time times
5 Dump water on
6 Jemima, e.g.
7 Art print: Abbr.
8 About
9 Evanston, to Chicago
10 "Original Gangster" rapper
11 Whip
12 Sugar suffix
15 Novelist Anita
20 Smidgens
21 Deep mud
24 Out-and-out
25 ___-cochere (carriage entrance)
26 Occupied
27 Statesman Root
28 Check for embezzlement, perhaps
29 Author Calvino
31 Dwight's opponent in '52 and '56
32 Car security device
33 Part of a cassette tape
39 Rapscallion
40 ___ Day (November 2)
42 Duck's home
45 Timmy's dog
47 What CD players don't require
49 Nick at ___
51 Hive dwellers
52 Nobleman
53 Beanery sign
54 Beethoven piano piece
55 Capitol site, with "the"
56 Restaurant with waffles and such
57 ___ Scotia
58 "What happened next . . ."
59 Blooming neckwear?

by John Greenman

ACROSS

1 Setting for the lingo in today's theme
6 Brick material
10 Cutting remark
14 Titlark
15 Bonheur or Parks
16 Birthplace of seven Presidents
17 NASA satellite launcher
18 Thomas Moore's land
19 Indicates assent
20 Begin's peace partner
21 [.] [.]
23 Oral Roberts University site
25 Tarzan portrayer
26 Request sweetener
29 Entertained
33 Physics unit
34 Elephant Boy of 30's film
37 Hippodrome
38 [::] [::]
42 Contemptuous look
43 Certain Ford, for short
44 Call ___ day
45 Saw-toothed
47 Reduce
50 Midafternoon on a sundial
51 Luxurious
53 [.] [..]
57 Cassettes
61 Concert halls
62 Trick
63 R-rated or higher
64 Large bell sound
65 Writer Bagnold
66 T, in physics
67 Otherwise
68 Pixels
69 Calvin Trillin piece

DOWN

1 Auditors
2 Baltic port
3 Copied
4 It may be beaten at a party
5 Prestige
6 Salad greenery
7 "___ Doone"
8 Where the Gobi is
9 New Englander
10 Cemetery, informally
11 Hail, on the briny
12 Carnival attraction
13 Supervisor
22 "Pomp and Circumstance" composer
24 "___ we forget . . ."
26 Iron
27 Frankie who sang "Moonlight Gambler"
28 Gardening tool
29 German industrial region
30 Union leader John L. ___
31 Growing outward
32 Six-Day War leader
35 "Sigh!"
36 Spell-off
39 Birthright
40 Hiker's spot
41 Org. that defends the Bill of Rights
46 Layered
48 Manor
49 Sunglasses
51 Propose
52 City on the Aire
53 Ear part
54 Person with fans
55 Counting method
56 Jupiter's wife
58 Cat
59 Scat lady
60 "Don't move!"

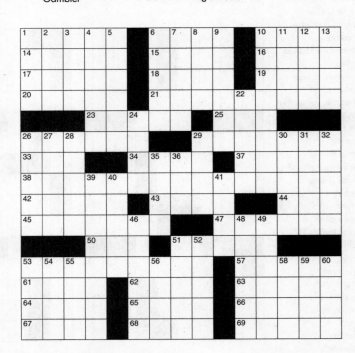

by Stanley B. Whitten

ACROSS
1 Opera house box
5 Geography book
10 Golfer's alert
14 Gung-ho
15 Aplomb
16 Missing from the Marines, say
17 Trio in Bethlehem
18 Kindergarten adhesive
19 Onionlike plant
20 Noël Coward play
23 Dobbin's nibble
24 Postsurgical program
28 "Total ___" (1990 film)
32 Set free
35 Internet messages
36 "You'd ___ Nice to Come Home To"
37 Trouble
38 "Ho, ho, ho" sayer
42 Ike's W.W. II command
43 Flunky
44 Disney mermaid
45 Arts and crafts class
48 Garb
49 Secret rendezvous
50 Sold-out sign
51 Nickname for Hubert Humphrey, with "the"
59 On ___ (without commitment)
62 Knight's wear
63 Not working
64 Prefix with bucks
65 Drink served with marshmallows
66 Grain for farm animals
67 Atop
68 Get used (to)
69 Town NNE of Santa Fe

DOWN
1 Gentle one
2 Skating rink, e.g.
3 Lerner and Loewe musical
4 Rewrite
5 Sex ___
6 Wedding offering to the bride and groom
7 Daffy Duck's impediment
8 Italian wine region
9 Psychic
10 Stumble
11 Be in arrears
12 Future flounder
13 Big game animal
21 Christmas decoration
22 Indignation
25 Michener novel
26 Penitent
27 Ladybug, e.g.
28 Veto
29 Ham
30 Dieter's unit: Var.
31 Be bedridden
32 Yorkshire city
33 "Uh-huh"
34 Rock's ___ Jovi
36 ___-a-brac
39 Moo goo ___ pan
40 University of Florida student
41 N.Y.C. subway
46 Waste receptacle
47 N.Y.C. subway overseer
48 Genesis mountain
50 Hawk's descent
52 White-spotted rodent
53 Egg on
54 Community org. with a gym
55 Break in friendly relations
56 Notion
57 Parkay product
58 Cincinnati nine
59 Home of the Mustangs, for short
60 Oomph
61 It may need massaging

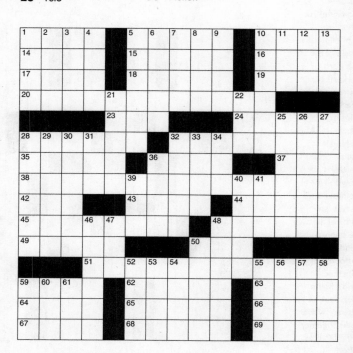

by Gregory E. Paul

ACROSS

1 Literary lioness
5 Open a crack
9 Seeing red
14 Painter of limp watches
15 Rational
16 Elicit
17 Road, for Romulus
18 Signs
19 "Drove my Chevy to the ___ . . ." (1972 lyric)
20 1991 feminist movie
23 Old photo
24 Skin layer
25 Radical 60's org.
28 For the taking
30 Give a licking
31 4:00, in Kent
32 300-pound President
35 Dog's drink, or resting spot
37 Bikini alternative
39 Cousin of the English horn
40 Work, as dough
43 Approximately
44 Valerie Harper series
46 "Much ___ About Nothing"
47 Certain grains
48 It thickens the plot
49 Snowball in "Animal Farm"
52 Rounds, say
54 Mythical monster
55 Eye opener
57 Balance sheet plus
61 Cartoon magpies
64 Reluctant
66 Zeno's home
67 Takes care of the squeaky wheel
68 Come together
69 Armed Forces option
70 Sunburn woe

71 It's all in the family
72 Fires
73 Ferber of "Show Boat"

DOWN

1 Blue-pencils
2 Shop tool
3 Result of counting sheep
4 Delivered by a Huey Cobra
5 Home of 3.5 billion
6 "Surf City" singers, 1963
7 It's just over a foot
8 Martha's Vineyard, in the summer
9 Trustful
10 Singer Burl
11 41-week best seller, 1970-71
12 Barely manage, with "out"
13 Gidget portrayer Sandra
21 Deface
22 Actress Thurman
26 Thickheaded
27 Powdered starches
29 Lodge member
32 Common sculpture
33 Hate
34 Ecological succession
36 Princess tormentor
38 Some check it daily
41 Early outcasts
42 Suffix with star or tsar
45 Side in many a western
50 Type
51 Lead ore
53 Screen siren West

56 "Chill!"
58 Went down a slope
59 "Sea of Love" star Barkin
60 Physicist Nikola
62 "___, Brute!"
63 Noisy birds
64 Blockhead
65 Early afternoon

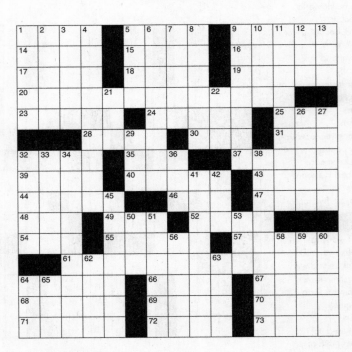

by Randall J. Hartman

ACROSS

1 Put one's foot down
6 Not stiff
10 Without: Fr.
14 Prefix with anthropology
15 Eye part
16 "Here comes trouble!"
17 Arctic or Indian, e.g.
18 Flees
19 Noose material
20 "Yes!"
22 Ogled
23 Name for many a theater
24 Totally absorbed (in)
26 Bright and bouncy
29 "Get ___ of yourself!"
33 Easter bloom
37 Managed
38 Often-welcomed part of the week
39 Suffix with switch
40 Bara of the silents
42 Lymph ___
43 Interstellar cloud
45 Diamond ___
46 Alum
47 Southwestern home material
48 "___ of Two Cities"
50 Atlantic Seaboard, with "the"
52 Egyptian's tongue
57 Quick
60 "Yes!"
63 Prez
64 So long, in Soho
65 Utter fear
66 Engineer's school
67 Western Indians
68 Court TV coverage
69 Nick and Nora's dog
70 Attention-getter
71 Because

DOWN

1 Mar
2 Tasteless
3 Kind of acid
4 Civil War general
5 Pay
6 One of a kind
7 "Terrible" czar
8 Computer capacity
9 Ziti, e.g.
10 "Yes!"
11 Hey there, at sea
12 Nah
13 Outbuilding
21 Mafioso's code of silence
25 Golfer's goal
27 Cheerleader's cry
28 Genuflected
30 Aroma
31 Terhune's "___ Dog"
32 Like Easter eggs
33 Songstress Horne
34 Enraged
35 Gray wolf
36 "Yes!"
38 Bit of finery
41 A day in Spain
44 Lowing herd's place
48 Baseball stat
49 Gives way to rage
51 ___ and took notice
53 Early name in video games
54 African republic
55 Ending with sacro-
56 Rinse or dry, in a dishwasher
57 Goat cheese
58 Gives the heave-ho
59 Splinter group
61 Holy Fr. ladies
62 Malt kiln

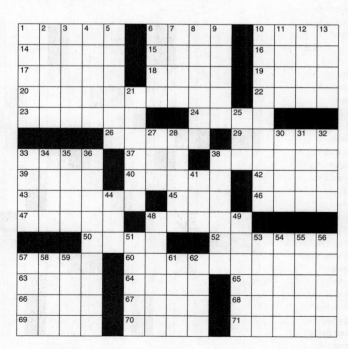

by Eileen Lexau

ACROSS

1 Prelude to a duel
5 Not hearing
9 Competitor for a Clio
14 Seat of Allen County, Kan.
15 Unattractive fruit that sounds that way
16 Upright, e.g.
17 Taking radical action
20 Kiss mark
21 Lamb's kin
22 Wonderment
23 "Bye!"
24 Much too bright
27 Romulus's brother
29 Rundown in appearance
33 Words of woe
37 "Buddy"
38 "23 ___": Var.
39 Holing up
42 Expired
43 Princess of operetta
44 "___ boy!"
45 One who can't go home
46 Give quarters to
48 Laotians, e.g.
50 Mowed strip
55 Breakfast staple
58 Have some tea
59 Sound investment?
60 Civil War story
64 Disconcert
65 Theater award
66 Peak in the "Odyssey"
67 "Same here!"
68 Fishing area
69 Lack

DOWN

1 Lovers' sounds
2 Sarge's boss
3 Restaurant owner of song
4 Hanky-___
5 Scout's pledge word
6 I, to Claudius
7 Inn drink
8 Repairmen
9 Like some mountain lodge activities
10 Conk out
11 Nursery call
12 Freshly
13 It smells a lot
18 Equipment
19 Prefix with light
24 Dillinger fighter
25 Setting for this puzzle's theme
26 Alpine heroine
28 Give off, as light
30 Redo, as text
31 Puts on
32 Eastern discipline
33 Grimm character
34 Martian invasion report, e.g.
35 60's dress style
36 ___ Gay (W.W. II plane)
38 Mass of hair
40 Caller's playful request
41 3 : 1, 5 : 2, etc.
46 Portable computer
47 Renaissance name of fame
49 Certain grandson
51 Champions' cry
52 Get up
53 Edgy
54 Nonsurfer at the beach
55 "Omigosh!"
56 Mongolian desert
57 Flying pest
59 Tool repository
61 N.C. and S.C. zone
62 Cable channel
63 Type of type

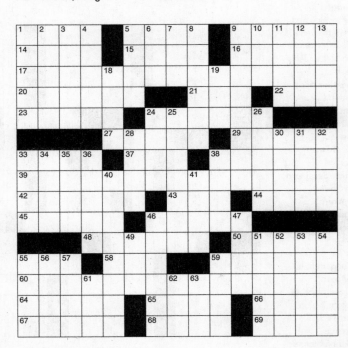

by Manny Nosowsky

ACROSS

1 Cleopatra's love ___ Antony
5 Scrabble play
9 Cosmetician Lauder
14 On the briny
15 Verdi's "D'amor sull'ali rosee," e.g.
16 Con man
17 List component
18 Datum
19 Bronco catcher
20 Good-time Charlie
23 Norway's capital
24 Embarrassing sound, maybe
25 Mouse catcher
28 Airedale, for one
31 Volcanic fallout
34 Playing marble
36 Building wing
37 Forearm bone
38 Best
42 Mishmash
43 Coach Parseghian
44 Kingdom
45 Fishing gear
46 Chicago newspaper
49 "Treasure Island" monogram
50 Wilt
51 Use Western Union, e.g.
53 Noble one
60 Diamond weight
61 Bit of thatching
62 Like hen's teeth
63 Martini garnish
64 ___ Spencer, brother of Princess Diana
65 Stadium section
66 Passover meal
67 "If all ___ fails . . ."
68 Child's Christmas gift

DOWN

1 Pony Express load
2 ___ spumante
3 Coral ridge
4 Alfred Hitchcock film appearance, e.g.
5 Breakfast dish made on an iron
6 Patrick Henry, for one
7 Rolling in dough
8 Whom one goes out with
9 Cream-filled pastry
10 Astute
11 Dry run
12 "No problem"
13 Ike's W.W. II command
21 Bone: Prefix
22 Suave competitor
25 Dinner rooster
26 Like a gymnast
27 Implied
29 Recovery clinic
30 Suffix with percent
31 Where "I do's" are exchanged
32 Tackle box item
33 Injures
35 Ring result, briefly
37 Indian with a sun dance
39 North Dakota's largest city
40 The first "T" of TNT
41 "Goodnight" girl of song
46 Make ragged
47 Wedding workers
48 Pine leaf
50 Spartacus, e.g.
52 Pub game
53 December 26 event
54 Rainless
55 At no cost
56 Dabbling duck
57 Banister
58 Arbor Day honoree
59 Group of cattle
60 Comedian Bill, to friends

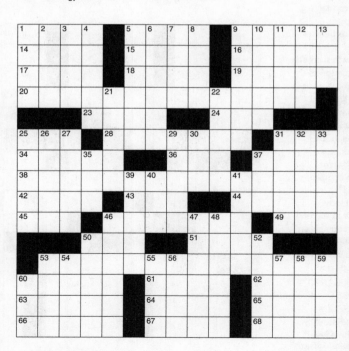

by Gregory E. Paul

ACROSS

1 Irene of "Fame"
5 B.A. and B.S., e.g.
9 Try to avoid a tag
14 Throat clearer
15 Eye amorously
16 Kitchen counter?
17 1996 Clinton challenger
18 Stand in line
19 More slippery
20 How to succeed as a stripper?
23 Opposite WNW
24 Letterman's network
25 Heir's concern
28 Vandalize
30 Start with down and out
32 Fourposter, e.g.
33 Stops
35 Areas between hills
37 How to succeed as a retailer?
40 Voting districts
41 Go light (on)
42 Getting on in years
43 Govt. book balancers
44 Lucky plant
48 Puts in office
51 "Tsk!"
52 First lady
53 How to succeed as a demolition crew?
57 Fine dinnerware
59 Ready and willing's partner
60 Finito
61 "Prizzi's ___"
62 Hit alternative
63 Just in case
64 They're cutting, sometimes

65 Sports figure?
66 Greek god of love

DOWN

1 Bummed
2 What Richard III offered "my kingdom" for
3 Load off the mind
4 "You can say that again!"
5 Somewhat pessimistic
6 "Yikes!"
7 Smooth-talking
8 ___ good example
9 Mudholes
10 On the up and up
11 Worthy of copying
12 "Look at Me, I'm Sandra ___"
13 Miscalculate
21 Means of approach

22 One of Lee's men
26 Ball props
27 Asner and Begley
29 Kind of test or rain
30 Addict's program
31 Takes advantage of
34 Flower supporter
35 Jumps with a pole
36 Brand for Bowser
37 Room connector
38 Bossing
39 Most safe
40 Grief
43 Sugar suffix
45 Presidential nixer
46 Nonetheless
47 Racks the pins again
49 Trapper transport
50 Russian autocrats: Var.
51 Oklahoma city
54 Thanksgiving potatoes

55 Passing notice
56 In neutral
57 ___ Guevara
58 Coal carrier

by Nancy Salomon

ACROSS

1 Labyrinth
5 Murders, mob-style
9 Numbers on baseball cards
14 ___ Brothers of 40's–50's music
15 Pink, as a steak
16 Sign in an apartment window
17 Head honcho
19 Think out loud
20 Michaelmas daisy
21 Prefix with metric
22 Like most sumo wrestlers
23 Kind of preview
25 Carpenter's machine
26 Droop
29 Roadhouse
30 Nuisance
31 More smooth
33 Medieval weapons
37 Lima's land
38 Relatives of the English horn
40 Pharaohs' river
41 Shivered
43 Persians, today
45 Slippery
46 "___ Mir Bist Du Schoen" (1938 hit)
47 Bombast
48 Gets the 7–10 split
51 Sheriff's symbol
53 Gypsy's deck
54 Have title to
55 Beginning
59 "Don't tell ___!"
60 Head honcho
62 "What ___ to do?"
63 Presently
64 Tickle-me doll
65 Tapes sent to recording companies
66 Classic political cartoonist
67 Card game start

DOWN

1 Doll's cry
2 Writer Kingsley
3 Piquancy
4 Adlai's 1956 running mate
5 Bobby of the Bruins
6 One-named 50's–60's teen idol
7 Search, as for weapons
8 Kind of lily
9 Informer
10 Head honcho
11 Nonnational
12 Uptight
13 One of the cattle in a cattle drive
18 Actor Kovacs
24 Signs up
25 Shaky
26 Mo. when Libra starts
27 Swear
28 Richard of "Primal Fear"
30 "Rue Morgue" writer
32 Head honcho
33 Pea container
34 Ped ___ (traffic caution)
35 Director Kazan
36 Meeting: Abbr.
39 Old Turkish pooh-bah
42 June bugs, e.g.
44 Severity
46 Folk music instruments
48 Conservative
49 Out of style
50 "___ With a View"
51 Master, in Swahili
52 Closed
54 Neighbor of Yemen
56 Shoe bottom
57 Jane Austen novel
58 Hammer or sickle
61 Toronto's prov.

by Robert Dillman

ACROSS

1 Pilgrimage to Mecca
5 Weather vane turner
9 It may have its own registry
14 Lamb's pen name
15 Champagne bucket
16 Pep ___
17 Catalogue abbr.
18 Twins player in "Big Business"
20 Gathered, as berries
22 Spinks of the ring
23 Suffix with Japan or journal
24 French father
26 Bronx cheer
28 Models of excellence
32 "The Crimes of Love" author Marquis ___
36 List-shortening abbr.
37 Recital piece
39 Betray, in a way
40 Terhune's "___ Dog"
41 Upright
43 Region
44 Lively Highland dance
46 Parcel (out)
47 Aspersion
48 Pizza portions
50 City on San Francisco Bay
52 Coup d'___
54 Late Chinese leader
55 Attorneys' org.
58 Soprano's song, maybe
60 Get ready
64 Twins player in "Start the Revolution Without Me"
67 Skeleton part
68 Part of UHF
69 Pound of poetry
70 Skip over
71 Shelley's "Adonais," e.g.
72 Tailor's meeting place
73 Assign an "R," say

DOWN

1 Rope fiber
2 Et ___ (and others)
3 Kind of jockey
4 Twins player in "House of Numbers"
5 Sweetbrier
6 Here, to Héloïse
7 "The Old Curiosity Shop" girl
8 Clothesline alternative
9 Get-tan-quick application
10 Zodiac animal
11 Supermodel Macpherson
12 Ivy League team
13 Bit of force
19 Warty hopper
21 Brain-wave test, briefly
25 Vast, in the past
27 Twins player in "The Girl in the Kremlin"
28 Ill-gotten gains
29 To any extent
30 Wheel spokes, e.g.
31 Catch some Z's
33 Ring around a lagoon
34 Cruller's cousin
35 January, in Jalisco
38 Group of eight
42 Pre-fax communiqué
45 Vacation spot
49 Rani's wrap
51 A wee hour
53 Scrabble pieces
55 Chills and fever
56 Dinger
57 Chip in chips
59 Axlike tool
61 "Arrivederci ___"
62 Condo division
63 Tennis's Sampras
65 Bit of work
66 Time to remember

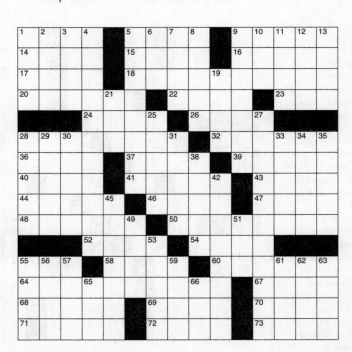

by John Greenman

ACROSS

1 From a distance
5 Zeal
10 Wrestling surfaces
14 Writer Ephron
15 Chessman
16 Here, in Honduras
17 ___ Alexander (Hall-of-Fame pitcher)
20 Surgery tool
21 Zsa Zsa's sister
22 Slander's counterpart
23 CBS logo
24 It makes the heart grow fonder
27 Is for more than one?
28 Middle of a simile
29 Last number in a countdown
31 ___ Duke (tobacco magnate)
38 Police officers
39 Yankee manager Joe
40 Common dog's name
42 Dadaist Jean
43 ___ non grata
45 Also
46 ___ Yello (soft drink)
48 Snooze
49 Gown
51 "The magic word"
53 Portuguese islands
54 ___ Toole (Pulitzer-winning novelist)
58 Tiff
60 Golfer's gouge
61 Corp. bigwig
64 Circle parts
65 Best of a group
66 Requirement
67 Stopped sleeping
68 Meted (out)
69 Sounds of disapproval

DOWN

1 What a protractor measures
2 Quick raid
3 Got out of bed
4 Great review
5 Busy mo. for the I.R.S.
6 Reduces to bits, as potatoes
7 Search (into)
8 Pacific, for one
9 Gun the engine
10 Niger's western neighbor
11 Gulf between Saudi Arabia and Egypt
12 Piano fixer
13 Move furtively
18 Clear the chalkboard
19 Actress Verdugo
25 Moisten the turkey
26 Former Maine Sen. William
28 Mornings, for short
30 Naval rank: Abbr.
31 Superman's father
32 Fermented cider
33 Brought to life
34 ___ Major (Great Bear)
35 Riding whip
36 Kiwis
37 Gallows loop
38 Pitch a tent
41 Light throw
43 Fancy-schmancy
44 Axlike tool
47 Noted Chinese philosopher
50 Mouse or beaver, e.g.
52 Finished
53 Chipped in chips
55 Amount in a drug shipment
56 Wicked
57 Memo
58 Trite saying
59 In favor of
62 Mouse hater's cry
63 Record store purchases

by Peter Gordon

ACROSS

1 Site of St. Peter's
5 Leg muscles, for short
10 Swindle
14 "Jeopardy!" host Trebek
15 Reversed
16 California Gov. Wilson
17 Itsy-bitsy skirt
18 Precalculator calculators
19 Corrida cheers
20 "Dallas" ranch
22 Fountain servings
23 Union letters
24 Airline seating class
26 Matzohs lack it
30 Early screen star Power
32 Axis foes
34 At any time, in poetry
35 Physics units
39 Teen hangout
40 50's bandleader Perez ___
42 Cross inscription
43 East European
44 ___ Lingus
45 Samples
47 Off the mark
50 A century after the Wright brothers' first flight
51 Like an old oak tree
54 G.I. entertainers
56 Cinema chain
57 Diving maneuver
63 First name in gymnastics
64 City south of Bartlesville
65 Point after deuce, maybe
66 ___ dire (legal process)
67 Have ___ of tea
68 Karate school
69 Start of North Carolina's motto
70 Catapult missile
71 Muhammad and others

DOWN

1 St. Louis 11
2 Hodgepodge
3 Carte
4 Kind of poll
5 Hearty draft
6 Open, as a barn door
7 Month after Shebat
8 Haggled
9 Star Wars, initially
10 "Hoobert Heever," e.g.
11 Rostropovich's instrument
12 Mr. T's TV show, with "The"
13 Cluttered
21 Bigot's emotion
22 Swindle
25 French landscape painter
26 Thanksgiving bowlful
27 Mideast carrier
28 ___ breve (2/2 time)
29 Theme of this puzzle
31 Pine
33 Alley score
36 Part of ABM
37 Three of a Kind?
38 Asunción assent
41 Adapt anew
46 One way to run
48 19th-century literary inits.
49 Arizona territorial capital
51 Fielder's aid
52 Legal pleas, informally
53 Umbrella
55 Play for the N.H.L.
58 Gravy Train competitor
59 Zippo
60 Pop star
61 South Seas getaway
62 Genesis son
64 Univ. instructors

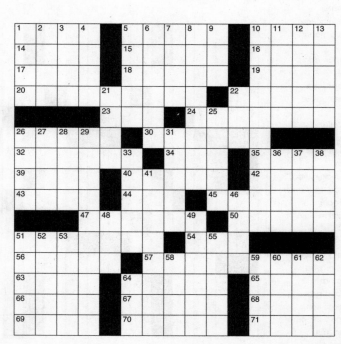

by Mark Elliot Skolsky

ACROSS

1 "Dear old" guy
4 Where Nome is
10 Nick and Nora's pooch
14 N.Y.C.'s ___ of the Americas
15 ___ to go
16 Urban haze
17 Tiny bite
18 Pat
20 Pet
22 ET's craft
23 Patriot Allen
24 Ozs. and ozs.
26 Facial spasm
29 Lucy's hubby
30 Kid's reply to a taunt
33 Cousin of "Oy!"
34 Della of "Touched by an Angel"
36 Suave actor David and others
38 Pit
40 Virginal
42 Unclouded
43 Sentry's "Stop!"
44 Europe's "boot"
46 Hounds
50 Yale student
51 ___ glance
52 Jazzman Blake
53 Spoil
55 Pot
59 Put
62 Chinese leader Sun ___-sen
63 "___ That a Shame" (#1 hit for 18-Across)
64 Scottish children
65 Opposite of WSW
66 Methods
67 Refuse to yield
68 Decimal point

DOWN

1 Tangoed, e.g.
2 Fly a plane
3 Ocean bottoms
4 Fire-setting crime
5 Lion's home
6 Florence's river
7 Ink a contract
8 Prepares to pray
9 Farming: Abbr.
10 Beginning on
11 Not so bumpy
12 Coal delivery unit
13 Grow older
19 City transit
21 Most equitable
25 Billy the Kid's surname
27 Country restaurant
28 Fortune 500 listings: Abbr.
30 Falseness
31 Common language suffix
32 Bing Crosby's record label
33 Add extra music to, as a vocal tape
35 Chow down
37 "Give ___ rest!"
38 Ex's payment, modern-style
39 Right-angled bend
40 Guerrilla Guevara
41 Falstaff's prince
45 Alternative to Maytag or KitchenAid
47 Followed orders
48 Jeans brand
49 Six-line poem
51 Biblical boat
52 ___ & Young (accounting firm)
54 Play parts
56 Elevator innovator
57 Opera's ___ Te Kanawa
58 Geologic periods
59 Observed
60 Spanish aunt
61 Japanese sash

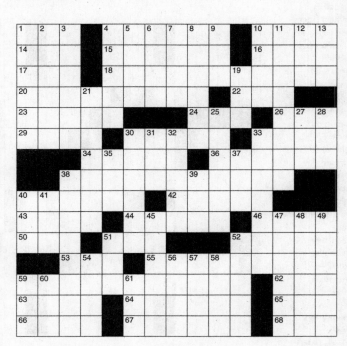

by Mark Danna

116 ★

ACROSS

1 What jazz ends with, in England
5 Leaves in, editorially
10 One who's decamped?
14 Linen color
15 Formerly one of the Dow Jones 30
16 Elizabeth of the Red Cross
17 With 39-Across, often-quoted work of 1923
20 Sot
21 Oval
22 Campus mil. org.
25 90 degrees, on a compass
26 Unit of oil production: Abbr.
29 Matter to go to court over
31 Linen colors
35 Statement from Pinocchio
36 Old-fashioned music hall
38 River to the English Channel
39 See 17-Across
43 Evil one
44 Common dice roll
45 Expected
46 Single-celled organisms
49 Austin-based computer company
50 Knight
51 More than a snack
53 Stir up
55 Tropical woe
58 Israeli native
62 What 17- and 39-Across is
65 Rainbows
66 Rips to pieces
67 Saroyan's "My Name is ___"
68 TV sleuth Fletcher, to friends
69 Wear away
70 Abysmal test score

DOWN

1 Part of an orange
2 Prefix with plasm
3 Tiniest bit
4 Marvelous
5 Schuss, e.g.
6 Quite a load
7 Advantage
8 Coffee ___
9 1973 NASA launch
10 Alternative to pregnancy
11 Coaxes
12 Kind of shoppe
13 "___ Miz"
18 Subatomic particle
19 Judicious
23 List heading
24 Ships' handlers
26 Rarity for a century plant
27 "That's it!"
28 Absorb facts
30 Played (with)
32 Diagrams
33 Ho-hum feeling
34 Rocker Bob
37 "Well, I ___!"
40 Like some stockings
41 Prefix with -drome
42 Sign up
47 Expensive
48 "Les Mouches" dramatist
52 One with no hope of getting out
54 Capital of Bolivia
55 Extra
56 The basics
57 Cartoonist Peter
59 Reduce to tears, maybe
60 Stern
61 BB's and such
62 The Brits in colonial India
63 Unusual
64 Atlanta-to-Tampa dir.

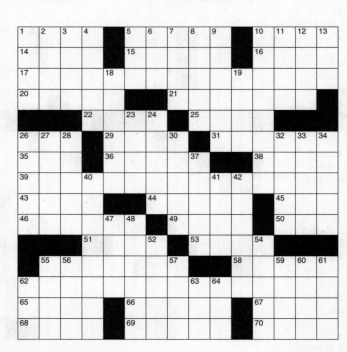

by Bill Ballard

ACROSS

1 Reply to a ques.
4 Wisecrack
8 Youngster
13 Brag about
15 Wrist-elbow connector
16 Cowboy contest
17 Defeats
19 Traveler's reference
20 Composer who wrote "The Magic Flute"
21 "Don't go out!"
23 Speaker's spot
25 Medicinal herb
26 Become motionless out of fear
30 Pass, as time
34 Thin fish
35 "This ___" (shipping label)
37 Unprepared comment
38 Actor Guinness
40 Plants used to make poi
42 Without: Fr.
43 Discipline
45 Popular athletic footwear
47 Golf bag item
48 Baroque and rococo, e.g.
50 Opposite of 26-Across?
52 Apollo astronaut Slayton
54 Suffix with gang
55 Unwanted art
59 Fanatic
63 U. S. Grant opponent
64 Opposite of 17-Across?
66 Deduce
67 Gloomy
68 Bubbly beverage
69 Castles' barriers

70 TV deputy from Hazzard
71 Armenia or Azerbaijan, once: Abbr.

DOWN

1 Tiny particle
2 Porto-___ (Benin's capital)
3 Canal that leads to the Red Sea
4 Division result
5 German city on the Danube
6 Chemical endings
7 Macaroni and such
8 Colorful brand name?
9 Rash people
10 Not busy
11 Shakespearean king
12 Prescription amount

14 Barter
18 Mania
22 Bubbly beverage
24 Land south of Egypt
26 Is afraid of
27 On again, as a lantern
28 Poem of lament
29 Jewish festival
31 Philosopher who wrote the "Republic"
32 Tendon
33 Actor Buddy
36 Nudges
39 Opposite of 9-Down?
41 Bubbly beverages
44 Illegal cigarettes, slangily
46 Turn the wheel
49 Do slaloms
51 Pulls

53 Conservatory assignment, perhaps
55 Bleak
56 Clinton Attorney General
57 ___ Romeo (Italian auto)
58 Let ___ a secret
60 Facilities, in Falmouth
61 Multivolume ref. works
62 Pre-1917 ruler
65 Twosome

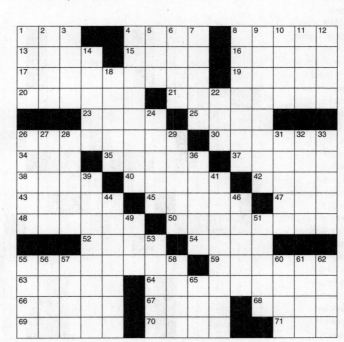

by Jeremy Thomas Paine

118 ⭐

ACROSS

1 Religious scroll
6 Coat, as with plaster
10 Group with the 1976 hit "Fernando"
14 Solo
15 Fare for Fido
16 Medicinal weight
17 Domingo, for one
18 Smack
19 Indian music
20 1991 best seller by Jim Stewart
23 It laps the shore
26 Trump's "art"
27 ___ de Cologne
28 "___ soul man" (Blues Brothers lyric)
29 Trains on high
31 Circumference
33 Sheepish response
34 Neighbor of Mex.
37 Lowbrow sitcom staple
41 Bro's counterpart
42 Lend a hand
43 Nattering type
45 Scandalous 80's initials
46 "___ Compères" (1984 film)
48 Suffix with Sudan
49 Hon
53 All over the place, as paint
56 Secret diet-breakers
58 Western Indians
59 Lévesque of Québec
60 Out-and-out
64 Elder, for one
65 Midmonth date
66 Info-packed
67 Pronounces
68 "Hey, you!"
69 American-born princess

DOWN

1 Work on a doily
2 ___ Miss
3 Director Howard
4 Where to connect one end of a jumper cable
5 Enclosed, in legalese
6 Noted Big Apple residence, with "the"
7 "Get ___!"
8 Against the current
9 Hooey
10 See eye to eye
11 Accolade for Von Stade
12 Deli item
13 Accumulate
21 Site of 60's tour of duty
22 Bouncers check them: Abbr.
23 Parlor drink
24 Poetic feet
25 Mideast emirate
30 "Well, ___-di-dah!"
32 The "I" of T.G.I.F.
33 Ogler's target
34 Actress Thurman
35 Clearheaded
36 Left one's seat
38 Lab runner
39 Sesame paste source
40 Discomposed
44 Rest stop?
45 Nuptial starter
46 Most recent
47 Season in Bordeaux
49 Aberdeen folk
50 Extremist
51 Like hot fudge
52 Dolts
54 Glazier's items
55 Fragrant compound
57 Stumble
61 J.F.K. terminal
62 Computer key, for short
63 Popular toast

by Elizabeth C. Gorski

ACROSS

1 "___ Howdy Doody time!"
4 Bit of gravel
9 "Falstaff" or "Fidelio"
14 Singer ___ King Cole
15 Lecture hall platforms
16 Boxcars, in dice
17 Barbecue dish
19 Open, as a bottle
20 Weird
21 "Cómo ___ usted?"
23 Enlivens, with "up"
24 Developments
26 One "E" on a scoreboard
28 Street urchin
32 Nay canceler
35 Load for Jack and Jill
36 Madcap
38 9-Across solo
40 Fairy tale figure
43 Bird on a beach
44 Malden and Marx
46 Scores 72 on a 72 course
48 Lair
49 Kind of timing
53 Slowdown
54 Deep Throat, e.g., in the Watergate scandal
58 Kill, as a dragon
60 Not slack
63 Smells
64 Birchbark
66 Nolan Ryan specialty
68 Bread spreads
69 Pale purple
70 NNW's opposite
71 Hornets' cousins
72 Very, very thin
73 Word before "more" and "merrier"

DOWN

1 Map within a map
2 Become narrower
3 Gawk (at)
4 Acceleration
5 Craggy peak
6 Garfield's canine pal
7 Bird beaks
8 It ends Lent
9 The Buckeyes: Abbr.
10 Locate exactly
11 Quoted (from)
12 Sow's opposite
13 Nile snakes
18 Bathtub detritus
22 Horace's "___ Poetica"
25 Without women
27 Genetic initials
29 Kind of foil
30 Skip the usual wedding preparations
31 Land of the leprechauns
32 Tibetan ox
33 Paleozoic and Mesozoic
34 Hangar contents
37 Larry King employer
39 Cartoon caveman
41 Rock's Fleetwood ___
42 Son of Aphrodite
45 Take a chair
47 Pub game
50 Egyptian boy king
51 Muscle tics
52 Surfer's sobriquet
55 Barnyard perch
56 Puppy love
57 Cosmetician Lauder
58 Flat-bottomed boat
59 Singer's refrain
61 Beehive State
62 Loyal
65 Super G curve, in the Olympics
67 "___ Got a Secret"

by Randall J. Hartman

ACROSS

1 Remote control button
5 Secure a ship
9 Hunter's trail
14 Pinnacle
15 Poet Pound
16 Mare : foal :: cow : ___
17 Sicilian spouter
18 Arabian Sea adjoiner
19 Hit the + key
20 Mrs. Morgenstern player on "Rhoda"
23 Watchdog's warning
24 Japanese dog
25 Explorer who named Louisiana
27 ___ Plaines, Ill.
28 Barnes & Noble habitué
32 Hi's helpmate, in the comics
33 Witchy woman
34 Buenos ___
35 Marxist exiled by Stalin
38 ___ Valley, Calif.
40 Out of dreamland
41 Saws
42 Cafe or cabaret
44 Pompous sort
47 Listened to again, as legal arguments
49 16 drams
51 Unusual shoe width
52 "Guys and Dolls" writer
56 Visit the registrar
58 Concept
59 Dairy airs?
60 Screen star Keaton
61 Wander
62 Poker pot starter
63 Man of La Mancha
64 Pulls a boner
65 "Untouchable" Eliot

DOWN

1 Attendant on Dionysus
2 Slow on the ___ (thickheaded)
3 With 44-Down, court query
4 Obtain by demand
5 Siamese sound
6 Baum princess
7 Kind of exam or history
8 Irritate
9 Surgical souvenirs
10 Hippie's hangout
11 The Stars and Stripes
12 Be situated atop
13 Set right
21 Peter of Peter, Paul & Mary
22 Pitcher part
26 Comparable
29 Long, long time
30 Cupboard crawler
31 Rid of vermin
33 Put an end to
34 "Now I ___!"
35 Like most Danish churchgoers
36 Have bills
37 Old salt
38 Lengthy discourses
39 Hattie McDaniel's "Show Boat" role
42 The Roaring Twenties, e.g.
43 Look up to
44 See 3-Down
45 Moves along quickly
46 Taste and touch, for two
48 Freud contemporary
50 Deprive of one's nerve
53 Scent
54 Approach
55 Namath's last team
57 Lennon's widow

by Patrick Jordan

ACROSS

1 Thumb-twiddling
5 Leapfrogs
10 ___ Bator, Mongolia
14 Make airtight
15 ___ a time (singly)
16 "Cleopatra" backdrop
17 "Yes!"
19 Darling
20 Sendak's "Where the Wild Things ___"
21 Composer Satie
22 Soviet leader Brezhnev
24 lightweight weapon
26 Land of the llama
27 Red-white-and-blue inits.
28 Information bank
32 Passing notice?
35 King of the jungle
37 What a lumberjack leaves behind
38 River to the Rio Grande
40 SSW's opposite
41 Like a haunted house
42 Skyward
43 Persian ___
45 Person to go out with
46 Round Table knight
48 C.I.O.'s partner
50 Skip
51 "Don't move!"
55 Snake-haired woman of myth
58 35-Across's sound
59 ___ de France
60 Walkie-talkie word
61 "Yes!"
64 Needles' partner
65 Train making all stops
66 Med school subj.
67 Otherwise
68 Manicurist's board
69 Optimistic

DOWN

1 Writer Asimov
2 Actress Winger
3 Tattoo remover
4 "Xanadu" rock grp.
5 Diary
6 Loosen, as a knot
7 Overly docile
8 Chum
9 Sharp-pointed instrument
10 "Yes!"
11 Mortgage
12 Jai ___
13 Uncool one
18 Arrival gifts in Honolulu
23 Remove, as marks
25 "Yes!"
26 See 51-Down
28 Coffee break snack
29 Glow
30 Slugged, old-style
31 Sportsman's blade
32 October's birthstone
33 Composer Bartók
34 PC picture
36 Fort Knox unit
39 Cherries' leftovers
44 So as to cause death
47 Apt
49 Raise crops
51 With 26-Down, a rooftop energy device
52 Elton John's instrument
53 Arm bones
54 Not handling criticism well
55 Brood
56 Like Darth Vader
57 Cub Scout groups
58 Derby
62 ___ Kippur
63 Something to lend or bend

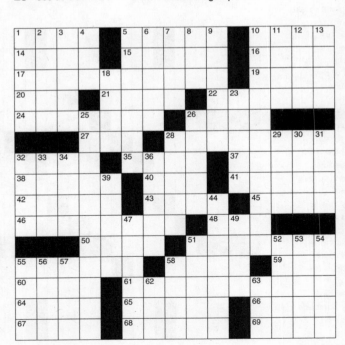

by Gregory E. Paul

122

ACROSS

1 Auntie, dramatically
5 "La Classe de danse" artist
10 Birds in barns
14 Quizmaster Trebek
15 Humble
16 Cookie since 1912
17 Asset for 34-Across?
20 Bee activity
21 Classical lyric poet
22 Creative work
23 Book after Nehemiah: Abbr.
24 Sites of crosses
27 Meadow sounds
28 ___ Na Na
31 No longer on the plate
32 Doughnut shapes
33 Extent
34 Circus act
37 Place for a revival
38 Kind of desk
39 Flowerless plants
40 Before, in poetry
41 Rules out
42 Not yet sunk
43 Common hello or goodbye
44 Habeas corpus, for one
45 Spicy cuisine
48 Takes advance orders for
52 Liability for 34-Across?
54 The Urals are west of it
55 Dinner bird
56 Witty Bombeck
57 Put salt on, maybe
58 Bridge positions
59 Time of decision

DOWN

1 Handy computers
2 "There oughta be ___!"
3 Southwest sight
4 Glad-handing type
5 Father of Xerxes
6 Dark shades
7 Thieves' group
8 Numbskull
9 Leaves the dock
10 Zing
11 Saran, e.g.
12 Preyer
13 London or New York district
18 Be about to happen
19 Feedbag feed
23 Jumping the gun
24 Romantic adventure
25 More cold and wet
26 Agreeing (with)
27 Marina sights
28 Veep Agnew
29 ___-Barbera (big name in cartoons)
30 Feeling of apprehension
32 Coil
33 Took the heat badly
35 Search like wolves
36 Aloof
41 Island near Java
42 Rugged ridges
43 Actor Tom of "The Dukes of Hazzard"
44 Extract by force
45 Symbol of noncommunication
46 Trick
47 Oscar winner Jannings
48 Light: Prefix
49 Byron or Tennyson
50 Tibetan monk
51 Corset part
53 ___ fault (overly so)

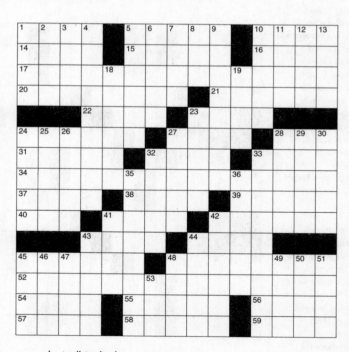

by Lyell Rodieck

ACROSS

1 Begin, as school
6 St. Peter's Square figure
10 Broadway "Auntie"
14 Peter of "Casablanca"
15 Cards up one's sleeve?
16 Muslim holy man
17 Any one of God's creatures
18 Classic Bette Davis line from "Beyond the Forest"
20 Second-place finishers
22 Call forth
23 WNW's opposite
24 DiCaprio, to fans
25 Lock opener
26 Proceeding easily, at last
31 Dallas's locale
32 Metal to be refined
33 Res ___ loquitur
37 Tempers
38 Flogged
40 Underground vegetable
41 Miss America wears one
42 ___ de Janeiro
43 Word on mail from Spain
44 Oscar-winning role for Tom Hanks
47 Greyhound, e.g.
50 Slalom curve
51 It's perpendicular to long.
52 Golden Delicious and others
54 1966 Simon and Garfunkel hit
59 High school parking lot fixture
61 Religious law
62 Soho socials
63 Responsibility
64 Blackjack phrase
65 Flubs
66 Sage
67 Run off to the chapel

DOWN

1 Exile site for Napoleon
2 Christmas
3 Speaker of Cooperstown
4 Cube inventor Rubik
5 Brief turndown to an invitation
6 Oklahoma Indian
7 Newspaperman Adolph
8 Stew morsel
9 Highly regarded
10 Skirt style
11 Frenzied: Var.
12 Mrs. Eisenhower
13 Running on ___
19 Not straight
21 Fire remnant
24 Tackle box item
26 Mayberry jail habitué
27 Actress Miles
28 Alimony receivers
29 Poison ivy woe
30 Courtroom addressee, with "your"
33 "___ to differ!"
34 Lima's land
35 Appear
36 Surmounting
38 Medieval weapon
39 Broadcasts
43 Diplomat's aide
44 Corn, to chickens
45 Run out
46 Uncle ___
47 Sew with loose stitches
48 Certain berth
49 Weapon that's thrown
53 More or ___
54 Radio man Don
55 Train track
56 Word after catch or hang
57 Free ticket
58 Bouncing baby's seat
60 Single: Prefix

by Randall J. Hartman

124

ACROSS

1 Nabisco cracker
5 Respond to seeing red?
9 Central highway
14 Brainstorm
15 Not taped
16 Former
17 Summon Warsaw citizens?
19 Hint of color
20 Opposite of masc.
21 F.B.I. workers
23 The I's have them
24 Mileage testing grp.
25 Undercover operation
27 Small change for a Brit
32 Unimagined
35 Broadcast studio sign
36 Any hit by Elvis
38 Hubbub
39 Artificial locks
40 Summon the elected?
42 Hit on the knuckles
43 Sorbonne summer
44 Bottle capacity
45 Common nest locale
47 Fine point
49 Under pressure
51 ___ Nile
53 Opponent of D.D.E.
54 Songstress Vikki
56 Dressed, so to speak
59 Trendy
62 Talk a blue streak
64 Summon actress Sharon?
66 ___ football (indoor sport)
67 Cartoonist Peter
68 "A Clockwork Orange" hooligan
69 Cattail's locale
70 Made a bubble, in a way
71 Crème de la crème

DOWN

1 Jazz phrase
2 Goofing off
3 Broncos or Chargers
4 Veer suddenly
5 Campaign ad feature
6 Scrabble piece
7 Broiling locale
8 Pains in the neck
9 To the point
10 The East
11 Summon Michael Jordan and John Stockton?
12 Take-out words
13 War god
18 Office fastener
22 Gravy spot
24 Prefix with center
26 Glaciers
27 Like illegally parked cars, sometimes
28 Get together
29 Summon a cable magnate?
30 Derby prospect
31 French fashion magazines
33 "Waste not, want not," e.g.
34 Ran
37 Malicious gossip
41 Was bedbound
46 Snaky letter
48 Chefs' wear
50 Was almost out of inventory
52 Get-well site
54 Study late
55 Ambiance
57 Baseball's Yastrzemski
58 German article
59 Links target
60 Washington bills
61 Student's book
63 "No dice"
65 Bill

by Nancy Salomon

ACROSS

1 Playwright William
5 Some Pennsylvania Dutch
10 Carol
14 That, in France
15 Division of a long poem
16 Hard rain?
17 Best Picture of 1995
19 Tex. neighbor
20 Car that was always black
21 Catch red-handed
22 Swerve
23 Arctic bird
25 Goalie's job
27 Bed turner?
31 ___ and anon
32 "I didn't know that!"
33 Appliquéd
38 Enticed
40 Crow's cry
42 Barber's work
43 ___ of Capricorn
45 Brit. fliers
47 Roman road
48 "Cracklin' Rosie" singer
51 "Shane," e.g.
55 "Last one ___ a rotten egg!"
56 Robust
57 Much of 35-Down's terr.
59 Melodious
63 With defects and all
64 Group that makes contracts
66 Fasting time
67 Drive away
68 "The African Queen" screenwriter James
69 Organization with a lodge
70 One of the Astaires
71 Slothful

DOWN

1 Part of a nuclear arsenal, for short
2 Fiddling emperor
3 Pleased
4 Listen in (on)
5 German warning
6 Fannie ___ security
7 ___ instant (quickly)
8 Italian road
9 Centers of activity
10 Push
11 Like some old buckets
12 Frasier's brother on "Frasier"
13 Harsh reflection
18 Actress Sommer
24 "Hold on ___!"
26 Payments to doctors
27 Moola
28 Assert
29 Fix up
30 Oyster's center
34 Capricious
35 Org. formed to contain Communism
36 Bread chamber
37 One who's socially clueless
39 Prime-time hour
41 Desert stream
44 Parts of brains
46 Wangle
49 Accustomed
50 Suffix with million
51 Humpback, e.g.
52 Stand for something
53 Go furtively
54 They may come in a battery
58 Ready to be picked
60 Korbut on the beam
61 Egyptian canal
62 Mind
65 The first of 13: Abbr.

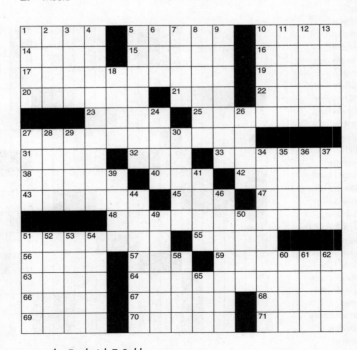

by Frederick T. Buhler

ACROSS

1 Penniless
6 Frank of the Mothers of Invention
11 Pharmaceuticals overseer, for short
14 Whose 1961 record Mark McGwire beat
15 Hägar the Horrible's dog
16 ___ Lingus
17 Part 1 of a song parody
19 ___ tai
20 Funny old guy
21 Bog
22 Hilarious jokes
25 Book after Job
27 "Put a lid ___!"
28 Song parody, part 2
31 Cuban coins
33 "I don't believe it!"
34 Song parody, part 3
40 Tiny bit
41 Tartish plums
43 Song parody, part 4
48 Spy's secret
49 Kvetch
50 Stalemate
52 Pleasant tune
53 Clean the hands before dinner
55 A Gardner
56 End of the song parody
61 Singer Shannon
62 Jack of "The Great Dictator"
63 It's positively electric
64 Time in history
65 Stimulates
66 Attach a patch

DOWN

1 Maker of the 5-Series
2 "Yay!"
3 Dig it
4 Jamaica's capital
5 "Terminal Bliss" actress Chandler
6 A Gabor
7 Upfront amount
8 Equal
9 Start with school
10 Pac.'s counterpart
11 Zoological classification
12 "Stars above!"
13 Bold, impatient type, astrologically
18 Ginseng, e.g.
21 West of Hollywood
22 Republican
23 Once more
24 Enthusiastic reply in Mexico
25 Gasp
26 Snooty types
29 Attire at fraternity blasts
30 "Be still!"
32 Burlesque bits
35 After-bath cover
36 Resident: Suffix
37 1931 convictee
38 Talks amorously
39 Shoes introduced by the United States Rubber Co.
42 Match in poker
43 Golf club
44 "How luxurious!"
45 Screwball
46 Snake sounds
47 Jewish youth org.
49 Forest clearing
51 Big cats
53 Boat follower
54 Arguing
56 Pull along
57 "That'll show 'em!"
58 It's one thing after another
59 Stir
60 Hankering

by Kelly Clark

ACROSS

1 Entr'___ (theater break)
5 Word repeated before "pants on fire"
9 Turns from ice to water
14 Daily delivery
15 Press for
16 Best
17 Italian wine province
18 Ring-tailed critter
19 Pause for a rest
20 Permanent military procedures
23 Lady of Lima
24 "___ geht's?" ("How goes it?"): Ger.
25 Plumbing convenience
32 Flower starter
35 They wrap their food well
36 Intake problem?
37 Part of a list
39 Coal box
41 Not a permanent employee
42 Reversible fabric
45 Wordsmith Webster
48 Wrestling site
49 Wishers' object
52 Chicken ___ king
53 Park features
57 Tree-to-tree traveler
62 Unearthly
63 Zap
64 "Othello" villain
65 Beatrice's adorer
66 Toward shelter
67 Threaded metal fastener
68 Recording sign
69 Fling
70 Puppy cries

DOWN

1 Pile up
2 Hindu social division
3 Giant
4 Romance novelist ___ Glyn
5 Tenor Pavarotti
6 Vitamin tablet supplement
7 Highly excited
8 Celebrity
9 Funguses
10 90's singer Brickell
11 Unpleasant look
12 Day planner features
13 Foxy
21 Clobber
22 Latvia's capital
26 Collar
27 Gershwin's "Of Thee ___"
28 Big inits. in long distance
29 Not us
30 Oscar winner ___ Thompson
31 Deeply absorbed
32 Auction actions
33 Orrin Hatch's state
34 It's just for show
38 Longtime Chinese leader
40 Rebuffs
43 Dye worker
44 Brick oven
46 Puts into harmony
47 Mata ___
50 Pesters
51 Blue moon, e.g.
54 Teheran native
55 Slight advantage, so to speak
56 Atlantic City machines
57 Sweetened custard
58 Director Wertmuller
59 Abominable Snowman
60 D-Day invasion town
61 Opposite of an ans.
62 Ruckus

by Fran and Lou Sabin

ACROSS

1 Airline founded in 1927
6 Garden smoother
10 Bygone Mideast leader
14 D-Day beach
15 "Make it quick!"
16 Showed up
17 "Look who just showed up!"
20 Uncle of rice fame
21 Court game
22 Cluckhead
25 Marooned motorist's need
27 Scouting job
28 ___ Gras
30 Perpendicular to the keel
34 "___ With a View"
35 Where cold cuts are cut
36 "This ___ fair!"
40 Popular basketball shoe
43 Midleg point
44 Rudely abrupt
45 Escape detection of
46 Expire
47 Eagle's home
48 Pitcher Hideo Nomo's birthplace
52 Popular oil additive
54 "Spy vs. Spy" magazine
55 Intern in the news
59 Spooky sighting
61 Rutgers, e.g.
66 Raison d'___
67 Numbskull
68 Blast from the past
69 Drifts off
70 Leave be
71 Thugs

DOWN

1 Not neg.
2 Sound booster
3 Highland negative
4 Captain of the Pequod
5 Provide (for), in a schedule
6 "A Yank in the ___" (1941 war film)
7 Regarding
8 Actress Madeline
9 Fencer's blade
10 Public row
11 Ruinous damage
12 Protein building block
13 Her face launched a thousand ships
18 Lennon's lady
19 Quad building
22 Impact sound
23 Baseball's Hank
24 Lying facedown
26 Crumples into a tiny ball
29 Peacenik
31 A round at the tavern, say
32 Delights
33 Do poorly
36 Castaway's spot
37 ___ und Drang
38 Gymnast Comaneci
39 In a corner
41 Company with a dog in its logo
42 Quaint children's game
46 Shady route
48 Sportscaster Merlin
49 Brawl
50 O. Henry, in the literary world
51 Toys with tails
53 Wed. preceder
56 Brewski
57 Shoelace problem
58 Cry of pain
60 1993 peace accord city
62 November honoree
63 Joining words
64 Food container
65 "Right"

by Brendan Emmett Quigley

ACROSS

1 "Damn Yankees" seductress
5 Thick piece
9 Where Rome's home
14 Frosted
15 Jay who chins with guests
16 Wanderer
17 Not much
18 Say positively
19 Brawls
20 Company with high personnel turnover
23 Dictation taker
24 "New Look" designer
25 Sweet potato
28 Graceful bird
31 Winnie-the-Pooh's creator
33 Lawyer: Abbr.
36 Regret
38 Mystery writer Gardner et al.
39 Eastern dancer
44 Bicker
45 Umpire's call
46 Home for Babe
47 Show, as a historic battle
50 Stands in the way of
53 Always, to a verse writer
54 Verse writer
56 Partner of pains
60 Yarn-making device
64 Pageant winner
66 Something the nose knows
67 Chorus syllables
68 Lovers' lane event
69 Popular sauce
70 Lacking bumps
71 Take care of
72 Messy dresser
73 Sprightly

DOWN

1 Whopper tellers
2 Eight-man band
3 "Get out!"
4 Extensions
5 Pole, e.g.
6 ___ Strauss & Co.
7 Put ___ to (finish)
8 Infamous Italian family name
9 Tattletale
10 Bullfight bull
11 Lilylike flower
12 Song played on a mandolin
13 Football gains: Abbr.
21 Daily temperature extreme
22 ___ good turn
26 "___ of robins in her hair"
27 Having an open weave
29 Jackie's second
30 Convent dweller
32 TV personality Kupcinet
33 Not in a fog
34 Perpetual time on the clock at Independence Hall
35 Ornamental stone
37 "I" problem
40 Operate
41 Enter full force
42 Nickname
43 Guesstimate letters
48 Jailbird
49 Pavarotti and Domingo
51 Green
52 Lug
55 Kind of wave
57 Throw
58 Specialist in fishing
59 Viewpoint
61 Botherer
62 Failed attempt
63 Chow
64 Parts of gals.
65 Suffix with press

by Dorothy Smitonick

ACROSS

1 Con game
5 Given an R or PG
10 60's do
14 Standard
15 Elicit
16 It may be entered in a court
17 Request for artist Georgia's forbearance?
20 ___ Tin Tin
21 Enticed
22 Washing jobs
23 They're apt to get into hot water
25 Sweetie
26 1952 and '56 campaign name
27 Grand
32 Like ___ out of hell
35 Drives off
36 Of the congregation
37 Mexico City portrait painter?
41 Behave
42 Western "necktie"
43 Revival meeting cry
44 Deficiency
46 Pale
48 OPEC export
49 Filled in
53 "Beat it!"
56 Plait
58 Eggs
59 "Georges paints as he pleases"?
62 Exploit
63 Appropriate
64 Marquis de ___
65 Recipe amts.
66 Schnozzes
67 Ogled

DOWN

1 [Hmmph!]
2 Newswoman Roberts
3 Scene of the action
4 Lady de la maison: Abbr.
5 Sanctuary
6 Swears
7 Heavy reading
8 ___ out a living (scraped by)
9 Org. involved in raids
10 Blacksmiths' wear
11 Kind of market
12 Study
13 Slow-growing trees
18 Antiaircraft fire
19 It may be worn under a sweater
24 Bridle parts
25 Catcall
27 Them there
28 Sharpen
29 Astringent
30 Specify
31 Actress Cannon
32 Epiphanies
33 "Art of the Fugue" composer
34 Choir part
35 Air apparent?
38 Punctual
39 Farm delivery
40 Author Grey
45 Lies in the summer sun
46 Places for watches
47 Adjutant
49 Shower
50 Incursion
51 Skirt
52 Saw
53 Room meas.
54 They're waited for at a theater
55 Glean
56 Vivacity
57 Tatters
60 Ashes holder
61 "___ as directed"

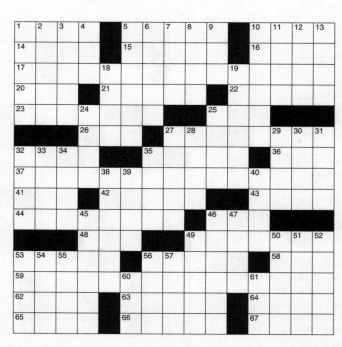

by Norma Steinberg

ACROSS

1 England's ___ Downs
6 Secluded vale
10 German philosopher Immanuel
14 Summa cum ___
15 Lifesaver, say
16 Hand cream ingredient
17 Tootsie
19 One of Columbus's ships
20 Implore
21 Pathetically inept person
23 Baptism, e.g.
25 Places for camels to drink
26 Two quarters
30 Kick-around shoes
33 Florida city
35 Sellout shows, for short
36 Building wing
39 Occasion for roses
43 Suffix with Canton
44 Country way
45 Sign by a free sample
46 Bullfighters
49 Nile vipers
50 Under way
53 March tourney sponsor
55 Way of thinking
58 Compel obedience to
63 Inter ___
64 Love note
66 Space on a schedule
67 Margarine
68 Delivery person's path
69 "Auld Lang ___"
70 Insect's home
71 Comic Johnson and others

DOWN

1 Otherwise
2 One on the way to a promotion?
3 Bird feeder food
4 River to the Baltic
5 Olympics measure
6 Area needing urban renewal
7 Meadow
8 Misses the mark
9 ___ care in the world
10 Topeka's home
11 Spy's name, possibly
12 Time being
13 Shipbuilding woods
18 Salute with enthusiasm
22 English county known for sheep
24 "We earn our wings every day" airline
26 Fire truck attachment
27 Book after John
28 Wash
29 Neighbor of Ga.
31 Thurs. follower
32 Long, long time
34 Apportions
36 Ice cream brand
37 Den light
38 Caustic materials
40 Order of corn
41 SSW's opposite
42 Mme., in Spain
46 Until now
47 Cousin of a leopard
48 Playing with a full deck
50 Stockpile
51 Colt's counterpart
52 Burger topper
54 Media workers' union
56 Black
57 Easy-to-clean floor
59 Scent
60 Win in a runaway
61 Baby-faced
62 Partners who called it quits
65 "___ Misérables"

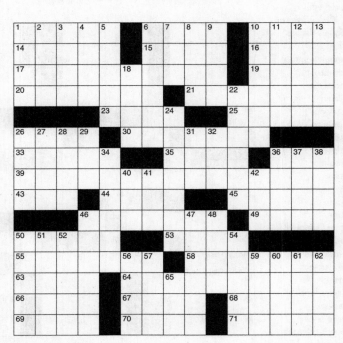

by Sidney L. Robbins

ACROSS

1 Does a standard dog trick
5 Flock members
9 Actor Cary of "Twister"
14 To be, in Toulon
15 Ernie's "Sesame Street" pal
16 ___-lance (pit viper)
17 Kind of instrument
18 The "B" of N.B.
19 Nourishes
20 Country club employees
23 Ink for une plume
24 Sulky state
25 Lao-___
28 Originally named
29 Coral formation
33 Long John Silver, e.g.
35 Ironed
37 ___-majesté
38 Col. Klink player on "Hogan's Heroes"
43 Certain util.
44 Channel swimmer Gertrude
45 Remove the pits from
48 Capt. Hook's companion
49 Martians, e.g.
52 Glimpse
53 Animal doc
55 Assail
57 Peppermint liqueur
62 Hinder
64 Actress Campbell
65 "God shed His grace on ___"
66 News subject
67 Large number
68 Projector load
69 Gives up
70 They're seven positions after this puzzle's theme
71 Scots Gaelic

DOWN

1 "Murphy Brown" star
2 Timeless, to a poet
3 Where Zeus was worshiped
4 Passover meal
5 Recedes
6 Time span
7 Sea eagle
8 Brew
9 Decadent
10 Playboy's gaze
11 Hulk Hogan, for one
12 Hall-of-Famer Roush
13 His or her, in France
21 Audacity
22 Energy
26 Late ruler Mobotu ___ Seko
27 River through Bavaria
30 Poetic contraction
31 Three-time speed skating gold medalist Karin
32 Circus impresario Irvin and others
34 Mirth
35 Suffix with exist
36 Consider
38 Joins in holy matrimony
39 Gen. Robt. ___
40 Completely excised, in surgery
41 G.I. chow in Desert Storm
42 Military academy freshman
46 Turns inside out
47 Rep. foe
49 Book after Nehemiah
50 Giggles
51 TV's "Remington ___"
54 High-strung
56 ___ nous
58 Actress Russo
59 Place for a farmer?
60 Daredevil Knievel
61 British stables
62 Jan. preceder
63 Night before

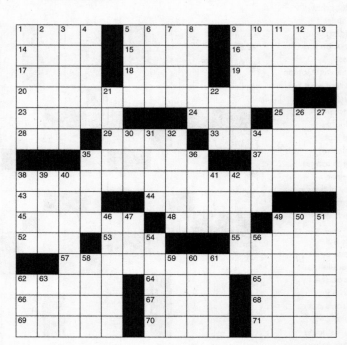

by Janet R. Bender

ACROSS

1 Pedicurists work on them
5 Ship's front
9 Old Venetian magistrates
14 Cutlass or 98, for short
15 Architect Saarinen
16 Give the slip
17 Sarcastic remark
19 Neighbor of Nigeria
20 New Year's ___
21 Mystique
22 Devastated
23 Backslide, medically
25 Imagination
26 Questionnaire response
28 Soak (up)
31 Bid
34 Falsehoods
35 Lawyers' org.
36 Select a winner in a sweepstakes
37 Base before home
39 Person whose name begins "Mc-," often
40 ___ Moines
41 Elvis's middle name
42 "Land ___!"
43 Word between ready and go
44 Hike
47 Pickup, e.g.
49 Stockpiled
53 Equality
55 Epithet
56 Actor Wallach
57 Precise
58 Title character in 1970's cult films
60 Corner
61 Skin softener
62 End in ___
63 Propositioned
64 Civil wrong
65 Mount Olympus dwellers

DOWN

1 Radio station facility
2 Martini item
3 Ford flop
4 Opposite NNW
5 Leaf through
6 Brought up
7 Killer whale
8 Moo goo gai pan pan
9 Exposes, as a false claim
10 Kind of acid
11 Grain holder on a farm
12 Chanteuse Adams
13 Dispatch
18 Prank
22 Competed at Daytona
24 Not many
25 Blond
27 Go on and off, as a light
29 Hand-held musical instrument
30 Butter servings
31 "What are the ___ . . . ?"
32 Gratis
33 Accelerated path to success
37 "Dick ___"
38 Leave at a pawnshop
39 ___ Fifth Avenue
41 Bordered on
42 Creepy
45 Whiteness
46 Lucky charm
48 Nouveau ___
50 Old defense pact
51 Spanish hero played on film by Charlton Heston
52 Dutch sights
53 Ex-Secretary Federico
54 Allies' foe
55 Farm building
58 Stand at the plate
59 Binge

by Randall J. Hartman

ACROSS

1 Wind ___ (pilot's problem)
6 Comic actor Jacques
10 Ali ___
14 How to play a dirge
15 Composer's work
16 Mimic
17 Woolf's "___ of One's Own"
18 Peacekeeping force in Bosnia
19 Not strict
20 Infallible fact
23 "There but for the grace of God ___"
24 Copacabana site
25 Westerns
27 Small tropical lizards
31 Arrest record
33 Jai ___
34 Eisenhower's boyhood home
36 Biblical sin city
38 Klutz
39 Woods on the fairway
43 Paramaribo is its capital: Var.
46 Achy
47 Halite
50 "Paper Roses" singer Marie
52 Strands, as by a winter storm
53 Just ducky
54 Speed: Abbr.
55 Rural route
62 Pub stock
64 Calf's meat
65 Fret
66 Grandparents' stories, e.g.
67 English essayist
68 Prince Valiant's wife
69 Name on which ancient oaths were taken
70 Brother, aunt, etc.: Abbr.
71 Southernmost part of Arabia

DOWN

1 Smelting residue
2 Long lunch?
3 Son of Seth
4 On
5 The Joker's portrayer on TV
6 Kemo Sabe's sidekick
7 On ___ with
8 Ballerina's skirt
9 U-235 or C-14, e.g.
10 ___-relief
11 Orbital high point
12 Prior to
13 One who makes a scene?
21 Actress Bonet
22 Lacks, in brief
26 Belief in one God
27 Neon, e.g.
28 "Shine a Little Love" rock grp.
29 Ungentlemanly sort
30 Newsstands
31 Laughing
32 Code word for A
35 Seethe
37 Orchestra output
40 Sticky stuff
41 Sea eagle
42 Badly chapped
44 Trampled
45 "The Hound of the Baskervilles" locale
47 Competes equally with
48 Yellow and black cat
49 Salad stalk
51 Bridge between buildings
53 Library volume
56 Congo river
57 Catch but good
58 Part
59 City near Provo
60 Museo holdings
61 Actress Cannon
63 Gender

by Randy Sowell

ACROSS

1 Surrounding glow
5 Big name in daytime TV
10 Certain herring
14 Swamp critter
15 Appalachian Trail's northern terminus
16 Turkish bath decoration
17 Flee
19 Pulitzer writer James
20 Tee preceder
21 Deplaned
22 Stockpile
24 Actor Vigoda and others
25 Father
26 Item in a magician's hat
29 Steep, as meat for barbecuing
32 Over 21
33 Determined to follow
34 Apr. 15 letters
35 Bog
36 Flung
37 Like the world to pre-Columbians
38 Site of ink . . . or oink
39 Russian range
40 It's shown on a projector
41 Dutch Guiana, today
43 The "S" in O.A.S.
44 Loosen, as laces
45 Gush forth
46 Dry martini with a pearl onion
48 Sneaker, e.g.
49 Tempe sch.
52 Judge's wear
53 Flee
56 Water pourer
57 Open-eyed

58 Cheese on crackers
59 Witch's facial blemish
60 Hard up
61 Fax, say

DOWN

1 Result of overexercise
2 "Exodus" author
3 Decomposes
4 One of five in "Othello"
5 Brunch entree
6 Capital on the Seine
7 Civil uprising
8 Santa ___, Calif.
9 Living "fence"
10 ___ Island Ferry
11 Flee
12 Away from the storm
13 Bucks and does

18 Custom
23 Opposed to, in the boondocks
24 Skilled
25 "Psycho" motel name
26 Wheelchair-accessible routes
27 French farewell
28 Flee
29 Haggard who sang "Okie From Muskogee"
30 Lifework
31 1950's candidate Kefauver
33 Embarrassment
36 Casey Jones, e.g.
37 Imperfection
39 "Do ___ others as . . ."
40 Animal in a roundup
42 Advertising section

43 Erratic
45 Piece of broken pottery: Var.
46 Sprouted
47 Des Moines is its capital
48 ___-Ball (arcade game)
49 Farm division
50 Scrape, as the knee
51 Like hand-me-downs
54 Pub pint
55 Stomach muscles

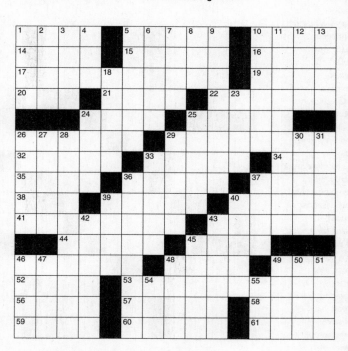

by Gregory E. Paul

ACROSS

1 It's catching
5 Tenor-soprano combos, e.g.
10 "Look out . . ."
14 Downs once of "20/20"
15 Sleeper's breathing problem
16 Figures in tables
17 B-1 insignia
18 1964 Beatles hit
20 Pressed for cash
22 Black-ink item
23 Northwest European
24 Rembrandt works
26 Royal home
29 Mosquito fleet craft
32 Fancy tie
33 Appraiser
34 Dine
36 Injury's aftermath
37 Paint base
38 El ___, Tex.
39 "2001" computer
40 Partner of onions
41 Ex-Gov. Cuomo
42 Adam Dalgliesh's creator
44 One very funny joke
45 ___ empty stomach
46 Microscopic
47 Mrs. Gorbachev
50 Bus passenger's request
54 Rating for the risqué
57 Yarn
58 Speechless
59 Target
60 Highland dialect
61 Simon ___
62 Divisions of municipal govt.
63 Repast

DOWN

1 Sic
2 Reddish-brown
3 Food thickener
4 How acid-base properties affect the body
5 Spotted horse
6 Discomfit
7 Author Bagnold
8 Address book no.
9 ___ Paulo
10 "Battleship Potemkin" locale
11 Makes bales on the farm
12 Western Indian
13 High, in the Alps
19 Heroism
21 Bombard
24 Sleek swimmer
25 Wild goat
26 Payment option
27 Songwriters' org.
28 Heat to just short of boiling
29 Crowns
30 Bygone dictators
31 "Wake Up Little ___" (1957 hit)
33 Poe visitor
35 D
37 Andes capital
38 Auditorium fixture
40 Hawaiian isle
41 "Death in Venice" author Thomas
43 Kids
44 Met Life Stadium team
46 Pick up the tab for
47 Tach readings
48 Spanish water
49 ___-bitty
50 Day worker, maybe
51 Bus token, e.g.
52 Hostess Maxwell
53 Lively dance
55 "Far out!"
56 Dead heat

by Robert Zimmerman

ACROSS

1 Places to pitch tents
6 BMW rival
10 Dr Pepper, for one
14 Dress fold
15 Restaurateur Toots
16 Golf or tennis championship
17 Designer Oscar de la ___
18 Slugger Sammy
19 For fear that
20 Deeply hurt
23 Nope's counterpart
24 Force
25 D.D.E.'s 1952 and '56 opponent
28 Award for a good student
31 Scorch
35 Blunder
37 Neighbor of Pakistan
39 Buenos ___
40 Visa alternative
43 Skylark, for one
44 ___ fide
45 Simplicity
46 What the fashion-savvy watch for
48 Cry at the doctor's office
50 Home for cubs
51 Goes out, as a fire
53 "Am ___ time?"
55 Gulliver's creator
61 Russian parliament
62 Scarlett's home
63 Pungent
65 Man with a spare rib?
66 Prepare for publication
67 River through Lyons
68 Exhausted, with "in"
69 Not bogus
70 "The Rehearsal" painter

DOWN

1 Paramedic's work, in brief
2 One of the Baldwins
3 Computer's option list
4 Raw quarter-pounder
5 Word with symbol or seeker
6 Mgr.'s aide
7 Apprehension expression
8 Administered medicine to
9 Invaders of Kuwait, 1990
10 Game in which players famously cheat
11 Oil cartel
12 Work space
13 Hill resident
21 Some nerve
22 Flip one's lid?
25 Make ___ buck
26 Fictional Gantry
27 Soft leather
29 Spirited horse
30 Talked and talked and talked
32 Auto tire necessity
33 Novelist Hermann
34 Ruhr industrial center
36 Subject of a trademark
38 Hawaiian goose
41 Neighbor of Pakistan
42 Horizontal line on a graph
47 Hunting dog
49 Facing
52 Sun protection
54 Recess for a statuette
55 Black belt's activity
56 Muscat is its capital
57 Diva's song
58 Part of N.F.L.: Abbr.
59 Budweiser ad creature
60 Actress Louise
61 June honoree
64 ___ Plaines, Ill.

by Ed Early

ACROSS

1 Parachute ___
5 "Animal House" party wear
9 Ham it up
14 In midvoyage, maybe
15 "___ restless as a willow . . ." (1945 movie lyric)
16 Morocco's capital
17 Have on
18 Fissure
19 Ready for anything
20 Sage advice, part 1
23 Got fresh with
26 Pennsylvania city
27 "___, two, three, four . . ."
28 Wide shoe specification
30 One making picks and pans
35 The Little Mermaid
37 Bills and coins
40 Aborted mission words
41 Sage advice, part 2
44 Part of Q.E.D.
45 Not masc. or fem.
46 Uncomplaining servant
47 Sandwich meat
49 ___ Tomé (island on the Equator)
51 Exist
52 Thingy
55 Abba's home country
57 Sage advice, part 3
62 Lasso
63 Thrilled
64 Jodie Foster's alma mater
68 Inquired
69 Author Wiesel
70 Say the paternoster
71 Pasta sauce with basil
72 Lairs
73 Test proctor's declaration

DOWN

1 Leno's got a big one
2 Exploit
3 ___ culpa
4 It was liberated in August 1944
5 Rant
6 Skip over
7 Faux pas
8 Moving
9 Pencil topper
10 Soda fountain choice
11 Follow the rules
12 Starch source
13 "___, Brute?"
21 Seems
22 Nouveau ___
23 Ray-Bans, e.g.
24 The dawn
25 Kind of cord
29 Behold, in old Rome
31 ___-European
32 "Tsk, tsk"
33 Tune out
34 Actor Joseph of "Citizen Kane"
36 Songstress James
38 Prefix with pressure
39 Where movies are made
42 Togetherness
43 Go under for the third time
48 Gilbert and Sullivan emperor
50 Digressions
53 Bordered
54 A thousand, in France
56 Pharaoh's land
57 Police sting
58 Get up
59 Beasts of burden
60 Editor's direction
61 Stuck on oneself
65 Mr. Onassis
66 Leave in a hurry
67 CBS symbol

by Stephanie Spadaccini

ACROSS
1 German river to the North Sea
5 Houston N.L.er
10 Fictional captain with an ivory leg
14 Fishing rod attachment
15 Oarsman
16 Malcolm X, for Denzel Washington
17 Where the President works
19 Minute amount
20 Jeans material
21 Regarding
22 Dick and Jane's dog
23 Skipped the wedding
25 Coin flips
27 High-hatter
29 Cockeyed
32 Seldom seen
35 Zoo inhabitants
39 Ill temper
40 Meyers of "Kate & Allie"
41 Sewing groups
42 L.B.J.'s successor
43 Bed-and-breakfast
44 Scrabble unit
45 Yards in passing, e.g.
46 Accepted doctrine
48 Shrink-___
50 Yellowbelly
54 Draw out
58 Auto racer A. J.
60 Sticky stuff
62 Hole ___ (ace)
63 "That hurts!"
64 Camelot fixture
66 Iwo Jima, e.g.
67 Hot coal
68 Study for finals
69 Lustful look
70 ___ Park, Col.
71 Makes bales for the barn

DOWN
1 Wear away, as earth
2 Carpenter's tool
3 Community gambling game
4 Area south of the White House, with "the"
5 Poodle's bark
6 Davenport
7 Chubby Checker's dance
8 Front of a sheet of paper
9 Nabisco cookies
10 Crops up
11 Dress for Scarlett O'Hara
12 Choir voice
13 Tuckered out
18 Harbinger
24 "The Many Loves of ___ Gillis"
26 Words of disrespect
28 Lahr of "The Wizard of Oz"
30 Humorous Bombeck
31 "What ___ wrong?"
32 Narc's bust
33 Cartoonist Peter
34 Wagner work
36 Have work in Hollywood
37 Lot
38 ___ Haute, Ind.
41 Falcon feature
45 Popeye's muscle builder
47 May honoree
49 Came down to earth
51 Be in harmony
52 Motel units
53 Harbor suspicions
55 Snake charmer's snake
56 Dental filling
57 Abounds
58 Aluminum sheet
59 River in England
61 Where gramps jounces junior
65 A.M.A. members

by Gregory E. Paul

ACROSS

1 Went airborne briefly
6 Sitcom set in Korea
10 Weary workers' exclamation
14 Eskimo home
15 Division word
16 "___ Rock" (Simon & Garfunkel hit)
17 Musician at a dance?
19 Egyptian cobras
20 Vitamin bottle info
21 Delaney of "NYPD Blue"
22 Address part
24 Shade of blond
25 "No" vote from a horse?
28 Funky musical genre, for short
29 Rock singer ___ Bon Jovi
30 Julie, in "Doctor Zhivago"
32 Needlefish
33 Jack who ate no fat
36 "What's your sign?," for example?
38 The hunted
39 Parson's home
40 Peruvian native
41 Booze for a 50's bash?
43 Fraternity man
44 Time of anticipation
45 Opening amount
46 Shoe part that may pinch
47 Gads about
49 Hells Canyon state
51 Modus operandi
54 Treat badly
56 "Praise be to ___!"
57 ___ brisk pace
58 Spring feature
59 Critique of an all-night teen dance?
63 Beheaded Boleyn

64 "Terrible" czar
65 MacLeod of "The Love Boat"
66 Relay segments
67 Superman's alter ego
68 Secluded valleys

DOWN

1 The Scales
2 "Holy smokes!"
3 Leader of Islam
4 Washington wheeler-dealer
5 Bun
6 Dolphins' home
7 Whichever
8 Sault ___ Marie
9 ___ d'oeuvre
10 Miss America's prize
11 Internal combustion device

12 Obstacle
13 Basketball strategy
18 Lender's claim
23 Cafeteria carrier
26 Peeked (at)
27 Unduly severe
29 Blue birds
31 66, e.g.: Abbr.
33 Sun-shaped
34 Smoked Italian cheese
35 Undoing an act
36 LuPone or LaBelle
37 Old Italian cabbage?
39 Back-to-work time: Abbr.
42 Singing Mama
43 Friendly, reliable sort
46 Norse bolt maker
48 Symbols of stubbornness

50 Publicity person
51 Forgo
52 Enjoyed home cooking
53 Shows signs of boredom
55 Estrada of "CHiPs"
60 Blvd.
61 Delivery vehicle
62 Kilmer of "At First Sight"

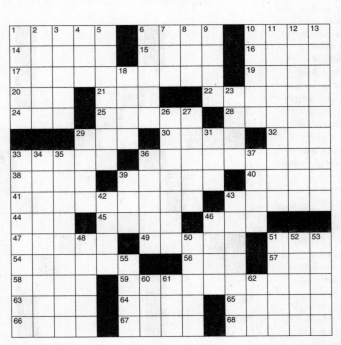

by Harvey Estes and Nancy Salomon

ACROSS

1 Sounds from pounds
5 Place for a massage
10 Bit of vocal fanfare
14 Lionel track layout, maybe
15 Big house
16 Pink-slipped
17 Madly in love
18 Curly-haired comics heroine
19 TV's Warrior Princess
20 Egotistical George Bernard Shaw drama?
23 Hot time in Haiti
24 When repeated, a first name in Hollywood
25 Egotistical James Bond caper?
33 Correctly sung
34 1989 Literature Nobelist
35 Nth degree
36 Zoo barrier
37 They're S-shaped
39 Dermatologist's concern
40 Bit of brandy
41 Half of Mork's sign-off
42 Central opening?
43 Egotistical 1977 pop smash?
47 ". . . __ quit!"
48 "Hail, Caesar!"
49 Egotistical 1948 Cole Porter tune?
56 Isinglass
58 Biology lab stain
59 Painter's estimation
60 Nose wrinkler
61 Emmy winner Lucci
62 Gung-ho feeling
63 Custom
64 #, to a typesetter
65 "Nana" author

DOWN

1 Contemplative sort
2 Dr. Pavlov
3 Webmaster's creation
4 Bulgarian or Croat
5 Person who mouths off
6 A.T.M. button
7 Magnani of "The Rose Tattoo"
8 Beef buy
9 Bar freebies
10 The Stamp Act, e.g.
11 Leap for Lipinski
12 Iniquity site
13 Critic __ Louise Huxtable
21 Hard to hold
22 Are, in Aragón
25 How sardines are packed
26 Cousin of a giraffe
27 Bottom line
28 Become slippery, in a way
29 Churchillian sign
30 "Toodles!"
31 Garçon's list
32 Pres. or treas.
33 Prefix with potent
37 Quality of bran muffins
38 Bearded antelope
39 Islands dish
41 Dragsters' org.
42 Did in
44 Miniature racer
45 Raving lunatic
46 DeCarlo of "The Munsters"
49 Clickable symbol
50 Make spiffy
51 Greek peak
52 Give the Bronx cheer
53 Hydrox look-alike
54 "Hud" Oscar winner
55 Big bash
56 Shorten, in a way
57 Witness stand oath

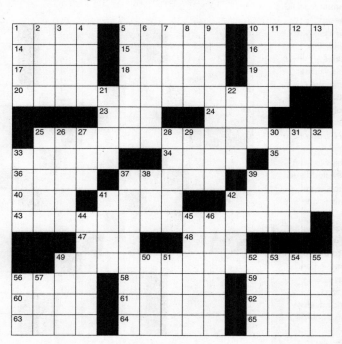

by D. J. DeChristopher

142 ★ ★

ACROSS
1 Gists
5 Forbes 400 list topper
10 #1 spot
14 Words said with a nod
15 Summing up
16 Kicker's target
17 Choir site
19 Beat (off)
20 Prison rebel, perhaps
21 Haberdashers' items
23 Lover of Eurydice
25 Baby bird?
26 St. ___ fire
28 Overloads
31 Bell ___
34 A purebred it's not
36 Capt. Hull who commanded Old Ironsides
37 ___ Lilly & Co.
38 Title for this puzzle?
40 Certain cross
41 One of the Flintstones
43 Safari
44 Hair curler
45 Fliers' frustrations
47 "Ditto"
49 Genius
51 Badly slandered
55 March sound
58 Number one Hun
59 Jai ___
60 Full of small talk
62 Laura of "Jurassic Park"
63 "Like it ___"
64 Proceed
65 Scotch diluter
66 Does a muffler's job
67 Politically incorrect suffix

DOWN
1 Funny-car fuel
2 Name on jetliners, once
3 Dizzy Gillespie's genre
4 Does a slow burn
5 Cause of some knocking
6 Santa ___ winds
7 Knowing when to be silent, e.g.
8 ___ Island National Monument
9 Makes roads slippery, say
10 To the extent that
11 Defeat
12 Fine fur
13 Pulls the plug on
18 Quaint dance
22 Namely
24 Bygone voting bloc, with "the"
27 Make music, in a way
29 1950's–60's NBC star
30 Lowlife
31 Off-color
32 "I cannot tell ___"
33 Pitch off the road
35 Believe it!
38 Pioneers of a 365-day calendar
39 Draws
42 Tennis star Hingis
44 Big catalog company expense
46 "Friends," e.g.
48 It might be bleeped out
50 Kind of jacket
52 Make a pass at
53 Pop's John
54 Singer Taylor ___
55 Teletubbies and others
56 Nondairy spread
57 Ice cream purchase
61 Little piggy

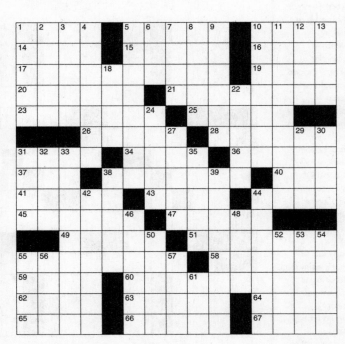

by Nancy Salomon and Harvey Estes

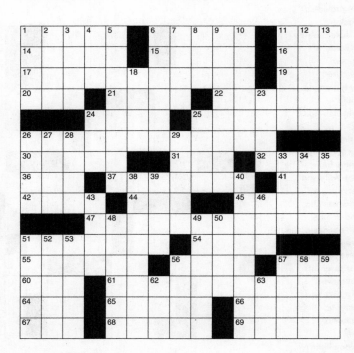

ACROSS

1 Sign language communicator, maybe
6 Myanmar, once
11 Muscles used in situps
14 Winter warmer-upper
15 Pisces' follower
16 Not even half-baked
17 Evidence of a royal thief?
19 ___-Wan of "Star Wars"
20 Harsh review
21 Pub stock
22 Wing-footed one
24 LAX guesstimates
25 Handbooks
26 Birthday camping gear?
30 Stand for something
31 Classic card game
32 Times past
36 Dadaism founder
37 In general
41 Baseball bat material
42 Gambling game
44 Sink
45 Signal interference
47 Recreation for Gregorian monks?
51 Like a beautiful night sky
54 Kick back
55 Response to a knock, maybe
56 Tough
57 Montgomery sch.
60 Nile slitherer
61 Pennies made in the 1990's?
64 Start of a Brewers line score
65 Tale of the Trojan War
66 Bud Grace comic strip
67 Season opener?
68 How long it takes mountains to form
69 Loved ones

DOWN

1 Letters on old Soviet rockets
2 Circle dance
3 Trash can, for one
4 Fell with a blade
5 Popular cigar
6 Slightest
7 "QB VII" author
8 ___ Tin Tin
9 Antifreeze additive
10 What a stamp may indicate
11 Bouquet
12 Gibberish
13 Watch word?
18 Work out
23 Subterfuge
24 Hamburg-to-Berlin dir.
25 Children's ___
26 Point on a graph
27 Like a no-hitter
28 Locker room shower?
29 Powerful engine
33 Reason for postponement
34 Mgr.'s aide
35 Tom Jones's "___ a Lady"
38 Florida State athlete
39 Aid's partner
40 Like some digital pictures
43 Fiend
46 Klutz
48 Actress Silverstone
49 Annual Nile events
50 Woodland critter
51 Rogue
52 "___, With Love"
53 Good-sized
56 Pulp novel hero
57 "The King and I" role
58 Flap
59 "Has 1,001 ___"
62 "O Sole ___"
63 Earlier than

by Greg Staples

144 ⭐ ⭐

ACROSS

1 It's south of Georgia
5 They may be run off base
10 A.L. or N.L. city
13 Role in "The Coronation of Poppea"
14 Traffic directors
16 Crew member
17 Silver-haired comic
19 White alternative
20 Industry leader
21 Postage
23 Wind dir.
24 Foolhardy
28 Monte ___
30 Hodgepodge
32 Broadway great Jerry
33 Line providers
35 Crack
36 California-based horticulturist
41 Flipper
42 Powdered
43 Away from the mouth
47 Fighter's weak spot
51 Express discontent
52 Sun spot?
53 School founded by Thos. Jefferson
54 Get ready for Judgment Day
56 Kind of tube
58 Cal. opener
59 Perennial name on best-seller lists
63 Got down
64 Four of a kind
65 Energetic
66 Double or twin
67 Saloon lights
68 Engendered

DOWN

1 Marching together
2 Skin cream ingredient
3 Products of glaciation
4 PBS classic
5 Predicament
6 Pitcher's stat
7 Be off base
8 Batches of stakes
9 Reset
10 Army medic
11 Needle holder?
12 Temper
15 Catch
18 Add value to
22 Former Russian orbiter
25 Entr'___
26 Shy
27 Silo contents
29 Wed
31 Rat-a-___
34 Roman dictator, 82–79 B.C.
36 Free
37 Sealed
38 Some TV's
39 Words before "show" or "class"
40 Zappers' targets
41 A long way
44 Go fast
45 "___ of robins . . ."
46 In fast time?
48 Word ending this puzzle's theme
49 Get even for
50 Mars, for one
55 Head, to Henri
57 1940's Soviet secret police org.
58 Punch
60 An athlete might turn this
61 Solo in space
62 Comic Wynn and others

by A. J. Santora

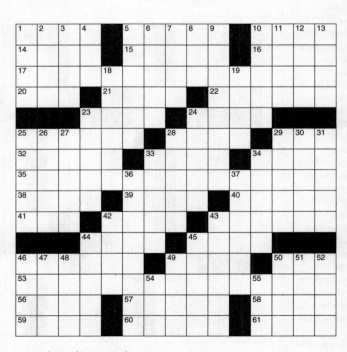

ACROSS

1 Worrisome car sound
5 Rant and rave
10 Part of a Racine play
14 Patent prerequisite
15 Nintendo's Super ___ Bros.
16 Polo Grounds replacement
17 Start of a story? (1977)
20 Ring count
21 Some floor votes
22 Deem appropriate
23 Mitchell's plantation
24 Winter Palace resident
25 Flattering, in an oily way
28 Nitty-gritty
29 Director Craven
32 Lofty abode
33 Take to the cleaners
34 Flu fighters
35 More of the story? (1987)
38 Sooner city
39 Chablis sediment
40 Nomadic mob
41 U.S.P.S. employee's beat
42 The Carpenters, e.g.
43 Carpenter's need
44 Like many a cellar
45 It may be struck
46 Cousin of a guinea pig
49 Sal's canal
50 Dickens alias
53 End of the story? (1964)
56 Uncle of Enos
57 Labor leader's cry
58 Trading center
59 Peccadilloes
60 Photo finish
61 "Nolo," e.g.

DOWN

1 Early Briton
2 Like some threats
3 Broadway brightener
4 Dentist's administration
5 Like wet ink
6 Roberts or Tucker
7 Ogres
8 Hope/Crosby film destination
9 Greek dish
10 Late bloomer?
11 Dish maker
12 Garr of "Tootsie"
13 Magi origin
18 Canine's coat
19 Sans ice
23 Simple chord
24 Goes like the dickens
25 One-time cohort of Rather
26 Intended
27 Ava's second
28 Choral work
29 Spooky
30 Eat at
31 Not as dotty
33 Causing sticker shock
34 Sling ammo
36 Bauxite yields it
37 Beer, at times
42 Numbers to crunch
43 Evening affair
44 Some showdowns
45 Brooklyn institute
46 "Ah, me!"
47 Mongolian expanse
48 It's within your range
49 Put out
50 False god
51 Meanie
52 Epsilon follower
54 Some trial evidence
55 Bart Simpson, typically

by Arthur S. Verdesca

146 ★ ★

ACROSS

1 Roguish
5 Has chits out
9 Less than right?
14 Concerto features
15 Get ready to fly
16 More sound
17 Speller's phrase
18 Svelte
19 Where the action is
20 Eastern flycatcher
22 Debaters' need
24 Big ___, Calif.
25 Seven, e.g.
29 Some protests
32 An itemized deduction
34 Same, by the Seine
35 "Take ___ the Limit"
36 Turns state's evidence
37 Marquee filler
38 Jazzman Getz
39 Pamplona parent
40 Chug-___
41 Ticket
42 Arab leader
43 Let off steam
44 A Baldwin
45 Heart of a Baldwin
46 D or EEE
47 Wool fat
49 Dyslexic's deity?
50 Sign of neglect
52 Isn't inert
56 Neighbor of Curaçao
59 Saharan land
61 He had a hammer
62 Gardner created him
63 Writer Turgenev
64 Hawkeyes' home
65 Influences
66 It may be stuck out
67 Confesses, with "up"

DOWN

1 Order request
2 ___ Hashana
3 Saatchi & Saatchi award
4 Headless horseman?
5 Brown fur
6 Former Cabinet department
7 Way out
8 Heartless villain?
9 Expect
10 Endless journey?
11 Milk, in a way
12 Half a score
13 Prohibition ___
21 Shuttle, perhaps
23 QB, at times
26 Staggered
27 Total, say
28 Derby victory margin
29 Kind of year
30 Fifth-century scourge
31 ___ Island, N.Y.
32 Bottomless pit?
33 Prefix with line or mine
36 Coins
46 Anguish
48 Lists
49 Manhattan, for one
51 Set aside
53 Grub
54 Hamlet's cousin
55 Mmes., in Madrid
56 Some rush-hour periods: Abbr.
57 Wet behind the ears
58 Cable network
60 Fond du ___, Wis.

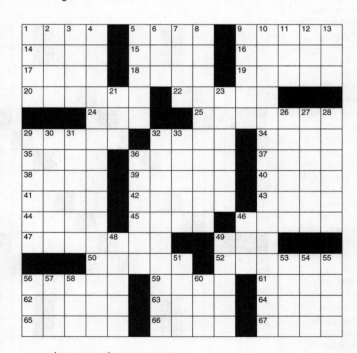

by Jeremy Thomas Paine

ACROSS

1 Figurehead's place
5 Broadway's Verdon
9 "My teacher," in Hebrew
14 Gad about
15 Adriatic resort
16 Silas Marner's creator
17 Sneaking suspicion
18 Teller's stack
19 Smooth thread
20 What Agassi does?
23 Highway interchange sights
24 The "A" in A.D.
25 Corneal repository
29 School org.
32 Cookbook phrase
36 School org.
37 Kind of function
38 What Hingis does?
41 Potluck choice
42 Ancient theaters
43 Stops on a sales rep's rte.
44 Manual communication syst.
45 Mistakenly
47 Bridge position
49 Oft-cluttered rooms
54 What Sampras does?
58 "Goosebumps" author
59 "It's either you ___"
60 Au naturel
61 Be silent, in music
62 Stand at a wake
63 Football play
64 "___ Dream" ("Lohengrin" piece)
65 Understands
66 Half a matched set

DOWN

1 Spectrum maker
2 Chute site
3 Manifest
4 Build a web site?
5 8 × 10, often
6 Skid row sort
7 First place?
8 Margin of victory, maybe
9 Join again
10 True up
11 Diocese
12 Hightail it out
13 Ore suffix
21 1985 Kate Nelligan film
22 Dressing choice
26 Eat into
27 A bungler might pull one
28 Fragrant oil
30 Sunglasses feature
31 Many moons
32 Co-star of Farrell and Swit
33 Roaster's spot
34 Ones who exchange rials for liras?
35 Sort of: Suffix
37 Letters of compassion
39 Sidekick of early TV
40 You are here
45 Specks in the sea
46 Gabby Hayes films
48 Sleep disorder
50 Tithe portion
51 Accustom
52 Insect-repellent wood
53 Arthur Murray lessons
54 List finish
55 Knocks over, so to speak
56 Ashtabula's lake
57 "Peter Pan" role
58 Jeanne d'Arc, e.g.: Abbr.

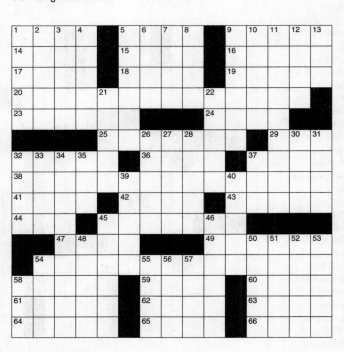

by Dan Reichert

148 ⭐ ⭐

ACROSS

1 Applies lightly
5 Greetings
8 Ice cream drink
14 Kind of engr.
15 "Shoot!"
16 Trojan War warrior
17 Everything
19 Hens
20 Palace display, maybe
22 Flashed sign
23 Copious
24 Anonymous fellow
26 Coleridge character
29 Russell Cave Natl. Mon. locale
32 Not the first recording
33 What some grads do
37 One of the Seven Wonders of the World
40 Colonial territory now reunited with China
41 Honors
42 Second letter addendum
43 Made a cocoon
45 Like fish sticks
48 Kind of ray
53 Above, poetically
54 Bullies
58 The W's in LLWWWWWL
60 Request for clarification
61 Words intended to instill fear
62 Lansing-to-Detroit dir.
63 Big name in oil
64 Let a slip pass
65 Co. that makes 29-Downs
66 Wistful sort

DOWN

1 Bing Crosby's record label
2 Auto option
3 Jazz genre
4 Glower
5 One of the Pillars of Islam
6 Coconut palm site, maybe
7 Warp
8 Drill sergeant's order
9 Pushes forward again
10 "___ questions?"
11 Pet item
12 Kitchen gadget
13 Big-selling 1920's car
18 Together
21 Dubai, e.g.
25 Family map
26 1950's–70's pitcher Drabowsky
27 Green shade
28 Bring new supplies
29 Place to enter a PIN
30 Grazing spot
31 Jeep maker, once: Abbr.
32 Matter of interest for a pilot
34 Person in a mask
35 Tweak
36 Formula 1 maneuver
38 Role model for a lad
39 One end of the visible spectrum
44 Brightened, with "up"
45 Particle physics subject
46 Fashionably old-fashioned
47 Was at fault
48 "No ___!" (Spanish cry)
49 Petal extract
50 Kind of jacket
51 Hint
52 Mary of "Don Juan," 1926
55 "Say ___"
56 Pear type
57 It has a big mouth
59 Round Table time

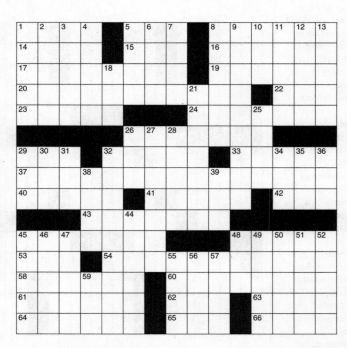

by David Ainslie Macleod

ACROSS

1 Medina resident
5 Rand McNally blowup
10 Flappers' hairdos
14 Newshawk's asset?
15 De ___ (actual)
16 He sang of Alice
17 Beginning of a quip
20 Right or fright preceder
21 Bricklayer's carrier
22 Gentle slopes
23 View from the Riviera
25 Depends (on)
27 Quip, part 2
31 Regis, to Kelly
35 Dance setting, perhaps
36 Imposing entrance
38 Auditor, briefly
39 Outback runner
40 Fla. neighbor
41 Uneven?
42 Knock (over)
43 Jungle swinger
44 Mustang's home
46 Dry as dust
47 Sportscaster John
49 Quip, part 3
51 Emcee's task
53 Craving
54 Bit of broken pottery
57 1996 Olympic torch lighter
59 Adlai's 1956 running mate
63 End of the quip
66 "I'll Be Around" composer Wilder
67 Didn't take part, with "out"
68 Flag
69 Undiluted, at the bar

70 Almost perpendicular
71 Precable problem

DOWN

1 Wee workers
2 Dig like a pig
3 Out of port
4 "Gaslight" Oscar winner, 1944
5 "___ were you . . ."
6 "Bronx"/"thonx" rhymer
7 Librarygoer
8 Exercise in musical dexterity
9 Tough turkey?
10 Cast out
11 Eyes, in poetry
12 Bummed out
13 Breathalyzer test flunkers
18 Smell something fierce
19 Noted traitor
24 Move, as marigolds
26 Plebe's place
27 Construction girder
28 Gulf city
29 Brought into alignment
30 Take wing
32 Good-sized combo
33 Cathedral topper
34 Diminish gradually
37 Like some lunch orders
40 To-do list
45 Priest's assistant
46 Romantic sights
48 Nonstop
50 Source of pressure, maybe
52 Peace Nobelist Bunche

54 Kenton of jazz
55 Pocket problem
56 Neighborhood
58 Words of understanding
60 Castor, to Pollux
61 Mark replacer
62 Gush out
64 ___ Alamos, N.M.
65 Naval off.

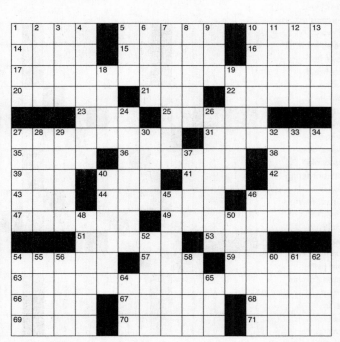

by Richard Chisholm

150 ★ ★

ACROSS
1 Guitar accessory
5 Unoriginal
10 Land where Moses died
14 Tiptop
15 Kitchen utensil
16 Playwright's dream
17 Darrow client
18 Maître's place
19 "Bill & ___ Excellent Adventure"
20 1960's sci-fi series
22 So far
23 Reasons
24 Copy to a floppy
26 S.&L. offerings
29 McCowen of "Frenzy"
31 Foursome
35 Allow to pass
37 Wild about
39 Princess loved by Hercules
40 Third man
41 Do detective work
42 Solitaire item
43 Jorge's hand
44 Alaska radar station site
45 Hägar's dog
46 Long-winded
48 Linen hue
50 Classified abbr.
51 Rising locale?
53 County bordering London
55 N.F.L. QB Young
58 Arrives ahead of schedule
63 Colleague of Dashiell
64 Square (with)
65 Onetime Korean president
66 Move, in Realtor lingo
67 Warms up
68 Reverberation
69 Doctor's ___
70 Rowing crew
71 Satirist from Canada

DOWN
1 Ripken, Jr. and Sr.
2 Per unit
3 Sunburn result
4 U-shaped river bend
5 Vinegar radical
6 Example
7 ___-Z (auto)
8 Three-time French Open winner
9 Domain of Otto I: Abbr.
10 Start, as a chain of events
11 Observe
12 Flunky
13 Bet or buy lead-in
21 Traveling carriage
22 Old greeting
25 Superimposed on
26 Get tough, with "down"
27 Preclude
28 Gregg grad
30 Exchange for 10 sawbucks
32 Cowboy
33 Sleep spoiler
34 Shoulder muscles, briefly
36 Jack Benny's theme song
38 Write or call
41 ___-Coburg-Gotha
45 Arizona N.B.A.'ers
47 "___ got it!"
49 Take back to the lab
52 Inamorata of Valentino
54 Diamond protection
55 Drought-ridden
56 "The Lost World" menace
57 "___ in London" (jazz album)
59 Hurler Maddux
60 Actress Perlman
61 Mrs. Rabin
62 Cheerleader's routine
64 Bruiser

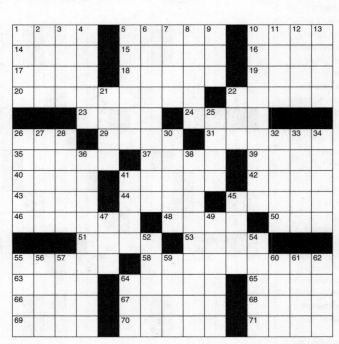

by Thomas W. Schier

ACROSS

1 Dilemma features, figuratively
6 Take measures
9 Starbucks offering
14 Up's partner
15 London facility
16 Pierre's girlfriends
17 With 37- and 61-Across, a 1936 title
20 Monogram of '52 and '56
21 Crumb
22 Prohibited
23 Rap sheet items
25 Amenhotep IV's god
26 Florida city, informally
29 Rockies' div.
31 Script ending
32 Author of 17-, 37- and 61-Across
34 Borodin's "Prince ___"
36 1995 Stallone title role
37 See 17-Across
39 Ephesus' land
42 Take down
44 Category of 17-, 37- and 61-Across
46 Reunion grp.
48 Woman in Fitzgerald's "Tender Is the Night"
50 ___ Stanley Gardner
51 Mont Blanc, e.g.
53 After-hours job, maybe
55 Be confident of
57 Really bad coffee
58 ___ soda
61 See 17-Across
64 "___ as I can see . . ."
65 Antipollution org.
66 Injun Joe creator

67 "___ It" (1983 Tom Cruise film)
68 Wasn't active
69 Brief brawl

DOWN

1 "Very funny!"
2 Reed section member
3 Spreadsheet components
4 Weirdo
5 An acoustic guitarist may use one
6 European carrier
7 Bamboozle
8 Peanut brittle base
9 Retreat
10 Amorphous critter
11 Singer born Anna Mae Bullock
12 Hay spreader
13 Dead Sea Scrolls scribe

18 Dry, in a way
19 Martini & ___
23 Supermarket chain
24 "Benson" actress
26 Three before E
27 Galley need
28 Easy questions, so to speak
30 Cry of relief
33 Shangri-la
35 Aaher's partner
38 Salami or bologna
40 Taken ___
41 Copy
43 Popular toy since 1964
45 Relax
46 Beauty parlor treatment
47 "The Tempest" king
49 Film festival site

52 Zhou ___
54 "Golden Boy" playwright
56 Go sour
58 Petty quarrel
59 Touched down
60 Late-night name
62 Busy bee in Apr.
63 Be light, in poker

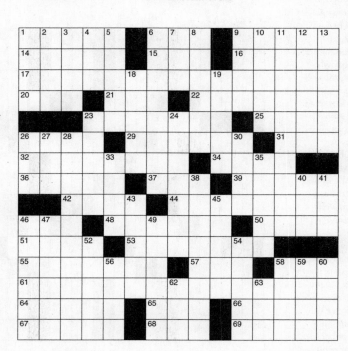

by Charles E. Gersch

152 ⭐ ⭐

ACROSS

1 Get rid of
8 Loser
15 City on Lake Ontario
16 "Well, I ___!"
17 & 18 Spendthrift's motto (which cracks ME up!)
19 W.W. II combat area: Abbr.
20 Lender's recourse
22 Military mission
23 Stage assistant's job
25 Phnom ___
26 Goldman ___ (brokerage)
29 Noggin
31 Latin lover's word
34 They keep people off beaches
36 Khartoum-to-Nairobi dir.
37 Gray
38 & 40 American novelist (who cracks ME up!)
42 Staffs
43 Neediest cases site?: Abbr.
45 Swinging
46 Gamy
47 It might be involved in a police roundup
49 Beer delivery
50 Settles with certainty
52 Lore
54 "___ what you say, but . . ."
56 Sludge
57 Break
60 & 62 Runner-up (who cracks ME up!)
65 End-of-book matter
66 Major coca producer
67 Spouse's meek response
68 Unity

DOWN

1 Suit to ___
2 Tug, say
3 Estimator's phrase
4 "The Thin Man" co-star
5 Business letters?
6 Popular vodka, familiarly
7 Zeroing (in on)
8 Yemeni city
9 Linda ___, Supergirl's alias
10 One way to run
11 Novelist Tillie
12 "Unchain My Heart" singer
13 Ship to Colchis
14 Brightly-colored
21 Prima donna problems
23 Buddies
24 Packinghouse stamp
25 Shampoo since 1947
26 Jerk
27 Shake like ___
28 Crows' hangouts
30 It may be temporary or practical
32 Director Louis
33 Follows
35 Shows of irritation
37 Stars on stage
39 AT&T competitor, once
41 Gambling, e.g.
44 "Do ___ others . . ."
47 Pacific
48 Park feature
51 Surrendered, with "in"
53 Enticed
54 Words to an "old chap"
55 Harbor
56 Actor Sharif
57 "___ Me a Break" (title for this puzzle?)
58 Sales term
59 Grps. that liaise with principals
61 Dietary abbr.
63 Order at the Green Dragon
64 China's ___ Piao

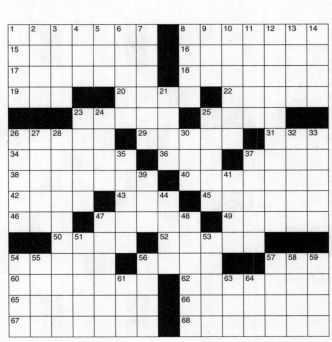

by Manny Nosowsky

ACROSS

1 Low-lying area
6 Dept. of Labor grp.
10 A&P part: Abbr.
13 "Three's Company" actress
15 Dazzles
16 River inlet
17 Start of a quip
20 English maritime county
21 Core
22 Matterhorn, e.g.: Abbr.
23 Reason for imprisonment, once
25 Satyr's kin
26 Prettify oneself
29 War room items
31 Recipe amts.
32 Not participate
34 Beauty's admirer
36 Part 2 of the quip
40 Covalent bond formers
41 Like firewater
43 One of Henry's Catherines
46 Concrete
48 Irritated moods
49 Meg's "Prelude to a Kiss" co-star
50 I-80 et al.
52 Stat that's good when it's low
53 Sony rival
56 Beethoven's "Pathétique," e.g.
59 End of the quip
62 Follower of Christ?
63 Eighty Eight, for one
64 Nero's tutor
65 N.J. clock setting
66 Tammany skewerer
67 Radiation quantities

DOWN

1 St. Louis-to-Little Rock dir.
2 Carpenter's finishing touch
3 Ancient resident of Jordan's present-day capital
4 Wanton look
5 Coastal raptors
6 Symbol of might
7 Fragrant climbing plant
8 Pianist Myra
9 [No return allowed]
10 Scenes of action
11 1996 golf movie
12 Gets dark
14 It has runners
18 Bit of gossip
19 No-no at some intersections
22 G.I. constabulary
24 Played the nanny
27 Saudi Arabia is one
28 Any miniature golf shot
30 Talk trash to
33 Son of Odin
35 Transporters since '76
37 Beryl varieties
38 Halves
39 Hypnotize
42 Fed. management agcy.
43 Flat peppermint candy
44 Warm hellos
45 Take offense at
47 More, in a saying
51 Dipsos
54 It may be pumped
55 Gymnastics coach Karolyi
57 Cry out for
58 ___ Domini
60 Musician's suffix
61 Jabber

by Gene Newman

154 ★ ★

ACROSS
1 Stand-up's payoff
6 Libreville's land
11 Jam ingredient?
14 Play ___ in (influence)
15 Last in a series
16 Metallurgist's subject
17 Winter sounds
19 Computer amount, slangily
20 Court sport
21 "Play it again!"
22 It may be caught
23 "Delaware Water Gap" painter
24 Big belts
25 High time?
26 Line part: Abbr.
27 Playwright Bogosian
29 Sinker
30 Home health hazard
32 Candy known as "The Freshmaker"
33 Mowgli's medium
36 Boot tip
37 Ancient Greek city-state
38 Zeal
39 Netanyahu, informally
40 "Holy cow!"
43 Element in Geiger counters
44 Game winner's cry
45 Joseph Conrad's "The Secret ___"
48 Consanguine folks
49 Kind of law or order
50 Ill-considered
51 "Wheel of Fortune" buy
52 Nitty Gritty Dirt Band hit, 1971
54 Football positions: Abbr.
55 Washington's ___ Stage
56 Former heavyweight champ Jimmy
57 Address component, these days
58 Part of a 1997 telecommunications merger
59 Like a pomegranate

DOWN
1 Some pilgrims
2 French satellite launcher
3 Perfecting
4 With fungi, they form lichens
5 Hawks
6 Much of Mongolia
7 Letters in many black church names
8 Noted French-born English writer
9 Good looks?
10 Harper's Weekly artist
11 Make a pass at
12 Post-accident question
13 College board
18 Relaxed
24 Cartel leader
25 They aren't done
28 Ex-Yankee Guidry
29 Actress Mazar
30 Satellite's job
31 Cracked open
32 Grammy winner Manchester
33 Assailed
34 Pleasure seeker
35 Alternative to a passing shot
36 Stein relative
39 1856 installation
40 Gate design
41 Tale of a journey
42 Fancy
44 TV producer Marshall
46 "Tap" star
47 Devious plan
49 Fed
50 Trojan War hero
53 It's better than nothing

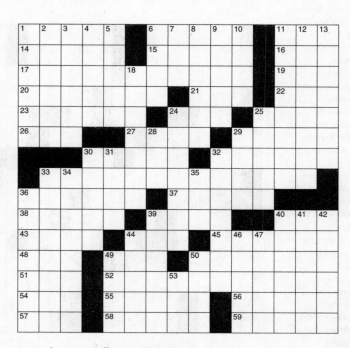

by Matt Gaffney and David Bianco

ACROSS

1 Windshield sticker
6 Employee's move, for short
10 Cries heard around cute babies
13 Dupe
14 Quark's place
15 Headlight setting
16 Spotted wildcat
17 Loafers don't grow on this
19 Musical markings don't grow on this
21 Oscar winner Davis
22 Ceiling spinner
23 Mileage rating org.
24 Supermarket checkout item
26 Cupid, to the Greeks
28 Hiker's route
30 "Try me" preceder
31 Clears of vermin
34 Slip through the cracks
36 It might make you see things
37 Baby fowl don't grow on this
40 Accomplished
43 Pennsylvania port
44 Like a wake-up time on an alarm clock
48 "___ first you don't . . ."
50 Pulls the plug on
52 "Comin' ___ the Rye"
53 Obsolescent term of address
55 Confucian truth
58 Dawn goddess
59 Deadly snake
60 Morays don't grow on this
62 Henhouse products don't grow on this
65 QB Doug
66 Maiden name preceder
67 Plane measure
68 Like horses at blacksmiths
69 Ave. crossers
70 Bastes
71 Krupp Works city

DOWN

1 "I do ___!"
2 1930's first lady
3 Kind of film
4 Pueblo brick
5 Abate
6 Too hasty
7 Addis Ababa's land: Abbr.
8 John, to Ringo
9 Certain sorority girl
10 Kind of gland
11 Ballpark purchases
12 Slung mud at
13 Tipped, as a hat
18 Watch
20 Chucklehead
24 Meat-and-vegetables fare
25 Canary's call
27 Midwest Indian
29 Appealed
32 Everyday article
33 Fathered
35 According to
38 Motion picture
39 N.Y.P.D. investigator
40 Devil
41 "Hmmm, it's not coming to me"
42 Compensation in a lawsuit
45 Protect in a cover
46 Shoreline problem
47 Deep-sixed
49 Dancer's woe
51 Sault ___ Marie
54 Shoreline shower
56 Actress Woodard
57 Gawks at
60 Hellenic H's
61 "tom thumb" star Tamblyn
63 Live and breathe
64 Just out

by Fred Piscop

156 ★ ★

ACROSS
1 Den denizen
8 Littermates
15 "Look Back in Anger" playwright
16 Asleep at the switch
17 Toothpaste tube direction
18 Classic exile site
19 Kayoed
20 Kind of tax
22 Dovetail
24 "___ Love You"
25 Chilled drink
26 It delivers the goods
28 Place for court battles?
30 Make permanent
34 Three-time Oscar-winning director
37 Leading
39 "I know what you're up to!"
40 Former name of Belize
43 High rollers?
44 Plant twice
45 In escrow
46 Traipse
48 Prune
49 ___ Accord (1998 peace agreement)
50 Cartoon utterance
52 Nashville-to-Chattanooga dir.
54 Flatboat
58 Thrifty traveler's stop
63 Toothpaste box letters
64 Pest
65 Red Skelton catch phrase
67 Fake
68 Running a temperature
69 In a coarse manner
70 Supermarket section

DOWN
1 Kind of buddy
2 Suffix with Roman or arab
3 Is adjacent to
4 Preschoolers?
5 Work party
6 Releases a fly?
7 Borscht basics
8 Midwife's exhortation
9 Local personality?
10 Poet Neruda
11 Security
12 Yesterday, in Italy
13 ___ go bragh
14 Certain partygoer
21 1959 Academy Award song
23 Offended
27 One and one
29 "Ouch!"
31 Topological shapes

32 Its capital is N'Djamena
33 57-Down carrier
34 Semi conductor?
35 Alice's chronicler
36 Galileo's birthplace
37 Mock phrase of insight
38 "Saving Private Ryan" depiction
41 Be one's own doctor
42 Aspirin has several
47 Tools (along)
49 Hoer
51 "Indeed!"
53 Blotto
55 Spanish seaport
56 "Swan Lake" role
57 Puzzle's theme (shown in 20-, 40- and 58-Across and 21-Down)
58 Bright side?

59 ___ about
60 "Render therefore ___ Caesar . . ."
61 Site south of Paris
62 Ring setting?
66 Bauxite, e.g.

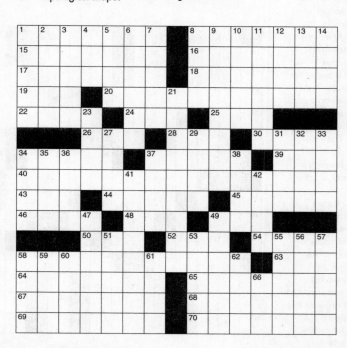

by Manny Nosowsky

ACROSS

1 It's just one of those things
5 "Aw, shucks" expressions
10 More
14 Jealous wife in Greek myth
15 Slackened
16 A portion
17 "The moan of doves in immemorial ___": Tennyson
18 Campbell of "Martin"
19 Winter Palace ruler
20 Ready to swoon
23 "Go on . . ."
24 Clan emblem
25 Straight start?
27 Orbital periods
29 Actor McKellen
31 Birth control device
32 C.P.R. administrator
34 It ends in Mecca
35 Brit. legislators
36 Good-looking
40 Insulation ingredient, for short
41 Cooperstown nickname
42 Wool source
43 Bolo, for one
44 Michael Jordan's alma mater, in brief
45 Have it ___
49 Place for rings
51 Gives the gate
55 Genetic letters
56 Seedy-looking
59 ___ fide
60 Baptism and bris
61 L.A. gang member
62 Need a bath badly
63 Awaited a dubbing
64 Surrealist Magritte
65 Charger, to a Cockney
66 Lowly ones
67 Took habitually

DOWN

1 Tao, literally
2 Curtis of hair care
3 Loser of 1588
4 What to do?
5 "I ___ kick . . ."
6 Grammy winner Bonnie
7 Joe Jackson's "___ Really Going Out With Him?"
8 Book after Ezra
9 Minn. neighbor
10 Fruity-smelling compound
11 Experience a delay
12 They attract rubberneckers
13 Musket attachment
21 "C'mon, I wanna try!"
22 Gentile
26 Some E.R. cases
28 ___ judicata
30 "Song of the South" song syllables
33 Unable to decide
34 Shaker ___, O.
36 Satanic sort
37 Colorless solvents
38 Addictive stuff
39 Japanese capital
40 School grp.
46 Strasbourg siblings
47 Like lots of shopping now
48 Sang like Satchmo
50 Not out
52 Complete
53 Cliff projection
54 They may come in batteries
57 Torah holders
58 L'eggs shade
59 Term of address in the 'hood

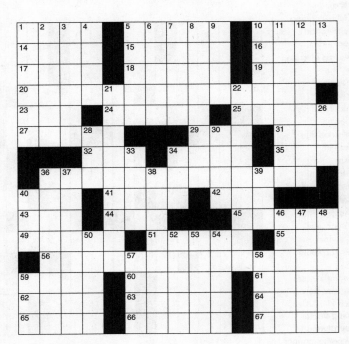

by M. Francis Vuolo

158 ★ ★

ACROSS

1 Embargoed country
5 Medicinal side effect, maybe
9 Hairpieces
14 "Up and ___!"
15 Keyboard instrument
16 Like some swarms
17 Operatic city created by Brecht and 64-Across
19 Actress Lotte, wife of 64-Across
20 Record player
21 Records
23 Mo. of the year
24 Musical comedy scored by 64-Across
27 Mason's burden
29 Part of a yen
30 River boat: Abbr.
31 The tops
33 Waikiki wingding
36 Discrimination
40 Brecht and 64-Across offering, with "The"
43 1920's auto
44 Ally (with)
45 Piccadilly Circus statue
46 Hotel floor sign
48 Suffix with Caesar
50 Tiny forager
51 Hit by Maxwell Anderson and 64-Across
57 Fire truck item
58 Jungle vine
59 Virginia colonist John
62 Like some illnesses
64 Composer born March 2, 1900
66 Skip a syllable
67 Clever Bombeck
68 Farm soil
69 Excised
70 Musical interval
71 Former parts of the Air France fleet

DOWN

1 Extravagantly theatrical
2 Rainbow Bridge locale
3 Eyewitnesses
4 Appliance maker
5 One of a Latin trio
6 Maintains course
7 Chengchow's province
8 Moses' birthplace
9 Something funny to sing in
10 Copy
11 Blair or Evans
12 Stratum
13 Potential diet-breaker
18 Olympus residents
22 Interrogatives
25 Puppy's cry
26 Cover, in a way
27 "Unimaginable as ___ in Heav'n": Milton
28 Newspaperman Adolph
32 "Now you ___ . . ."
34 Black cuckoo
35 Places for crutches
37 Harems
38 1982 Disney film
39 Whence the Magi, with "the"
41 Got all A's
42 Some votes
47 Big record inits.
49 Neighbor of Swed.
51 Redeemed
52 Napoleon, twice
53 Jeopardy
54 One whose job is a piece of cake?
55 Harden: Var.
56 Holiday entertainments
60 Fizzless
61 Popular street liners
63 Fruity drink
65 Tit for ___

by Frances Hansen

ACROSS

1 Bogus
6 Greeting with a smile
11 S.A.T. takers
14 Chosen ones
15 "Cry, the Beloved Country" author
16 10th-anniversary gift
17 [Hint] Apple on the head
19 Self center
20 Comparison figure
21 Lowest deck on a ship
22 Swear
23 VCR button
25 Water measurement
27 It might keep a shepherd awake
30 Pollen producer
32 Old Ford
33 Symbol of freshness
35 Kind of key
38 Come out
40 Pitch
42 The "greatest blessing" and the "greatest plague": Euripides
43 Little belittlement
45 Vaudeville dancer's prop
46 Not born yesterday
48 String decoration
50 Hiker, in a way
52 Refuse
54 Tramp's partner
55 Walpurgis Night figure
57 ___ Jones of old radio comedy
61 "You ___ here"
62 [Hint] Apple off the head
64 Annual awards giver
65 High points of a trip to South America?
66 Quartet member
67 A ship, to crew members
68 It raises dough
69 G.I. wear

DOWN

1 Sinn ___
2 What's more
3 Cordelia's father
4 Seafood dish
5 Busy person's abbr.
6 Copyists
7 Wild
8 Football legend Graham
9 Hype
10 "Barbara ___" (1966 hit)
11 [Hint] Apple in the head
12 Demanding standard
13 Buffaloes
18 Fannie Farmer treat
22 Mr. T's group
24 Slowly and evenly
26 Base
27 Squandered
28 Sphere starter
29 [Hint] Apple? Went ahead!
31 Classification
34 Superlative suffix
36 Missouri River tribe
37 Card-carrying
39 Foul
41 Image site
44 Cuddles
47 Bearish
49 Scheduled
50 Shuts (up)
51 Solid ground
53 Midsection
56 "M*A*S*H" star
58 Dissolve
59 Chili pot
60 Plug away
62 Kind of station
63 Former AT&T rival

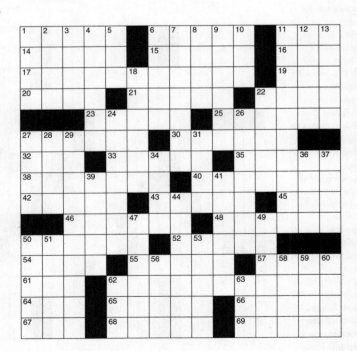

by Greg Staples

ACROSS

1 Pastoral pipe
5 Living daylights
10 "I Do, I Do, I Do, I Do, I Do" group
14 Assert
15 Class ___
16 Take the low road, in a way
17 Star of "The Producers"
19 Needing some sun
20 One who marries in haste?
21 Chapter titles
23 Pop choice
25 Ilsa's love
26 When tripled, a storeowner's asset
29 Gossiped
32 It gives the eye color
33 Revelries
35 Singer's syllable
36 Peaks
37 Cake container
38 Author John Dickson ___
39 Part of a sneaky response
40 Jungle vines
43 ___ Trask ("East of Eden" character)
44 Herculon's fiber
46 Sheep farmer's need
48 Distinctive horse
49 Spicy stews
50 Dr. Pangloss's doctrine, in "Candide"
53 Music assignments
57 Shed things
58 Dangerous area
60 Right after
61 Possible cause of goose bumps
62 Icelandic literary classic
63 Baseball's Mel and family
64 Loudness units
65 Mont. neighbor

DOWN

1 Level
2 First name in daredeviltry
3 Architect Saarinen
4 Hockey or soccer maneuver
5 Aggressive, moody type, they say
6 Commuting aids
7 Possible title for this puzzle
8 ___' Pea
9 Swell
10 Salad jellies
11 Hardly a sign of intelligence
12 Balkan land: Abbr.
13 Leon of "Mister Ed"
18 Contest
22 "Buenos ___"
24 Somewhat, colloquially
26 It's a work of art
27 Cantilevered window
28 XPINPU LPXXOJP, e.g.
30 Computer announcement
31 Fixes a toe?
34 Together
38 Some spacecraft
40 Former Irish P.M. ___ Cosgrave
41 Scoreboard divisions
42 "The Tramp" and "The General," e.g.
45 Forces (on)
47 Certain congratulations
50 "Not that!"
51 One who works with feet
52 Manhattan neighborhood
54 Some of Duchamp's art
55 They can be tight
56 Mont. neighbor
59 Peer Gynt's mother

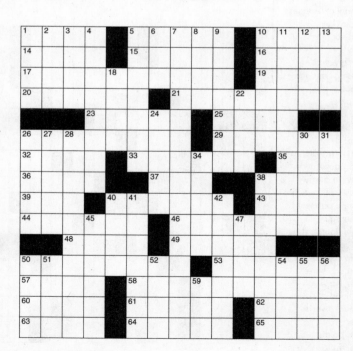

by Myles Callum

ACROSS

1 British sex symbol Diana
5 Tortilla, to a burrito
9 Food often cut in eighths
14 Plimpton book subtitled "An American Biography"
15 Good sign?
16 "Up the creek," e.g.
17 Eskimo prospector?
19 1,000 kilograms
20 Like some coffee orders
21 Feeling of pain
23 Dark time for poets
24 Defatted, as a whale
26 Not quite yet
28 Eskimo hot dog topping?
33 Have hands-on experience?
37 Tram filler
38 Suppress
39 More than suggest
40 Waits on
43 Sight from the crow's-nest
44 Maggie's mate, in the comics
46 "Well, lah-di-___"
47 Cows and sows
48 Eskimo words of enlightenment?
52 Attire worn with sandals
53 Was of use
58 Wanted-poster letters
61 Hang
63 Salad green
64 Remove errors from
66 Eskimo street?
68 Mississippi's ___ State University
69 Vogue competitor
70 Designer Gucci
71 "The sweetest gift of heaven": Virgil
72 Critic Rex
73 Look of a wolf

DOWN

1 Joltless joe
2 Two-time batting champ Lefty
3 Lunar valley
4 Roomy vehicle
5 Impassioned
6 Showed
7 Pub potables
8 Way in
9 Casino honcho
10 Swearing-in words
11 Fans' publication, for short
12 Defense type
13 "You said it!"
18 Junk drawer abbr.
22 "___ takers?"
25 Calamitous
27 Epitome of toughness
29 Three-time U.S. Open winner Ivan
30 Zion National Park home
31 Dunce cap shape
32 Winds up
33 Honshu peak
34 Grid great Dickerson
35 Like zabaglione
36 Kosher
41 Andrews or Carvey
42 Cleared of snow
45 Temporary fix
49 Ripen
50 Cavalry member
51 Tinker Bell prop
54 Worth a ten
55 Fine cotton thread
56 Give the slip to
57 Furnishings
58 Throws in
59 Boat's backbone
60 Fully qualified
62 Loser in 1996
65 Western Amerind
67 Pamplona cry

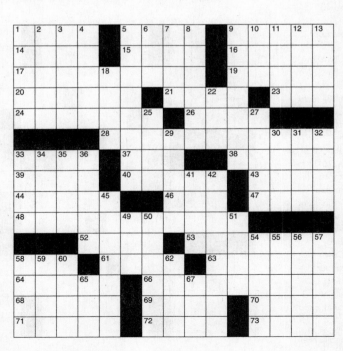

by Fred Piscop

162 ★★

ACROSS

1 One of the Three Bears
5 Shouts with both hands raised, maybe
10 Cowboy, informally
14 First-rate, slangily
15 Like an old apartment
16 Ties with bows
17 With 38-Across, poem by 24-Down
20 Rossini opera
21 U.S.-Mexico border city
22 Very, musically
23 "The Woman ___" (1984 film)
25 Tanner
27 Small bone
32 Bump
35 Gift ___
37 Unpleasant guest
38 See 17-Across
42 British royal
43 Akron AA baseball team
44 Durocher, astrologically(!)
45 Ailing
48 Local political div.
49 Home to 33 mil.
51 Shampoo instruction
56 A Virgin Island
60 Not so good, as a photo
62 Poem by 24-Down
64 Squander
65 Fighting ___
66 Certificate
67 What tags may produce
68 Methods: Abbr.
69 Baseball's Slaughter

DOWN

1 Noodles, maybe
2 Serve in the capacity of
3 Hardly bigwigs
4 It may have a pet project
5 Racer Luyendyk
6 Poem by 24-Down
7 ___ Marbles, British Museum magnet
8 Colo. neighbor
9 Does salon work
10 D
11 Kin to a clarinet
12 Noted captain
13 Petrol seller
18 "Fidelio" setting
19 Bankrolls
24 Much-quoted poet
26 Amateur video subject, maybe
28 Arab name part
29 Kind of spring
30 Isolated
31 Therefore
32 Rivers of New York
33 ___ Domini
34 Bombast
36 "Yes, Scottie"
39 Wrap (up)
40 "I shall return," e.g.
41 Lively wit
46 She loved Narcissus
47 Oahu verandas
50 Roman fire
52 Silly
53 Popular camera
54 Look after
55 Sea birds
56 1944 battle site
57 G
58 Bit of banter
59 Malachite and others
61 Olympians: Abbr.
63 No longer producing

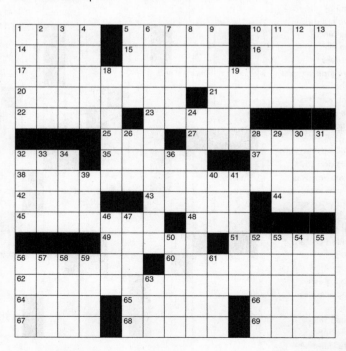

by Nancy S. Ross

ACROSS

1 Big blowout
5 Little dent
9 Candidate's concern
14 1977 movie in which Bo Derek's leg is bitten off
15 Snack item since 1912
16 Rover
17 Statement from actor Rob's debtors?
19 Hot trend
20 Rock's Brian ___
21 Disney's Ludwig ___ Drake
22 Make more attractive
24 Dr. Dre, for one
26 Columbia Pictures founder
27 Monochromatic rock?
33 Up to snuff
36 Junior, to Senior
37 Holy ___
38 Plunders
40 Took in
42 College bigwigs
43 Water channel
45 Slalom track
47 Lotion ingredient
48 Aged, unemotional shrew?
51 Pointer's word
52 "A Hard Day's Night" director
56 Reports by phone
60 Hail, to Caesar
61 Stowe girl
62 Self-evident truth
63 Question from an uncertain Osiris?
66 It may be about a yard
67 Casing
68 Prelude to a duel
69 First name in rock since 1970
70 Put up
71 A zillion

DOWN

1 Shady spot
2 Kind of football
3 Lois Lane exclusive
4 Turn left
5 Del Rio of film
6 Tend to pressing business
7 Just out
8 Keeps at it
9 Hopping mad
10 "Encore!"
11 Latin I word
12 A crystal ball user has it
13 Worry-free locale
18 Roulette bet
23 Put an edge on
25 Like some justice
26 Dispute
28 Words in a dedication
29 Radial surfaces
30 Viva-voce
31 Dessert, say, to a dieter
32 Limerick language
33 Besides
34 Weevil's target
35 Garish
39 Followers of Robert Bruce
41 PC key
44 Like some schoolbook publishers
46 What you're doing now
49 Coffee accompaniment, maybe
50 Wine sediment
53 Colleague of Edison
54 Perrier alternative
55 Hoarse
56 Soup and sandwich spot
57 Jump on the ice
58 Kind of trap
59 Nuts
60 Speller's phrase
64 Reggae relative
65 Doctrine

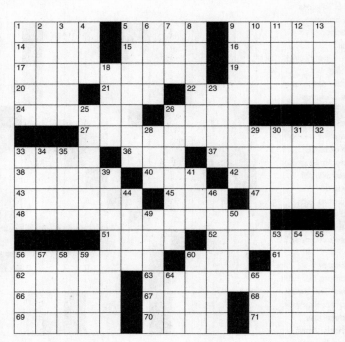

by Richard Silvestri

164 ★ ★

ACROSS

1 With 63-Across, author of the quip starting at 17-Across
6 Chicago sights
9 Baltic country: Abbr.
13 Rest against
15 Waikiki gift
16 Cruising
17 Start of a quip
19 "___ be a cold day in hell . . ."
20 Routing word
21 Add spice to
22 Jazz trumpeter Baker
23 To be, at the Sorbonne
25 Where the U.N. is in Manhattan, with 27-Across
27 See 25-Across
28 Like Salome
31 In motion
33 Soak
34 "Yours truly" and the like
35 Middle of the quip, with 37-Across
37 See 35-Across
38 Rears
39 Name for a king or a queen?
40 About three grains of troy weight
41 Deli order
45 Columbia, e.g.: Abbr.
46 Rare string
48 Santa's reindeer, e.g.
49 Pelvic parts
51 Baltimore N.F.L.ers
54 When "77 Sunset Strip" aired: Abbr.
55 Batter's base, maybe
56 End of the quip
58 Once, once
59 Electric ___
60 Beachgoer's burden
61 Sleek fleet
62 Cunning
63 See 1-Across

DOWN

1 Major producers of oil
2 Mideast native
3 False rumor
4 Enero to enero
5 Falls apart
6 Hard to pin down
7 Name immortalized by Poe
8 Indications
9 Secular
10 "Really?"
11 Watch a monitor, say
12 They hold your horses
14 Actress Carrie
18 Hardly refined
24 Author Welty
26 Address
29 Dracula and others
30 They have a lot of pull
32 Speech sound
34 Langston Hughes's "___ Unashamed"
35 Online merchants
36 Most gutsy
37 Like caresses
38 Writers' bloc
39 With refinement
41 Commit a court infraction
42 Bar order
43 Spun, as a story
44 Solzhenitsyn, e.g.
47 They're for the birds
50 Liberal pursuits
52 212 initials
53 Put belowdecks
57 ___ polloi

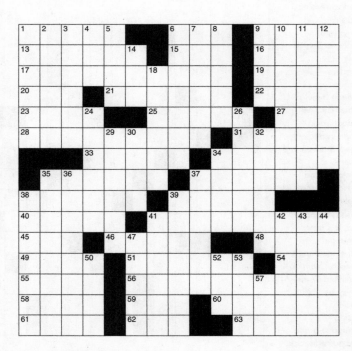

by Elizabeth C. Gorski

ACROSS

1 Like many a wrestler
6 Balance sheet item
10 One of a great quintet
14 ___ Rogers St. Johns
15 Alice's chronicler
16 Beasts in a span
17 Purple shade
18 Plowman's need
19 Cutlass maker, briefly
20 Start of a quip about middle age
23 "Star Wars" walk-ons
24 Kachina doll makers
25 Embellish, in a way
28 It may be upside-down
31 Fireplace
35 Org. with a much-cited journal
36 Needing patches
37 Micromanager's concern
38 Middle of the quip
41 Grand
42 It's insurable
43 Ike's command, once: Abbr.
44 Small songbirds
45 Blackthorn fruit
46 Ruse
47 Blame bearer
49 Smoker or diner
51 End of the quip
58 Steinbeck hero
59 Scads
60 When repeated, an Ivy League tune
61 Social introduction?
62 Baltic port
63 Packing heat
64 "___ here long?"

65 Object of blind devotion
66 Aggressive sort

DOWN

1 Java neighbor
2 Tinker with, in a way
3 Fish lacking ventral fins
4 Full of holes
5 Spinnaker's place
6 Extremely, informally
7 ". . . ___ saw Elba"
8 Cheerful
9 Old TV sidekick
10 Investigate
11 Linchpin's place
12 Reebok competitor
13 Pulver's rank: Abbr.
21 Accompanist?
22 Pricing word

25 Bochco TV drama
26 Love affair
27 Place to practice driving
29 Class in which posers are presented
30 Small hill
32 Court attention-getter
33 Be still, at sea
34 N.F.L. great Hirsch
36 Smith's partner
37 Cause for a recall
39 Kipling classic
40 Earth Summit site
45 Stone-faced
46 Monk's home, maybe
48 Arcade name
50 Chance to swing
51 Calisthenics improve it

52 Motive for some crime
53 Full of energy
54 List ender
55 Win big
56 Virginia's Robert ___
57 Arp movement
58 Front end of a one-two

by Alan Arbesfeld

166 ⭐ ⭐

ACROSS

1 Actor Green of "Buffy the Vampire Slayer"
5 Chicken order
10 "Bury the Dead" playwright
14 Soothing color
15 Football commentator ___ Long
16 Long green
17 Exposé of a lithographer's bad hangouts?
20 Word repeated in "___ always begets ___": Sophocles
21 "Vamoose!"
22 Supporter
23 Boils down
24 Old Clara-Clarence romance?
28 Bring up
29 "___ out?" (dealer's query)
30 Actress Hurley, for short
33 Urge
34 "Personal Injuries" author Scott
36 Pet name
37 "Shame on you!"
38 "Don't you just ___ it when . . . ?"
39 Biblical miracle-maker
40 Book subtitled "Cowgirl Evans's Favorite Desserts"?
43 Dispositions
46 Give up
47 Mafia code of silence
48 Polish sausage
52 Paradise with shortcomings?
54 Wind instrument
55 Serve
56 "Later, gator!"
57 One in custody
58 Nez ___ War of 1877
59 Title girl of a 1918 hit song

DOWN

1 Pink-slip
2 Prefix with lateral
3 Part of driving directions
4 Ready money
5 Finis
6 Played (around)
7 "As ___ saying . . ."
8 Bermuda highball ingredient
9 Common property boundary
10 Way to get to the top
11 Disorder
12 Northerner
13 Bridge positions
18 Poppycockish
19 Better Homes and Gardens concern
23 Villain at Crab Key
24 Subject of Elizabeth
25 Stable diet?
26 Part of a cigarette lighter
27 Cao da Serra de ___ (dog breed)
30 Money in the banca
31 Pagoda sight
32 Basketball defense
34 Rest
35 Western Indians
36 Prepare to pass, maybe
38 Poker Flat chronicler
39 Mix up
40 Like a boomerang
41 Like sour grapes
42 Pester
43 With zero chance
44 Life on a slide
45 "Coffee, ___ Me?"
48 Wood blemish
49 Bellini work
50 Right away
51 Call to a mate
53 Fifth, e.g.: Abbr.

by Manny Nosowsky

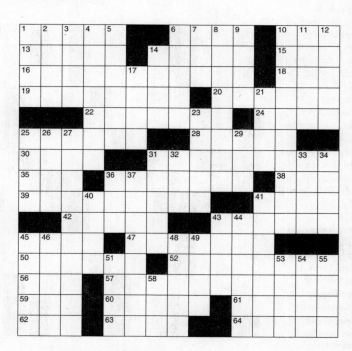

ACROSS

1 Cracker toppers
6 "Dirty" activity
10 Director's call
13 Javelin, for one
14 Having a strong resemblance
15 Botanist Gray
16 Nurse's office supply
18 Difficulty, to the Bard
19 Like a gardener's pants
20 Stellar
22 "Rocky II" climax
24 Links unit
25 Light reflection ratio
28 Bomb squad worker
30 Modeling medium
31 Believing that the universe has a soul
35 Thunder Bay's prov.
36 Place to put the feet up
38 Lennon's love
39 Uncages
41 Semicircular recess
42 Theater name
43 Victim of hair loss?
45 Austen heroine
47 Water current in the same direction as the wind
50 Windy one
52 Gun manufacturers
56 Mentalist Geller
57 Millionaire makers
59 Cacophony
60 Capone rival
61 Plume source
62 Legal conclusion?
63 Jump over
64 Places for forks

DOWN

1 Amount of trouble?
2 Bristol's county
3 Head overseas
4 Penetrated
5 Put on board
6 Mole, maybe
7 A little squirt?
8 "I Cain't Say No" musical
9 Minus
10 Redheads
11 Bar order, with "the"
12 Spreadsheet section
14 Start of a magician's cry
17 Pitcher Hideo __
21 Jefferson or Edison: Abbr.
23 Whodunit start
25 Roll call misser
26 Hermitic
27 Bean counter's concern
29 Bargain basement unit
31 In total agreement (with)
32 Dissenting votes
33 __ many words
34 Filmdom's Ethan or Joel
36 Relative of "Hurrah!"
37 Shop area
40 Nebr. neighbor
41 Explorer Vespucci
43 Fool
44 Quite the fan
45 Schumann work
46 Slugger in 1961 news
48 Bother
49 Suffix in nuclear physics
51 Adm. Zumwalt
53 University founder Cornell
54 Marsh plant
55 Members of a fast fleet
58 Prefix with angular

by David Ainslie Macleod

168 ★ ★

ACROSS

1 Is in another form?
4 Rodin sculpture at the Met
8 Best and others
13 Accident scene arrival: Abbr.
14 Hindi relative
15 Brewers' needs
17 See 32-Across
18 Morse T's
19 Parisian palace
20 Method of plant propagation
22 ___ Simbel, Egypt
23 Cartesian conclusion
24 Apiary?
26 Mr., in Mysore
27 Saved on supper, perhaps
28 Winglike appendages
29 Make doilies
30 Shaky problem
31 Court target
32 With 17-Across, Dijon's department
33 Decongestant, maybe
36 Mountain
37 Saharan sights
38 Like ___ of sunshine
39 ___ Avivian
40 Three Stooges prop
41 "The One I Love" singers
42 Golfer Ballesteros
43 Ax
46 Ninny
47 Danny's allowance?
49 "Do ___ Diddy Diddy" (1964 hit)
50 Justice Fortas
51 Fast, informally
53 Rabbitlike rodent
55 Fictional terrier
56 Prefix with athlete
57 Gist
58 Took too much, briefly

59 Cabinet dept.
60 Boxer's threat
61 "White Christmas" dancer ___-Ellen
62 Ambient music pioneer

DOWN

1 Makes one
2 It forms food vacuoles
3 It may be curbed
4 Nerve
5 Chinese parade features
6 Leigh Hunt's "Abou Ben ___"
7 Some fraternity chapters
8 Superman's revealing piercer?
9 Very fine
10 Formal refusal
11 Help with, as a project
12 Zinc ___ (ointment ingredient)
16 Arabs, e.g.
21 Time to honor Sandra?
22 Bushed
25 One out?
32 Pool ball hitter?
33 Malaysian state
34 Harbingers
35 It's blown on Yom Kippur
36 "If I Were a Rich Man" singer
37 Tab, e.g.
39 Charge for an afternoon social?
40 Cornrow creator
42 Ice lander?
44 "Roman Elegies" author

45 Like some ball games
48 ___ Island
52 Prank
54 "___ voce poco fa" (Rossini aria)
55 Mazel ___

by Robert H. Wolfe

ACROSS

1 Ship's complement
5 Atlas feature
10 Call's mate
14 Lifesaver
15 Former Yankees manager Joe
16 Nobelist Wiesel
17 Tech sch. grad
18 Beginning of a quote by W. C. Fields
20 Paparazzo's purchase
22 Place for the undecided
23 Hawaii County's seat
24 Military assaults
26 Quote, part 2
30 Napoleon, notably
31 Debatable
32 It'll take your breath away
35 Easy stride
36 Settle, in a way
38 L.B.J. in-law
39 Coast Guard off.
40 Outstanding
41 Cliffside dwelling
42 Quote, part 3
45 Got bored stiff
49 Bond foe
50 Galloping
51 Astronomer Copernicus
55 End of the quote
58 It towers over Taormina
59 It may be belted
60 Asian capital
61 Actor ___ Patrick Harris
62 ___'acte
63 Midway alternative
64 Kind of case

DOWN

1 Word in French restaurant names
2 Betting setting
3 Thus
4 Unwelcome sight on an apple
5 ". . . is fear ___"
6 "Later!"
7 Sp. ladies
8 Go off
9 Holiday in 60-Across
10 Feature of a miter joint
11 Film role for Kate Nelligan
12 "Odyssey" enchantress
13 Conservative Alan
19 Note in the C minor scale
21 Long sentence
24 Ancient colonnade
25 Mariner's cry
26 Typographer's strike
27 Neurotransmission site
28 Sounds in pounds
29 Drive forward
32 Five-time Wimbledon champ
33 Big Apple award
34 "Not on ___!"
36 1960 Olympics site
37 An OK city
38 Like perfume
40 Half of a 45
41 Part of A.D.
43 Slate.com employee
44 Comics character with an "R" on his sweater
45 Pen
46 Like many kitchens
47 Nautical direction
48 Banks hold it
51 Notable caravel
52 Suit to ___
53 Colleges, to Aussies
54 It may be shaken
56 Sorority chapter
57 Baby's cry

by Jon Delfin

170 ⭐⭐

ACROSS

1 Volvo rival
5 Nez ___
10 Longfellow bell town
14 Soup vegetable
15 Modern husband or wife
16 "The Black Camel" detective
17 63-Across film, 1931
19 Marie Antoinette lost hers
20 Place du Casino locale
21 Choose
23 Russian station
24 Bizet opera priestess
26 Dimwit
28 Egypt's Nasser
32 Some fund-raisers
34 "Billy, Don't Be ___" (1974 hit)
35 "You don't say!"
36 Where jetsam may be thrown
38 63-Across film, 1939
43 Half of a familiar Chinese duo
44 Hipster
45 Reach
46 Where a plane's engine is housed
49 Gluey plaster of Paris
50 Search for water
52 Football Hall-of-Famer Link ___
54 "Yay, team!"
55 Water of Oise
57 Like some dancers
61 "How sweet ___!"
63 Actor born 2/1/1901
66 Greek cheese
67 Freight
68 Fashionable 60's dress
69 Low part of a hand
70 One ordered to stop?
71 Leprechaun's land

DOWN

1 Chip off the old block
2 Old-time actor Tamiroff
3 Ship of myth
4 Road to Rostock
5 English tips?
6 Pertaining to primitive horses
7 Capek drama
8 Clicker
9 Zeno's home
10 Take steps
11 63-Across film, 1961
12 Connecting gears have it
13 Comatose
18 Soapmaker's need
22 Epitome of easiness
25 Without due concern
27 Party to a financial transaction
28 [That's awful!]
29 Salty shout
30 63-Across film, 1934
31 Where gladiators performed
33 O.T. book
37 Demolition supplies
39 Pilot's worry
40 Bankhead of "Lifeboat"
41 Drink that's stirred
42 Ski-___ snowmobiles
47 Average grade
48 Come forth
50 Implication
51 "Outlaws of the Range," e.g.
53 ___ the covenant
56 Billing abbr.
58 Unexciting
59 Structural beam
60 Year Marcus Aurelius became emperor
62 "By the way . . ."
64 Jackie's second
65 Die Welt article

by Frances Hansen

ACROSS

1 Short haircut
4 Check out, so to speak
8 Deaden
14 Bush spokesman Fleischer
15 Stationery quantity
16 Grim one?
17 Treat for a pup
19 Pooh pal
20 "That's ___ ask!"
21 Thin toast
23 Something to pick
24 Singer Sumac
26 Nevada senator Harry
27 The Internet's ___ Drudge
28 Baseball's first Hall-of-Famer
31 Introduction to economics?
33 Suffix with president
34 New England state sch.
36 Floppy disk?
40 Makes aware
42 1993 Earp portrayer
43 Groups within groups
44 Letters on many black churches
45 "Shoot!"
46 Simple chord
48 Prepares for a crash
50 Actress Russo
53 Deliberate affront
55 Theater admonition
56 "Xanadu" rock band
57 Painter Matisse
59 No room to swing ___
62 Tout's tidbit
65 W.W. II missile
67 Summary
68 Stick ___ in the water
69 Soccer standout Hamm
70 Smear
71 Foxx of "Sanford and Son"
72 Cold comment?

DOWN

1 Cake with a kick
2 Pitcher Hershiser
3 Copper's bopper
4 Trombonist Kid ___
5 Idea's beginning
6 "Headliners & Legends" host
7 Hammer and sickle, e.g.
8 Tidbit for a bird feeder
9 Superwide
10 Nonpro?
11 "Once ___ Honeymoon" (1942 film)
12 Reason for a raise
13 Quarterback Favre
18 Long ride?
22 1967 seceder
25 Addict, e.g.
27 Shaded growth
28 Rapid blinks, maybe
29 Manchurian border river
30 Where to have a banger
32 Staircase parts
35 Cuckoo
37 Scavenge, in a way
38 Otherwise
39 Fraternal group
41 Family of patrons of the arts
47 "The Sport of the Gods" author
49 Fictional whaler
50 Get-well center
51 Bond on the run
52 Prominent
54 Savage sort
58 Classic shirt brand
60 Gulf States bigwig
61 Winter lift
63 Chorus syllable
64 Hosp. section
66 The end, to 'Enry

by Kent Lorentzen

172

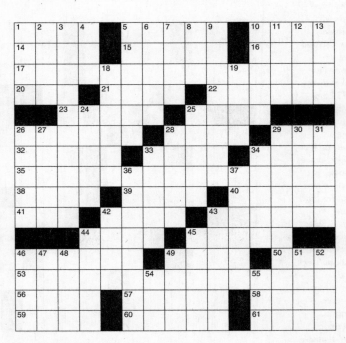

ACROSS

1 Lower, south of the border
5 Deck out
10 It may be made by a stargazer
14 Chug-___
15 Cook in a wok, perhaps
16 Not duped by
17 Where God is King of Kings?
20 Source of suds
21 Litigant
22 Like some auctions
23 Second baseman called "The Crab"
25 Flier
26 Fairy tale figure
28 Diversify
29 "Prince Valiant" cartoonist Foster
32 Lionesses lack them
33 One of a couple
34 Fashion
35 Tongue-twister phrase hinting at this puzzle's theme
38 So
39 Glazed unit
40 "Adam and Eve on a raft," e.g.
41 It may be tipped
42 Have too little
43 Like some salad dressings
44 Airborne unit?
45 Sea
46 Passionate
49 Plating material
50 No exemplar of grace
53 Wine-flavored espagnole
56 Quaint outburst
57 Stage presence?
58 Bit of planning
59 Ding-a-ling
60 Complaining
61 The bulk

DOWN

1 Burglar's deterrent, maybe
2 Natural balm
3 Crushing force
4 21, for one
5 Hearten
6 Hotel listing
7 Essen's region
8 Had something, so to speak
9 Emphatic affirmation
10 ___-be
11 Memo opener
12 Blow out of the water
13 Central computer
18 Burundian biter
19 Light
24 Scenes
25 Irrigate
26 Metalworker
27 Ottoman title
28 Safe place
29 Hi
30 Pitching pros
31 Guarded
33 Acadia National Park locale
34 San Rafael's county
36 Not driving while intoxicated, e.g.
37 Washington team, informally
42 25-Across's perch, perhaps
43 Stubborn as a mule
44 Buddy
45 Protected animal
46 Follow
47 Scrubbed
48 Donnybrook
49 Tubes on the dinner table
51 Tennis statistic
52 Bit of derring-do
54 Cry in Kiel
55 Cry before firing

by Manny Nosowsky

ACROSS

1 Stored, as honey
6 Name prefix meaning "son of"
9 Make provision (for)
14 Where drachmas were once spent
15 "Son ___ gun!"
16 Sponger
17 Start of an idle question
20 Many namesakes: Abbr.
21 State tree of New Jersey
22 "Psst! Pass ___!"
23 ___ Affair
24 Baseball's strikeout king
26 Scharnhorst admiral
29 Yokels
31 Decline
34 Big name in philanthropy
37 Bologna's place
39 Question, part 2
41 Pressure, in a way
42 Surmounted
43 Person who knows the drill?: Abbr.
44 Slingshot item
46 Much binary code
47 Joint tenant's place?
48 Way to stand
50 Spanish ayes
53 Brings out
56 Cross shape
59 End of the question
62 Deborah of "Days of Our Lives"
63 Sign of aging
64 Prepare for reuse, perhaps
65 Parable's message
66 Old pronoun
67 No longer in

DOWN

1 Muslim pilgrimage
2 Operatic prince
3 R.S.V.P. part
4 East ender?
5 Holstein's home
6 Anticipation or sadness, e.g.
7 Onetime Michael Jackson do
8 Trans Am rival
9 "Aladdin" prince
10 Red Square figure
11 Riga resident
12 ___ Rios, Jamaica
13 Declaration of Independence starter
18 Shriner topper
19 Go into free-fall
23 Hard-to-combine gas
25 Up and about
26 Burn
27 Skinned
28 "Aunt ___ Cope Book"
29 Massenet's "Le ___"
30 Deceived
31 Name in 2000 headlines
32 Ecological community
33 Deadly poisons
35 Irregularly notched
36 Made tame
38 Cravat's cousin
40 "___ seen enough!"
45 Guinness adjective
47 Paramecium propellers
48 Its tip may be felt
49 Set, as a price
50 Chang and Eng's homeland
51 ___-European
52 Mark for life
54 Jazz home
55 Shrewd
56 Precisely
57 Nave neighbor
58 Played for a sap
60 Net location
61 La-la starter

by Robert Dillman

174 ⭐ ⭐

ACROSS

1 One getting a cut
6 Tout's tabulation
10 1968 folk album
14 Mother of Perseus
15 Lug
16 Animal house?
17 Producer of Eazy-E and Eminem
18 Item used in basement waterproofing
20 Sonja Henie's debut film, 1936
22 Methodical
23 Commencement dangler
24 Bully
27 Geographical connectors
29 Truth, old-style
31 Inability to speak
35 Pro ___
36 1971 James Taylor/Warren Oates cult film
41 Perfect
42 Politically incorrect coat
43 Adjust, as a brooch
45 They may have shorts
50 24-time Ryder Cup winner
51 Kind of soup
55 When tripled, an old war cry
56 1932 Bette Davis melodrama
59 "The Thin Man" producer Hunt ___
61 Hi from Ho
62 Nautical nose
63 Senate accusation
64 TV or radio station
65 Cheerleaders' practice
66 Split in the cold, perhaps
67 Marble-producing Italian city

DOWN

1 Annexes
2 Relative of cerise
3 Take to one's heart
4 Airport near Tokyo
5 New driver, maybe
6 Rembrandt, for one
7 Socialite Duke
8 Some exhaust systems
9 Subway station sight
10 Kind of flute
11 Shower apparel
12 Diminutive, in Dogpatch
13 It's fine for a refinery
19 Guitarist Lofgren
21 Harmonize
25 Sgt. Snorkel's dog
26 Larrup
28 Ogden Nash's "___ Stranger Here Myself"
30 Mork's planet
32 ThinkPad producer
33 Cutting repeatedly
34 Malacañang Palace locale
36 By way of, briefly
37 Troubles
38 Like a beat cop
39 Haole's souvenir
40 The 900's, e.g.: Abbr.
44 Benchmark
46 List ender
47 Drives (along)
48 Parts of feet
49 Most of Mauritania
52 Mediterranean ship
53 Canines
54 Cardiological concern
57 Ginsberg poem
58 Word with yes, no or thank you
59 Good looker?
60 Half of sei

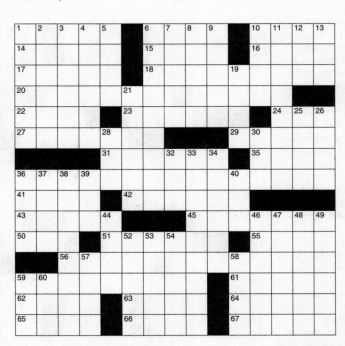

by David Ainslie Macleod

ACROSS

1 Pocahontas's husband
6 Invitation to duel, perhaps
10 Close to closed
14 Intense hatred
15 Tabula ___
16 Ankle-length skirt
17 Nearing the hour
18 James Bond beauties?
20 Titan orbits it
22 St. ___ (spring break spot)
23 Drop in on
24 Bar choices
26 Feather's mate
27 Where to order un thé
30 Luau staple
32 Back from dreamland
37 ___ above
38 "Alfred" composer
40 Cameos, e.g.
41 Marine creatures with unneeded limbs?
44 Masked critters
45 L.B.J. son-in-law
46 Barrie pirate
47 Buchholz of "The Magnificent Seven"
48 H.S.T.'s successor
49 Kickoff preceder
50 Absorbed, as a loss
53 Part of UHF: Abbr.
55 Pole worker
58 Kind of stand
60 Statement of the obvious
64 Emulate Prometheus?
67 Veep John ___ Garner
68 Word processor command
69 Custard concoction
70 "___ Marner"
71 Scraped (out)
72 Itches
73 Winter Palace residents

DOWN

1 Goes bad
2 Concert halls
3 Suit jacket buildup
4 2004 Olympics stars?
5 Atlanta university
6 A.A.R.P. members
7 Reindeer herder
8 So far
9 Elbows, but not knees
10 Horner's last words
11 Shakes up
12 Linchpin's place
13 Court order?
19 Actor Depardieu
21 Sherpa's home
25 More tender
27 Come down with
28 Allergy season sound
29 Uproar
31 ___ we trust
33 Least desirable wharves?
34 Something to remember?
35 "Dinner at Antoine's" author
36 They're common in Mississippi
39 Treble clef lines
42 What you will
43 Thumb-raising critic
51 Chewy candy
52 Send to Siberia
54 Surrealist Max
55 In ___ (actually)
56 Security lapse
57 Half a sawbuck
59 OPEC member
61 "To Live and Die ___"
62 Permanent marker?
63 Quantico cuisine
65 Zodiac's start, in England
66 U.S.N.A. grad

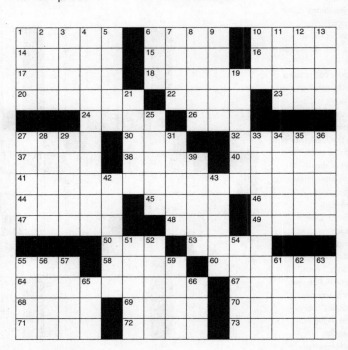

by Karen Hodge

176 ⭐ ⭐

ACROSS

1 XXX
5 Unnatural, in a way
10 Place for some icons
14 Up-to-the-minute
15 Opponent for Ike
16 Brown-and-white
17 What is more
18 What old enemies may do
19 Window-rattling
20 Start of a quip
22 "___ be in England . . ."
23 "Cheerio!"
24 Flop
26 A pop
27 Measures of some losses: Abbr.
28 Gymnast's place
32 Big leagues
34 When things don't go right
36 Who "is alone" in a 1987 Sondheim title
37 Middle of the quip
40 Seed coverings
41 Volleys
42 Jack and the missus
44 Go back and forth (with)
45 Kind of mask
48 Book after Philemon: Abbr.
49 Soak (up)
51 Fifth- or sixth-grader
53 Bumper ___
55 End of the quip
59 Take ___ (rest)
60 Spanish 101 verb
61 "An Essay on Criticism" writer
62 Microwave
63 "Veni"
64 Idle fellow?
65 Hearty dinner
66 Colossus
67 Go on and on

DOWN

1 Swank
2 Having a certain glow
3 Time releases
4 Alibi
5 One of Henry VIII's six
6 Old music halls
7 Sound before "Thanks, I needed that!"
8 Dog-___
9 Chinatown offering
10 Singer Guthrie
11 Diminish
12 Semisweet white wine
13 Sign on the dotted line
21 Bull sessions
25 William ___, who founded Ralston Purina
29 A lot of fluff
30 Hullabaloos
31 Half of a 60's quartet
33 Tittles
34 Kans. neighbor
35 Cry out
37 Monocled advertising figure
38 Mechanical device that operates by compression
39 Eggs
40 Waste holders
43 "Very well"
45 Woman of la casa
46 Constrain
47 Treehopper, e.g.
50 "Lethal Weapon 2," ". . . 3" and ". . . 4" actor
52 Rain check
54 Shoot
56 Sportscaster's tidbit
57 Author Janowitz
58 Songbird

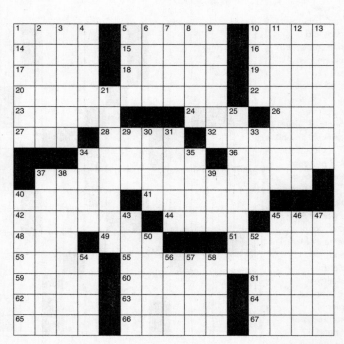

by Elizabeth C. Gorski

ACROSS

1 White House nickname
4 Reaches a peak
10 Be a nag
14 Pother
15 Milk-related
16 Western Hemisphere abbr.
17 1984 Democratic keynoter
19 ___ doble (Spanish dance)
20 Come forth
21 Commit to another hitch
23 Small pointer
24 Have status
25 "Catch a Falling Star" singer
27 Queen, maybe
28 Throughway
30 Walk-ons, e.g.
31 Not averting one's eyes
33 Blatant deception
35 With 36-Across, a depiction of Jesus
36 See 35-Across
37 On a branch, maybe
40 Do Little?
44 "___ man with seven wives"
45 Sailed through
46 Something to flip
47 Chief steward
50 Adriatic seaport
51 Rocker Brian
52 Break up with, and not nicely
53 Numbskull, to a Brit
55 Nice evening
57 Hypes a movie, perhaps
59 Word in many college names

60 Concern of 43-Down
61 "___ Rosenkavalier"
62 Margarine
63 Farmer, at times
64 Nus, to us

DOWN

1 Shooters' needs
2 Unyielding
3 Hot Lips portrayer
4 Plunger's target
5 Derby
6 Euro forerunner
7 On disk
8 Track official
9 Use elbow grease on
10 Salary limit
11 #1 hit for Jimmy Dorsey, 1941
12 Began again
13 Ask for a hand?

18 Choler
22 Cheops construction
25 Beeped
26 Barbizon School painter
28 One of two Plantagenet kings
29 Back then
32 Page 1, 3 or 5, e.g.
33 Harpo's interpreter
34 Directive to James
37 Olive stuffer
38 Common temple name
39 Exult
41 Apple-pie order?
42 Radial makers
43 Staff of Life
45 Fuse unit
48 Guys, slangily
49 Samuel Lover's "Rory ___"

50 Prickly seedcase
53 Game ending
54 On ___ with
56 Howe'er
58 Bummed

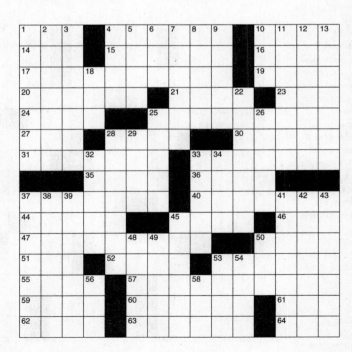

by A. J. Santora

178 ★ ★

ACROSS

1 "Goldberg Variations" composer
5 Like Beethoven
9 Crisp cookies
14 "The Intimate ___" (1990 jazz album)
15 Empire builder
16 Zipped, so to speak
17 Start of some campus graffiti
19 Extreme
20 Spode item
21 Lands, as a fish
23 TV inits.
24 Doctor's cupful, maybe
25 Teachers' org.
28 Graffiti, part 2
34 First and second
36 Wharton's Frome
37 To the ___
38 Du Pont trademark
41 Music box music
42 City whose name is derived from a Timucua Indian name
44 Rubber stamp
46 Graffiti, part 3
49 Canton ender
50 1960's revolutionary Mark
51 Snack
53 Collage, e.g.
57 Not so valuable furs
61 Experts
62 End of the graffiti
65 National competitor
66 In ___ (not piecemeal)
67 Beef ___
68 Oppose
69 Coloraturas' performances
70 Till compartment

DOWN

1 Inclination
2 "___ of the Mind" (Sam Shepard play)
3 "The Alexandria Quartet" finale
4 Deck opening
5 Kitchen sink device
6 Business letter abbr.
7 Essen interjection
8 ___ Islands, between Scotland and Iceland
9 Very narrow fit
10 Valueless
11 River isles
12 Prefix with scope
13 Cartoonist Drake
18 Maestro Mehta
22 D.C. is on it
24 It's not part of a play
25 Adverb disdained by English teachers
26 Author ___ Maria Remarque
27 Ike challenger
29 Layer
30 Manche capital
31 Relative of a leek
32 Compels to go
33 ___ nous
35 "___ never work!"
39 Employee's wrap-up: Abbr.
40 Time for le déluge?
43 Pfffsss producer
45 Gaucho's rope
47 Big ___
48 Shows honesty, in a way
52 Gallery installation
53 Thickening agent
54 Do or don't
55 Fat mouth
56 Cause for opening a window
58 Business letter abbr.
59 Ring site
60 Wraps (up)
63 ___ Canals
64 N.L. Central team inits.

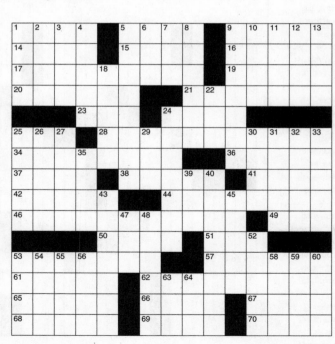

by Nancy S. Ross

ACROSS

1 Inventory's place
6 Opposite of baja
10 Singer Redding
14 University in Beaumont, Tex.
15 Wagered
16 Polite encl.
17 Like rams and lambs
18 Iris's locale
19 Religious image: Var.
20 Figured out a British royal
23 Word with drum or trumpet
24 Good times
25 Inventor Otis
27 Make way
31 Daisylike bloom
32 PC key
33 Capp and Green
35 Hoped-for low number: Abbr.
36 Invoiced a British royal
41 Fictional detective ___ Pym
42 The Reagan boy
43 Geologist's measure
44 Food of the gods
47 Aide's job
52 Crosses the threshold
54 G-man: Abbr.
55 Land's end
56 Discarded a British royal
60 Celestial hammerer
61 Area code 801 area
62 Is a bibliophile
63 Prefix with globin
64 Point of intersection
65 Identification
66 First place
67 Hitch, e.g.
68 Show of contempt

DOWN

1 Isn't flat
2 Go for
3 Displaced person, maybe
4 Country singer k. d. ___
5 Skydiver's start
6 Donor's group
7 Hawaiian bubbly?
8 Level
9 Saw
10 Underworld leader
11 Has an afternoon break
12 Line on a weather map showing equal temperatures
13 Clinton, e.g.: Abbr.
21 1970's Plymouth
22 ___ mode
26 Coach Parseghian
28 Friend
29 Occurs to, with "on"
30 Yalie
34 Toy holder?
36 Split
37 Avoids callers, say
38 1950 noir classic
39 Making daguerreotypes, and other things
40 Acct. earnings
41 Fr. woman
45 Synapse neighbor
46 Waterspout trajectory
48 Potpourri bag
49 Makes others wait
50 Rib
51 Quite a joke
53 Shut out
57 Harrow's rival
58 Carpenter's groove
59 Pull (in)
60 Many a 65-Across starter

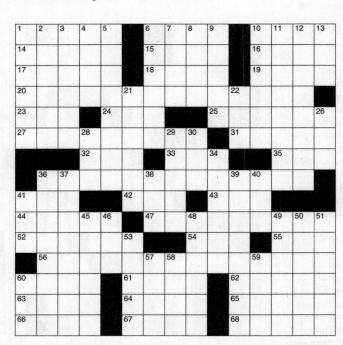

by Noah Dephoure

ACROSS

1 "One Man's San Francisco" author
5 ___ doble (Latin dance)
9 Some Olympians, nowadays
13 Stare impertinently
14 Slogan
16 Algebra topic
18 Like some rats
19 "You there?"
20 Org. that banned DDT
21 Knock over
24 Critic, at times
25 Pay the entire check
28 Fertilizer sources
31 What a cedilla indicates
33 Talk incessantly
34 Turnstile part
37 It can be found in oil
40 Game in which jacks are highest trumps
41 Inflammatory diseases
42 Radiate
43 Ripens
45 Monterrey jack?
46 Pinch-hitting great Manny ___
49 Super ___ (old video game standard)
50 Washington, to Lafayette
52 Fed
54 Chafing dish fuel
57 1947 Best Picture nominee
62 Waste away
63 Answer to the riddle "Dressed in summer, naked in winter"
64 1980's Davis Cup captain

65 Hits a fly
66 City on the Gulf of Aqaba

DOWN

1 Serving with vin
2 Río contents
3 Airline with King David Lounges
4 "Nashville" co-star
5 Outdoor dining spot
6 N.C. State plays in it
7 H. Rider Haggard novel
8 Alphabet trio
9 They talk too much
10 Angrily harangue
11 "___ Mio"
12 "Sí" man?
14 Break activity, perhaps

15 "What's that?"
17 Saw with the grain
21 Knocking noises
22 Kind of triangle
23 Louis Botha, notably
25 Recipe abbr.
26 Fleece
27 Black key
29 Guarantee
30 Blender setting
32 The Rhumba King
34 Together, in music
35 Some mail designations: Abbr.
36 San ___, Calif.
38 Something in writing?
39 An American in Paris, perhaps
43 Dugong's cousin
44 Half of quattordici
46 A Gabor sister
47 Cruel people

48 Choppers
51 Part of a baby bottle
53 Artist Gerard ___ Borch
54 Flies away
55 "Me neither"
56 1977 Scott Turow book
58 Greek letters
59 "Ker-bam!"
60 Quod ___ faciendum
61 Subway wish

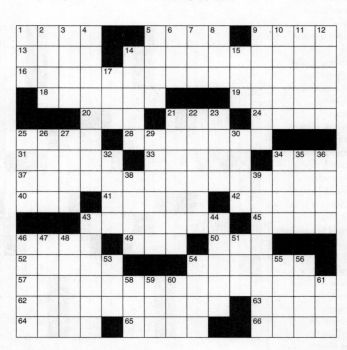

by Peter Gordon

ACROSS

1 Balkan capital
6 "Black Beauty" star ___ Freeman
10 Under the weather
14 Uniform hue
15 K-6: Abbr.
16 Topology figures
17 Support person
18 Colorful mount
19 Mil. truant
20 Common darning spot
21 Hide boredom, in a way
24 Part of a boilermaker
25 Lays out
26 Sot's state
29 Used a peephole
31 Hunt like a cave man
33 Interview bit: Abbr.
36 Down ___ (Maine)
37 Small island
38 "Phooey!"
39 Child advocacy org.
40 Make peace
44 Anouk of film
45 Gad about
46 Wellesley grad
49 Years and years
50 They're hidden in 21-, 31- and 40-Across
53 "Vamoose!"
56 Like many fans
57 Seine sights
58 Roomy cut
60 Winks
61 Aloha State bird
62 Some six-shooters
63 Q.E.D. part
64 Breyers rival
65 Praise

DOWN

1 Three-player game
2 Home to Columbus
3 Falter at the finish
4 Likable prez
5 Blue Angels display
6 Reason for a raise
7 Former Swedish P.M. Palme
8 "Hud" star
9 Knock-on-the-noggin consequence
10 Didn't fold
11 Hawkeye
12 Three, they say
13 Hops driers
22 ___ Bora (Afghan region)
23 Mimic
24 "X" may mark it
26 Put one's foot down
27 "How about ___?"
28 Celestial bear
29 Title holder?
30 Anti-fur org.
32 Solomonic
33 Kaffiyeh wearer
34 One of the major leagues: Abbr.
35 Lid swelling
38 F.D.R. and L.B.J., e.g.
40 ___ Fein
41 "Think of it!"
42 Meadowlands pace
43 Turn upside-down
44 In the thick of
46 Bring down
47 Onions partner
48 City near Syracuse
49 Slalom paths
51 Said "no contest," e.g.
52 Counting-out bit
53 Embellish richly
54 A fan of
55 Tracy's Trueheart
59 Bud's bud

by Sarah Keller

182 ⭐ ⭐

ACROSS

1 Boeuf à la Russe ingredient
4 Chord type
9 Chicago Cubs spring training site
13 Actress Long
14 Novelist born in Thornton, Yorkshire
15 Smackers
16 Author-turned-radio personality?
18 H.S. helpers
19 Really enjoys
20 1950's political inits.
22 Knock the socks off
23 Win by ___
24 Psychologist-turned-N.F.L. runner?
27 Child pluralizer
28 King of the Bullwhip
30 Man in search of meaning?
31 Less risky
32 Toronado or Starfire
33 Writer-turned-physician?
37 Turkish dough
39 Put off
40 Pessimist's reply
42 Dumps
43 Lettuce serving
46 Author-turned-coroner?
48 58-Across feature
50 Tiny wriggler
51 Gleeful cry
52 Quit
53 Settled down
55 Adventurer-turned-alien?
58 Spanish lady
59 Light shades
60 Present time: Abbr.
61 Hosp. charts
62 Expand
63 Preaction fig.

DOWN

1 Win the love of
2 1997 Demi Moore title role
3 Alphonse's partner in old comics
4 Spill
5 Actor Moody of "Oliver!"
6 Mozart's Sonata ___ for Keyboard and Violin
7 Resting
8 Batting whiz Jeter
9 Bad hairdo
10 Jumble
11 Iodine source
12 Puts forward
14 Sabbath proscription
17 Donkey's uncle
21 Paul McCartney, for one
24 Neighbor of Lucy and Desi
25 Lab tube
26 Knotted rope
29 Request for Vanna, maybe
31 Joe of "Apollo 13"
33 Greenhouse operation
34 Wig
35 Overseas honour: Abbr.
36 Winter coats
37 Citrus mixer
38 Ross Sea sight
41 La la lead-in
42 Explicit
43 One who's fair
44 Draws out
45 Make out
47 Yemen, once
49 Suffix with favor
52 Poet Harwood
54 Univ. workers
56 Top
57 Years ___

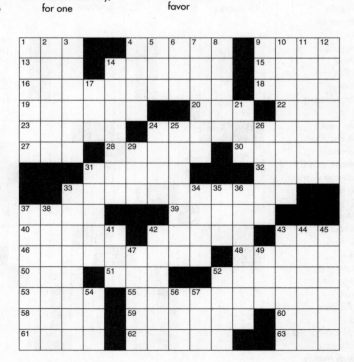

by Randolph Ross

ACROSS

1 Skinny tie
5 Specimen holder
9 Barely maintaining, with "out"
14 Jannings of "The Blue Angel"
15 "That ___ excuse!"
16 "Long time ___"
17 Start of a thought by 29-Across
19 Trough diners
20 Upright
21 Imitated a peacock, maybe
23 Tedious business
25 ___-Magnon
26 Start of a Doris Day song title
29 See 17-Across
33 Java holder
34 ___-dink
36 Pythagorean triangle?
37 German article
39 Thought, part 2
41 "Titanic" soundtrack singer
42 It'll make you sweat
44 Silas Marner's foundling
46 Green light
47 Thought, part 3
49 Major keys?
51 Prov. bordering Hudson Bay
52 Fancy-dress dos
53 Light into
57 Seat of Parliament
61 Jump for joy
62 End of the thought
64 Path in Paris
65 "My Life as ___" (1985 film)
66 Ural River city
67 Exploits
68 Golf's Ballesteros
69 One of Maris's overtakers

DOWN

1 "Little Women" woman
2 Sequel to Melville's "Typee"
3 MGM icon
4 Mexican natives of old
5 "We are not amused" speaker
6 Suffix with bull or bear
7 Win by ___
8 Send up
9 Guaranteed
10 Bowed and scraped
11 "From where ___ . . ."
12 Hawaiian goose
13 Made a right turn
18 Family name in a Poe story
22 Camcorder maker
24 Extends
26 Pilgrimage
27 Bathsheba's husband
28 Lassitude
29 Mr. Magoo's problem
30 Name in 2000 headlines
31 Prepared for the anthem, say
32 Aquariums
35 Keystone fellow
38 Exalted
40 Knock loose
43 Relatives on father's side
45 Make happy
48 Roy Orbison's "___ Over"
50 Nolan Ryan and others
52 Sparkly paperweight
53 Front-runner's edge
54 Wheel shaft
55 Stubborn sort
56 Start of a Yuletide reading
58 1970's coif
59 Weak one
60 ___-Seltzer
63 Remembrance Day mo.

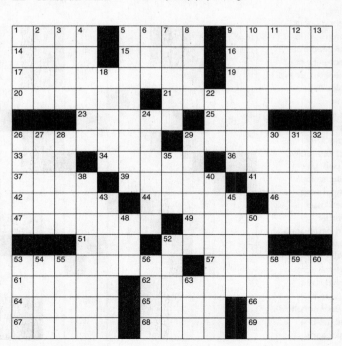

by Susan Harrington Smith

ACROSS

1 It may follow U
5 Leather, essentially
9 Scales up?
14 Year in dates
15 Lepton's locale
16 Wind section
17 Historical zenith
19 Puppy protests
20 Barely hit
21 What "there's gonna be," in a "Funny Lady" song
23 Body of eau
24 Warriors' grp.
26 "Purty" one
27 Cone source
28 Stretches, with "out"
30 Tattered Tom's creator
32 Legal scholar Guinier
33 Dragon puppet
35 Rulings
36 What people in relationships need together . . . or this puzzle's title
39 Spring
41 Cat's comment of understanding
42 Geraint's wife
43 React to a really bad pun
45 Smelter stuff
49 Big Apple ave.
50 Hottie's asset
51 On target
53 Word before long or now
54 Big Akron employer
57 Like some patches
59 Giant in chips
60 Bar promotion
62 City on the Mohawk
63 Shrek, for one
64 Highlander's tongue
65 Avian chatterbox
66 Plaintiff
67 Detached ends?

DOWN

1 Wrangle
2 Arctic cover-up
3 Loosen, in a way
4 Polish birthplace of Arthur Rubinstein
5 Off-the-wall pastime?
6 Spanish female suffix
7 Rapper Snoop ___
8 Come forward
9 Not running
10 Skeptic's remark
11 Dark characters?
12 Brighten up, maybe
13 Semiramis's domain
18 Sundown, in sonnets
22 A hoop may hang from it
25 Et ___
29 Ping or pong
31 Be admitted
32 Barely gets (along)
34 Cub scout, say
35 Sixth-century date
36 Hardly practical
37 Pool provider, often
38 Proverbial payee
39 King Albert II's land
40 City on the Susquehanna
43 Trouble
44 Some spuds
46 1831 Poe poem
47 Work up
48 Sci-fi and mystery
50 Bit of internal governance
52 Tax
55 Numerical prefix
56 It has 11 "Robusto!" flavors
58 Expressed surprise
61 Affix with fix

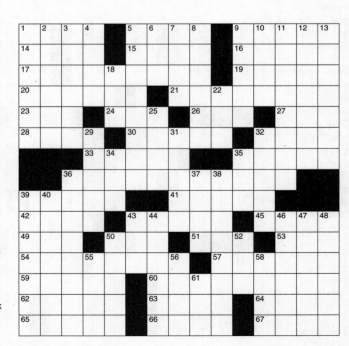

by Alex Vaughn

ACROSS

1 Read (through)
5 Guanaco's cousin
10 Singing style
14 Harbinger
15 See 70-Across
16 "Heaven forbid!"
17 Like most of Aeschylus' plays?
20 Quaker
21 Like a mandolin
22 Diplomatic to-do
24 Turn one way
25 Position
28 Breakable things
30 Dojo teaching
35 God defeated twice by Hercules
37 Response to "Shall we?"
39 Paris, to Romeo
40 Round cameo?
43 Sacred text
44 Caffeine-rich nut
45 Lawn sculpture, maybe
46 Says unpleasantly
48 Marrow
50 Govt. org. that employs mathematicians
51 Triumphant cry
53 Goon
55 201, e.g.
60 Bump result
64 Students' objections to a big exam?
66 Walt Kelly creation
67 Promotional campaign adjunct
68 Unwanted e-mail
69 Check
70 With 15-Across, 1950's "Tonight Show" host
71 Daly of "Judging Amy"

DOWN

1 Bolt (down)
2 Omnia vincit ___
3 TV's Arnaz
4 Log
5 Crow's-nest sighting
6 M.L.K.'s honorary deg. from Yale
7 Skiing mecca
8 Fred or Ethel of "I Love Lucy"
9 Hooded jacket
10 Presently
11 Perform a bar dare
12 Sister of King Arthur
13 Mrs. Lincoln's maiden name
18 Shrub that yields indigo
19 Mozart's "Le Nozze di ___"
23 Fine-tune
25 Game with a ball
26 Betelgeuse's constellation
27 Hall of Fame catcher
29 Barbershop band
31 Improvised bit
32 Of interest to bird-watchers
33 Anklebone
34 Tennis player Dementieva
36 Rocky outlook
38 Gymnast's feat
41 Loosen, in a way
42 1940's Holmes player
47 Features before main features
49 Smart
52 Concede
54 Talk show interviewee
55 Concert gear
56 Laugh ___
57 Margin
58 Speck
59 Foil alternative
61 1960's Cosby show
62 Satirist Freberg
63 Salinger heroine
65 "6 Rms ___ Vu" (play)

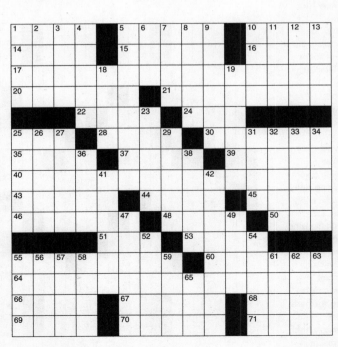

by Linda Bushman

ACROSS

1 Reworking of old material
5 Look closely
10 Vaulted area, perhaps
14 Comics canine
15 Barbara of "Gone With the Wind"
16 Five-time U.S. Open champ
17 Fighting words
20 Threaten to fall
21 Dove with a Pulitzer
22 ___ particle
23 Separates
25 Ropes
27 See 52-Down
28 ___ Pensacola (mil. center)
30 Smelly smoke
31 Christmas wish
33 They may fill yards
34 What 17- and 54-Across indicate
37 Sofer of soaps
38 "The Tempest" sprite
39 Rah-rah
41 Sushi selection
42 Base of a crocus stem
46 It may be shown on a tree
48 One with a yen
50 Feminizing suffix
51 Old radio's "My Friend ___"
53 Go with the wind
54 Fighting words
57 Donizetti's "Tornami a dir che m'ami," e.g.
58 Rest stop sights
59 Having southerly breezes
60 Lieutenant: Abbr.
61 Beehive, e.g.
62 Hand demand?

DOWN

1 Place to feel a jet stream?
2 Classical symbol of wisdom
3 Toughens
4 Shackle
5 Necessity for an opening act?
6 It may get stuffed: Abbr.
7 48-Across's look
8 Stop-off
9 Doesn't just please
10 Cause of some spots
11 Jane Goodall, to Louis Leakey
12 Trips overseas
13 Flow out
18 Football Hall-of-Famer Dawson
19 Kind of comb
24 Yemen's capital
26 Evergreen oak
29 South American capital
31 Just barely
32 Raced down?
34 Lewis Carroll and others
35 Haloed one, in Le Havre
36 Air
37 Catastrophic
39 Good witch of note
40 Bad witch, e.g.
42 Big California industry
43 Wellspring
44 Product
45 Stevenson scoundrel
47 Hanged Irish patriot
49 Algonquian-speaking people
52 With 27-Across, Fort Lee, e.g.
55 The Little Giant
56 Nonexistent

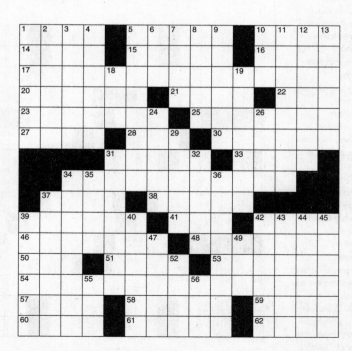

by Sherry O. Blackard

ACROSS

1 Lively
5 "Get outta here!"
10 Shock
14 Ruthless boss
15 Aromatic herb
16 Sondheim's "___ Like That"
17 Singer's football tackles?
19 Invitation letters
20 Prognosis
21 Leavenworth and others: Abbr.
23 Souvenir shop item, for short
24 Completely
25 Prefix with terrorism
27 Reproductive needs
29 Cardinal's nest?: Abbr.
30 Sounds of a broom-beating?
35 Play the host to
36 Scream
37 Moore of film
40 Skip
42 1970's Chevy
43 Person who switches lines?
45 Whoopi's role in "The Color Purple"
47 Expensive carpeting supplies?
49 USA alternative
52 Pollution control grp.
53 2001 Will Smith title role
54 Mr. Moto portrayer
56 Quirky
58 Test locale
60 Stone work
62 Globes
64 Truckers' cry?
66 Passion
67 City on the Seine
68 First president of South Korea
69 Tense
70 Minute Maid Park player
71 Pinings

DOWN

1 Dialect
2 Old-fashioned stage direction
3 Blockbuster transaction
4 Sing
5 El ___
6 Traveling medicine show purchase
7 Sot's sound
8 Requisition
9 Wild ___
10 Shake
11 Roadblock
12 15 preceder
13 Sort
18 Husband of Pocahontas
22 Manhattan neighborhood
26 Like a tepee
28 Pipe feature
31 Hesitant
32 Marine snail
33 It's tapped
34 Madrid Mme.
35 Exercise unit
37 Atl. Coast state
38 Web address ending
39 Mélange
41 Figure out
44 Kind of argument
46 53-Across's faith
48 Bans
49 Medicine lozenge
50 Kaput
51 Noted quintet
55 Eared seal
56 Sludge
57 Harriet Beecher Stowe novel
59 Gillette product
61 Late-night name
63 Tricky
65 His tomb was found in 1922

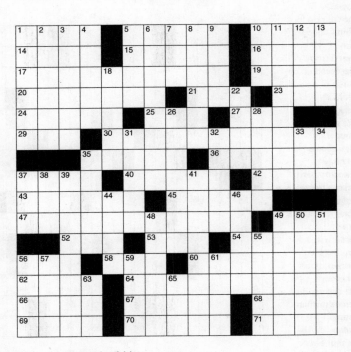

by Alan Arbesfeld

188 ★ ★

ACROSS
1. With 5-Down, Microsoft co-founder
5. ___ unto itself
9. Naval Academy newcomer
14. "The Weakest Link" host Robinson
15. ___ land
16. Play against
17. Laissez-faire doctrine
20. Kay Kyser's "___ Reveille"
21. Earthshaking?
22. W.W. II vessel: Abbr.
23. "Music for Airports" composer
24. It may be bitter
25. Article in Le Monde
26. Board mem., maybe
27. 1916–18 post for Calvin Coolidge: Abbr.
29. Concert array
31. It may wind up on the side of a house
32. Motor City monogram
34. 1940's Giants manager
35. Belle's counterpart
36. Wet blanket
39. Housecat's perch
41. Snicker syllable
42. Piece activists?: Abbr.
43. Piece
44. What it is in Italy
46. Surround snugly
50. One that shoots the breeze?
51. Sixth-century date
52. Electric's partner
54. Margin
55. Director ___ Lee
56. City near South Bend
58. Actress/singer Tatyana ___
59. Minor obsession
62. Some Mideast dignitaries
63. Guesstimate words
64. German border river
65. Matisse's "La ___"
66. Small dam
67. Nobelist Morrison

DOWN
1. Many a Degas
2. Consecrate
3. Open, in a way
4. Souvenir with a scent
5. See 1-Across
6. Oh-so-genteel
7. Cry after failing
8. Become friendly with
9. Tag line?
10. China's ___ Piao
11. A saint he ain't
12. One of the strings
13. Bay State emblem
18. Invariably
19. Nascar sponsor
28. Challenging tests
30. Depression, with "the"
31. Letter-shaped girder
33. Murderous Moor
36. Begin impetuously
37. "That's nothing new to me"
38. Magic word
39. Overnight guest's spot
40. Beach in a 1964 hit song
45. 1999 U.S. Open champ
47. 1972 Oscar refuser
48. Soprano Farrell
49. Composer Shostakovich
51. Doltish
53. Shady plot
57. Now's partner
60. C.P.A. hirer
61. Word in a denial

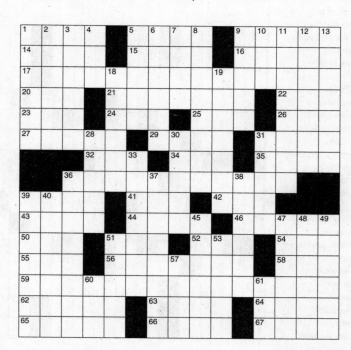

by Brendan Emmett Quigley

ACROSS

1 Targets for snakes
6 Arena shouts
10 Sec
14 Dumpy digs
15 It may be outstanding
16 Chanteuse Adams
17 Capital of Guam, old-style
18 Finito
19 Finito
20 Either way, the letter carrier's work not appreciated
23 Pickled delicacy
24 Clavell's "___-Pan"
25 Rather's former network
28 Prefix with sweet
31 Zero in acting
36 Zuñi's cousin
38 Protuberance
40 "M" star
41 Either way, Cupid recognized my pain
44 Nosy Parker
45 Time for eggnog
46 The gamut
47 Court battle?
49 Sine language?
51 Mexican Mrs.
52 Estuary
54 Aurora's counterpart
56 Either way, country star shunned hip-hop
65 Jerusalem's Mosque of ___
66 Hoopster Bryant
67 Like some accents
68 Act the expectant father
69 Hibernia
70 Warren of "Dillinger"
71 Charon's river
72 Take five
73 60's poster genre

DOWN

1 It may have a dimple
2 Stadium section
3 Caplet shape
4 Wish granter
5 Breaks one's back
6 Household spray target
7 Tax
8 Critic Roger
9 Place to fish
10 Skywalker, e.g.
11 Elvis, once
12 Dandy
13 Satellite transmission
21 "Maria ___" (hit of 1941)
22 Early strings
25 Highboy or lowboy
26 Shouldered
27 Three wood
29 Like a neat yard
30 Blockhead
32 Cub with a club
33 Brings (out)
34 Overthrow, e.g.
35 First name in daytime talk
37 "The Heat ___"
39 It may have a fat lip
42 Veep before Gerald
43 1979 sci-fi thriller
48 Tricky pitch
50 Baby talk
53 Really dig
55 Holster part
56 Daddy-o
57 Part of a Latin trio
58 Risqué
59 Natural history museum display
60 Nile bird
61 Mar, in a way
62 Pro ___
63 Maintain
64 Dennis, to Mr. Wilson

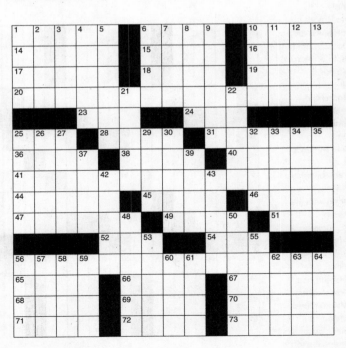

by Randall J. Hartman

190 ★ ★

ACROSS

1 "An instructor of great sagacity": Emerson
5 Radar unit?
9 Rectory
14 Dog dish filler
15 Shivering fit
16 Something to shoot for
17 Sidesplitter
18 Self-titled WB comedy
19 ___ Kea
20 Men went to the moon in it
23 Sounds of pain
24 Sugar suffix
25 What "V" means to a string player
28 "That ___ lie!"
29 Dish manufacturer
32 Our planet, grandly
35 Adriatic port
36 Yucatán natives
37 Capo ___ capi (big boss, in 35-Across)
38 Dried out
39 Reps.
40 Billboard line
42 Formerly
43 Cereal plant portion
44 Nets
45 One of Mickey's exes
46 City southwest of Bogotá
48 It began with the Big Bang
55 Spill source, perhaps
56 Info
57 Interlace
59 Voters' surprise
60 Sicilian smoker
61 De Valera's land
62 Peter and Paul
63 Owner's acquisition
64 Mythological ferry locale

DOWN

1 Outlying
2 "A Chapter on Ears" essayist
3 Each
4 Old newspaper part
5 "Tamburlaine the Great" playwright
6 Words with Reason or Aquarius
7 Areas within areas
8 Bunch
9 Brunch drink
10 Saw
11 Prefix with -algia
12 Arab capital
13 Biblical kingdom
21 Roller-coaster features
22 Beginning, in Hebrew
25 What a meter might measure
26 Plant: Suffix
27 Bent
28 Suffix with arthr-
29 Peace agreement signer of 9/13/1993
30 Salad green
31 Planes need permission to enter it
32 One on a mission, maybe
33 Shevat follower
34 Abbr. after an officer's name
35 Pioneer in quantum theory
38 Get a bad mark on?
40 W.W. II server
41 Landing place on a roof
43 Turns inside out
45 Arabic for "commander"
46 Franklin is on it
47 Compensate (for)
48 Enter la-la land
49 Sirloin parts
50 Mrs. Victor Laszlo
51 Modern newspaper part
52 Little strings?
53 Knot or watt
54 Boglike
58 Cowboy's moniker

by Bruce F. Adams

ACROSS

1 With 34-Down, an ordering option
4 Paul or Brown
7 "Them"
10 England's Queen ___
13 Earmark
15 Fit
17 "Well, sorr-ry!"
18 Woodworker, at times
19 Offer for campus visitors
21 Place to share a tub
24 Pack neatly
25 Marquis name?
26 Common shift
31 Detective Pinkerton
32 Do some tub-thumping
33 Sprint rival
36 Figure-skating maneuver
39 Business end of a missile
41 Giant Giant
42 One way to ring
44 Bizarre
45 Ruminations
48 Prefix with culture
51 Daffy Duck or Elmer Fudd
52 Gel
53 Famous place with a hint to this puzzle's theme
58 Not exactly tidy
59 Access
63 At work
64 Drained
65 Get hitched
66 "Amen!"
67 It may have an E.I.K.
68 Called the shots

DOWN

1 Much spam
2 Writer Rosten
3 Jerk
4 Place
5 Catch, as in a net
6 Takes care of
7 Third-rate newspaper, slangily
8 "I'm ___ you!"
9 Isaac's eldest
10 Craze
11 Overthrow
12 Cause of a traffic tie-up
14 Jerk
16 Kind of fit
20 Big concert news
21 Org. abolished in 1977
22 It may be within your range
23 Lace tip
27 Golfer Sutton
28 Govt. security
29 Chain letters?
30 "Just look ___!"
33 Unwanted closet items
34 See 1-Across
35 In other words
37 It's picked out
38 Soldiers pitch them
40 Car nut?
43 English prep school
45 Where rye is "whiskey"
46 Chinese restaurant offering
47 Cloverleaf part
48 Shining
49 Raise a stink
50 Carried on
54 Time to attack
55 Motion picture
56 Date with a dr.
57 Three sheets to the wind
60 Zip
61 Course requirement?
62 "That's ___ . . ."

by Joe DiPietro

192 ★ ★

ACROSS
1 Bargaining ploys
7 Mathematician Charles
14 Ring out
16 Worn down
17 Barking up the wrong tree
18 Kind of vowel in "loop"
19 Cartoon millionaire created by Harold Gray
21 Well-chosen
22 1987–91 Mideast hostage Terry
23 Blinking light, maybe
26 Regulus's constellation
27 Golf course adjunct
29 Squeegee
31 Fuzzy-skinned fruits
32 River formed by the Congaree and Wateree
33 Chingachgook, for one
36 Casting choices?
37 Voters' problem
38 Something to remember, with "the"
39 Capital successor to Calcutta
40 Particular strength
41 Agreed upon
44 Little one
45 Jim's portrayer in "Gentleman Jim"
47 It might be broken into quarters
48 Cartoon millionaire created by Carl Barks
53 Displeased spectator's cry
55 Anticipated
56 Unauthorized
57 Maria ___ (Hungarian queen)

58 Shade trees
59 E-mailer

DOWN
1 Kind of gown
2 Delaware Indian
3 Unfazed by
4 Crossing point
5 Wrath
6 It's not seen on cable TV
7 Toy since 1959
8 More or less
9 Cartoon millionaire created by Bob Kane
10 C.D. seller
11 Signifies
12 "Oh, my!"
13 Baseball Hall-of-Famer Roush
15 Attracted
20 Glad ___
24 Rancher's purchase
25 They're often unearthed
27 Cartoon millionaire created by Alfred Harvey
28 On vacation
30 Concerning
31 Friends and neighbors
32 Cut open
33 Fashioned
34 German automaker
35 Worn part of a shoe
36 One end of the political spectrum
38 Synthesizer innovator Bob
40 Makes translucent
41 Blotto

42 Protect, in a way
43 William Shatner sci-fi novel
46 Archetypical W.W. II metalworker
49 Nattily dressed
50 ___ scale
51 Ontario natives
52 Actress Laura
53 It's hung around the neck
54 "Bravo!"

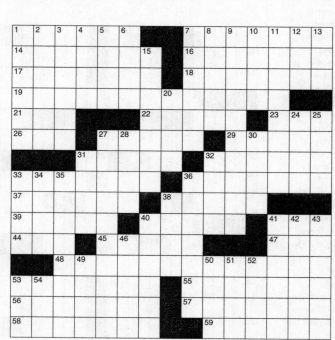

by Patrick Berry

ACROSS

1 High-hatter
5 "Where's ___?" (1970 film)
10 Smooch
14 Lift
15 Hearing-related
16 Blunted blade
17 "I'll get ___!"
18 Bundle-of-joy bringer
19 Peak near Taormina
20 Start of a quip
23 Actress ___ Marie Saint
24 Part of a poker pot
25 Washington site
27 Add luster to
29 Hide-hair link
32 Brief fight
33 Hipster's eyewear
35 Military inits., 1946–92
37 Make out
38 Middle of the quip
42 Bear greeting?
45 Hirsute Himalayan
46 Least furnished
50 Habituate
53 Mouse's place
55 Buttinsky
56 Church laws
58 Southern constellation
60 Downing Street number
61 End of the quip
65 Diva's moment
66 They may be mowed down
67 Conductor Klemperer
68 City on the Aare
69 Steps over a fence
70 Yucca plant cousin
71 They often begin with "To"
72 Like many brandy casks
73 Jersey group?

DOWN

1 April forecast
2 Assyrian capital
3 Pacific battle site
4 ___ noire
5 Easy stroll
6 Beat to the tape
7 Some Olympians, nowadays
8 Prefix with graph
9 Durable resin
10 Retro car
11 Raises, in a way
12 Having feelings
13 Swell place?
21 Foxy lady
22 Showy moths
26 Future fish
28 Flap
30 Honshu city
31 Cleaning need
34 Like Reynard
36 Hack
39 Big, fat mouth
40 Uxmal builder
41 Poetic preposition
42 Lush sound?
43 Never broadcast
44 Oater sound effect
47 Make a baron, say
48 Loud speaker
49 Practiced an Arthur Murray lesson
51 Mountain ashes
52 Wind dir.
54 Lollygag
57 Final authority
59 Out of bed
62 Pro ___
63 Composer Satie
64 Ham's father
65 Blood-typing system

by Steven Picus

ACROSS

1 Was a crew member
6 Tooth site
10 Pack it in
14 Projection, maybe
15 Ruler with a throne
16 Ruin
17 Popular gift
20 Tofu base
21 Time and time again?
22 Rebounds
23 New Mexico tourist site
24 Delighted
25 Like a 17-Across, often
29 Arrest
32 Doesn't let the issue die
33 Like some love
34 Where the heart is
35 In districts
36 Elevator part
37 Not too hot
38 German river
39 "I'm ___ in Love" (1975 hit)
40 European satellite launcher
41 Ayres of "Don't Bet on Love"
42 It may lead to romance
44 Decision makers
45 Manhandles
46 Willows
49 Love story?
50 Wane
53 Romantic time
56 Bank transaction
57 Scanned
58 Scarlett's love
59 Has
60 Desires
61 Feeling

DOWN

1 Barbecue entree
2 1847 novel about a mutiny
3 Like some floors
4 It may be massaged
5 Beat
6 Same old stuff
7 Biblical prophet
8 Attack word
9 Go
10 Almost a liter
11 "Do ___ others . . ."
12 As previously mentioned
13 Start of a football game
18 Religious symbol
19 Touch down
23 More devoted
24 Nautical yard
25 Eye shade
26 Wear away
27 Running mate of '68
28 Noted violinmaker
29 Like some stock
30 Kind of acid
31 Moisten, in a way
34 Kings and queens want them
36 Fake
37 Eskimos, e.g.
39 Place for plants
40 Native of any of the "49-Downs"
42 Weightlifter's lift
43 Robots, for short
44 Casual attire
46 City ESE of Bergen
47 Put away
48 Catcher Rodriguez
49 See 40-Down
50 Place of bliss
51 Loony
52 A computer processes it
54 Born
55 "___ Loves You"

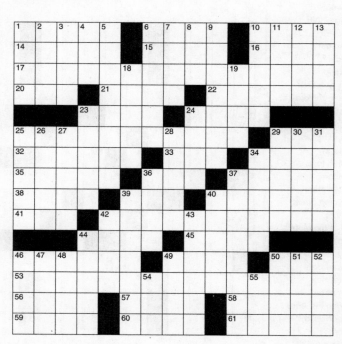

by Janet R. Bender

ACROSS

1 The pyramids of Giza, e.g.
6 Newspaper's essay forum
10 "Invaders From ___" (1953 sci-fi)
14 Jamaican witchcraft
15 Leaf opening
16 Baseball's Moises
17 Business statistic
20 River that was notably crossed on Christmas 1776
21 Was jealous of
22 Soccer star Hamm
23 How spaghetti may be cooked
24 Teacher training institution
29 2004 Olympics site
30 "X Games" airer
31 ___ choy
34 Painter Mondrian
35 Waitress at Mel's Diner
36 "___ Lisa"
37 Simile's middle
38 Freshwater duck
40 Peanut butter choice
42 Starting point of the Freedom Trail
44 Says yes to
47 Place for a stud
48 Hubbub
49 Walked through a puddle
54 Benefit of a steady job
56 "___ Tu" (1974 hit)
57 Sales rep's goal
58 "Gigi" star Leslie
59 ___ terrier
60 Debate side
61 How eccentrics behave

DOWN

1 Sondheim's "Sweeney ___"
2 Reed instrument
3 Whimper
4 Mexican peninsula
5 P. T. Barnum, for example
6 "Norma" and "Don Carlos"
7 Sit
8 Historical period
9 Add detail to
10 Publisher of "X-Men" comics
11 French author Robbe-Grillet
12 Man of many words?
13 Fancy leather
18 They may be polished
19 Finish with
23 Comment from Mr. Moto
24 California winegrowing county
25 ___ & Carla, 60's singing duo
26 Emmy winner Perlman
27 Bumped into
28 Yo-Yo Ma's instrument
31 Prosperous time
32 Not fooled by
33 "Ain't We Got Fun" lyricist
35 Saturated substances
36 Popular tattoo
38 "Fiddler on the Roof" star
39 Officer Poncherello's portrayer
40 Like a lizard's skin
41 Fine leather
42 Addle
43 Gurkha or Sherpa
44 Farm units
45 Court employee
46 Not forthcoming
49 Uttered contemptuously
50 Roe source
51 Driven group
52 Environmental sci.
53 Fashion initials
55 Cartoon chihuahua

by Marjorie Richter

196 ⋆⋆

ACROSS
1 Natl. Hot Dog Mo.
4 House of Commons members: Abbr.
7 Charged
12 "Season of Glass" artist
13 Where football's Pro Bowl is played
15 California wine town
16 Start of a quip by Alfred E. Neuman
18 Clowns
19 Quip, part 2
21 "Tristram Shandy" author
22 Half of a half-and-half
23 Poetic preposition
24 ___ room
25 Fruit in a mixed drink
27 Highlander
28 Common place for a sprain
31 Titanic
33 Quip, part 3
35 Railroad support
37 Wrung out
41 Rust sprinkled with white
42 "Deutschland ___ Alles"
43 Greenwich Village sch.
44 Three months from 1-Across: Abbr.
45 Mexico City Olympics prize
46 Degraded
49 Quip, part 4
53 Star in Aquila
54 End of the quip
56 Old Spanish coins
57 Statistics calculation
58 Elton's john

59 Eastwood's "Rawhide" role
60 Human Genome Project topic
61 Laboriously make

DOWN
1 Old Testament book
2 Like leftovers
3 Décolletage
4 Fool
5 Dolley Madison's maiden name
6 Pump, e.g.
7 Roulette bet
8 Not pro
9 Beaujolais ___
10 Current units
11 Fez attachment
14 Cesar Chavez's org.
15 Hanks's "Bosom Buddies" co-star

17 Historic Scottish county
20 Queen Victoria's royal house
21 Sp. woman's title
25 Natural fuel source
26 Film not made by a Hollywood studio
27 Attendee
29 City on the Rhone
30 Daughter of Hyperion
32 Year that Chaucer died
34 Some sharks
35 Part of the inner ear
36 Knocking sound
38 Trendy
39 Simple fastener
40 Turkey
41 Traffic circle
45 Tony's cousins

46 Dam that formed Lake Nasser
47 Safari head
48 Luxury car standard feature
50 Yarn that is spun
51 Deep Blue maker
52 Poverty
55 Adversary

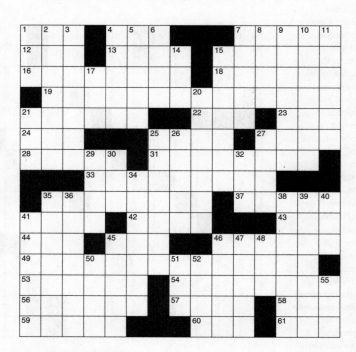

by Peter Gordon

ACROSS

1 Possible title for this puzzle
5 1990–92 French Open winner
10 Cattle rancher's tool
14 Long, for short
15 Ready to joust
16 Ashcroft's predecessor at Justice
17 Gulf port
18 Earl Hines, familiarly
19 Promise, e.g.
20 Noted celebrity photographer
23 Cross letters
24 Fake drake
25 Switch from plastic to paper?
28 Digital document outputter
32 Abbey Theatre playwright
34 Alive with talk
38 One reggae fan to another
39 Santa ___
41 "Sprechen ___ Deutsch?"
42 The Rock
45 Broadway producer Liz, Tony winner for "Elephant Man" and "Amadeus"
48 Let off
50 Monteverdi opera
51 Hive's head
54 "Alfred" composer
56 Ornette Coleman genre
62 Dancer's dress
63 HCl and others
64 Chicken ___
66 Winglike parts
67 Singer Tucker
68 French 101 word
69 "Doggone it"
70 Provide with funding
71 New Look designer

DOWN

1 Doc bloc
2 "I did it!"
3 Big bovines
4 Showy annuals
5 Not so chancy
6 Phrase of inclusion
7 For dieters
8 K–12
9 Try
10 Nugget for Franklin
11 Excavation find
12 "Takes ___ know . . ."
13 Lulu
21 "Where's Daddy?" dramatist
22 Ancient concert halls
25 Alitalia destination
26 E.P.A. concern: Abbr.
27 Court seat
29 Indian corn
30 Computer key abbr.
31 David Bowie genre
33 Kitten's plaything
35 B-2 letters
36 Fan mag
37 Paradoxical Greek
40 Basketball coach Holman
43 Fifth and others
44 Fair spot
46 And, e.g.: Abbr.
47 Sounded old
49 Cool cat
51 Oil-rich land
52 Throat dangler
53 Bother
55 Further shorten, maybe
57 Box office take
58 Open ___ of worms
59 Melon protector
60 Tubes on the table
61 Goose egg
65 Part of a chap.

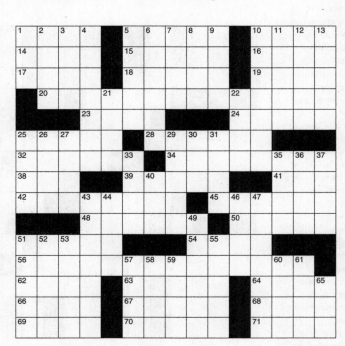

by Brendan Emmett Quigley

Note: In a letter bank, the letters of one word are used (and repeated as necessary) to spell a longer word or phrase. For example, IMPS is a letter bank of Mississippi.

ACROSS

1 Loudspeaker sound (and a letter bank for 60-Across)
6 Planets and such
10 Steamy
14 Howled
15 Raise a stink
16 Isaac's firstborn
17 See 71-Across
19 Hoosegow
20 Freshwater duck
21 Sporty Fords
23 What's more
27 Going strong
29 Became an issue
30 See 13-Down
33 Neigh-sayer
34 Educator Horace
35 Company with a dog in its logo
38 Applicable
41 Do away with
43 ___ Moines
44 Harmony
46 They have long tails
47 See 50-Down
50 Many states have them
53 Mrs. Chaplin
54 "___ Breckinridge"
55 Present from birth
57 Knock for a loop
59 Dutch cheese
60 See 1-Across
66 Queue
67 French cheese
68 Singer Abdul
69 Monopoly card
70 Sound
71 Ludicrous (and a letter bank for 17-Across)

DOWN

1 London's ___ 1 or ___ 2
2 "Love Story" composer Francis
3 "The Fountainhead" author Rand
4 VCR button
5 Touch up
6 More than fancy
7 Seeing things as they are
8 "Wanna ___?"
9 "Saturday Night Live" staple
10 It's often burning
11 Jeff Bagwell, notably
12 Hotel staff
13 Derby prize (and a letter bank for 30-Across)

18 Getting warm
22 Without exception
23 Orchard pest
24 Sierra ___
25 Lord's workers
26 Approximately
28 Ruler until 1917
31 Hang tough
32 Popular card game
35 Rootin'-tootin'
36 More adorable
37 Out of it
39 Dancer Charisse
40 Opposite of ecto-
42 Abound
45 Pen up
47 Made to take the fall
48 Main course
49 Spread (on)
50 Football locale (and a letter bank for 47-Across)

51 Actress MacDowell
52 Mindless
56 Goes back out
58 Vintners' valley
61 Pitcher's stat.
62 Skedaddled
63 Track feature
64 Ivy Leaguer
65 ___ Leman

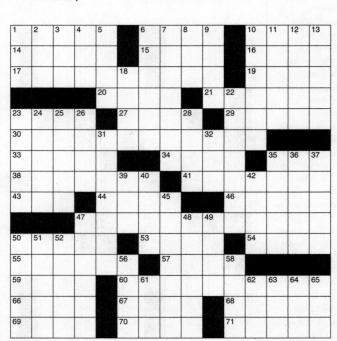

by Greg Staples

ACROSS

1 90 degrees
5 Place for a cypress
10 Attempt
14 Be a monarch
15 Staples Center player
16 Hack
17 "Magnet and Steel" singer Walter
18 Word to a knight
19 Aspirin, e.g.
20 Reduce one's feelings of weariness?
23 Check for fit
24 Looped handle
25 Actress Campbell
28 Heavenly edible
33 Court decision
36 Play baseball with cheeses?
40 Water color
42 Seafood entree
43 Perplexity
44 Badly bruised president?
47 Rock producer Brian
48 Kind of bean
49 Over
51 Dutch export
55 Canadian peninsula
59 Master at wielding a tongue depressor?
64 Monopoly square
65 Piano specialist
66 Cut, as film
67 Pac 10 school
68 Grimalkin
69 Steam up
70 Keep at it
71 King of Judea
72 Sibyl

DOWN

1 Be constructive?
2 Foreshadow
3 Dark bluish-gray
4 Muscle/bone connector
5 Common side order
6 Put on notice
7 Japanese dog
8 Elementary particle
9 Urge
10 Dateless
11 Dial on the dash
12 Central line
13 Didn't pass
21 First-floor apartment
22 Shakespeare's foot?
26 Bud holder
27 Make an artistic impression
29 Famous holder of pairs
30 1982 Tony musical
31 Broadway brightener
32 Regarding
33 Arctic native
34 Prefix akin to iso-
35 Change colors
37 Singing syllable
38 Georgetown athlete
39 Adam's apple area?
41 Fitting
45 MGM Studios founder
46 Utah's state flower
50 Thin treats
52 Get rid of
53 Lapis lazuli
54 House of lords
56 "Sexy" Beatles girl
57 Audio attachment?
58 Any acetate, chemically
59 Food whose name means, literally, wadding
60 Hawaiian port
61 Zing
62 Attorney general from Miami
63 Stowe book
64 Water carrier

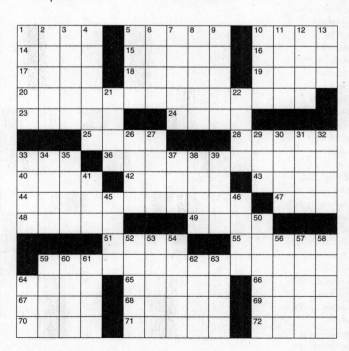

by Richard Silvestri

200 ⭐ ⭐

ACROSS

1 Sachet scent
6 Resting place
10 Harbinger
14 Pitcher Hideki ___
15 Epps of "The Mod Squad," 1999
16 De ___ (from the start)
17 Top of the military?
18 They may make great comebacks
20 Aylesbury actress?
22 Majors on TV
23 Vacation time in Valois
24 Nutritional stat
25 With 61-Across, river of Québec
26 Snake's sound
27 Michelangelo sculpture
29 Snorkeling areas
31 Dust collector?
32 Court fig.
34 Oversupply
35 Corinth cartoon character?
39 Implored
40 Arles assent
41 10th, 20th, 30th, etc., in N.Y.C.
42 West Wing workers
44 Spud
46 Self-titled 2001 #1 album
49 Loan-making org.
50 Is down with
52 A.C. stat
53 Muffin material
54 Pamplona playwright?
58 ___ Day (Holy Thursday)
59 Publisher ___ Nast
60 Essential
61 See 25-Across
62 "Lou Grant" star
63 Bookie's concern
64 First to vote
65 Converges on

DOWN

1 Puts down
2 Dunne and Ryan
3 Certain soft drink buys
4 1960's–70's steelworkers' chief
5 Attractive one
6 Long-tailed finch
7 Pass over
8 Sports car since 1926
9 Challah, e.g.
10 Storybook beginning
11 In a sulky way
12 Busy
13 Most curious
19 Fruit spray
21 Ripped
28 Sly's "Rocky" co-star
30 Inflatable things
31 Eliot's "Adam ___"
33 Idiot boxes
35 Saw
36 Embarrassed
37 Upstage
38 Ancient Italian
39 Pal
43 Clamber up
45 Steakhouse orders
46 Title girl in a 1983 Kool & the Gang hit
47 Storage room
48 Frisky critters
51 Analyze
55 Beatty and Rorem
56 "The Best Little Whorehouse in Texas" woman
57 Thoroughly wet, with "down"

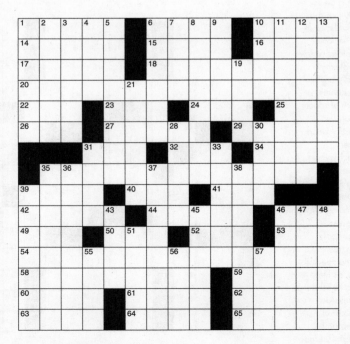

by Elizabeth C. Gorski

ACROSS

1 Santa Anna at the Alamo, e.g.
9 "Dixie" composer
15 Judge too highly
16 Like a big grin
17 Start of a comment on a popular adage
18 Cries of pain
19 Papas on the screen
20 "The Mikado" accessories
22 "What was ___ do?"
23 To be, to Bernadette
24 Comment, part 2
27 It may be raw
29 Hind, e.g.
30 C.S.A. state
33 Response to an insult
35 Hammett pooch
39 Comment, part 3
44 Rest area sight
45 Favor one side?
46 Thus far
47 "You betcha!"
51 South Vietnam's Ngo Dinh ___
53 Comment, part 4
57 Certain column
61 Just fine
62 Regarding
63 Hand warmer?
64 Ascended
66 End of the comment
69 Not so remote
70 Bombarding
71 Take stock of
72 Brunch order

DOWN

1 Alamo defender
2 Three-time Wimbledon champ
3 Setting for a famous "Les Misérables" scene
4 Smoothed (out)
5 Seaside raptor
6 Flit about
7 Hot time in Paris
8 Arrange into new lines
9 Star of France
10 Chilled dessert
11 Soft shoe
12 Set of principles
13 Certain sorority woman
14 Iron Mike
21 Oyster's home
24 Circle overhead?
25 Norwegian king
26 Part of Q.E.D.
28 Sigmoid shape
30 They may be crunched in a gym
31 Get prone
32 Usher's offering
34 Bud
36 Short
37 Pipe joint
38 Frick collection
40 45, e.g.
41 Friend of Rover
42 Send forth
43 Bad way to go?
48 Czars' edicts
49 Stair parts
50 Young newt
52 Mark with blotches
53 Zoologist's study
54 Bounds along
55 Podded plants
56 "___ fast!"
58 Like seven Ryan games
59 Marathon, e.g.
60 Conductor Koussevitzky
63 It may be hard or soft
65 Vein find
67 Resistance unit
68 "I'm impressed!"

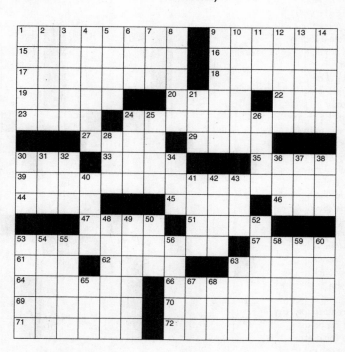

by Ed Early

202 ★ ★

ACROSS

1 Diagnostic data, informally
5 "Chitty Chitty Bang Bang" screenwriter
9 Office correspondence
14 Gas's partner: Abbr.
15 1958 Pulitzer winner
16 Rod Stewart's ex
17 Tropical tuber
18 Botch
19 Wrap up
20 It may allow you to make an entrance
22 Single-named supermodel
23 Woody Guthrie's "I Ain't ___ Home"
24 Football Hall-of-Famer Ford
26 Some people pass on them: Abbr.
28 Suffix with verb
29 "___ there?"
33 Update a factory
35 Pipe problem
37 Data
38 Focus of an interplanetary search
42 It may be abstract
43 Remove roughly
44 Took pains
46 In stitches
47 South-of-the-border title: Abbr.
50 Go for the bronze?
51 Some speeding vehicles' destinations, briefly
53 Drive forward
55 Ordination, e.g.
57 Comeback, maybe
61 High hat
62 December 13th, e.g.
63 Act like an ass
64 Like some skies
65 They can get rough
66 "___ cost you!"
67 Halfhearted
68 Vigorous
69 Misses

DOWN

1 "C'mon!"
2 Los ___
3 Dress down
4 Pooh-pooh
5 Ste. Jeanne ___
6 Mexican water
7 One who has it coming?
8 Tennis great who never won Wimbledon
9 Devil dog
10 Ca, Ga or Pa
11 Tubes on a plate
12 Intermittently
13 Aphid's sustenance
21 Spa handout
25 Heretofore
27 Member of the rose family
30 Revealing top
31 Dust Bowl figure
32 No quick reads
34 Feature of the Earth
35 NBC host
36 "American Gigolo" star
38 Part of V.M.I.: Abbr.
39 Stamp and sign, perhaps
40 "Louder!"
41 Cover-up in 47-Down
45 Didn't go straight
47 Ancient military hub
48 Amnesiac's lack
49 Univalent chemical groups
52 Cager's favorite sound
54 Head honcho
56 Actress Polo
58 Guess
59 Navy commando
60 "___ est percipi" (old Latin motto)
61 Yoga class need

by Elizabeth C. Gorski

ACROSS

1 Clipper feature
5 "Hogwash!"
10 Coventry cleaner
14 Cousin of a hawk
15 Up the ante
16 Take on
17 Improve one's golf game?
20 Marbles, so to speak
21 Jukebox favorite
22 Barely miss, as the golf cup
25 Hatcher of "Lois & Clark"
26 Grammy-winner Black
27 Meter reading
29 Son of Cain
32 Heads downtown?
34 Sticky stuff
35 Like some noodle dishes
39 Inexperienced golfers?
42 Links rarities
43 Cheer
44 Hardly cheery
45 1996 A.L. rookie of the year
47 Composer's basis
48 Bewildered
52 First name in Polish politics
54 Mach 1 breaker
55 Common fraternity activity
56 Friend of Pooh
58 Taking one's time on the green?
63 Wanton look
64 Olympics broadcaster Jim
65 Mary Kay competitor
66 Little spin
67 Edges (out)
68 Duchamp's movement

DOWN

1 Schuss, e.g.
2 Cause of inflation?
3 Midori on the ice
4 Place for a cap
5 Kind of danish
6 Many a Swift work
7 Playing golf
8 Unhealthy-looking
9 Minute
10 "Relax, bro!"
11 Language from which "thug" is derived
12 Alan of "Gattaca"
13 PlayStation button
18 Horse operas
19 "How'm I doin'?" asker
22 Arthur Murray lesson
23 Father of Esau
24 Noncommittal response
28 Takes off
30 "That's amazing!"
31 Like Vassar, now
33 Beget
35 Brit's "Baloney!"
36 Zeroes (in on)
37 First vice president
38 ___ of Langerhans (pancreas part)
40 Rebellious Turner
41 Become wizened
45 Hemingway's Barnes
46 Rasta's music
48 iPod maker
49 Made level
50 Beyond full
51 Diary bit
53 Potter's buys
56 Trillionth: Prefix
57 Warty hopper
59 Loser to J.F.K.
60 Charlottesville sch.
61 Approval of sorts
62 Genomic matter

by James Rogers

ACROSS

1 Prepares for a bout
6 Easter serving
10 A lot
14 John Lennon's last million-selling single
15 String puller
16 Bibliophile's label
17 Apologize and then some
18 Commercial prefix with bank
19 Big furniture retailer
20 Start of a quip by hockey commentator Don Cherry about his autobiography
22 Pain in the neck
23 Boy-girl
24 "___ So Easy"
26 Muckraker Tarbell
27 Settings for some TV dramas: Abbr.
28 Quip, part 2
32 Dignified
33 Federation
34 Carryall
37 Top
39 Match parts
40 Brightest star in Aquila
43 Pizazz
46 Quip, part 3
48 Top
51 Souvenir from Aruba?
52 English ___
53 "I've had enough"
55 Trash can, perhaps
57 End of the quip
60 Pickable
61 Kind of doctor
62 Countenance
63 ___ even keel
64 Farm cry
65 Upholstery fabric
66 Bump on a branch
67 Hungary's Imre ___
68 "+" site

DOWN

1 Bandage
2 Uproar
3 Loan payment schedules: Abbr.
4 Bombay royal
5 Ridicule
6 Life's founder
7 Sri Lanka's locale
8 ___ system
9 Connecticut city that's home to ESPN
10 Traffic chart
11 Institute of Nuclear Studies site
12 Mexican tree with large, edible seeds
13 Navigable channels
21 Series of postures, basically
25 Go after
29 Bribe
30 Dunderhead
31 Eye protector
32 Eskimo's catch
34 Not subject to change
35 "Heat" star, 1995
36 Place for shorthand
38 Play-___
41 Out of sorts
42 More than dampens
44 Author Simpson
45 How refunds may be made
47 More work
48 "Gangsta's Paradise" rapper
49 Traitor's name
50 Little one
54 It's opened with a knife
56 Island bird
58 Faction
59 Black

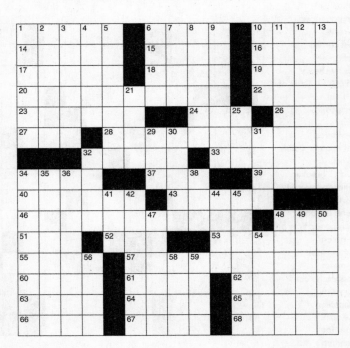

by David J. Kahn

ACROSS

1 Not telling
4 Drink before bed, maybe
9 Belt clip-on
14 Part of a World Cup chant
15 Sister of Terpsichore
16 Squirreled-away item
17 Merkel of old movies
18 Irish symbol
20 Time off, briefly
22 Fuller than full
23 Bottom line
27 Something to draw from
30 ___ fille (French girl)
31 Society Islands island
34 Item in a thimblerig game
37 Fixes, in a way
39 Exorcist's quarry
40 Like a snap decision
44 Lines man?
45 "You've got a deal!"
46 Huge expanse
47 Tastelessly affected
49 Christina of "The Opposite of Sex"
52 Letters at a Nascar race
53 Commodity in the old South
58 Strand in winter, maybe
61 Grenoble's river
62 Informal discussion
67 Subj. of this puzzle's theme
68 Healing plants
69 Leave out, in speech
70 "Get comfy"
71 "Same here"
72 In shape
73 D.D.E.'s W.W. II command

DOWN

1 Opposite of celebrate
2 Carpi connectors
3 Stood for
4 It's the law
5 Palindrome center
6 Nutritional fig.
7 A.B.A. member: Abbr.
8 Impose (on)
9 Munich ___ of 1938
10 One to grow on?
11 Esther Rolle sitcom
12 Hosp. areas
13 12-Down staffers
19 Start angling
21 Basketball Hall of Fame nickname
24 Beach lapper
25 Condos, e.g.
26 Chicken breed
28 Make amends
29 Ship commanded by Pinzón
32 Hubbub
33 Confine, with "in"
34 Jrs.' exams
35 ___ Center
36 Cockpit aid
38 Baseball's Bud
41 Baloney
42 Montana's motto starter
43 1700
48 "The Grapes of Wrath" figure
50 Invented
51 T.G.I.F. part
54 Atlas feature
55 High-strung
56 Go around in circles?
57 "Cool!"
59 1963 role for Liz
60 Big name in petrol
62 "Batman" sound
63 Relative of -let
64 Highway warning
65 "Boy, am ___ trouble!"
66 Lofty lines

by Brendan Emmett Quigley

206 ⭐ ⭐

ACROSS

1 With 5- and 10-Across, need for 69-, 70- and 71-Across
5 See 1-Across
10 See 1-Across
14 "___ off?"
15 Earthling
16 Vargas Llosa novel "___ Julia and the Scriptwriter"
17 Ye follower
18 Blue dyes
19 Atlases, e.g.: Abbr.
20 Cruelty
22 Hebrew prophet
24 Milk provider
25 P.D. alert
27 Cheated
30 Div. of a former union
31 They have big bills
34 Outside: Prefix
35 Relating to life
36 Philips product
38 Label on many an advertising photo
41 Washington State's Sea-___ Airport
42 Pantywaist
43 Adherent in Iran
44 Work boot feature
46 Clockmaker Terry
47 How some rebukes are made
49 "Life ___ cabaret"
52 Creepy-crawlies
54 38-Down was the second one
55 R.N.'s treatment
56 Rarely
59 Unconcerned retort
61 Kind of bag
63 Period
65 Surrounding light
66 Litigious one
67 "And then again . . ."
68 Desktop marker

69 With 70- and 71-Across, what the middle of this puzzle is
70 See 69-Across
71 See 69-Across

DOWN

1 Snares
2 Marriage byproduct
3 Yes-man, perhaps
4 "___ Sleep, for Every Favor" (old hymn)
5 It might be next to a bar of soap
6 Bit of wit
7 Provençal pal
8 "Safe" or "out"
9 Academy graduate
10 ___ Abdel Nasser
11 Unfeeling
12 Place to lay over
13 Skid row ailment
21 Like Britain's Private Eye magazine
23 Antidrug mantra
26 Fit up against
28 Split personalities?
29 Feeble-minded
32 Informal goodbyes
33 Ins have it
35 She played Maude on "Maude"
37 Limo passenger
38 See 54-Across
39 Scottie in the White House
40 Craved
45 Nearly
48 Ted Williams and others
49 Cornell's home
50 Winter Olympics event
51 Broadway opening?
53 Turns
57 Other, in España
58 "Death in Venice" author
60 Antiroyalist, in the Revolution
61 Scolding sound
62 Ja, across the Rhine
64 Vishnu, e.g.

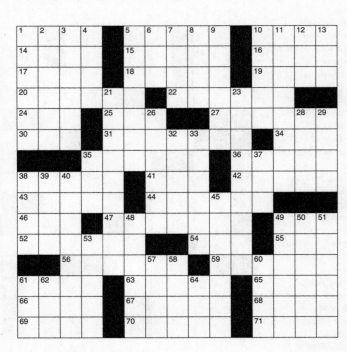

by Patrick Merrell

ACROSS

1 Followers of Tyler and Taylor
6 One-inch pencil, say
9 To boot
13 So out it's in
14 Home to José
15 Place
16 See 48-Across
17 Hurl a barb at
18 Sacred creatures of old
19 Woodworker's own tool?
22 Oxy-5 target
23 Takes off
24 Main lines
26 Boxing Day's mo.
29 Place for a ring
30 Deliver by chute
31 Son of Aphrodite
33 City north of Nancy
35 Trash hauler
38 1990's civil war site
40 Losing purposely
42 Jam producer?
43 Voice mail prompt
45 Use binoculars, say
46 P.T.A. and N.E.A., for two
48 With 16-Across, places to pull over
50 Baseball stat
51 Slain
53 Kansas motto word
55 Cellular ___
56 Apt title for this puzzle
61 Label info
63 Visitor to Cathay
64 Talks nonsense
65 Neutral shade
66 Assist, in a way
67 Concerning
68 Letter opener
69 French possessive
70 They're verboten

DOWN

1 End of shooting
2 Epitaph starter
3 Road to old Rome
4 Llano growth
5 "Already?"
6 Home builder's tool
7 Jimmy Carter's coll.
8 City on the Tigris: Var.
9 Cookbook phrase
10 Cost of a 19th-century composer's work?
11 Brown pigment
12 Gives the boot to
14 Winter Palace throne?
20 Campbell or Judd
21 1964 Anthony Quinn role
25 They may have forks
26 Fam. tree member
27 Switch add-on
28 Undistinguished poet Pound?
32 Le ___ (Buick model)
34 Photo of the Panama Canal, once?
36 Sports stuff
37 Peak near Taormina
39 Aristotle's forte
41 Bunting places
44 Wise counsels
47 Be short with
49 "Iliad" warrior
51 Gave medicine to
52 In reserve
54 ___ acid
57 Soliloquy starter
58 Flush
59 Paradoxical Greek
60 Fast fliers
62 Where It.'s at

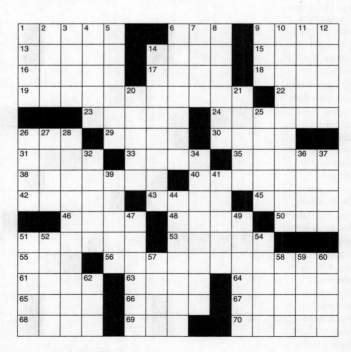

by Michael Shteyman

208

ACROSS

1 Spanish eyes
5 Jots
10 News anchor Paula
14 Hitchcock title
15 Black-necked goose
16 Award started by the Village Voice
17 Reducing the autopsy staff?
20 Crime for which one takes the heat
21 Barely flows
22 Captain of science fiction
25 Alias
26 Jokester
29 Dyed trick-or-treat costume?
35 Emotionally charged
37 Subject for il poeta
38 ___-Honey (candy name)
39 High-hats
42 Ovaltine ingredient
43 People travel only one way on them
45 Permanent spot on a dress
47 Lively state?
50 Spotter
51 Prefect ending
52 Knock off
54 Growing post-W.W. II environs
59 Swing and a miss
63 Politician on a spree?
66 Pipsqueak
67 Many a McDonald's promotion
68 Stuff on slides
69 "Vamoose!"
70 Famous bucktoothed dummy
71 Longtime Susan Lucci quest

DOWN

1 Sea World attraction
2 Day at the Louvre
3 Decides
4 Decided about
5 "Son of," in Arabic names
6 Domain name suffix
7 Public relations need
8 Parka
9 Sound, as the hour
10 Stupefy, slangily
11 Explorer Tasman
12 Engage
13 Role for Stack and Costner
18 Like helium
19 City SSE of Gainesville
23 They lap France's coasts
24 God who gave up an eye to drink from the spring of wisdom
26 Home entertainment option
27 Way out
28 Imply
30 Ambit
31 Literary matchmaker
32 Warty jumpers
33 Fourth deck of a ship
34 Meshlike
36 Mrs. Dithers in "Blondie"
40 Cranberries thrive here
41 Place on a schedule
44 Bad etiquette at the dinner table
46 Famous
48 Flies around
49 Curb
53 Part of growing up
54 Estonia et al., once: Abbr.
55 Nope
56 Rock star with many causes
57 Machinating
58 Onetime Mets slugger Tommie
60 Particular
61 1040, for one
62 Scuffle
64 Hardly an ordinary Joe
65 Apt answer for this clue

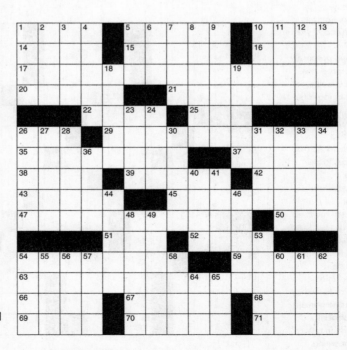

by Cathy Millhauser

ACROSS

1 Much of the back of a baseball card
6 Mac, e.g.
10 Genesis victim
14 Piece of cave art
15 Hawaii County's seat
16 Our Gang pooch
17 Yemeni thieves' hangout?
19 Keen about
20 Jockey Turcotte
21 Wrecker's job
22 Marketing lures
24 Blond hair, hot temper, etc.
26 Pouts
27 Chaucer pilgrim
29 Nebraska river
33 Fine fiddle, for short
36 Musket attachment?
38 Obie or Edgar
39 "Indeed!"
40 Sing-along syllable
41 Racer Luyendyk
42 Strengthens, with "up"
44 Schuss or wedel
45 Dish's partner in flight
46 Disassembler
48 Dwight licked him twice
50 Flinch, say
52 Give power to
56 Greek city-state
59 On vacation
60 Galley tool
61 Eggs order
62 Why the tourist departed for Africa?
65 Actress Ward
66 P.D.Q.
67 Tore to the ground
68 Quotation attribution: Abbr.
69 Shrimpers' gear
70 John of plow fame

DOWN

1 Eligible for Mensa
2 Henry VIII's house
3 Fight locale
4 Whip but good
5 Like a revealing skirt, maybe
6 Plug of tobacco
7 Suffix with fact or planet
8 Oldsmobile model
9 Get into shape
10 Actress Zadora visited Samoa's capital?
11 Out of shape
12 Kitchen annex?
13 Thirteen popes
18 Schnozzola
23 Gymnastics coach Karolyi
25 Mideast Olympic marathoner's claim?
26 African mongoose
28 Docs for dachshunds
30 Poi base
31 Rock's Cream, for instance
32 Perfect place
33 "Elephant Boy" boy
34 Some feds
35 Marsh growth
37 Fridge foray
43 "As __ on TV!"
45 Fred played by Redd
47 Wicker material
49 Hit the road
51 X'd, as a candidate's name
53 Likker
54 Stein contents
55 Chip away at
56 __ Nostra
57 Place for a cake
58 Move, in the realty biz
59 "So sorry!"
63 Gun moll's gun
64 __ kwon do

by Fred Piscop

210 ★ ★

ACROSS

1 Pool pull-over
5 Shooters
9 It may let you see a hearing
14 Fawning target
15 Buckets
16 1939 Best Actress role
17 The "T" in Britain's ITV
18 Cause for alarm?
19 Millionairess portrayer in "The Millionairess"
20 Shoots for a salad
23 Poorest
24 Bank acct. info
25 Accident scene arrival, for short
26 Fog
30 Big name in TV journalism
34 Stadiumgoer
35 Mrs. McKinley
36 Approximate number of weeks in a Roman year
37 Rose buds?
44 Spick-and-span, now
45 Vardalos of "My Big Fat Greek Wedding"
46 Global positioning meas.
47 Checks out
52 Sacagawea, for one
55 Like some curves
56 Elated
57 Old newspaper section
58 12/25, e.g.
59 "Coriolanus" setting
60 Mix
61 Quire member
62 Ablutionary vessel
63 Sign of overexertion

DOWN

1 Colossus
2 Dance partner for Fred
3 Husband of Pocahontas
4 One on bended knee, maybe
5 Crisp fabric
6 A thief may go under one
7 Get the better of
8 Measure to take
9 North, for one
10 Really let have it
11 Separate
12 Spear carrier of myth
13 Photographer Goldin
21 Bird's perch
22 "Rubyfruit Jungle" novelist ___ Mae Brown
26 Acronym on a police jacket
27 Card game declaration
28 "The Haj" novelist
29 ESP and such
30 It may be skipped or jumped
31 Frank or Francis
32 Orange coat
33 Inits. on a toothpaste tube
34 Broadcasting overseer: Abbr.
38 Pepsi One's one
39 Up the creek
40 Neighbor of Ger.
41 No typical stock trader
42 Nothing, in Nantes
43 Fashionable pendant
47 Simmering
48 Former New York mayor
49 Orchestra seat
50 Have something at home
51 High-hat
52 Pahlavi, for one
53 Can't take
54 Mean man
55 L.S.A.T. takers

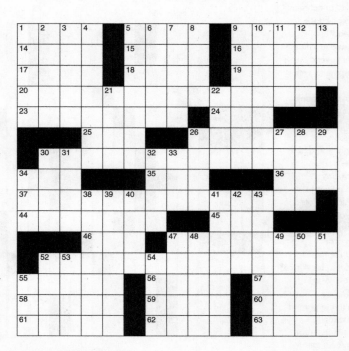

by Alan Arbesfeld

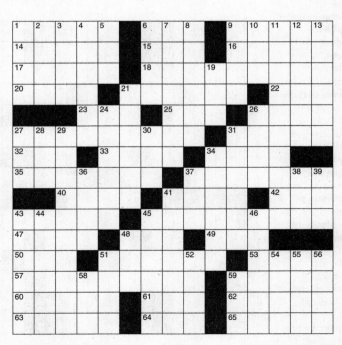

ACROSS

1 Airborne toy
6 "The Simpsons" storekeeper
9 Loafers holder
14 Après-ski drink
15 Zip
16 Spacious
17 Native on the Bering Sea
18 Sea lion, e.g.
20 Horseshoer's tool
21 Sports page summary
22 Purge
23 Sinuous swimmer
25 Galley tool
26 Fall off
27 Like the verb "to be"
31 Bigot
32 Society page word
33 "Step ___!"
34 Bamako's land
35 Theater receipts
37 It shouldn't be stuffed
40 Boozehound
41 Smidgens
42 Dundee denial
43 French seaport
45 Food device
47 10K, for one
48 "You stink!"
49 Triangle part: Abbr.
50 CPR giver
51 Tune player
53 Scads
57 "Come to think of it . . ."
59 A-1
60 Pitchfork wielder
61 Actor Billy ___ Williams
62 Emerson piece
63 Excellent viewing spot
64 Comics bark
65 Transmission

DOWN

1 Part of a freight train
2 ___ nut (caffeine source)
3 Boardwalk treats
4 False top
5 Chow down
6 Zoo animals
7 Naval attire
8 Commotion
9 One-named singer from Nigeria
10 Pinafore letters
11 Organ transplants, e.g.
12 "Seinfeld" pal
13 Tree of the maple family
19 Blunder
21 Meal-to-go
24 Self-interested one
26 Mural site
27 Correspondence collector
28 Antique auto
29 Like a mirror
30 Get prone
31 W.W. II U.S. admiral nicknamed "Bull"
34 Miniature auto brand
36 It may be blown
37 Life story, in brief
38 Chinese "path"
39 Filmdom's Rocky, e.g.
41 Range part
43 Classic item in size comparisons
44 Any of several Egyptian kings
45 Spanish inn
46 Meager
48 Florida N.F.L.er
51 Become soft
52 Staff leader
54 Actress Kudrow
55 Mullah ___, former Afghan leader
56 Place for playthings
58 River inlet
59 Hard throw, in baseball

by Ron O'Hair

212 ⋆ ⋆

ACROSS

1 "All I ___ Do" (Sheryl Crow song)
6 Singer in Bob Dylan's Rolling Thunder Revue
10 Clinches
14 Afghan, e.g.
15 Director Wertmuller
16 Clammy
17 Number one assistant, strictly speaking?
20 Some degree
21 Posted
22 Orwell's "Animal Farm," e.g.
23 Lbs. and ozs.
25 Pain
27 Instruction for casual dress
28 Going around a clock every minute?
31 Sheikdom of song
32 Regarded guardedly
33 Enlivens
35 Shrimp dish
41 Bric-a-___
45 Diamond situation after a single hit
46 Nonchalant gait?
51 Trap
52 Hubbubs
53 Without limit
54 Doo-wop hits, e.g.
56 Has markers out
58 Cleveland ___, O.
60 Where farm workers take a dip?
63 Indigo plant
64 Chip in
65 Place for a hawk
66 Burns and Allen: Abbr.
67 Doldrums, for one
68 "Texaco Star Theater" star

DOWN

1 Tip off
2 So to speak
3 Second half of a doubleheader
4 "No way"
5 Aardvark's prey
6 "A Streetcar Named Desire" role
7 Is of value, slangily
8 Eliminate
9 Eliminates by remote control
10 Words of agreement
11 Per ___
12 Chef Lagasse
13 Wild time
18 Cattle rancher's unit
19 Called
24 Sad sounds
26 Suffix with ethyl-
28 Weaken
29 School situated at Washington Sq.
30 Person with a practice: Abbr.
34 Alley org.
36 Bunko game
37 "The King and I" character
38 Hamburg honorific
39 Barbie feature, at times
40 Like Mahler's Symphony No. 4
42 Carrier of genetic info
43 Expand
44 Packed
46 Reading e-mail, e.g.
47 Movie technique
48 Gimcrackery
49 Take note of
50 Exploits
51 TV room features
55 Only make-believe
57 Poke holes in
59 "Peter Pan" pirate
61 Pitch ___-hitter
62 Riddle-me-___

by Manny Nosowsky

ACROSS

1 Diplomat Deane
6 Lancia competitor, for short
10 Tee off
14 Prepared to be dubbed
15 Cash in Qom
16 1950's British P.M.
17 Advice to a driver, part 1
20 Hardly genteel
21 Court feat
22 Hardly genteel
23 Literary monogram
24 ___ Park (Manhattan neighborhood)
27 Barcelona title
29 One-in-a-million
30 Botanist Gray
33 Advice, part 2
37 Clear of the sea bottom
40 Moulin Rouge performance
41 Advice, part 3
45 Buck's mate
46 Long story
47 Reasons to cram
51 Garden ornamentals
54 Beer may be on it
55 Waters on stage
58 Polo Grounds legend
59 "Dumb" comics girl
60 End of the advice
64 Director Rohmer
65 Tech support caller
66 Actress Anne
67 "Why not?!"
68 Nuclear fuel holders
69 Mountain nymph

DOWN

1 Evades
2 Imbue (with)
3 Dutch cheese
4 Lotion ingredient
5 1950's-70's senator Symington, for short
6 Small toucan
7 One of the front four
8 500-pound, say
9 Apiece, in scores
10 Put in hot oil again
11 Brainchild
12 "Why not?!"
13 Son of Seth
18 "This means ___!"
19 Watchdog agcy. beginning 1887
24 Some shorthand
25 Pitching stat
26 React violently, in a way
28 Final notice
30 Sector boundary
31 Rwy. stop
32 Writer Rand
34 Write for another
35 Clotho and others
36 Jet black
37 Tag on
38 A suitor may pitch it
39 Suffix with ethyl
42 Mer contents
43 Disregarded
44 Skiers' leggings
48 A.S.A.P.
49 First first lady
50 Neutered
51 British coppers
52 Bridge guru Culbertson
53 J.D. holder: Abbr.
55 Farm females
56 Like some traffic
57 One who's got it coming
59 Shy creature
61 Start of many a Catholic church name
62 G.I. entertainer
63 Telephone interrogatory

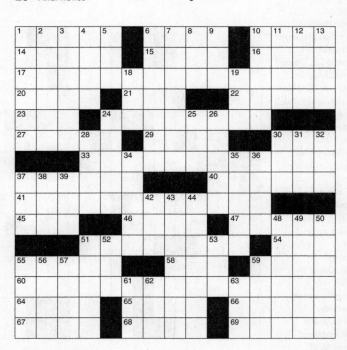

by Ed Early

214 ⋆ ⋆

ACROSS
1 No-loss, no-gain situation
5 Modeled
9 Bleed for
13 Sermon's conclusion?
14 Lost
15 Chocolate source
16 A man's "better half"
18 Ivy League school, familiarly
19 LOER-PRICED BOOK
21 Better
22 Bring action against
23 Intraoffice linkup: Abbr.
25 Walker, for short
26 Gilbert & Sullivan princess
29 It may come in buckets
32 Where water is poured on the rocks
34 1985 Literature Nobelist ___ Simon
35 SAIN LOUIS BASEBALL SQUAD
38 Fish preparer's task
39 Booze
40 Worked in a judge's office
42 Due before five?
43 Where, to Caesar
46 Morse E
47 "___ pro nobis"
49 Range rover
51 ACCOR
56 Ancient assembly area
57 Indicated
58 Early 20th-century leader
59 Like some batters
60 Immensely
61 Kind of course
62 1998 National League M.V.P.
63 Bar ___

DOWN
1 Moist towelette
2 Not out
3 Three sheets to the wind
4 Confine
5 Target of some humor in The New Yorker
6 Peak in Thessaly
7 Signs on again
8 Relax
9 Hemingway sobriquet
10 Cirrus, say
11 Ale holders
12 "Silent Night" adjective
15 62-Across, e.g.
17 Lettering liquid
20 Come again?
24 Storm heading: Abbr.
27 Castle section
28 Symbol of industry
30 Money put on a horse to finish second
31 Meticulousness
32 The cooler
33 Sighed sounds
35 Opposite of "from now on"
36 Kind of correspondence
37 Chow down
38 Alphabet trio
41 Room darkeners
43 In the habit of
44 High society
45 Chant
48 As much as you like
50 Start of a clarification
52 Stalactite producer
53 Golfer Woosnam
54 Convoy lineup
55 "A Day Without Rain" singer
56 Mont Blanc, for one

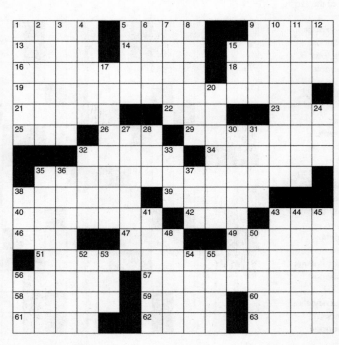

by Joe DiPietro

ACROSS

1 The Charleses' canine
5 Circus employee
10 Full of energy
14 Slick, in conversation
15 "I'd walk ___ for . . ."
16 Saharan
17 Doesn't keep
18 Hoarder's supply
19 Provide pro tem
20 Start of a quote by 53-Across, when asked to name his favorite song
23 Carbolic acid
24 Moving about
28 Quote, part 2
33 R.p.m. indicator
36 Lacks, in brief
37 Go for the gold?
38 Nickname of radio shock jock Greg Hughes
39 Monte ___
40 Chops, e.g.
41 Bobby on the ice
42 Slur over
43 Rainbows, e.g.
44 End of the quote
48 What "dis" is
49 Self-assured
53 Speaker of the quote
58 Chamber phenomenon
61 TV producer Spelling
62 Verve
63 Channel marker
64 Amount wagered
65 "Fashion Emergency" host
66 Buzzers
67 High bridge card
68 Talk back to

DOWN

1 "Get ___ on yourself!"
2 Sluggard's sin
3 Share with the church
4 Green liqueur
5 Angler's gear
6 Nanjing nanny
7 Flexible mineral
8 Like some textbook publishing
9 Item of 5-Down
10 Overshoe
11 Lode load
12 Card player's shout
13 Like all primes but one
21 Kabuki kin
22 1920's chief justice
25 Put darts into, as a garment
26 Singer Hayes
27 Carries on
29 The Andes, e.g.
30 Start to go?
31 Speck on a map
32 Rock's Brian
33 Characters in cels
34 Patriots' Day month
35 Approximately
39 Middle of the second century
40 Early shows
42 Hence
45 Relishes
46 Game one
47 H+, e.g.
50 1965 march city
51 Dutch treats?
52 Units of force
54 Talk (over)
55 Expanding grp.
56 Ollie's human friend
57 "The Mikado" character
58 Flow's partner
59 "The Hustler" prop
60 Ground breaker

by Sarah Keller

216 ★ ★

ACROSS

1 Pampering places
5 Pronunciation indicator
10 See 40-Across
14 Minor stroke
15 Loads of fun
16 Word with Bay or gray
17 Gray
18 Something not to talk about
19 Naval position: Abbr.
20 Leaves a center for cereal abuse?
23 Bard's nightfall
24 AWOL chasers
25 Go online
27 An hour of prime-time TV, often
29 Back muscles, for short
32 Grp. vigorously backing the Second Amendment
33 It's not the norm
36 @
37 Makes cereal more flavorful?
40 With 10-Across, place to get milk and bread
41 Divide, as Gaul
42 TV puppet voiced by Paul Fusco
43 Asian cookers
44 Kind of bulb
48 Mrs. Ceausescu of Romania
50 Galoot
52 Whole
53 Master cereal-maker's knowledge?
58 Spirit, in Islamic myth
59 42-Across, for one
60 Crowning
61 "I Want ___" (Rodgers and Hart song)
62 Kitschy film monster
63 Loafer, e.g.
64 Depend
65 Low-rent, maybe
66 Rancher's concern

DOWN

1 Went blank in the head
2 Narc's target
3 Armored Greek goddess
4 River to the underworld
5 Stayed awake
6 Heart-to-hearts
7 Wanderer
8 Rough bark
9 Ending with comment or liquid
10 Swaggering
11 French brandy
12 Good wood for cabinetry
13 Pit contents
21 Muscat dweller
22 Chicago transports
26 "Nope"
28 Skirt for the modest
29 Blue stone
30 Regrettably
31 Northumberland river
34 Palindromic guy's name
35 Gloom
36 Accusatory question
37 Play solitaire, perhaps
38 Hellish
39 Certain jazz combo
40 Al Capp's Daisy ___
43 Salon job
45 Abhor
46 Like some pools
47 Complained slightly
49 Fool
50 Having the most points
51 Copper
54 Galley workers
55 Arctic sight
56 Lunar effect
57 Unheedful
58 Food container

by Peter Sarrett

ACROSS

1 Composer whose music is often heard at graduations
6 Word on some diplomas
11 TV sked abbr.
14 Take for a while
15 When the Boston Marathon is held
16 It comes with a charge
17 Nondefensive military move
19 Shine, in product names
20 High dudgeon
21 Baby's ring
23 There are six of these in the middle of 17- and 56-Across and 11- and 25-Down
28 Razor brand
29 Hand or foot
30 "Well, well!"
31 Reassuring words
32 High muck-a-mucks
34 Of the flock
35 Ending of the Bible
36 Medium settings?
38 Punishment, metaphorically
41 Base tune
43 Garage figure
45 Old-hat
47 Santa ___ (hot winds)
48 "Paradise Lost," e.g.
49 Roguish
50 Jam producer
52 Scam artist
54 1995 court V.I.P.
55 Eastern way
56 "Just do it," e.g.
62 Lennon's lady
63 Sun Valley locale
64 Mirage sight
65 Theologian's subj.
66 Dot in the ocean
67 On the dot

DOWN

1 Tiny toymaker
2 Hula hoop?
3 Long-snouted fish
4 Basketball stat
5 Back in?
6 Place for a pin
7 Financing abbr.
8 Like sandpaper
9 "Just do it" shoes
10 Away from the wind
11 Fix
12 "10" music
13 Eskimo garb
18 Tour for Nicklaus
22 "Mon Oncle" star
23 1, 8 or 27
24 "Step ___!"
25 Some adult education
26 Dog star?
27 Emerging
31 Capital of old Moldavia
33 Crosby partner
34 Reveal accidentally
37 Future J.D.'s hurdle
39 Auricular
40 Knock flat
42 Connors contemporary
44 Hanukkah item
45 Flock leader
46 Like federal tax laws
47 From the heart?
50 Sweat units
51 Group values
53 Early 12th-century date
57 Leader in a beret
58 On a roll
59 ___ rule
60 Lady's man
61 Unproven ability

by Greg Staples

218

★ ★

ACROSS

1 Miffed
5 Early in the morning
11 Bit of sugar, say: Abbr.
14 Historical chapters
15 Big ___ (German gun in W.W. I)
16 Olive ___
17 Slangy dissents
18 Vinegary
19 Baton Rouge campus
20 A driver may come to it
23 Pay back?
24 Number of weeks per annum
25 Brownish-orange
27 "28 Days" subject
29 Funny Philips
32 Great plays may be seen in it
33 TV dial: Abbr.
35 Sportscaster Cross
37 Far or down follower
38 Sound on a winter's night
41 Apple not for eating
43 Sawbones
44 Word repeated in the Beatles title "___ Said ___ Said"
45 Teasdale and others
47 Bridal-notice word
49 Robert Devereux's earldom
53 Stick one's nose (in)
55 Fed. construction overseer
57 Second person
58 Five-foot wading birds
62 Potpie morsel
63 Shell figure
64 "Look ___ hands!"
65 Superlative finish
66 "Newhart" actor Tom
67 Old accusation
68 Scores: Abbr.
69 Flunky
70 Catbird seat?

DOWN

1 Motion detector
2 One with a vision
3 Gung-ho
4 In ___ (actually)
5 Adders
6 Computer whiz
7 Afternoon hour in Bonn
8 Memo abbr.
9 Old bloc in Parliament
10 Cheesy snacks
11 It's not free of charge
12 A 6-Down may oversee them
13 Opposite of sing.
21 Piece of pipe
22 Francis and Dahl
26 Home land?
28 Shade of green
30 Not use plainly
31 Web address ending
34 Legal scholar's deg.
36 Bugs, briefly
38 Construction crew
39 It's not free of charge
40 "What's this ___ . . . ?"
41 Philosopher's study
42 "Myra Breckinridge" star
46 Single-masters
48 Yuletide offering
50 Nomination approver
51 Doings
52 Cancels
54 Center of Florida
56 At times it's stolen
59 "Wishing won't make ___"
60 Defense grp.
61 "You said it!"
62 Get-up-and-go

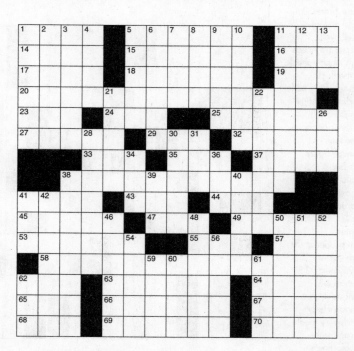

by Elizabeth C. Gorski

ACROSS

1 Domini preceder
5 ___ prof.
9 Aisle walker
14 Penury
15 Member of a bygone empire
16 School assignment
17 Approach the gate, say
18 Corner piece
19 Poison
20 Roman rebuke
22 Poet's Muse
23 A drawbridge spans it
24 Wrong
26 Selling very well
29 With 46-Across, an observation about the game in this grid
31 Folder labels
35 Jubilant
37 Musical sensitivity
38 That Spanish girl
39 Social
40 Tel. no. addition
41 55-Down under a flame
42 December 24 and 31, e.g.
43 Historical division
44 Instant
45 Viper's home
46 See 29-Across
48 ___-blue
49 Planning detail
51 It's 5 for B and 6 for C: Abbr.
53 Record company that rejected the Beatles
56 Where dirty clothes go
61 Sag
62 Inflict upon
63 Montreal player
64 Ancient marketplace
65 "So I ___!"
66 63-Across, for short
67 Bumpkin
68 Goes off
69 All wrapped (up)

DOWN

1 What you may do to get a hand
2 Spiffy
3 Waiting room call
4 Execration
5 Cause of a W.W. II siren
6 Porcine features
7 Sean Connery, for one
8 Cry during a duel
9 Total
10 For the immediate future
11 Prefix with -gon
12 Give off
13 Gambler's destination
21 Arena antagonist
25 ". . . ___ the fields we go"
26 Macho guys
27 Oil source
28 Colonists' annoyances
30 Bush, for one
32 Soothing plants
33 Lose a staring contest
34 Like pretzels, typically
36 Datum for college applications
40 "Monty Python" player
41 Carried
43 Woolly mama
44 Ways
47 Yak
50 Kind of court
52 Athlete Jesse
53 40's turning point
54 So
55 Prepare
57 Black, as la nuit
58 Wagon part
59 Erupt
60 It may be French

by Tyler Hinman

220 ⭐ ⭐

ACROSS

1 Chickens
6 Subject for Fermi
10 Chinese image in a shrine
14 Kind of box
15 Mother of Castor and Pollux
16 Dr. Dre contemporary
17 Words from young George Washington?
19 Collapsed
20 Sit (down)
21 Petrol purchase
22 Exultation
23 Some tournaments
25 Prince Edward, e.g.
27 Director's cry
30 Penn State branch site
31 What might have a person spinning?
34 "Doctor Who" airer
37 Pop singer Mann
38 Sound heard during a massage
39 "Vive ___!"
41 Nitrous oxide, e.g.
42 Like a stressful job?
45 Through
46 Latke ingredients
47 Charmingly odd
50 Precept
52 Press
53 From the beginning: Lat.
55 In-line skating gear
59 "Not returnable"
60 Outlaw's limit?
62 Possible result of bankruptcy
63 The Phantom of the Opera
64 Something to go under
65 Obedience school command
66 Writer Isak Dinesen, e.g.
67 Costa del Sol feature

DOWN

1 Bit of a cloud
2 "American ___"
3 Catalan painter Joan
4 Victim of a drift net
5 Farm pen
6 French actor Delon
7 Libretti
8 River of Brandenburg
9 Dessert wine
10 Shake a bit
11 Seat of Marion County, Fla.
12 Evening hour
13 Mount
18 Graff of "Mr. Belvedere"
24 Japanese game figures
26 Wide, in a way
27 Like gossiping tongues
28 Herbal "pet"
29 Allen and Conway
30 For grades K through 12
32 Lock maker
33 Unnecessary part
34 Esprit
35 Beethoven's birthplace
36 Weeds
40 Voters' survey
43 Wild
44 Like a ___ bricks
45 Engine type
47 Suppress
48 Star bears
49 Catlike
50 Snake venom, e.g.
51 Summon mentally
54 Theda of silents
56 Andrea Bocelli piece
57 Sideless wagon
58 1998 N.L. M.V.P.
61 Stun

by Cathy Millhauser

ACROSS

1 Second in a series
5 Ship to remember
10 Saudi citizen
14 Singular person
15 Spirit
16 Showroom sample
17 S
20 Squab alternative
21 Shortstop of fame
22 Significant period
23 Started moving
27 Sea or way ending
29 Screenwriter James
30 Sister of Thalia
31 Sexy person
37 Scream or be rowdy, as a child
38 Strapped
39 Signature tune
44 Spill consequence
45 Solo for Renata Scotto
46 Sort of cuisine
47 Snaps again
52 Select
53 Skirt style
54 Schaffhausen's river
57 's
63 Sporting blade
64 Stockpile
65 Scoreboard postings
66 Series of legis. meetings
67 See eye to eye
68 Sour fruit

DOWN

1 Seckel's cousin
2 Single-named singer
3 Soothing, weatherwise
4 Site where trees are displayed
5 Start to function?
6 Sandy's sound
7 Swearing-in words
8 Scand. land
9 Sounds of hesitation
10 Stella who founded an acting conservatory
11 Send for information
12 Slay, in a way
13 Sick and tired
18 Soap may be found like this
19 Spoon-bender Geller
23 Scrooge's cry
24 Sense of self
25 Salon offering
26 Scale's top, sometimes
27 Skillful act
28 St. Louis sight
32 Still woolly
33 Similes' relatives
34 Stunning
35 Shorten, in a way
36 Sandberg of baseball
40 Stood no more
41 Smeltery input
42 "Seduction of the Minotaur" author
43 Station ration
47 Sprints
48 Split to unite
49 Speeders' penalties
50 Stud fees
51 Sun. talk
55 Spanish boy
56 Seneca's being
58 "So that's it!"
59 Slot filler in a gearwheel
60 Seaman
61 Spleen
62 Shelley work

by Richard Silvestri

ACROSS

1 Eyes
6 Marx brother's instrument
10 Says further
14 An element, to the ancients
15 Turkish official
16 Dinette spot
17 The plain in Spain
18 Turn
19 One of TV's Sopranos
20 Fixes a flat, like a supermodel?
23 Outlaw
24 Bulletin board item
25 Sporty imports
29 Trim to fit, maybe
31 D.C. setting
34 Management course subject?
35 Oral, e.g.
36 Literally, "I forbid"
37 Cleans a windshield, like a snake?
40 Baseball rarities
41 Betting group
42 Ward off
43 Zeta follower
44 Whoop
45 Plays loudly
46 Cel character
48 ___ de vie
49 Eliminates a blind spot, like a cosmonaut?
55 'Hood
56 It may get plastered
57 Roberts of "Everybody Loves Raymond"
59 Do in
60 Double Stuf, for one
61 Poor Richard's Almanack item
62 Folks in smoke-filled rooms
63 Blouses and sweaters
64 Lacking slack

DOWN

1 Wise one
2 Math class, for short
3 Jazz home
4 "Beany & Cecil" boat Leakin' ___
5 Jail fixtures
6 Safe place
7 Census data
8 Mother of Zeus
9 Ineligible for benefits, say
10 Bit of slapstick
11 Guard
12 Ready to serve
13 Blue shade
21 Driver's need
22 Tit for ___
25 Photo finish
26 Arctic native
27 Lots and lots
28 Super scores
29 Laud
30 Willy Wonka's creator
32 Metric volume
33 Law school subject
35 Organic compound
36 Cheer starter
38 Hirer's posting
39 Worth on the open market
44 Cry before "Over here!"
45 Dickensian outburst
47 "Love Train" singers, with "the"
48 Cultural values
49 Singer Guthrie
50 Poi source
51 Going together, after "in"
52 Fashion
53 Shah's land, once
54 Teamsters' vehicles
55 Egyptian cobra
58 "Savvy?"

by Mike Torch

ACROSS

1 European capital of 2½ million
5 Part of N.A.A.C.P.: Abbr.
9 Business school subj.
13 Mouth site?
15 Endangered goose
16 Prefix with magnetic
17 Love
18 Nursery offering
19 Certain rug worker
20 Like LP's
22 Latin 101 verb
23 Appropriate
26 Comic strip set in Coconino County
28 Messes up
29 Article in Die Zeit
30 Around
33 Hosp. picture
34 Not worth debating
35 Birthplace of Hans Christian Andersen
36 Pioneer in vaccination
38 Rampaging
39 Watching
40 Copycat
41 Computer units: Abbr.
42 Commercial prefix with foam
43 Careered
44 U.S.S. ___, ship in 2000 news
45 1933 RKO hit
47 0 letters
48 Plant with pods
50 Doesn't ignore
52 Crawl (with)
53 "Beetle Bailey" dog
54 "Me, too"
58 San ___, Italy
59 Mouselike animal
60 Order beside a car door
61 About half of binary code
62 Milk dispensers
63 Certain race . . . or a cryptic title to this puzzle

DOWN

1 Spectra maker
2 Polit. designation
3 "Xanadu" rock group
4 Greeting card features
5 Frontal, to an anatomist
6 Reynaldo, to Polonius
7 Blessed act?
8 Not self-sufficient
9 Wagered
10 Classic comedy figure
11 "___ bien!"
12 Reason for an R rating
14 Business card abbr.
21 Barely make
23 Presto and others
24 Out-and-out
25 It opened its first store in Winston-Salem, N.C., in 1937
27 1950's–60's Hungarian premier János
31 In working order
32 Less wordy
34 Physics particle
35 Tense
37 "1000 Oceans" singer, 1999
38 Some women's shoe features
40 Peter or Paul, but not Mary
43 One way to the top?
44 Baby
46 Boxing need
48 Other: Sp.
49 Neato
51 Bother
55 Downed
56 Bit of time: Abbr.
57 Publicity

by Michael Shteyman

224 ★ ★

ACROSS

1 Like a Thanksgiving turkey
6 Some of this and some of that
10 Met star
14 Boarding areas
15 Commotion
16 Lena of "Chocolat"
17 Friendship
18 Descartes's "therefore"
19 Hurl an insult at
20 Truce after a fistfight?
23 Short flight
24 Smoothing tool
25 Court cutup
29 Terrier type
31 Site for cyberbidders
32 Point after deuce
34 Intensified, as sound
39 On the outs with a relative?
42 ___ tube
43 Tallow source
44 Nut job
45 Cool treats
47 Leaving no remainder
49 Caterer's heater
53 Dundee denial
54 Genetic engineer's observation about his pet?
60 Designer Gucci
61 Villain's work
62 Islamic holy war
64 Pull (in)
65 Boring way to learn
66 Come to mind
67 Arboretum sight
68 Ornamental vessel
69 Title role for Streisand

DOWN

1 Links org.
2 Souvlaki meat
3 Gas, e.g.: Abbr.
4 Intro to physics?
5 It contains the id
6 Tough to climb, perhaps
7 Whig's rival
8 Add a fringe to
9 Suggestive of a forest
10 Egg purchase
11 Tale of Troy
12 Coach Lombardi
13 Rile up
21 Imam's book
22 Song of praise
25 "Star Wars" warrior
26 Black, poetically
27 Cut, as a log
28 Newcastle's river
29 Skull cavity
30 Where pants may be worn
33 Two caplets, say
35 Distance not run in the Olympics
36 Working stiff
37 Tree hugger's subj.
38 Declare untrue
40 Circular gasket
41 Super bargain
46 Stick together
48 MTV figure
49 Like some bombs
50 Tippecanoe's mate
51 Vaudeville's ___ Foy and the Seven Little Foys
52 TV exec Arledge
53 N.Y. Jet or Phila. Eagle
55 Admit openly
56 Place to build
57 Home for the Murphys and O'Connors
58 Gossip
59 Biblical star locale, with "the"
63 Actor Benicio ___ Toro

by Fred Piscop

Note: There are ten errors in this puzzle. Can you find them?

ACROSS
1 Often-told truths
5 ___ facto
9 Tricky shot
14 Racer Luyendyk
15 Gardener's purchase
16 Some saxes
17 Lava geese
18 It's passed on
19 Contents of some John Cage compositions
20 Start of a question
23 Adjusts
24 Big ___
25 Whomps, briefly
28 Old Mideast combine: Abbr.
29 John Dean, to Nixon
32 Sure way to lose money
34 "Gosh!"
35 Ruined
37 A star may have one
38 Middle of the question
41 Place
43 Discernment
44 Common ratio
46 Sample
50 Chamber piece?
49 Dispatched
51 Monk's title
52 Driver's aid: Abbr.
54 Track racer
56 End of the question
60 Like workhorses
62 Arcade name
63 V.I.P.'s opposite
64 It's passed on
65 Compelled
66 Wading bird
67 Ottawa-born singer/songwriter
68 Turned up
69 Cry that might be appropriate at this point in the puzzle

DOWN
1 Retreat
2 Passage between buildings
3 Bingo announcement
4 "Toodles!"
5 Mirage
6 Magician's sound effect
7 Draped dress
8 Things to be read
9 Om, e.g.
10 Cream ingredient
11 Malodorous pest
12 Coded message
13 Language suffix often seen in crosswords
13 Compass dir. often seen in crosswords
21 African grazer
22 Put words in someone's mouth?
26 Anthem contraction
27 Platform place: Abbr.
30 Is hip to
31 1995 country hit "Someone ___ Star"
33 "Dagnabbit!"
35 Latched
36 Affectedly dainty, in England
37 Extinct Namibian shrub genus: Var.
38 Coordinated effort
39 Like some seats
40 First
41 Trip producer
42 W.W. II Pacific battle site, for short
44 Appropriate
45 Blazing
47 Cat
48 Desired response to "Take my wife . . . please!"
50 Open-sided shelter
53 Perfume source
55 Noted archer
57 What a germ may become
58 Good sign
59 Ticks off
60 Hearst kidnapping grp.
61 Dear

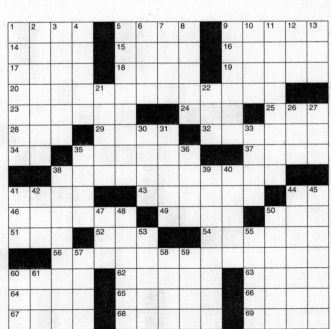

by Patrick Merrell

226

★ ★

ACROSS

1 Nerd
6 "When it's ___" (old riddle answer)
10 Corp. money managers
14 Midway alternative
15 Fix up
16 In ecstasy
17 See 36-Across
20 Modem termini?
21 Icky stuff
22 No-goodnik
23 Smoked delicacies
24 One of the Gulf States
25 See 36-Across
29 Inventor Swift
32 Feet, of sorts
33 Take in
34 Helen, to Menelaus
35 Ancestry record
36 Clue for 17-, 25-, 43- and 55-Across
38 Weight
39 Impart
40 Shine, in ad-speak
41 Jack ___ ("24" agent)
42 Relative of -trix
43 See 36-Across
46 Starlet's dream
47 Winner of a posthumous Pulitzer
48 Sydney señorita
51 Son of Seth
52 Jazz grp.
55 See 36-Across
58 Is addicted to, maybe
59 Actress Skye
60 Steve of country music
61 Swiss chard, e.g.
62 Did a sendup of
63 Golden Hind captain

DOWN

1 Former North Carolina senator
2 "Kapow!"
3 Canal sites
4 Fraction of a joule
5 "Night Fever" group
6 Melodic passage
7 Yo-yo
8 Put on
9 Utility bill sharer
10 Debate airer
11 Spore producer
12 "That's ___ haven't heard"
13 Sebaceous gland woe
18 Flax pod
19 Cause of cold sweat
23 Fell away
24 Shimmering stone
25 Dame, e.g.
26 Things to hawk
27 Signs to heed
28 "___ the Beat" (1982 Go-Gos hit)
29 Highway headache
30 Have for sale
31 Big-city newspaper department
34 One known for spouting off
36 Many a dictator's problem
37 Balm ingredient
41 Like holy water
43 Onetime White House pooch
44 Prohibited
45 Wide-eyed
46 Mark McGwire's position
48 Much-used pencil
49 Engine attachment
50 Abbé de l'___ (pioneer in sign language)
51 German article
52 Writer Ephron
53 Like some mail
54 To ___ (exactly)
56 Keystone ___
57 DeSoto, e.g.

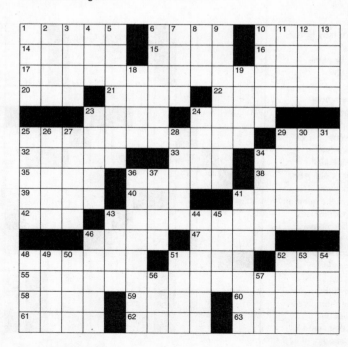

by Barry Silk

ACROSS

1 Séance happening
4 Wows, in comedy
9 Pub decoration
14 Put one past
15 Out of port
16 Home without a refrigerator
17 Post office delivery: Abbr.
18 Represent
19 Israeli party
20 "Whatever!"
23 Chores
24 Active sorts
25 King's home
28 Roman emperor after Galba
29 Cook, as beans
30 Premier under Mao
31 Union with 2.7 mil. members
32 Out of shape
33 "Look, ma, no cavities!," e.g.
34 Padlocks, say
38 Finnish architect Alvar ___
40 Irish girl's name
41 The Paper Chase topic
44 Capital south of Chernobyl
45 Sleep: Prefix
47 Memorable kicker
48 MGM motto word
49 "Ditto"
50 Name that means "beloved"
51 Sales rep's need
53 Company famous for Centipede and Battlezone
56 Tangle
57 Muscle car
58 "Eat!"
59 "Don't ___ soul!"
60 Modern: Ger.
61 Astronauts experience it

62 Computer bulletin board administrator
63 Most Mets games are on it: Abbr.

DOWN

1 Pet food brand name
2 Get going
3 Grocery items
4 Doesn't run
5 Bananas
6 Top of the class
7 2004 . . . with a hint to the starts of 20-, 34- and 51-Across
8 Back-talker
9 Red-haired soprano
10 Weekend-starting cry
11 Member of an order
12 Slip in a pot

13 Go-ahead
21 Bout stopper, briefly
22 Trick ending
25 Eighth-century king
26 Tel. book contents
27 Plumber's piece
29 Hi-___ monitor
30 It's chaos
32 Pal
33 Encouraging French word
35 Off-road transport, briefly
36 Golfer from South Africa
37 Sixth-century year
38 Alias
39 One mode of travel
42 On one's toes
43 Eliminate
45 Certain smoke signal

46 Keats and others
47 Kodak print
49 Seeking damages
50 "It's ___!" ("Simple!")
51 Vivacity
52 Prairie building
53 Wood shaper
54 20-20, e.g.
55 Cabinet dept.

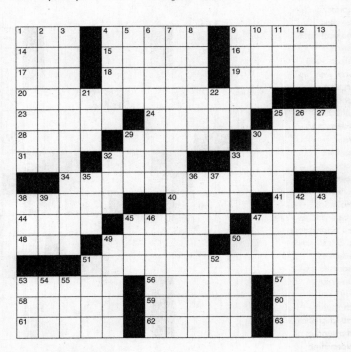

by Roy Leban

228 ⭐ ⭐

ACROSS
1 Ford or Chevrolet
5 Far from cordial
10 Waffle House alternative
14 Tel ___
15 Kind of toast
16 In the altogether
17 Event advertised in the classifieds
19 Clean Air Act target
20 Constriction of the pupil
21 Stumpers?
23 One of the Chipmunks
24 Spark plug, e.g.
26 Electrical glitch
30 Basilica part
33 Slippery ___
34 Time piece?
35 Jungfrau is one
36 Fighters at Lexington
39 One past due?
40 Actress Witherspoon
42 Enjoy, with "up"
43 Part of Air France's fleet until 2003
44 Place to buy wine
48 Boarders
49 Crop up
53 Sportscasting position
55 Web mags
56 It has a pocket
57 Time appropriate for 17-, 26- and 44-Across?
60 Nebraska tribe
61 Robin player of 1938
62 Rich source
63 "The King and I" co-star
64 Fits together
65 Charon crossed it

DOWN
1 Source of igneous rock
2 Benefit
3 Bolshoi rival
4 Hard to pin down
5 Skunk River city
6 Guitar great Paul
7 Commercial suffix with Rock
8 Shaped like a fish stick
9 Spenser's "The ___ Queene"
10 Parts of feet
11 Will Rogers and others
12 A hound may pick it up
13 Tent holders
18 1992 Heisman winner ___ Torretta
22 Cruising
24 "___ never work!"
25 Most off-tasting
27 Gift that's hung around the neck
28 Go-___
29 Peepers
30 50+ org.
31 "Nolo," for instance
32 Eventgoer
36 First A.F.L.-C.I.O. president
37 Makes lace
38 1995 trial name
41 Helter-___
43 Soaps, e.g.
45 Some meter readers
46 Unbroken
47 Bulldoze
50 Bullion unit
51 Like a fleabag
52 Reo contemporary
53 Out of control
54 Marquee time
55 Conduit bends
58 E.R. workers
59 Ellipsis part

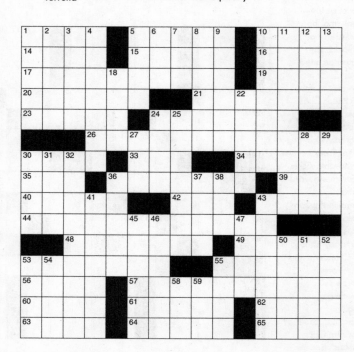

by Jim Hyres

ACROSS

1 Ready to work
8 "Now where ___?"
12 Kennedy adviser
13 End ___ era
14 Start of a definition of "elbonics" (a word that doesn't exist but should)
16 Greek god sometimes pictured as blindfolded
17 Novelist Seton
18 Each
20 Delighted reaction
21 Gathering place: Abbr.
23 Delilah player in "Samson and Delilah"
25 Definition, part 2
29 Israel-based bank
30 Kind
31 Kind of history
33 Actor Herbert
34 Definition, part 3
39 1961 Literature Nobelist ___ Andric
40 Drill
41 "___ fallen . . ."
42 "Siddhartha" author
44 Definition, part 4
49 Oil worker?
51 Alway
52 Cry of dismay, in poetry
53 Roll maker?
54 Came down
57 Token look-alike
58 End of the definition
62 Some bills
63 Do some stock speculating
64 Station name in England
65 How "Waltzing Matilda" is to be played

DOWN

1 Holiday cheer?
2 Cholers
3 Confederate
4 "Wheel of Fortune" request
5 C, alternatively
6 Not very profitable
7 "A kind of praise": John Gay
8 Try to win a hand
9 House with a steep roof
10 Caesar Park International Airport site
11 Sell out, in a way
12 Kind of vote
15 Proverb ending?
16 Have something
19 Choice
21 Former name of Sulawesi
22 Ginza locale
24 Everywhere
26 Teledyne Water ___
27 One keeping one's own company
28 Work unit
32 Blazing
34 Holy war
35 Make too much of
36 Hollywood studio department
37 Something that may be rolled over: Abbr.
38 Court matter
43 Paul and Carly
45 CH3
46 The Rockets of the Mid-American Conference
47 Accustom
48 Holiday quaff
50 ___ chi ch'uan
55 Castor's mother
56 Big World Cup power: Abbr.
57 Diva, e.g.
59 Letters on a brandy bottle
60 Season in Haiti
61 Big World Cup power: Abbr.

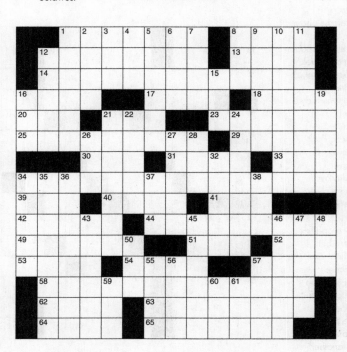

by David J. Kahn

230 ★ ★

ACROSS

1 Country's McEntire
5 Professional pitcher
10 Atomic groups: Abbr.
14 Trash can, e.g., on a computer
15 Lollapalooza
16 What Hamlet called Polonius
17 Late beloved entertainer
19 Steak order
20 Some diner orders
21 Prince ___ Khan
22 Suffix with prank
23 Up to now
25 Be in the red
26 Home, sweet or not
27 17-Across's alias
30 California's San ___ Dam
31 Like some phone nos.
32 Flight board abbr.
33 Part of a hookah
34 Least amount of caring
35 Longtime record label
36 Dandy
39 "My country" follower
40 "Nice!"
41 Wine: Prefix
42 Where 17-Across was inducted in 1990
47 3-D graph line
48 Last: Abbr.
49 Violinist Zimbalist
50 Declines
51 ___-Magnon
52 Like community property
53 Lit ___ (college course, slangily)
54 17-Across's first national TV show
58 Repeated call to a dog
59 Crop up
60 Biblical shepherd-turned-prophet
61 Former Iranian president Bani-___
62 Sportscaster Jim
63 Handshake's meaning, maybe

DOWN

1 Tease
2 Author Umberto
3 Hair holder
4 Low socks
5 Juice drinks
6 Haircuts
7 Nontraditional haircuts
8 Pretty shrub
9 Part of a Mad. Ave. address
10 Chocolate and almond treat
11 One with a silver tongue
12 1960's TV western
13 Dorm room staple
18 James of jazz
23 Scopes trial grp.
24 Suffix with ptero-
25 Normal force felt on earth
26 Taj Mahal city
28 Like the "Too-ra-loo-ra-loo-ral" lullaby
29 Cheesy snack
34 Five-spots
35 Ale ingredient
36 Dreaded
37 Treater's phrase
38 Pound piece
39 Popular party game
40 Permit to enter
41 Like some vehicles
42 Moravians, e.g.
43 California fossil site
44 Variety of sandpiper
45 Light show
46 Family problem
51 Actor Jackie
52 Court cry
55 Summer clock setting: Abbr.
56 ___ favor
57 Designer inits.

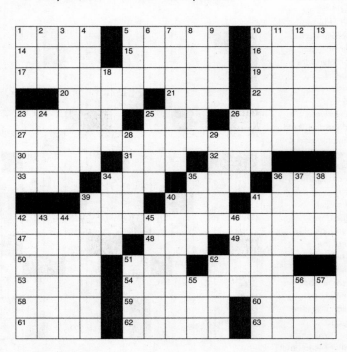

by Roy Leban

ACROSS

1. Six-time Best Actress nominee
5. Score
10. Move slowly
14. Onetime newsman ___ Abel
15. Flip over
16. Air-cooled machine gun
17. Cave explorer's need
18. Where explorer John Cabot was born
19. Take to mean
20. Road repair tools
23. Barbecue items
24. Test for some srs.
25. Program begun under Kennedy
28. "Thou pleasing, dreadful thought," to Addison
33. Western hoopster, for short
34. Gillette product
35. Norma Webster's middle name
36. Shrink
40. Ike's command in W.W. II
41. "Armageddon" author
42. Film producer credited with discovering Sophia Loren
43. Woody Allen-like
46. Snags
47. Two-time U.S. Open winner
48. "No problem!"
49. Classic geocentric theory
57. Certain sitar piece
58. Cant
59. "___ Road" (1999 Oprah's Book Club selection)
60. ___ house (down-home music site)
61. TV exec Arledge
62. Tennis score
63. Silent parts of 20-, 36- and 49-Across
64. Schlepper
65. R-rated, maybe

DOWN

1. Sustenance for a sea urchin
2. Joie de vivre
3. White coat
4. Plato's ideal
5. Where Jonny Moseley won a skiing gold medal
6. "Golden Boy" playwright
7. N.B.A.'s Kukoc
8. Bigmouthed critter
9. Helmets and such
10. Rockne player
11. Former Dodger Hershiser
12. Enthusiasm
13. Periods
21. Nursery buy
22. Elementary letters?
25. Town near Snowmass
26. Mail, in Marseille
27. "Shame ___!"
28. Reason to be good
29. ___ chic
30. Figure skater Slutskaya
31. Toothsome
32. Himalayan sightings
34. Longfellow's bell town
37. Fool
38. Silly trick
39. Guiding light
44. Circuit breakers
45. Adjective sometimes used with 60-Across
46. 1970's Plymouth
48. Bakery treat
49. Brace
50. Mending stuff
51. Blackguard
52. Buck chaser?
53. Jerome Kern's "___ Love"
54. Cry before applause
55. Pop singer Carmen
56. Countless

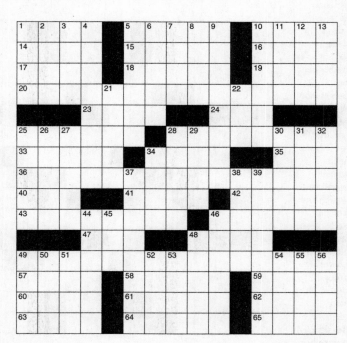

by Alan Arbesfeld

ACROSS

1 Lagoon locale
6 Triumphed
9 Former Montreal N.L.'er
13 Amos of "Amos 'n' Andy"
14 Cow chow
15 Terrify
16 Start of a quote by Anton Chekhov
19 Friend of Fido
20 "Go, team!"
21 Stopped
22 Idle fancy
24 Slugger Gonzalez
25 Quote, part 2
31 Phantasm
32 Hypnotist's imperative
33 ___-friendly
34 Boot
35 Windows preceder
36 Smile
37 It's an honour: Abbr.
38 Horse's motion
40 South Seas attire
42 Quote, part 3
45 6:1 or 3:2, say
46 Canned
47 Educate
50 Appropriate
51 Blowtorch fuel
54 End of the quote
58 Composer Copland
59 Like Burns's "tim'rous beastie"
60 Penned
61 Verve
62 Young 'un
63 Furnish with a fund

DOWN

1 Open a bit
2 Strengthen, with "up"
3 Cameo stone
4 Flower wreath
5 Something that's illegal to drop
6 End of many a riddle
7 Courtroom affirmation
8 Home of the IRT and BMT
9 ___ terrible
10 Yule
11 Horse's motion
12 Flat
15 Restless
17 Kind of whiskey
18 Obtuse's opposite
22 Habeas corpus or mandamus

23 Event on "The Sopranos"
24 Some sails
25 Island in a Beach Boys lyric
26 "___ at the Bat"
27 Like a chimney sweep
28 Graceful bird
29 Medium for writing "Happy Anniversary"
30 Dance partner?
31 Grove
35 Los ___ de los Muertos (Mexican holiday)
36 Electrical network
38 Descend
39 Discombobulate
40 A mile a minute
41 "Hail!," to Horace
43 Overly

44 Ended, as a subscription
47 Attempt
48 Scorch
49 Spy Mata ___
50 Zone
51 Saintly
52 A factory worker might make a dash for it
53 Dish cooked in a pot
55 Hole maker
56 Be in the hole
57 Ashes holder

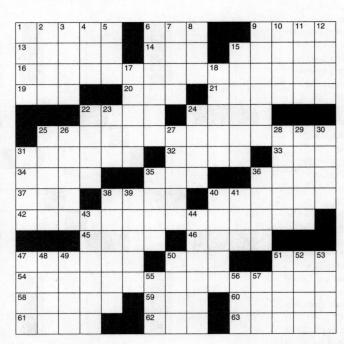

by Ethan Friedman

ACROSS

1 Sidepiece
5 Sockeroo
10 Some noncoms: Abbr.
14 "Gewehr ___!" (German military order)
15 Befuddled
16 "American Pie" actress Reid
17 Michael Jordan or Dr. J
19 "Ohhhh . . ."
20 Big Twelve powerhouse
21 Former beau or belle
23 Type spec: Abbr.
25 Opera ___
26 Workshop fixture
30 Opposite of whole
33 Film director Resnais
34 Dial-up ___
36 10¢ picture
37 Actress Sorvino
38 Title character of TV's "The Pretender"
39 Female singer who was Grammy's 1985 Best New Artist
40 Wash out to sea
41 Clubs, say
42 Steps over a fence
43 Tiara
45 Metric measures of area
47 Dance from Cuba
49 "Phooey!"
50 Person with a figure like Olive Oyl
53 "Uh-uh"
57 Apple variety
58 Interactive part of some Web pages
60 Have some fancy provisions?
61 Edit
62 Cousin of an org.
63 Stops: Abbr.
64 Opera that climaxes with a firing squad
65 "Toodles!"

DOWN

1 Attic buildup
2 "Take a Chance on Me" group
3 Lowdown
4 Capital on the Paraná
5 Dances to "Cali Pachanguero," e.g.
6 Parts of a range: Abbr.
7 Regarding
8 Barkers
9 Set
10 Leader born in Georgia
11 Soiree
12 Disneyland sight
13 Convenience for an ed.
18 Grow dark
22 Born in
24 Truman's Missouri birthplace
26 Docile, now
27 Suspect eliminator
28 Title girl of a 1966 pop hit
29 Goodness
31 Confuse
32 Ashes, e.g.
35 Administered, as medicine
38 Big flier
39 Not change
41 Burlap material
42 Barber's accessory
44 Knuckleheads
46 Home of six N.H.L. teams
48 Memorable mission
50 Sellers' solicitations
51 Send out
52 Abbr. after some telephone numbers
54 "Casablanca" role
55 "___ la vie"
56 Peak near the Gulf of Catania
59 Mandela's onetime org.

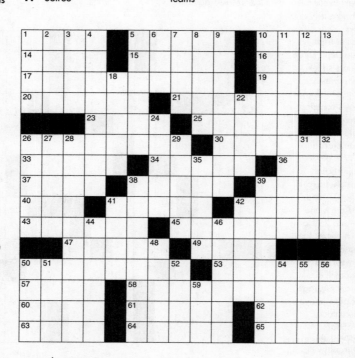

by Craig Kasper

ACROSS

1 Shout from the sidelines on TV
6 "Monty Python" airer
9 "Concentration" puzzle
14 Expo '70 site
15 "Seinfeld" uncle
16 Visibly shocked
17 Casino slickster
19 Caddie, basically
20 Dangerous cargo, in modern lingo
22 Humble reply
23 "Charlotte's Web" author
27 Sheriff's party?
29 Snickers
30 Like some eels or catfish
33 Genesis firstborn
34 Sleek, in car talk
35 "I'm so glad!"
36 Elevs.
37 Toaster treat
40 State Dept. figure
41 Comics shriek
42 Met number
43 Opposite of endo-
44 Shows contempt for
46 Potential retiree
48 Gold rush territory
49 Shamefaced
50 W.W. II ally
52 Major fiction
54 "Go ahead, ask!"
56 What 17- and 37-Across and 11- and 25-Down each comes to?
61 Two-door conveyance
62 Aladdin's sidekick
63 Instant message recipient, maybe
64 Like unlucky toreadors
65 Iron-pumper's unit
66 Writer who's in the minority

DOWN

1 Ad ___
2 "Love ___ Sickness" (Daniel poem)
3 Deface
4 Gave the go-ahead
5 Five iron
6 Mark, as a trail
7 Road shoulder
8 Accede to the district attorney, perhaps
9 Blow the whistle (on)
10 Self-server
11 Bad coffee, informally
12 Manipulator
13 Light-footed
18 Panama and porkpie
21 "___ is human . . ."
23 Makes aquatints
24 Much traveled
25 Sugary cocktail
26 Clucker
28 Nae sayer
30 Trouble constantly
31 "You are not!" retort
32 RoboCop, e.g.
37 Bench locale
38 Mork's leader on "Mork & Mindy"
39 Place for cocktails
43 Chang's twin
45 Low Countries locale
46 Margarita feature
47 Ratify by stamping
49 In a lather
50 Maritime grp.
51 "Buzz off!"
53 Sensation, slangily
55 Sitcom newsman Baxter
57 Lobster eggs
58 Brownie
59 Take captive
60 Like some wells and lectures

by Mitch Komro

ACROSS

1 Film, in Variety
4 Pant
8 Neighbor of Orlando
14 Call ___ day
15 What un lago holds
16 Card game for two
17 Like some memoirs
19 Bad news from a credit card company
20 Patron saint of goldsmiths
21 Have the lead
23 Outdated
24 Wind-borne deposits
26 Hindu incarnation
28 Pressured
30 Musical aptitude
33 High nests
36 Insult, slangily
37 Goya's "Duchess of ___"
38 Porter classic
40 Close cousins
42 "Come here often?," e.g.
43 Queue after Q
45 Certain foundation
46 "Evil Woman" band, for short
47 Humors
49 Chicago university
50 Like some physical tests
54 Creepy one?
57 Caged
59 Beak
60 Playoffs
62 Abandon
64 Handsome youth
65 Architect Saarinen
66 Used
67 1973 Peace Nobelist
68 Lozenge
69 ___ in Thomas

DOWN

1 Computer bit
2 ___-Greek
3 Birchbark
4 Hood's gun
5 Wrinkles, say
6 Harem keeper
7 Chitchat
8 Checked, as a box
9 Bygone deliverer
10 Estate
11 Hosp. testing techniques
12 Announcements from the cockpit, briefly
13 Hard to hold
18 Can't stand
22 Plant root
25 "Did You Ever ___ Dream Walking?" (1933 hit)
27 Themes

29 Off the mark
30 Lodge group
31 Rose's love, on Broadway
32 Carry on
33 Mandrel
34 Pianist Gilels
35 Splitsville
37 Dragging on the shore
39 Bar at the bar
41 Part of N.B.
44 Sent before e-mail
47 Sheep gatherer
48 Person with binoculars
49 Chinese weight unit
51 Unpaid servant
52 Refuges
53 Yorkshire city
54 Tunisian port once a stronghold for Barbary pirates

55 Spiders' nests
56 Soon
58 Corrida beast
61 Lith., once
63 "Alley ___"

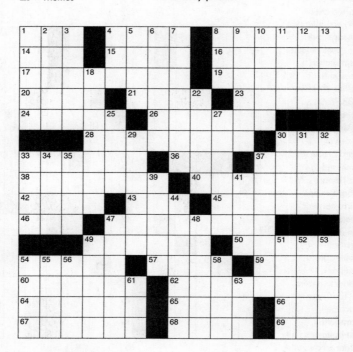

by Alfio Micci

236 ⭐ ⭐

ACROSS

1 5-Across handle
5 Sharp weapon, slangily
9 Rope fiber
14 Mozart composition
15 Animal with a scut
16 Shiraz native
17 Start of a message on a Lincoln Center T-shirt
19 Honor, in academe
20 See 13-Down
21 Wedding reception ritual
23 Clan emblems
24 T-men, e.g.
25 Cathedral city
28 Great balls of fire
29 "The Immoralist" author
30 Liberate
31 Walked over
33 Butchers' offerings
35 Message, part 2
39 Doings of Hercules
40 Table section
41 Cross to bear
42 Mother of Horus
44 1938 Physics Nobelist
49 Sword conqueror
50 Aware of
51 Word processing command
52 ___ Lama
54 Babar's queen
55 Spiral-horned antelope
57 End of the message
59 Tubular pasta
60 Jam-pack
61 Morlocks' victims in "The Time Machine"
62 Fragrant oil
63 Does some tailoring
64 Can blemish

DOWN

1 Things to kick
2 "Am too!" rejoinder
3 Cinco de Mayo event
4 Tear to shreds
5 Round at a bar, maybe
6 Keep
7 Tick off
8 Discharged, as gases
9 Eliot's Marner
10 S. & L. offerings
11 Sweet wine
12 What's more
13 With 20-Across, receive a posthumous honor
18 Cage-wheel runner
22 One-named singer
24 Opera that inspired the T-shirt slogan
26 Popular jeans
27 Sycophant's word
29 Statehouse V.I.P.
30 Pro
32 Soprano in "The Barber of Seville"
34 Stymie
35 What a groom may groom
36 Plentiful
37 John ___ Passos
38 Realtor's abbr.
39 Prune
43 Zigzag, e.g.
45 Smoothed out
46 Fix, as a pump
47 Women's prison figure
48 "Looky there!"
50 Grayer, maybe
51 Appears to be
53 "___ Karenina"
54 Secretive sort
55 Rater of m.p.g.
56 Court cry
58 Bonanza find

by Nancy S. Ross

ACROSS

1 Musically detached: Abbr.
5 Capital examiners, briefly
9 Fairy tale brother
14 Bleeper's target
15 See 32-Across
16 Asian currency
17 Psychic's furniture?
20 Beast of burden
21 Gets a move on
22 Something big in front of the sofa?
26 Bowls
27 Laugh sound
28 Barrett formerly of Pink Floyd
31 Madrid mousers
32 With 15-Across, a noted London theater
34 Chiang ___-shek
35 Vamooses
36 Plus ___ (theme of this puzzle)
37 Big name in sneakers
38 Richmond-to-Virginia Beach dir.
39 Breakfast item
40 "Left ___ own devices . . ."
41 Like a lobster
42 Ingredient of black bottom pie
43 One way to sort a list
44 Savings of a German opera star?
47 Disinclined
50 Auxiliaries
51 Two features of a hurried golf game?
56 The least bit
57 Helen's mother
58 180° turns, slangily
59 Virile
60 Helen's land
61 See 47-Down

DOWN

1 Covering for a bald spot
2 ___ chi (martial art)
3 Off-road goer, for short
4 Mexican-Americans
5 Shinnies
6 Cartoonist's drawing
7 White, informally
8 Sabbath msg.
9 Freezer locale
10 Buzz
11 ___ facto
12 Come across
13 1986 World Series champs
18 Grannies
19 Herr Schindler and others
22 Blade
23 Poker phrase
24 Checked for accuracy
25 One without manners
28 Top of the Alps?
29 Washington city
30 Gas station choice
32 Believer's belief
33 Way in Québec
36 Some early 20th-century French artists
37 Matter of little importance
39 Irascible
40 Supercompetitive
43 Down time
44 Dryly amusing
45 Having more reason
46 Friendly term of address
47 First resident of 61-Across
48 Ars longa, ___ brevis
49 Hunter of fiction
52 PC key
53 "If only ___ listened . . ."
54 View finder?
55 Fig. in identity theft

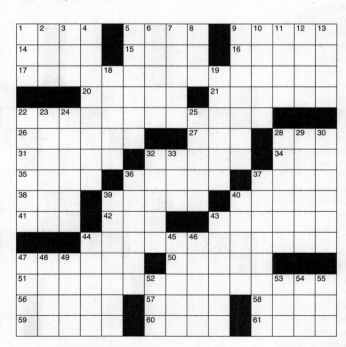

by Manny Nosowsky

238 ⭐ ⭐

ACROSS

1 Check, as the horizon
5 Pick out
9 Home feature
14 Lotion additive
15 Walk in water
16 They may be spent in France
17 Restaurant lines?
18 Atlas section
19 Some transportation stocks
20 End of a line
23 Swamp goo
24 Charged particle
25 Move with stealth
28 The Merry Men, e.g.
30 Like a wallflower
33 "___ as good as another"
34 Symbol of stubbornness
35 Race in an H. G. Wells story
36 Ending for a line
39 Curved lines
40 2%, maybe
41 Tolerate
42 #26 of 26
43 Up for something
44 Film components
45 Quadrennial conventiongoer
46 Sci-fi writer Frederik
47 Ending line
53 Bond before Dalton
54 Joint problem
55 Creep (along)
57 Oktoberfest air
58 "When in ___ . . ."
59 Clothing line
60 Hint of light
61 Parishioner's line
62 One getting a decoration

DOWN

1 1950's–60's singer Cooke
2 Staff symbol
3 Top-of-the-line
4 Ones getting "worry lines"?
5 "Dirty Dancing" co-star
6 Stickum
7 Garfield's pal
8 Go lickety-split
9 Certain 36-Across
10 Greg Evans comic strip
11 Diva's lines
12 Car payment
13 Curved line
21 Settle down for the night
22 Sal of "Exodus"
25 Shade of yellow
26 Harden
27 London coppers
28 Montana city
29 "It's a Sin to Tell ___" (1936 hit)
30 Done in
31 Bunch of people
32 "Omigosh!"
34 What to call a lady
35 Add frills to
37 Russian range
38 Snack chip
43 Stadium cheer
44 Tone down
45 Winter wear
46 Feather in one's cap
47 Hammer or tongs
48 Doughnut's center
49 Taj Mahal city
50 Weaving machine
51 Kind of pad
52 Operation memento
53 Auto ad stat.
56 Med. care plan

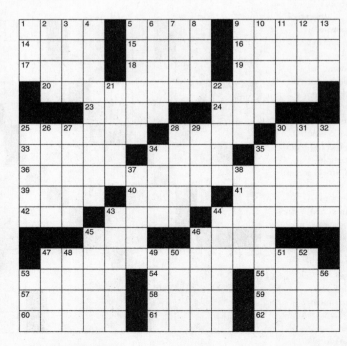

by Mark Diehl

ACROSS

1 Mandlikova of tennis
5 Narrow
9 Cold response?
14 Any of the Beatles, once
15 Rolling rock
16 Language akin to Tahitian
17 Kind of system
19 Ones quick with a line?
20 Washington V.I.P.'s
22 Secretary, e.g.
23 Sci. facilities
24 Antiknock fluid
26 Obsolescent suffix
27 Mr. Bumble's position in Oliver Twist
30 Verb with thou
33 Cronus or Oceanus
35 Salad option
37 Cause for swearing
42 Band
43 The Brady Bunch girl
44 Milk source
45 Danger signal on the prairie
48 "Caught ya!"
51 Paper towel hawker, in old TV ads
53 Mitchum competitor
55 Ragamuffin
57 Prior to the 20th Amendment, what 20-Across would do on 37-Across, or when they would do it
61 Of an old empire
63 Like Congress
64 Limelight milieu
65 Turkish chiefs
66 In any case
67 Sighed (for)
68 Hand-over-mouth reaction
69 Dry

DOWN

1 One with a pad, maybe
2 Trims
3 At least
4 Party desirables
5 Declined
6 Mennonite decoration
7 Former Wall Street insider Boesky
8 Fountain order
9 Org. for an OB/GYN
10 One who's left holding the bag
11 Old country, maybe
12 Meteor materials
13 Pen sound
18 "___ Autumn" (Woody Herman hit)
21 N.L. Central team: Abbr.
25 Biblical king
27 A.C. letters
28 Stalk outgrowth
29 Put on ___
31 VCR maker
32 Lord's Prayer pronoun
33 Primitive percussion instrument
34 Roles in "Frankenstein" movies
36 Even one
37 Harbor problem
38 When, for an eager beaver
39 Cheese type
40 Dusk-___-dawn
41 Chemical suffix
46 "Fire" preceder
47 It gets in hot water
48 Achieve success
49 One trying to run from home
50 Cling
52 Adult
53 A continent: Abbr.
54 37-Across oaths, e.g., [or] 37-Across parades follow them
55 Trace
56 Oppositionist
58 Capital occupied by the Germans in 1941
59 Figureheads?
60 Lock securer
62 "The Simpsons" neighbor

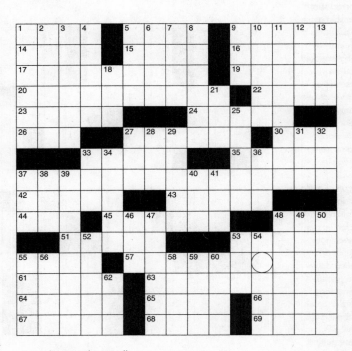

by Patrick Merrell

240 ★ ★

ACROSS
1 Crash site
4 Babe in the woods
8 Black rock
14 Language suffix
15 "Would ___ to you?"
16 Alchemist's concoction
17 Apiece, at Wimbledon
18 Jungle woman
19 With subtlety
20 Wedding man lookin' at the newspaper?
23 Late-night host
24 Tripe
29 Surgeon's request
32 Spill material
33 Man, for one
34 Gasket
36 Sacred spot
37 Durable piece of boxin' equipment?
42 Rubbernecked
43 Russian alternative
44 Largest of seven
45 Commencement wear
46 Mix movies
51 Name trump, in bridge
53 Jai ___
54 Result of a silo tippin' over?
59 Nimble
63 Fit for service
64 Newspaper supply
65 Batten down
66 The gamut
67 Genealogy word
68 Warming device
69 Not a lick
70 Muff

DOWN
1 Choker components
2 Slumbering
3 Presidential middle name
4 Where Suva is
5 Presidential middle name
6 White House section
7 Poetic adverb
8 Soil
9 Out on ___
10 Mortal thing
11 What Carry Nation carried
12 Diamond ___
13 Take a shot at
21 Slip on
22 Ancestry
25 Check
26 Analogy phrase
27 Montenegro native
28 "Take this!"
30 Olympian's quest
31 Years of note
32 Ready for use
35 David, "the sweet psalmist of ___"
36 Turkish title
37 Old oath
38 Carnation container
39 Grist for DeMille?
40 MTV's "___ World"
41 Lt. saluter
45 Copernicus, for one
47 Pit contents
48 Marilu Henner's "Taxi" role
49 Best Actress of 1936 and 1937
50 Tackle box item
52 All lit up
55 Help for some students
56 Concerned with
57 Light stuff
58 Use a crystal ball
59 Camel's end?
60 River to Solway Firth
61 Company with a dog logo
62 Call at first

by Richard Silvestri

ACROSS

1 Blast from the past?
6 Artsy Manhattan area
10 Pest control brand
14 ___-off coupon
15 Pizazz
16 It's west of the Isle of Man
17 Ad come-on #1
20 Suffix with buck
21 The Virgin Is., e.g.
22 Lace into
25 Washington's ___ Stadium
27 Moon of Mars
31 See 23-Down
34 Left Bank locale
35 Fine arbitrarily
36 Fair-hiring abbr.
38 Show off one's biceps
39 Fallen Russian orbiter
40 Men's accessories
43 Young newt
44 "How sweet ___!"
46 Cable Superstation
47 Arrow poison
49 Israeli desert region
51 With 29-Down, ad come-on #3
53 Lover of Aphrodite
55 Mouse's place
56 2.0 grades
57 Knotted, scorewise
59 Grow tiresome
61 Ad come-on #4
68 "Hold it ___!"
69 Shade provider
70 Nary a soul
71 Carol time
72 Short hours of operation?
73 Ohm's symbol

DOWN

1 Coolers, for short
2 Sri Lanka export
3 Ltr. container
4 Clambake clam
5 Mikhail Romanov, e.g.
6 Detonate
7 "That ___ Devil Called Love"
8 Doe's mate
9 Right turn ___
10 Get intelligence from
11 Intelligence grp.
12 Table scrap
13 Born in France
18 Surrender
19 "___ Tu" (1974 hit)
22 Endurance
23 With 31-Across, ad come-on #2
24 Explorer Vespucci
26 Stays current
28 Car rental info
29 See 51-Across
30 Hockey teams, e.g.
32 School mo.
33 Louis XIV, e.g.
37 Makes unreadable, in a way
41 Fall back
42 Catch some rays
45 Get older
48 Ping-Pong locale
50 In ___ (occurring naturally)
52 Opened wide
54 Navratilova rival
58 Fargo's state: Abbr.
60 "___ extra cost!"
61 Roll-call call
62 Buckeyes' sch.
63 Rolodex no.
64 "___ got an idea"
65 Underwater eggs
66 It's east of the Isle of Man: Abbr.
67 Bounding main

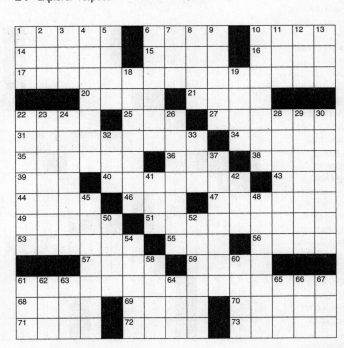

by Michael Shteyman

242 ★ ★

ACROSS

1 Like the hair under a comb-over
7 Rare blood type, informally
11 Illicit drug inits.
14 Soup holder
15 Ex-attorney general
16 ___-di-dah
17 Vigilant
19 Brown, e.g.
20 Sheet music instruction
21 Rebel-turned-national leader
22 Stir
23 Carol contraction
24 Certain design transfer
27 Caterer's aid
29 Cheri of "Scary Movie"
30 Doesn't work anymore, informally
34 Self-replicating things
35 Quickly . . . and a hint to 17-, 24-, 45- and 55-Across
37 Cowboy's domain
39 Foreign correspondent?
40 Seriously winded
41 Cheaper now
45 Top-rated sports group
50 Ancient law
51 Pack ___ (quit)
52 Siouan Indian
53 Little dog of old Disney cartoons
54 Western defense grp.
55 Was victorious, but not by a knockout
58 "Lord, is ___?"
59 Pharaoh's deity
60 Behind, so to speak
61 Google's realm, with "the"
62 Chapeau holder
63 Stimulates, slangily

DOWN

1 Not highly valued furs
2 "Meet the Press" guest, maybe
3 Excite
4 Actor Auberjonois
5 Realize
6 Coast Guard officer: Abbr.
7 Brown bear
8 "Cool!"
9 Noted bankruptcy of 2001
10 Jupiter, e.g.
11 Epoch from two to five million years ago
12 Expensive hors d'oeuvre: Var.
13 1970's sitcom
18 Ronnie & the Daytonas hit
22 Iterates
24 Arch sites
25 ___ Hashana
26 Plant with a bitter root
28 Welcomes, as a new year
31 Cool, once
32 Lines of homage
33 Bridge capacity unit
35 Stopping by to say hello
36 Over
37 Call to police headquarters, maybe
38 Stir
42 Some dresses
43 Undisturbed
44 Lives
46 See 47-Down
47 With 46-Down, words finishing "Ready ___, here ___"
48 Not a soul
49 Have
53 Cousin of Rover
55 Angkor ___ (Cambodian landmark)
56 Slob
57 "It's Alright" singer

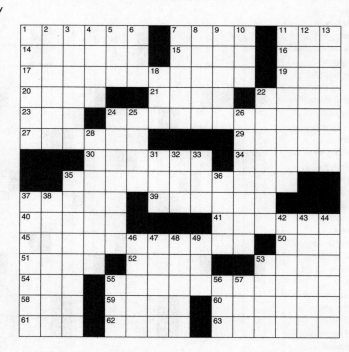

by Robert H. Wolfe

ACROSS

1 "Sex and the City" airer
4 Big dos
9 Varnish ingredient
14 It's measured in minutes
15 Multiple choice options, perhaps
16 Come up
17 Oscar Wilde, notably
18 College basketball coach who was the subject of "A Season on the Brink"
20 Alpine event
22 Have an impact on
23 "Fooled Around and Fell in Love" singer, 1976
26 Piggy
29 "The Witches" director Nicolas
30 ___ Jeanne d'Arc
31 Some N.C.O.'s
32 Celerity
35 Gym wear
37 "Different Seasons" author
39 Inferior, slangily
41 Directly show where
42 Tusked beast
43 Mideast grp.
44 Black-and-white predator
48 Arrange
49 Pseudonym in detective fiction
53 Spade player, familiarly
55 It begins with an equinox
56 Half a famous dance team
60 44-Across's milieu
61 Slippers of sorts
62 Attire for Mr. Peanut
63 Like 31-Across
64 ___ four

65 One of the black keys on a piano
66 Skid row affliction

DOWN

1 Mooring rope
2 S.O.S alternative
3 Staff interval
4 Libreville's land
5 "Little Boy" in 8/6/45 news
6 Shot having a 14-Across
7 Wall St. worker
8 Reaper's tool
9 Incurred, as charges
10 Journalist Sevareid
11 Red Skelton specialty
12 Sort of: Suffix
13 Take home
19 Hootchy-___
21 Match alternative

24 Panama, e.g.: Abbr.
25 Ring site?
27 The Little Giant
28 20-Across path
31 Dispatched
33 1950's political inits.
34 Wire wearer
35 Do a 20-Across
36 Sports datum
37 It'll keep you in your place
38 Queen who wrote "Leap of Faith"
39 The so-called Tiffany Network
40 Weeder's need
43 "The magic word"
45 Got more life from
46 Dental compound
47 They're history
49 Discharge, in a way
50 Form of ID: Abbr.

51 W.W. II conference site
52 Jason's journey, e.g.
54 "The ___ Love" (R.E.M. hit)
56 Devilkin
57 Wish undone
58 Coppertone rating: Abbr.
59 1960's chess champ

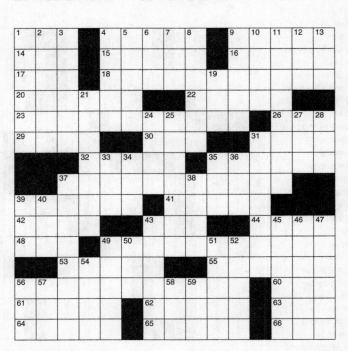

by Alan Arbesfeld

244 ★ ★

ACROSS

1. Visibly wowed
5. Hindu noble
9. Interest of Fermi
13. Teed off
14. ___ Bator
15. Big brand of office labels
16. Setting for a romantic dinner
18. Roman household deities
19. Plugs
20. Cushion site
21. Guinness adjective
22. It may be made by a falling rock
23. Microscopic menace
25. Sunning spots
28. Seamstress' cry upon making a mistake?
29. 5 Series or 6 Series
32. Hick
33. Top-notch
34. Manfred B. ___, half of Ellery Queen
35. Uris hero
36. Key to answering 16- and 58-Across and 10- and 27-Down
39. Bygone polit. cause
40. Bowler
41. Unwonted
42. Move a little
43. Smith and Gore
44. Vicious
45. "Look, ma, no cavities!" and others
47. Spill
49. Sidekick
50. What water in a pail may do
52. Uncle's heir, perhaps
54. Evil, to Yvonne
57. Not wandering
58. Start of an appeal for privacy

60. Chips in
61. English actor Bates
62. ___ Fein
63. Thai money
64. Lorgnette part
65. It puts on a really big show

DOWN

1. 1934 film canine
2. Provoke
3. Christmas bulbs, e.g.
4. Salon supply
5. Red-haired
6. Not sotto voce
7. Pusher's foe
8. Red-handed
9. Be useful
10. Difficult stage
11. Some rocks
12. Classic computer game

15. Royal grandfather of Spain's Juan Carlos
17. She loved Narcissus
22. Secure
24. Pilot with flight attendants
25. European capital, to natives
26. Of sound
27. Quarter's value
28. Adventured
30. Kind of raise
31. Has on
36. Bad-mouths
37. Datum
38. Rug choice
42. Elegiac
45. Kevin and Francis
46. Provo neighbor
48. It's a plus
49. Pie choice
50. Stick

51. Olin of "Chocolat"
53. Skye, for one
54. Wing, say
55. Poet Akhmatova
56. Big cat
59. Inflation measure?: Abbr.

by Robert Zimmerman

ACROSS

1 Guy Fawkes Day mo.
4 Flora and fauna
9 In a lather?
14 Big time
15 Translator's obstacle
16 "Alfie" actress, 2004
17 Path to enlightenment
18 Place to take off in lighter-than-air craft?
20 Mid seventh-century year
22 Caught, in a way
23 50's monogram
24 Like some wonders
27 Like W. C. Fields's nose
30 Community news source in Belgium?
33 July 1944 battle site
34 "Agnus ___"
35 Name in plastic
38 Animator?
42 Early Chinese dynasty
43 Ode title starter
44 "Must've been something ___"
46 Row of cavalry barracks?
50 Street cleaner
53 Pick up
54 Omega symbolizes it
55 "A.S.A.P.!"
58 Just out
59 Satirical blog item?
63 Stanford-Binet figs.
66 Cornhusker city
67 Xbox user
68 Whole bunch
69 Formal turndown
70 "Them"
71 Med. insurance group

DOWN

1 ___ Percé Indians
2 It's extracted
3 Martha's 1960's backup group
4 Book lover's prefix
5 Gilbert & Sullivan princess
6 Some museum hangings
7 Painted metalware
8 Organism with pseudopods
9 Railroad stop: Abbr.
10 "Alley ___!"
11 Brazilian novelist Jorge
12 Concealed
13 "Holy cats!"
19 "Movin' ___" ("The Jeffersons" theme)
21 Salt, for one
24 Cries of pain
25 "Certainly"
26 List heading
28 Strauss of denim
29 Nielsen of "Rocky IV"
31 "The Matrix" role
32 Old Ford
36 Give some to
37 Web site?
39 Ballpark rollout
40 Syllable from Curly
41 Cape Town coin
45 Capable, slangily
47 Prefix with -drome
48 1990's rock genre
49 Halter?
50 Wise old head
51 Frisbee maker
52 Lazarus and Goldman
56 Ending with time or life
57 ___ office
60 Key letter
61 Toil in a trireme
62 Half of a yr.
64 Iranian city
65 ___-cone

by Leonard Williams

246

★ ★

ACROSS

1 Appear
4 KLM competitor
7 Promulgate
10 Help the crew
11 Paprika-powdered serving
15 One doing checks and balances?
16 Election day: Abbr.
17 "Not true!"
18 TV cartoon dog
19 Stain
21 Bicycle maker since 1895
23 Some sports cars, for short
24 "Out of Africa" novelist Dinesen
26 Niche at Notre Dame
27 Baltic Sea viewer, maybe
28 Rudiments
29 Cleaning cloths
30 Letters in Icelandic
31 "Yay, team!"
32 Patronizes, as a restaurant
33 Make compact, with "up"
35 Groups on horseback
39 Parking place
40 Particle flux density symbols
44 Quechua-speaking
45 79 for gold, e.g.: Abbr.
46 Neither this nor that, in Peru
47 Rob Reiner's father
48 Chichén ___ (Mayan city)
49 Hearts
50 Gossipy group
52 Lug
54 In place
55 Horace's "Ars ___"
57 What's brewing, perhaps
58 Tolkien monster
59 Tempers
60 Knave
61 ___ degree
62 Lily Tomlin character Edith ___
63 Shaker ___, O.

DOWN

1 Gallery event
2 Terse verse
3 Like L, alphabetically
4 Where to order tekka maki
5 Like
6 Some dips
7 Newspaper publisher who founded the United Press
8 Briny expanse
9 Most pale
11 Beats it, out of the city
12 Not needing a prescription: Abbr.
13 Twisted
14 Restrained laugh
20 Some are wild
22 "You're going too fast for me!"
25 "Hogan's Heroes" sergeant
28 Meteor paths
29 "Do ___ Diddy Diddy" (1964 #1 hit)
32 Opposite of endo-
33 Upper body: Abbr.
34 Occidental, e.g.
35 Harasses
36 Ready for anything
37 No-go at the track
38 A dash, maybe
40 Kitty
41 Time for one doing time
42 Words of emphasis
43 Some pot scrubbers
45 Acropolis figure
48 Pointer's target
49 The New Yorker cartoonist Addams
51 Marienbad, for one
53 D with 50% off
56 Number of one-voweled, seven-letter words in this puzzle

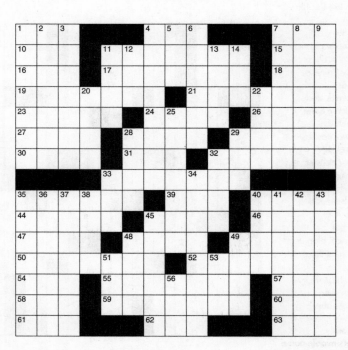

by Manny Nosowsky

ACROSS

1 Evergreen trees
5 Hammer part
9 Fit for a king
14 Massage target
15 Inauguration highlight
16 Dress type
17 . . . Boo or yoo follower
19 Jazz singer Carmen
20 "I should say ___!"
21 Actress Gaynor
22 Leaves high and dry
23 Certain OPEC minister
25 Gravity-powered vehicle
27 Lorraine's neighbor
29 Online activity
30 Functioned as
33 Unwitting tools
34 Snowy locale in a Frost poem
35 Currently "in"
36 Hightailed it
37 Manifests
38 Kind of package
39 B & B
40 Up
41 "I ___ Right to Sing the Blues"
42 Wolf's home
43 After the whistle
44 Green eggs and ham profferer, in Dr. Seuss
45 Rigatoni relative
46 Puzzles solved with a pencil
47 Circular dinner order
50 Actor's minimum
52 Atomic
55 Lies against
56 . . . Reagan's first interior secretary
58 Camp craft
59 Tall story
60 Elvis's middle name
61 Steps lightly
62 New York county
63 Lucy Lawless role

DOWN

1 Open wide
2 Cavern feature
3 . . . Oldtime radio station in a 1990's AMC series
4 Prepared
5 Trig function
6 "Chicago Hope" actress
7 Completely
8 . . . Inventor of the sewing machine
9 Certain plane engines
10 Charlton Heston title role
11 Lass
12 Art sch. class
13 Venerable Virginia family
18 Some Apples
24 Sperry's partner
26 Little shavers
27 Sap sucker
28 "Mule Train" singer, 1949
29 Onetime "Masterpiece Theatre" host
30 . . . Massachusetts birthplace of the 19th-century feminist Elizabeth Packard
31 Cardiology concern
32 Robert Fulton power source
34 . . . English river, site of the ruins of Tintern Abbey
37 Big blow
38 Rain or shine preceder
40 Pen names
41 Stares
44 Like some solutions
45 Alphabetically last top 40 rock artist
46 Polynesian language
47 Warsaw ___
48 Construction beam
49 New Mexico Indian
51 Scorch
53 George Orwell's alma mater
54 Sicilian peak
57 Candle dripping

by Stanley Newman

248 ⭐ ⭐

ACROSS

1 Dairy morsel
5 Brainy
10 Liven (up)
14 1997 Peter Fonda role
15 Certain chairmaker
16 ___ d'amore
17 Sked guesses: Abbr.
18 The Three Link Fraternity
20 City whose newspaper is the Daily Planet
22 Flip remark?
23 Jackie's second
24 Hwys.
25 Expands
26 Most October babies
28 Turner of film
29 Western wolf
30 Devotees
33 Place to play the start of 18- or 52-Across or 3- or 32-Down
37 Pokes fun at
38 "I can't ___ thing"
40 Home of the White Sands Natl. Mon.
41 It has rocks and rolls
43 Pump feature, possibly
47 Bill offerer: Abbr.
48 Optima maker
49 Lowly assistant
50 Battery type
52 Tied
54 They're usually first to raise their hands
55 It's messy
56 Behind
57 Lancelot player, 1995
58 Suffix with fabric
59 Egg containers
60 She, in Italy

DOWN

1 Breaker?
2 Hidden
3 Silver medal equivalent
4 Editor's ___
5 Lets have it
6 Hot spot
7 Williams of song
8 Ring figure
9 "N.Y.P.D. Blue" setting
10 La ___, home of the Salk Institute
11 Like ___ from the blue
12 "Holy smokes!"
13 Livens
19 "I'm not listening to you!"
21 Low fig. for Randy Johnson
25 Traditional international powerhouse in badminton
27 Womanizer
28 Surgical glove material
30 N.J. city on the Hudson
31 Above, in Berlin
32 Marks of shame
34 Slow musical passages
35 Northernmost city in North America with more than half a million people
36 Merchants not seen on the street
39 Body of water south of Orsk
41 Humans
42 "Anything else?"
43 The end
44 Turning point
45 Start of el año
46 Montana, notably
47 Lead provider
50 Enterprise rival
51 Rat's place
53 Female Wiltshire

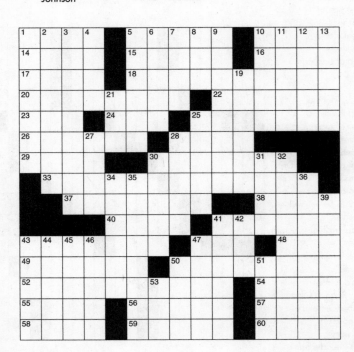

by Jim Hyres

ACROSS

1 Exemplar of grace
5 Bidder's site
9 Fancy duds
14 Stay near the shore, say
15 1963 film "___ la Douce"
16 Eyeball benders
17 Pierce portrayer on TV and film
18 C
19 Raggedy Ann and friends
20 What a scary Doris Day did on the film set?
23 Cried a river
24 Congressional committee subject
27 Slippery sort
28 Nursery noise
30 Lather
31 More miffed
34 Talking birds
36 60's muscle car
37 What the lexicographer/dairy expert did?
40 Ring master?
41 Family nickname
42 Adam of "The O.C."
43 Air ball, e.g.
45 Math ordinal
46 RR depot
47 Sounded like a chick
49 Oracle site
52 What the paranoid C.I.A. publicist did?
56 Diet guru Jenny
58 Temple University team, with "the"
59 Snack with a lickable center
60 In reserve
61 River Kwai locale, formerly
62 Gem for some Libras
63 More together

64 Hill inhabitants
65 Auditioner's goal

DOWN

1 Give and take
2 Dylan Thomas's home
3 Build on
4 Weak brew
5 Tower designer
6 Hair twist
7 Gallic girlfriend
8 Prison exercise area
9 Beckett's no-show
10 Historical periods
11 Stern lecture
12 www bookmark
13 N.B.A. stats: Abbr.
21 Land south and west of the Pyrenees
22 Post-op program
25 Referred to

26 Bedtime request
28 See 29-Down
29 With 28-Down, noted 20th-century American artist, informally
31 Little rascal
32 Kukla's puppet pal
33 Scream and holler
34 Breath freshener
35 Understated
38 Bankrolls
39 Magician's secret exit
44 Repair, as film
46 Quakes
48 Fired up
49 C sharp equivalent
50 Comedic horn honker
51 Ultimate goal
53 Sluggin' Sammy

54 Victor's cry
55 Fish dish
56 Comedian Bill, for short
57 Some strands in a cell

by Richard Leva and Nancy Salomon

250 ☆ ☆

ACROSS

1 Semiprecious stone
5 Railroad fixtures
9 Searches (through)
14 Declare
15 Progress slowly
16 Siouan language
17 Characteristic carrier
18 Plantation of literature
19 The opposition
20 Some legal tender
23 One going back and forth
25 Route abbr.
26 Short walker?
27 Time of anticipation
28 Extreme action
32 "Peer Gynt" dancer
33 Company that had a 64-page "Code of Ethics"
34 13-stringed Japanese zither
35 Urban transportation
36 "Get the lead out!"
40 Home of the Atlantic 10's Black Bears
43 Alfred ___ of 2004s "Fiddler on the Roof"
45 Court conclusion
49 Bedevil
50 Stuff in a pit
51 Middle of the 11th century
52 Cry at a light show
53 Goal of most games (and a hint to this puzzle's theme)
57 Renaissance ruler
58 Bugs
59 Primo
62 Bad treatment
63 Fuzzy Wuzzy features
64 Country cousin
65 Leveled, in London

66 College endower Cornell
67 ___ glass

DOWN

1 Sporty car, briefly
2 Park in N.Y.C., say
3 "Act now!"
4 Subject of some still lifes
5 "A Midsummer Night's Dream" queen
6 Not exactly now
7 Like raw silk
8 Whets
9 One who shall remain nameless
10 "___ Angel" (1933 comedy)
11 More round
12 Lift, so to speak

13 Answers with an attitude
21 ___ 'acte
22 Oenophile's concern
23 Mt. Rushmore's place: Abbr.
24 Ligurian Sea feeder
29 Endured
30 Breakfast or dessert dish
31 Family man
35 Perk up
37 Sushi bar order
38 Not duped by
39 "The Turtle" poet
41 No longer in service
42 In the wink ___ eye
43 Girl's name from Greek for "a bee"
44 "Mourning Becomes Electra" role

45 Johnny Carson, notably
46 "Iliad" wife
47 Major departure
48 One working on a puff piece?
54 Pink potable
55 Firm honcho
56 South Seas starch source
60 Warriors' grp.
61 Sushi bar order

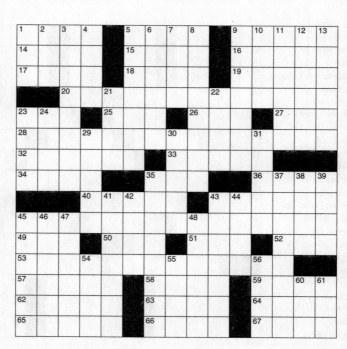

by Elizabeth C. Gorski

ACROSS

1 Actress Thompson
5 Dye-yielding plant
9 Humble in position
14 Baseball great ___ Speaker
15 Paradoxical Greek
16 Far from 9-Across
17 Actors Holm and McKellen
18 Annual Broadway event
20 Travolta musical
22 Woolly, e.g.
23 Met debutante of 1956
26 Talking computer of film
29 Bikini, for one
30 War stat.
31 Coin rating
32 Aware of
34 Baffin Islander
36 Theme of this puzzle
40 Dunk, e.g.
41 Sp. miss
42 "The Time Machine" people
43 Mattress problem
44 "Vive ___!"
49 Pick up
50 Football's Gang Green
53 Play too broadly
55 Online newsgroup system
56 Predatory players
60 Follower of H.S.
61 Crop up
62 Trusses
63 Shuttle protector
64 Like Waldorf salad apples
65 Goofball
66 Cheap digs: Abbr.

DOWN

1 Scarlet letter, e.g.
2 Genesis landfall
3 Moolah
4 Tear into
5 Cortez's victim
6 Start of some movement names
7 "Vacancy" shower
8 New Orleans campus
9 Defeater of Holyfield, 1999, for the world heavyweight title
10 Pearl Buck heroine
11 Terrier type
12 India inc.?
13 "Indeed"
19 Moira's player in "On the Beach"
21 Respectful greeting
24 Mine, in Marseille
25 Tennis's Davenport
27 ___ brat
28 Bossy but generous type, supposedly
31 "Suspicion" studio
33 Wash. setting
34 Erhard movement
35 Menaces, in a way
36 Corduroy rib
37 Understood by few
38 Hit the trails
39 So
40 Pray
43 Having had a good workout
45 Spits out
46 Painter of bathers
47 Verdi opus
48 Yucca fibers
50 Beat (out)
51 Ordinal ending
52 ___-Finnish War
54 Gds.
56 Dirty dog
57 "Exodus" hero
58 "Road" film destination
59 G, e.g., but not H

by Alan Arbesfeld

252 ★ ★

ACROSS

1 Terrif
4 "Ain't Too Proud ___"
9 Saunter
14 Education, initially?
15 Amtrak offering
16 Like some panels or flares
17 Emissions inspector's concern
19 Southern sound
20 Messenger ___
21 "Remington ___" of 1980's TV
23 Union agreement
24 "___ go!"
26 Dog option
28 Head of England
29 Sharp competitor
32 Lucy Lawless title role
33 Midway around a diamond
36 Betty ___
40 Wine that doesn't age
44 Literary governess
45 It can take the long or short view
46 Toast
50 Frederick's of Hollywood offering
51 School of tomorrow?
52 New York lake that flows into the Allegheny
56 Abrades
58 Place for many a PC
59 Limy libation
62 Degree in mathematics?
63 Very little, in recipes
65 "la Orana Maria" painter
68 Circus supporter
69 Wrinkly fruit
70 Wing it?
71 Pitiful
72 Treat unfairly
73 Doctor's charge

DOWN

1 Teutonic title
2 Hall-of-Fame football executive, longtime Steelers owner
3 Jurassic giant
4 Custom
5 "Draft Dodger Rag" singer
6 Doozy
7 "Someone ___ America" (1996 film)
8 Light, rich sponge cakes
9 Back at sea
10 Annihilate, with "down"
11 Major's successor
12 Carriage with a fold-down top
13 Cereal killer
18 Listen to your gut?
22 See 57-Down
24 It'll show you the world
25 Exxon alternative
27 Asian capital
30 Mustard, e.g.: Abbr.
31 Santa ___
34 Throw out
35 Gillespie, to fans
37 Cram
38 40-Across fancier
39 Lulls
41 Break down
42 Easter lead-in
43 ___ Torrijos Herrera, former head of Panama
47 Like a snob
48 Atmospheric pollution meas.
49 Hullabaloo
52 Seniors, e.g.
53 Couldn't help but
54 Domestic . . . or a title for this puzzle
55 What jokes are good for
57 With 22-Down, noted Taiwan-born film director
60 Ex-governor Grasso
61 Office cry
64 Camera inits.
66 Neighbor of Ger. and Hung.
67 Nevada county

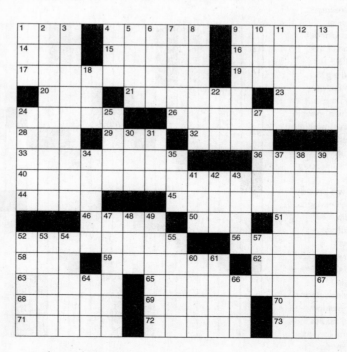

by Frank Longo

ACROSS

1 Fraternity letter
4 Battery contents
8 Oldtime actress Todd
14 Personal
15 Goof off
16 Attack
17 Stop on it
18 No neatnik
19 Anxiety
20 Cartier's Christmas creation?
23 In any way
24 Stat for Sammy Sosa
25 Thimblerig thing
27 Meal
30 Ones soon to leave the ivied halls: Abbr.
31 Subcompact
32 American Revolutionary portraitist
34 Illegal act, in slang
35 Capote's least favorite road sign?
39 Olympus competitor
40 "I'm in!"
41 Just
42 "Noble" element
43 Woven fabrics
48 Narc's employer: Abbr.
49 Fall from grace
50 12 chimes
51 Songbird's lament?
57 Sounded like a Persian
58 Point to the right
59 Driver's org.
60 Shed
61 Shade of green
62 Comic strip cry
63 Didn't go straight
64 Scored the same
65 Like few counties nowadays

DOWN

1 Drink at the Duke's Head
2 Deviate
3 Completely committed
4 Likewise
5 Massage target for a runner
6 Popular shirt maker
7 Actress Mazar
8 All ___
9 City on the Hong River
10 Tied
11 Absolute
12 "Le Cid" composer
13 Got the fare down
21 Chapter of history
22 Collar
26 Run on TV
28 Hand measure
29 Hué New Year
30 Swings around
31 Wild West
33 Big name in fashion
34 Montana Indian
35 Johnny Unitas wore it
36 Norman's home
37 Diminutive, as a dog
38 Rug rat
39 Silent agreement
42 Prepared for action
44 Gerund maker
45 Lit
46 More protracted
47 Sly
49 Computer honcho Wozniak
52 Jedi ally
53 Play Shylock
54 Hideaway
55 Man, but not woman
56 Be hot and bothered
57 Miss after marriage

by Richard Silvestri

ACROSS

1 Attention getter
5 Former company with a globelike logo
10 Pronto
14 Start of a treasure hunt instruction
15 Bone cavities
16 Area of expertise
17 Mercutio and Roméo, in Gounod's "Roméo et Juliette"
18 Stay away
20 Makes a cross for, maybe
22 Twisted, in a way
23 React badly
25 Like many a gen. or maj.
26 AOL, e.g.
27 Catch
28 "The ___ the Deal"
30 Pro in the sticks
31 Popular Don
35 Digress
39 ___ prof.
40 Unpleasant illness
41 Broadcasting
42 Credit card no.
43 "Red state" grp.
45 F.D.R. plan
46 What "Pay Toll 1 Mile" implies
52 Trojan leader who survived the fall of Troy
53 Like a defendant
54 They fill pressing needs
56 Powerful engine
58 Abba of Israel
59 C.I.A. director under Clinton and Bush
60 Opposite of morns
61 Sch. periods

62 Start of the year, to a 63-Across
63 Mex. title

DOWN

1 Sports org. since 1916
2 Big tops
3 Daggers
4 Where ships go
5 Author John Dos ___
6 Get in the game
7 Event outlawed by intl. treaty
8 It may come after you
9 Pasta topper
10 ___ nothing
11 Tuscan city
12 Diarist Nin
13 Bar in a cage
19 Rock climber's handhold
21 Solo racing boat
23 Sonia of "Kiss of the Spider Woman"
24 "Oh, sure!"
29 Thomas Moore poem "___ in the Stilly Night"
30 Quick message
31 Starter: Abbr.
32 Coyote, e.g.
33 Unpaired, as a chromosome
34 Pricey set of strings
36 Like the prepositions in 23-, 35- and 46-Across
37 Swed. butter?
38 Kind of stock
42 Grandfather of Enos
43 Artillery unit member
44 Decides one will
46 Postal conveniences: Abbr.

47 Not touch
48 When "S.N.L." ends
49 Gradually removes
50 Who discovers the perfect crime
51 Sign of an allergy
55 TV chihuahua
57 Hush-hush grp.

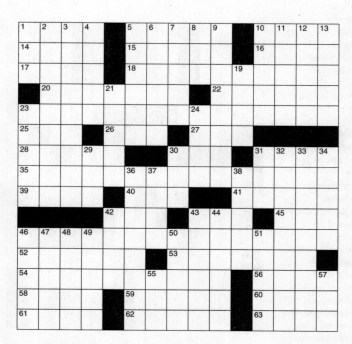

by Patrick Merrell

ACROSS

1 Chest adornment
6 Candidate for rehab
10 Somewhat, in music
14 Really go for
15 Boffo review
16 Apricot-shaped
17 Valentine's Day pastries?
19 Make rhapsodic
20 Top of a suit?
21 Mrs. Chaplin
22 Hardly suited for Mensa
23 Director Craven
24 Rainy months?
27 Sword handles
29 Pickled delicacies
30 A lot of binary code
32 Asian nurse
33 ___ mater (brain covering)
36 Subtly added mistakes? . . . or a title for this puzzle
41 Part of marbling
42 Wild revelry
43 Rainfall measure
44 Suffix with buck
45 Areas usually decorated with stained glass
48 Attempt to score in hockey?
52 New Deal inits.
55 Viking attire
56 Teen spots?
57 Sibling, e.g.: Abbr.
58 "Yikes!"
59 Fork in a mountain pass?
62 Zola heroine
63 ". . . ___ sum"
64 Try to bite
65 They lack refinement
66 It's held at eateries
67 "Later, dude!"

DOWN

1 Colorful parrot
2 Draw forth
3 Horse player's buy
4 "Exodus" hero
5 Went first
6 Father of the Titans
7 Port south of Osaka
8 Time to revel, perhaps
9 Hi-___ graphics
10 Pretend to be
11 Pizza places
12 Playground retort
13 Bygone
18 Stallion, once
22 Indian metropolis
25 2004 Boston conventioneers, informally
26 One of a Navy elite
28 Sun Devils' sch.
30 Clocked out
31 Anti-Brady Bill org.
32 In the least
33 Line of suits?
34 "Monsters, ___" (2001 animated film)
35 Bone china component
37 Column style
38 Will or fist preceder
39 Really eager
40 Pizza
44 Nike rival
45 Blessing evoker
46 Swimming site
47 Suds holders
48 Minutes taker, maybe
49 Former Indiana senator Richard
50 Really dumb
51 Needing a lift
53 5/8/45
54 Prince Valiant's lady
59 Hesitation sound
60 Public radio host Glass
61 Compete

by Lee Glickstein

256 ★ ★

ACROSS

1 Prefix with industry
5 Pace
9 Malfunction
14 City whose major league baseball team was once named the Naps
16 Dirt
17 Domestic animal thought to bring good luck
18 Persian Gulf noblemen
19 Quiet end?
20 Was outstanding
21 Charge for cash
22 Country for which a cat was named
24 Readies for drilling
26 Mrs. Victor Laszlo
27 "___ With Love"
29 Singer Edith
30 Back lot lot
31 "Little House on the Prairie" family name
33 Airplane wing parts
35 Southern titleholder
40 Adagio and allegro
41 Scalding, as coffee
42 Job for a barber
45 Snookums
47 Fastens, in a way
48 Words that are a treat to hear?
49 Archangel of salvation
51 One available in Mex.
52 Pays off
54 Newbery-winning author ___ Lowry
56 Mother: Var.
57 Personality
58 Plan for vacations
60 Directly from the side
61 Vaudeville performances
62 Seed's exterior

63 Old talk show host Joe
64 Johann who wrote the Swiss national anthem

DOWN

1 Habituate
2 Flowers with sword-shaped leaves
3 Studio output
4 Egg: Prefix
5 Rodeo sight
6 Prepare to skate
7 Cause for suppression of evidence
8 July hrs. in Vegas
9 Adopt-___
10 Post-disaster appointments
11 Hardly anything

12 Discord
13 Stand in for
15 Prefix with system
21 Of equal speed
23 Blow it
25 Vacation isle
28 Center of a former empire
32 Aura
34 General ___ chicken
36 Rigging support
37 Site for people in white coats
38 Kellogg's brand
39 Words in "The Little Mermaid" after "The human world . . ."
42 University of Ohio athlete
43 Prepare for a massage, perhaps
44 Flexes one's zygomatic muscles

46 Royal's attendant
50 Monarch's loyal subject
53 Aretha Franklin's Grammy-nominated sister
55 Dir. for a ship
58 Recipe amt.
59 Turn left

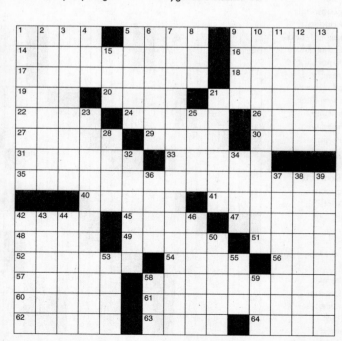

by Patrick Merrell

ACROSS

1 Strip ___
5 Favored by God
10 Wielding a peeler, maybe
14 Locket shape
15 Instant message sender, perhaps
16 Disney lioness
17 Purse item
18 Popular group dance
20 Like dessert wines
22 Top-2% group
23 "Ich bin ___ Berliner"
24 Travelers' org.
26 Plod along
28 Toasters do it
34 River islet
35 Farmer's letters?
36 Salinger title girl
40 Desk set item
44 Van ___, Calif.
45 Enter again
46 Neighbor of Braz.
47 Four-runner?
51 Break into parts, as a monopoly
54 Hoo-ha
55 Notebook maker
56 Unwelcome forecast
60 Potter's potions professor
64 One with a half-interest
67 Laundry item
68 Earthen pot
69 Commercial prefix with liner
70 Grant for a film?
71 Lone Star State sch.
72 Rodeo critter
73 Girl or boy lead-in

DOWN

1 Comfy footwear
2 Swear to
3 ___ duck
4 Lands' End competitor
5 Dickensian epithet
6 Warp-and-weft machine
7 Actress Sommer
8 Glimpsed
9 Soap opera meetings
10 A Beatle bride
11 In one's natural state
12 Movie set light: Var.
13 John of "Miracle on 34th Street"
19 Peel
21 1970's Japanese P.M. ___ Fukuda
25 Not "fer"
27 Worked with
28 ___ Crunch
29 Place
30 Humble response to praise
31 Pick up
32 Felt under the weather
33 Taints
37 Most of it nowadays is filtered
38 ___ mortals
39 Many an M.I.T. grad: Abbr.
41 U.S.A.F. rank
42 "Nana" author
43 Old oath
48 Sign of disuse
49 Self-assurance
50 Friend on "Friends"
51 Exquisite trinket
52 Letter-shaped fastener
53 Prepare to get shot?
57 Water holder
58 Course on insects, for short
59 Fork-tailed flier
61 "I smell ___"
62 Left side
63 "Only Time" singer
65 Quick rest
66 Bird in the "Arabian Nights"

by James M. Jenista and Dana McLemore

258 ⋆ ⋆

ACROSS

1 Chicken coop material
5 Idiosyncrasies
9 Where captains go
14 Others, in Latin
15 Suffix with depend
16 Not upright
17 Aardvark feature
19 With 13-Down, "I'll get those guys!"
20 Makes a dazzling entrance
22 Furrow maker
23 Revolutionary leader
24 Pact
27 Saucy
28 Garden party?
31 Calculus calculation
32 French author who co-founded La Nouvelle Revue Française
33 Epitome of grace
34 Screens, filters and such
37 Spheres
38 Major success
39 Échecs piece
40 Kind of cross
41 Expensive box
42 Word with salt or root
43 Kay who sang "Wheel of Fortune," 1952
45 City on the Oka
46 "Indiana Jones" genre
52 With 12-Down, fiery guy?
53 Common football spread
54 Granny and Windsor
55 Dagger part
56 Fax button
57 Horse ___

58 Part of Y.S.L.
59 Western tourist destination

DOWN

1 Washington locale, with "the"
2 "The Time Machine" race
3 Belt, perhaps
4 Sinatra standard
5 Got tight
6 "Peace ___ time"
7 Bra spec
8 Squared accounts
9 Scout's find
10 Cheri of "S.N.L."
11 "Waiting for God" philosopher
12 See 52-Across
13 See 19-Across
18 Squirrel, to 35-Down

21 "___ stand" (Martin Luther declaration)
24 Kind of tie
25 Santa ___, Calif.
26 It may be spontaneous
27 It comes in fits
29 Famous phrase-turner
30 Long key
32 Place settings, collectively
33 Quick appraisal of legitimacy
35 Proverbial start of great things
36 Acts like a peacock
41 Taoism founder
42 Family matters?
44 Salon supply
45 Reproductive cell
46 Names a price
47 Punish, in a way

48 Mid sixth-century year
49 Iris container
50 Western vacation destination
51 Pulls the plug on

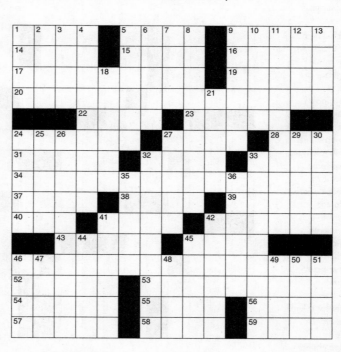

by Byron Walden

ACROSS

1 Light ___
6 Defender of some unpopular causes, in brief
10 "Jabberwocky" starter
14 Father ___ Sarducci of "S.N.L."
15 Game delayer
16 "I can't ___ thing!"
17 Comedy troupe since the 60's
20 Org. with bomb-sniffing dogs
21 Gull-like predator
22 Enter cautiously
23 The Joads, e.g.
25 Features of some cell phones
26 Breakfast bowlful
28 "Really?!"
29 Milk: Prefix
30 Gives a rap
31 Hogwarts letter carrier
34 Bellicose god
35 Propelled a shell
36 Peau de ___ (soft cloth)
37 Part of w.p.m.
38 Orbital point
39 ___ nova
40 Slips on a slip
42 Housekeeper, at times
43 Lights into
45 Margaret Mead study site
46 From there
47 Geeky sort
48 Nashville sch.
51 Momentous
54 Double contraction
55 Egyptian Christian
56 Bubbling over
57 Poetic adverb
58 Gas brand in Canada
59 Like unwashed rugs

DOWN

1 Fuji competitor
2 Exec
3 Military part-timers
4 Chemical suffix
5 "William Tell" composer
6 Giant slain by Hermes
7 Water-to-wine site
8 Beyond tipsy
9 Cold
10 Prickly plant
11 London rail hub
12 Places in the heart
13 Composer Camille Saint-___
18 Swedish chain
19 Chair designer Charles
24 Hobby shop stock
25 Nuclei
26 Brouhaha
27 Bern's river
28 MTV teen toon
30 Broadway rosters
32 Cheeky
33 Shakespearean king
35 Shimmer
36 Passable
38 "If I Were ___ Man"
39 Short end of the stick
41 Blusterer
42 1960's–70's Dodge
43 Had home cooking
44 Parasol's offering
45 Brief tussle
47 Drops off
49 Piqued state
50 Beyond homely
52 Sounds from Santa
53 Baseball card stat.

by Rob Richardson

ACROSS

1 Airspeed ratio indicator
10 Full of activity
15 One way to repent?
16 Soprano Fleming
17 A commitment must be made here
19 Gracious loser
20 "Sad ___ . . ."
21 Low
22 Support for a bill
24 Tsuris, so to speak
26 Pacific arm
32 Lexicon topic
36 Post-O.R. stop, perhaps
37 Catalog abbr.
38 Made waves?
39 They're spotted on beaches
43 Kind of acid used to make soap
44 Russia/China border river
45 Prefix with conscious
46 More terrible
47 Cause for pause
50 By the agency of
52 Take in slowly
53 It'll never fly
56 "When We Were Very Young" writer
60 Old film vamp Pola
64 Stuffy stretch
67 1990's sitcom
68 Worthy of respect
69 Primed
70 Gulfweeds

DOWN

1 Route revealers
2 Straddling
3 Madison Avenue award
4 Son of William the Conqueror
5 Hand holder?
6 Pamplona pronoun
7 Goatee, e.g.
8 Rubik of cube fame
9 Essex contemporaries
10 Question after an accident
11 Track transaction
12 "One" on a one
13 Bubkes
14 Philosopher for whom a paradox is named
18 Unseasoned
23 Seasoned
25 Morales of movies
26 Certain rifle stand
27 Source of some stomachaches
28 Schoolbag item
29 Athenian meeting places
30 Wonderland message
31 It contains tracks
33 Cellulose fiber brand
34 Big name in insurance
35 Pelé's given name
40 Capital on the Dnieper
41 Bitterness
42 Camera component
48 Place for a concession
49 High-culture entertainment
51 Put on
53 It can come before after
54 Square ___
55 Pac Ten powerhouse
57 Sprawls
58 Pathfinder's parent
59 ___ 'acte
61 Wedgelike metal strips in a machine shop
62 Caramel candy from Hershey
63 Midmonth time
65 "First Blood" director Kotcheff
66 Nonsharing type

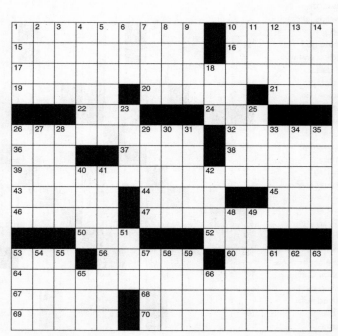

by Ed Early

ACROSS

1 Writing that lacks objectivity
16 Purveyors of spicy cuisine
17 "Hurry, you'll be late"
18 Tpks.
19 Full house sign
20 Patriot, e.g.: Abbr.
21 Old map abbr.
22 "Look ___!"
24 One going back and forth to work
26 Replacement raiser
30 Loses
34 When Nora leaves Torvald in "A Doll's House"
35 Man wearing une couronne
37 Follow
38 It's often hit at night
40 Musicians whom orchestras tune up to
42 Work unit
43 Daughter of Hyperion
45 Beat in November, perhaps
46 It's on the Rhone delta
48 Some tracks
50 Kind of cart
52 Sticking point?
53 Elicitors of little dances, briefly
56 Wing
58 Alternative to Rep. or Dem.
59 67-Across citers: Abbr.
62 August comment
66 Like Scorsese, but not Fellini
67 It begins "A well regulated Militia . . ."

DOWN

1 Member of the Allies in W.W. II: Abbr.
2 Expressed surprise
3 R.F.K. Stadium team, briefly
4 Proactiv target, informally
5 Aeschylus trilogy
6 Legendary 49ers receiver
7 Charles of CBS News
8 Uintah and Ouray Reservation inhabitant
9 Madrid maze-runner
10 Ices, maybe
11 Bakery output
12 John
13 "Last one ___ . . ."
14 Boarding places: Abbr.
15 Religious title: Abbr.
22 Start of an Ella Fitzgerald standard
23 Old map abbr.
25 Reply to "The phone's for you"
26 Mullah's decree
27 Fall shade
28 Composition of some nerves?
29 Ski-___
31 "The Other Side of Oz" autobiographer
32 Coup follower
33 Ways: Abbr.
36 Osteoarthritis treatment
39 Silent lawman?
41 Public
44 It might be filled with ink
47 Like guests at home
49 Message on a dirty car
51 Tons
53 "I'm pointing at it"
54 Act feeblemindedly
55 Disconnected, in mus.
57 Large moth
59 Inits. on many A.T.M.'s
60 Sheepskin leather
61 Volunteer babysitter, maybe
63 Inits. in 70's-80's rock
64 Leg that gets whistled at
65 Net holder

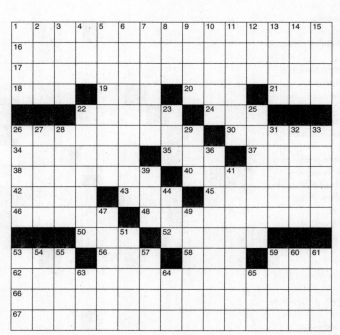

by David Levinson Wilk

262

★ ★ ★

ACROSS

1 Some pizza slices, e.g.
8 They employ speakers
15 Army E-7
17 One good at making faces
18 Moved like molasses
19 Plant holder?
20 Needles
21 1971 U.S. Open winner ___ Smith
22 Launch
24 It's sold in bars
25 A abroad
26 Modern company category
28 A abroad
29 Modified
31 Like British bishops
33 Time to attack
34 2004 P.G.A. Player of the Year
35 Dreamliner developer
37 Miss Gulch miffed her
40 Ovidian openings
41 Contact lens solutions
43 N.L. West team, on scoreboards
44 Home on the range: Var.
46 Moselle feeder, to Moselle natives
47 South-of-the-border spouses: Abbr.
48 End of ___
50 36-Down, por ejemplo
51 Island in the East China Sea
52 1995 Annie Lennox hit
55 "Maybe yes, maybe no"
56 Be made up
57 Worried about, slangily

DOWN

1 Anti
2 Satan, to Scots
3 Fictional swinger
4 When some people retire
5 Sud's opposite
6 ___ T
7 Whiny one
8 Infected
9 Chorus bit
10 Sponsorship
11 Lessor's list
12 Gloater's remark
13 Narrow, in a way
14 Lineate
16 Not impromptu
22 Caviar fish
23 Potential vote-getter
26 Pluto and others
27 Change places?
30 "___ get it!"
32 ___ Friday's
34 Auto options
35 Like some gardens
36 Ciudad Bolivar is on it
37 With lightness
38 Wipeout?
39 Bullyragged
42 Driving aid, of sorts
45 Hotel room amenities
47 ___ lot (is telling)
49 First drawing class, perhaps
51 Only
53 Mountain road section
54 Binding declaration

by Jim Hyres

ACROSS

1 See
5 Flexible prefix
9 Cries for attention
14 Summoning
16 With 13-Down, places for shooting stars
17 Bit
18 Take ___ (break)
19 They have African cousins
21 An eagle is on its flag
22 Pattern of scanning lines on a TV
23 They can be choppy
24 Bill for fine clothing?
27 Argonaut who slew Castor
29 "Bob & Carol & Ted & Alice" co-star
32 Hard-rock center
35 One in a shelter, maybe
36 ___ particle
37 Is in charge
40 Beautiful people of literature
41 "___ in the Park" (Rodgers and Hart song)
42 He wrote a hit Broadway musical with Weill
46 Parts of some joints
48 ___ ready
49 Rank last attained in 1950
53 Imminent, old-style
54 Harmless reptile with a dangerous-sounding name
55 "Somebody's Knockin'" singer ___ Gibbs
56 Wannabe's efforts
57 Easy ___

58 Auto performance factor, informally
59 Start of Massachusetts' motto

DOWN

1 Beards
2 Repay, in a way
3 "See?!"
4 Dwarf
5 Piles
6 Entangle
7 Not merely warm
8 Like some commerce
9 Far Eastern female servants
10 "Good night, sweet prince" speaker
11 Now level
12 Cold northerly winds of southern France
13 See 16-Across

15 ___ lot (very little)
20 Late
24 Sans subtlety
25 Jedi protector
26 Many a surfer
28 Cold war abbr.
30 Abbr. in a birth announcement
31 Med. specialty
32 Whiz
33 Premium product
34 Mediterranean succulent
38 Early form of Greek
39 Understanding, of sorts
43 Transportation in a 1941 hit song
44 Military toppers
45 Amazon warrior killed by Achilles
47 One of Hamlet's courtiers

48 Novelist Tina McElroy ___
49 ___ morgana (mirage)
50 Behind
51 Down
52 Some bent pipes

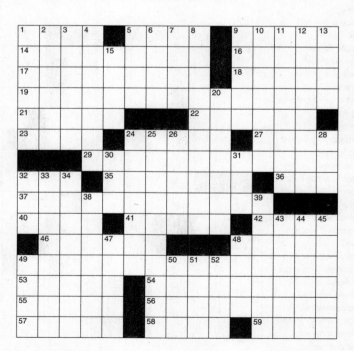

by Eric Berlin

264

★ ★ ★

ACROSS

1 Soup line
9 Erased
14 One might request help getting started
16 Inclined . . . or flat
17 Makes something up
18 Roman land
19 Company once taken over by Carl Icahn
20 "So sorry"
22 Mr., abroad
24 Southwestern sign-off
25 Reminds a bit too much
26 Like Indians
28 Suffix with jardin
29 Irish Sea feeder
30 Jazz fan, most likely
32 Rubens painted her
35 Decor finish?
37 Figs. in identify theft
38 Goes off
42 Like a lottery winner, typically
46 Boomer's kid
47 He played J-Bone in "Johnny Mnemonic"
49 Quaint schoolroom item
50 "No ___!"
52 Beau's belle
54 Carmaker since 1949
55 Layabouts
58 Opposite of always, in Augsburg
59 Round window
60 Tender shoot?
62 First name in TV talk
63 Whip snapper
64 They're perfect
65 Cross the line?

DOWN

1 Best Supporting Actor for "The Fortune Cookie," 1966
2 She served eight days in jail for public obscenity
3 Sub-Saharan scourge
4 Year for Super Bowl LXXXIV
5 Exploit
6 Where the Enola Gay plane was built
7 Start of a Beatles title
8 Olympic team?
9 Vision: Prefix
10 DuPont trademark
11 Made impossible
12 Steams up
13 Hypersaline spot
15 In places
21 Sub-Saharan scourge
23 1986 Indy 500 winner
27 ___ forces
31 "Ixnay"
33 Italian province
34 Gets back to, quickly
36 Foosball locale
38 Look into
39 Like some copies
40 Mentor's companion
41 Manager's terse order
43 It's a short walk from Copacabana
44 Celebrity-spotting eatery
45 "A diamond is forever" sloganeer
48 "Key Largo" Oscar winner
51 Fee to enter a poker game
53 Daughter of Zeus
56 Period in sch.
57 Out-of-commission cruisers
61 Feather holder?

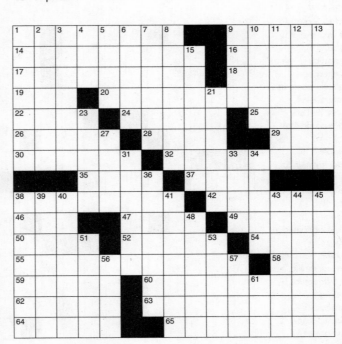

by David Quarfoot

ACROSS

1 Antique store?
7 Violin components
15 Make a ball
16 Ladle
17 Secrets
18 Holder of an afternoon service
19 French flag color, in France
20 "Shoot!"
21 Where workers may do the daily grind?
22 Excited pointer's comment
24 1999-2001 Broadway musical revue
25 Editorial cartoonist Rall
28 Listener
29 From, in some names
30 Former Washington duo
37 Stepped in like Superman
38 Somehow
39 Resort of a sort
40 Old TV control abbr.
41 Old protest grp.
42 2000 Olympic gymnast ___ Ray
45 Rhoda's sister on "Rhoda"
48 Passiontide time
49 Dogsbody, so to speak
50 Mark of distinction
54 Isabel Allende's birthplace
56 Meet, as expectations
57 Child's cry at a parade, perhaps
58 "Harrumph!"
59 Kids' game sites
60 Preceder of many a goal

DOWN

1 Unpopular worker
2 Cast
3 Sea predator
4 National headquarters of J.C. Penney, Dr Pepper and Frito-Lay
5 Paper strip for old computer data
6 Energy Star org.
7 Toledo twinkler
8 Command to a dog
9 Just so
10 Fail to keep
11 Surrounded by
12 "Dona ___ Pacem" (Latin hymn)
13 Plays for a sucker
14 Ancient burial stone
20 Popular snack chip
23 One of The Jacksons
24 Fates
25 Kind of salad
26 Zip
27 British title
29 Castle with many steps
31 Paper carrier
32 Part of a sentence: Abbr.
33 Showy bird's mate
34 Famous name in newspaper publishing
35 Like many a mistake
36 Kin of -ists
42 Fashion designer Perry
43 Olympus alternative
44 Hero of Charles Frazier's "Cold Mountain"
45 Topper with a tab
46 Voluptuaries
47 Places for many stained-glass windows
49 Tender in Tijuana
51 First name among clothiers
52 Huntsman Center players
53 Work with mail
55 Old TV's ___ Club
56 Narrow waterway

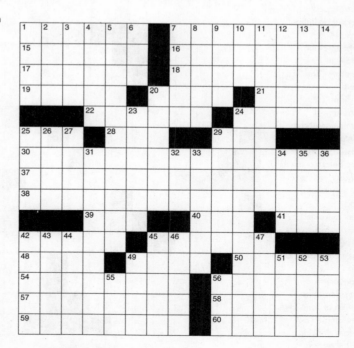

by Harvey Estes

266

★ ★ ★

ACROSS

1 Accusatory words
5 Certain red algae
12 Potting materials
14 Clicker
15 Native up north
16 Essayist whose motto was "Que sais-je?"
17 10 kilogauss
18 It has many soap slots
19 Plans to get back at
21 "Dog Barking at the Moon" painter, 1926
22 Comes back
23 Name on some briefs
24 Provide with new squares, perhaps
25 Insults wittily
26 It isn't repeated
28 Land at an Italian airport?
31 Captain of the Ghost, in Jack London's "The Sea Wolf"
34 William ___, secretary of commerce under Clinton
35 Casserole dishes
37 Day before a Jewish holiday
38 Passing legend
40 Go
42 They're treated by veterinarios
43 Turned over
44 Floor coverings, to a Brit
45 Pronunciation considerations
46 Cousin of Jane Eyre
47 One singled out before drinking
48 It's full of slots, briefly

DOWN

1 Martyred Carmelite nun ___ Stein
2 Music critic's bane
3 One tying up a turkey, say
4 Exercise, in Exeter
5 Brazilian port known for coffee
6 Artificial flavor base
7 Petal product: Var.
8 Number one
9 Not stopped
10 Many Madrileños
11 They're good at taking things down
13 Legally punishable
14 Starbucks slip-ons
16 Make a mess of
20 Woman in Chekhov's "The Sea-Gull"
23 Chart climber
25 Literary character who debuted in "The Curse of Capistrano"
27 Beat up
28 City on the Salentine Peninsula
29 Warner Music Group label
30 Looks up to
32 Involves
33 Order lover
34 Not be able to take
35 One way of fitting
36 Big bore
38 Pop singer McCartney
39 Leader of a 1970 military coup
41 Theme of Nabokov's "Lolita"

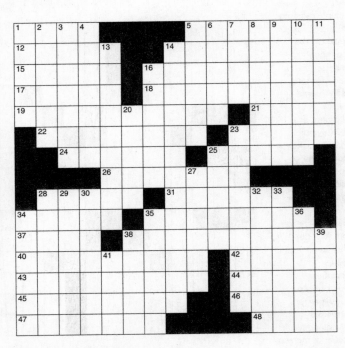

by Brendan Emmett Quigley

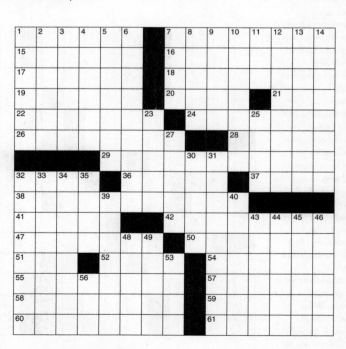

ACROSS

1 Didn't immediately go on
7 "Don't fall for that"
15 Title bandit in a Verdi opera
16 Postseason event
17 Some fertile regions
18 Bottle label
19 Disorderly type?
20 It doesn't require a full deck
21 Yvette's years
22 G.P.S. device, at times
24 Botanical beards
26 Shout to a cabbie
28 "Scarface" setting
29 Back together
32 Locks up
36 Comic introduction?
37 Figs. in bank records
38 Teller's area
41 Teaser
42 Not in harm's way
47 Best
50 "With Reagan" writer
51 Wall St. purchase
52 Better writing
54 Seven of 1,000,000
55 Arduous
57 Quickly
58 Checking one's territory
59 Beat one's gums
60 Antiphon
61 Like patent leather

DOWN

1 Piano trio
2 Playground retort
3 Loosen
4 Ruthless governor
5 One passing
6 Not straight
7 Native Nigerians
8 Big name in small trucks
9 Not just say
10 Record
11 ___ Friday's
12 Rappers' sounds
13 Emphatic concurrence
14 Annual celestial display
23 Kitchen aid
25 Sets a setter on, say
27 Spelling and others
30 Calling
31 "Is that a fact?!"
32 Wolf in sheep's clothing, e.g.
33 Something auto-dialed?
34 Star treks?
35 ___ Hills (edge of the San Fernando Valley)
39 Totals
40 Primary
43 Smooth, to Solti
44 Many of the Founding Fathers
45 Actress Chandler and others
46 Catch sight of
48 Gild
49 Long rides?
53 Cast leader?
56 Sometime PC supporter

by Sherry O. Blackard

268 ★ ★ ★

ACROSS

1 Easily swindled sort
5 Baby with big eyes
10 They're not good
14 Like some hurricanes
15 ___ Island
16 Secluded spot
17 Fine-tuner
18 Midlevel math course
20 Some important decisions
22 Really let have it
23 Wreathes
24 Loud succession of sounds
25 It's debatable
26 Mouth burner
29 Goes over
32 Fictional mariner and others
34 Dam, e.g.
35 You might get into it before going under
37 Jet pump for fluid withdrawal
39 Carrier with Tokyo hdqrs.
40 George ___, German-American artist known for vitriolic caricature
42 Some wines
43 13-Down creator
45 Old empire member
47 Singer Cantrell
48 Leaves in the kitchen
52 Academy offering
54 Picture tube
55 Historic ship that sank on Christmas Day
57 Ned Beatty's role in "Superman"
58 Bureau: Abbr.
59 River through Newark, England
60 1955 Tony winner for "Quadrille"
61 Source of some pressure, maybe
62 Go (along)
63 Lummoxes

DOWN

1 It may hang on a pot
2 Like Filipinos
3 Not inadvertent
4 Some pianos
5 Appendixes, e.g.
6 For what purpose
7 Quick survey
8 Teachers' degs.
9 It's ball-bearing
10 Advance
11 Stalwarts
12 Two-time Newbery winner ___ Lowry
13 Funny number
19 Ones keeping a firm balance?
21 African beauty
24 Get going
27 Place for a tap
28 "___ to Hold" (1943 film musical)
29 Spoils
30 1990's transportation secretary
31 Just by scanning
33 Department store area
36 Soap opera creator ___ Phillips
38 Corporation whose stock symbol is KO
41 They send things up
44 Real bitter-ender
46 Compact
49 Mustered
50 Imagine
51 Animal shelters
52 Order ender
53 Carry on
54 Syrup brand
56 Big inits. in 1970's TV

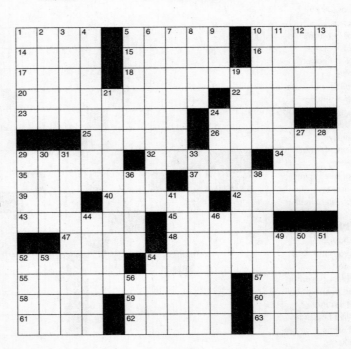

by Dana Motley

ACROSS

1 "Regarding what was just said . . ."
16 Make it louder
17 "C'est la vie"
18 Hotfoots it
19 Milk sources
20 ___ gratia (in all kindness): Lat.
21 Newspaper section
22 Some computer messages
24 Like la mer: Abbr.
25 Windy City rail inits.
26 Twist of the head?
27 It's read online
29 Large-minded
31 Family that founded America's first theme park
32 Some course requirements
33 "For ___ be Queen o' the May": Tennyson
34 The right stuff
37 Stuffed sole stuffing
41 Like a good turkey
42 It comes with laurels
43 Member of a corp. board
44 Directional suffix
45 Bone brace
47 Like a mudhole
48 Dries, as hay
50 Loaded
51 Outcomes of some talks
52 "Possibly"
55 Set the record straight on something personal
56 Like a done deal

DOWN

1 Have some pull
2 1960's-90's Indonesian president
3 Like some mathematical curves
4 They're usually placed in the middle of the table
5 Sen. Feingold
6 Quick
7 Noted erupter of May 18, 1980
8 Wagon train locale
9 Choppers
10 Nautical imperative
11 Play cat and mouse (with)
12 Very smooth
13 Unconscious
14 Distinguished
15 Chicken flavorers in a Chinese restaurant
22 Ishmael's people
23 On a mission for
26 Missionary writings
28 Whiz
30 Some Connecticut collegians
31 Store first opened in Detroit in 1962
33 Firm control, metaphorically
34 Ipecac and others
35 Italian violinist Giuseppe ___
36 Kicker
37 Choose, as an icon
38 Like some rules
39 TV sponsor's concern
40 What Romeo and Juliet did
42 The Witch of the South
46 Used leverage
47 "Mountain," in Hawaii
49 "Land," in central Asia
51 Model behavior?
53 Hapsburg domain: Abbr.
54 Wanna-___

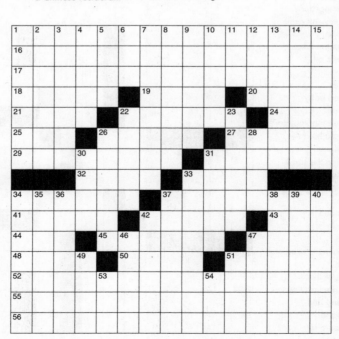

by Manny Nosowsky

270

★ ★ ☆

ACROSS

1 Sheets
7 Rub
15 Flowering plant with prickly leaves
16 Funnelform flora
17 Like part of the heart
18 Periods of decline
19 Garage sale?
20 Neighbors of Indians
21 Breadwinner
22 Circus pioneer Ringling and others
23 Magazine contents
25 "___ Secretary," Madeleine Albright's 2003 autobiography
30 Lie very, very still
35 Wolfish
36 Be on the take
38 Throws off
39 Secret
40 Slaves
41 Bullied baby, maybe
42 Mouse manipulator?
43 It might hold the solution
49 Having the same concentration of salt as mammalian blood
54 Pounded
55 Cousin of a sego
56 "Fighting" collegiate team
57 Is older than
58 ___ Sea between Ireland and England
59 Concurring comment
60 O.K.

DOWN

1 Put on
2 Prefix with syllabic
3 Like rhinos vis-à-vis elephants
4 Like some elephants
5 Ride
6 They can cause eruptions
7 It's simple to solve
8 Inclines
9 Recipe parts
10 Kind of steak
11 Shrub of the genus Indigofera
12 Film
13 Trails
14 Latin infinitive
24 Its currency is the dirham: Abbr.
25 Number associated with a boom
26 Emblem of life
27 Prayer addressee, in Paris
28 Unwelcome dining discovery
29 Work well together
30 Surveyor's map
31 Italian island reef
32 Follower of myself
33 Cry
34 Travels at a speed of
35 Home of San José
37 It may involve a homophone
41 Yeast, e.g.
42 "Benjamin"
44 Drones, say
45 Dispensary stock
46 Pool
47 "The State and Revolution" writer
48 A famous one was issued at Nantes
49 Parenting challenges
50 1980's Geena Davis sitcom
51 City once named Provo Bench
52 Tendency, as of events
53 Moonfish

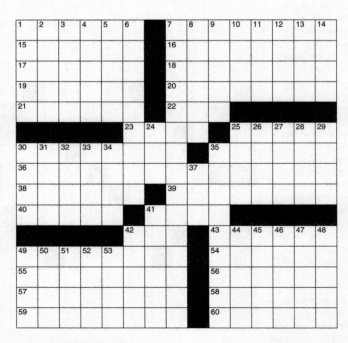

by Philip C. Ordway

ACROSS

1 Light show?
16 Small player
17 Big 12 team
18 Math ratio
19 It's made in Japan
20 Press
21 Bit of shrink rap?
24 Frequent portrait subject
26 Incoming clutter
29 Vet's memory, maybe
31 Rest of the afternoon
35 Coin with 12 stars on it
36 Often-dunked item
38 "I don't buy it"
39 Bug elimination
42 In danger of snapping
43 Belafonte catchword
44 Fool on the ice
45 Evergreen shrubs
47 Casual states?
48 European tongue
49 Jabba the ___ of "Star Wars"
51 Match maker?
53 Navy noncom
55 Farm butter
57 Quintillionth: Prefix
60 Kingdoms by the sea
65 Hogan's hero?
66 Pet expression?

DOWN

1 Pou ___ (vantage point), from the Greek
2 Tees off
3 Bones connected to fibulae
4 One whom everyone is for
5 Contents of some urns
6 Brother of un padre
7 Follower or Lenin or Stalin
8 "Our Gang" assent
9 They're often held under water
10 Cacklers
11 It might be struck south of the border
12 Annexation justification
13 Hebrew for "delight"
14 Highlander's weapon
15 Attention-getters
22 Form of ether
23 Like cornstalks
25 T'ang dynasty poet
26 Otto preceder
27 Relatively white
28 Rice-___
30 Road Runner cartoon backgrounds
32 More likely to retire
33 Does very poorly, in slang
34 Coy compliment response
37 "Now I remember!"
40 Steady
41 Move imperceptibly
46 Pace
50 Certain Sri Lankan
52 Kristy's "Little Darlings" co-star
53 Italian term of endearment
54 P.E.I., e.g.
56 Dramatic opening?
58 Mary in the White House
59 ___ cat
60 Year in the reign of England's King Stephen
61 Fictional uncle
62 Sparks setting: Abbr.
63 Drink additive?
64 Line part: Abbr.

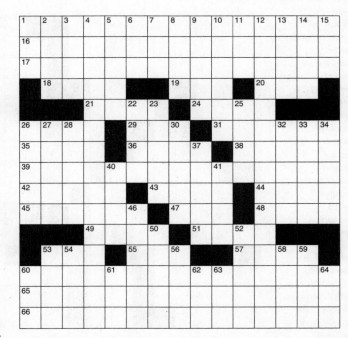

by Harvey Estes

ACROSS

1 You may pretend to pick one
10 Chewed stimulant
14 He had a 2004 #1 hit "Drop It Like It's Hot"
15 Capital 12,000 feet above sea level
16 Willful ones?
17 "Take ___" (office order)
18 NPR reporter Shapiro
19 Title boy genius of a 1991 film
20 It might be neutral
21 Gets hot
23 "Who'da thunk it?!"
24 One of Bolivia's official languages
26 Campus grps.
28 Surprises with a call
30 Adenauer's successor as German chancellor
32 Word of admonishment
33 Native New Yorkers
35 Taker of two tablets
36 No-parking area
39 Preferably
42 "Kiss Hollywood Good-by" memoirist
44 Introduction to chemistry?
45 Virtuoso
46 Idyllic spot
48 Keypad locales
49 Dickens
50 Middle-of-the-roaders: Abbr.
52 Multiple of VI
53 Baked, in Bologna
54 Erroneous claim about a superhero
56 Fatty liquid
57 Hoi polloi
58 Sable or Montego, for short
59 It's graded subjectively

DOWN

1 "Shall We Dance" co-star
2 Not right
3 W.W. II icon on a 1999 stamp
4 Landed
5 "___ Oxford" (Ved Mehta memoir)
6 Name holder
7 Blew the whistle
8 Yes-men
9 QB protectors
10 Twinings offering
11 It gets little consideration
12 Best Director of 1997
13 Kind of dye
15 Dinner spinner?
22 Bluff, maybe
24 "That's ___ excuse for . . ."
25 Word with white, red or black
27 Rupee earner
29 Volt per ampere
31 Gave out
34 ___-Off (windshield cover brand)
36 Fourth steps in some sequences
37 Stuck
38 Prehistoric stone chips
40 Some royal coats
41 Like the best outlook
43 They can be overloaded
47 "Battlestar Galactica" commander
51 Fix
53 Modern address part
54 Rock suffix
55 E.T.O. transport

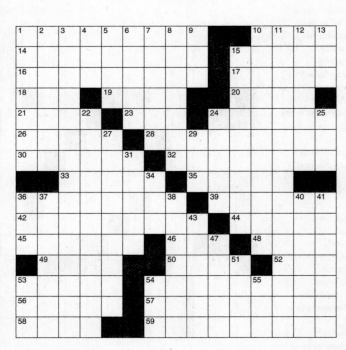

by David Quarfoot

ACROSS

1 Royal protection
12 Swift quality
15 Vitamin C, e.g.
16 "Another Green World" musician
17 1990's White House chief of staff
18 Largest U.S. youth org.
19 Certain connection makers
20 Gets the word out?
22 Whom auditors audit
23 Remiss
25 Hangouts
26 Spherical cereal
27 Little jingle
28 Custom
29 Representation of tuning fork sounds
31 List
33 Route markers
35 RR place
38 Infrangible
39 Directory data: Abbr.
40 Solara, for one
42 Friend of "Ralphie boy"
44 Words of resignation
45 Person who's authorized to shorten a sentence
46 Former New York senator
47 Tanning need
48 Alternative to eBay
52 Sight seer
53 1996 Emmy-winning role in a sitcom
54 Lottery-running org.
55 Game that involves opening a door

DOWN

1 Political columnist Thomas
2 Lacks of energy
3 One who sings but maybe shouldn't
4 Inflammatory stuff
5 Runners
6 What cribs are used for
7 Array on a bar shelf
8 It's fruit-flavored
9 Inked art, for short
10 Key word
11 Steadily took in
12 It always has a home
13 Raid targets
14 Warmed by the fire
21 Animate
22 Bird ___
23 Consumes with flair
24 Puts forth
26 It literally means "thing to wear"
29 Slangy greeting
30 Verb for a historian
31 Victorian-era novelist
32 Indiana-born composer/writer
33 Busy times at fast-food restaurants
34 Sets off
35 Composer of the opera "Brandenburgers in Bohemia"
36 Eight-line verse form
37 Newspaper inits. since 1851
38 Former Falcons coach Dan
40 Acquire
41 Put down
43 Word immediately preceding some signatures
44 More like a swami
46 The Great ___ (Victor Borge's nickname)
49 Some Eng. majors get them
50 Alma mater of NPR's Tom and Ray Magliozzi: Abbr.
51 Storm dir.

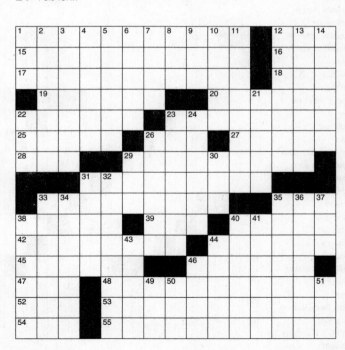

by Trip Payne

274 ★ ★ ★

ACROSS

1 2005's "Bad News Bears" and the like
14 Firm up-and-comers
15 Saw about frugality
16 Wildcats' sch.
17 TV Guide listings: Abbr.
18 Johnny Cash's "___ Picture of Mother"
19 Pauperize
21 Resting places
24 They're game
25 Something rattled
27 Identi-Kit options
29 Church with elders: Abbr.
30 Commander at the Alamo
32 Brings in
34 Modern inhabitants of ancient Aram
36 Fast movement
40 Have bad posture
42 Material for some sheets
43 Legal V.I.P.'s
46 "That's ___!"
48 Woman with une nièce
49 It might be stuck to a dish
51 Longtime first name in South Carolina politics
53 Peter Gunn's girlfriend
54 Megalopolis with about 30 million people, for short
56 Pianist Maisenberg
58 It may finish second
59 Realize there will be no resolution
63 "Don't put words in my mouth"
64 Not here

DOWN

1 Place to get rolls
2 Letters of discharge
3 Turnabouts, slangily
4 Proscriptions
5 Like some transfers
6 Picks
7 Damp and chilly
8 Great time
9 People may take a pass on them: Abbr.
10 Chose to play
11 Lab locale
12 Like badlands
13 Cool red giants
14 When many resolutions are broken
15 Certain links
20 One of the Leeward Islands
22 Unable to get one's feet on the ground?
23 Makes an impression on?
26 It's twirled on a trail
28 Smash production?
31 Puts one over on
33 Caterpillar features
35 Breed
37 French copper
38 Many a senior
39 King of diamonds feature
41 Like Mad
43 Tests
44 Loving, as eyes
45 Backbone part
47 Gentlemanly
50 Bel ___
52 Intervening, legally
55 Proceed impulsively
57 Canterbury can
60 Up to
61 Ladies' room
62 Some racecars

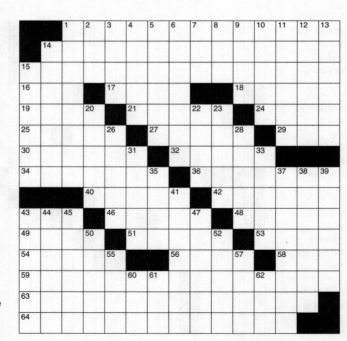

by Eric Berlin

ACROSS

1 Tanglewood's ___ Hall
11 Wet blanket?
15 Winslow Homer's "The Reaper," e.g.
16 After
17 Certain secretary
18 When repeated, a taunt
19 Standard of living?
20 Place that may suit you
22 After
24 ___ bourgeoisie (gentry)
25 "It will come ___ surprise . . ."
28 Within: Prefix
29 Prefix with business
30 End of many a riddle
32 Isn't just a licensee
34 The Seminoles, in coll. sports
36 Hardly an independent thinker
38 Fail
40 But, to Brutus
41 Prefix with drama
43 Political convention activity
44 Tow job
46 Mark of a ruler
48 It may have a big head
49 ___ bar
50 Anago, in a sushi restaurant
52 Hideous
54 One thrown at a rodeo
58 Immoralist
59 Big blow to the Japanese?
61 "This one's ___"
62 "Well, bless my soul"
63 Forks
64 Place to wait for a couple of minutes, maybe

DOWN

1 ___' Pea
2 Marco Polo's heading
3 Zinc oxide may treat it
4 Giant bottle
5 Maya Angelou's "And Still ___"
6 Mo. with United Nations Day
7 Get very close
8 Not recognizable by
9 Wearied
10 Trojan ally, in the "Iliad"
11 Wiesbaden weekday
12 Confrontational
13 Cicatrix
14 Ticklee's utterance
21 Mount in Siskiyou County
23 Poet who wrote "Don't send a poet to London"
25 Cobblers' tools
26 Does it ever hurt!
27 Voltaire, e.g.
31 Brunch beverage
33 Time to see estrellas
35 Former empire inits.
37 Ballet step
39 For all to see
42 Club with a nearly vertical face
45 Check list?
47 Home of the 1988 and 2010 Winter Olympics
49 Best-selling author of "Personal Injuries"
51 Stiff-backed
53 Pass on
55 Starbuck's orderer
56 Bilbao bull
57 Top
60 Application form datum: Abbr.

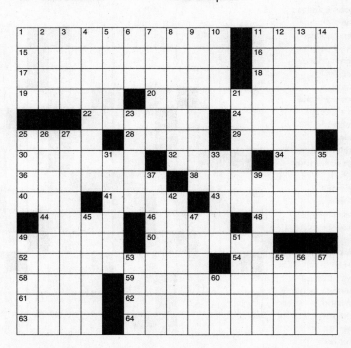

by Manny Nosowsky

ACROSS

1 Boarders' spots
9 Excites, with "up"
13 Declaration from Mama Rose in "Gypsy"
15 Seethe
16 Resolution phrase
17 Nitwit
18 Italian TV channel
19 Sleuth's outburst
20 Richard's longtime partner on Broadway
22 Down-home entertainment
24 High, in a way
26 Served as
28 Drop off
29 Shade of bleu
30 Kind of infection
32 One and the same
34 Bygone epidemic cause
35 Asian peppers
38 Shared sleeping accommodations
39 Serengeti creature
40 Some are made with chocolate
43 Pie chart dividers
44 Pardner's mount
45 Proves otherwise, briefly
49 Sugar amt.
50 Tell off in no uncertain terms
52 Burrow
53 Letter opener
55 Series of articles, maybe
57 "Give ___ hug"
58 Bannister's length
59 Overhead
62 Big hearts?
63 Bums
64 "Over here"
65 "Not necessarily"

DOWN

1 Guide
2 Bar
3 Vitamin C provider
4 1999 best seller "___ Road"
5 208 people
6 Dress material
7 Supportive org. since 1965
8 Bluejackets
9 Lane with smooth curves
10 Michael Jackson autobiography
11 Can you top this? Why, yes!
12 Mo preceder
13 Following
14 L train
21 Like the "Wheel of Fortune" wheel, again and again
23 Mocha native
25 Turkey
27 Booted, maybe
31 Renal : kidney :: amygdaline : ___
33 Getting up there
35 Q*___ (vintage video game)
36 Office holders
37 Larval amphibians
38 Split
40 Flex, for example
41 Squirt
42 One-named singer with the 2002 #1 hit "Foolish"
46 One known for a bad hair day
47 Phil who was a five-time Gold Glove winner
48 Photocopier selections
51 Feat
54 Cold war faction
56 In and out, quickly
58 "The Amazing Race" prop
60 -esque
61 Hamburger's one

by Henry Hook

ACROSS

1 Rejected
10 Food whose name means, literally, "ring"
15 Personal
16 Title place in a Francesco Rosi film
17 Whistle blower?
18 Reach
19 Hit daytime show
20 Eustachian tube site
21 Mixer with O.J., popularly
22 In public
23 Ancient writers of hieroglyphics
25 Plunder, slangily
26 Chicken soup ingredient
28 Org. with a House of Delegates
29 Rankles
33 Sunken
35 Profits
36 Peppermint ___
37 Means of introduction
39 Bad thing to be at
40 Calculator: Abbr.
41 Almost spills
43 Knights of ___
45 Chasing
46 Buster?
50 "I Remember Mama" aunt
52 Swedish coins
53 It goes over the wall
54 Abominable
55 Not car-share
57 Space Invaders maker, once
58 "The devil's tools"
59 Joint part
60 Classic subject for rock 'n' roll lyrics

DOWN

1 "Gremlins" co-star, 1984
2 Fred's dancing sister
3 Shelf material
4 Game piece
5 Word said just before opening the eyes
6 "Make yourself comfortable"
7 Broken up
8 Travelers' headaches
9 ___ City of book and film
10 Mendicates
11 Encourages when one shouldn't
12 Rot
13 1942 Allied victory site
14 Didn't settle
23 Sicilian dessert wine
24 More oozing
26 Attacks from a snow fort, say
27 "Sailing to Byzantium" poet
29 "Oho!"
30 Disappear
31 Good one
32 A winner may break it
34 Sports stat.
38 "I won't stand in your way"
39 Inveigle
42 Usually you try to hit yours
44 Julio's opposite
46 Family name in "A Tree Grows in Brooklyn"
47 ___ friends
48 Divides
49 Trough's opposite
51 Score just before winning, maybe
53 Ditch with a retaining wall used to divide land
56 ___ tho

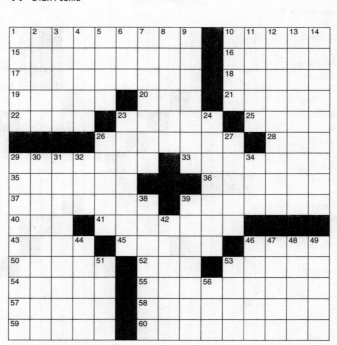

by Tyler Hinman

278 ★ ★ ★

ACROSS

1 Working together
10 Level connectors
15 Ready to take off
16 Arita porcelain
17 Dig in one's heels
18 Risk
19 N.Y.C. subway line
20 "The X-Files" org.
21 The "R" in Edward R. Murrow
22 Cleaner
24 Item with a long spout
26 It follows directions
27 Plains natives
29 Schedule
30 Sheet of matted fabric used in quilting
31 Staging area for the Crusades
33 Post-accident inquiry
35 Dated database
37 Rare occasion
40 King's bane
44 Abu ___, first Muslim caliph, 632-34
45 Turns down
47 Drug agent
48 Part of the sch. year
49 Tick off
51 Stage lead
52 Vegetable holder
54 Depilation brand
56 Common gift of welcome
57 Newswoman Gwen
58 Frequent raid target
60 View
61 Green light
62 Beginnings
63 Really big job

DOWN

1 1994 literary autobiography whose first chapter is titled "Infant Prodigy?"
2 River pollutant
3 Meal replaced by M.R.E.'s
4 Grass part
5 Bricklayers' equipment
6 Monteverdi opera
7 Common childhood malady
8 Epic 1975 showdown, popularly
9 N, O or P, in chem.
10 Bad-mouth
11 Rachel of "General Hospital"
12 "Art of silence" performer
13 Ahead of
14 Start to knit
21 Very violent, say
23 Ethylene glycol product
25 Chip ingredient
28 Hustle
30 Railyard sight
32 Lost ground
34 Birth
36 "Act!"
37 Grill sites, briefly
38 Visa charge
39 Largest country wholly in Europe
41 Ignis fatuus, the fair maid of ___
42 Learning
43 Handle
46 Don who directed "Invasion of the Body Snatchers," 1956
49 Idiots
50 Copier setting
53 Responded in court
55 Trainee
58 Loan figure: Abbr.
59 Except for

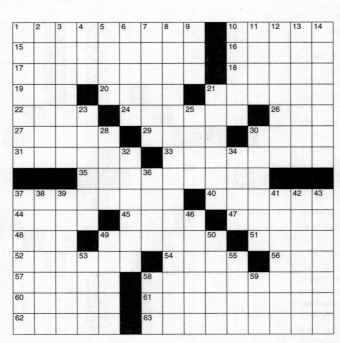

by Bob Peoples

ACROSS

1 Idle
8 Crusade
15 One who might be in for a fall
16 Away
17 Err
18 Lacking the usual oomph
19 Shelley's fairy queen
20 Common alarm clock setting
22 Montemezzi's "L'Amore dei ___ Re"
23 Noted Americana lithographer
25 Storage site
26 Analyze
28 Strings run along one
29 Bob's partner
31 Good place to sit
32 Many a sled driver
34 Fibulae
36 Entrance part
38 MGM co-founder
39 Teetotalers
43 Environments
47 Official required to have a beard
48 Jefferson's portrayer in "Jefferson in Paris"
50 Old German duchy name
51 Actress Hedren
53 Gus who wrote "Dream a Little Dream of Me"
54 Broadcasting option
55 An agt.'s take
56 Awful, and then some
59 It may be raised by a rabblerouser
60 Belfast bloke
62 The Fonz, for one
64 Set against
65 Resonated
66 Worked
67 Speed-read

DOWN

1 Light yellow
2 Staff sizes?
3 Classic quartet leader
4 Sellers co-star in "A Shot in the Dark," 1964
5 Goes out
6 Avon peddlers, traditionally
7 1978 Glenda Jackson title role
8 "Isn't that unusual!"
9 Most fit to serve
10 Member of the Camelidae family
11 The Beatles' "___ Blues"
12 Serves
13 Ho-hum
14 Result of lack of sleep, maybe
21 Company famous for its safety record
24 Winter Olympics sight
27 A bit dense
30 Having I-strain?
33 They're often asked to look
35 ___ air
37 Negotiated
39 Not be satisfied, perhaps
40 A fraternity chapter
41 Afternoon, often, for a toddler
42 High-five, e.g.
44 Peak in New Hampshire's Presidential Range
45 Nth
46 Cut off
49 Exercise targets
52 "___ to Be You"
57 Hither
58 ___ place for
61 Masseur's workplace, maybe
63 "Kung Fu" actor Philip

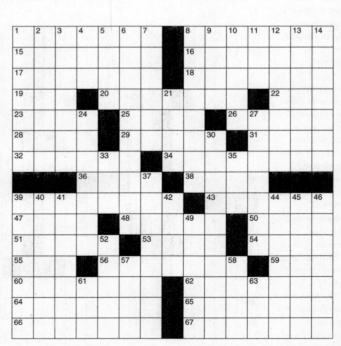

by Kevin McCann

280

★ ★ ★

ACROSS

1 Fair trade
11 Words with "move on" or "life"
15 Baby shower
16 Draft choices?
17 Spaghetti sauce slogan
18 Actively trading
19 Through
20 Its highest possible score is 180: Abbr.
21 Inflict upon
22 Many are trained in childbirth: Abbr.
24 Slugger Williams and others
25 Looking frightened
26 It was uncommon at the Forum
27 Way to direct a helm
28 They might offer support in prayer
29 Unité politique
30 Ready for mounting
32 Characterize
34 "The nerve!"
38 Love, e.g.
42 First of a noted trio
43 First name in 19th-century outlawry
46 Grandson of Leah
47 Philadelphia's Franklin ___: Abbr.
48 Asian au pair
49 Plagues, with "at"
50 "Breezy" star, 1973
51 Ram home?
52 Pituitary hormone
53 Historic Thor Heyerdahl craft
54 Little Thief, for one
55 Snubbed person's comeback
59 Kids' TV character with a thick unibrow
60 Wipes out
61 Goddess who wed her brother
62 Physical component

DOWN

1 Shook
2 Last
3 Heads-up cry
4 Abbr. after Sen. Jack Reed's name
5 Label a bomb, perhaps
6 Letter run
7 "So-o-o sexy!"
8 Searched a trail, as a dog
9 Like some advertised films
10 "The Country Girl" playwright
11 Sides in an age-old battle
12 Smoke out
13 Go from 0 to 20 in three years?
14 Gets to

23 Luxury items for a king or queen
24 Pair from a deck, maybe
28 Knowledge
31 Property lawyers' concerns
33 Iowa college since 1851
35 More than look up to
36 Catches
37 Superlatively swank
39 Music critic's assignment
40 Raising Cain
41 Whip material
43 Star of the 1976 miniseries "I, Claudius"
44 Cries too easily, say

45 Zen enlightenment
49 Some cause laughter
56 Hi-___
57 Suffix with robot
58 Habitual scratcher

by David Quarfoot

ACROSS

1 Modern, efficient matchmaking process
12 Alimentary particle?
15 One who got held up, maybe
16 Old Testament book: Abbr.
17 Sensor
18 TV schedule letters
19 Director Craven
20 Pleads
21 Drawer freshener
23 Record collection?
24 Soothing art
25 "Nope"
28 Something you might part with overseas
29 Kmart acquisition
30 Popular wedding gift
31 N.F.L. Hall-of-Famer ___ Barney
32 Sans warranty
33 Slate evaluator
34 Biblical peak
35 Acre's setting: Abbr.
36 Stable parents
37 Like tigers vis-à-vis lions
38 Good as new
40 Washer setting
41 Arrives like a social butterfly?
42 Pinup's pride
43 Unspecified, but invariably unpleasant, alternative
44 Harry Belafonte cry
45 Regrettable
48 Fabled elephant abductor
49 "Impossible!"
52 The third to the fifth?
53 "Miss You Like Crazy" singer, 1989

54 Some tech. inst. grads
55 Worker around a furnace

DOWN

1 Raft
2 Like 24-Across
3 Are, in Alençon
4 Port. joined it in 1986
5 Old Japanese cars
6 "The Art of Arousal" writer
7 Northern constellation
8 Little jerks
9 "___ no idea"
10 Skeptical sort
11 Player of Joe the Bartender
12 Open-eyed
13 1974 David Bowie song

14 1953 hit that mentions "old Napoli"
22 Shipping unit: Abbr.
23 Mean types
24 You can see right through them
25 Falcon's home
26 Dessert with candied fruit, nuts and liqueur
27 Top secrets?
28 Placed
30 Oscar winner for "Two Women"
33 Like some wines
34 Bert Bobbsey's twin and others
36 Lost
37 Modernize
39 N.L. scoreboard abbr.

40 1960's–70's antidiscrimination movement
42 Residents of ancient Alesia
44 ___ told
45 Throw below
46 Au fait
47 Rural road sign image
50 Windy City rail inits.
51 PX shopper

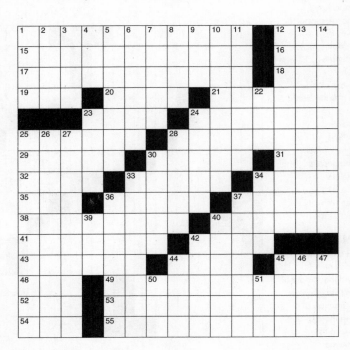

by Paula Gamache

282

★ ★ ★

ACROSS

1 Cranberry center
8 Runs through
13 Wears out
15 Inventories
16 Title for a duchess
17 Valuable fur
18 Settings for some TV dramas
19 Narcissists
21 Blame
22 Having very little kick
23 Protection
25 Not spontaneous
26 Make more sanitary, in a way
28 Sir Frank ___, historian of Anglo-Saxon England
30 People often leave them with cuts
32 Toast, after "a"
34 Vernacular
38 Handrail supporter
40 Halves of Córdoba couples
42 Legitimate
43 Relish
46 Two out of nine?
47 Like a string bean
48 Grunts
49 Postulate
50 Five-time Art Ross Trophy winner
52 Salad greens
53 Chiselers
54 To-do list
55 Asses with dorsal stripes

DOWN

1 Was logically consistent
2 Found the middle of?
3 Didn't stay dry
4 Tiny fraction of a British thermal unit
5 Tobacco farm employee
6 Some Siouans

7 Boils down
8 "The Rose Tattoo" Tony winner, 1951
9 Naval defense
10 Sevillian skills
11 Drafts, say
12 Some ID's
14 Leave
15 Apparently pleased
20 Fair selection
24 One being counter-productive?
27 They get punched
29 Result of a coup
31 Voiced bits of speech
33 Investigator who finds someone's birth mother, say
35 "I ___ you!"
36 Garden bouquet

37 Summons
39 Schoolwork
41 Get into easily
43 Tom Courtenay's "Doctor Zhivago" role
44 Characters in "Casablanca" and "Judge Dredd"
45 "___ roll!"
47 Poise
51 Line part: Abbr.

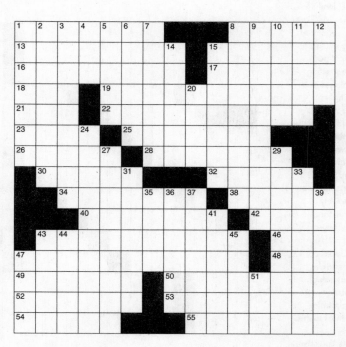

by Robert H. Wolfe

ACROSS

1 Declare one's intentions publicly
16 Job for one doing character studies?
17 Be in a very advantageous position
18 Old roadside name
19 Indication that one is being rubbed the right way
20 String along
21 Physics units
23 Deadlines on eBay are given in it: Abbr.
24 Verdi's "Un ___ in Maschera"
28 River in "The Divine Comedy"
32 Quadrennial observation
38 Locales of frequent injuries
39 "F Troop" role
40 Fire, to Flavius
41 Point (to)
42 Old cable inits.
45 They're not in
48 Like some mail or traffic
52 Amorous bit
53 Image: Var.
57 Longtime La Scala conductor
60 It can take a lot of heat
61 Summer resort area famous for recreational boating

DOWN

1 "Am ___ Man" (1960 Jackie Wilson hit)
2 Cramped urban accommodations, for short
3 "Do the Right Thing" pizzeria
4 Release
5 What that might be in Spain
6 Quiet
7 Where "Otello" premiered
8 Almost too late
9 Book between Ezra and Esther: Abbr.
10 Hot
11 Something that's often made up
12 Series ender
13 Some cough medicine: Var.
14 Lincoln in-laws
15 Kickoff
21 Sharp turn
22 Falling-out
24 Kind of crime
25 Ending to avoid?
26 Actor who roared to fame?
27 Brother of Nintendo's Mario
29 Rank
30 It's good to graduate with them
31 Transfuse
33 It means "red" in Mongolian
34 Kidney secretion
35 Village, in Würzburg
36 Tennis star ___ Huber
37 It flows in Flanders
42 Thomas Paine's "Common Sense," e.g.
43 Grammy-winning Jones
44 Cracked
46 Big name in wine
47 Joins in space
49 Cabriole performer's wear
50 Dwarf planet just beyond the Kuiper Belt
51 "Cannery Row" woman
53 On Wilshire Blvd., say
54 Furnace
55 Like a line, briefly
56 Quibbles
58 World
59 Not fare well

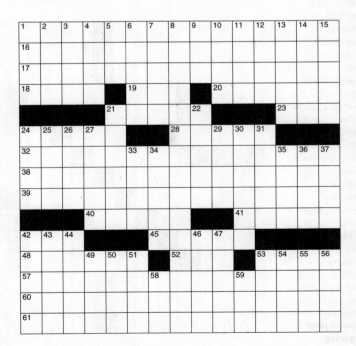

by Sherry O. Blackard

284

★ ★ ★

ACROSS

1 Blind, in a way
8 Spain's San Isidro and others
15 Children's author who was a regular contributor to Punch
16 Nation of 181 square miles
17 Introduce
18 "Just So Stories" author's first name
19 When there's no other option
21 Recommendations
22 Hospital dogsbody
23 Brickmaking company
24 Adirondack chair part
25 "Jabberwocky" opener
26 1956 cult film from overseas
27 Frost lines
28 Burdensome
29 It lays its eggs in others' nests
33 Ticks
34 Spanish rice ingredient
35 They make tracks
36 Device that contains an electromagnet
37 Seriously break the trust of, slangily
38 Chlorophyll-containing microorganism
42 Landscaping supplies
43 Some Tate Modern pieces
45 ___ 500, annual list of the fastest-growing private companies
46 One that picks up the kids?
47 Kerosene

49 Itch cause
50 French rococo artist Watteau
51 Court stat
52 Some chocolate
53 Free throw, e.g.

DOWN

1 Putts that might be conceded
2 Talking-to
3 God worshiped in ancient Thebes
4 Most widespread
5 Frosted
6 People in trees
7 Had a tough time deciding
8 Capacitance units
9 Condition
10 The Christian Science Monitor founder
11 Brown condiment

12 Got credit for
13 High-and-mighty
14 Elton John hit that begins "Guess there are times when we all need to share a little pain"
20 Country name retired in 1949
23 Folk wisdom
26 Brinks
27 Like some air fresheners
28 Aesop character with a country cousin
29 Napoleon, e.g.
30 Exclusive meeting
31 Kansas State athletes
32 Squeezers
33 National instruments of Guatemala
35 Insignificant
37 Cross references?

38 Detectives check them
39 Not quite on time
40 Blue ___
41 Still
43 Home of the Calendar Islands, once thought to total 365 in number
44 Teen affliction
46 Be angry
48 Gob

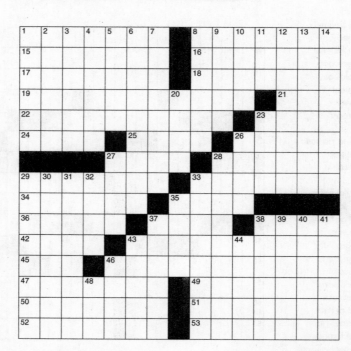

by Patrick Berry

ACROSS
1 Plot device in some science fiction
9 Expedient
15 Saint born in Newark, N.J.
16 Modern site of an ancient Egyptian capital
17 Fictional character who says "I have measured out my life with coffee spoons"
19 ___ Nuevo
20 Cardio choice
21 ___ Lacs, Minn.
22 Discoveries in Al Hirschfeld drawings
24 Off the market
26 Whammy
27 Rack holder
28 Merry
30 Spawn
31 It's a free country
33 Descend, in mountaineering
35 Movie buff: Var.
38 1993 Peace co-Nobelist
39 Night sticks?
40 Western party
41 Computer key
42 Homer's home
44 One of the Bush brothers
48 Word with legal or lower
50 Home of the Hmong
51 Part of a French toast
52 Pan
54 Thomas formerly of the N.B.A.
56 Flagstaff-to-Tucson dir.
57 Early Jesuit
60 Moving vehicles
61 Wagner opera setting
62 One side in the Battle of Thermopylae
63 Drill command

DOWN
1 Music style that often includes an accordion
2 "Terrible" czar
3 Longtime TV role for Danson
4 Generator output: Abbr.
5 Partner of all
6 Specialty
7 Weathers
8 National car care chain
9 ___ particle
10 Switch letters
11 Trinidadian, e.g.
12 The Barsetshire novels novelist
13 Doing very well moneywise
14 Sure thing
18 Popular caramel candy
23 Dealers' requests
25 Browbeating
28 George of old vaudeville
29 "Mame" director of stage and screen
32 Biblical verb
34 Joint assemblies
35 Busts a gut
36 First opera to premiere at London's Savoy Theatre, 1882
37 Rather close
38 Parent's stern order
40 Like some consonant stops
43 Flock member
45 Store, in a way
46 Word of emphasis
47 Eye libidinously
49 Some lampshade shades
51 Abbas I, II and III
53 Wife of Shiva, in Hinduism
55 Toll unit
58 "The Puzzle Palace" org.
59 One of the Ewings on "Dallas"

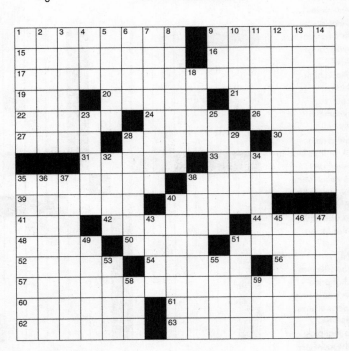

by Karen M. Tracey

286 ★ ★ ★

ACROSS

1 Lock locale
6 Licks
11 Some rocket fuel
14 One lost through divorce
15 He said "Marriage is nature's way of keeping us from fighting with strangers"
16 Not disparate
17 Pooh-bah
18 Matching, with "the"
20 Chat room info
21 Mournful
22 Potluck panfuls
23 Words before a sarcastic "ha ha"
24 Now
26 Part of a pound
32 Put on again
33 Review unfairly
35 Political leader from Georgia
36 Driving range device?
43 Name in high fashion
44 Trigger, e.g.
45 Nickname in tabloids
46 Eyelet creator
47 Deux or trois lead-in
48 Chewed on
49 Of a pelvic bone
50 Some store officials
51 Knight's list
52 Peter and Paul, but not Mary

DOWN

1 In opposition to
2 Kind of price
3 American painter of sports scenes
4 Half of an old comedy duo
5 Deck chair part
6 Radial alternative
7 Supplements
8 Most vile
9 Breaks with service?
10 Producing bullets?
11 World capital on a river of the same name
12 Woman in a "Paint Your Wagon" song
13 Shows no sign of abating
19 Otto's preceder
25 Lions and tigers and bears
26 U.N. beachhead during the Korean War
27 Stout
28 Water
29 Part of an Ethiopian emperor's title
30 Columbus discovery of 1498
31 The Big Easy
34 Most coveted position
37 Brazilian beach resort
38 Crumble
39 Foreign dignitaries
40 British chemist's solution strength
41 Maze marking
42 Chancel symbols

by Harvey Estes

ACROSS

1 Multiple-choice choices
6 "Then again" follower
14 More within reason
15 Something to get sent off with
16 100 öre
17 "Possibly"
18 Ford's predecessor
19 Band's lineup
20 Collectible sheet
21 Begin to form
22 Drive away
23 Where to go for a cup
25 Bourbon flavorer
26 Response to an impatient person
27 Dating service datum
28 Broadcaster from 1995 to 2006
29 Hardly windy
30 Ships
33 Exclamation in a locker room talk
37 River of Troyes
38 "Phooey!"
39 Through
40 Single or double, say
41 Tenor Bostridge and others
42 Form 1040 fig.
43 With 10-Down, ocularist's offering
46 Old boom makers
47 Choice for the indecisive
48 What "-" may signify
49 A sigh
50 Olympics event
51 Having no match
54 Emerge
55 It may be password-protected
56 Derby wear

57 They've been on the road many times
58 Heretofore

DOWN

1 Display some interest in
2 Frequent USA Today features
3 Like people in the front row of a group photo, often
4 Get further Details?
5 Company
6 Suit request
7 Stop or touch follower
8 Rocher of cosmetics
9 Cannonball Adderley's specialty
10 See 43-Across
11 "Eraserhead" star Jack

12 Home to Hill Air Force Base
13 Transformer creator
15 Yellowstone feeder
22 Lit
23 Receivers of cuts
24 It helps one keep one's place
26 Trailer makeup
27 Indians, e.g.
31 Behind someone's back
32 His self-titled book has 24 chapters
34 Cookout fare
35 In heat?
36 Some problems to solve
43 Infomercial cutter
44 Winds
45 Period of douze mois
46 Cut

47 Bottom
49 Geometric figure
50 You can get a charge out of it
52 Landing site
53 Boxer's org.

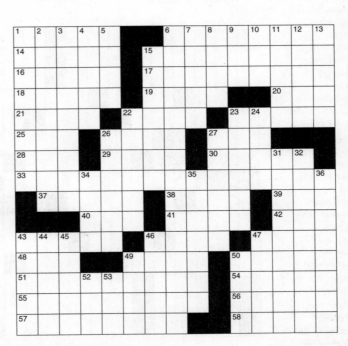

by Mike Nothnagel

288

★ ★ ★

ACROSS

1. Flooring?
10. Main character of TV's "The Pretender"
15. Occasion to reserve a table for two?
16. Singer/songwriter ___ Mandell
17. Greeting spot
18. Ready to be used again
19. Volcano part
20. Old cereal brand
21. "Wow!"
23. Boosler of stand-up
25. "___ for That" (1939 hit song)
26. Output of Tintoretto, e.g.
27. Small force
28. Dud of an idea
31. Slated
33. Reasons for some delays
34. Notice
35. Indicators of comfort and handling
38. Hall of introductions
41. British officer's wear
42. Patriot Putnam
46. Tournedos, e.g.
49. Part of a Latin trio
50. Eric who played Hector in "Troy," 2004
51. Temple player
52. Bank donation?
54. Mischievous
56. Saturn S.U.V.
57. Pig stealer, in a nursery rhyme
58. Literally, "first generation"
59. Key
62. Some gowns
63. Old World pigeons with markings around the neck
64. Contemporary of Arp and Miró
65. Prada alternative

DOWN

1. Marinara alternative
2. Andy Warhol subject
3. Superhero of 1960's TV
4. Kind of state
5. N.B.A. star Brand
6. American coot
7. Short-lived TV spinoff of 1980
8. Chevron sporter: Abbr.
9. Neighborhood in the Bronx
10. Actress Ryan of "Star Trek: Voyager"
11. Sour, fermented liquid
12. Getaways
13. Ragtime dance
14. Highly agitated
22. Eye irritants
24. Wine info
25. O.K., maybe
29. Locale in a classic Frank Sinatra song
30. Heavenly field?: Abbr.
32. Some ironware
36. Jam ingredients?
37. Capital of Fiji
38. Refluent phenomenon
39. Formal introduction
40. Eisenhower's Texas birthplace
43. Old Ford model
44. Dry-eyed
45. Like some connections
47. Stunning slaps
48. Poinsettia's family
53. Tips
55. Word with Star or Sun in product names
56. Means of escape
60. Writer ___ Pera
61. Tee, e.g.

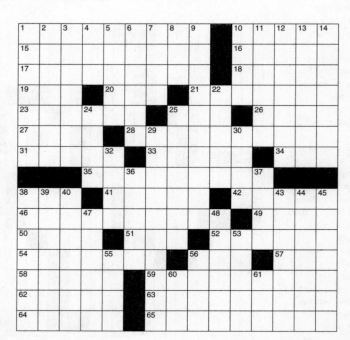

by Karen M. Tracey

ACROSS

1 Basic teaching
4 Sirens
9 Ruthlessly competitive
14 Start of a Tennessee Williams title
15 Red as ___
16 Spendthrift's joy
17 ___ de guerre
18 Whip on the high seas
20 Slows down
22 ___ Tech
23 Airline with the King David Lounge
24 Slander, say
26 Like "Brokeback Mountain"
30 Fix, as a pump
32 Org. with the annual Junior Olympic Games
34 Nosh
35 Hotter than hot
37 Stooge
38 Vandal
41 See 25-Down
43 Underhanded
44 Orchard Field, today
46 Buzz
48 Film pooch
49 Kind of party
50 Drug used to treat poisoning
54 Place of disgrace
56 E.T.S. offering
58 Unaccompanied
59 Spot for Spot?
60 Takes in
62 Unplanned
67 Word between two names
68 Get around
69 Military operation
70 Loaf on the job
71 Six Flags features
72 To the point
73 Some city map lines: Abbr.

DOWN

1 Lowly post
2 Something that may need boosting
3 Inner selves, to Jung
4 Annul, as a legal order
5 Apollo 13 astronauts, e.g.
6 Organization that no U.S. president has ever belonged to
7 Designer from China
8 Stop: Abbr.
9 Guiding light
10 Some fed. govt. testing sites
11 N.L. West team, on scoreboards
12 Business card abbr.
13 Venice's ___ Palace
19 Light shade
21 Cook up
25 With 41-Across, title for this puzzle
27 Reward for waiting?
28 List ender
29 ___-eyed
31 Track down
33 Arith. process
36 Still red inside
37 Burger topper
38 Show-off
39 "Here comes trouble"
40 Org. with troops
42 Ones going home after dinner?
45 Meat dish with a filling
47 100 centavos

49 Jazz buff
51 Carnival treats
52 Notwithstanding
53 Mathematical groups
55 MS. enclosures
57 Slot car, e.g.
61 Old dagger
62 Serve, as a banquet
63 Year in Trajan's reign
64 Kept
65 St. Paul hrs.
66 Rush

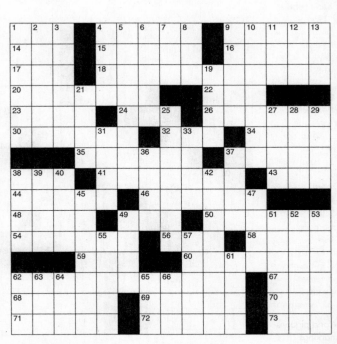

by David J. Kahn

290

★ ★ ★

ACROSS

1 Faucet with a rotating plug
9 Top with a quip, maybe
15 Convenient, in a way
16 Observer
17 Kids
18 Bibliographer's term
19 Tolerate
20 Product with the old jingle line "One little can will keep you running free"
21 Curved nails
22 The 80s, say
23 Time up
25 Chow fixer
26 Whips
28 Some Oscar-night gowns
29 Rig-___, Hindu sacred book
30 "The Sand Pebbles" actor, 1966
32 See
33 Lacking light
36 "Speaking personally . . ."
38 Ones with gifts who don't care about presents
39 Embryonic sac
41 Air ___, discount carrier
42 Top-___ (sports brand)
43 Banff Natl. Park locale
47 It's in the neighborhood: Abbr.
48 He wrote "A man cannot be too careful in the choice of his enemies"
49 Seaside flier
50 Olympic competitors since 1900
52 ___ Strait, east of Canada's King William Island

54 Nabokov novel
55 Soon
56 "Really?!"
58 Form of boxing using both the hands and feet
59 Tiger's quality
60 Wailed
61 Genetic condition known medically as ephelides

DOWN

1 Guitar strings, e.g.
2 Ballerina Karsavina
3 One of 2.7 million Japanese
4 "Here Is Your War" author
5 Mil. rank
6 Punch lines?
7 Bow-making time

8 Gas in fluorescent lamps
9 Angle symbols, in geometry
10 Go after
11 Knit, maybe
12 Enthusiastic response
13 Checked
14 Conjoined area
24 Knot
27 Belittling act
28 ___ gratia
29 Actress Bloom of "High Plains Drifter"
31 Some football linemen: Abbr.
32 "Ick!" evoker
33 Indication to look down
34 Forum characters

35 Stretch in the 90s, say
37 Word of disgust
40 Area under a halter
42 Two-___ (strong)
44 Protein source
45 Sad
46 Bugs
48 Parting request
51 "Voice of Israel" author
53 Being abroad
54 Lies together?
57 Latin pronoun

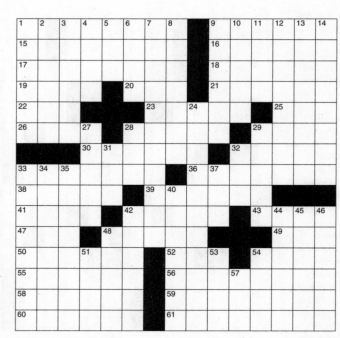

by Rich Norris

ACROSS

1 Steps up
10 Treasured instrument
15 Strike out
16 Goes down
17 Polka heard frequently on "The Benny Hill Show"
18 Part of a chronicle
19 Frustrate
20 1950's political slogan
22 A, B or C, often: Abbr.
23 Part of a telephone worker's routine
24 Baseball's Vizquel
27 Hunter of literature
28 Part of CORE
31 Marks off
36 Doesn't puff idly
38 Subject of the biography "All or Nothing at All"
39 Develops anacusis
41 Spurs
42 Pollster Roper
43 ___ the Great (detective of kids' books)
44 One end of a canal
48 Chemical ending
50 Frequent area of auto damage
51 Symbols
55 Lord's realm
56 Boeing employee
58 "He seemed like such ___ boy"
59 Chance
60 When to see la luna
61 Votaries

DOWN

1 Country rocker Joe and others
2 You might run for it
3 Forming clumps
4 Parts of some services
5 Admit
6 "I understand now"
7 Set-___
8 Like spam
9 Masters topics
10 Realization
11 "Un bar aux Folies-Bergère" artist
12 "Maybe" musical
13 Durable woods
14 Dot on a map, maybe
21 How a snake may be caught?
24 Before being retitled: Abbr.
25 War preceder
26 Flu symptom
29 Bearer of catkins
30 Actress Sobieski
32 Make attractive
33 Words with shame or boy
34 Order at a horse show
35 Levelheaded
37 TV witch
40 A bad way to be left
44 "The Rights ___"
45 Heavens: Prefix
46 Nervine, for one
47 Methuselah's father
48 ___ least
49 Like some stocks
52 Brio
53 Cartoonist Walker
54 Criteria: Abbr.
57 Geom. figure

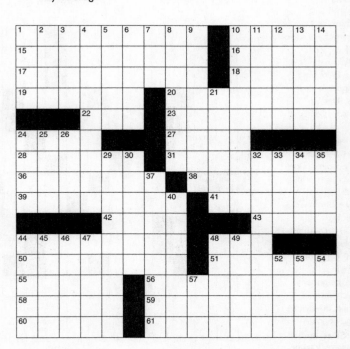

by Eric Berlin

ACROSS

1 Top in a certain contest
10 1988 Olympics superheavyweight gold medalist
15 Reply on a ship
16 Transcontinental railroad city
17 Tanzanian tourist destination
18 It has a cap in the kitchen
19 Hesitate in speaking
20 One of two N.T. books
21 Coastal feature
23 Tell
24 ___ Bank (U.S. loan guarantor)
26 Wire: Abbr.
28 Wrong
29 Expired
31 "I think," succinctly
32 Georgetown athlete
33 Soil
34 Artist on the cover of a 1969 Life magazine
36 "___ Her Go" (Frankie Laine hit)
38 W.W. II city on the Vire
39 Brest friends?
43 TV producer Don
47 Prefix with -stat
48 Puck
49 Key of Brahms's Fourth
50 C.D., e.g.: Abbr.
51 "Peter ___ Greatest Hits" (1974 release)
53 Tot minder
54 Afg. neighbor
55 Catch in a pot
56 While, briefly
58 It may be AM or FM: Abbr.
59 Crony of Tony on "The Sopranos"

61 One of the five major circles of latitude
64 Up to
65 Become disconnected
66 Coasts, say
67 Hot-blooded ones

DOWN

1 They have loads of work to do
2 Task to focus on
3 Extreme ends
4 Inventor's inits.
5 See 27-Down
6 With 22-Down, disgruntled remark about a failed partnership?
7 Alpine feeder
8 Score abbr.
9 Ancient vessels
10 Glen Gray's "Casa ___ Stomp"

11 Rock genre
12 Center for strategic planning
13 "Right on, brother!"
14 Oppressive measure that helped spark the French Revolution
22 See 6-Down
25 French Impressionist Berthe
27 With 5-Down, match, in a way
28 Add
30 Ralph Bunche's alma mater
35 Basic: Abbr.
37 Delays
39 Ones doing push-ups?
40 1959 Neil Sedaka hit
41 Windsor, e.g.
42 A season: Abbr.
44 Bothered

45 Annuity scheme
46 Spells
52 10th-century emperor known as "the Great"
55 Hosp. procedures
57 "Trionfo di Afrodite" composer
60 Poll abbr.
62 Alphabet trio
63 Height in feet of the Statue of Liberty, expressed in Roman numerals

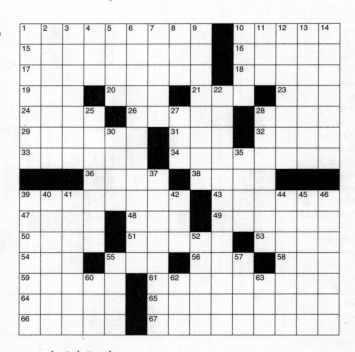

by Bob Peoples

ACROSS

1 Bristly
7 Sports anchor's offering
12 Henry Clay's estate in Lexington, Ky.
14 1997 Michael Douglas film
16 Unexplained phenomena
18 Quai d'Orsay setting
19 Possible sentence in the slammer
20 Unfriendly
21 Whom Pocahontas married
23 U.K. award
24 "___ and Louis" (1956 duet album)
26 It doesn't stay in for long
30 Like silhouettes, typically
32 Subject to debate
33 1950's–90's singer called "The High Priestess of Soul"
34 Ones forging
36 Congregation location
37 Finish a hole
39 There are no plans for this
43 18-Across feeder
44 "Of course!"
45 Footballer Haynes
47 Former state: Abbr.
48 Some misses
52 On the other hand
54 Classic 1894 swashbuckler, with "The"
56 Bound
57 Satisfied customer's request
58 Send another invitation
59 Sharp

DOWN

1 Relatively smart
2 George's mother on "Seinfeld" and others
3 HBO showing of 1975
4 1937 Oscar role for Luise Rainer
5 Less likely to lose it
6 College dept.
7 Torn
8 Kellogg's brand
9 Epic achievement?
10 Blob
11 Put down
13 Let down
14 Carroll creatures
15 Scoot
17 Some PC image files
22 Conjectures

25 Two-time A.L. home run champ Tony
27 Exempt
28 "___ can't be!"
29 Stevie Wonder's "___ Have You"
31 Something often fallen out of
34 Supporter
35 Falls off
38 Threefold
39 The "blood" in bloodstone
40 Brian of "Juarez," 1939
41 Full
42 Bridge piece
46 Close cutter
49 Cub bearers, in Spain
50 Swing alternative

51 Glass finish
53 "The Cotton Club" star
55 Put paper into

by Charles Barasch

294

⭐ ⭐ ⭐

ACROSS

1. Facility with many schools
9. One using the metric system?
13. Way over the line
15. Less likely to reconcile
16. Further stirring
17. Very small serving
18. Jude, e.g.
19. Toys, for tots
21. Mine shaft borer
22. Put a ceiling on
23. Telemarketing need: Abbr.
24. Eponymous Scottish inventor
25. High-rise, e.g.
27. Habitations
29. Don Juan
30. Saturnine
31. Some sprouts
32. Ski resort sights
36. Soft, transversely ribbed fabric
39. Unfeminine
40. ___ of Court
41. Where tests are often given: Abbr.
42. Angus rejection
43. Medical school course
46. Supplement
48. Daring adventurer
50. See 20-Down
51. Advanced point
53. Defeater of Holyfield and Tyson
54. Decorate
55. Eremitic
56. Sullies

DOWN

1. Captain's command
2. Feckless
3. Landing place
4. Miss in a derby?
5. Step on it
6. Not merely like
7. Chafes (at)
8. Pronoun for Pliny
9. Givers of unfriendly hugs
10. Like some poisoning
11. Go back
12. Valets, at times
14. Director's cry
15. Clueless
20. With 50-Across, acted
26. Sharer of both parents
27. Spider producer
28. Torches
30. Hunter's lure
33. Lessens the force of
34. Tony's player on "NYPD Blue"
35. Pasta variety
36. Galician galas
37. It's across the Albert Canal from Liège
38. How decisions shouldn't be made
44. "Charlie ___ Secret" (1935 film)
45. "On a similar note," e.g.
47. Jazz singer Anderson
49. Ones with talent?
52. "I ___ shepherd of those sheep": Millay

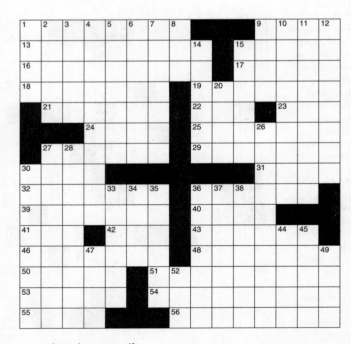

by Robert H. Wolfe

ACROSS

1 Kind of blocker
5 Clay defeater
9 Standard jacket feature
14 Conference intro
15 26 on a table
16 Girl's name meaning "born again"
17 Dangerously
19 8 ½-pound statue
20 Comment of abandon
22 ___ Bad Wolf of comic books
23 Cement layer
24 "Hey, just a second!"
26 W. Coast airport
28 ___ horn
30 It works as a translator
31 Tragic figure of literature
33 Splash guard
37 1960's TV dog
38 Head
40 Like some myths
41 "No more"
43 High-waisted to the extreme
45 Psych 101 topic
46 Poet/cartoonist Silverstein
47 Affliction
48 "Who knows?!"
52 Pioneering 1940's computer
54 Business card abbr.
55 Modern phone display
59 ___-Car
61 Event souvenirs
62 Island shared by two countries
63 Eastern queen
64 Study of figures: Abbr.
65 Spirited
66 Partner of letters
67 Business page inits.

DOWN

1 Lay up
2 Phnom ___
3 ___ Springs, Fla.
4 Former Los Angeles and New York Philharmonic conductor
5 It admits very little light
6 Like the Mikado and Nanki-Poo
7 Shetland Islands sight
8 They're often found under desks
9 Difficult means of communication
10 Article in a French magazine
11 Poseidon, to Athena
12 Show over
13 Star of "Always Leave Them Laughing," 1949
18 "Too much to go into now"
21 Early "What's My Line?" panelist
25 Red River city
26 Game in which jacks are the highest trumps
27 Seek at random, with "for"
29 Grad student's hurdle
32 Welcome
34 Star of a former self-titled sitcom
35 Onetime distributor of free maps
36 Nerve network
39 Very strong
42 Hemisphere
44 Creation
48 Common sugar source
49 No longer working for the Company
50 Smithereens
51 Part of a crowd, maybe
53 "It's ___" ("Maybe it's meant to be")
56 Do 80, say
57 Sporty cars
58 Salinger dedicatee
60 Directory data: Abbr.

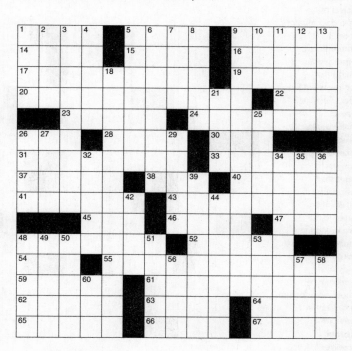

by Patrick Merrell

★ ★ ★

ACROSS

1 Sensational news format
10 In line with
15 End of a challenge
16 Was a star?
17 "The Prisoner of Zenda" setting
18 Seat of generative power
19 Those, in San José
20 "___ say it is good to fall": Whitman, "Song of Myself"
22 ___ for peace
23 Place to sleep
24 Is ready for the task
27 DVD viewing option
28 Census designation
31 Common tater
34 Subject of the 2006 documentary "Toots"
35 Japanese ___, bonsai plant
37 Entertainer who owns Big Dog Productions
38 Derelict
39 Hanky-panky
41 Calliope filler
44 Place for a pin
46 Bikini-to-Fiji dir.
49 Lesser star designation in a constellation
50 Query to the Lord in Matthew
51 Symbol of gracefulness
52 Study aid?
54 Flimflammery
57 Schoolroom feature
58 It's brilliant in handicrafts
59 Succulents for salves
60 Bond dealers?

DOWN

1 With 5-Down, run down
2 Words with light or blow
3 Originator of the phrase "truth is stranger than fiction"
4 "Family Guy" mom
5 See 1-Down
6 Ballerina Rubinstein, for whom Ravel wrote "Boléro"
7 As a 16-year-old actor, youngest nonroyal with an individual portrait in Britain's National Portrait Gallery
8 First step in division?
9 Italian entrees
10 Not flat
11 Cable option
12 Vitriolic
13 Lassitude
14 Tamper with, as an odometer
21 Big ___
24 Festivity
25 Ancient rival of Assyria
26 Webers per square meter
27 Last king of Egypt
28 Seat, quickly
29 P
30 N.B.A. scoring leader, 1974–76
32 A.C.C. school
33 One who remains nameless
36 ___ Style Awards
40 Neighbor of Mo.
42 Commandeers
43 "Baby ___ You" (1962 hit)
44 Popular block game
45 It has a certain ring to it
46 Cop
47 More sound
48 Corps personnel: Abbr.
51 Pole classification
53 U.K. honor
55 ___-American
56 School fig.

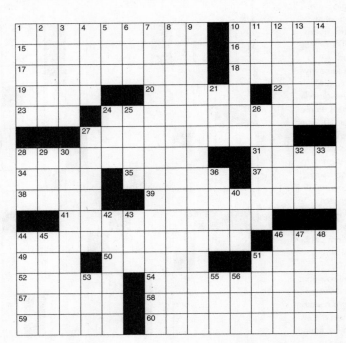

by Byron Walden

ACROSS

1 Waylay
7 Object of ailurophobia
10 Penny : pound :: ___ : krone
13 Bug's midsection
14 "Hollywood Homicide" actress, 2003
15 Box to check on a form
16 TV show that earned Jane Wyman a Golden Globe
18 Protestant denom.
19 Handy thing to know?: Abbr.
20 Like some church matters
21 List heading
22 Try
24 Band components
26 Polo of "Meet the Fockers"
27 Archaeological handle
28 Out of this world
29 The Oscars, e.g.
31 What two zeroes after a dot may mean
33 1978–80 F.B.I. sting that forced a U.S. senator to resign
35 Big bills
36 Green shade
37 First name in architecture
38 One not pure of heart
39 Boss for agents Youngfellow and Rossi
41 Object of a scout's search
45 Alcohol-laced cookie
47 Blue prints?
48 Play bit
49 "Willow Song" opera
51 Cost
52 Here, over there
53 Common and cheap
55 French pronoun
56 Certain asst.
57 Snap out of it
58 Bygone flier
59 Animal with a white rump
60 Destroys

DOWN

1 Equally quick
2 Pure
3 Arrest
4 Dungeons & Dragons beast
5 Adaptable aircraft
6 Sandwich filler
7 End-of-season event
8 It divides people
9 "We know drama" sloganeer
10 Rocker with the 1981 triple-platinum album "Diary of a Madman"
11 Signs back in
12 Some "60 Minutes" pieces
14 Ocean threats
17 Dessert garnish
21 Dangers for paragliders
23 Hoo-ha
25 Ornamentation
30 "What ___!"
32 It's to the left of a dot
33 Misers' feelings
34 Plant supervisor?
36 Words of contentment
40 Other side
42 Floors
43 France's F.B.I., formerly
44 Some assistants
46 Tyrolean refrain
50 Must, say
53 Peer Gynt's mother
54 Medical suffix

by Eric Berlin

298 ★ ★ ★

ACROSS

1 Rapper with an MTV show . . . whose name sounds like a word meaning "show"
7 Total
15 Defiant dare
16 Weigh
17 What some bars provide
18 Any of the teens, say
19 Ducky
20 Madrilenian madams
21 Maker of many sprays
22 Woodbine or twinberry
25 Special favor providers
28 With 8-Down, "Happy Trails" songwriter
29 Steps on a scale
31 Jolly exclamation
33 Manuel de Falla opera "La ___ Breve"
35 Cow's first stomach
36 Items in many a still life
38 Cuff link companions
40 "Since Marie Has Left ___" (Sinatra song)
41 They make charts
43 Start to date?
44 Poultry preparation tool
46 Fabric features
48 Setting at 0° long.
49 Singer who wrote the poetry collection "The Lords and the New Creatures"
52 Terminal abbr.
53 Electrolysis particle
54 Pioneer in the development of nuclear power
58 Baja California port
60 "Oryx and Crake" novelist, 2003
61 One once again
62 Modernize, as a factory
63 What a lot may have a lot of
64 Intricate

DOWN

1 Marvel Comics comic
2 "The Phantom" star Billy
3 Big name in furniture
4 Slip
5 "Nothing for me, thanks"
6 Writer Josephine
7 Lured
8 See 28-Across
9 Freeboot
10 Something that has long needed settling
11 Him, in Le Havre
12 "Chitty Chitty Bang Bang" author
13 Showers of purchases
14 Not allowed to go
20 Finger-lickin' good
23 Place for a flock
24 He had a 1941 hit with "Drum Boogie"
25 They offer hot links
26 Her "Don't Know Why" was 2002's Record of the Year
27 Initial public offering, e.g.
30 Atlas feature
32 Two bells, in the Navy
34 Make
37 Like the Danish language
39 Some surfers' choices, briefly
42 Forays
45 Liszt wrote only one
47 Cushion
50 Amendment
51 Hardly an old pro at
52 Its flag has a vicuña on it
55 Etymologist's concern
56 Kind of point
57 One way to sit
59 Last
60 Sanctuary

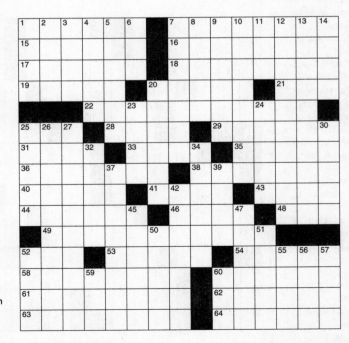

by Karen M. Tracey

ACROSS

1 He appointed the first chairman of the A.E.C.
4 Secretive places
14 Simple choice
16 What a standard deviation measures
17 Oscar-nominated actress for "Leaving Las Vegas"
18 Like some fears
19 Hint
21 City at the confluence of the Lehigh and Delaware rivers
22 Team member
24 Without a break
28 Christmas at St. Peter's
30 First lady before Eleanor
31 2000 best seller on social epidemics
37 Climax at Daytona
38 Title boy in a nursery rhyme
39 Ability to let a pitch go by
41 Historic beginning?
42 Budget item
43 Doesn't follow the party line
47 Pension supplements
51 Make good progress
53 Yellow bloomer
54 Artful gossip
58 Crackerjack
59 Common elevator stop
60 Hedge fun?
61 Communist collectives
62 Bit

DOWN

1 Precipitate
2 1987 BP acquisition
3 Jack's place
4 Program introduced by R.W.R.
5 Person of intelligence?
6 Begin, say
7 Body shops?
8 Row
9 Singer/film composer Jon
10 In harmony
11 "Henry & June" role
12 Big inits. in camping
13 Broadcast from Rockefeller Ctr.
15 "Go easy"
20 Office communications
23 How some stock is bought
25 Go straight
26 Kind of section
27 Person in a class of one
29 Part of a ship
31 Cookbook amts.
32 Compassion
33 Hall-of-Fame Viking Carl
34 Tales of derring-do
35 Baseball, in slang
36 Dental routine
40 Cicero or Publius
44 Feed for a fee, as cattle
45 Fictional matchmaker
46 Things
48 Be a bad winner
49 Where you may have a yen for shopping
50 1994 Sandra Bullock film
52 Start of a Christmas chorus
54 Possibilities
55 Picked peeve
56 Mme. of La Mancha
57 Traffic at Union Sta.

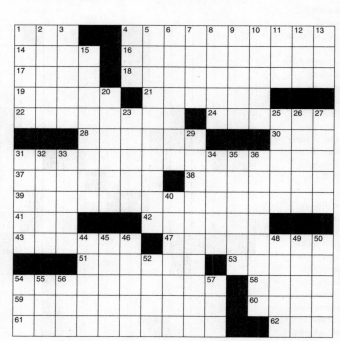

by Randolph Ross

300 ★ ★ ★

ACROSS
1 Real name of a Disney title character
6 Small drawing?
10 15-ml unit
14 Broadcasting
15 Falls into decline
17 With the help of
18 Providers of tip-offs?
19 Laurel and Hardy film with the line "Well, here's another nice mess you've gotten me into!"
21 Middle-earth resident
22 Gene ___, 1932 U.S. and British Open champ
23 Nikola Tesla, for one
25 Information for the record
30 Becomes an issue
32 Total
33 Rock group whose members all assumed the same last name, with "the"
35 Flip alternative
37 Eclipses, to some
38 At the back
39 Headmaster's faculty
42 "I must have missed the ___"
45 Concern for a hostess
47 Part of a certain college course
48 Desserts from the South
53 Wild-haired stock character
54 One of the Traveling Wilburys
55 Prepared to strike, perhaps
56 Coat hangers-on
57 Bristle (with)
58 Outfit
59 Lets fly

DOWN
1 Pickles
2 It's often underfoot
3 "Big iron," in hacker slang
4 Plastic containers
5 Greek city that remained neutral during the Persian Wars
6 Grocery stores
7 What many Latter-day Saints are
8 Architectural element often decorated with bas-reliefs
9 Computer desktop icon
10 Radio's "___ American Life"
11 Ill will
12 Amphilochus, in Greek myth
13 Sound from a test cheater, say
16 Divisions of a mark
20 Made-up
24 Unbroken mount
26 Witching hour follower
27 Laundry that's often food-stained
28 "Strange Magic" band, for short
29 Designing
31 Demand
33 Retinal cell
34 Any of the Three Musketeers
35 Narrow-bladed weapons
36 "___ we all?"
38 Said the same
40 ___ AC (pharmacy purchase)
41 "Truthful words are not beautiful; beautiful words are not truthful" espouser
43 Female bacchanalian
44 Take hold of, in a way
46 Follows a course
48 Scuzz
49 Flag
50 Warhol actress Sedgwick
51 Birthplace of Herod the Great
52 One of Carter's charges, on TV

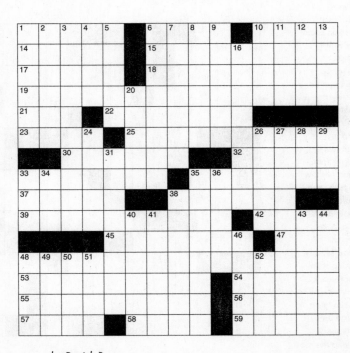

by Patrick Berry

ACROSS

1 Like the reading on a thermometer
7 Molly who wrote "Bushwhacked"
12 Facility
15 Camp sight
16 Relations of Homer?
18 ___ river
19 Service for filmgoers
20 "I almost forgot . . . !"
21 Unwavering
22 Candlemas dessert
23 Private
25 "In a hurry, are we?"
28 Puts down, in a way
29 Forensic indicators of the presence of blood
30 Makes a fraidy-cat (out of)
32 Cause
33 Put two and two together
34 Modern marketing aid
40 Deborah who starred in "Tea and Sympathy"
41 Decorate
42 Give praise
44 Observatory doings
45 Strength of a chemical solution
46 Parts of mountaineering trips
47 Grippers
48 Having the most social anxiety

DOWN

1 Could be
2 Horse of the Year that won the 1949 Preakness and Belmont
3 "___ said many times . . ."
4 Soprano Albanese
5 Put in to start
6 Plant on after a wildfire, say
7 Post-O.R. post
8 Producing some clouds
9 Fit
10 Ones without a chance in the world
11 "Now listen!"
13 London locale of Prada, Dior, Gucci and Giorgio Armani

14 Wits
17 Gets ready for dinner
22 ___ de fraise
24 Olivia de Havilland film of 1949
25 Pilferers from ships and port warehouses
26 Alabaman who wrote the Best Novel of the Century, according to a 1999 Library Journal poll
27 Foreign title meaning "commander"
28 Part of Act IV where Marc Antony resolves to kill Cleopatra
30 "The first network for men" sloganeer, once

31 Overplayed?
35 Claudia ___, 1984 Olympic gold medalist in shot put
36 Tigres del ___, Dominican team that has won the Caribbean World Series ten times
37 "What have ___?"
38 Fall times: Abbr.
39 Meet away from prying eyes
43 ___-80 (classic computer)

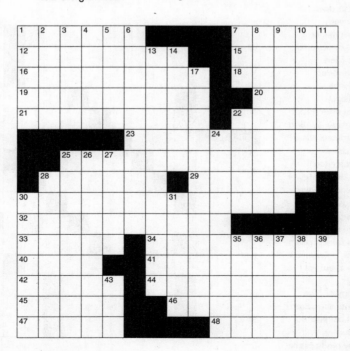

by Raymond C. Young

302

★ ★ ★

ACROSS

1 Saucily titled best-selling diet book
12 Center starter?
15 It's featured in "A Night at the Opera"
16 Tickled user's response
17 Target of a school bully
18 ___-de-four (hemisphere-shaped vault)
19 3,280.84 ft.
20 Suspect's request: Abbr.
21 Internet site graphics
23 Chooses by divine election
25 Ice remover
26 Fig. on a 1970s dollar
27 Enamel strengthener
28 Has confiscated
31 Slip fillers
32 T preceder
33 Alliance
34 College bookstore stock
35 Château ___-Brion (Bordeaux wine)
36 Arizona senator Jon
37 Yes or no follower
38 Abundant sources
39 Lands in the Persian Gulf
41 John of Lancaster
42 Ben Jonson poem
43 N.F.L. salary limit
47 Like 1, but not I
48 Rest
49 Peggy of "The Dukes of Hazzard"
50 Not be generous with
51 They really ought to be kicked
54 Next to nothing?
55 Sign of stress?
56 An alien may take it: Abbr.
57 Is a hero

DOWN

1 University of Alaska Southeast campus site
2 Anne of fashion
3 ___ disco (European dance music)
4 Reactor overseer: Abbr.
5 Cry from a daredevil cyclist
6 1884 short story by Guy de Maupassant
7 St. ___ (Caribbean island, familiarly)
8 Wee, to a wee 'un
9 Foremost
10 Private dos?
11 They're straight
12 Yosemite Valley peak
13 Dumped
14 Harms
22 Manhattan's place
24 Every month has one
25 Ticket
27 Babes
28 Where Fredo Corleone gets shot
29 Passive-aggressive and the like
30 Common desiccant
31 Kentucky college
34 Body found high in the Andes
35 Where to hang, in slang
37 Steinbeck's birthplace
38 Apiece
40 No Yankee fan
41 Light into
43 Governor who helped found Ohio State University
44 Called out
45 UnitedHealth rival
46 Like plaster
48 Suffix with super
52 Explorer, e.g.
53 Dating letters

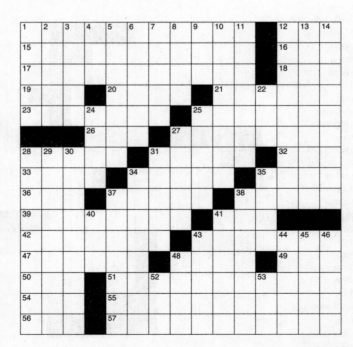

by Paula Gamache

ACROSS

1 Kind of year
6 Fed up with
13 It can be scary to go under this
14 Key
16 How some ashes are scattered
17 GQ figure
18 Detente
19 Dried out
20 Sound of contempt
21 Indication of feigned fright
22 They act on impulses
24 Like smooth-running engines
26 Black birds
27 Airport uniform abbr.
30 Mathematician famous for his incompleteness theorems
31 Pasta choice
32 One guarded in a soccer game
33 What you take when you do the right thing
36 Co-worker of Dilbert
37 Start of the Boy Scout Oath
38 Innovative chair designer
39 Innovative
40 Natural fluid containers
41 Backyard Jul. 4 event
42 Decision time
44 Fill-in
46 "Bummer"
49 Shortened word on a yellow street sign
50 It follows Shevat
51 "Win some, lose some"
53 Historic capital of Scotland
54 Concerning
55 "Outta sight!"
56 "Outta sight!"
57 ___ Landing (Philadelphia area)

DOWN

1 Pass superficially (over)
2 Free
3 Ditsy waitress player on "Mad About You"
4 Rough estimate
5 "Guilty," in a Latin legal phrase
6 Exchange of thoughts?
7 Burn up
8 Name of 11 ancient kings
9 Some collars
10 "White Flag" singer, 2003
11 Recovered from
12 Believed
14 Sign
15 Transition to a heliocentric model of the universe, e.g.
19 Late rocker Barrett
22 Auction
23 Draft
25 Nut cracker, perhaps
27 Negative sign
28 Requirement
29 They make connections
30 Fed
31 Sunburn preventer
32 Really take off
34 Winter coat?
35 Moon unit?
40 Minds
41 Drive nuts
42 Some sisters
43 ___ cat
45 Practices zymurgy
46 Toiletry brand introduced in 1977
47 Nail-biter's cry
48 Loud outburst
50 Long
52 Moon unit
53 Bribe

by Mike Nothnagel

304

⭐ ⭐ ⭐

ACROSS

1 Energize
10 Food fight noise
15 "Tom Jones" beat it for Best Picture of 1963
16 Singer Bryson
17 Cocky competitors might take them on
18 Star Steeler Stautner
19 Sends off again
20 Beards
21 Not do anything about
24 Basketmaker?
28 Touristy resort borough SE of Scranton, Pa.
32 Christmas story bad guy
33 Record holder
34 Writer of a five-volume Henry James biography
35 Curling setting
36 Young 'uns
37 Much unscripted fare
39 High hideaway
40 Acquisition before becoming a resident
41 Comparatively close
42 Fits behind the wheel?
44 1984 Cyndi Lauper hit
47 House style
52 Middle Eastern dish
53 Recording session starter
55 Stampless I.R.S. submission
56 Sultana-stuffed treat
57 Exercise
58 Showed

DOWN

1 Plymouth Reliant, for one
2 River at Rennes
3 Frames a collector might frame
4 "Citizen ___" (1992 autobiography)
5 Having turned
6 Monkey
7 Historically significant trial
8 Elementary school trio?
9 Univ. helpers
10 Small trunks
11 Achievement by 30-Down that had been previously unattained
12 Legal scholar Guinier
13 Rose's beau on Broadway
14 Web sites?
20 Take a bit of one's savings, say
22 Place of refinement
23 State second: Abbr.
24 Col. Potter on "M*A*S*H," to pals
25 Turned over
26 Mountain nymph
27 Title sport in a 1975 James Caan film
29 "Laborare est ___" ("to work is to pray")
30 Big name at the 1976 Olympics
31 1987 world figure skating champion
33 Having spokes
35 Leave in difficulty
38 Acknowledgment on a slip
39 Sterile
41 1994 U.S. Open winner
43 Sharp
44 Shoot out
45 Record holder
46 Designer Saab
48 View from Catania
49 Hands are under one: Abbr.
50 Steinbeck figure
51 Title
53 Many workers look forward to it: Abbr.
54 Golfer Woosnam

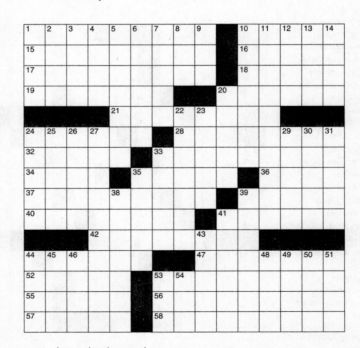

by Frederick J. Healy

ACROSS

1 Drawing power
10 Soigné
14 Suddenly
15 Stereo receiver button
16 Steely Dan hit of 1972
17 Villain in the Book of Esther
18 T formation participant
19 Cunning
21 ___ clue
24 Georgia ___ of "The Mary Tyler Moore Show"
25 Perishable fashion accessory
26 Certain sale item: Abbr.
28 Six-time All-Star third baseman of the 1970's Dodgers
29 Ancient fragrance
30 Molière comedy
33 Canadian equivalent of the Oscar
34 Filled treat
35 Properly filed
37 "Cooking With Astrology" author
38 "Moon Over Parador" star, 1988
40 "Buona ___"
41 You wouldn't sit for a spell in this
42 No-goodnik
43 Suffix with Darwin
44 "Divine" showbiz nickname
46 Motivational cries
49 Classic mystical book by Khalil Gibran
52 Brood : chicken :: parliament : ___
54 Asian title
55 Gulf of Taranto's locale

58 Echo, e.g., in Greek myth
59 Guided missile sections
60 ___ Atomic Dustbin (English rock band)
61 Have as an appetizer

DOWN

1 Not natural
2 Lengthwise
3 Skate
4 R.F.K. Stadium player, for short
5 ___ Carinae (hypergiant star)
6 Attire
7 Witless
8 Journal with an annual "Breakthrough of the Year" award
9 Where the wild things are?
10 Detective in "The Shanghai Cobra"
11 Pilgrims leave them
12 Not randomly arranged
13 Weigh
15 "The Amazing Race" host Keoghan
20 Thing on a ring
22 Earth, en español
23 Hard-to-break plates
27 18-wheeler
29 "Ode to Broken Things" poet
30 Beach house arrangement, perhaps
31 No longer gloomy
32 Rotary motions
33 Be a big success
34 Beta decay emission, sometimes

36 Subway Series locale, for short
39 Directorial demand
41 Thing with a life of its own?
44 TV star who said "Stop gabbin' and get me some oats!"
45 Prometheus Society alternative
47 Egypt's Mubarak
48 Honeybun
50 Potpie ingredients
51 Top-___ (leading)
53 Secure, in a way
56 & 57 Commercial entreaty

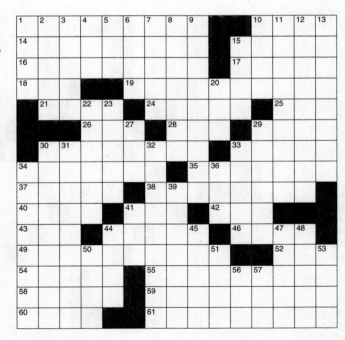

by Trip Payne

ACROSS

1 Mesoamericans of old
7 Mekong River sights
14 Warm up, as leftovers
15 Freak out
16 Small cavity, as around a cactus spine
17 Embassy issue?
18 Short cut
19 Look at a Playboy Club?
21 1993 rap hit with the repeated lyric "Bow wow wow yippy yo yippy yay"
22 Big name in sportswear
24 Concordat
26 Role in a Tchaikovsky ballet
27 Battlers, at times
29 Fiat headquarters
31 Part of many cultural venue names: Abbr.
32 Shrill
34 Long rides?
36 See 15-Down
40 Rise partly
41 Echelons
43 Gridiron stat: Abbr.
46 "Dead Souls" novelist
48 Platters' platters players
49 Indisposed
51 Gulf of ___, body of water next to Viet Nam
53 Bring down
54 Lit
56 Jim Beam and others
58 Univ. of ___, alma mater of Joe Namath and Bart Starr

59 Infer
61 Higher-priced
63 Put on the line, perhaps
64 Sportscaster with the catchphrase "Oh, my!"
65 Superlatively derogatory
66 Having one's feet up, say

DOWN

1 Mideast expert, maybe
2 Love all
3 Simon & Garfunkel hit after "Mrs. Robinson"
4 Affirmative action letters
5 ___ letters
6 Acclivitous

7 Adolphe with an instrument named after him
8 Not blasé
9 New York City transportation option
10 Hard-top
11 Sharp
12 Certain diet restriction
13 Influential one
15 Noted 36-Across passenger
20 Down
23 Actress Mazar and others
25 Rabbit food?
28 Christmas song favorite since 1949
30 Little terrors
33 Prefix with parasite
35 Letter finisher
37 Water towers?

38 Refuge
39 Father-and-son comedic actors
42 Comparatively bulky
43 Groups of plants
44 Entered
45 What a game plan leads to?
47 Romantic narrative
50 Helped, in a way, with "over"
52 Title role for Maria Callas in her only film
55 Mercury-Atlas 5 rider
57 Turned on
60 When repeated, an old-fashioned cry
62 ___ Lyman & His California Orchestra, popular 1920's–40's band

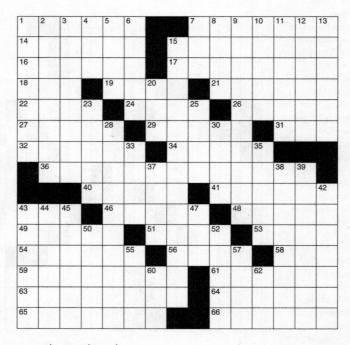

by David J. Kahn

ACROSS

1 War-torn Baghdad suburb
9 23-Across and others
15 One and only
16 Weather Channel topic
17 Fleet runner of myth
18 Key that doesn't include 58-Across
19 Up to
20 Ape
22 Habit
23 Shade shade
25 Biblical miracle setting
26 Powerful piece
27 Boarding spot
29 Call from home
31 1936 N.L. leader in slugging percentage
33 Brooklynese pronoun
34 Pilot's place
37 Part of Manhattan's Alphabet City
39 "Be honest"
41 Onetime Serbian capital
42 Show some spunk
44 Drops in a theater
45 Japanese model sold from 1970 to 2006
47 Meccan pilgrim
48 Some speakers
51 Abbr. before a date
53 Underhand?
54 Zip
55 Spotter's confirmation
57 Polit. label
58 It's almost a B, scorewise
60 Pilot's place
62 Apple application
63 Fancy haberdashery item
64 No longer in
65 Judge of films

DOWN

1 Henry Clay or William Jennings Bryan
2 It forbids religious tests for political office
3 Versatile actors may play them
4 Person found in a tree: Abbr.
5 Buck
6 Corinthian alternative
7 It might hold a couch potato's potato
8 Really hoped to get, with "for"
9 It can be drafted
10 ___ bark beetle
11 Stuck
12 11½" soldier
13 Online memo
14 Archaeologist David who found the lost Roman city of Kourion
21 Made some waves?
24 Word in some British place names
26 Put out
28 School exercises
30 Zoo de Madrid beasts
32 Shade of blue
34 Enter gently
35 Head of state known to his people as "Dear Leader"
36 "Of course"
38 Exclamations
40 Piehole
43 Swee' Pea's creator
45 Edmond Rostand hero
46 Calm
48 Composed
49 Dirección sailed by Columbus
50 British poet Tate
52 Track-and-field equipment
55 ___ dixit
56 1982 film title role for Bruce Boxleitner
59 Traffic stopper
61 School dept.

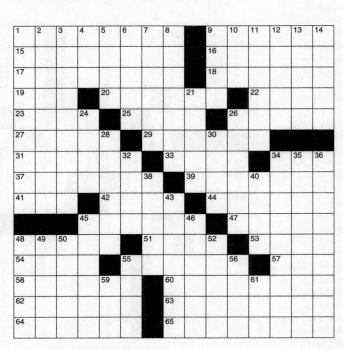

by David Quarfoot

308

★ ★ ★

ACROSS

1 Cash cache, often
10 No surprise outcomes
15 Happy
16 Liner threat, once
17 Well again
18 Spanish table wine
19 "Isaac's Storm" author Larson
20 Player of the Queen Mother in "The Queen," 2006
21 Determined to execute
22 Wanton type
24 Please, to Pachelbel
26 Shout across the Seine?
27 Green vehicle
29 They don't stay hot for very long
30 It's prohibited by the Telephone Consumer Protection Act of 1991
34 Vitamin A
36 Toughens
37 Kind of party
38 General equivalent
40 "New York City Rhythm" singer
41 Bills
42 "Turandot" composer Ferruccio ___
44 Sr.'s test
45 Dad's rival
46 Iranian filmmaker Kiarostami
51 Weasley family's owl, in Harry Potter books
53 Breaking sticks
55 Minnelli of Broadway
56 Biblical woman who renamed herself Mara
57 What kids might roll down
59 Old lab items akin to Bunsen burners
60 Darkroom equipment
61 Cold weather
62 Blues guitarist Vaughan

DOWN

1 They're seedy
2 Glass work
3 Ibid. relative
4 Crackpot
5 Hip-hop producer Gotti
6 "Vous ___ ici"
7 Peer group setting?
8 Peaked
9 Dwarf, maybe
10 Ill-prepared worker?
11 Drama honor
12 Potential canine saver
13 Personal manager
14 Playwright/painter Wyspianski
23 Direct
25 Mine shaft tool
28 Honeydew alternative
29 The Yasawa Islands are part of it
30 "The Thief's Journal" author
31 Review unfairly, maybe
32 Tops
33 Cheryl's "Charlie's Angels" role
35 ___ Raymonde, player of Alex Rousseau on "Lost"
39 Reels
40 Light white wine
43 Look askance
45 Rapture
47 Eight-time Grammy winner Mary J. ___
48 Patient one
49 Hyundai sedan
50 Fresh
52 It has an exclave on the Strait of Hormuz
54 Pomeranian or Dalmatian
58 Asian honorific

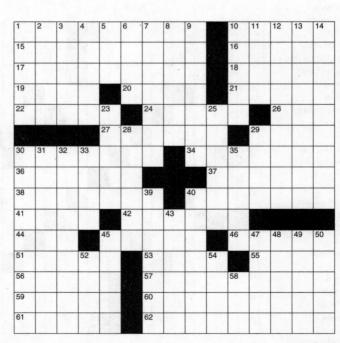

by Karen M. Tracey

ACROSS

1 Temper
8 Ape wrestlers
15 Be negative about
17 Hobbes in "Calvin and Hobbes"
18 Went to a lower level
19 Prefix with 6-Down
20 Body part above la bouche
21 Frames found in frames
22 Clubs: Abbr.
23 Señora's step
24 "A little ___ the mightiest Julius fell": Shak.
25 Actress Kimberly of "Close to Home"
26 Give away
27 Intimate
28 Tahini base
29 Well activity
32 Domesticates
33 Dramatic beginning
34 With 44-Down, Cajun dish with giblets
35 Polynomial components
36 Subject of some conspiracy theories
37 Prez's first name on "The West Wing"
40 Shot near the green
41 Little piggies?
42 Staff note
43 Ad follower
44 Playboy's plea?
45 She's dangerously fascinating

46 They're not easily overturned
49 Stereotypically smarmy sorts
50 Without much wind
51 Tickled the most?

DOWN

1 For one
2 Not at all sunny
3 Fit to be tried?
4 Id output
5 Mordant
6 Suffix with 19-Across
7 Going by
8 Fred of "The Munsters"
9 Hosts
10 Brand in a bathroom
11 Linguist Mario
12 Before being delivered
13 Unfrequented
14 Chief goals?
16 Smart
22 Exclusively
23 British meat pie
25 Actress Gray and others
26 ___-crowd (attendance booster)
27 Make like Pac-Man
28 They're bound to work
29 "Heads up!"
30 It stocks blocks
31 Less lax
32 Prepare for a shower, maybe
34 Foundations, often
36 Aggressively ambitious

37 Basso Hines
38 Hosts
39 "Who ___?"
41 August
42 Belarus's capital
44 See 34-Across
45 Longtime columnist who coined the term "beatnik"
47 Cloverleaf composition: Abbr.
48 Second-century year

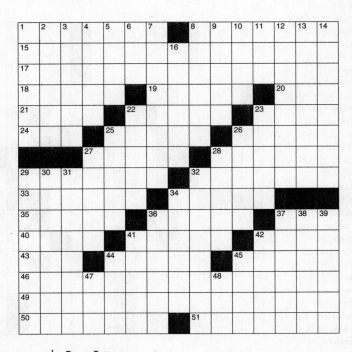

by Doug Peterson

310 ★ ★ ★

ACROSS

1 "The County Chairman" playwright, 1903
4 Hershey brand
8 Tree
14 Spinners, for short
15 Southern university whose campus is a botanical garden
16 Interstice
17 Having the most pizazz
19 Cap and bells wearer
20 Convict
22 Meter readers?
23 Kind of batting stance
24 Nos.
25 Reddish-brown
26 Al-___
27 Big bang creator
28 Fifth qtrs.
29 Enforce the rules
31 Italian mine
32 Has as a foundation
33 "Rugrats" dad
36 Easter-related
37 "___ now the very witching time of night": Hamlet
38 Norm of "This Old House"
41 Coup d'___ (survey made with a glance)
42 Part of a moonscape
43 No longer under consideration
44 Tetris objectives
45 Like clayware
46 Seemingly silent types
49 Burns
50 "She's gonna blow!"
52 Ferris Bueller's girlfriend
53 Spoils

54 Where the utricle is
55 Like haunted houses, compared to ordinary houses
56 Good-looker
57 The Wildcats of the Big 12 Conf.

DOWN

1 Hoelike cutting tool
2 Neighbor of Somalia
3 Brewed drink
4 Checks
5 Two-time figure-skating Olympic gold medalist Protopopov
6 Snapped
7 Ecstatic
8 Option for wings
9 Smeltery input
10 Paraphrase, say
11 A jiffy

12 Decides
13 Least spotted
18 British P.M. when the U.S. Constitution was signed
21 Quality that's hard to express
22 Event for a king and queen
26 Father of Harmonia
27 Former Giant Robb ___
30 Gymnastics move
32 Butt
33 1979 film with sequels II to VI
34 Prophet of Thebes, struck blind by Athena when he accidentally saw her bathing
35 Drew on

36 Popular dish in an Asian cuisine
38 Guide
39 Zyzzyva, e.g.
40 Malignity
42 Protein-rich paste
44 Certain softball pitch
45 Amendment that prevents being subjected to double jeopardy
47 Oscar-winning French film director ___ Clément
48 Article in Hoy
51 Robert Morse Tony-winning role

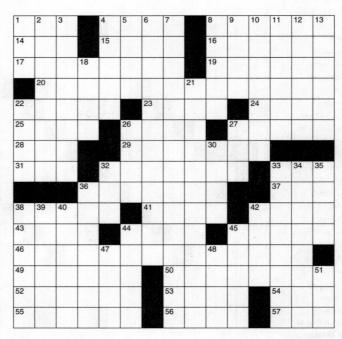

by Natan Last

ACROSS

1 Ways to get inside hip joints?
5 Results of compliments
14 Is not misused?
15 Invention convention
16 Bad mark
18 Opening on an environmentalist's agenda?
19 Wrangler rival
20 Pay stub data
22 Person after a lifestyle change, self-descriptively
23 How a goose acts
25 Charge
26 Lug
27 Modern vent outlet?
29 You may pass on these: Abbr.
30 Underachievers are not up to it
31 Old hippie hangout, with "the"
33 "Start doing your job!"
37 Restaurants are full of them
38 Singer Lennon and others
40 ___ shop
43 Where a tongue can be found
44 "No more!"
45 Rolls over, in a way
47 Probably will, circumstances permitting
48 Fragrant resin
49 Cornerback Sanders
51 Torch-lighting skater at the 1998 Winter Olympics
52 Africa's westernmost point
54 Woozy
56 Like some salesmen and preachers
57 Ryan of "Boston Public"
58 Brushes off
59 Club: Abbr.

DOWN

1 Laugh-producing game popular since 1958
2 What ethylene may be used for
3 Conspiring
4 Longtime Lakers commentator Lantz
5 Kind of resin
6 See stars?
7 Natives of Noble County, Okla.
8 Big ___
9 Short-term relationship
10 Alternate
11 Less apt to learn
12 Much-studied religious writings
13 May TV event
17 Ultra-obedient companions
21 Mugful, maybe
24 Measure that resulted in multilingual labeling on goods
25 They're hard to see through
27 Sect governed by the Universal House of Justice
28 Storyteller's pack
31 Web code
32 Attach
34 They're not positive
35 Turns over
36 Jersey workers
39 Pinch-hit
40 Abstract
41 Have a connection
42 Spare part?
44 Pitch preceder
46 Correct
47 It brings many people to church
49 Duel action?
50 "The Facts of Life" housemother ___ Garrett
53 Silent ___
55 1977 double-platinum album with the hits "Peg" and "Deacon Blues"

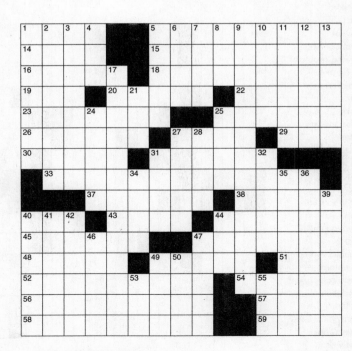

by Mike Nothnagel

312 ★ ★ ★

ACROSS

1 It can really bite
8 Warrant
15 See 33-Down
16 Late afternoon, typically
17 Nothingness
18 Temporary
19 Former major-league pitcher___Seo
20 Home of Clarke College
22 Plymouth-to-London dir.
23 1847 tale of the South Seas
25 One of the losers in the War of the Pacific
26 Asian bowlful
28 Hot spots
30 Night table
32 Key word
33 Glut
34 Home of Waterloo: Abbr.
35 Growing problem?
38 Pick-up and drop-off point: Abbr.
40 French mathematician Cartan
41 Grain sorghum with stout, leafy stalks
45 Mush
47 It covers six time zones
48 Asked too much?
49 Sport
51 It's pulled by una locomotora
52 Plasma component
53 Foundation with ties
56 Dummy
57 It doesn't help much when it's cold

59 Where Mt. Suribachi is
61 Middle third of a famous motto
62 Puts down
63 Cicero, e.g.
64 Factor

DOWN

1 Latin American capital
2 Founding member of the Justice League
3 Prevent
4 Title robot in an Isaac Asimov short story
5 Lacking interest
6 Basic exercise routine
7 Fence-sitter's answer
8 Post codes?
9 Dish describer
10 Some prayers
11 Taxonomic suffix
12 Electrician
13 Standing out
14 Set right again
21 Built up
24 ___ wonder (athlete known for a single great play)
27 Hanna-Barbera character
29 Agent Gold on HBO's "Entourage"
31 Capo ___ capi (Bologna boss)
33 With 15-Across, sites for some corals
36 Come together
37 Kingston pop
38 Pinchpenny
39 Classic 1934 novel set in Prohibition-era

New York City, with "The"
42 The moon has one
43 Madison Avenue types
44 Zipped by
45 Zip providers
46 Clever
47 Yarn variety
50 Bear
54 ". . . outrageous fortune, ___ . . .": Shak.
55 "Paradise Lost" illustrator
58 State with the lowest high point (345 feet): Abbr.
60 "The Gift of the Magi" hero

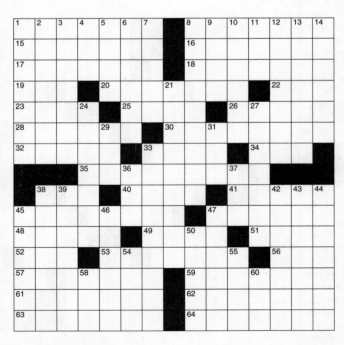

by Shannon Burns

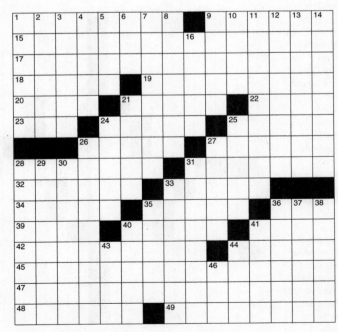

ACROSS

1 Didn't take advantage of
9 Muscleheaded
15 He conducted the premiere performances of "Pagliacci" and "La Bohème"
17 Bands of holy men
18 Become one
19 Newspaper column separators
20 ___ Elliot, heroine of Jane Austen's "Persuasion"
21 Star of "Gigi" and "Lili"
22 Put on an unhappy face
23 Revival movement's leader?
24 Strand at the airport, maybe
25 Maker of Coolpix cameras
26 Stray animals don't have them
27 ___ Couple (yearbook voting category)
28 "Field of Dreams" actress Amy
31 1979 #1 hit for Robert John
32 More of the same
33 Like St. Basil's
34 Incite
35 Center
36 Yielding ground
39 Young cowboy in "Lonesome Dove"
40 Ships on the seafloor
41 Roofing choice
42 Compliant
44 Gives up responsibility
45 Sometime soon
47 One with a guitar and shades, stereotypically
48 Bathe in a glow
49 Most mawkish

DOWN

1 Game featuring Blinky, Pinky, Inky and Clyde
2 Photographer/children's author Alda
3 Jelly seen on buffet tables
4 Kind of protector
5 Pennsylvania's Flagship City
6 Vet, e.g.
7 Stage actress who wrote "Respect for Acting"
8 Pilot light?
9 Treat badly
10 Albee's "Three ___ Women"
11 Vast
12 One that gets depressed during recitals
13 Awaiting burial
14 Files a minority opinion
16 Boxy Toyota product
21 Some emergency cases may be found in them
24 Steely Dan singer Donald
25 Some Degas paintings
26 1939 film taglined "Garbo laughs"
27 First African-born Literature Nobelist
28 "Is There Life Out There" singer
29 Titular mouse in a classic Daniel Keyes novel
30 1600 to 1800, on a boat
31 Big hit
33 Number to the left of a decimal point, maybe
35 Unlikely to rattle or squeak, say
36 Trifling
37 Political extremists
38 Roughly a third of the earth's land surface
40 Carthaginian statesman who opposed war with Rome
41 Rwandan people
43 Blue shade
44 Great literature's opposite
46 Possible work force reducer

by Patrick Berry

ACROSS

1 Bristles
8 Post boxes?
15 Thinner option
16 Piece of silver, say
17 Lab tube
18 A lot of foreign intelligence intercepts
19 Relatively remote
20 Many-sided problems
21 Ready to be put to bed
22 "Rugrats" baby
23 Isn't O.K.
25 One of the Gandhis
26 Golden fish stocked in ornamental pools
27 Christening spot
28 Nottingham's river
29 Dirt
31 One protected by a collie
32 Patron of Paris
35 One making calls
38 Schubert's "Eine kleine Trauermusik," e.g.
39 Demand
43 Some apéritifs
45 Mother of Hyacinth, in myth
46 Hindu sage
47 Certain alkene
48 Incubator
49 Slew
50 Anti-ship missile that skims waves at nearly the speed of sound
52 Touch-related
53 Part of a special delivery?
54 Be quite enough for
55 Amscray
56 Hamlet, notably
57 Give a bad name
58 "On Your Toes" composer

DOWN

1 "The View," essentially
2 Home to Mount Chimborazo
3 Earthen casserole dish
4 Letting stand
5 Decayed
6 Put in up front
7 Skittish herd
8 Small, deep-fried pork cube
9 C_2H_4
10 Size up
11 Bait
12 Singer of "A Foggy Day" in "A Damsel in Distress"
13 Isn't very visible
14 Shooter that may be digital, for short
22 Caused to be scored, as a run
24 European Union member: Abbr.
26 Means of public protest
30 Was broad on the boards
33 Big Mac request
34 Real
35 Island entertainer
36 Kind of water
37 Nearest, to Nero
40 Lessen
41 One using a crib
42 They work the earth
44 Apply messily
49 ___ Nurmi, nine-time track gold medalist in 1920's Olympics
51 Chowderhead
52 Peter or Paul, but not Mary
53 Picture producers

by Tony Orbach

ACROSS

1. Awfully accurate?
11. California wine center
15. Salade niçoise ingredients
16. "The company for women" sloganeer
17. Providers of exceptional service?
18. Neural network
19. With 50-Across, surmount
20. Turn out to be
21. Presidential middle name
22. Queen in a long-running comic strip
24. "What's ___?"
26. Pal
27. Disconcert
28. Strip alternative
30. Change from two to one
32. They might indicate hunger
33. "Centuries"
34. Where to find pop art?
37. Turns up
38. Start of some how-to titles
39. One who brings bad luck
40. Childish comeback
41. Some are manicured
42. NATO member: Abbr.
45. Boulogne-sur-___, France
46. Response of feigned innocence
48. Lose successfully
50. See 19-Across
52. Parry
54. Holder of many tracks
55. ___-Mints (Rolaids rival)
56. Singer of the 1967 hit "California Nights"
58. Incomplete picture?
59. Subject of the 2004 book "Dancing Revelations"
60. Jarrow's river
61. Outdoor toy that attaches to a garden hose

DOWN

1. Mil. V.I.P.
2. Eye component
3. Where I-25 and I-70 meet
4. Poet who won a Pulitzer for "The Dust Which Is God"
5. Prefix with directional
6. Shortening in the kitchen?
7. Level
8. Kinkajou's kin: Var.
9. 1883 Maupassant novel
10. Dine, in Düsseldorf
11. Caper
12. Bit of kitchen wear
13. Execute exactly
14. Over, with "of"
23. Suffered a blow to one's pride
25. Magazine holder
29. Creation of 31-Down
31. See 29-Down
32. "Underboss" author Peter
33. Smythe of hockey
34. Cause of colonial unrest
35. "You don't say!"
36. Hide in the woods
37. It's out for a pout
39. Ruler of Scotland, 1567–1625
41. Hanks's "Apollo 13" role
42. "That's Amore" setting
43. Scented
44. Photo flaw
47. Papa Bear of the N.F.L.
49. Watch
51. What some people get caught on
53. Home of Davy Crockett: Abbr.
57. Title syllables in a 1961 Lee Dorsey hit

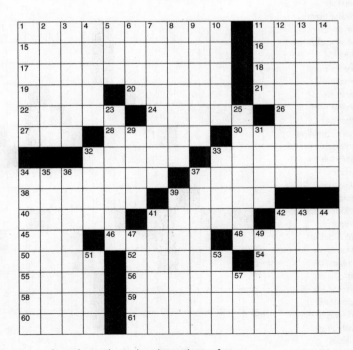

by Mike Nothnagel and David Quarfoot

316

★ ★ ★

ACROSS

1 Lard source
8 Service with a queue
15 G.P.S. receiver display
16 Explanatory tool
17 Uses a certain iron
18 Ousting
19 What flamingos often stand on
20 Reunion moniker
21 Vision de nuit
22 They travel by air
24 Part of some Muslim households
25 Ltr. recipient pinpointer
28 Candidate supporter, briefly
29 First to be admitted?: Abbr.
30 Frequent business traveler
33 Flow stopper
36 One who didn't say no?
38 Abbr. in some city names
39 They hang from the roof
40 Indications of good bowling
41 ___ Beach, Hawaii
42 What's left
43 Home to Al Jazeera
46 "Oh, right"
48 ___-Ude (Russian city on the Trans-Siberian Railroad)
49 Game intro?
50 Trust
54 An ace is a good one
56 Chin-wag
57 County west of Dublin
58 Some oilseeds
59 Subsequent
60 Things that wear well?

DOWN

1 Burkina ___
2 "East of Eden" twin
3 MTV segment?
4 South Dakota's ___ National Park
5 Robed ruler: Var.
6 Wear for rough outdoor activities
7 Some G.I. duties
8 Nostril
9 Chemical endings
10 Laddie's lid
11 Like some prints
12 Gallant
13 Donation declaration
14 Botanical nutrient conductor
20 Profanity
23 Atlanta commuting option
24 Afghan province or its capital
25 Mischievous
26 Sound of impatience
27 Some vacationers' acquisitions
29 One who might pick up toys
31 River formed by the junction of the Fulda and Werra
32 Amazed
33 Cordage material
34 Potent round
35 ___ Helens
37 Where you might get into a rut
40 Exotic estate
43 Faultfinder's concern?
44 Gridder Harper
45 Heads-down view
46 Like some bad goods: Abbr.
47 "___ sorry!"
49 Feelthy stuff
51 Space hog in a library
52 Israel's Weizman
53 Much ___
55 Sea bream, in a sushi bar
56 Birmingham-to-Montgomery dir.

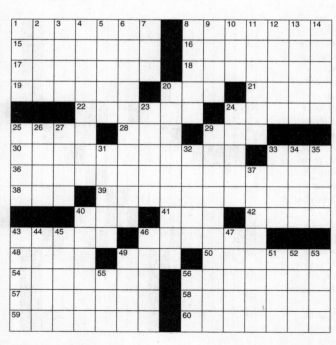

by Barry C. Silk

ACROSS

1. Product once advertised with the catchphrase "There's no step 3!"
5. Barely mention, as something one doesn't want to discuss
14. Putting regular gas in a diesel engine, e.g.
15. One abandoned at the altar?
16. Presently
17. In-house debugging
18. Person at the wheel?
20. Most useless
21. "Rich gifts wax poor when givers prove unkind" speaker
23. Snazzy
24. Region bordering Mount Olympus
26. Sound of a dropped scoop of ice cream
29. Certain chess piece, informally
30. Edward who created the Gashlycrumb Tinies
32. Coca-Cola creation
34. "Caribbean Blue" singer
35. Candle holders
36. Ford or Lincoln
37. "Notorious" setting
38. Dispel a curse?
39. Man
40. Unit of radioactivity
42. It protects car buyers
44. In the distance
46. #1 Beatles hit with the only known vocal contribution by Linda McCartney
47. Soft spread
51. Hang it up

52. 1990 #1 rap hit that starts "Yo, V.I.P., let's kick it"
54. Mystical indicator
55. Bernard Malamud's debut novel
56. Ball boy?
57. One who refuses to shake hands, maybe
58. Poses

DOWN

1. Agitated
2. Like most 1950's recordings
3. Final Gene Wilder/ Richard Pryor comedy
4. Neapolitan noblewoman
5. ___ volatile
6. Goes to bed, in Britspeak
7. Having a single purpose
8. Flowers named for their scent
9. Tendency toward chaos
10. "The Great God Brown" playwright
11. Classical art medium
12. Lifesavers, for short
13. Others
15. "___ Full of Grace" (2004 film)
19. Other
22. Pool owner's nuisance
25. Clodhopper
27. Continuously
28. Stop working
31. Push off
33. "Don't spread this around, but . . ."

35. Tightly embrace
36. Home for the Ojibwa and Cree
38. Split right before your eyes?
39. Go for a party, say
41. Wisconsin city that's home to S. C. Johnson & Son
43. Actress Streep
45. Picture writing, of a sort
47. Atoms
48. Comeback
49. Pullers of the chariot of Artemis
50. Practically unheard-of
53. Rule out

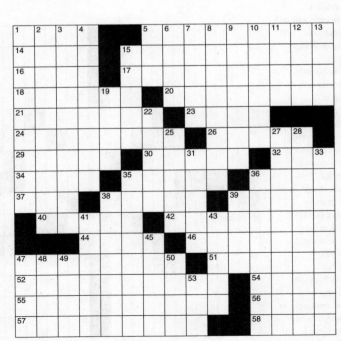

by Patrick Berry

318 ★ ★ ★

ACROSS

1 Event in which teams may drink rounds during rounds
8 Comb
15 Minimal, with "of"
16 Broke out
17 Conditioning system
18 Dumpling dish
19 Defeats easily
20 Doesn't stick around
21 1920's birth control advocate Russell
22 Author of "Save Your Job, Save Our Country: Why Nafta Must Be Stopped ___ Now!"
24 Name on some euros
25 They may be found in sneakers
27 "___ vindice" (Confederacy motto)
28 Chairperson?
29 Big name in flight
31 Place on a game board?
33 A.L. home run champ of 1950 and '53
35 Mop holder?
38 Often-minimized thing
43 1966 Grammy winner for "If He Walked Into My Life"
44 Focus of some ball-handlers?
46 Spanish mistress
47 Samoan capital
48 Cuts into a pie, often
50 Field fare, briefly
51 Distribution slip
53 Ostensible composer of "The Abduction of Figaro" and "Oedipus Tex"
55 Summit goal

56 Bennett of the Ronettes
57 Worker doing a desk job?
58 Bright planet, sometimes
59 "First . . ."
60 Information technology subject

DOWN

1 Leader who claimed to have put a fatal curse on J.F.K.
2 Cousin of Ascii
3 Dances in waltz time
4 Some radio sources
5 "'___ Me?' I do not know you" (Emily Dickinson poem)
6 Get slippery, in a way

7 Zipped up
8 Boho-chic footwear
9 Big combo
10 Old marketplace surrounder
11 Saints, e.g.
12 Function whose domain is between -1 and 1
13 Not-so-new work crew
14 First pitcher to have defeated all 30 major-league teams
23 Having a better bottom?
26 Part of a certain kit
28 Wolf, e.g.
30 H.S. subject
32 Faster, maybe
34 "Danger!"
35 Enter for a spin

36 Bristly appendages
37 Words after "Whew!"
39 Least sensible
40 20th-century German leader's moniker
41 Part of a fin?
42 Load-bearing things?
43 Most intrepid
45 Man and others
48 Zagat contributor
49 Opinion opener
52 Italian province or its capital
54 Amts.

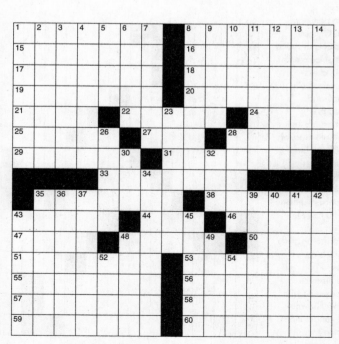

by Brendan Emmett Quigley

ACROSS

1. Climbing Mt. Everest, for Sir Edmund Hillary
12. 1937 Paul Muni drama
14. Art, metaphorically
16. History
17. Probe
18. Manfred ___ Earth Band
19. Roman well
20. Basic verse option
21. Whacked
22. Drum containers
23. Site of the siege of Candia
24. Feaster on frogs
25. Legato indicator
26. Coast Guard boat
27. It's hard to recall
29. Cowboys, but not Indians
32. Fitting decision?
33. Clued in, once
36. Stains
37. Delicate
38. Singer who is part owner of Forbes magazine
39. First name in fragrances
40. "In that area"
41. Cousin in a Balzac title
42. Cut across
44. Reminiscent of the 1890s
45. Census Bureau data
47. Only if it's worth the trade-off
48. London Zoo locale

DOWN

1. Remote access?
2. Stanford of Stanford University
3. Base runners?
4. Evidence that one is short
5. A foot has 305 of these: Abbr.
6. Like most medicine bottles
7. Things in rings
8. Big name in college guides
9. Old one, along the Oder
10. Holmes fought him
11. 50-50 proposition
12. Hand holding
13. Passing subject?
14. Artist Wyeth
15. Not lit
19. Princess Ozma's creator
22. Nine ___ (London district)
23. Bug zapper?
25. "Dear" ones
26. Under a quilt, say
27. Set off
28. "Blue II" painter, 1961
29. It's headquartered in the G.E. Building
30. Sacramento suburb
31. Global positioning system, e.g.
33. Bit of jazz improvisation
34. Bait
35. Meter makers
37. Certain inverse function
38. Get going
40. Honduras-to-Guatemala dirección
41. City bombed in the gulf war
43. Waste
44. Rockne protégé
46. Country singers England and Herndon

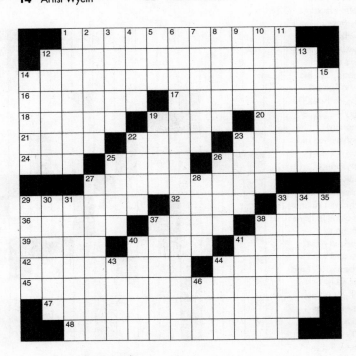

by Paula Gamache

320

★ ★ ★

ACROSS

1 Big flap on the road?
12 Yearbook div.
15 Song sung by Mehitabel in Broadway's "Shinbone Alley"
16 Treaty of Rome org.
17 Traitorous
18 First Fiesta Bowl winner: Abbr.
19 Since
20 Algorithm component
21 Forgoes a cab, say
23 Nickelodeon nut
24 Rijksmuseum subject
26 Ready to be driven
30 Poetry Out Loud contest org.
31 Vandals' target
32 Tennis's Ivanovic
33 Est., once
34 ___-Ball
35 Sketching
39 She's entertaining
41 Abba's "___ the Music Speak"
42 Subj. of the 2006 film "The Good Shepherd"
44 Identification aid in an obituary
45 Sponsoring publication of TV's "Project Runway"
46 Prefix with culture
47 The Danube flows through it
51 People in a rush
54 Host and winner of the 1966 World Cup: Abbr.
55 With 59-Across, it lasted from about 3500 to 1000 B.C.
56 Defeater of Schmeling in 1933

59 See 55-Across
60 Slogan ending
61 Dedicatee of "The Muppet Movie"
64 Flow checker
65 Dish with coddled egg
66 ___-Mère-Église (D-Day town)
67 Order of ants

DOWN

1 Prolific suspense novelist Woods
2 Soft, thin silk cloth
3 2006 Tony-nominated "Sweeney Todd" actress
4 1977 Steely Dan title track
5 They're often fried
6 Offended
7 Member of the 1960's Rams' Fearsome Foursome
8 Sports biggies
9 Insurance fig.
10 Cornelius Vanderbilt and Jay Gould
11 Cook, at times
12 Dangerous swimmer with an oarlike tail
13 Bathtub rings, e.g.
14 Deep-sixes
22 Card
25 Be in harmony
27 Bizarrely hellish
28 Aussie's place of higher learning
29 Mardi Gras, in the U.K.
35 Early-birds' opposites
36 Ride roughshod over
37 "Born to Be Blue" singer

38 Yield some
40 Lead-in to a sheepish excuse
43 Home to some fighters
48 Charles Darwin's ship H.M.S. ___
49 Ready to be driven
50 Steering committee's creation
52 Language in which "k" and "v" are the words for "to" and "in"
53 Kitchen gripper
57 It rises in the Cantabrian Mountains
58 Plaintiff's opposite: Abbr.
62 Beauty
63 Turncoat

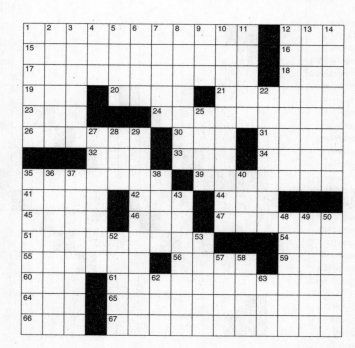

by Brad Wilber

ACROSS

1 Problem in closing?
16 Just before it's too late
17 1984 JoBeth Williams comedy/adventure film
18 Ouija option
19 Bucket seat feature
20 Seventeen people, briefly
21 One whose deposits are often collected
22 Hit-making group?
24 Gazelle, at times
27 Beetle's need
30 Grounded
34 One way to kick a bad habit
37 It's a shore thing
38 Alice who wrote the short-story collection "Open Secrets"
39 Utter collapse
40 Preview crowd
43 ". . . ye shall ___ more vanity": Ezekiel 13:23
44 Social group member
45 Social group
46 Instinctive
48 1980's N.B.A. guard Matthews
49 They look better when they're ripped
52 Like some cookie sheets
56 I have, in Le Havre
59 Pressure points?
62 Who said "A hungry man is not a free man"
63 One who'd like to put you in your place

DOWN

1 Supporting piece
2 World-weary words
3 Refuse
4 Poet's ending with what or how
5 They might be full of baloney
6 Brief scouting outing?
7 ___ and Jaron (identical-twins pop duo)
8 Posted
9 Prefix with Germanic
10 Not be picky with an instrument?
11 First film in CinemaScope, 1953
12 Word associated with a light bulb
13 It's on Norton Sound
14 Given a line
15 Goes off
21 Whitebait, e.g.
23 Rodeo trio
24 Stone, to Caesar
25 Like a shepherd's charges
26 Really get to
27 City NE of Rotterdam
28 Ban succeeded him in 2007
29 Supporting piece
31 Luxury hotel amenity
32 Big pictures
33 ___ per centimeter (surface tension measure)
35 George Harrison's "___ Mine"
36 V-shaped carrier
41 Real poser
42 Brewer's product
47 They have certain rings to them
48 Zigzag
49 Start ___ (be extremely aggressive)
50 Eliot hero
51 A room with una vista?
53 Formerly archaic?
54 Fictional wirehair
55 Decide to leave
56 Cuban patriot Martí
57 Like some sources: Abbr.
58 Abba's "Love ___ Easy"
60 Jazz guitarist Farlow
61 Like Mahler's Symphony No. 4

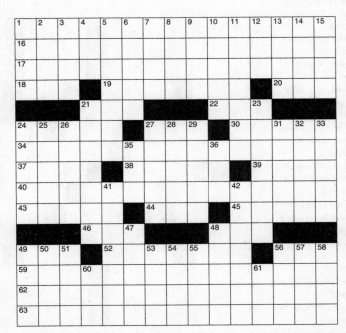

by Martin Ashwood-Smith

322 ★ ★ ★

ACROSS

1 Brewer Joseph
8 "America This Morning" outfit
15 "Comin' through loud and clear"
16 Region south of Silesia
17 Database search option
18 Curt comment to an ogler
19 Border line?
20 Hard bop, e.g.
22 Surpassed
23 Clothing store bargain fodder: Abbr.
25 Dwindle, as support
26 Greek goddess of youth
27 Move stealthily
29 Record letters
30 Like the Topoxte archaeological site
31 Setting for Joshua trees
33 Permits
35 Mistress of Charles II
37 Can
38 Where things get checked
42 Passed pleasantly
46 No place for a big rig
47 The following: Abbr.
49 Current terminus
50 Mixture
51 Magellan visited it
53 Participated in a pool, say
54 Suffix that may appear in a record
55 Language of central Mexico
57 About 20 pinches: Abbr.
58 Noted Venetian army general
60 People who may be removed
62 Potential cause of a wrongful conviction

63 Singer of the 1974 hit "I've Got the Music in Me"
64 Made with 39-Down, maybe
65 Stage production

DOWN

1 It rejects the caste system and idolatry
2 English toast
3 1993 hit for the R&B duo Zhané
4 Counselor's area
5 Hard stuff
6 David who caught a key pass in the 2008 Super Bowl
7 "Butterfly" star, 1981
8 2005 Best Supporting Actress nominee for "Junebug"
9 Hard stuff
10 Cristiano symbol
11 1986–93 war-themed Marvel Comics series, with "The"
12 Supposed bringer of bad luck
13 Bouquet setting
14 Gets down
21 Cause for winking
24 Not on the level
26 "Treasure Island" hero
28 ___ other
30 Latte variety
32 "Eldorado" grp.
34 Nail site
36 Become despondent
38 Appeared (as)
39 Ingredient in some chips
40 Something great, informally

41 See 51-Down
43 When some sea creatures are exposed
44 Santa Claus player in a 2003 comedy
45 "Honey, I just forgot to duck" speaker
48 They treat people badly
51 With 41-Down, cheap fast-food offerings
52 Immovable type
55 Giant, e.g., briefly
56 Patron saint of surgeons
59 Energy expressed in volts: Abbr.
61 You might pay for it later

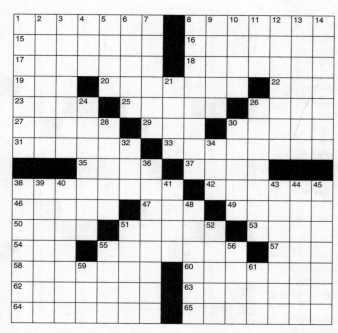

by Peter Wentz

ACROSS

1 A looker might give it . . . or get it
12 Partner of a certain rabid sports fan
14 "Please?" elicitor
16 Native home of the canary
17 Lion, tiger or shark
18 Wankel engine component
19 Winner of 11 Grand Slam tournament titles
20 ___ de boeuf
21 Goose
22 Computer hookup point
23 Infer from data
24 Local borders?
25 19th-century engineer with a star on the St. Louis Walk of Fame
26 Forgers
27 Something to turn on
28 Ruler crowned in 1953, informally
29 Bouncy kid-lit character
32 Blood sausage ingredient
33 Rock-___
36 First name in erotica
37 Saucy
38 With 15-Down, hangs on the line
39 Matted cotton sheet
40 Dylan was once her protégé
41 Shorts material, in München
42 Prefix in parentheses
44 Department store founder who pioneered credit unions
45 Habitués of art galleries, theaters, etc.

47 Nursery rhyme title fellow
48 Once-common monochrome PC display

DOWN

1 Some hybrids
2 Fast accelerator
3 Clear sky
4 U.K. awards
5 "We Were Soldiers" setting
6 Raises an outcry
7 "Hooked on Swing" jazzman Larry
8 Seeing red?
9 Gambling too much, e.g.
10 Loser in the Battle of Bannockburn, 1314
11 Find and destroy

12 Italian beans, in a Dean Martin standard
13 Base person
14 Base person?
15 See 38-Across
19 Figures, informally
22 See 25-Down
23 Ooze
25 22-Down that has split
26 Ooze
27 One stirring the pot
28 It can be frightening when one is popped
29 The French smoke it
30 Bug's place?
31 Drop leaf supporter
32 They're short on T's
33 Call for delivery
34 One with a mortgage, e.g.
35 Opposite of avant

37 Many an opening shot
38 Cataclysm
40 The Great Dane of entertainment
41 Petrol purchase
43 Smoke, e.g.
44 Thing with pétalos
46 Lines at a checkout counter?: Abbr.

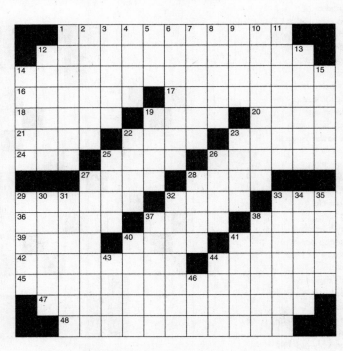

by Paula Gamache

324

★ ★ ★

ACROSS

1 Deserter
9 Main engagement?
15 Kind of fin on a fish
16 Person at home
17 Safecrackers, slangily
18 Corrupting influence
19 Oft-repeated words
20 Foot-long stretchers
22 Dyslexic TV host with a college degree in speech therapy
23 Cotton Club standout of the '30s
24 252-gallon measures
25 Doesn't bother
27 Computer prefix meaning 2 to the 40th power
29 "___ che penso" (Handel aria)
30 Dress cuts
32 Rigel, for one
34 "The Good German" actor, 2006
37 Area between forest and prairie, e.g.
39 Bushy-tailed?
40 Nero's homeland
42 River to the Yangtze
43 Fire
45 Best in one's position
49 "Ha!"
51 Remain close
53 Cant
54 Oil-rich South American basin
56 Kites, e.g.
57 C relative
58 Food carried by doves
60 Manage
61 Style of envelope for greeting cards
62 Irreparably cracked
63 Water

DOWN

1 Scandalize, e.g.
2 River with an alphabetical-sounding name
3 Piece of pie, often
4 Literally, "roof lizard"
5 Flew
6 Magazine article
7 Regimen with "cardio bursts"
8 The United States, to some prospective immigrants
9 Early South Carolina senator Thomas
10 Let off
11 Cut off
12 See through at last
13 Member of the first state to adopt Christianity as its religion
14 Calm, say
21 Quick round of tennis
23 Scion
26 Defeat quickly and overwhelmingly
28 Furious
31 Asian language with 14+ million speakers
33 Studs
34 Brilliantly colored food fish that changes hues when removed from the water
35 Hank Williams or Nat King Cole
36 No-names
38 Bit of a bluff
41 Morgiana's storied master
44 Game played with a piquet deck
46 One side in the Battle of Marathon
47 Like sunbeams
48 Ready to move
50 Poem of 31 syllables in five lines
52 Land rover
55 Eagle, e.g.
56 ___ Bones of "The Legend of Sleepy Hollow"
59 It's under a top

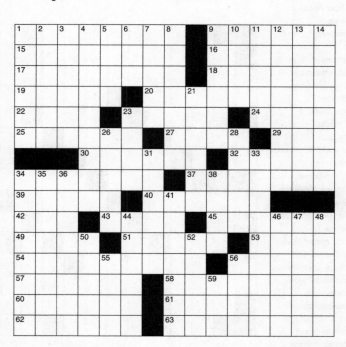

by Bob Klahn

ACROSS

1 Romp
6 Scotch flavorer
10 Soprano ___ Huang
14 A raise may raise it
16 Novel about its author's experiences on Tahiti
17 When many shots are taken
18 ___ snuff
19 Not letting go
20 Many a Kirkuk native
21 Some livestock
22 Regatta setting
24 "A Writer's Life" writer, 2006
28 Some singing villains
30 PBS station with a transmitter on the Empire State Building
31 Spin cycles?
33 Uppland inhabitant
36 Response to "I have a question for you"
38 Tinseltown is part of it
40 Cul-___
41 He fought Robin on an episode of "Batman"
43 "An Enquiry Concerning the Principles of Morals" philosopher
44 Since
46 Verne of Austin Powers films
48 Reno's county
50 Break
52 Michigan's ___ College
53 Arnold Schwarzenegger, four times
59 Somewhat dense
60 Match point?
61 Government largesse
62 It requires spin control
63 ___-Ball
64 See 48-Down
65 Ringer of some necks

DOWN

1 Steward's domain
2 Poet who wrote "Hope springs eternal in the human breast"
3 Penitent
4 Birds with "meat cleaver" bills
5 "The Two ___" (Martha Finley children's book)
6 Run on
7 Passes gingerly
8 Greatly
9 Addition column
10 Unnamed individual
11 Many an item at a checkout line
12 Our counterpart in France?
13 Small perk
15 Reply to "Have you got that in stock?"
23 Brand named after the pronunciation of its parent company's initials
24 Flat
25 Huber of women's tennis
26 "Keep it simple"
27 Oscar nominee for "Training Day," 2001
29 Kind of ed.
32 Aleutian island
34 Torch site
35 Israel's Weizman
37 Prefix with -pod
39 Béchamel sauce ingredient
42 Adapts
45 Confines
47 Leak
48 With 64-Across, sight under the eaves, at times
49 Perfectly good
51 Not just jitters
54 Force through a sieve
55 Is in Spain?
56 Sluggers' stats
57 ___ fil (wireless, in Paris)
58 Conclusion lead-in

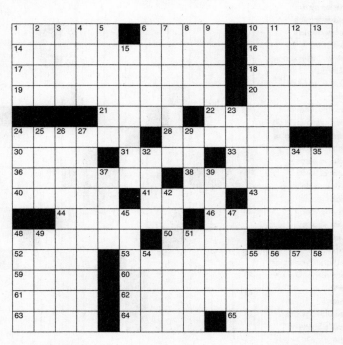

by Mike Nothnagel

326 ★ ★ ★

ACROSS

1 Stadium stands
10 It's sometimes ribbon-shaped
15 They have extensions
16 His tribute to Marilyn was remade for Diana
17 Vents
18 Pant
19 2004 U.S. Women's Open winner Mallon
20 100 sen
21 Future egg
22 Pricing words
24 Bracing
26 Cardsharp's goal
27 Brown and others
29 Futile search
32 Ace
34 Range accessory
35 What 16-Across has been called since 1998
36 64 crayons, e.g.
37 Gave away an intruder, maybe
41 Military districts
45 Glare
47 Whence some spaniels and terriers
48 N.C.A.A. rival of Vassar
49 Like some weaves
51 Legendary athlete on the 6/23/75 cover of Sports Illustrated
52 Landslide election winner of 1945
55 Player in a docking station
57 Gerrymander
58 Lipstick shade
59 Player of Pat Nixon in "Nixon"
61 Word after Vanilla or Chocolate, at Dunkin' Donuts
62 Forward
63 Head of Hogwarts School's Slytherin House
64 34-Across sporter

DOWN

1 Artist's tone-blending technique, used in the "Mona Lisa"
2 Part of some splits
3 Spent
4 Communist leader?
5 Trunk protuberance
6 Not advanced
7 Where Hampshire College is
8 Try to land
9 Certain card issuer: Abbr.
10 One-named Belgian cartoonist who created the Smurfs
11 "The Black Stallion" lad
12 Go nowhere
13 Dessert garnished with crumbled macaroons
14 Only Mouseketeer personally chosen by Walt Disney
21 Try to block
23 Volkswagen model
25 Kindred
28 Sharply irritating
30 Governor or mayor follower
31 Buzz generator on Wall Street
33 Words often accompanied by a 45-Across
37 Music store array
38 Player of Richard Nixon in "Blind Ambition"
39 Its flag features an olive branch inside a wreath
40 1950 film that opens with a man reporting his own murder
41 What to flash when you need a lift?
42 First U.S. coed college
43 Spell
44 Wallace ___, Pulitzer winner for "Angle of Repose"
46 Idle
50 Certain jazz combo
53 Miner's aid
54 Part of a noted reb's signature
56 Show pluck
59 Yak
60 Photocopier abbr.

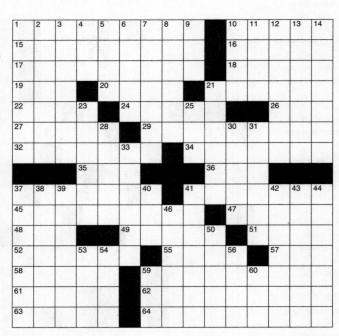

by Brad Wilber

ACROSS

1 Creek Confederacy tribe
8 "The Appeal" novelist
15 Two-time foreign minister of the U.S.S.R.
16 Clio maker
17 Film with the line "By the authority vested in me by Kaiser William II, I pronounce you man and wife. Proceed with the execution"
19 Equipment for strokes
20 ___ lot (was telling)
21 Observing things
22 Home of Sault Ste. Marie: Abbr.
23 Recipient of a trade discount
25 Withdraw
26 Not be generous
30 King of Naples in "The Tempest"
33 One way to recoil
35 Sported
36 Ill-gotten
38 Prefix with marine
39 Jesus, Mary or Joseph
41 Like some DVDs in DVD players
43 Burning evidence
44 Evidence that one is an alien
46 Opening for an anchor
48 Toy store inits.
51 Asian au pair
54 Have ___ (not be trapped)
55 U.S. org. with over 39 million members
56 Fantastic flight
59 Cheat
60 August

61 Ignition problem
62 Big East team with six N.I.T. basketball championships

DOWN

1 Childish comeback
2 "I Know Who Killed Me" actress, 2007
3 Word often preceded by a color
4 Givers of unfriendly hugs
5 Justice Dept. division
6 A ham might use it
7 Focus on one's approach, say
8 Inclination
9 Kind of artery
10 Govt. probe
11 Frank request
12 U.S. military chopper
13 One way to turn a ship
14 Chain links?: Abbr.
18 George H. W. Bush, once
23 Apt., e.g.
24 Panamanian pronoun
25 Lifter
27 Ticks off
28 Glutton's desire
29 Driving tool
30 Beards
31 The good earth?
32 Pasta eaten with a spoon
34 Web connection means
37 Trapped
40 Franklin contemporary
42 Word with longer or minute
45 Body types
47 Apparently anxious person
48 Hill in Nashville
49 "As You Like It" setting
50 Subjective pieces
51 Switch letters
52 Where Bambara is spoken
53 All ___ (words on a game box)
55 One of a comic-strip married couple
57 Third-century year
58 Atlantic City hot spot, with "the"

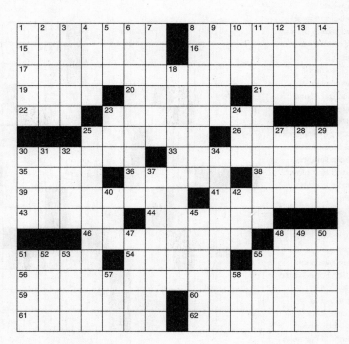

by Barry C. Silk

328 ★ ★ ★

ACROSS
1 Brand for preparation on a stovetop
9 Like some misguided remarks
15 Tourist booth handouts
16 Hebrew title for God
17 Appliance numbers
18 "The Crimes of Love" author
19 Buy in
20 Call for
22 Old atlas inits.
23 Where pins are made
24 Use leverage on
25 Bakery container
27 Not stiff at all
29 Fifth-year exams at Hogwarts
31 Jambalaya need
32 Land where the air is thin
33 Press
34 Black as night
35 Lines for liners
38 Moccasin sound
41 Brings in
42 Workout reminders
46 Funny papers pooch
47 Longtime North Dakota senator Gerald and others
48 Certain charity event
49 Hanger-on
51 C.S.I. tasks
53 Give-to-go filler
54 "I knew it!"
55 Loose overcoat
57 Pitcher Saberhagen
58 Civic club
60 Just too cute
62 "Aaargh!"
63 Sushi bar order
64 Weightlifting move
65 Indy, for one

DOWN
1 Early hominid
2 Early period
3 Kind of pen
4 Them's the breaks
5 Peruvian Sumac
6 Cell alternative
7 "Look, bonehead!"
8 Discreet call
9 Ham's rig
10 Writer ___ Rogers St. Johns
11 Amex listings: Abbr.
12 Twirling
13 Born loser
14 "Laura" star, 1944
21 Dressed to the nines
24 Sports star with an accent in his name
26 '67 Summer of Love locale
28 ___ Volcanic National Park
30 Set down
36 Nominee for Best Supporting Actress in "Mildred Pierce," 1945
37 Hammer holders
38 "___ End"
39 Sarah Palin, by birth
40 Sands part-owner, once
43 Girlish accessory
44 She was a pip to Pip in "Great Expectations"
45 Like elm trees
50 Golden
52 Go on and on
56 Needlework, for short?
57 Minstrel
59 Colony member
61 English singer Corinne Bailey ___

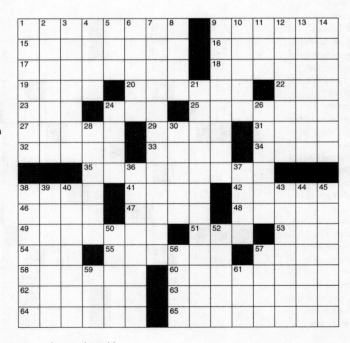

by Mark Diehl

ACROSS

1 Woolly bear, eventually
5 City at the foot of Mount Entoto
15 Cross letters
16 Sludge buildup sites
17 Like falling off ___
18 Brownish orange
19 Early 20th-century New York City mayor
21 Many a defender: Abbr.
22 Rule that ended in 1947
23 Journalist with a widely read "Report"
25 Newbie: Var.
26 Maintains
27 Not overseas
28 ___ moment
29 Not at all wet
30 Be visibly disconsolate
31 Steakhouse order
32 Foundation maker
34 It may be mined
35 Warnings, to Juan
38 Peter Pan rival
39 "The Emperor's Snuff-Box" novelist John Dickson ___
43 1980's Big Apple nightclub with a chemical name
44 Mattress problem
45 Cliffside detritus
46 ___ outing
47 Cry when you don't think you'll make it
49 Some linemen: Abbr.
50 ESPN analyst Pasquarelli
51 Hits a line drive
52 Gardener or landscaper
55 "Women and Love" writer
56 Some forms are filled out in it
57 City south of West Jordan on I-15
58 1993 Emmy winner for "Seinfeld"
59 Asian lang.

DOWN

1 Noxious vapors
2 Ashore, maybe
3 Horse in harness
4 It has made many people lose their heads
5 Person in an apron
6 Tapped
7 ___ el Beida (Casablanca, to its natives)
8 Destitute-looking
9 Work on one's figure, say
10 A.T.M. receipt abbr.
11 ___ Dai (last emperor of Vietnam)
12 One way to sit on a chair
13 Tritium output
14 Facetiously
20 Denom. with elders
24 Touch
25 Briar locale
28 Young fox
30 911 call, e.g.
31 Org. involved in the gulf war
33 From, in some names
34 Computer-savvy crowd
35 Salamander variety
36 Classic Pontiac
37 Excited
38 Big bump
40 Dresser alternative
41 Verify, as a password
42 Saves
44 "Phoenissae" playwright
45 Offering of appeasement
47 "___ it!" (cry of accomplishment)
48 Had a 31-Across, e.g.
50 Asparagus's family
53 May days?: Abbr.
54 Big D cager

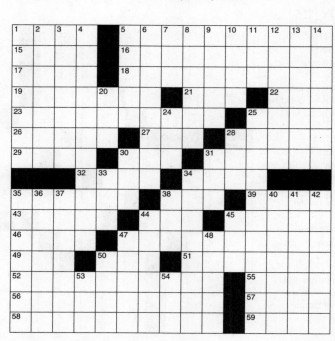

by Brendan Emmett Quigley

330 ★ ★ ★

ACROSS

1 Seek change?
11 Southern appellation
15 Between wings
16 Showy wear
17 Ad pitcher who's really a pitcher
18 Some familia members
19 College of the Redwoods locale
20 ___ Archer, with whom Sam Spade had an affair
21 Red state?
22 They have their ups and downs
23 Weapons once produced extensively by the Royal Small Arms Factory
25 Chicago Fire's sports org.
26 Satyajit Ray's "The ___ Trilogy"
27 Dish with cornhusks
29 Trials
35 Big name in cells
36 Blood drive quantity
37 Player of the first Bond girl
39 Actor Jack
40 No place for a lady
42 Hold up
44 "Thrilla in Manila" airer
45 Timetable listing: Abbr.
46 Combinations' locations
48 Badger
53 Yak
55 It has its ups and downs, with "the"
56 Kind of beef or chicken
57 Fungal spore cases
58 Evolutionary process

60 Diagonal
61 Marquee name
62 They're near temples
63 Toy with blueprints

DOWN

1 Dawdling sorts
2 Have ___ (not be trapped)
3 Link in a chain?
4 Cart
5 Trees of the verbena family
6 Early Chinese dynasty
7 Capt.'s announcement
8 Hot-dog
9 Pita source
10 Kind of farmer
11 Short orders?
12 Indian tribe V.I.P.
13 Spammer's resource

14 Stops stewing
23 Hot rods?
24 Market yardstick, for short
26 Yellowfin, on Hawaiian menus
28 Last name of father-and-son N.F.L. coaches
29 Copper head?
30 Bergman title role
31 Terminal offering
32 Italian leader
33 Bygone stickers
34 Automotive debuts of 1949
38 ___ Dinh Diem (first president of South Vietnam)
41 Stand-up routine?
43 One of a couple at a French restaurant
47 Travel writer Eugene

48 Swell
49 Still no longer
50 They're shown at horse shows
51 Whac-___ (carnival game)
52 Something a believer believes
54 It's often planted
56 Keep in
59 Shot

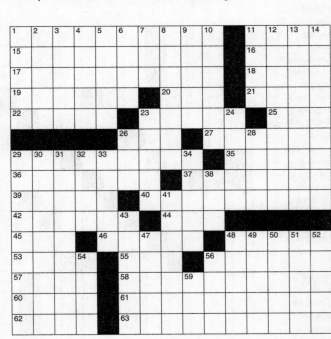

by Ken Bessette

ACROSS

1 Big name in exercise
10 Firm parts: Abbr.
15 Dessert skipper's declaration
16 Big-eyed baby
17 Valuable piece of time?
18 Sofia, por ejemplo
19 It's sometimes pulled while running
20 1966 hit from the album "Sounds of Silence"
22 Keep
23 Track has-been
25 It's passable
26 Transports near stairs
27 Like pigs
28 Game with many balls
29 Topple
30 Zulu's group
31 Sci-fi hero whose home planet is Corellia
34 Most economical
36 Bits of créativité
37 Derby attire
38 Many a 21-Down celebrant
39 Amuse
41 Lays out
44 Knob on old TVs: Abbr.
45 They might be in stitches
46 "Home Improvement" actor Richard
47 Yakut, e.g.
49 Modern home of ancient Ebla
50 Feather: Prefix
51 Term of address used during an argument
54 They're often found in tubs
55 Zip

56 They're green
57 "Sure"

DOWN

1 Shake
2 Unlikely to be judgmental
3 "It won't be missed"
4 Split up
5 Forest issue
6 Certain ladies' room
7 Small beef
8 Unquestionable
9 Near
10 It might be worn under a cap
11 It has a lip and a mouth but never speaks
12 Epoch when the landmasses of North and South America joined

13 A call used to go out for this
14 Plan to catch a criminal
21 Kentucky Derby time
23 City founded by Ivan IV
24 Star viewed at night
27 Mailing ctrs.
28 Where Manhattan is: Abbr.
29 Handled
30 Oven dial word
31 Climax
32 À la an expert
33 Drink for a designated driver, maybe
34 Not far from
35 Direction-changing pipes
37 Blockhead
39 ___ chi

40 Rally speaker's emphatic response to his own rhetorical question
41 Site in ancient Thebes
42 A.L. East player
43 Cross
45 Total amount
46 Former capital of Japan
48 Sock attachment?
49 Atlantic catch
52 Armagnac article
53 18-Across's partner

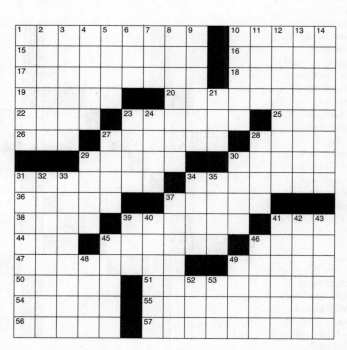

by Frederick J. Healy

332 ★ ★ ★

ACROSS

1 Unoriginal order, with "the"
5 Enhancers of cognitive abilities
15 Raven
16 Places to live the high life?
17 Lawless vehicle
18 Follower of an extra-long workday
19 Meal bit
20 Extravagant display
21 Comes up to
22 Rambler's lack
24 Acts clownishly
26 "Grease" co-writer Jim
27 Maggie's dog in "Bringing Up Father"
28 Trumped-up bit
31 The Louvre's Salles des ___
32 Drink with a bite
34 Glazed, waxy fabric finish
35 Sounds unsound
36 Move caller for a round dance
37 Produced 28-Acrosses
39 Kind of cycle
40 ___ Balls (snack brand)
41 Somewhat open
42 It doesn't have an obvious answer
43 Uncooked side
44 Headed out for the drink
45 Open
48 Give up
49 Original Dungeons & Dragons co.
50 Upper-class luxury
53 W.W. II partisan leader
54 Like bottles with S O S messages, typically
55 Muddy
56 Spot to show off alpine plants
57 Letter abbr.

DOWN

1 Idols, often
2 Anomaly
3 Solitaire game of matching pairs of cards
4 Disney doe
5 Cheerleaders' display
6 Substantial
7 Animated film featuring the voices of Gene Hackman and Sylvester Stallone
8 G.P.S. request
9 Seminary deg.
10 Icing
11 Old character set
12 John McCain's alma mater: Abbr.
13 Emmy winner Will
14 Bygone Black Sea borderers: Abbr.
20 Rack parts
23 Supported a runner
24 Those whose actions speak louder than words?
25 Potential hoax subjects
27 Pyrexia
28 Something to build on
29 Not real-world
30 Aerobatic maneuver
32 Hit NBC series succeeded in its time slot by "ER"
33 Gulf war weaponry
35 Asian royal
38 Activity avoided by 24-Down
39 Miller option
42 Betray shame
43 Choice for third and short
44 It's under the Pont Neuf
45 Rosa or violeta, por ejemplo
46 First baseman Brogna
47 Matisse's "Jeune fille ___ tiare"
48 Jester
51 Org. with guards
52 Neighbor of Alg.
53 Amount past due?

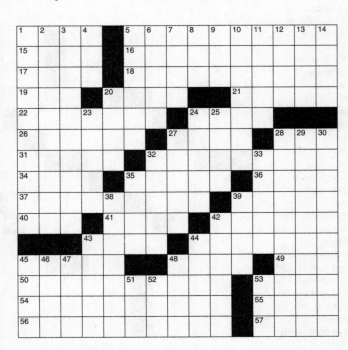

by Pete Muller

ACROSS

1 Activity involving a needle
10 Expression of praise
15 Household help?
16 Flavor of Calvados brandy
17 Wave measurement
18 Unusually high 17-Across
19 Closest to nil
20 Potential sucker
22 Wretched
23 Gallimaufry
24 One getting pinned?
27 Even's counterpart
28 It's hard to penetrate
29 "Desperate House-wives" housewife
30 "Point taken"
31 Out-of-the-way spots
32 Big draw of early Broadway
38 Putters
39 Ray in pictures
40 Dispensary stock, for short
41 Cat's-eye alternative
43 Furry sci-fi figure
47 Self-starter's equipment?
49 Something that's picked up
50 Field of field workers: Abbr.
51 Small dabbler
52 Grinder in an Italian restaurant
53 Indication of a job well done
55 Getting ready to make one's move?
58 Crane, e.g.
59 Command
60 Act unprofessionally
61 Merrie Melodies regular

DOWN

1 Peace
2 Thick-skinned fruit
3 Debilitate
4 "The Simpsons" bully
5 Set down
6 Choosing method
7 19th of 24
8 Locale of Krypton in the Superman saga
9 Feigned
10 Madrid's ___ del Prado
11 Useful piece of code, briefly
12 Series kickoff
13 1955 A.L. batting champ
14 Gratuitous
21 Part of N.Y.C.: Abbr.
24 Boughpot
25 City liberated during the Battle of Kursk
26 Hollow
30 Hypotheticals
31 ___ Worm (1980s light-up toy)
32 Victoria Falls forms part of its border
33 "No smoking" symbol, e.g.
34 Poe poem about a knight's lifelong quest
35 Exploit
36 Disrespectful
37 Expressions of praise
41 Bolted things down
42 Balsamic vinegar source
43 Composition of some chains
44 Ad-lib
45 Thick
46 Big-enough catch
48 Browser setting?
52 Very serious
54 Clinic worker
56 Person in the fourth grade: Abbr.
57 "The Wonder Years" teen who loved Winnie

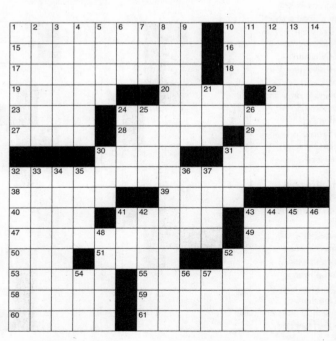

by Doug Peterson

334

⭐ ⭐ ⭐

ACROSS

1 Unpleasant face covering
4 "O Fortuna" composer
8 Notice in a restaurant
13 Battery, e.g.
15 Fifth-century pope called "the Great"
16 1973 musical for which George S. Irving won a Tony for Best Actor
17 Stat for a state
18 "Can-Can" song
20 Unexpected info source
21 Edgy?
22 Member of a NATO land since 2004
23 Manual component
25 It's all relatives
26 Old Mideast org.
27 A long one is 12% "longer" than a short one
28 Emulate a woman, in "I Am Woman"
32 Aggressive guarding option
37 Bad thing to drive into
38 What some dogs and flaming daredevils do
39 Winter Olympics maneuver
40 Get into
41 From left to right: Abbr.
42 Plasma alternatives, briefly
43 As required
45 It's taken in court
49 Was compelled
51 Added power, in slang
53 "Tell me more . . ."
55 Coin with 12 stars on both the front and back
56 It's often filtered

57 Fee-faw-fum
58 Company V.I.P.'s: Abbr.
59 Do nothing worthwhile
60 Minuscule part of a 34-Down: Abbr.
61 Surprise winner of 1948: Abbr.

DOWN

1 Citation abbreviation
2 Tusks, e.g.
3 Lionel to Drew Barrymore
4 Number between scenes
5 1941 Disney film based on a Kenneth Grahame story, with "The"
6 They're sold in oversize rolls

7 Bygone emporium
8 Autumn arrival
9 Like some confessions
10 Simple
11 Tizzy
12 Adventure
14 Result in serious damage
19 It follows directions
24 Many an ad
28 Shakes off new distractions
29 Away, in a way
30 Clarifying link
31 Invoice abbr.
32 Third baseman Melvin
33 "He eateth grass as ___": Job 40:15
34 See 60-Across: Abbr.
35 Tiny fraction of a foot-pound
36 F on a physics exam

42 1969 Omar Sharif title role
44 Nomadic dwellings
45 Piece of punditry
46 Book of Mormon's longest book
47 Cousin of a greenwing
48 Approve enthusiastically
50 "Currently serving" military designation
52 Blog bit
54 Apt to trick

by Joe Krozel

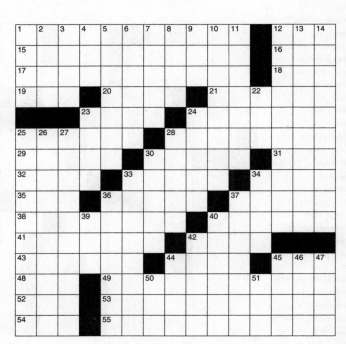

ACROSS

1 Aids in artful deception
12 Knowledge base?: Abbr.
15 Correctly positioned
16 Org. in the 1982 film "Enigma"
17 Babble
18 Where people wear gowns, for short
19 "The Daughter of Time" novelist
20 Big Daddy player on 1950s Broadway
21 Gabfest
23 Hit
24 Sink
25 How Viola is disguised in "Twelfth Night"
28 Crude dwellings
29 ___ of Galadriel (gift to Frodo Baggins)
30 Go for ___
31 "Livin' Thing" group, in brief
32 Like some details
33 Antigen attacker
34 Year of the last known Roman gladiator competition
35 Plot line
36 Street show
37 2003 memoir of a TV executive
38 Back out?
40 One may be backed up
41 Wrote
42 Something fit to be tied?
43 Center of learning
44 Switch
45 Followers of closings: Abbr.
48 Duct opening?
49 1970s–'80s sitcom putdown/ catchphrase

52 Loch ___, on the River Shannon
53 Recyclable
54 Not be on target
55 Components of some alarms

DOWN

1 Bailiff's concern
2 Strauss's "___ Nacht in Venedig"
3 Part of 16-Across: Abbr.
4 "The Tudors" airer, briefly
5 Like straight shooters
6 Square, in 1950's slang, indicated visually by a two-hand gesture
7 High on amphetamines

8 Dedicated compositions
9 TV pooch
10 Decoy accompanier
11 Cave
12 Pet with short legs and a hard coat, informally
13 Big Apple excursion operation
14 Reviews repeatedly
22 Court figure: Abbr.
23 Words after "if" or before "as well"
24 Slate, originally
25 Measure of a newborn's health, named for its developer
26 Extension of the terms of a marine insurance policy
27 American, for one
28 "Nice!"

30 Bitter
33 Wealthy Cayman Islands resident, maybe
34 Juniper product
36 One of Judaism's four matriarchs
37 It can be a stunner
39 Slowing, in mus.
40 Private detective Mike of Brett Halliday novels
42 Round of four
44 Real-estate ad abbr.
45 ___ Rivera, Calif.
46 Lead
47 Hyphenated IDs
50 ___ sponte (of its own accord, at law)
51 Real-estate ad abbr.

by Paula Gamache

336

★ ★ ★

ACROSS

1 Item with clear face value?
6 One who may have connections
14 Certain blues
16 Cry of relief at an accident scene
17 "Haw"
18 Provoked
19 Roadside stand offering
20 NATO member since 2004
22 Grp. with the debut single "10538 Overture"
23 Rectangular array that's identical when its rows and columns are transposed, as this puzzle's grid
27 Stud alternative
28 Fruity
29 Fruit salad waste
30 Where pizza originated
31 Some collectible Dutch prints
34 Round-bottomed vessels
35 Split and boned entree
36 A choli is worn under it
37 Kind of paper
40 Pondering, informally
43 Many a goddaughter
45 "Collage With Squares Arranged According to the Laws of Chance" artist
46 Revealed the end to?
48 One involved in future deals?
49 Who wrote "I dwelt alone / In a world of moan, / And my soul was a stagnant tide"

50 Some early "astronauts"
51 Lecture, in a way
53 Magazine sales
55 Courtside seats?
56 Honey
57 Cockamamie
58 Automaker Maserati
59 Tots

DOWN

1 Hindu musician's source material for improvisation
2 Methyl orange or Congo red
3 Woman's name meaning "peace"
4 Elementary stuff
5 They may be seen on a lake's surface
6 1963 Elizabeth Taylor/Richard Burton drama
7 Dinosaur, so to speak
8 Turkey setting
9 A little cleaner?
10 "Hostel" director Roth
11 Completely straightforward
12 Title woman of a story from James Joyce's "Dubliners"
13 Electron-transferring reactions, briefly
15 Country music's ___ Brothers
21 Prunes
24 1990's HBO sketch comedy series
25 Obi-Wan's apprentice
26 Some are heaping: Abbr.
31 Dido
32 German chancellor, 1998-2005

33 Specialty cookware item
34 Drop off
36 End of many business names
37 Trough
38 Polish stripper
39 Some dupes
41 Brand of insecticide strips
42 Doesn't skip
44 Self-response to "Must we put up with this?"
47 Believer in al-Hakim as the embodiment of God
52 Home of Presque Isle Downs racetrack
54 Be a different way?
55 Wrench part

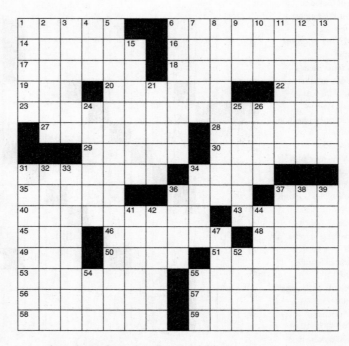

by Mike Nothnagel and Byron Walden

ACROSS

1 Bygone flag
16 Think a certain way about
17 Make a call
18 New York's Bear ___: Abbr.
19 Ballyhooed new product of 1998
20 Name repeated in a nursery rhyme
21 Short dog, for short
22 It's nothing
23 Before the races
25 Kind of depth finder
27 Bit of noise pollution
28 B and O figures: Abbr.
29 Brilliant moves
30 Roll
33 Bubbly name
34 Loosens (up)
35 Big copper exporter
36 Cover girl, e.g.?
37 Laid-back
38 Time being
39 Mammonism
40 "Something to Talk About" singer, 1991
41 Words starting a simple request
44 1960s–'70s touchdown maker
45 Mission statement part
47 First name in conducting
48 Actress Mazar
49 Lab subj.
50 Much of Central America, once
54 "This would be a first for me"
55 Trading posts?

DOWN

1 Beat but good
2 Can't continue
3 A tossup
4 Not hurting for cash
5 Pastes in Mideastern cooking
6 Hardly hearty
7 Relating to wheels
8 You might not get paid while working on it
9 Hurt
10 Dayton-to-Toledo dir.
11 Ladles
12 "Scènes de la Vie de ___" (novel on which a Puccini opera is based)
13 Make ___ of it
14 Actress Blakley
15 Comics dog
23 Downright
24 Emulates Eve
26 With 41-Down, shrunken
27 Yet to be engaged?
28 Early times, for short
29 "The Insect Play" playwright
30 Withdrew quietly
31 It's a little over 65 degrees: Abbr.
32 Deserved
34 Things that open and close yearly?
35 Maui mouthful
37 Coach
38 Home of Walvis Bay
39 1997 Demi Moore flick
40 Co-firing technique used to reduce pollution from electrical power plants
41 See 26-Down
42 Furlough
43 Chambermaid's charge
44 Pennies : dollar :: ___ : drachma
46 Producers of sunbows
48 Skin: Suffix
51 Palindromic girl's name
52 Bill of Rights subj.
53 Kicker

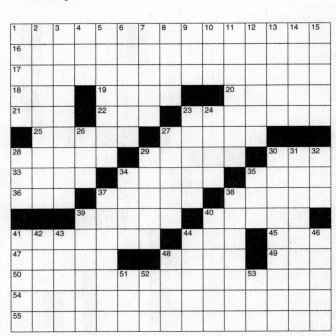

by Joe DiPietro

338 ★ ★ ★

ACROSS

1 Hindenburg's predecessor as German president
6 Cousin of an alewife
10 Longtime name in news-gathering
14 Drive participant
15 Heads of Italy
16 Gifford's talk-show replacement
17 Place for a tie
19 Magnitogorsk's river
20 Summer cooler
21 Biblical trial word
22 Manages to get through
23 Roger of "Cheers"
24 Multiplied
25 One doing fitting work
27 Hue similar to cyan
33 Miss at a rodeo
36 Off for a stretch
37 Brand of octane booster
38 Oscar winner for "The Bridge on the River Kwai"
41 Water-skiing variety
42 She, to Schiaparelli
46 Credit report tarnisher, briefly
47 First holder of the title Supreme Governor of the Church of England
53 Calls for passage
54 Governing group
55 Origination point
56 Epithet coined for the 2002 State of the Union address
57 Toe trouble
58 Recommend highly
59 Toy with tassels
60 Dr. Foreman's portrayer on "House"
61 Title aunt in a 1979 best seller
62 Plant ____

DOWN

1 The rough vis-à-vis a green
2 Summer headgear
3 Bring to the boiling point
4 2001 Emmy nominee for "The West Wing"
5 Quality
6 Elaborate solo vocal composition
7 It might be kicked after being picked up
8 With celerity
9 Like some tracts
10 Sternum attachment
11 Alveoli, e.g.
12 Enter la-la land
13 Spiel preparer
18 Cheerful, in Châlons
26 Sports winners
28 Stationery topper
29 Count
30 Second-century year
31 Phil Rizzuto, on the Yankees
32 Headed up
33 Burner locale
34 Court crowd-pleaser
35 Executed part of a 34-Down
39 Shuts up
40 Group with the 1967 #2 hit "Georgy Girl," with "the"
43 English poet Smith
44 Butcherbird or woodchat
45 Like supermarkets
48 Locale of Theban ruins
49 Part of the body next to the sacrum
50 Ritz rival
51 Catullus's "Odi et ____"
52 U.K. equivalent to an Oscar

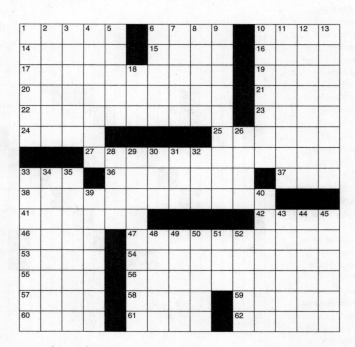

by Frank Longo

ACROSS

1 Tetanus symptom
7 1980's–90's action/adventure series
15 Square off against
16 Being borrowed by
17 The world, per the Bard
18 Be in a fix, say
19 It may be glassy
20 Key
21 Low reef
22 Sender of the Calydonian boar
24 Insignificant injury
26 Prefix with -polis
27 "The Great Broxopp" playwright, 1921
29 1989 French Open winner and others
31 Academic area
35 Name tag?
36 "Cómo es ___?" ("How come?" in Cádiz)
38 Follower of drop or shut
39 It includes mayo
40 Doctor who's friends with Matthew Mugg
43 Prize
45 New Jersey setting of "Coneheads"
47 "All You Need ___" (2008 Morrissey song)
48 Dance around a high chair?
49 It doesn't include a bonus
51 Annual stretch of trois mois
53 Physicist Ampère
55 Noted role for Maria Callas
57 With 60-Across, hypocrite's mantra
59 Cry that may forestall a lame excuse
60 See 57-Across
61 Backpedaler's words
62 Forward and back, e.g.
63 "St. Elsewhere" actor David

DOWN

1 Stepping-off points: Abbr.
2 Yellow-green shade
3 Place to receive communion
4 Tackle
5 1966 Tony winner for "Marat/Sade"
6 Julie, e.g.: Abbr.
7 Philosophies that regard reality as one organic whole
8 Without ___ (daringly)
9 It's next to 10-Down, both in an adage and literally in this puzzle
10 See 9-Down
11 Derisive cry
12 Feature of some shirts
13 See 28-Down
14 Thickly fibrous
20 Using
23 One way around town
25 What few people live for: Abbr.
26 Breakdown cause
28 With 13-Down, here and there, to Henri
30 Start pulling down more?
32 Certain section
33 Barry B. Longyear novella that won Hugo and Nebula awards
34 Certain
37 Brazilian greeting
41 Subject for a W.S.J. article
42 Early developments
44 Upset
46 Sharjah's fed.
48 Ledger with lines
50 As a friend, to Frédéric
51 Mom in "Hairspray"
52 Blow
54 ___ City, Fla.
56 Pro in briefs?: Abbr.
58 Paradise in literature
59 Family member

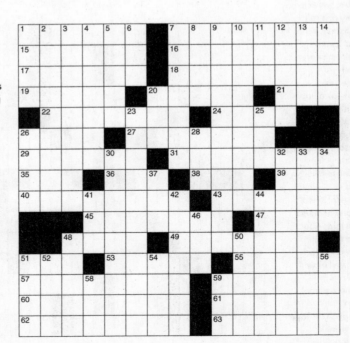

by Corey Rubin

340

★ ★ ★

ACROSS

1 Drug combination?
15 Many a vigilante
16 Call for dishes
17 Going for
18 Unspoken language
19 Not in the dark
20 Scent
22 River that meets the Thames at London
23 Very hot star
25 Insinuating
26 No walk in the park
27 Players that replaced Minis
29 Base pay recipient?: Abbr.
30 Title holder
31 Pitcher Orlando Hernández's nickname
33 Undercover Playboy bunny of 1963
35 Continuous series
36 "Lost" Emmy nominee Henry ___ Cusick
37 Sans strife
41 Break, as a habit
44 Started
45 ___ Morris College, in Jacksonville, Tex.
47 Electric guitar model, familiarly
48 Mind
49 Praise for Nero?
51 Bygone boomers
52 Gate info: Abbr.
53 Bebe who co-starred in "The Maltese Falcon," 1931
55 Act on a primal urge
56 "Krapp's Last Tape" playwright
58 Chew out
60 Be postponed
61 Dweller along Lake Volta
62 Doesn't get wrapped up well?

DOWN

1 Not taken to the cleaners?
2 Not perfectly round
3 Come back
4 Major downer?
5 Money-changer's profit
6 Splits
7 W.W. I battle locale near the Belgian border
8 Hoedown moves
9 It may be received after sweeping
10 Sedative target, with "the"
11 Beltway fig.
12 Longtime columnist for The Nation
13 Phone system starting point
14 One set for a future wedding?
21 Pro wrestler Flair
24 "Walk on the Wild Side" singer
26 Upright relatives
28 Platoon part
30 They make lasting impressions
32 Family moniker
34 Roofing material
38 Legalese adverb
39 Like some navels
40 Hyundai model
41 Bear
42 First name in late-night talk, once
43 Automatic sound
46 Réponse affirmative
49 Round midnight?
50 Root of law
53 Band that famously remade "Satisfaction" on its first album
54 Work to help one get 57-Down
57 See 54-Down
59 Night spot

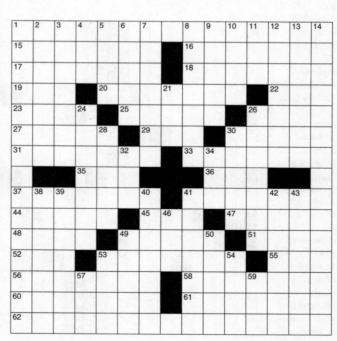

by Joe Krozel

ACROSS

1 Part of a horse between the shoulder blades
8 Xanax maker
14 Quaint game with a giver and a striker
15 Valerie of "The Electric Horseman"
16 Like broken things
17 Pros at projecting
18 Ready to be fired
19 Pot cover
21 Basketball Hall-of-Famer Holman
22 Resistance leader in Woody Allen's "Sleeper"
23 Eldest of a trio of comic brothers in 1930's–40's films
24 Neil Sedaka's "___ Ape"
25 Williamson who played Hamlet and Macbeth on Broadway
27 Its chapel was designed by Eero Saarinen, briefly
28 Processing time unit: Abbr.
29 Foul territory?
30 Pas de deux part
33 Dostoyevsky's exile city
34 Coarse, as stucco
36 Plantation creation
39 Dieter's concern
40 Org. whose emblem features an eagle and a crown
43 She's a paradigm of patience
44 Notable head-turner
45 Bouillabaisse go-with
47 I
48 Like some love
51 Time of Obama's swearing-in

52 First Across word in the world's first crossword
53 Einstein, notably
54 Elk's enemy
55 His opening statement is famous
57 Uniform adornment
59 New Testament miracle recipient
60 Great Dark Spot locale
61 Blackmailer's words
62 Record producers

DOWN

1 Some winter wear
2 Sure to be grounded, say
3 Matter of lease concern?
4 Bring bad luck to
5 Coin depicting Louis XVI
6 One with a dreaded style?

7 Play set entirely in a beauty parlor
8 Choate ran with him in 1996
9 Half of a recurring "Saturday Night Live" duo
10 N.Y.C. transportation debut of 1904
11 Movement Herman Wouk called "a single long action of lifesaving"
12 Sets off
13 Do a store chore
15 City hall, often
20 Clown's over-the-top topper
26 Mekong River native
28 Zinger
31 Police blotter abbr.
32 One of Iowa's state symbols

34 & 35 Mocha is on it
36 Mix on the range
37 Far from Rubenesque
38 Put on a pedestal
40 Abductor of the Sabine women
41 Sustaining stuff
42 Obsesses
46 Ascribe
48 Psychotherapy topics
49 Suffuse
50 New Testament miracle recipient
56 Credit card statement abbr.
58 Credit card statement abbr.

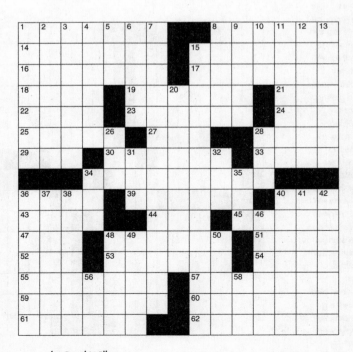

by Brad Wilber

342

★ ★ ★

ACROSS
1 Early 1990's first lady's first name
6 Cross
13 Group member from the time of Jesus
15 Chosen as a career
16 Mushroom supporters
17 Without any wood or plastic, say
18 Repetitive rebuke
19 Untrustworthy
20 What goes on?
21 A conductor may have it memorized
22 Units in nuclear physics
23 Serves
24 They may be full of hot air
25 Sigmoid architectural feature
26 Rubber stamp
28 One getting hit on?
33 Skipping syllables
35 Acoustic measures
37 Momentum
41 Play the flute
42 Kings Henry I and Stephen
43 Oxide used in television tubes
44 Spasm-relieving alkaloid
45 Feast
46 Mexican and Indian, e.g.
47 Spinachlike potherb
48 People working with logs?
49 Parents' hiree
50 Folks going through leaves
51 Its openings are often studied

DOWN
1 Fill positions differently
2 With sapience
3 "Really?"
4 Defensive fencing positions in which the top of the blade is pointed at the opponent's knee
5 Arterial problem: Var.
6 They're not green
7 New face on base
8 Congregation location
9 Dapper Dan's doodad
10 Destine
11 They're often drawn on the street
12 Like an 8-Down
14 Eleanor who wrote "The Hundred Dresses"
15 One full of hot air
25 How most sleds are mounted
27 Goal getter
29 Way out there
30 Way to walk
31 Dramatic break
32 Fancies
34 Value
36 Those who put you in your place?
37 Pleasant way to play
38 Swank's co-star in "The Next Karate Kid"
39 Wrote an essay, say
40 Persia, e.g., once
41 Pros' opposites
44 One not allowing a volley

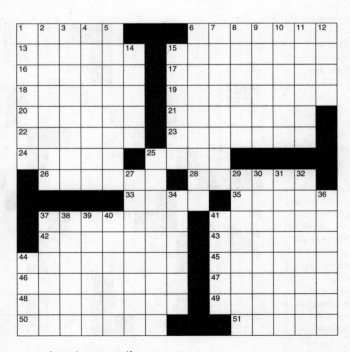

by Robert H. Wolfe

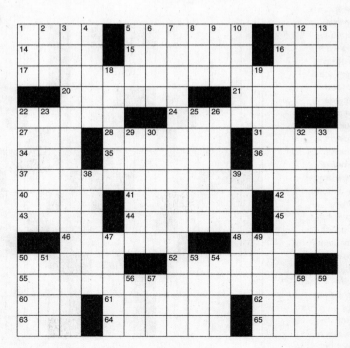

ACROSS

1 Repeat offenders?
5 Cover
11 Ask too much?
14 Sarcastic reply
15 Unsuitable for mixed company
16 Note traded for bills
17 "That's how it looks to me, anyway"
20 Cheers
21 Weak heart, for example?
22 Does badly at the box office
24 Rubber
27 Org. that awaits your return
28 Hightail
31 In the vicinity of
34 John no one knows
35 Like some glasswork
36 13th-century literary classic
37 Night light used by Sherlock Holmes
40 Therapist's comment
41 King defeated at Châlons
42 Disembarrass
43 Cricket match
44 Eye shadow?
45 Put in one's ___ (interfere)
46 Mason's assistant
48 "South Park" boy
50 1950's-60's actor known as the Switchblade Kid
52 White robe wearers
55 Crows and others
60 French dip's dip
61 Chevy model discontinued in 2001
62 Deadfall, e.g.
63 Jack, for one
64 Docile marine mammal
65 Daring, in a way

DOWN

1 Plame affair org.
2 Things used during crunch time?
3 Extreme exposure
4 Follow closely
5 "Vamoose!"
6 Cheat, slangily
7 Clive Cussler best seller made into a 1980 film
8 Member of Sauron's army
9 Miss ___
10 Dings
11 Charles IX's court poet
12 It may be played for money
13 ___ Ball, quinquennial dance in Harry Potter
18 Irritated reactions
19 1995 thriller about identity theft
22 Chocolate chip, e.g.
23 Stir to action
25 Land
26 Speedy Gonzales cry
29 Words that affect one's standing?
30 Father Time's prop
32 Monk's first name on "Monk"
33 Stopped flowing
38 Thorn, once
39 Acted as an informant
47 Muddies up
49 Carriage trade
50 Goya's "La ___ Desnuda"
51 1989 Radio Hall of Fame inductee
53 Italian boxer Benvenuti
54 Not just nibble
56 Prompter action
57 Practice overseers: Abbr.
58 Not just nudge
59 Invisible ink user

by Patrick Berry

344

⭐ ⭐ ⭐

ACROSS

1 Fugitive-hunting Fed
10 2000 U.S. Open winner
15 "E.T." follower
16 Free sample, say
17 Local assessment
18 Plume hunter's prey
19 Antisocial type
20 Type with finesse
22 "How ___ is the candle of the wicked put out!": Job 21:17
23 Like some thin fibers
26 Not quite none, in Naples
27 Yacht spot
29 Reason for a lighter conviction?
30 Like many smoothies
31 View spoiler
33 Chronicle
35 Crutch
36 Social type
37 Get down
41 Where some touchdowns are made
45 Detriment
46 Popular piercing site
48 Orchestra alternative
49 Where organs may be repaired, briefly
50 It stores fish in a pouch
52 Set of utensils
53 It has a dark side, in sci-fi
55 "___ My Family" (Cranberries song)
57 Corral
58 Its logo is a rubber-band ball
61 Spring
62 Counted raised hands, say
63 See 7-Down
64 Like many avenues

DOWN

1 In one's face
2 Pennsylvania Dutch pie
3 Enduring symbol of Canada
4 Last of the Stuarts
5 In once more
6 Lacking
7 With 63-Across, 1972 Rolling Stones "greatest hits" album
8 Knight of medieval literature
9 Defining work
10 What a 9-Down might help you do
11 Galley of myth
12 H_2O, e.g.
13 "For real!"
14 Opposite of destined
21 Smoke that's not thick
24 "The Canterbury Tales" charlatan
25 26-Across and 26-Across and 26-Across
28 The last one begins "Praise ye the Lord"
30 Percival caught sight of it
32 Permian Basin yield
34 Sister's study: Abbr.
37 Met the course standard
38 Bronze Star recipient
39 One of the metalloids
40 Literature Nobelist Derek
41 TV's "___ Ramsey"
42 Collectible card creatures
43 Shake
44 Quit using
47 Try to win
50 Dixie cakes
51 Lite as can be
54 1972 A.L. Rookie of the Year
56 Supreme Hindu goddess
59 One to go up against
60 Memorable 2008 Gulf hurricane

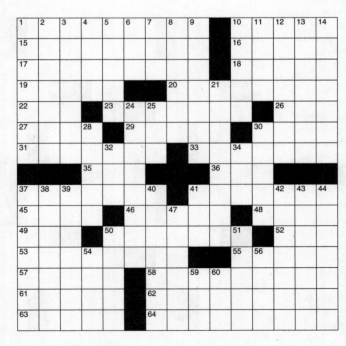

by Chuck Deodene

ACROSS

1 Ticketed
6 Chilled
15 Chilling
16 Constellation once called the Dragon's Wing
17 Tenor Mario
18 The Who's "Quadrophenia," e.g.
19 Microscopic protists
21 Part of a picket fence
22 Docs who've paid their dues
23 Lettuce variety
24 Japanese code word meaning "tiger"
25 Tandoori-baked breads
26 Singer of the Leoncavallo aria "Vesti la giubba"
27 Organ repair sites, for short
28 Like some coats
29 Fine point
30 Land of a Million Elephants
31 Bill
32 Printing press parts
35 A cappella group part
36 Joe-___ weed (herbal remedy)
39 Perfume, in a way
40 Suffix with techno-
41 1930's Royales
42 ___ milk
43 Be fourth in an order
45 Union and others: Abbr.
46 "Well done!"
47 Reveled
49 In Key West it's known as the Overseas Hwy.

50 "You're probably going to get me, but go ahead"
51 They result from catching bugs
52 Set sail
53 Break off a relationship

DOWN

1 School in the Patriot League
2 Well-suited?
3 Bad traits for conductors
4 Aloe target, perhaps
5 Silas who was the United States' first foreign diplomat (1776)
6 Bicep builders' accessories
7 Process of mountain building
8 Walt Disney has more of these than anyone else
9 Great ___
10 Post-punk genre
11 Returns, as from a high level
12 Makeup of some jokes
13 Briefly
14 Stereotypical college drinker
20 OB's perform them
26 Bye for an Italian soccer team?
28 Suffix after kitchen
29 Irk
30 Factor in a more healthful diet, perhaps
31 Food item once used as currency in Mongolia
32 Event with pairs and eights
33 Fresh angle
34 Add gradually, as to dough
35 Virtuoso
36 Certain table tennis grip
37 1941 Glenn Miller hit that spent five weeks at #1
38 Zener cards are used in it
40 City on the Strait of Dover
41 Outs, in a way
43 "The Hobbit" character
44 Draw forth
48 It can come on white, briefly

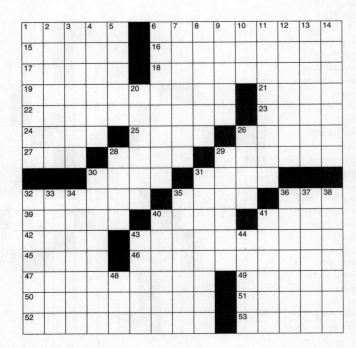

by Joe DiPietro

346

★ ★ ★

ACROSS

1 One very concerned with how a kid acts
9 Edible mold
14 Plant disease similar to blackleg
16 Comic actress who co-starred on "Archie Bunker's Place"
17 1968 soul album with the hit "Think"
18 Plague
19 Boarding house?: Abbr.
20 "That's completely wrong!"
22 Medical suffix
23 Got together
26 Like the coats of 25-Down
27 ". . . who hath begotten the drops of ___?": Job 38:28
28 South of Brazil?
30 Not just reworked
31 Lay an egg
32 Driver's problem
35 Limerick scheme
36 A bowl of cherries, in Chelsea
38 Sheets are sold in them
39 Gender-neutral phrase
40 "___ White Season" (André Brink novel)
41 Cost increaser
42 Not even once, to Nietzsche
43 Mil. authority
44 Change (into)
46 Org. that tracks numbers
50 It was split in 1948: Abbr.
51 #1 hit from the album "J.Lo"
53 Mimicking
54 How some foods are packed
56 To the extent that
59 Dividers of 35-Down
60 A caddie may hold it
61 A caddy may hold it
62 Sonnet feature

DOWN

1 Jerk
2 Nutty nosh
3 Troubled
4 Rod
5 End of the Bible?
6 Evidence of paranormal activity, perhaps
7 Speculation follower
8 1919 novel set in Paris and Tahiti, with "The"
9 The ___ Dukes (1960's–70's band)
10 Go with
11 Dance based on bullfight music
12 "Time was . . ."
13 Carolina natives
15 What an angry employee might give a boss
21 Kansas City-to-Omaha dir.
24 Company man's grp.?
25 Deer stalkers
29 Orderly supervisor, maybe: Abbr.
31 Engages in hydrotherapy
32 Entrepreneur's request
33 They may fall when you're down
34 Jackson Pollock's player in "Pollock"
35 They're fed by venae cavae
36 Neither freshwater nor marine
37 What "+" may indicate
41 Kenyan leader Mboya whom Obama called his "godfather"
44 Biblioteca Ambrosiana locale
45 Sports
47 Sportscaster with the autobiography "Holy Cow!"
48 Cell phone feature
49 ___ bourrée (ballet move)
52 One who minds his manors?
55 Contemporary of Baiul and Yamaguchi
57 Élément #26
58 Exclamation in Ems

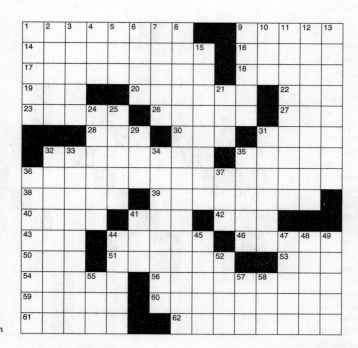

by Ned White

ACROSS

1 Pad producers
12 Name in many suit cases
15 Cry before a disappearance
16 Saturn's wife
17 Something that's just too cool
18 Recharging aid
19 Musician who was a trailblazing Rastafarian
20 European wine center
22 Matching ring recipients: Abbr.
23 Small part of an archipelago
25 Ben Franklin
26 Follower of directions
27 Cry upon being fleeced?
29 Grateful Dead bassist Phil
31 One exploring deeply?
35 Longtime name in auto parts
36 Ramen brand
38 It's sometimes forbidden
39 Free
40 Classic record label for the Bee Gees and Cream
41 M., in Milan
42 Monitor setting, briefly
43 Nickname in pioneering jazz piano
45 38-Across variety
46 "Grey's Anatomy" hookups
49 Hushed
52 Mother of the Gods
53 Big name in flooring?
54 So-called "baby busters"
57 Pronoun in 20-Across
58 Song that mentions "the Father, Son and the Holy Ghost"
59 Unit in astronomy
60 Well-known TV evangelical

DOWN

1 There are 746 in a single horsepower
2 Can't stomach
3 Bun bit
4 Up
5 Producer of some dishes
6 Muscle strengthened in rowing, in brief
7 Opinion opener
8 Skedaddles
9 "Uh-huh"
10 Work that marked the start of musical Romanticism
11 Admitted politely
12 "St. Mark" artist
13 Is like a moonstone
14 Make out
21 Finely tempered blades
23 Item next to a salad bowl
24 Jamaica's St. ___ Bay
26 E.T.'s pal
27 Opposite of clarify
28 The Ponte alle Grazie spans it
30 You may work out its kinks
31 Common crash site?
32 What an art student builds
33 Cabinet department
34 First name in international diplomacy
35 Passed (out)
37 En ___ tiempo (formerly, to Felipe)
41 Help line?
44 Navajo home
45 You're in it if you cry 41-Down
46 Bit of wishful thinking
47 To come, in Cádiz or Caen
48 Instruments in Ravel's "Boléro"
49 Matching
50 Superficial, briefly
51 Vint ___, the Father of the Internet
52 38-Across covering
55 Here, in Honduras
56 Result of exposing oneself at the beach?

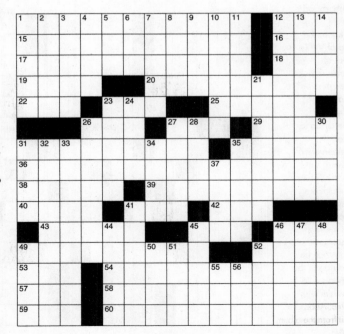

by Natan Last

348 ★ ★ ★

ACROSS

1. Acted impulsively
6. Unofficial "Main Street" of New York's Chinatown
10. They might prevent getaways, briefly
14. He starred as himself in "Cuban Pete," 1946
15. Treat with a "Golden" variety
16. Doubtful
17. Wife of Augustus
18. Smoke with straight sides
20. Like
22. Agenda
23. Wins easily
25. Nest down
26. Archer of literature
28. ___ Plateau (U.S. region)
31. They're in the neighborhood: Abbr.
33. Capital on the island of Viti Levu
34. Source of valuable deposits
35. Self expression?
37. Responses of confusion
39. One may be in stitches
40. Chairmen often call them: Abbr.
42. Calls
44. Potential hiding places
46. Respectful greeting
48. Stern playing?
50. Old song with the lyric "When he would ride in the afternoon / I'd follow him with my hickory broom"
55. Not withdrawn
56. 1-Down counselor Ann

57. Hot
59. Living proof?
60. Italian well
61. River with historic flooding in 1966
62. Goober
63. A.M.A. member?: Abbr.
64. B'way buys
65. Inclines

DOWN

1. "ER" replaced it on NBC's schedule in 1994
2. "Traffic" actress Christensen
3. Aid in forging
4. One canvasing?
5. Gyro sauce
6. One with a replaceable head
7. Their addresses are moving
8. Near the hour
9. Grunting, slimy-skinned swimmer
10. Fielding and Menotti title heroines
11. Lenin's body
12. Lenin, for one
13. Saves, say
19. Some emergency services
21. It has hundreds of thousands of meanings: Abbr.
24. Curt summons
27. Swimmers do them
28. Resistor measures
29. "Chicago" Oscar winner

30. Book of Common Prayer readers
32. Actress Allen
36. Kid with no hometown, often
38. Scene of horror and confusion
41. Instrument played with a spatula
43. Major pest in the South
45. Block
47. One of a loving trio?
49. "Oh, no!"
51. Court figure
52. K. T. of country
53. Do some green maintenance
54. 11-Down dissents
55. Nagasaki noodle
58. Takes down

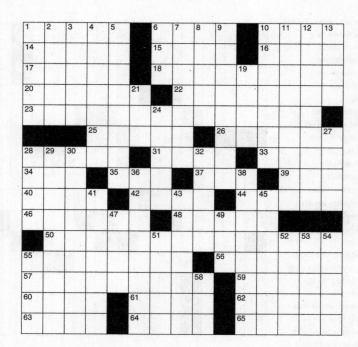

by Karen M. Tracey

ACROSS

1 Red choice
10 Decide to use
15 "The Hitch-Hiker" director, 1953
16 Old Indian infantryman
17 Resin sources
18 Weenie
19 Appropriate game
20 Ram
22 Dostoyevsky's exile city
23 Dessert fruit
24 It's grounded on the Sabbath
26 Many reality shows
29 Star followers
32 Precious
33 Streaked
34 Nat stat
35 Endures
38 Spare part?
39 Pat makeup
41 Sir ___, foster brother of King Arthur
42 Hero described as "Eyeless in Gaza"
44 "Are you nuts?!"
46 Right fielder, on a scorecard
47 It merged with Tanganyika in 1964
49 Get down quickly
53 Managed to obtain
55 One thing on top of another?
56 It has 95 printable characters
57 Not currently
59 Tubular snacks
60 What might come as a relief at night?
61 Tracking aid
62 Noted Volstead Act enforcer

DOWN

1 Diddly
2 Hit the ceiling, say
3 Spoilers, often
4 Like a strawberry roan's coat
5 Bibliography abbr.
6 "Science Friday" carrier
7 Motor ship driver
8 Hostile
9 City near San Jose
10 Breathtaking condition?
11 Most childishly pure
12 Results of some labor laws
13 Computer connection
14 Four for for, for one
21 Loud drill bit?
23 Vodka cocktail
25 Electronic gag reflex?
27 The Jimi Hendrix Experience, e.g.
28 A diagram bears his name
29 Parts of it may be revealed in biology class
30 Fit
31 "Übermensch" originator
32 "Watch it!"
36 Confirm
37 Chicken tikka go-with
40 Keynote, e.g.
43 4.184 petajoules
45 Win the support of
46 Campania's capital, in Campania
48 Tear-resistant synthetic rubber
50 Worth keeping
51 Has a hitch
52 Metric system output?
53 Words of support
54 Org. with a SportsMan of the Year award
55 Digs cash?
58 Conservative front?

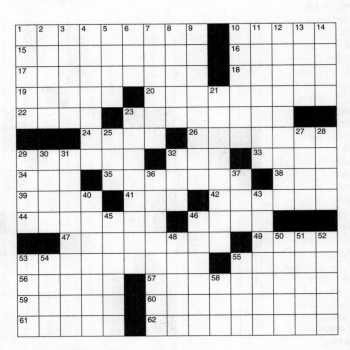

by Doug Peterson

350 ⭐ ⭐ ⭐

ACROSS
1 Allergy source
9 "Steve Canyon" cartoonist
15 Small planted bulb
16 Lacking a signature, say
17 Diamondback, for one
18 Church room
19 Group whose 1972 debut album "Can't Buy a Thrill" went platinum
21 Plenty
22 Robin Hood, the ___ of Huntington
23 Indian barter item
25 No. usually figured to two decimals
26 Toyota pickup named for a U.S. city
29 Giocondo and Angelico
30 Make a person feel good
33 Shock-and-awe strategy
34 Sources of some Zimbabwean exports
35 Alternative to Beauvais
36 "Who ___?"
37 Substantial hit: Abbr.
38 Hardly balmy
39 Part of una salsa
43 Co-winner of the first Albert Einstein Award, 1951
45 Late entertainer who was known for his laugh
49 Like Chekhov's "The Cherry Orchard"

51 Overthrows, e.g.
52 Head-scratcher
53 Not together
54 Certs ingredient
55 Absents oneself

DOWN
1 Small stand
2 One of the Pointer Sisters
3 Strength of a solution
4 Neighborhood eyesore
5 Navy relative
6 Game with a spotter
7 English horn, e.g.
8 Get ready for chow
9 Ohio pro, for short
10 Worried
11 Little something
12 Limits of some sums

13 Nowhere near an agreement
14 Go by quickly
20 Macduff, to Macbeth
24 California peak
26 The witches in "Macbeth," e.g.
27 Cross of mysteries
28 Pub pull
29 Long row
30 Blame-diffusing words
31 Major employer
32 Pull up
33 Not grounded
34 Relatively hard to pin down
38 Vile
39 ___ States
40 Thackeray's "Vanity Fair: A Novel Without ___"

41 What a loser may be out of
42 First sign
44 Many Caltech grads: Abbr.
46 M.'s counterpart
47 Judging point at a dog show
48 Comfy wear
50 Preserve . . . or get rid of

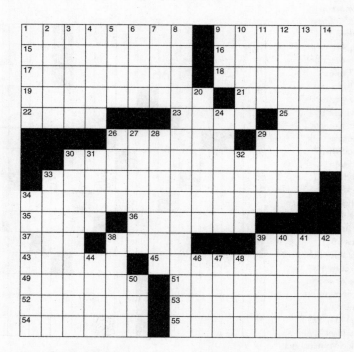

by Mark Diehl

ACROSS

1 Mexican play places
8 Cry of accomplishment
15 Very rarely indeed
17 They're often tipped on sidewalks
18 Home of Samsung Tower Palace
19 Astra and Antara
20 Often-improved thing
21 P.D. rank
22 "Let's take ___"
23 Italian province or its capital
24 Windows options
25 Title town in a 1945 Pulitzer-winning novel
26 Drop by quickly
27 Arrive
29 [Yawn!]
30 They may get belted
31 Lane in a mall
32 Charges
33 Quick surveys
35 "O naked Moon full-___!": Browning
36 Tell
37 ". . . ___ will!"
38 Podiatric problem
39 Heave
40 Spanish conquistadora ___ de Suárez
41 Mgmt. member
42 Loggers' contest
43 "___ of Simple Folk" (Seán O'Faoláin novel)

44 Stored something for future use?
47 Big-top worker with a big responsibility
48 Maid in "The Merchant of Venice"
49 Drawn-out dissertations

DOWN

1 Sign of fitful sleep
2 Summit success
3 Like an extradition transition
4 Start a hole
5 Indochinese currency
6 Bruce Peninsula locale: Abbr.
7 Some tearoom equipment

8 Hardly ignorant of
9 Option for one's return
10 Fourth qtr. enders
11 "That's ___ quit!"
12 Calls for a quick dispatch
13 "Try someone else"
14 "1, 2, 3" lead-in
16 "Gypsy" Tony winner
22 More than capable
23 Unseen surroundings
25 Jamal of jazz
26 1972 Pulitzer winner for Commentary
28 Current device for a cop?
29 Stock option

31 Doesn't buy, in a way
32 Marine Corps candidates, it's said
33 Scarcely visible fingerprint
34 Residents of some campus houses
36 1993 Grammy winner for Best Mexican-American Album
39 Some tomatoes
40 About 90% of people have one
42 Fan sounds
43 Poison apple creator?
45 Something left of center?
46 Compass creation

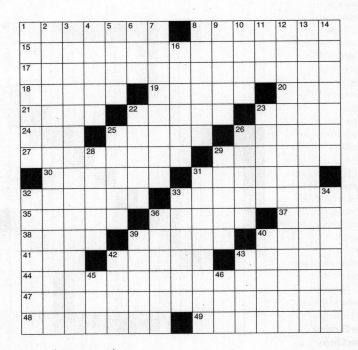

by Joe Krozel

352

★ ★ ★

ACROSS

1 Savage
6 Present
11 Alpine feature
12 Get in the can early
16 Tasty torus
17 Heavily corroded
18 "Not bad at all!"
20 Cavaliers' home, for short
21 "Cheers" alternative
22 Calculating bunch, briefly
23 Relief pitcher Craig
24 Day-care charges
25 Like some wrongs
27 "Blue II" and "Harlequin's Carnival"
28 Run on
29 ___ Mae
30 Less approachable
31 Magic acts?
32 Safety org.
33 King's middle name
34 Poison
35 Observance made official by President Wilson in 1914
39 N.F.L. passing stat.
40 Prominently featured
41 "The lady in red" betrayed him
43 Pulitzer-winning poet Mark Van ___
44 Samaritans' doings
45 Have no life
46 ___ año (in the course of the year: Sp.)
47 Socialite who inspired "Call Me Madam"

DOWN

1 Career diplomat Philip
2 Mild-flavored seaweed in Japanese cuisine
3 Denver university
4 Slow an increase
5 Heading for classified information?
6 Grant consideration
7 Goose, in Spain or Italy
8 Lacking sufficient desire
9 Levee breaches
10 "Hairspray" mom and others
12 Iron-handed one?
13 Hasty
14 Ruhr Museum locale
15 Lines: Abbr.
19 A dead one looks like something else
22 Place to get milk
24 Whit
25 Opposite of sluggishness
26 Something to build on
27 Lothario
29 Confession receivers
31 Stopped being a 38-Down, with "out"
33 What opens easily?
34 Scout's honor
35 Mysterious word repeated in Daniel 5:25
36 Isn't too yellow
37 Chemical ___
38 Blabbermouth
40 Killer ending?
42 C.E.O., e.g.: Abbr.

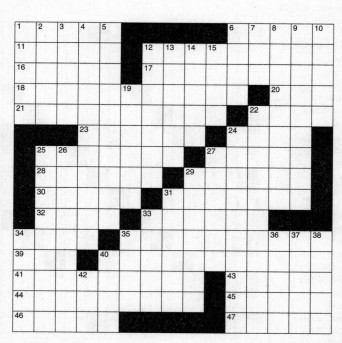

by Frederick J. Healy

★ ★ ★ 353

ACROSS

1 9 + 3 + 1 + 1/3 + 1/9 + . . ., e.g.
16 Dating service questionnaire heading
17 Seminal naturalistic work
18 They're dishwasher-safe
19 Main character?
20 Tree-line tree
21 Some 21-Downs
25 Tir à ___ (bow-and-arrow sport: Fr.)
27 Punch lines?
30 Thunderstorm product
31 Fit by careful shifting
32 Help in hunting
33 Routine statement?
36 ___ francese
37 Puttering
38 Fish garnish
39 Novelist who was a lifelong friend of Capote
40 Ducky
41 What the ugly duckling really was
42 Tipping point?
43 Where one might keep time?
44 Heart and brain
53 Doesn't hedge
54 A lot may be on one's mind
55 13-time Grey Cup winners

DOWN

1 Hoods may conceal them
2 German "genuine"
3 "Cup ___" (1970's Don Williams song)
4 Trend in 1970's fashion
5 "Sure, but . . ."
6 10-kilogauss units
7 Potato preparation aid
8 California's Mission Santa ___
9 Milk holders: Abbr.
10 Spares
11 Sizzling, so to speak
12 Point (to)
13 "This ___ . . . Then" (Jennifer Lopez album)
14 Citation abbreviation
15 Govt. database entries
21 One with subjects
22 Nitrogen compound
23 Physicist James who contributed to the laws of thermodynamics
24 He had a #4 hit with "It's Time to Cry"
25 Hanukkah nosh
26 Visibly horrified
27 Odysseus saw him as a shade in the underworld
28 Animated character who likes "Hello, Dolly!" songs
29 Lane pain?
31 Sci-fi's Chief Chirpa, e.g.
32 One of the Palins
34 Creator of some illusions
35 Time of awakening
40 Dan ___, 1994 Olympics speed-skating gold medalist
41 "Alistair ___ America" (1973 book)
42 Need for some shots
43 Top-___ (sports brand)
44 To be in a faraway land
45 Basis of development
46 Compliment's opposite
47 Hand ___
48 Lightman who wrote "Einstein's Dreams"
49 1958 Best Song Oscar winner
50 "Lemme ___!"
51 Chile child
52 Fleet fleet, once

by Kevin G. Der

354

★ ★ ★

ACROSS

1 1968 hit musical with the song "Life Is"
6 Former transportation regulation agcy.
9 Hot: Fr.
14 "Caesar, now be still: / I kill'd not thee with half so good ___": Brutus
15 Whirl
16 Stop from running, maybe
17 One making waves in the news business?
20 What 36-Acrosses and 7-Down appreciate
21 Gray and others
22 Sworn ___ (officially given the role of)
23 Charter of Punta del Este grp.
25 Omne vivum ex ___ (all life [is] from eggs: Lat.)
26 "For the life ___ . . ."
30 Make plans to tie the knot
34 Like Cuba and Venezuela, e.g.
36 You, e.g.
38 Clear out
39 Mozzarella alternative
40 Cavort
41 Pen
42 Community coll. prerequisite, maybe
43 Big Utah export
45 It's written right to left
48 Ones with reading schedules
55 "It was the best of times, it was the worst of times . . . ," e.g.
56 50-Down holder
57 John who pioneered time-lapse photography

58 Some porcelain
59 Patisserie order
60 Intelligence grp.
61 Parties with a whole lot of shaking going on

DOWN

1 Cup holder
2 Man ___
3 Endure difficulties, with "out"
4 Paradise
5 Welcome to paradise?
6 "Was ___ hard . . . ?"
7 You and others
8 Rostand hero
9 Santa ___
10 Long way?
11 It's west of the Sea of Okhotsk
12 Former part of 11-Down: Abbr.

13 Feeble-minded
18 Certain H.S. teams
19 Draft org.
23 Academy offering
24 ___ di linea (flier to Italy)
25 Iowa relative
26 Pot on a fire
27 Like an old English coin worth 21 shillings
28 Reagan cabinet member
29 Conqueror of Northumbria in 946
31 Express letters?
32 It ends in the fall: Abbr.
33 Dazzle
34 It's sometimes seen in the corner of a TV screen: Abbr.

35 Prune
37 ___ mother
41 Brand for the bath
43 Singer profiled in "Sweet Dreams"
44 Vintner's prefix
45 Holder of a "leaf-fringed legend," to Keats
46 Honey badger
47 Sch. in Madison, N.J.
48 ___ of all
49 Prefix with -metry
50 Contents of a 56-Across
51 Questionnaire datum: Abbr.
52 Not fully tested
53 Soft shade
54 Part of a committee sched.

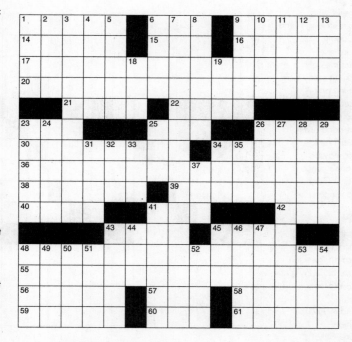

by Ashish Vengsarkar

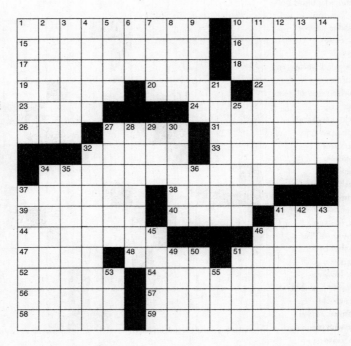

ACROSS

1 Male gopher
10 People travel only one way on them
15 "The Broken Tower" poet
16 The senior Saarinen
17 "Beautiful" things in a 1951 hit song
18 See 7-Down
19 Orlando's ___ Center
20 Capital largely surrounded by high clay walls
22 Sportscaster Collinsworth
23 Uncle ___
24 City at the mouth of the Fox River
26 They make cents.
27 Cards
31 Homage
32 Dress down
33 Cat's-eye relatives
34 Metaphor for a middle-class American
37 Host of a self-titled 1990's talk show
38 Las ___ Filipinas
39 Ancient Macedonian capital
40 Abbr. at the top of a memo
41 Abbr. for the Prince of Wales
44 Hair salon activity
46 New range rover?
47 Freedom fighter, for short?
48 Their faces have spots
51 Secretary on "Hogan's Heroes"
52 Weapon for Wonder Woman
54 When women may get in for less
56 Put through the system?
57 Rush hour, to radio programmers
58 Some flying saucers
59 Fleet type

DOWN

1 "Man alive!"
2 One with growing concerns
3 Displays displeasure
4 "___ my pleasure"
5 Big Apple sch.
6 Ahead of, in verse
7 Parts of planes in which to put 18-Across
8 First to be called up
9 Answerable with a nod or a shake
10 Sherlock
11 They have chocolate relatives
12 Overhead corridor
13 Need for checking people out
14 Applies carelessly
21 Blitzkrieg
25 Ewing player
27 Twist alternative
28 Oregon Shakespeare Festival locale
29 Former AT&T rival
30 Crayola color in a 64-crayon box
32 Encouraging statement start
34 Kind of appointment
35 Like most bars
36 U.S.N. craft
37 Downgrades, e.g.
41 "Whoa!"
42 "___ Sans-Gêne" (Sardou play)
43 Offer?
45 Brightens
46 Sock deliverers
49 Complaint
50 Lou Grant's ex on "The Mary Tyler Moore Show"
51 Not brush off
53 FAQ part: Abbr.
55 It may be added to excess

by Victor Fleming

356

★ ★ ★

ACROSS

1 Product with a secret sauce
7 Muff
14 Pitcher's charge
15 Like many student jobs
16 "___ in bloody thoughts, but not in blood": Richard III
17 Like the drummer for rock's Def Leppard, amazingly
18 First Japanese infielder to sign with a major-league team, familiarly
20 Naja naja, familiarly
21 Writer of the 1950 Tony-winning play "The Cocktail Party"
22 Letter after Juliet in a phonetic alphabet
24 ___ Éireann (Irish legislative assembly)
25 Ran-tan
26 Energy converters of a sort
28 Bourbon and others: Abbr.
29 Certain suckling
30 Note from one who's shy
31 Exposure warning?
36 Catchy thing?
37 Some bushes, for short
38 I.M. not sent through AOL?
40 Alcohol or drugs, it's said
44 See 1-Down
45 Be-all and end-all
46 "___ doch!" (German reply)
47 Emasculates
48 ___ Zagora, Bulgaria
50 2008 Olympics sensation
52 Heat
54 Model for Machiavelli's "The Prince"
55 Person making a check mark?
56 Come (to)
57 Nereus and Proteus
58 Bridge problem

DOWN

1 With 44-Across, it may lead to a seizure
2 Perfection
3 Elegantly, to Brahms
4 Burrower with a bushy tail
5 Bugged
6 Superior court writ: Abbr.
7 The Pearl of the Orient
8 Extreme soreness
9 Disconnected, in music: Abbr.
10 Approached purposefully
11 Kettledrum
12 "The Essence of ___," Food Network show
13 Goes by foot, in a way
15 Chardonnay from Burgundy
19 Copenhagen alternative
23 Prayer
26 Liking romantically
27 Talks romantically
29 Neck piece
32 Cartoon hero with a blue cape
33 ___ Spalko, Indiana Jones villainess
34 Words after "The end"
35 Some provocation
39 Tuition classification
40 Breakouts
41 ___ rating
42 "Finding ___," 2008 comedy
43 Participates in a class action
44 James of the court
47 Diminutive chthonic figure
49 Prefix with biology
51 Building piece
53 Foreign exchange abbr.

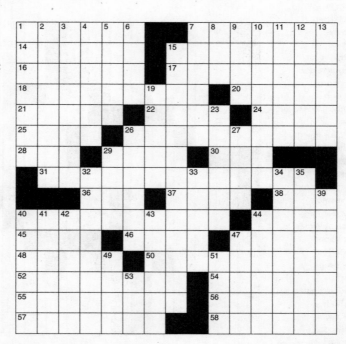

by Paula Gamache

ACROSS

1 Releaser of "1921" in 1969
7 Author of the best-selling investment book "You're Fifty—Now What?"
13 Participate in drag?
14 Thing turned while speaking
15 Source of the word "avatar"
16 Words of intimidation
17 They get many saves
18 Shout about Paris?
19 Something below the bar
20 Diet of Worms concern
21 Lewis Carroll's birthplace
23 "___ Growing" (Temptations hit)
24 One against another
25 Soeur de la mère
26 One concerned with entrances and exits
31 Stalemate
35 Start of a traditional love story
36 They rock, sometimes
39 Far-away connection?
40 "The Art of Hitting .300" writer Charley
41 A diva may throw one
43 Not splurge on a 48-Across, say
46 Inits. by a dateline
47 Tony's consigliere on "The Sopranos"
48 It's often taken down Broadway

49 Make the rounds?
51 Completely in the dark
52 Cell assignment
53 Sci-fi smuggler
54 R-rated, say
55 Mean

DOWN

1 Band member with a bent neck
2 1946 Literature Nobelist
3 Tennis's Clijsters and others
4 Cause of fitful sleep
5 Sartre's "___ clos"
6 Target of Durocher's "Nice guys finish last" sentiment
7 Body in a case
8 Breaks a bottle on, maybe
9 It ended in 1806: Abbr.
10 Capacious closet
11 Hold
12 Member of the 27-Down group
13 Item used for studio mixing
15 Big break
18 How a gull might feel
21 O.K.
22 What Greece has that Germany doesn't
24 Means of reaching the stars
27 Brothers who sang "Stayin' Alive"
28 Biodiversity setting

29 Period named for an earth goddess
30 Option for a hit
32 Setting for big rigs
33 "Yep, unfortunately"
34 Orchestra section
36 Dairy equipment
37 Remove, as carpet
38 A question of introspection
42 Very hot
43 Go to a lot
44 Very upscale?
45 DuPont discontinued it in 1990
48 Group sharing a coat of arms
50 Utah Stars' org.
51 City with both A.L. and N.L. teams, informally

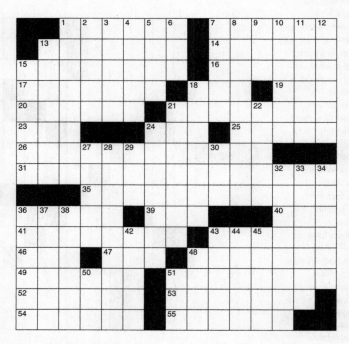

by Josh Knapp

358

★ ★ ★

ACROSS

1 Big-time kudos
9 Film about the Statue of Liberty?
15 Exasperated cry
16 Response to a good dig
17 Hidden danger
18 Preparatory stage
19 Subject of the biography "King of the World"
20 Bright spot in architecture?
22 Saison de septembre, mostly
23 Deal killers
25 Sets right
26 Honoree on the third Friday of Sept.
27 Like many old series, now
29 Grammy-winning Gnarls Barkley, e.g.
30 Bats are smaller than normal in it
32 Disco or swing follower
34 Mascot that's a shell of a man?
36 Slinky and stealthy
40 What's-his-face
41 Demi Moore was in it
43 ___ factor
44 Springtime arrival
45 College football coach Miles
47 Wiesbaden's state
51 Application datum: Abbr.
52 It's under the Host
54 Torpedo
55 Eponymous general
56 Be cut down to size
58 Mute neighbor, maybe: Abbr.
59 Dot-com with an asterisk in its name
61 Words at the outset
63 Picture receiver
64 Moved out?
65 Official's helper
66 Opening used before opening a door

DOWN

1 Lombardia's capital
2 "Operation Bikini" co-star, 1963
3 Robbed of
4 Goal of some candidates
5 Means of forced entry
6 Bad blood
7 Immobilized, in a way
8 What sticks to your ribs?
9 Tops of golf courses?
10 Subtle warning sound
11 It goes through lots of luggage: Abbr.
12 Hot
13 Captain Nemo's final resting place
14 Beseech
21 Things that disappear in the shower?
24 Modelesque
28 Namby-pambies
30 Do school work
31 One concerned with checks and balances
33 Street name lead-in
35 One side of Hawaii
36 Common toy go-with
37 One being printed at a station
38 Customize for
39 Kudos
42 Dog's coat?
46 Still
48 Definitely gonna
49 Film critic Joel
50 Protect, in a way
52 Triumphant song
53 Like some mythology
56 "Laverne & Shirley" landlady
57 Emulate Niobe
60 "Ready" follower
62 Crib note?

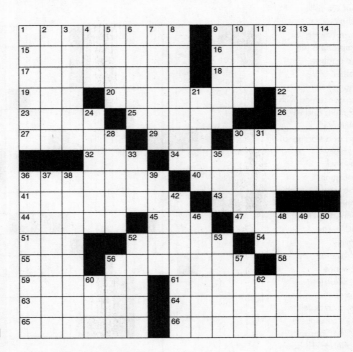

by Patrick John Duggan

ACROSS

1 Crescendos
7 Eye-opening things
13 In the database, say
15 Not look upon favorably
16 Brutal force
17 Nice thing to cut through
18 It's not hot for long
19 They're not hot
21 Lifesaver, briefly
22 Plains folk
23 Rankled
24 Goalkeeper's guarded area
25 People may be put out if they're not put up
28 Part of an exchange
29 Engine sound
30 Figure seen on the lunar surface
33 Multitasking, e.g.
34 Like some cruises
38 Conceived in a nonstandard way
39 Badge holder: Abbr.
40 White House girl
42 Revolting bunch
43 Setting for everything
45 X-ray spec?
46 ". . . __ woodchuck could chuck wood?"
47 Worker in the medium of torn and pasted paper
49 Will be present?
50 Sword or dagger
52 Yaps
54 Part of a board
55 Safari jacket feature

56 Give some relief
57 Marathoner's concern

DOWN

1 Not just request
2 Left on a plate
3 "There!"
4 It gets replayed
5 Gunslinger's cry
6 Quaint photo
7 Caffeinated?
8 Tom and Huck, e.g.
9 "A lie that makes us realize truth," per Picasso
10 Try to steal a basketball from another player, e.g.
11 Cartography

12 "Journal to Eliza" author, 1767
14 Early flag warning
15 West Jordan is near it
20 Semi professionals?
24 Second of January
26 They were brought down by Olympians
27 Move furtively
29 Members of the genus Troglodytes
31 Times for wake-up calls, briefly
32 Longtime power provider: Abbr.
34 Cruise vehicle
35 Drumming sound
36 Arab-__

37 Like some steaks
38 Sorrowful
41 Carol's first word
43 Stock to hawk
44 Jobs for plumbers
47 Roles, figuratively
48 It has two critical reading sects.
51 That Mexican?
53 Charge lead-in

by Louis Hildebrand

360

★ ★ ★

ACROSS

1 They're highly reflective
8 Misses
15 Ned Buntline dime novel subject
17 Signs of unavailability
18 The Iron Horse
19 Composer Janácek
20 It. was part of it
21 San Francisco street or theater
23 Skeleton part, in Padua
24 Defensive end Antwan
28 Ski resort forecast
30 Crude, slangily
32 Paternal relative
36 Beckerman who wrote "Love, Loss and What I Wore"
37 Poe title character
39 "The Hoosier Folk-Child" poet
40 Screen setting
42 "Easy now . . ."
44 Farmwork
46 #1 honor
47 Where lederhosen are worn
50 Woolly
52 Many a Playbill paragraph
53 Not baring one's sole?
54 Least sound
59 Costs of admissions?
62 Alaska area almost half the size of Rhode Island
63 License
64 Sequoias, e.g.

DOWN

1 "___ of you . . ."
2 Sight near a lagoon
3 What I will follow
4 One way to travel
5 Tricks
6 Opposite of coarse
7 What a person goes by in Paris
8 Relatives of flies
9 City near Horseshoe Curve
10 Shooters for pros
11 High school dept.
12 Actress Skye and others
13 Nips
14 Food service Fortune 500 company
16 Private consultant to the federal government, in slang
22 Go out very slowly
23 Totally dominating
24 ___ suspension (ear medication)
25 Supermarket work station
26 Some team members
27 Certain portraits of Zola, Chabrier and Mallarmé
29 One may put a damsel in distress
31 Formal introduction?
33 It's high in the Sierras
34 Sing
35 Took in
38 Bit or hit lead-in
41 Cry of respect
43 Don
45 Ancient philosopher whose name means "old master"
47 Brook
48 Like some shirts
49 "What's your ___?"
51 "Viva ___!"
53 What may accumulate in the mouth
55 Slimming option, briefly
56 One of 31 in Mexique
57 Some medicines
58 Shows disapproval
60 Red sushi fish
61 Stable particle

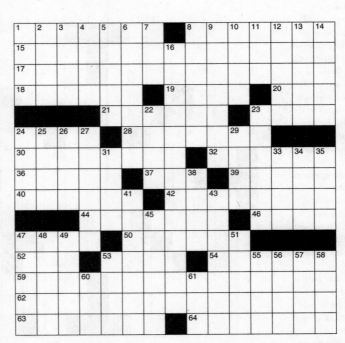

by Barry C. Silk

ACROSS

1 Star of India, once
5 Concert spectacles
15 29-year Knesset member
16 "Prêt-à-Porter" actress
17 Material for a suit?
18 Convention fighter
19 Ring bearer
21 "Roots" name
22 It's free in Paris
23 Hazardous obstruction
25 Humidifier output
26 It often gets fed
27 Where the biblical lost tribes were held captive
30 N.Y.P.D. descriptor
32 Cry to get 40-Across
37 What Taft, Hoover and Carter each had
39 Gave a face-lift
40 People with saving accounts?
42 "Rock Me ___" (1984 hit)
43 One worthy of emulation
45 Simon & Schuster's parent
46 Opposite of 4-Down
50 Tunnel creator
51 Leaving lines
53 Order in a rush order
55 Barn dance accessory
57 Onetime Chevy Blazer competitor
59 Mythological trickster who was punished by being held to a rock
60 Steam roller?
61 Peck, e.g.
62 What loaded people have
63 Strings used in payroll depts.

DOWN

1 Take, finally
2 Native
3 Far from frilly
4 Opposite of 46-Across
5 Spot of seclusion
6 Racks up
7 Dingbats
8 Dug in, with "down"
9 What stops swings, briefly
10 Give the heave-ho
11 Area where blood vessels enter an organ
12 Sur citizen
13 Bridge openers
14 Rip into
20 Make stand on end, as hair
24 "That's it!"
28 Course
29 Pad
31 "That sorta thing"
33 Pumpkin
34 People are not 35-Down after these occur
35 See 34-Down
36 Publicists' preparations
38 Hit from the 1983 platinum album "Kilroy Was Here"
41 Sultan who captured Jerusalem in 1187
44 Palais des Nations setting
46 Not worthless
47 Yanks' foes
48 Drawn-out chemical
49 It may cut things close
52 Educational ideal
54 Arizona county or its seat
56 Bouncing baby
58 Kind of chip

by Mark Diehl

362 ★ ★ ★

ACROSS

1 Rome's ___ Choir
8 Didn't go out
15 Iron-deficient?
16 Subject of 2002 Senate authorization
17 Unstable
18 Going by
19 Glycerides, e.g.
20 Actress Mazar of HBO's "Entourage"
21 Prefix with biology
22 Complaint
23 Fine-tuning
25 Gambler's opening?
26 Person with dreads
27 Bust
31 Privy to the gag
33 Source of the line "Midway upon the road of our life I found myself within a dark wood . . ."
35 Brief online messages
36 Apply with force
37 Saber rattlers
39 Place name in 1960's TV
40 Dom Pedro's ill-fated wife
41 It's probably played first
43 P.M. counterpart
45 Loud horn
47 Stayed out?
48 Palindromic girl
51 Departure info?
52 Match venues
53 Seeks
55 Better, as cuts of meat
56 Bit of change in Cuba
57 Source of heat
58 Bulk up
59 Bristles

DOWN

1 Pressure, metaphorically
2 Overseas fabric spun from flax
3 Prime seating area at sporting events, maybe
4 Censured
5 French department or a river that runs through it
6 Pulls in
7 Ice cream eponym
8 Carriage part?
9 Indus outlet
10 Hard-to-miss shot
11 Command ctrs.
12 Boo-boo
13 ___ cat
14 Consequently
20 Mohawk and others
23 Lid
24 It's known as "the Prairies" in Canada
26 Transcends
28 Robber's target
29 Unbroken
30 Get into
32 Toshiba competitor
34 Zipper hider
35 Owner of Capitol Records and Parlophone
38 Spade mashie
39 Cooler
42 Point
44 Acted rudely, in a way
46 Diet
47 Lay up
48 Indirect lines
49 Puccini's "O Mimi, tu più non torni," e.g.
50 ___ mundi
52 Actor Andrew of 1990's TV
54 Poker legend Ungar
55 Ty Cobb and Willie Mays, positionally: Abbr.

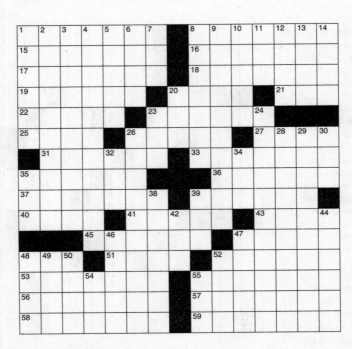

by Joe DiPietro

ACROSS

1 Balderdash
10 1981 best seller set in Castle Rock, Me.
14 Midwest city in the middle of the I–70/I–71/I–75 triangle
15 Satisfy
17 "Shoot!"
18 Neuter
19 Operculum
20 Result of some heavy lifting
22 Dashboard Confessional's genre
23 It lost to "Born Free" for Best Song of 1966
26 What a plus sign may indicate
27 Grammy-nominated film composer Brion
28 Minderbinder of "Catch-22"
29 Woodstock artist
32 Red state
33 Israel's foreign minister during the Six-Day War
34 Prime
35 Golfe setting
36 See 52-Across
37 "Hamlet" composer
38 What bugs are often found in
39 Some academicians: Abbr.
40 It's the same old story
41 Transfusion amount
42 Thing to get pinned on
43 Rally figure
44 Internet ___
45 "Rockaria!" grp.
46 Jazz piece?
47 Bothered
48 Site of some 60's tours
49 "Get ___ Up" (John Mellencamp hit)
51 Long way to go?

52 With 36-Across, school gathering equipment
54 Swiftly written?
59 Like spots in which nails are often used
60 1902 Kentucky Derby winner that was named after a fictional character
61 Central Asia's Tien ___ Mountains
62 RadioShack stock

DOWN

1 Second-century year
2 Post-retirement occurrence
3 Suffix with railway
4 A ton
5 Bush or Cheney, once
6 Square-___ (prim)
7 "Of course!"
8 Pound of Turkey?
9 Highest mountain in Australia
10 Virtuosic improvisation
11 Explorer or Navigator, briefly
12 He pitched a no-hitter in 1999
13 Over
16 No longer charged
21 Place for a hanging piece
23 Its first word is "Congress"
24 They're not technical
25 Result of good middle management?
29 ___ buckle (eye surgery procedure)
30 Doesn't get any higher than
31 Tears into
38 Hitch

40 Calvin's baby sitter in "Calvin and Hobbes"
47 Measure associated with Leyden jars
50 Many an opening event
51 All right
53 "Huh?"
55 Shoe add-on
56 Fashion designer Posen
57 Buckskin source
58 "Porte ___ Lilas" (Oscar-nominated 1957 film)

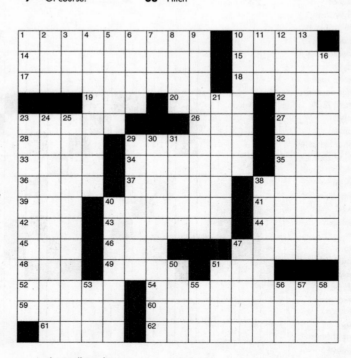

by Will Nediger

364 ★ ★ ★

ACROSS

1 It's now called "Periodicals"
16 Uppity
17 Dangerous thing?
18 Muchacho
19 Cross letters
20 Pandemonium
21 Blu-ray relative
22 Interject
25 Part of a farm harrow
27 Go out with
28 "The Poverty of Philosophy" author
30 Peaty places
32 Hot
35 Blueprint feature
37 Ward of Hollywood
38 Hotel waiters?
40 Genealogist's study
42 Robotic rock group popular in the 1980's
44 Frosty's relative
46 Cost of living?
48 Kind of bean
49 Std.
50 Auburn competitors
52 Survey check-off
53 Ace
54 "That's nasty!"
57 Time starter
59 R.I.P. part
60 Navigator's aid
65 Broad appeal
66 Union of 1284

DOWN

1 Jerks
2 Spiced up
3 One who knows the value of a dollar
4 Not had by
5 Pocket
6 Cable alternative
7 1969 biopic starring 10-Down
8 Taylor of "The Haunting"
9 Means
10 Star of 7-Down
11 Fez wearer
12 Calendar abbr.
13 Mex. neighbor
14 "This ___ joke!"
15 Big name in construction
22 Quantity: Abbr.
23 Zip
24 Overnight sensation
26 Violinist/ bandleader ___ Light
29 Base line
31 Green energy source
33 Pack rat
34 Bust finds
36 Argue (for)
39 Island along Cuillin Sound
41 Overlooks
43 100 centesimi
45 Musical instrument inventor Adolphe
47 Bird on a Kellogg's cereal box
51 Burn
54 "Good Luck, Miss Wyckoff" novelist
55 Normandy city
56 ___ fu
58 "All Fool's Day" writer
59 Chute opener?
61 ___ el Amarna, Egypt
62 Author Beattie
63 Former Ford
64 Small gull

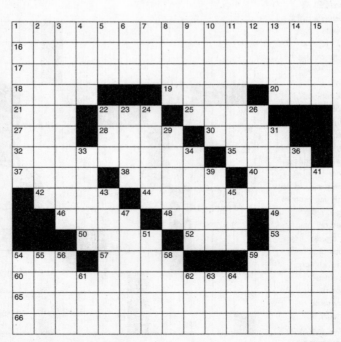

by Martin Ashwood-Smith

ACROSS

1 Notes' counterparts
6 They have soles
10 "What are you waiting for?!"
14 It's like -like
15 Growing part of the economy
17 Good thing to end a close race with
18 "Whatever"
19 Deviled
21 Nuprin alternative
22 Plant toxic to sheep and goats
23 Stable stock
24 "Frost at Midnight" poet
27 Like a fig
28 Cabell who was the 1978 N.L. at-bats leader
29 Byzantine weaving output
31 Place to litter
32 Arizona national monument with Pueblo ruins
33 Office of Small Business Utilization agcy.
36 One way to be married
37 Churn
38 Not release, as bad news
41 Item of current technology?
43 Knot
45 LSD and others
46 They have major bifurcations
47 Grilling demand
49 Rifle shot, so to speak
51 Kol ___ (Yom Kippur prayer)
53 No wear for waifs
54 "___ in a sentence"
55 Bribes
56 Discrimination fighter: Abbr.
57 Plastic surgery may change it

DOWN

1 Flat, e.g.: Abbr.
2 Sports-themed restaurant chain
3 Rat out
4 They have retractable heads
5 Passer and blocker's teammate
6 Santos rookie of 1956
7 Eating stuff
8 Food is often tossed in it
9 Bad mark
10 They take years to end
11 Very wise one
12 1954 Patti Page hit, whose title is sung three times before "Please, don't go"
13 Minute
16 Bit of bunny slope gear
20 Out of action
22 Nailed
23 Memorable J.F.K. arrival
25 Smart
26 Priority Inbox offerer
30 Overhead shooter
32 Idle people may scour them
33 "That just might work!"
34 Cruise option
35 They're often tapped
36 Eater seater, sometimes
37 Like a 23-Down
38 Crown covers
39 Port on the Panay Gulf
40 Appear
42 Countdown term
44 Paranormal, say
47 Chevy model
48 Fam. tree member
50 Organ finale?
52 Côte d'Ivoire's rainy season

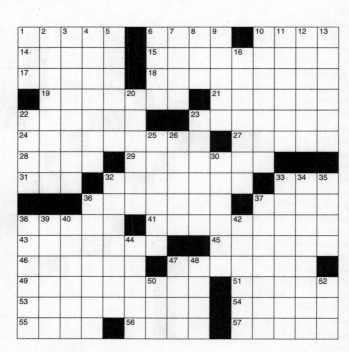

by Barry C. Silk

366 ★ ★ ☆

ACROSS

1 Aflac ad figure, facetiously
11 Omegas represent them
15 She played Appassionata von Climax in Broadway's "Li'l Abner"
16 Janus-faced
17 Chinchillas and boas, e.g.
18 Words before expert or fool
19 "The Gene Krupa Story" title role player
20 Pamplona pronoun
21 Bygone N.Y.C. punk club
22 Handles
24 Literary inits.
26 Chocolate __
27 Ace pitcher's reward?
30 Epoch when bats first appeared
32 Starbucks offering
36 Homebuyer's "bargain"
38 Quiche ingrédients
40 "__ Ferienreisen" (Strauss polka)
41 Cool
42 Result of a permanent failure?
45 Basis of growth
46 Jockey wear
47 Ones concerned with custody
49 Put down a can?
50 Telecom techies
52 Profanable
57 "__ on the Line" (Thomas the Tank Engine story)
59 Residencia
62 Bit of a grind
63 Byron poem
64 Outrageous
66 Clarifying words
67 Bad blood
68 Totally not happening
69 Make a spectacle of oneself, say

DOWN

1 Watch things
2 User of a 58-Down
3 When a quick snap may happen
4 Bush and Jackson
5 Writer known as Old Possum, and his family
6 Lib. Arts major
7 Suck in
8 They're hung across roads
9 __ Optics (telescope maker)
10 Laura Bush biographer Ronald
11 Like some poetry
12 Crow
13 Iron's preceder on the periodic table
14 Acted like a baby, in a way
23 Palooka
25 Introductory course?
28 Many an interrogee
29 Radiate
31 Navy equivalents of S.F.C.'s
32 High-fat dish with greens
33 Sit on the bench
34 Assembly places
35 "__ Should Ever Leave You" (Tom Jones song)
37 High-tech transmission
39 Trustworthy
43 Motion approval
44 "That's what I'm talkin' about!"
48 Bag in a trunk
51 Make last, maybe
53 Crayfish claw
54 Wankel engine part
55 Jagged
56 Secretaries' charges: Abbr.
58 Item used by a 2-Down
60 One of Swoosie's co-stars on "Sisters"
61 Shoulder-to-shoulder
65 They often hang around sports bars

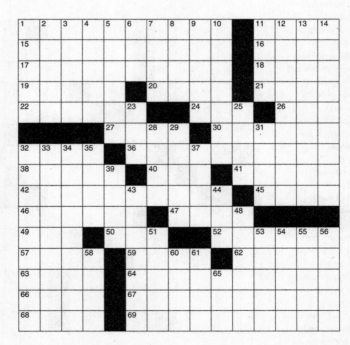

by Pete Mitchell

ACROSS

1 Papers and such
10 Many people surf on them
15 When trading ceases
16 A point is a division of one
17 Feature of many tires
18 Big name in coverage
19 Firm acceptances?
20 Blast source
22 Delivered piece: Abbr.
23 Develop ruts, say
24 Bit of aid
25 With 43-Down, storied Bronx station house
26 Count
27 Like Russ., once
28 Eames lounge chair feature
30 Gather
32 "Die Fledermaus" maid
33 She's no naïf
38 By surprise
39 What's now in Mexico?
40 "In My Own Words" missionary
42 Suffix with ethyl
43 Basic travel path
47 Apt to snap
48 Stick with it
50 Chicken's lack
51 Cove's cousin
52 13 religious heads
53 Gothenburg's river
54 One wished long life, overseas
56 Sound bite in bytes?
58 With no break
59 It's left during a digression
60 Physics Nobelist Stern and others
61 Used wastefully

DOWN

1 Advance man?
2 Invitation information
3 Kind of ester
4 Ally of New York City
5 Hockey game highlight, for many
6 Is refluent
7 Gold finish?
8 Regular's request
9 Glenn Miller's real first name
10 Declaration of determination
11 Murray of silents
12 Gallery fixture?
13 Singer Blu with the 2001 hit "Hit 'Em Up Style (Oops!)"
14 Taken 38-Across
21 They may develop ruts: Abbr.
24 He was declared dead in absentia in 1982
25 Spot follower, perhaps
27 ___ Mountain (Pennsylvania ski resort)
29 Thirsty tot's request
30 Tattooist's supply
31 Neighbor of Loire and Ain
33 Undoing
34 Like good pointers
35 Court on the court
36 ___-deucey
37 "___ thou and peace may meet": Shelley
41 Get saggy, say
43 See 25-Across
44 Name provider
45 Flight status
46 Sounded the alarm?
49 Compost ingredients
50 Opposite of industry
52 Tupperware stock
53 Guinness measure
55 "Walking on Thin Ice" singer
57 División del mes

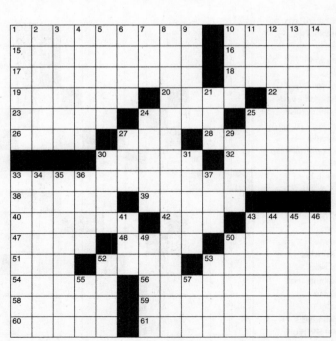

by Victor Fleming

368 ★ ★ ★

ACROSS
1 Run in two places at once
10 Savannah growth
15 Nut's suggestion
16 Home of Creighton University
17 Station finder
18 Iron Age people
19 Mythical mortal who helped raise Dionysus
20 Aye's opposite, poetically
21 Used the name
22 See 49-Down
24 Out of top form
26 1925 Literature Nobelist
27 Cartoon series
29 Middle of summer?
31 Frog-eating bird
32 Tangle
33 Temperature, e.g.
36 Herpetologist's supply
38 Some island dwellers
41 French for "clog"
45 Washington Irving hero, informally
46 Father, e.g.: Abbr.
47 Vigil locale
48 What some veterans recall
50 Japanese brew
53 Burst
54 X'd
56 More than surprise
58 What you may do when you're beat
59 Sunbathing spot
60 Bob Fosse specialty
62 Not rounded
63 Minor restrictions
64 Two-bit
65 Dead duck's cry

DOWN
1 Doesn't blow dough
2 Like much oil
3 One often seen with her child
4 Magazine holder
5 Lord ___ (overseer of Scottish heraldry)
6 Press releases?
7 Literally, "to God"
8 Brands . . . or carrier of brands
9 ___ vez (Mexican "maybe")
10 Take place
11 Forecaster's concerns
12 Dish topped with crushed peanuts and lime
13 Ball of wax
14 Romp
21 Longtime Rolling Stones bassist
23 Trim, in a way
25 Parisian thinkers?
28 Like the Bay of Rainbows
30 Washing machine sound
33 Glasses for a scientist
34 It creeps up
35 Upper-class?
37 Small change
38 Like rice in some cereal treats
39 On-demand flier
40 One of 300 at Thermopylae
42 Stretches between Ryder Cups
43 Plays without a break
44 Nautical danger
47 Thing often heard in short order?
49 With 22-Across, genius's asset
51 It may become a cliché
52 "Animal House" figure
55 President after Auriol
57 Better papers?
60 Hook connection point
61 "Just ___" ("Hold on")

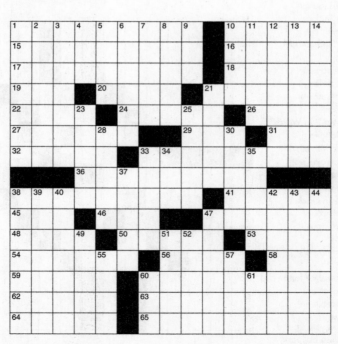

by Kevin G. Der

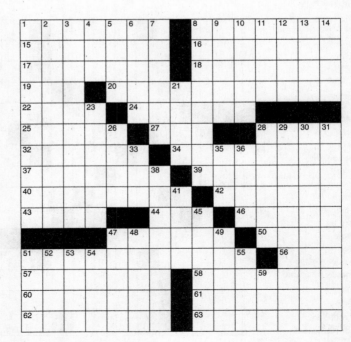

★ ★ ★ **369**

ACROSS

1 Eric ___, Google C.E.O. beginning in 2001
8 Period between Shaban and Shawwal
15 "It doesn't matter . . . anyone's fine"
16 Home of Nascar's longest oval
17 It may be free or attached
18 Title for Columbus, in the Indies
19 Start of some picture books
20 They can make people break up
22 More than un peu
24 Rags
25 Firth class?
27 Soapmaking compound, chemically
28 Make clean . . . or dirty
32 Expect that one will
34 Something handed down
37 Turn into a chestnut
39 Keeps cruising
40 Present day figure in Paris?
42 Cheap cigar, in slang
43 They have maridos: Abbr.
44 Glass part
46 One kneeling at work
47 More than ruffles
50 Sheep genus
51 A runner who loses may still win it
56 With 36-Down, cocked
57 Works with steam?
58 Smallish ballpark, in slang
60 Clues from 7-Down
61 Lazuline
62 Camphor and such
63 Aids in preparing spots?

DOWN

1 Much of New York's Garment District, once
2 Upscale wedding reception amenity
3 Wild West show?
4 TV diner employer of 9-Down
5 English poet/composer Gurney
6 Checkout choice
7 TV host with a star on Canada's Walk of Fame
8 Sends
9 See 4-Down
10 Some big trucks
11 He had righteous blood, per Matthew 23:35
12 Say "You can't do that!" to, say
13 The love of Juan's life?
14 Passage blockers
21 County with the resort town Red River
23 Volume measures
26 Floor
28 Texas city near the Coahuila border
29 Like the equation "$x = x + 1$"
30 Case the joint
31 Staples of jazz music
33 Big creature in un zoológico
35 Aye's counterpart
36 See 56-Across
38 Freshwater plant also called wild celery
41 Actor Schreiber
45 Emmy-winning reality show host of 2008, '09 and '10
47 Not from around here
48 Inlay option
49 Driven supporter
51 Trough's opposite
52 D-Day invasion river
53 A Webmaster may approve it
54 Aircraft in 1960 headlines
55 Mononymous four-time Grammy winner
59 Volume measures: Abbr.

by Ned White

ACROSS

1 Unbeatable mark
6 Ne plus ultra
10 "Squawk Box" airer
14 Ship out
16 Ring event after exchanging rings
17 Affectionate utterance
18 Sharing
19 Sustenance for a fatigued person?
20 Name in old German duchies
21 Like many Scandinavians
22 Event at which reporters rub elbows?
24 One in an affair
28 Still no more
29 Parisian possessive
30 Like "10," but not "9"
32 Puncher's nickname
33 Life ___
34 Boss's address?
36 Chance to meet
38 "Fusses" is a form of it
39 It's not a very big story
41 Heavenly radio source
42 Like a Scottish young 'un
43 Asteroid belt orbiter
45 Harvester maker
46 Potentially paintable
49 Encrypt?
50 Stagger
51 Sister co. of Applebee's
55 Impoverish
56 E-tail detail

58 Poem referencing "the darker brother"
59 Modicum
60 Volunteer's place: Abbr.
61 It may change your perspective
62 Backing

DOWN

1 Tap-on-the-shoulder alternative
2 Paneling material
3 Old Fords
4 Mountain West team
5 Oldies syllable
6 It may include destroyers
7 Nice thing to do peacefully
8 Beast to beware
9 It starts in Mar. in D.C.
10 Its flag is red, white and blue
11 Plain and simple
12 Award won by Henry Fonda
13 Where suckers lure people?
15 Relative of Manx
21 Cold response?
22 Member of an extensive empire of the seventh century B.C.
23 Play matchmaker for
24 Maker of one's own rules
25 Under-the-wire
26 Chemistry
27 Slight
31 Direct
33 Noxious

35 Like a nudnik
37 As one entered the world
40 Keeper of the rings
43 Many a stray
44 Leg-building set
47 Joint part
48 Knot, say
51 Dictator's start
52 Watergate-era White House chief of staff
53 Westin alternative
54 Ringtoss equipment
56 Connection letters
57 Grant grp.

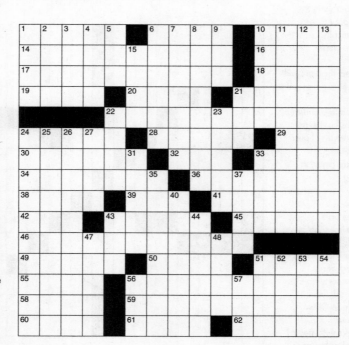

by Ashton Anderson

ACROSS

1 Food that makes a crunch
11 Means to ease withdrawals
15 Some Navy personnel
16 Eats
17 Potential offices
18 Cry with a swelled chest
19 Things sometimes seen on shoulders
20 Stay current (with)
22 Took the place of
25 Final
26 Future alums: Abbr.
27 Not just check out
29 Allan who directed "Sands of Iwo Jima"
31 Corn-filled state
34 Mineral in the form of quartz or flint
36 South-central U.S. city named for a woman in English literature
37 Common St. Tropez sight
39 Jade
40 About half of all dates
42 Actress who played Endora on TV's "Bewitched"
44 New varsity team member, maybe: Abbr.
45 Provokes
46 ___ 21, Intl. Day of Peace
47 4x4, e.g.
49 Icing tool
53 Operations are performed in it
56 Barbers shave them
57 Band whose self-titled 1982 album was #1 for nine weeks
58 Dramatic piano effects
61 Dot-___
62 "I'll be finished in a minute"
63 Sack starter
64 Cocktail attire

DOWN

1 They can be made with adobes
2 Shred
3 Provoked
4 Moved to the top, perhaps
5 A boulevard in Memphis is named for him
6 Saw attachment?
7 Company quota
8 Confusedly
9 Things that may be worn by someone sleeping with the fishes
10 Earliest stage
11 Book that begins in Jerusalem
12 "Not so!"
13 Nowadays, with "the"
14 Pulls the switch?
21 Many academics, for short
23 Choice word?
24 Ohio town where "there's a happiness" in an old Glenn Miller song
28 Red wear for Speedy Gonzales
30 Holds off
31 N.T. book
32 Run of TV's "My So-Called Life"
33 Korean-made sedan since 2001
35 Struck
38 Piehole
41 Nickname for a noted L.S.U. grad
43 Issue
46 X
48 Draw a little at a time?
50 Common prom coifs
51 West African currency
52 Zebra kin
54 Door fixture
55 Alcopop brand
59 The Old ___
60 Old atlas letters

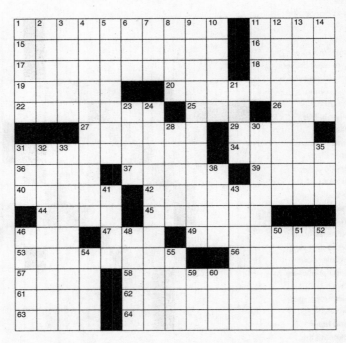

by Mark Diehl

372

★ ★ ★

ACROSS

1 Loser to Al Pacino for Best Actor of 1992
11 Simple folks don't put them on
15 Where pitchers are often placed
16 Get in a hold
17 Paparazzi targets
18 Scratch
19 Two out of twenty?
20 Wheels
21 "Let's Cook It Right" author Davis
23 "She ___ Dian's wit": Romeo
25 Cutting back
26 Sunshine State athletes
29 "Antigonae" opera composer
30 Honest ___ (drink brand)
31 Form a clandestine union?
32 Focused (on)
33 Référendum vote
34 They're often broken after being reached
35 Group seen in late-night hours?
36 Wildly positive
37 Onetime communications giant
38 Pesäpallo is their national sport
39 He broke Gehrig's 70-year all-time hits record
40 Like a series finale?
41 TV persona giving prank interviews
42 They're not allowed to travel
43 Service stripe sites
45 Protein-rich seed
46 Second hand
47 Creation on the sixth day
48 Oscar-winning screenwriter Tally and others
52 Title character of 1920's Broadway
53 Navel base?
56 Flooring option
57 Its newspaper is the Nugget
58 24-Down, in Dijon
59 Old Hollywood's method of promoting talent

DOWN

1 Squad leader: Abbr.
2 Something that's related
3 Fashion designer Saab
4 They offer lots of food that people won't eat
5 Cold war inits.
6 Causes to stand
7 Singer Jones
8 Cannon sound
9 First responder, for short
10 Cause of global panic in 1957
11 Pled
12 Like much Renaissance art
13 Renewed, in a way
14 Deal-closing aids
22 Crackers
24 Add up to
25 Onetime meringue-filled treats
26 Work out
27 Some
28 Not be a rebel
29 Taking credit?
32 Actor O'Hare of "Milk"
35 Wing parts
36 Sails events?
38 Top pick, informally
39 Big name in late-night
42 Dances with one person after another?
44 They often have pistol grips
45 Not so 22-Down
47 Remembered one?
49 "The even mead, that ___ brought sweetly forth . . .": "Henry V"
50 Hockey player's "dangle"
51 Rich layer
54 Bushwa
55 Minnesota city with Vermilion Community College

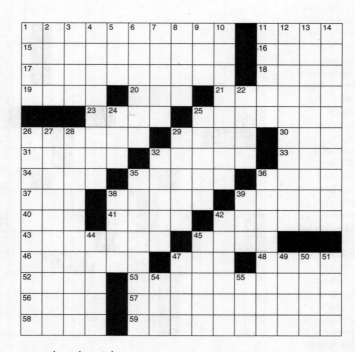

by Adam Cohen

ACROSS

1 Urban playground barb
11 ___ Cervin (11-Down, to French speakers)
15 All-purpose putdown
16 Keystone's place
17 Region with the highest concentration of national parks in the U.S.
19 "Don't forget about me"
20 "The best of animals," in a classic children's book
21 Curly rider?
22 Work's antithesis, briefly
23 "Football Night in America" host
27 It develops before your eyes
32 Like 21-Across's behavior
33 What runs ruin
34 Set of sheets
35 They're prepared for breaks
36 The redbud is one of its symbols: Abbr.
37 Try demonstrating that one can
39 Buttinsky
40 Fifth-century capital of the Visigoths
41 It's dangerous to do on the road
42 Bearded ___
43 What some A.L.'ers play for
44 1961 film scripted by Arthur Miller
49 Capping
53 They're the cutest in the world, per a hit song
55 Handful, maybe
56 "Ooh, aren't you special!"
57 Composition of some hedgerows
58 Education supporters

DOWN

1 Geneva-based org.
2 "I know that one!"
3 Father or son
4 Excitable one
5 Nick, say
6 Poplar trees
7 Foster child in 60's TV commercials
8 Some growlers, in Granada
9 Didn't surrender
10 "Out of the Silence" novelist Cox
11 It was first conquered in 1865
12 Its outsides are ornately embossed
13 Org. with a Hall of Champions
14 Fall's end
18 Variety
21 Leopard runner
23 100 points
24 Almost at the hour
25 Result of bill-passing
26 Features of many quiz shows
27 What a copier will often do
28 Seeing right through
29 Some police dept. personnel
30 It may have a single palm
31 Sugar
33 Spread things?
35 High-tech "guts"
38 Interior decorator's concern
39 27-Acrosses, slangily
41 Key phrase
43 Cousin of an avocet
44 Tastee-Freez alternative
45 Fabulous slacker
46 Pigtailed mothers?
47 Not rest easy
48 Visiting the Getty, e.g.
49 "Another Pyramid" musical
50 Honeycomb alternative
51 Quaint, quaintly
52 Some TV spots, briefly
54 Piece of the 'hood

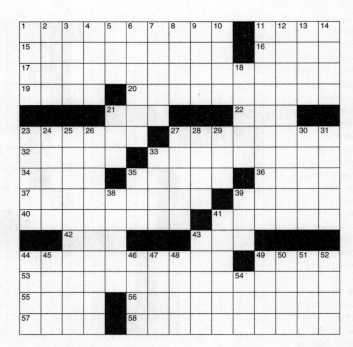

by Joel Fagliano

374 ★ ★ ★

ACROSS

1 Crossbar supporter
9 2009 "Survivor" setting
14 Attempt
16 Like wearing socks on your hands
17 "Be that as it may . . ."
18 Four-time presidential candidate
19 "Isn't that so?," to Rousseau
20 Roman leader?
21 Sci-fi beeper
22 Old doctor's supply
24 Milquetoast of old comics
28 Stop order?
29 Return a letter, say
32 Venezuela's ___ Margarita
33 2008 greatest hits album that includes the song "Proud Mary"
34 Palindromic name high on the Forbes billionaires list
35 Indicator of second thoughts
36 Statement of resignation
37 Peevish
39 Knife injury
40 Touch screen toucher
41 Certifies
43 They support TV viewers
48 Take temporarily
49 Creator of strange worlds
53 Unseen "Mork & Mindy" character
54 Totals
55 Common praenomen among Roman emperors
56 Bright school member
57 Blank ___
58 Considers beneath one's notice

DOWN

1 African soccer powerhouse popularly known as the Black Stars
2 Gun show?
3 Stop order?
4 Slower than adagio
5 Bird in a Sean O'Casey title
6 Baddie in Perrault's tales
7 It may be found in a dish
8 "Toodles"
9 Expose to flame
10 Disorderly sort?
11 Got a move on
12 Like early life
13 Balloon, e.g.
15 Early radio transmitter
23 1974 Billboard hit with Spanish lyrics
25 Run interference for, e.g.
26 Game animal?
27 Evasive answer
29 Involving both sides
30 1997 animated film set in Russia
31 Quits gambling
33 More than a quarter of native Filipinos, ethnically
38 "The Mambo Kings" co-star
42 Somehow know
44 Mixer maker
45 Handmade things?
46 Word in Kansas' motto
47 Fur source
50 ___ Research Center (NASA lab in Silicon Valley)
51 It comes before one
52 Make less sharp, maybe

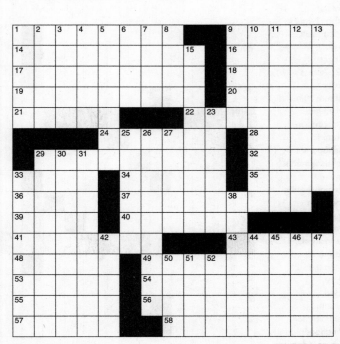

by Patrick Berry

ACROSS

1 Like a message in a bottle
11 What makes cats happy?
15 Needed to relax and unwind, say
16 Parisian possessive
17 Get in on the ground floor, perhaps?
18 Palma's place
19 "Wielding ___ Sword" (Piers Anthony novel)
20 Classic novel with biblical parallels
22 Old
23 Some office equipment
24 Flake
31 Language with 44 consonants
35 Kind of tart
36 With 37-Across, express freely, with "to"
37 See 36-Across
38 Not free
39 Unlike one
40 Aisle or window, e.g.: Abbr.
41 Do a wedding, maybe
42 Contents of some farm bushels
43 Eliminate lines of communication?
45 Shut up
46 Sam Adams alternative
50 Wear for some guards
57 Not knocked off
58 Controversial color enhancer
59 Reunion question
61 Source of current information?
62 Allows an adequate period
63 They've split
64 Many a police officer must pass one

DOWN

1 Key starter?
2 City of a Thousand Minarets
3 Tidying tool
4 "Billy the Exterminator" network
5 Drafting org.
6 Paper quantity
7 Some ancient halls
8 They're good stds. to follow
9 Santa drawer
10 Surprises
11 "Death in the Desert" writer, 1930
12 Opposite of much
13 Bus schedule specification
14 Utah's ___ Canyon
21 Grp. caring about airing
24 "Wannabe" hitmakers
25 Kind of code
26 Penetrating
27 Spade work?
28 Hissy-prone missy
29 Present opener?
30 Composition of some wads
31 "Seinfeld" designation
32 One may win a heart
33 Fresh
34 "I should have guessed as much"
44 Led
46 1980 A.L. M.V.P.
47 Takeoff point for many a flight
48 "The Colbys" co-star
49 Driving danger
50 Mass gathering place
51 Oil source
52 Pool or carpool concern
53 Shuffled things
54 Baseball's Minaya
55 "Le ___," Picasso painting of his sleeping mistress
56 Some Eur. ladies
60 First degs.

by Tim Croce

376

★ ★ ★

ACROSS

1 Spice mix used in Indian cuisine
7 "Far out!"
14 Pasqueflower, e.g.
16 Shade of green
17 Conditions
18 Proved to be quite a poser?
19 16th-century assembly
21 Winner of a famous 1938 rematch
22 Colonial captives
27 Becomes cracked
32 Brooklyn neighborhood
33 Construct
34 Kansas City university
35 Plot line
37 1988 animated action film set in 2019 Tokyo
38 "The Newlywed Game" contestants
39 Attractive
41 36-Down's locale
42 Site of Napoleon I's coronation
43 "Raging Bull" co-star
44 Detractors' comment concerning 19-Across?
53 Convert to pounds?
54 One who's withdrawn
55 Enormous statues
56 Say "Hallelujah!"
57 Short-___
58 Choice in bottled water

DOWN

1 Canvas holder
2 Lit. collection
3 Drought-stricken
4 In
5 1970s pinup name
6 "___ Ashes"
7 High priest in "Aida"
8 Swears
9 Dummy
10 Champagne bucket
11 0 on the Beaufort scale
12 Vitamin C providers, maybe
13 City near Ben-Gurion Airport
15 Member of the U.N. since 1991 and the E.U. since 2004
20 As far from the heart as possible
22 Roguish sort
23 Montreal suburb
24 Novelist Brookner
25 Jeeves, for one
26 Indulge in character assassination?
27 Washington Irving character
28 Followed a trail, maybe
29 Gut reaction?
30 Adar festival
31 Opportunity for privacy
36 Bench, for example
40 Mourned
42 Calypso, e.g.
43 Entourage
44 Architect ___ Ming Pei
45 Account
46 Liqueur flavor
47 Weapon for 21-Across
48 North American peninsula
49 Screen figure
50 Bankruptcy
51 Retro style
52 Discovered
53 Alternatives to Pepsis

by Henry Hook

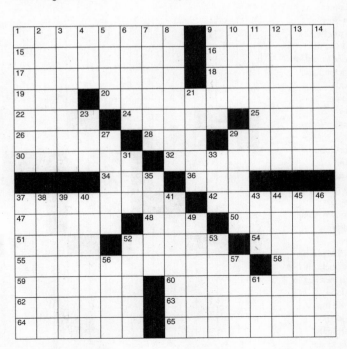

ACROSS

1 Glamorous, high-profile pair
9 Group worshiping at a teocalli
15 Make airtight, in a way
16 Shut in
17 Light pop
18 Remove some strips from
19 Ham preserver?
20 Red flag for the I.R.S.
22 Some deer
24 Olympus rival
25 Big Red rivals
26 Goofballs
28 Italian possessive adjective
29 Gregor's sister in "The Metamorphosis"
30 Lager brand
32 Band with the 1985 #1 hit "Broken Wings"
34 California river
36 Not too sharp
37 Shoot for the stars
42 Amphibious W.W. II vehicle
47 Decorating do-overs, for short
48 Pal
50 Longtime classical music label
51 Class with many makeup exams?: Abbr.
52 Avifauna
54 Routing aid: Abbr.
55 "She's as headstrong as an allegory on the banks of Nile" speaker
58 Documentarian Burns
59 Potpourri collection
60 Ex
62 Many a homeowner
63 Having a flush
64 "The Diary of Anne Frank" Oscar nominee
65 Optician's offer

DOWN

1 "Amen, bro!"
2 Spot for a spot
3 Set for driving
4 Needing no script
5 Ace's setting: Abbr.
6 Like some laws
7 Big dippers
8 Perfectly happy state
9 Maker of the ZDX crossover
10 Man-to-man alternative
11 Is close to failure
12 Fringe holder
13 Certain red ore
14 One-named fictional detective
21 Wishes one can get on a PC?
23 Inveterate brown-bagger
27 Bird-dogs
29 Curt command
31 Country with a tree on its flag: Abbr.
33 Italian possessive adjective
35 Hydra's neighbor
37 Crush
38 He played Laszlo in "Casablanca"
39 All anxious
40 Two, say
41 Opening for firing
43 Melodic bit
44 Exhausting thing to run
45 Intermittently
46 Accept as valid
49 Competitive lumberjack
52 Cub reporter of comics
53 Like some outfields
56 Chrysler Building architect William Van ___
57 Indication of a dud
61 ___-di-dah

by Bob Peoples

ACROSS

1 Certain contracts
16 Procrastinator's comment
17 Last of Nordhoff and Hall's "Bounty Trilogy"
18 East Germany and such
19 Infant follower?
20 Source of collectible deposits
21 "Please?"
23 What may be put on before spelling?
29 Prefaced
30 One of Frank's four wives
31 Book before Phil.
32 ___ times
33 Turn down
34 Get off the mark?
36 Philanthropist/art collector ___ Broad
37 "Fabien ___ Franchi" (Oscar Wilde poem)
38 ColorQube maker
39 Port terminal?
43 They may hold many pks.
44 Unknown name
45 Latin pronoun
46 Term popularized by Jesse Jackson
55 Much that has to get done
56 City on the Niagara Escarpment
57 Strain to see, in a way

DOWN

1 Uses a 39-Across
2 #3 hit from the 1997 album "Surfacing"
3 He followed Dole in the Senate
4 Pregnant
5 Casanova
6 Have ___ on (track the activities of)
7 "The Facts of Life" actress Jewell
8 It may be stabilized
9 Further
10 Wonder-working biblical figure
11 Buddy
12 Bond girl player in "The Man with the Golden Gun"
13 Smart
14 Point of eating?
15 Regular things: Abbr.
21 They're straddled in pits
22 Contribute
23 Film fish
24 Brown's group
25 Depth finder?
26 "La Cage aux Folles" Tony winner
27 Lhasa ___ (supposed good luck bringers)
28 "___ Factor" (TV talent show)
29 MGM co-founder
34 Clips
35 Go for
40 Make part of the manuscript
41 Lose momentum
42 Rough roof
45 Intervening, in law
46 Music to masseurs' ears
47 Needing to get keyed up?
48 See 52-Down
49 Hand-passing time
50 A dozen mesi
51 "Turnin ___" (2009 Keri Hilson hit)
52 One loved in 48-Down
53 Play to ___
54 Traditionalists' opposite, briefly

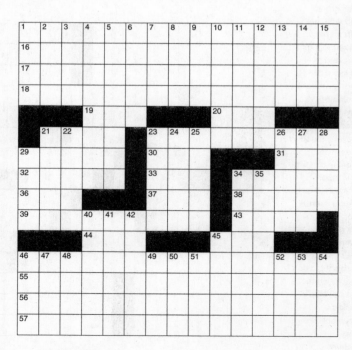

by Joe Krozel

ACROSS

1 Drawing room gathering
9 Yankee star who batted left and threw right
14 Went off on
15 Channel between mainland England and the Isle of Wight, with "the"
16 Place to stretch one's legs
17 Leg supports
18 It has two bridges in India
19 Homeostatic
21 Head-tail connection
22 Fathers, in the Bible
23 Jack-a-dandy
24 More often than not
26 Neil Diamond's "September ___"
27 It may be pulled on a field
30 Abided
31 Missing links, so to speak
32 Euphemizes
33 Figure in the high 60s
34 Things rolled over by cars
37 "___ of life, an imp of fame; / Of parents good . . .": "Henry V"
38 Like many an unsuccessful politician
39 It's perfect
40 Secret places
41 Title in Topkapi
44 Capital served by Faleolo International Airport

46 "A transient madness," per Horace
48 Audits, with "on"
49 Term of endearment
51 Getting ready, with "up"
52 Subway line
53 Piece of schoolwork
54 See 40-Down

DOWN

1 They're open on Saturdays
2 Took to the clink
3 Hook up with
4 Poorly explained
5 Specialty oven
6 Upset
7 Real-life opera composer who's a title character in a Rimsky-Korsakov opera
8 Arm of the British military
9 Churns
10 "Valentine's Day" co-star, 2010
11 Buttress
12 Trapped
13 Slope
15 Only one bears the name of a U.S. president
20 E.U. member
22 Place for a dance
25 Images on windows of une cathédrale: Abbr.
26 Area where Dalí, Monet, Picasso and van Gogh all painted
27 Sipped
28 McDonald's offerings
29 Black gemstones

30 Stand at a ceremony
32 Hugo's Thénardier and others: Abbr.
34 Word: Suffix
35 Toppled
36 Senator supporter
38 Rue Morgue murderer
40 Hit TV series featuring 54-Across
42 Goggles
43 Mushroom grower, for short?
45 Land shared by Iraq and Iran
46 Tapestry thread
47 Lots of laughs
50 Touchdown stat

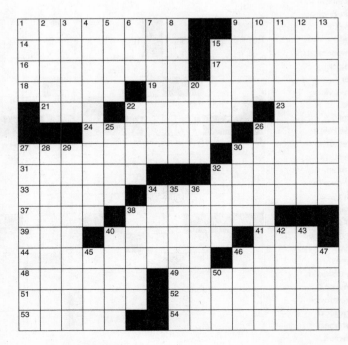

by Randolph Ross

⋆ ⋆ ⋆

ACROSS

1 Cosmonaut's craft
6 Runner, of a sort
15 Eat up
16 Suggestions
17 Signal withdrawal
19 Cabinet dept. since 1965
20 Range rovers
21 Mailing courtesy, briefly
22 Second-rate
25 Cows
27 Bulls, e.g.
28 Designer's deg.
29 Fields in which 6-Acrosses are found
38 Much to do
39 Concentration for an English major
40 Close
41 Glamour types, for short
42 Super ___ (1990's video game console)
43 Game keeper
47 Tipped off
51 Colorado's ___ Mountain
52 Food quality
54 Verdi's "___ giardin del bello"
56 They may keep you up
60 Outlines
61 Long-distance commuter's home, maybe
62 Pretty good poker hand
63 Superman, for one

DOWN

1 What the narrator "threw up" in "The Night Before Christmas"
2 Baseball's Lefty
3 "Seriously?"
4 Columbarium object
5 Letter in the Globe and Mail
6 Ben of Ben & Jerry's
7 Parry
8 Square type
9 Hooks, of a sort
10 Onetime owner of Sheraton Hotels
11 Backs
12 Close, poetically
13 One likely to get men's attention
14 Children's author Eleanor
18 Egyptian expanse
23 Etiolate
24 Made a comeback
26 High-tech auto device
28 Hallowed
29 ___ Pinto (Texas county or its seat)
30 Lena of "Havana"
31 French novelist Pierre
32 Bulblike bases of stems
33 Daughter in "The Cherry Orchard"
34 Cain, e.g.
35 Shaving alternative
36 "Lemme ___!"
37 Legis. period
43 Sailor's stopper
44 Russian alternative
45 Bartlett, notably
46 Slimming cut
47 Part of a stage
48 Good earth
49 Boredom
50 Raison follower
53 Tom T. Hall's "Mama Bake ___"
55 Novel ID
57 Daniel ___ Kim of "Lost"
58 Main
59 Rock's ___ Rose

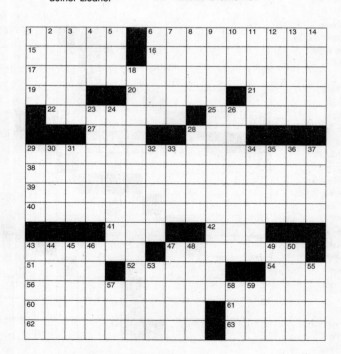

by Martin Ashwood-Smith

ACROSS

1 Company whose jobs are often changing?
10 Working group
15 Got to the bottom of
16 It takes a bow at a musical performance
17 1958 Buddy Holly hit
18 "Guaranteed relief every time" sloganeer
19 Historic leader?
20 "Dove ___" (Mozart aria)
21 Thing
22 Poetic contraction
23 Kind of strip
25 Workers' org. founded by Samuel Gompers
26 Farriers' tools
29 Letters signifying quality brandy
30 Grant-giving org.
31 Musical with the song "Written in the Stars"
33 Said "There, there" to, say
36 It makes the Statue of Liberty green
39 Guarantee
40 Very excited
42 The so-called Island of the Gods
43 Head for the hills
44 One can be tall
46 Jerry or Jerry Lee
50 Seine sight
51 Rappers' covers
53 Sign
54 Lane on Broadway
56 Attack
58 Telephone trio
59 Against a thing, at law

60 2010 Ke$ha chart-topper with a creatively spelled five-word title
62 Clichéd
63 Series of Nintendo games
64 Certain 49-Down
65 Watersheds

DOWN

1 18-footer, maybe
2 Measured two-dimensionally
3 Chickens for dinner
4 "Marvy!"
5 Surrealist Tanguy
6 Simon of Duran Duran
7 Russian ballerina Galina
8 Gets into Monk music

9 Eponym of a frozen food
10 It may be picked up in the woods
11 Do a driver's no-no
12 Axis, e.g.
13 Condition known medically as pes planus
14 1967 hit with the lyric "You know you're a cute little heartbreaker"
21 Wife, in Juárez
24 Sister of Helios
27 Sibling, at times?
28 Sound really good
32 007 player
34 Put to sleep
35 Auto racer Luyendyk
36 "Refudiate," e.g.
37 Mythical runner

38 1990's series initially set in the year 2193
41 Place for a plug
42 Mild Irish oath
45 Nike competitor
47 Move to and fro
48 Belong
49 Women's wear
51 Women
52 2005 horror sequel
55 Prefix with port
57 Fund-raising suffix
60 Iraq war subject, briefly
61 Volga tributary

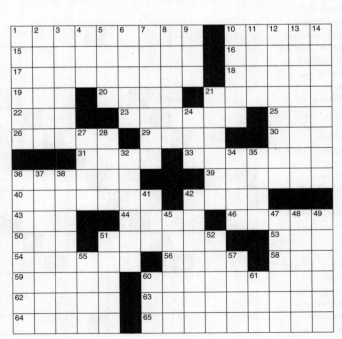

by David Steinberg

382

★ ★ ★

ACROSS

1 Like many a fairy tale princess
8 Craft with one mast and one sail
15 Offering for continuing education
17 Totally gone
18 "___ I might . . ."
19 Pretend
20 Papua New Guinea port
21 One with a glazed-over expression?
22 Plant related to pepper
23 Places for shooting stars
24 Finished
25 They've been splintered
26 Boiling point at Roman baths?
27 Number tossed out
29 Glacial pinnacles
30 Longtime "Guiding Light" actress Beth
31 Hellenistic-era galley
32 Is offensive, in a way
33 Lost it
35 Left unsaid
36 Waterwheel parts
37 Learning the ropes
38 Depression specialist's subj.
39 Fix
40 Bullfighter's cloak
41 Vietnam's Dien Bien ___
42 Lacking
43 Like some uncared-for closets
44 Mudslinger, say
47 Lacked any supervision
48 Strawberry, for example
49 Voiced letters

DOWN

1 Potential beach closer
2 Aid in scaling down?
3 Hung in there
4 It prevents things from becoming 43-Across
5 Some, in Seville
6 Southern leader?
7 Southern and such
8 Hundreds
9 "___ Million" (Nathanael West novel)
10 Like some muscles and tendons
11 Frank's place
12 Taxing educational hurdle
13 One traveling around India with a trunk
14 Progress by intelligent design
16 Proust's Parisian courtesan
22 Campout dangers
23 One whose head is turned
25 Take the lead from?
26 Roll of candy
28 Wack, in hip-hop
29 Blockage-busting brand
31 Job-hunting consideration
32 Pop from a different line
33 Lacked in freshness
34 Hockey player Roloson and wrestler Johnson
36 Like pocketed bills
39 Barbizon School painter Jules
40 Brown shade
42 Court hearing
43 Brooklyn Park setting: Abbr.
45 Municipal div.
46 Before-long link

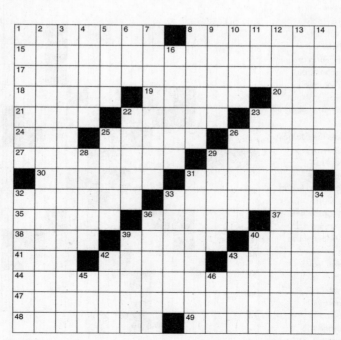

by Joe Krozel

ACROSS

1 Eaters of halal food
8 Like many mall fixtures?
15 Star of 2011's "Puss in Boots"
17 One shooting out on a golf course
18 Oil sources for oil paint
19 Mode
20 Mo. containing Constitution Day
21 Unhealthily light
25 From
29 It may be fat after a fight
32 Digs
33 Onetime Taliban stronghold
35 What twisty arrows warn drivers of
37 Bring into being
38 Hit film directed by James Cameron
39 Football linemen: Abbr.
40 Arctic or Antarctic fish-eater
41 It has left and right channels
42 Part of S.F.S.U.
43 How some hearts are broken
48 Car exhaust part
54 Potential pets
57 Worker whose charges may charge
58 Answer that avoids answering
59 Writer's field

DOWN

1 More, to a señor
2 Like surprises you'd rather not get
3 Youth
4 Chop source
5 They have keepers
6 Bit of D.J. equipment
7 Flat bottom
8 Hold hands?
9 Nav. position
10 Nestlé brand
11 Partridge family setting
12 Hanging out in galleries, say
13 Isle of Man man
14 "Nine Stories" title girl
16 Flat bottom
20 Web presence
22 "Natural Affection" playwright
23 Surgical aid
24 Big band
25 Done to ___
26 Foundering call
27 Black-and-white giants
28 Geologist's big break?
29 Couples' retreat
30 Rachel McAdams's "Sherlock Holmes" role
31 Choose to refuse
34 Big wheel at a party?
36 Beyond, to Browning
43 Put the finger on
44 Short plea
45 Some govt. raiders
46 Imitated Niobe
47 Dept. of Labor division
48 Stole option
49 Do one's part?
50 N.F.C. part: Abbr.
51 Concerning
52 Order
53 Except
55 Univ. helpers
56 Some 55-Down: Abbr.

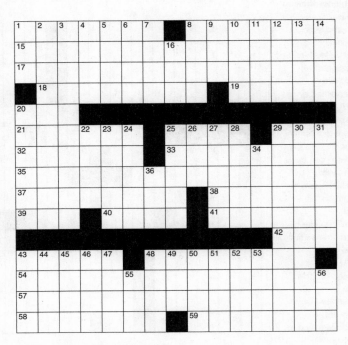

by Todd Gross and Doug Peterson

384 ★★★

ACROSS

1 Aldrin, Armstrong and Collins
10 Large parts of some support systems?
15 Bit of the magic of Disney
16 Increased
17 Start practicing, as bad habits
18 University next to the Centers for Disease Control headquarters
19 A.B.A. team that signed Moses Malone out of high school
20 Yellow fever carrier
21 "Vexations" composer
22 Cause people to disbelieve, with "on"
24 Flintstones vitamins maker
25 Pull up stakes, informally
26 U.S. United Nations representative, 2005–06
30 Pfizer brand since 1997
32 Dunce cap-shaped
33 "The Great Santini" author
34 Nutty as can be
36 Kept slightly open artificially, maybe
37 Storms on the road
38 Spanish uncle?
40 Anne Brontë's first novel
42 The U.S.S. Constitution has three
47 Grounation Day celebrant
48 Snack item next to a dip bowl
50 With lid rattling, say
51 These days
52 Waterfall or rapid
53 Feature of many a pizzeria
54 Builds up
55 Sticks firmly

DOWN

1 A little above average
2 Loop taken on a drive?
3 Gertrude Stein or Alice B. Toklas
4 "___ could" (expression of regret)
5 Thornburgh's predecessor as attorney general
6 Mine entrance
7 Makeshift cat dish
8 Animal that has escaped from its owner
9 Fox Business Network show
10 Horrible
11 Provider of relief for a finger?
12 Roman count?
13 All in the family?
14 Le Carré specialty
23 Flashes
24 Ominous
26 Coastal setting of "The Birds"
27 Bistro offering
28 Bathroom item on a honey-do list
29 Bit of retribution
31 Locust tree feature
32 Cuban remnant
35 From Land's End, e.g.
36 Aces, nowadays
39 Will, if intentions bear out
41 De-ices, perhaps
42 Rules of conduct
43 Lead-in to God or Congress
44 Trinity member
45 Post-marathon posts
46 Wiped out
49 "Best friend" from Germany?

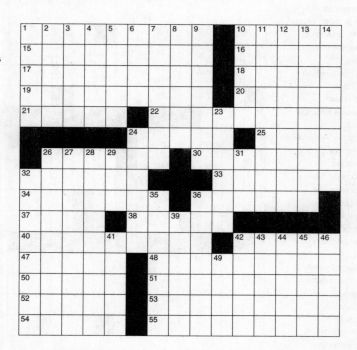

by Mark Diehl

ACROSS

1 Semimonthly tide
5 Mooring post on a ship
9 Head nurse on "Scrubs"
14 If you add up the pros and cons
16 Nautical direction
17 Pitcher of the only no-hitter in World Series history
18 Small truck manufacturer
19 Highly rated 1997 film with the song "Tupelo Honey"
20 Take in, possibly
21 Flogs
22 Like yoga instructors
23 Pink shade
24 Secures every share from
26 Early man?
28 Had some inventory problems
29 ___ lane
30 Berate profanely
33 Court
34 What mansions rarely are
36 "___ = Politics" (TV slogan)
37 Inventor given a gold medal by Titanic survivors
38 "Goodness me!"
41 U.K. Triple Crown racecourse site
42 Dance trio?
47 Suddenly took interest
48 Motivated
49 Go on
50 Communion place
51 Abject
52 Colorful Amazon swimmer
53 They're indispensable
54 Mrs. Charles Lindbergh
55 "The Lucy-___ Comedy Hour"

DOWN

1 "Well, of course"
2 Name on a famous B-29
3 Mammy's son
4 Adjective applied to ginger ale
5 Things towed along towpaths
6 Expanse beneath an arch?
7 Certain lymphocyte
8 Works behind a counter
9 Prompter
10 Get rid of
11 Like some store furniture
12 North American home of 30,000 islands
13 Tiramisu ingredient, often
15 Frequent photo prop for Will Rogers
25 "___ furtiva lagrima" (Donizetti aria)
26 Bourbon enemy
27 Blow out of proportion
28 Flat fish
29 Pleasantly rustic
30 The Village ___ (musical group with the 1963 hit "Washington Square")
31 Walked away with
32 Star of Ang Lee's "Hulk"
35 Looked for a phenomenon, maybe
36 Blackened
38 Leroux who created the Phantom
39 Premium number
40 What a dickey simulates
43 Lady of Paris
44 Junk car
45 Some funeral attendees
46 "We're Madly for ___" (old campaign song)

by Patrick Berry

ACROSS

1 Fiddlehead sources
6 Get chummy
11 Odeur detector
14 Phone query before a private conversation
16 Grp. with the top 10 album "Face the Music"
17 Emerge
19 Like many obscenities
20 Supporter of Yoda
21 Masters focus
22 Words before story or debate
24 Wrapped up
25 Dodgem feature
27 Euro forerunner
29 It first circulated in 2000
38 Great parking spot, slangily
39 Gate holder
40 Sultanas, say
41 Things often zapped
42 It shows many B&W pictures
43 South Georgia's Prince ___ Harbor
46 1960's TV actor whose name looks like a free offer?
50 Big revolver
53 "Mickey" singer Basil
54 Lighting problem?
57 Slice from beneath the ribs
60 Roquefort source
61 One of Washington's houses, e.g.
62 1976 Rodgers and Harnick musical about Henry VIII
63 Soft, meshed fabrics
64 Some are drug-induced

DOWN

1 Braves
2 Lose ground?
3 D.J.'s creation
4 Maxim's denial
5 Somme silk
6 "Cry, the Beloved Country" author
7 One way to pray
8 Match game?
9 America East sch.
10 Epi center?
11 Seti River setting
12 Opera's Obraztsova
13 Like a lot, maybe
15 Oppressed by the heat?
18 Kabbalah
23 Big leagues
25 Roosevelt established it as Shangri-La
26 Steeped in tradition
28 Vast

29 Pleasant treatment centers
30 Oberhausen opera highlight
31 Highly glazed fabric
32 Believers in raising spirits?
33 Sinks a sub?
34 Joltin' Joe, e.g.
35 "Lift Every Voice" author Guinier
36 ___ end
37 Genealogical line: Abbr.
43 Sleek fur
44 "The Little Prince" composer
45 Proposal for business expansion
47 "But not without ___": Pope
48 Golden Pavilion setting

49 Early New Yorkers
50 Early hour
51 Neck tie?
52 Is oppressed by the heat
55 Brief moment, briefly
56 He's 2, say
58 An expat may take it: Abbr.
59 One taken on a drive: Abbr.

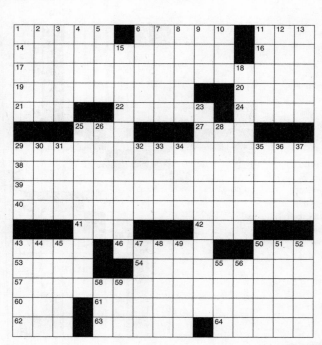

by Martin Ashwood-Smith

ACROSS

1 Actress Stone and others
6 "Just playin' with ya"
10 Base characters?
14 Meccan, e.g.
15 Ones sitting on pads
16 Cut off one's ears?
17 One asking questions he already knows the answers to
19 Cousin of contra-
20 Highness
21 "Figures I'd have this problem!"
23 French expert in body language?
24 Draw back
25 Education dissemination locations
30 Solidifying agents
31 Vase lookalikes
35 Bouncing off the walls
36 Enclosure . . . and an alphabetical listing of letters not appearing elsewhere in this puzzle's answer
37 Sylvester's "Rocky" co-star
38 A Ford
39 "___ Girl" ("Bells Are Ringing" tune)
40 One swimming with flippers
46 Logical ending
49 Accessible for shooting
50 Like pool racks
52 Host of PBS's "Scientific American Frontiers"
56 Baseball All-Star Kinsler and others
57 "1984" shelfmate
59 Ordeal for jrs.
60 Part of some pools
61 Rose partially
62 Clinic shipments
63 Henry James biographer
64 Least desirable parts

DOWN

1 A.B.A. members' titles
2 Wailuku's county
3 California's ___ Woods
4 Wood shop shaper
5 "Scrooge" star, 1951
6 "Likely story"
7 Lawn flamingos and such
8 Pop alternative
9 With 12-Down, lidocaine delivery option
10 Risk board territory
11 Stack at IHOP, say
12 See 9-Down
13 Like some punk hairstyles
18 Cracked open
22 Stocking-up time?
23 Lay claim forcibly
25 Weak
26 Quaint euphemism
27 Film holders
28 True companion?
29 Pundit
32 Highness: Abbr.
33 Mass action
34 Mosel tributary
41 Begin a conversation with
42 Cut back
43 Contact liquid
44 Nail topper
45 Home to a much-visited tomb
46 Sticks in a makeup bag
47 Sweep the board?
48 Mosul money
51 The Charleses' pet
52 Not close
53 Like fashionable partygoers?
54 It may knock you out
55 Concert pieces
58 54-Down for a trip

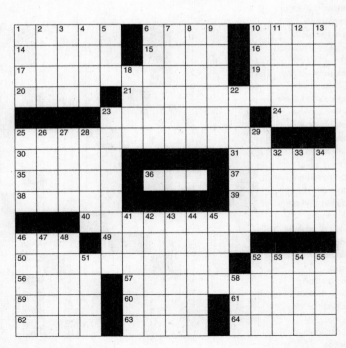

by Joe Krozel

388 ★ ★ ★

ACROSS
1 Concern for a dermatologist
5 They often come with eggs
15 Catalan article
16 What cuts power in half?
17 Sheila's welcome
18 Opposite of "dissuaded from"
19 Coulee
21 Messed up
22 Roster curtailer: Abbr.
23 Product of some decay
25 Non-Hollywood, say
26 Bit of wet-weather wear
27 Packed things
29 Touchdown letters
30 Something stuck in a freezer?
33 Five in the ninth inning?
35 Step
36 Prefix with 11-Down
39 Signs near a teller's window, maybe
42 Some proctors, briefly
44 Of the essence
47 Silverwing flier
49 Prepare to send some mail
50 Route through a park, maybe
52 The toe of a boot?
53 Schnapps choice
55 Declamation stations
56 Many a crash cushion at a construction zone
59 Get 44-Down
60 Affection
61 Bananas

62 Civil engineering vehicle
63 School in the Piedmont region

DOWN
1 It's checked before taking off
2 Ripple
3 Dieter's design
4 Like many horror flick characters
5 One of the subjects of the best-selling '02 book "The Conquerors"
6 King Hussein Airport locale
7 Disgrace
8 Cod relative
9 Java, for one
10 Like the Phillies' caps
11 Word with career or goal
12 Falls short
13 Manx trait
14 Some ermines
20 Securing device
24 Her help was solicited in a hit song
25 P.R., e.g.
27 P.R. releases
28 Passing comment at a poker table
31 Shared funds
32 Symphonic score abbr.
34 Backed up
37 "Sold!"
38 Universidad de las Américas site
40 "Children of the Albatross" novelist
41 Osmose

43 Like much of Niger
44 Not so remote
45 Swiss alternative
46 Big coffee exporter
48 Quick and thorough learner
50 Like some canine teeth
51 Daughter of Zeus and Themis
53 "The Incredibles" family name
54 Aretha's Grammy-nominated sister
57 Bit of 1-Down
58 Photocopier abbr.

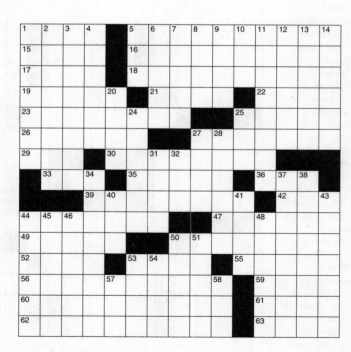

by Barry C. Silk

ACROSS

1 Title matchmaker of early 19th-century literature
5 Drifting type
9 Some help
14 With 21-Across, ship out?
15 Britain's Douglas-Home
16 Need for a 17-Across
17 Special delivery of a sort
20 Fluoride, e.g.
21 See 14-Across
22 Spots for rubs and scrubs
23 Is homesick, say
25 "Oedipe" opera composer, 1936
27 Response to being tickled
29 They often have quiet eyes
32 Moo ___
34 Santa's checking things
36 N.F.L. QB Kyle
37 Revolutionary Tribunal casualty
40 Verdugo of "Marcus Welby, M.D."
41 Oxford attachment?
42 Automne follows it
43 Fort's steep slope
45 Click beetle
47 Go at
49 98.6°, say
52 Korean War outbreak year
54 Starchy
56 African antelope
57 Discovery of Vitus Bering before his shipwreck
60 Paavo ___, track's Flying Finn

61 "Live at Red Rocks" pianist
62 Under tension
63 Some tides
64 City in Padua province
65 Shakespeare title contraction

DOWN

1 Steele work
2 Where "ayuh" is an affirmative
3 What 007 might shoot with
4 He declared "The planet has a fever"
5 Largest ethnic group in China
6 Pasternak mistress Ivinskaya
7 Implicatively
8 Large quantity
9 GPS screen abbr.
10 Curling rink line seven yards from the tee
11 Destination after a touchdown
12 Scholarship-offering org.
13 4-Down's grp.
18 Semicircular canals' locales
19 Burning solutions
24 2008 demolition target
26 Eolith or neolith
28 Fifth of fünf
30 Glam rock's ___ the Hoople
31 Old dagger
32 Hook helper
33 Dutch Golden Age painter
35 Dirty

38 Experiencing down time
39 Home of Sistan and Baluchestan
44 Spanish term of endearment
46 Printed slips
48 Really put out
50 "The X Factor" panelist, once
51 Things Santa checks
52 "Doctor Faustus" novelist
53 Footprint or fingerprint, say
55 Tears can create one
58 "Indeedy"
59 "___ Cried" (1962 hit song)

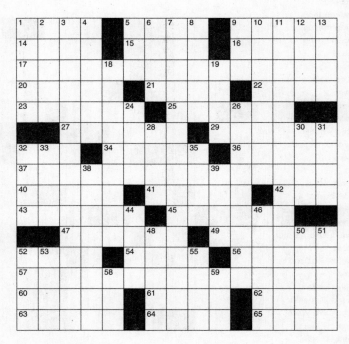

by Joel Kaplow

ACROSS

1 Navajo terrain
6 Chicken ___
10 Pack member, for short?
13 Top
14 What going 100 might result in
17 "You ___ one"
18 1980's–90's hip-hop show co-hosted by Fab 5 Freddy
19 Ingurgitate
21 Delectable
22 Joins
24 Food item whose name means "pounded"
25 "Patton" setting
27 Relieve
28 They often accompany discoveries
29 Congregation, metaphorically
32 Org. studying viruses
35 Be daring
39 Sound after "Lower . . . lower . . . that's it!"
40 Noted entertainer with a whistle
41 Site of a religious retreat
42 Oaf
43 Sneeze cause
46 Salad bar offering
49 Writer about a bear
51 "Julie & Julia" co-star
53 Amass
56 "Bad for bacteria" brand
58 Setting for the 1996 documentary "When We Were Kings"
59 "Funny People" actor

60 "Pietà or Revolution by Night" artist
61 Jerk
62 Zip
63 "L'Amateur d'estampes" painter

DOWN

1 Subjunctive, e.g.
2 Dutch chess grandmaster Max
3 First N.B.A. player to light the Olympic cauldron
4 Caution
5 French nuns
6 Liberal arts dept.
7 Midway, e.g.
8 Fratricide victim of myth
9 "Meet the ___" (major-league fight song)
10 Bye lines?
11 Data
12 Artist's supply
15 Line at a water fountain, maybe
16 Burned out
20 Échecs piece
23 Modern-day pointer
25 Part of a bar order
26 "Dream on!"
27 King, e.g.: Abbr.
30 Like 40's boppers
31 Colossal, to Coleridge
32 Christmas order
33 Alter ___ amicus
34 Follow
36 It rolls across fields
37 Gorgon, e.g.
38 Business that's always cutting back?
42 Disinclined
44 Put on
45 Like some doughnuts and eyes
46 Makings of a model, maybe
47 Billet-doux recipients
48 Some bump producers
49 Computer that pioneered in CD-ROMs
50 Onetime Moore co-star
52 Longtime Yankee moniker
54 Nocturnal bear
55 No ___ (store sign)
57 Rhinology expert, for short

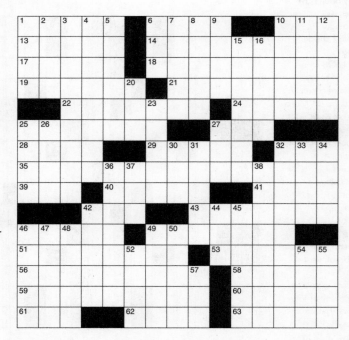

by Brendan Emmett Quigley and Caleb Madison

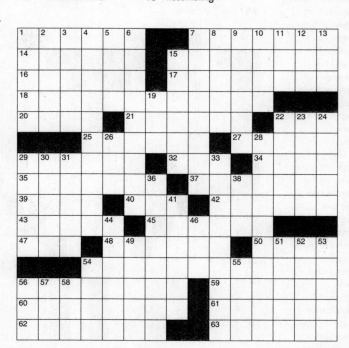

ACROSS

1 Like eaters of humble pie
7 Impossible dream
14 Clichéd company claim
15 Surveilled, say
16 Onetime pickling liquid
17 Pumpkin is rich in it
18 Party makeup?
20 Abbr. accompanying some dotted notes
21 Urban planting favorite
22 Half the time?: Abbr.
25 Makes less edgy
27 A weather strip may fit into it
29 Only Englishman named a Dr. of the Church
32 Tony's "Taras Bulba" co-star, 1962
34 Maneuver
35 Reckon
37 Producer of a blowout, maybe
39 Danny DeVito's "Throw Momma From the Train" role
40 Clock stopper, at times
42 Good dogs for pulling loads
43 Most negligible
45 Expect
47 Winged ___
48 Cobble, perhaps
50 More, in ads
54 Maker of fabrics with intricate designs
56 Tryst figure
59 Running quarterly, for short?
60 A 40-Across will watch for it
61 C_3H_8, e.g.

62 Like some words and swords
63 Reacted to a punch

DOWN

1 Alternatives to sales
2 Spartan toiler
3 ___ Express
4 What Jack got in exchange for a cow, in a children's story
5 Form of "sum"
6 Proper
7 Attributes (to)
8 Grand entrance?
9 Retort of contradiction
10 Longtime Dodgers coach Manny
11 Feta milk source

12 "Footloose" hero McCormack
13 Ending for AriZona flavors
15 Hardly abundant
19 N.L. Central city
22 Divvy up
23 Cabbage
24 Ocular irritants
26 "Bad" cholesterol, briefly
28 Inscrutable
29 Tiptoed, say
30 Spa handout
31 Subs
33 Body shop offering
36 Cheerleading outfit?
38 A 40-Across may call it
41 Like many bakers' hands
44 Walks heavily
46 Resembling

49 Collège, e.g.
51 Like the Navajo language
52 ABC's Arledge
53 Full of adrenaline
54 Shocks
55 World's largest fruit company
56 One-striper, briefly
57 Swiss stream
58 Spanish stream

by Barry C. Silk and Brad Wilber

392 ★ ★ ★

ACROSS

1 Fashion show disaster
4 Dated
7 Make a major decision?
9 Head honcho in baseball
11 Element in many semiconductors
13 Like galley slaves, typically
15 Late 1980's Cadillac
16 Literally, "the Stairway"
17 ___ Day
19 Makes a person less tense
20 Exceeds, as demand
21 Closet item, for short
24 Collection of Blaise Pascal writings
25 Middle of this century
28 Spanish queen and namesakes
30 Father-and-son Connecticut congressmen Thomas and Chris
31 Big ring
32 Buckle attachment
34 9-5 connector
35 Choice word?
36 With love
39 Long Island university
40 Like the relatives notified in emergencies, usually
41 Entices
42 Grass for some baskets
43 Economical
44 It might be tipped at a rodeo

DOWN

1 Fingers on a diamond
2 "That's my intention"
3 Quickly reproduces
4 Ship's boarding ladder
5 Keys and Markova
6 CeCe of gospel
7 Lavish events
8 Like John Kerry in 2004
9 Opposites of mansions
10 Food topping in France
11 Blast
12 Has no significance
13 They let traffic through after a crash
14 German article
18 Doesn't continue, as an argument
21 Maintainers of a sacred flame in ancient Rome
22 Made a commitment to play
23 Boxing Hall-of-Famer Primo
25 Sewers, often
26 Sends
27 ___ Hewitt, 2002 Wimbledon winner
29 Nascar driver Elliott
31 Eye
33 One side of a longstanding ad battle
35 Military encampment
37 Nose: Prefix
38 Sign for a musician not to play

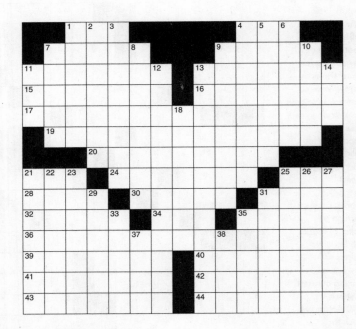

by Joe Krozel

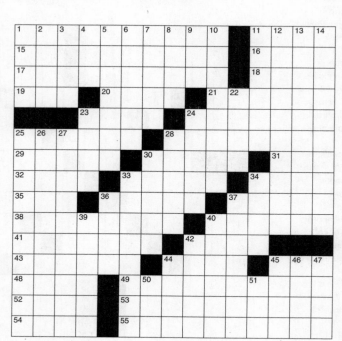

ACROSS

1 Stud, say
11 Court defendant: Abbr.
15 He played Don Altobello in "The Godfather Part III"
16 Fair
17 Side effect?
18 Hillbilly's plug
19 More, to a 37-Down
20 Eric of "Funny People," 2009
21 It's gradually shrinking in the Arctic
23 Lost traction
24 One punched in an office
25 Kitchen dusting aid
28 Admirable person
29 They might be left hanging
30 Not pussyfooting
31 1990's Indian P.M.
32 "Youth With a Skull" painter
33 Didn't use a high enough 45-Across, maybe
34 Carpenter's groove
35 Some E.M.T. cases
36 They stand for things
37 Kind of nut
38 Evenly matched
40 Employees at a ritzy hotel
41 Is routed by
42 Whiff
43 Hand holder?
44 Grain, e.g.
45 Ray blockage no.
48 Month whose zodiac sign is a fish
49 "Lady Baltimore" novelist, 1906
52 Prefix with 3-Down
53 "It'll be O.K." lead-in
54 Tummy filler
55 "Whoa, not so fast!"

DOWN

1 Appear thrilled
2 Two before Charlie
3 Computing 0s and 1s
4 Milk source
5 Sense, slangily
6 Aquila's brightest star
7 Secretive body part
8 Mariner's grp.
9 Outer: Prefix
10 Postapocalyptic best seller of 1978
11 Wraps up
12 Send
13 Flighty type
14 Drills, e.g.
22 League division
23 Criteria: Abbr.
24 Veers sharply
25 Friend one grows up with, often
26 "News to me!"
27 Reason for a track delay
28 "Faded Love" singer, 1963
30 Film with the tagline "Borat was SO 2006"
33 Where following a star might lead you
34 Shoulder press target, briefly
36 It's in front of the cockpit
37 South-of-the-border bad guy
39 Colorful additions to tanks
40 Beheld
42 Name in seven Shakespeare titles
44 Charges from counsel
45 They may be prayed to in Fr.
46 Graceful fairy
47 Part of a long neck
50 "Huh?"
51 "___ being Brand" (Cummings poem)

by Ian Livengood

Note: This puzzle has two bonus answers in appropriate places. Can you find them?

ACROSS

1 Big chickens
9 Seat cushions?
15 Loose
16 Like Fiennes's Shakespeare
17 Supply in a camper's first-aid kit
18 Actress Matlin
19 W.W. II inits.
20 British meat pies
22 Soviet accords?
23 Maine's ___ Bay
25 Locks
26 Kind of cloud
27 Vertical: Prefix
28 Anderson who wrote "My Life in High Heels"
29 1950's–60's singer Jackson, the Queen of Rockabilly
30 Forum : Rome :: ___ : Athens
32 Go on
33 Exchange
36 Talking-tos
37 "Save the ___" (conservationists' catchphrase)
38 A park may have one
39 No challenge
40 See 51-Across
41 Stoked
45 Grand
46 Stern contemporary
47 Massey of "Frankenstein Meets the Wolf Man"
48 "This is a test. For the next 60 seconds . . ." org.
49 Beats
51 Notable stat for 40-Across

52 Nickname for Warren Weber in an old sitcom
54 Rowdy
56 "I'm a walking, talking ___": Larry David
57 Resting
58 Bee wine
59 Veteran

DOWN

1 Plain's opposite
2 Commensurate (with)
3 "It's about time!"
4 Doo-wop syllable
5 Grave, for one
6 "Confessions of a Drunkard" writer, 1822
7 Didn't have enough

8 "The Brandenburgers in Bohemia" composer
9 Scrabble accessory
10 Final pharaoh of the Fifth Dynasty, whose pyramid is near Cairo
11 Canon type, briefly
12 Retain
13 Classic actress who played the principal in "Grease"
14 Reel
21 Junior Jr.
24 Hat
26 Dish eaten with a spoon
28 "___ on First" (1981 comedian's biography)
29 Tune (up)
31 Hiking snack

32 Aid consideration
33 Big house
34 Offensive formation
35 Uncommitted
36 Sacagawea, for one
38 "In actuality . . ."
40 Minnesota senator Klobuchar
42 Homer's "dread monster"
43 Not home?
44 Picked up
46 Gossip opening
47 Key chain?
49 Italian lyrical verse
50 N.F.L. coach Jim
53 ___ Friday
55 Bit of news in the financial sect.

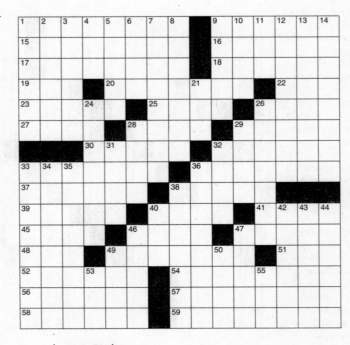

by Matt Ginsberg

ACROSS

1 Cuisine featuring nam prik
5 Identifies
9 Counterpart
13 Mezzo-soprano Marilyn
15 1968 Best Actor nominee for "The Fixer"
17 A blimp may hover over one
18 Induce squirming in, perhaps
19 Coat that's easy to take off
21 French loanword that literally means "rung on a ladder"
22 Colors
24 Perfect
25 It was MSNBC's highest-rated program when canceled in 2003
26 Antique shop purchase
29 Wizard's garment
30 Paper assets
36 Device with a hard disk
37 It has a denomination of $1,000
38 Homeric character who commits matricide
41 Weapons used to finish off the Greek army at Thermopylae
46 What a robot might resemble
47 To the left
48 Psychedelic 1968 song featuring a lengthy drum solo
51 What a whatnot has
52 Like molasses
53 Danger for a climber
54 President's daughter on "The West Wing"
55 Alternative to "your"
56 Company whose Nasdaq symbol is the company's name
57 Keep alive, as a fire

DOWN

1 Showed a bit more friendliness
2 Poet who gave us "carpe diem"
3 Singer at Barack's inauguration
4 Poor
5 Hymn sung to Apollo
6 Trees in Gray's country churchyard
7 Kaplan who co-hosted six seasons of "High Stakes Poker"
8 Acknowledge a commander's entrance, maybe
9 Pizza sauce
10 Not going with the flow?
11 Round-bottomed container
12 Letter on Kal-El's costume
14 One hanging at a temple
16 It's all in your head
20 Christmas green?
23 Gets the gist
25 Dimwit
27 "I hate it when that happens!"
28 Business often located near an interstate
30 Obstruct
31 Trunk item
32 Too accommodating for one's own good
33 Once-autonomous people of southern Russia
34 Sober
35 Nonwoody plant parts
39 Senate sheets
40 Make possible
42 Disobey the rule?
43 Baltimore's ___ Park
44 Begin with enthusiasm
45 Got a lot of laughs out of
47 1980's Tyne Daly role
49 Small quantity
50 Surrealism forerunner
51 Buddy

by Patrick Berry

396

★ ★ ★

ACROSS

1 Crowds around noisily
5 "In the Still of the Nite" doo-wop group, with "the"
15 Beginning of time?
16 Somewhat
17 Korean War weapon
18 Where to request a knish
19 "___ the brinded cat hath mewed": Shak.
21 Like sports cars, briefly
22 Reagan-era teen, e.g.
23 Modern-day stream
25 Burgeon
27 Like some shape shifters?
29 Cut bits from, maybe
33 What "-" means in a search query
34 Big ring rivals
36 Mark of a successful gunfighter
37 They cause blowups
39 Like many disabled vehicles
41 Positions
42 Helped supply a sushi restaurant, say
44 Promotions may require them, for short
46 Chile's main airline
47 Yarn identifier
49 Bar lines?
51 Washout
53 First bishop of Paris
54 "Looky here!"
57 ___ balls (chocolaty snacks)
59 1950 sci-fi classic
60 Medium relative
63 Mini successor
64 Spy's query at the start of a meeting
65 LeAnn Rimes's "Love ___ Army"
66 Like legal voters
67 Take out

DOWN

1 Like some top-10 people
2 Like bull's-eyes
3 One in a stag's litter
4 "Aah!"
5 Tricks
6 1969 Peace Prize agcy.
7 Certain stamp of approval
8 Fifth element, per Aristotle
9 Of atoms' spatial relationships
10 The Hebrew Hammer of the Cleveland Indians
11 J.F.K. speechwriter Sorensen
12 Horned mountain dweller
13 View from Memphis
14 Kerfuffle
20 Airport fleet
24 It's south of the Banda Sea
26 Hydroxyl compound
28 Tinkertoy bit
30 One of Henderson's record 1,406
31 Off-and-on
32 Bit of paste
35 2009 Tennis Hall of Fame inductee
38 Common portrait subject
40 Beat
43 Actress-turned-nun Hart
45 Abolhassan Bani-___ (first president of Iran)
48 Clawed
50 Russian playwright Andreyev
52 Guideposts magazine founder
54 "'Tis all a Chequerboard of Nights and Days" poet
55 Take on
56 Universal donor's type, briefly
58 Kitchen drawer?
61 Traffic violation, for short
62 Okla. City-to-Tulsa direction

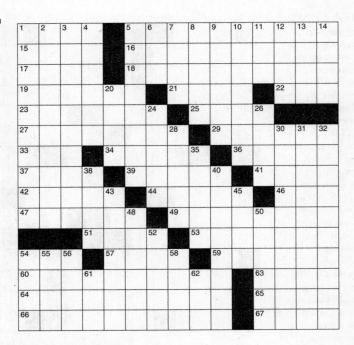

by Barry C. Silk

ACROSS

1 The miss in "Miss Saigon"
4 Burger go-withs
10 Big race sponsor
13 Dishes fit for astronomers?
16 Panglossian person
17 Asia-to-Africa link
18 Carmen ___ ("The Producers" role)
19 Interior decorator's suggestion
20 Southeast Asian holiday
21 Grp. concerned with bowls
23 Rout
26 Mean cur, typically
28 Ice cream mix-in
30 Place to go in Soho
31 See 32-Across
32 On the 31-Across side
34 ___ question
36 South Asian chant word
38 Had a lot to digest
40 Restless
41 Ear-related
43 Longtime Russian acronym
44 ___ Dogg Pound (rap duo)
45 Chihuahua scratch?
47 Adjust one's sights
49 Lays atop
51 Asset
53 King, in Cape Verde
55 Handy-andy's letters
56 Box-office take
58 SALT I and II, e.g.
60 Beloved "Immortal Beloved" piece
63 How this puzzle's black squares are arranged
64 They may have you in stitches, in brief
65 Gunsmith with Smith
66 One may say "I'm with stupid"

DOWN

1 "Take cover!"
2 Security requests
3 Star in Cetus
4 What an express often whizzes by: Abbr.
5 Hägar's wife
6 Polynesian farewell song
7 "Beau Geste" headgear
8 Responsibility for a groundskeeper
9 Grade sch. subject
10 Round-trip flight?
11 Tackles a tough task
12 W. Coast clock setting
13 Do some recharging
14 Center for cat-tails?
15 Highly decorated Bradley
22 Prefix with many fruit names
24 Georgetown athlete
25 Things worked under in a garage
27 "Sax All Night" New Ager
29 Mtge. broker's come-on
31 "SCTV" lineup
33 Hmong homeland
35 It is in Spain
37 It has a sticking point
39 Sandy shade
42 Pre-stunt provocation
46 Thing worked on in a garage
48 Second-largest city in Finland
50 Matched up, after "in"
52 Can
54 Exeter exclamation
57 Cut takers: Abbr.
59 Some kind of ___
60 6 letters
61 Fan setting
62 Apollo's chariot "passenger"

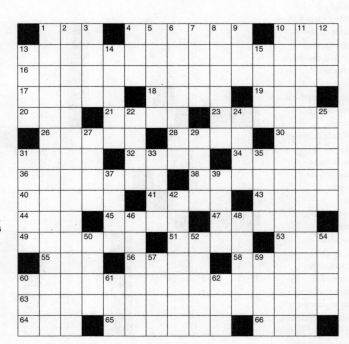

by Scott Atkinson

ACROSS

1 Gemini, Libra and Aquarius
9 Untrustworthy sort
15 Result of too much TV, it's said
16 Not bad, in Nantes
17 Common aquarium decoration
18 Promotional description for a coming show
19 Ancient key
20 Goat's call
21 "Green Book" org., familiarly
22 Home of the Dostoyevsky Literary Museum
23 Kitchen tool
24 Do stuff
29 Field marshals' commands
30 Thumbs-up
34 Monkey ladder vine
35 Holiday when sweeping and emptying the trash are considered bad luck
36 Vega of "Spy Kids"
37 Polyhedron part
38 Chaotic
40 Symbiotic partners of clownfish
41 "She is more precious than ___": Proverbs 3:15
45 Points
46 Garment originally made from caribou or sealskin
47 "___ Back" (2004 Kenny Chesney hit)
48 Tarzan trademark
52 Takes a powder
53 Steve Allen sidekick with the catchphrase "Hi-ho, Steverino!"
55 Cup alternative
56 Engaged, as a target
57 Keeping half the world down, say
58 Flock member

DOWN

1 "East of Eden" girl
2 Unrelenting
3 Pool accessory
4 Guru follower
5 "___ 500" (annual list)
6 Case study?
7 Cape Breton locale
8 Taco Bell offering
9 Dogs that ought to be great swimmers?
10 State of nervous tension
11 Test course challenges
12 Sphere of influence
13 Old country name or its currency, both dropped in 1997
14 "The Apostles" composer
22 Mrs. Václav Havel, the first first lady of the Czech Republic
24 Game part
25 "Celeste Aida," e.g.
26 Leopard's home?
27 Hall-of-Fame Cub Sandberg
28 Conniving
30 Imperial offering
31 "Smoke Gets in Your Eyes" composer
32 Wheelset piece
33 Exuberant cries
36 Byrd and others: Abbr.
38 Executive suite?
39 Fix up, in a way
40 Nobel-winning poet Heaney
41 Lacks a clear voice
42 "Say ___!"
43 Compound used to kill ants
44 Ramadi resident
48 River intentionally flooded in W.W. I
49 Michael who wrote "The Neverending Story"
50 Home of the international headquarters of Interpol
51 Time of forbearance
54 Reverend ___, onetime radio evangelist

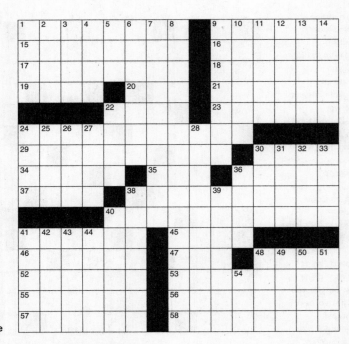

by Byron Walden

ACROSS

1 Many fans are running during this
9 Three-toed wading birds
15 Gets
16 Present-day cry?
17 A vegetarian isn't on it
18 Holds forth
19 Tycoon types
20 "Go ahead," to Shakespeare
21 Certain odor absorber
22 Tabulae ___
23 Storming-out sounds
24 Must-see
27 Spam protection items?
28 Like many bread knives
30 Grammy-winning Brian
31 Looks
32 ___ of Lagery (Pope Urban II's real name)
33 Brushing and such
35 Blood rival
36 Ivy supporters
37 It's developed in a sonata
38 Parts of kingdoms
39 Curtain fabrics
40 Needs for some games of tag
42 Noted 19th- and 20th-century portraitist
43 Flight from danger
44 Bump down
45 Immobilized during winter, say
46 "Not if my life depended on it!"
47 "Done"
48 Four-seaters, maybe?

DOWN

1 Clumsy
2 Queen Mary, for one
3 "Don't do it!"
4 TV Land staple
5 They often get depressed
6 Modern guest-list organizer
7 Onetime Virginia V.I.P.'s
8 Amphibious carrier, for short
9 Establishment where customers typically are seated
10 Singer with the 1994 #1 alternative rock hit "God"
11 Short, strong pan
12 They may be odd
13 Malcolm-Jamal's "Cosby Show" role
14 Plea for aid
20 Teases playfully
22 It hasn't yet been interpreted
24 Strikes out
25 What many crewmen carouse on
26 Deposited into a bank
28 Dancer who was a fan favorite?
29 Ones giving winner forecasts
31 Amass
34 Not belowdecks
35 Tiny biter causing intense itching
37 Sign of availability
39 "Swearin' to God" singer, 1975
40 Hardly a good looker
41 1966 A.L. Rookie of the Year
42 Ward on a set
43 Sock
44 Not quite make the putt, with "out"

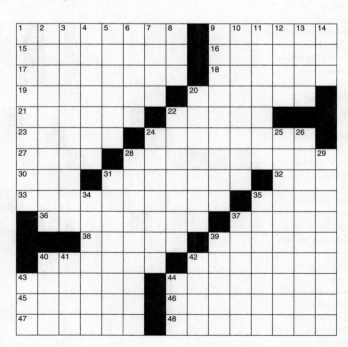

by Tim Croce

400

★ ★ ★

ACROSS

1 Regular fluctuation
11 Resourcefulness
15 Choose not to mess with
16 Stop shooting
17 Written between two rows of text
18 "But men are men; the best sometimes forget" speaker
19 Opposing
21 "Jelly Roll, Bix and ___" (1994 history of early jazz)
22 Lamb's "___ From Shakespeare"
23 Empty space
24 ___ of Denmark (James I's queen consort)
25 Fiber-rich fruits
26 Madrigal syllables
28 Crumbled ingredient in "dirt pudding"
29 Takes the big cheese down to size?
30 Surprising revelation
34 Superior facility
35 "You have been ___"
36 Salon selections
37 She bests Sherlock in "A Scandal in Bohemia"
38 Light
39 Snide remark
43 Items found in jackets
44 TV golf analyst who won three Masters
46 What tickets may get you
47 Some movies on TV are shown in it
50 Possible solution
51 Approximately
52 Film genre
53 Quick affair?

54 One attracted to vinegar
55 Terrible #2s

DOWN

1 "24" actress Cuthbert
2 Robert who won Oscars for both writing and directing "Kramer vs. Kramer"
3 1942 invasion site
4 Pay back
5 Square
6 "Burning Giraffes in Yellow" painter
7 More obdurate
8 Much earlier
9 Two stars of "Paper Moon"
10 One held in a trap

11 When the O.S.S. was formed
12 Reagan-era scandal
13 Subjects of many notices stapled to telephone poles
14 Part of a timing pattern on a football field
20 Winners of the longest postseason game in major-league history (18 innings, 2005)
25 Lead role in "Miracle on 34th Street"
27 Way to serve vegetables
28 1940's–50's tough-guy portrayer Dennis
29 Gandalf the ___
30 Drinking to excess

31 Brought up incessantly
32 Aeschylus trilogy
33 "This Week at War" airer
34 Mineral found in igneous rocks
36 Took a mulligan on
38 Typical lab rat, e.g.
39 Circumferences
40 Yardbird
41 Cylindrical vessel with a flat bottom
42 Compounds found in wine
45 Ancient Mycenaean stronghold
46 Do without
48 Pointed, in a way
49 Stymie

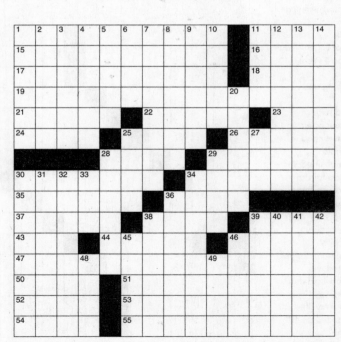

by Patrick Berry

Celebrate the 100th Anniversary of the Crossword Puzzle!

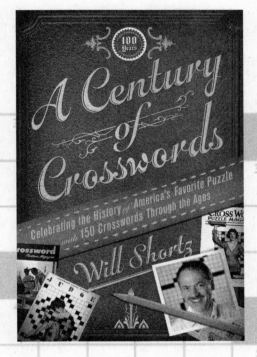

Available Summer 2013

1

```
GOT   OVALS   RATSO
ANA   AIMEE   OTHER
LEI   HOPOMYTHUMB
LAWFUL   NIECE
ITAL   CASS   NAVE
CANASTA       HACEK
   STARDATE   LYE
   SKIPTOMYLOU
ALE   REASONER
PERMS       RENDERS
TOFU   MAME   ELAN
   PIETA   HORACE
JUMPSTARTED   IKE
AGREE   LIKED   NEZ
WHITE   LOOPS   ERE
```

2

```
THAD   BATS   SOCKO
AARE   OLIN   ASHEN
ILKS   RICO   YEARS
LOSEONESWAY   IRE
   TEN   GIE   RST
INTOTO   MORSEL
HORNE   TAOS   BIND
ADAIR   OHS   ASFOR
DEVO   LURE   BETTE
   ENTICE   SENSED
GAR   OOH   AWL
OPS   UNDEVELOPED
TRIPP   OBOE   SPRY
TINGE   WRIT   SPEE
ALGAE   NODS   ASIS
```

3

```
MAGUS   HEMP   BASS
OCALA   ALAI   ARIA
THENUDISTCOLONY
   ELATED   TAR   LAS
   SET   SERAGLIO
ELF   DOOM   DNA
RARE   URIS   GLOB
GROVERCLEVELAND
   AMEN   HITE   OKAY
   RAF   NERO   SIE
IMCOMING   IDA
OAR   EGO   STELLA
THEBLARNEYSTONE
AREA   RACE   SOLTI
SEPT   ODOR   ANAIS
```

4

```
SELF   GAGS   PELE
OVAL   ACRES   LAOS
FIREESCAPE   URGE
ALDEN   NICEST
   SIR   DATE   HOR
OAS   DESI   LIMBO
CLUB   COLOR   TOLD
ULNA   ALONE   EVAN
LUGS   PIQUE   METE
ARLES   USSR   REY
REA   ASHE   EOS
   SATEEN   OPERA
GASP   WATERMELON
AGES   SPLIT   LIST
POSE   SYNE   LESS
```

5

```
MOSS   ATRIP   CARP
ATTU   MAUNA   OBOE
STUBBORNASAMULE
CONSORTS   TEETER
   CPAS   DIOR
LAUREL   LIMN   OAS
ARTIE   GAVE   INTO
SLIPPERYASANEEL
SECT   DAIS   RAISE
ONA   REIN   STUNTS
   PENN   MAID
ASSENT   CALLISTO
NAKEDASAJAYBIRD
OBIT   TUTOR   LAIR
NUDE   EMORY   EMMA
```

6

```
   CRAFT   FANTAN
EAGLED   ALERTED
STEELE   STEALER
STIRS   PETER   ADE
HMO   HALTER   ANIS
EONS   COED   ANTES
WISEGUYS   ROTARY
   RATS   LONI
AERATE   BEDECKED
GRAPE   FATE   SNEE
HATE   WONTON   IRA
ASA   PARSE   ASTIN
SETTING   REBATE
TRAINEE   SPODES
   STEEDS   ABORT
```

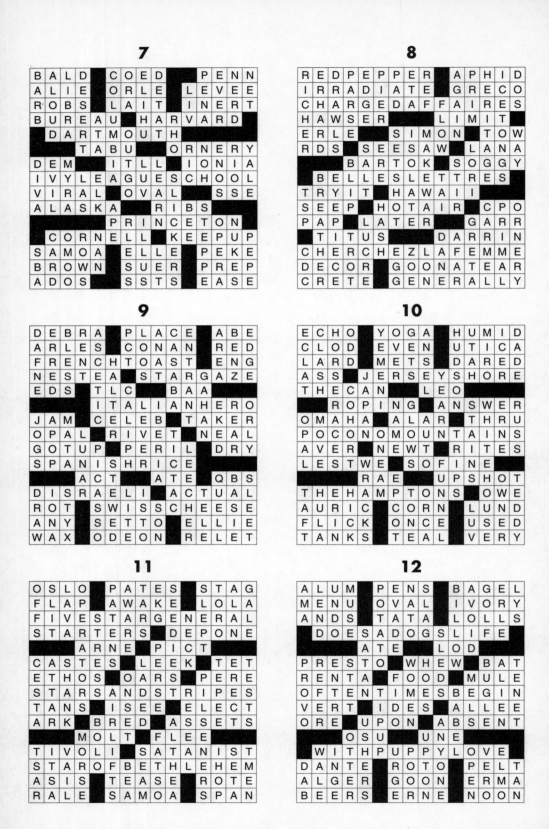

7

```
BALD  COED   PENN
ALIE  ORLE  LEVEE
ROBS  LAIT  INERT
BUREAU  HARVARD
 DARTMOUTH
   TABU   ORNERY
DEM   ITLL  IONIA
IVYLEAGUESCHOOL
VIRAL  OVAL   SSE
ALASKA   RIBS
    PRINCETON
 CORNELL  KEEPUP
SAMOA  ELLE  PEKE
BROWN  SUER  PREP
ADOS   SSTS  EASE
```

8

```
REDPEPPER  APHID
IRRADIATE  GRECO
CHARGEDAFFAIRES
HAWSER    LIMIT
ERLE  SIMON  TOW
RDS  SEESAW  LANA
   BARTOK  SOGGY
 BELLESLETTRES
TRYIT  HAWAII
SEEP  HOTAIR  CPO
PAP  LATER  GARR
 TITUS   DARRIN
CHERCHEZLAFEMME
DECOR  GOONATEAR
CRETE  GENERALLY
```

9

```
DEBRA  PLACE  ABE
ARLES  CONAN  RED
FRENCHTOAST  ENG
NESTEA  STARGAZE
EDS  TLC   BAA
   ITALIANHERO
JAM  CELEB  TAKER
OPAL  RIVET  NEAL
GOTUP  PERIL  DRY
SPANISHRICE
  ACT   ATE  QBS
DISRAELI  ACTUAL
ROT  SWISSCHEESE
ANY  SETTO  ELLIE
WAX  ODEON  RELET
```

10

```
ECHO  YOGA  HUMID
CLOD  EVEN  UTICA
LARD  METS  DARED
ASS  JERSEYSHORE
THECAN   LEO
  ROPING  ANSWER
OMAHA  ALAR  THRU
POCONOMOUNTAINS
AVER  NEWT  RITES
LESTWE  SOFINE
   RAE   UPSHOT
THEHAMPTONS  OWE
AURIC  CORN  LUND
FLICK  ONCE  USED
TANKS  TEAL  VERY
```

11

```
OSLO  PATES  STAG
FLAP  AWAKE  LOLA
FIVESTARGENERAL
STARTERS  DEPONE
  ARNE  PICT
CASTES  LEEK  TET
ETHOS  OARS  PERE
STARSANDSTRIPES
TANS  ISEE  ELECT
ARK  BRED  ASSETS
  MOLT  FLEE
TIVOLI  SATANIST
STAROFBETHLEHEM
ASIS  TEASE  ROTE
RALE  SAMOA  SPAN
```

12

```
ALUM  PENS  BAGEL
MENU  OVAL  IVORY
ANDS  TATA  LOLLS
 DOESADOGSLIFE
   ATE   LOD
PRESTO  WHEW  BAT
RENTA  FOOD  MULE
OFTENTIMESBEGIN
VERT  IDES  ALLEE
ORE  UPON  ABSENT
  OSU   UNE
 WITHPUPPYLOVE
DANTE  ROTO  PELT
ALGER  GOON  ERMA
BEERS  ERNE  NOON
```

13

L	A	D	D		R	I	V	E	R		C	H	E	R
A	W	A	Y		E	M	I	L	E		L	I	V	E
M	A	N	E	E	V	E	N	T	S		A	R	I	A
A	R	E		L	I	T		O	I	L	W	E	L	L
S	E	S	A	M	E		A	N	N	I	E			
		I	O	W	A	N		S	E	D	A	T	E	
W	E	A	R		E	X	E	S		S	M	I	R	K
A	L	D	A		D	E	M	O	S		O	D	I	E
F	L	A	P	S		S	O	F	T		N	A	P	S
T	E	M	P	U	S		N	A	I	V	E			
		A	M	P	L	E		N	I	T	W	I	T	
S	C	O	R	P	I	O		A	K	A		O	R	E
L	O	V	E		C	R	E	W	E	L	H	O	A	X
O	M	E	N		E	N	T	E	R		B	E	T	A
B	E	R	T		S	E	E	D	S		O	D	E	S

14

A	S	T	A		T	E	R	N		O	P	A	R	T
M	E	A	L		K	N	E	E		V	I	R	E	O
P	A	P	A	D	O	C	D	U	V	A	L	I	E	R
S	T	E	R	E		H	O	R	A		S	A	F	E
			M	Y	R	A		A	L	A	N			
S	O	B	S		U	N	C	L	E	R	E	M	U	S
A	T	E		M	E	T	H		T	I	R	A	N	A
M	A	G	D	A		S	I	P		E	S	S	A	Y
O	R	I	E	N	T		N	A	G	S		O	P	S
A	U	N	T	I	E	M	A	M	E		U	N	T	O
			H	A	L	O		P	L	A	T			
A	G	A	R		I	D	E	E		R	A	N	T	O
D	R	J	O	Y	C	E	B	R	O	T	H	E	R	S
D	I	A	N	A		M	R	E	D		A	N	I	L
S	T	R	E	P		S	O	R	E		N	E	M	O

15

	M	E	H	T	A		G	A	S	L	A	M	P	
M	A	Y	O	R	S		T	A	L	L	U	L	A	H
A	N	E	M	I	A		O	B	L	I	G	A	T	E
R	E	C	A	P		S	N	E	A	D		N	E	W
	A	G	E	I	N	G		Y	E	T				
R	A	T	E		D	A	U	B	S		A	J	A	R
U	P	C		L	E	P	E	R		R	I	A	T	A
M	P	H		C	A	S	T	O	F	F		W	I	N
P	L	E	A	D		O	W	N	E	D		B	L	T
S	E	R	B		O	N	I	C	E		A	R	T	S
			C	O	G		S	O	L	A	C	E		
A	S	K		F	L	A	T	S		S	C	A	R	S
D	O	E	S	T	I	M	E		K	O	O	K	I	E
D	A	R	K	E	N	E	R		I	N	S	E	C	T
S	P	R	I	N	G	S			M	E	T	R	O	

16

O	V	E	R		M	A	C	E	D		D	U	S	T
P	E	L	E		E	N	L	A	I		O	T	O	E
T	R	A	F	A	L	G	A	R	S	Q	U	A	R	E
S	O	L	E	N	O	I	D		A	U	G	H	T	S
			R	O	D	E		B	L	A	H			
R	E	M	E	D	Y		C	O	L	D		A	G	A
I	V	A	N	A		S	O	L	O		I	L	E	S
C	I	R	C	L	E	T	H	E	W	A	G	O	N	S
E	T	R	E		N	A	N	S		S	N	O	R	E
R	A	Y		E	G	I	S		S	T	O	K	E	S
			Y	S	E	R		F	E	H	R			
A	N	D	E	A	N		A	I	R	M	A	I	L	S
B	E	R	M	U	D	A	T	R	I	A	N	G	L	E
E	R	N	E		E	R	O	S	E		C	O	D	A
L	O	O	N		R	E	N	T	S		E	R	S	T

17

H	A	R	P	S		A	B	E	E		M	E	A	D
A	D	I	E	U		C	E	L	T		I	S	L	E
H	O	T	O	N	T	H	E	H	E	E	L	S	O	F
A	G	E	N	D	A		B	I	R	D	D	O	G	
			A	D	E			N	E	E				
H	E	R	H	E	A	R	T	W	A	S	W	A	R	M
A	R	O	O		R	O	I	L	S		C	I	A	
V	A	M	P	S		A	N	S		A	G	E	N	T
O	T	E		T	O	T	I	E		E	R	S	E	
C	O	O	L	A	S	A	C	U	C	U	M	B	E	R
		A	T	H			P	U	N					
	S	T	R	I	K	E	S		B	I	A	F	R	A
P	O	U	R	C	O	L	D	W	A	T	E	R	O	N
A	I	N	U		S	L	A	Y		E	R	E	C	T
S	L	A	P		H	A	K	E		S	O	D	A	S

18

E	A	R	T	H		A	N	T	I			C	A	R
A	R	O	O	M		L	E	A	N		A	R	E	A
S	T	A	R	S	E	A	R	C	H		L	A	R	D
T	E	N	T		S	M	O	K	E		A	S	I	A
				G	P	O			R	A	S	H	E	R
E	L	A	T	E			S	T	A	I	N			
S	A	B	E	N	A		O	U	T	D	O	E	S	
T	H	E	S	U	N	A	L	S	O	R	I	S	E	S
	R	E	T	I	T	L	E		R	E	S	T	E	D
			N	I	F	T	Y		W	E	E	P	S	
A	R	I	S	E	N		E	D	S					
M	I	R	E		O	P	I	N	E		B	R	A	S
P	L	E	A		M	O	O	N	S	T	R	U	C	K
L	E	N	T		I	S	L	E		B	E	L	I	E
E	Y	E		C	H	A	D		S	W	E	D	E	

19

```
M E L E E ■ F A C T ■ T A S K
A C A S E ■ A M O R ■ A R L O
T H I C K J U I C Y S T E A K
H O R A ■ U N D O ■ H A S T O
■ ■ P A D ■ ■ K I M ■ ■ ■ ■ ■
F R I E D O N I O N R I N G S
R A T E S ■ A S H O T ■ A H A
A N T S ■ B F L A T ■ G I A N
N C O ■ C A T E R ■ M E A N T
C H O C O L A T E S U N D A E
■ ■ A M I ■ ■ E G O ■ ■ ■ ■ ■
S H A R I ■ F I J I ■ V A N E
H I G H C H O L E S T E R O L
O R E O ■ E X I T ■ U S E R S
W E E P ■ N Y E T ■ B E A M E
```

20

```
P A T I E N T ■ H A I R D O ■
A D A G I O S ■ O R D A I N S
D E F E N S E A T T O R N E Y
S E T T E E ■ S T U ■ E G A N
■ ■ ■ ■ C O E U R ■ R O L E ■
G O I N T O L A B O R ■ ■ ■ ■
I N T E R N E ■ ■ A B A T E
M E A N I E S ■ A L T E R E D
P A L E O ■ ■ V E E R I N G
■ ■ ■ S H I P O F S T A T E
B U S T ■ I D O N T ■ ■ ■ ■
A N T I ■ T I O ■ T A I W A N
S C A L E S O F J U S T I C E
E A R D R U M ■ O R I E N T S
■ S T E E P S ■ E N T R E E S
```

21

```
A S P E N ■ D A L I ■ A M I D
T H E S E ■ E G A N ■ V I V A
T A S T E ■ M O T S ■ E L A N
■ G O O D N I G H T I R E N E
■ ■ ■ P L O ■ S E C ■ ■ ■ ■ ■
P A R ■ E L K E ■ P I E C E S
O R A L ■ A I L S ■ E R O D E
L O V E A N D M A R R I A G E
E M E N D ■ S E M I ■ S T E M
S A N D A L ■ R E S T ■ I R S
■ ■ ■ G A L ■ ■ E O N ■ ■ ■ ■
I L L B E S E E I N G Y O U
N E A R ■ T E R N ■ G L A R E
K A T E ■ E R I N ■ L O R D S
S K E W ■ D Y E S ■ E N S U E
```

22

```
A S H E S ■ A U R A ■ E R M A
S P A R E ■ E R I C ■ N O O N
P O I N T O F N O R E T U R N
S T R E A M ■ O S A G E S
■ ■ ■ E A R S ■ S P I E S ■
L A M B ■ R E C I T A L ■
A S I A ■ L E N I N ■ L I T
W E S T P O I N T C A D E T S
S A T ■ A R E T E ■ I N C A
■ ■ T R I D E N T ■ B O H R
■ S L A V E ■ D D A Y ■ ■
S T A L I N ■ R I F L E S
C O M E S T O T H E P O I N T
O R A N ■ A B I E ■ E R A T O
W E S T ■ L I E N ■ S T R O P
```

23

```
C O R M ■ I N C A ■ S C R A P
O L I O ■ M E L D ■ A H O M E
M E N U ■ P A I L ■ S I M O N
M I S S M A R M E L S T E I N
A C E T I C ■ B R A E ■ ■ ■
■ ■ ■ A T T U ■ T R E B L E
E V I C T ■ N A P E ■ T R O Y
W I S H Y O U W E R E H E R E
E L I E ■ L M N O ■ L O W E R
S E N S E D ■ N O E L ■ ■ ■
■ ■ ■ L I S P ■ S N O R E S
W H E N W E M E E T A G A I N
R O M E O ■ E T T E ■ I N D O
A M I N O ■ W A R N ■ S T E R
P O L E D ■ S L E D ■ T O R T
```

24

```
C A M P ■ S W A B ■ Q U A C K
O L E O ■ T I L L ■ U N C L E
W O R K I N G V A C A T I O N
L E V E R ■ G A I L ■ A D D S
■ ■ ■ R E A L ■ S A W N ■ ■
A S P S ■ N E V E R A G A I N
S T U ■ A I R Y ■ A L L U D E
C A P O N ■ S I C ■ S E D E R
A R A B I C ■ N O A H ■ R A F
P R E T T Y U G L Y ■ S A S S
■ ■ R A G S ■ L E F T ■ ■ ■
E S A U ■ N U D E ■ O R A T E
N O N D A I R Y C R E A M E R
D A T E D ■ E N T O ■ I M A N
S P I R E ■ R E S T ■ T O M E
```

25

```
D O R M ■ S E D E R ■ S A M P
A S T I ■ H A U T E ■ T R I O
T H E S P O R T O F K I N G S
E A S T E R L Y ■ A R R E S T
■ ■ ■ R A T S ■ A S I S ■ ■ ■
N A D I R S ■ P E T S ■ S T A
I D E A L ■ P A R E ■ O N E R
D A I L Y R A C I N G F O R M
E G G S ■ E P E E ■ A F O R E
S E N ■ S C A R ■ M I S T E D
■ ■ ■ A I R S ■ R I T E ■ ■ ■
S T A P L E ■ R E L E A S E S
W I N P L A C E A N D S H O W
A L T A ■ T R A D E ■ O O N A
P E E L ■ E I D E R ■ N O S Y
```

26

```
S I N S ■ H E R D ■ M A S T S
T M E N ■ E R I E ■ E X T R A
R A T E ■ W I L T ■ A L A I N
A R T L I N K L E T T E R ■
F E L L S ■ ■ S H Y ■ W I Z
E T E ■ R O T A T E ■ C A R E
■ ■ P A L E R ■ S C A R E D
■ F R E D C O U P L E S ■ ■
S T E A L S ■ O R I O N ■ ■
A I R Y ■ T A M E S T ■ C A M
L E O ■ Q E D ■ ■ H E A V E
■ C H A R L I E J O I N E R
I D I O T ■ I D L E ■ G A N G
M I T L A ■ B E A R ■ E D G E
P A Y E R ■ S A N K ■ R A E S
```

27

```
S E M I ■ G A L A S ■ A F A R
I R A Q ■ A L I C E ■ L U L U
F I R S T O F T H E M O N T H
T E E ■ A L I S ■ I N T E R
■ ■ F L E E ■ P I N E ■ ■
C A L L E R ■ S E A N ■ S F C
A L O E ■ C O N G O ■ P E R
M I D D L E O F N O W H E R E
E G G ■ A R R A Y ■ Y A M S
O N E ■ Y I P S ■ E S P R I T
■ ■ S O N S ■ L U C E ■ ■
W O O L F ■ T O G A ■ P I T
E N D O F T H E C E N T U R Y
S T O P ■ R O M A N ■ A M O R
T O R E ■ A P P L E ■ M A N E
```

28

```
H A V E ■ U S E S ■ S A G A
I M A G E ■ P O G O ■ A M O S
S I N G L E S B A R ■ T E R N
■ R E S A L E ■ D E R A N G E
■ ■ L I T ■ ■ E N D E R
U R S A ■ E S C A R P ■ ■
N I O B E ■ A R O U S E S
D O U B L E O R N O T H I N G
■ T R E M B L E ■ E E R I E
■ ■ O B E Y E D ■ D E P T
A A R O N ■ L O A ■ ■
G R U N T E D ■ A L L O U T
L U M S ■ T R I P L E P L A Y
O B O E ■ N O D S ■ C A N O E
W A R T ■ A P S E ■ L A S T
```

29

```
A L G A ■ I D E A ■ T A R P
S E E D ■ S E W U P ■ E L I A
C A R O L I N E K E N N E D Y
A G A ■ U S E ■ G O O S E S
P U L L S ■ B O L G E R ■ ■
■ E D I T H ■ R A Y S ■ L E E
■ F O R A ■ I N C ■ F E E L
L E O N A R D O D A V I N C I
E R R S ■ P A L ■ S I N N
X E D ■ A O N E ■ S L A Y S
■ E N M E S H ■ E L B O W
M T E T N A ■ E S L ■ R U E
R I C H A R D D R E Y F U S S
E T R E ■ X E R O X ■ I C E T
D O U R ■ B U S Y ■ T E D S
```

30

```
♥ I E R ■ G R A B ■ W A R M ♥
S T A Y ■ R E A R ■ A R E A L
H E R E ■ E C R U ■ S T A R E
A R A ■ S T E ■ C A P ■ L T S
P A C ■ T A N D E M S ■ T I S
E T H E R ■ T I L E ■ F O A L
D E E M E D ■ S E N ■ O R L Y
■ O P E N ♥ E D L Y ■ ■
B R A T ■ T O E ■ S I E G E S
R A R E ■ E T N A ■ A R E N A
O V A ■ D R E S S E R ■ N S C
K E N ■ E S P ■ P A S ■ O U R
E L T O N ■ A P E S ■ S E R E
N E X U S ■ D I C E ■ U S E D
♥ R A T E ■ S E T S ■ R E D ♥
```

31

```
B A H S   _   E N O S   _   T H Y
A L E E   _ A R E N A   _ W H E E
J O L L Y G R E E N G I A N T
A P P E A R S   _   _ O R R S   _
_   _ N R A   _ D I N E D   _
G R E E N I N J U D G M E N T
R E X   _ N E A R S   _ A S I A
E A C H   _ A S H   _ N E X T
A C H E   _ S T O A T   _ R I A
T H E G R E E N M O N S T E R
_ Q U I N N   _   L E T   _
_ F U M E   _   S E R I A L S
G R E E N B A C K D O L L A R
E A R N   _ M A R I O   _ L I S A
D T S   _ W H I T   _   S E T S
```

32

```
C H U M   _ A S S E T   _ A S S T
I O N A   _ G E E S E   _ B A T H
A R M S   _ E L A T E   _ A L E E
_ S E C O N D M A N A S S A S
S E R   _ A D O   _   _ S H A K E
C H I C K A M A U G A   _
R I T A S   _   _ T R A P   _ M V I
E D E N   _ A M E N D   _ G E O L
W E D   _ A C E S   _   _ S E L L S
_   _ C H A T T A N O O G A
A C T O R   _   _ A S U   _ D O S
F R E D E R I C K S B U R G   _
T I R E   _ A G R E E   _ P A R D
O M I T   _ P O E M S   _ O M A N
N E S S   _ T R E E S   _ N A D A
```

33

```
M A R I A   _ C A R A T   _ C A Y
A L O N G   _ O S A G E   _ A D O
T O M T E R R I F I C   _ T R U
C H A R   _ Y E S   _ T H E B A R
H A N O V E R   _ R A I L A G E
_   _   _ A S S   _ S T E A L   _
T I K I S   _ A V E   _ I L I E
O V I N E   _ L I P   _ A N O D E
W E T S   _ M A R   _ R E U S E
_   _ T O T E D   _ S A M   _
P A Y L O A D   _ A N S W E R S
O C H E R S   _ A W E   _ A L O E
P T A   _ P U S S Y W I L L O W
P O W   _ O R A T E   _ A L E N E
A R K   _ R E T A R   _ M A N E D
```

34

```
L I S P   _   _ P A T S   _ A B C S
O D O R S   _ A L O T   _ S L U E
B L U E C O L L A R   _ T U R N
_ E L M E R   _ D E A R E S T
_   _ I N I T   _ S N I P E   _
F I B S T E R   _ A S I D E   _
O G L E   _ N I P S   _ L E N D S
L O U   _ T O R S O   _   _ C O E
D R E G S   _ D O E R   _ S I R E
_ B R I B E   _ T A M A L E S
_ B O O Z E   _ S T A N   _
S I N C E R E   _ O R D E R   _
A N N E   _ B L U E R I B B O N
D E E R   _ E L S E   _ A A R O N
A T T Y   _ R E E L   _ R O M E
```

35

```
_   _ P A R S E   _ P E A R S   _
C R A N I U M   _ A E S O P S
R E R A T E S   _ C R E M A T E
A D E L E   _ R E O   _ A R A P
S O S O   _ P L E D   _ S I E N A
_   _ G A L E N   _ R A N   _
I M A   _ V A N E   _ E L E V E N
L A W   _ A N A G R A M   _ I W O
K I N D L E   _ A E R O   _ M E G
_ R O T   _ D A M N S   _
C H A I N   _ D E M S   _ C R O P
L O P E   _ S I S   _ P R A D O
U S E D C A R   _ S T R I P E D
_ T R U D G E   _ I S O M E R S
_ S P E A R   _ R E A P S   _
```

36

```
A W E D   _ I N C U R   _ G L E N
C A L I   _ G O O S E   _ L E V I
T H E S O U N D O F M U S I C
_ L E A D A   _   _ A I S L E
_   _ B I N D   _ A M I N   _
B E L L S A R E R I N G I N G
A D I E T   _ E A R L   _ M I R
S I N S   _ D A T E D   _ R E N I
I C E   _ I M U S   _ S E T O N
S T R I K E U P T H E B A N D
_   _ L I S P   _ S O R E   _
B R A I N   _   _ O I L E D
L A C A G E A U X F O L L E S
O V I D   _ G E N I I   _ E M M Y
W E D S   _ G R I S T   _ D O I N
```

37

```
C L O B B E R ■ S A L ■ F L O
D E S E R V E ■ C R A T I O N
S A L L I E D ■ I M P A S S E
■ P O L A R O P P O S I T E S
■ ■ ■ E N S ■ E I R E ■ ■ ■ ■
M A G S ■ ■ E G O ■ ■ M O N A
A P R ■ E A R L ■ M A D D O G
C H I L L Y R E C E P T I O N
H I P P I E ■ G A L E ■ U N E
O D E S ■ ■ M G M ■ A M E S ■
■ ■ ■ W H E E ■ I A N ■ ■ ■ ■
C O O L H E A D E D N E S S ■
O N G O I N G ■ R E D M E A T
K I R S T I E ■ L A R I A T S
E N E ■ E E R ■ E L E C T E E
```

38

```
A C T I ■ B L E D ■ T H R O W
L O R N ■ R O A D ■ H O O C H
F O O T L O O S E ■ W R O T E
A L P H O N S E ■ G A S T O N
■ ■ ■ E T T E ■ T O R E ■ ■ ■
G O P ■ T E N F O O T P O L E
C R A N E ■ A N D ■ L U I S
L O R E ■ M A T E S ■ A T N O
E N D S ■ A M S ■ ■ S Y R U P
F O O T I N M O U T H ■ E S S
■ ■ ■ L M N O ■ N E A T ■ ■ ■
T O B I A S ■ L E A D O F F S
A M O N G ■ P U S S Y F O O T
L A N G E ■ P A C E ■ F A R O
C R A S S ■ D U O S ■ S L A P
```

39

```
U S A F ■ C A S T ■ ■ A B B A
H A R I ■ R I P U P ■ P L O Y
F A T S D O M I N O ■ R A G E
■ R I C O ■ ■ K I T H ■ C I A
■ C H U B B Y C H E C K E R ■
■ T H E B A Y ■ S E R A ■ ■
C H O R T L E D ■ R E M O V E
O A K ■ ■ S O D ■ ■ R A T ■
D R E A M T ■ C A L A B A S H
■ ■ Y U R I ■ M A L O N E ■
S K I N N Y D I P P I N G ■
H E R ■ I S A R ■ B A E R ■
O N E S ■ T H E T H I N M A N
C Y S T ■ S O N A R ■ Z E R O
K A T E ■ S E N S ■ A N E W
```

40

```
A R O M A ■ F L E W ■ A P E D
M E S A S ■ I O N A ■ L I M E
P A S T P E R F O R M A N C E
S P A S ■ M E T S ■ A M E E R
■ ■ ■ S I D ■ S H O R E ■ ■
B A L L E T ■ I O T A ■ ■ ■
A L I E N ■ I N K E R ■ E M S
I S N O T A G U A R A N T E E
L O T ■ I V O R Y ■ N O R M A
■ ■ M O R E ■ M E T E O R ■
■ S I N E W ■ F O E ■ ■ ■
C A N O N ■ A L A D ■ L I E U
O F F U T U R E R E S U L T S
T E E N ■ S I A M ■ I R E N E
E R R S ■ O A R S ■ T E X A S
```

41

```
H A I F A ■ T H E E ■ O V A L
A S T E R ■ A I L S ■ P I L E
S H E E T M U S I C ■ A B B A
P E S T E R ■ ■ A S L E E P
■ ■ ■ T A D ■ L O S S E S
C A D R E ■ O R A L S ■ ■
O R I E L ■ R E M O ■ P E S O
B L A N K E T A P P R O V A L
S O L O ■ S A M E ■ A L I K E
■ ■ S T E E R ■ M O L E S
B O L E R O ■ D E N ■ ■ ■
I C E C A P ■ ■ C A U L K S
P A G O ■ P I L L O W T A L K
E L A L ■ E R I E ■ L A N A I
D A L E ■ L A D D ■ S H A N T
```

42

```
A R G O N ■ R O A M S ■ B V D
S O U S A ■ A F L A T ■ L E E
T W I S T O F F A T E ■ I N A
R E D ■ E L F ■ E A R N E D
O R E M ■ E L M S ■ M A D R E
■ ■ ■ A N G E R E D ■ D D A Y
■ A F R O ■ S R A S ■ A T E
L I T T L E M A N T A T E
F I R ■ A L T I ■ A L E S
R E S T ■ B E T T E R S ■
A N T I C ■ S H A Y ■ O B O E
M A R M O T ■ P E A ■ R A G
E T A ■ R O L L E R S K A T E
R E T ■ G A Y E R ■ H I K E S
S S E ■ I D E A S ■ E X E R T
```

43

```
MASH . SHAW . SHOES
OTTO . TAPE . AORTA
THEYLIVED . FAIRY
HOLLERED . MERGES
. SEEM . . TAR . .
. . MASKED . COAL
SPA . ASCOT . SABRA
TOGETHERHAPPILY
ARENA . NEEDI . SOS
REED . DEARER . .
. . WAS . . AWED
SNOWED . APPEASED
TALES . EVERAFTER
ATILT . RENE . TORE
BOOTS . ARTY . SPED
```

44

```
RAN . COMTE . ARMEE
AVA . OMAHA . NEARS
TIDEWATER . AVIAN
ADAMANT . LICENSE
. . CRIER . RINSES
NOSED . SEVENUP .
IMPELS . TON . ERAT
PER . YEARNED . IRE
SNIP . CSA . SINNER
. NEMESIS . SAGAN
BEGLAD . NEATH . .
LATIMES . CLOUDED
ARICA . WATERMAIN
SEDAN . APORT . IRA
EDENS . TORTS . LES
```

45

```
INCA . ARMED . SNCC
NERD . IHAVE . TORA
OMAR . REMIT . ITOR
NOBELPEACEPRIZE
. . AGO . TNT . CEE
COMMERCE . TAVERN
CHA . THERESA . .
CORE . ARI . SCLC
. . MARTINS . LEO
TABULA . EDUCTIVE
ORO . TIL . POI .
WESHALLOVERCOME
COTY . WADER . TAUT
ALOP . AMONG . ATTY
RENE . YARDS . CHEM
```

46

```
SWIPE . METS . AMEN
PALER . ATOP . NYRO
ARLEN . RATA . AFRO
MYSWEETLORD . AOK
. . ESPY . TAPIRS
COMETS . SCALER .
ORY . SOREL . INLAW
PALM . MYWAY . SAGE
SLEET . NEPAL . DEA
. FERBER . LAWYER
DOTTIE . PITA . .
ELF . MYTHREESONS
LEOS . OREO . RADIO
LAOS . NULL . ABIND
ANTS . DELE . LINES
```

47

```
. ACRE . MODEL . ELF
EARED . AROMA . VIE
GREENSTREET . EVE
GOTFAT . SNEERED
SNEE . ROB . DRAG .
. . RAIDERS . GRAB
PEG . OPERA . DEERE
SIREN . SAD . ERECT
IRENE . STILE . NSA
SEED . CAESARS .
. NASA . SHY . ARFS
WALTERS . EATERY
IRA . WINTERGREEN
TIN . ONION . HASTE
HAD . NAPES . APES
```

48

```
STS . VEEP . SCIPIO
LEA . IAGO . TABARD
OXYMORON . ETALII
BASIL . STERN . SSE
SNORED . NEAL . .
. . ONOMATOPOEIA
RAP . TRIER . STROP
ABET . ANTAS . SITE
JEERS . ANNAS . SAD
ALLITERATION .
. . GAME . SPEEDO
ACT . TOTEM . RATON
COOLIT . METAPHOR
ERMINE . MAIN . ANY
DEBUGS . ALPO . NEE
```

49

```
COP  CAPO  HOPES
ORAL ONEA  ORONO
MAKESHORTWORKOF
ENISLE CHIT  EST
RGS  ARN  DES
  TAKEASHORTCUT
BLAME  VIEW  ALSO
LINO  SADAS  GOER
AMIR  CHER  JESSE
HASASHORTFUSE
  LAI  YIN  TAO
IVS  CZAR  STRING
GETSHORTCHANGED
ORATE  GERE  AHME
RABAT  OSIS  TON
```

50

```
SCAPE  CASAS  SAT
ALLEY  UHHUH  TIE
WILKESBOOTH  USN
NOSALT  TWO  MALE
  NEAT  CLARET
TAJ  STEM  RECT
OMARS  REPAIRMAN
DICE  TRAIT  OISE
DEODORANT  INLET
  BARE  DORM  LAS
BEACON  NAPS
REST  CPA  MOCHAS
ART  PHILIPSOUSA
CIO  HELOT  TULIP
EER  ISLES  STANS
```

51

```
MEMO  SMACK  CRAB
AVID  TALON  HOME
JANEMARPLE  ALOE
ODD  ERIS  ARREST
RESERVE  EDEL
  LEE  LASSITER
JOEL  SCOT  TERSE
ULCER  HOE  SCENE
MICRO  ANNE  HEEL
POLYGAMY  AMA
  QUIP  GRENADE
ARGUER  ARTS  RED
CALE  MIKEHAMMER
TRUE  ARIEL  GORE
SEEN  NANNY  MRED
```

52

```
BORIC  ARC  LEAFS
AMINO  GEL  ALLOT
SANJOSECA  GOPRO
INSULT  REO  ALP
LIEN  RESETS  COP
SSS  FIXATE  JIVE
  LAPEL  SANER
  JOSECANSECO
TRACT  BUICK
RENO  BALLET  TOP
ADE  NOVELS  MONA
UTE  OWE  TRACER
MAYLE  NOWAYJOSE
APRIL  GAY  NOMEN
SEEPS  EKE  ERECT
```

53

```
REGO  FALL  COAT
ETON  ADUE  RAMBO
SHOE  DONTGIVEUP
TED  BELA  AGENTS
SLAVE  PTERO
  DOLPHIN  RUFUS
REVILE  COD  SORA
ELIDERS  SECURES
NICE  TAB  MORAYS
DEEDS  REGIMEN
  KOALA  ERATO
AFFAIR  LLBS  CAM
YOURDAYJOB  ITSA
ERNES  EARL  ROTH
SETS  TRES  AREA
```

54

```
ATIT  MELS  SPAIN
TONE  ARUT  PASTE
STEN  RICE  ERASE
EARTHSCIENCE
ALTHEA  DREI  MAA
  SAL  AARONS
ASH  DAILYPLANET
SMEE  RIO  GERE
WORLDRECORD  TAR
ATTLEE  IAN
NEZ  APED  CRESTS
  GLOBETHEATRE
WHALE  SLUE  TAIL
OILER  ETES  ELEE
OPENS  NAST  NESS
```

55

T	U	B	A		G	O	F	A	R			U	T	A	H
A	R	I	D		A	Z	U	R	E			R	O	B	E
P	A	L	M		M	O	R	N	I	N	G	D	E	W	
A	L	L	I		E	N	S		G	U	E	S	T	S	
		E	R	A	S	E		A	N	I	N				
I	N	T	A	C	T		S	T	I	T	C	H	E	D	
S	I	D	L	E		S	E	A	T		Y	O	R	E	
L	O	O		S	A	M	P	L	E	S		W	V	A	
A	B	U	T		N	A	T	E		L	E	D	I	N	
M	E	X	I	C	A	L	I		S	A	X	O	N	S	
		P	O	L	L		P	A	P	P	Y				
U	N	E	S	C	O		E	O	N		O	O	P	S	
P	O	S	T	A	G	E	D	U	E		S	U	E	T	
D	O	M	E		U	N	I	T	S		E	D	G	E	
O	N	E	R		E	G	E	S	T		D	O	O	M	

56

T	A	P	S		A	R	I	Z		S	A	L	A	D
A	V	E	C		B	O	C	A		A	M	A	T	I
B	A	T	H		B	L	I	P		C	A	N	O	E
	N	E	W	O	R	L	E	A	N	S	J	A	Z	Z
	T	R	A	Y		A	R	T	E					
A	G	E		L	O	W		A	L	B		E	S	P
M	A	D	D		I	A	N		S	V	E	L	T	E
B	R	O	O	K	L	Y	N	D	O	D	G	E	R	S
E	D	U	C	E	D		W	Y	N		O	M	O	O
R	E	T		A	R	P		S	S	R		E	N	S
			U	R	A	L		K	O	N	G			
B	A	L	T	I	M	O	R	E	C	O	L	T	S	
E	Q	U	I	P		F	O	X	Y		M	A	U	L
M	U	T	T	S		I	S	I	S		E	R	I	E
Y	A	Z	O	O		T	E	A	T		C	Y	T	O

57

B	I	T	E	S		B	R	O	W		R	A	P	S
A	R	I	E	L		L	A	N	E		E	D	A	M
J	O	L	L	Y	R	O	G	E	R		C	U	R	E
A	N	T	S		O	B	E	S	E		E	L	S	A
			L	O	S		W	A	S	T	E	R		
J	E	T	S	A	M		S	T	O	P	S			
U	N	I	O	N		S	H	I	L	L		S	P	A
J	O	L	L	Y	G	O	O	D	F	E	L	L	O	W
U	S	E		A	L	O	N	E		N	O	I	S	E
		P	R	A	T	E		S	T	A	T	E	D	
S	T	E	E	D	S		T	O	Y					
A	B	M	S		S	N	A	I	L		A	C	T	S
L	O	O	T		F	E	L	L	O	W	S	H	I	P
A	N	T	E		U	R	A	L		A	T	O	N	E
D	E	E	R		L	O	S	S		G	A	P	E	D

58

B	A	B	E	S		A	B	E	A	M		M	R	S
I	L	O	N	A		B	E	R	R	A		I	I	I
B	E	S	O	M		B	E	A	L	L		G	A	G
S	C	H	U	B	E	R	T	S	E	I	G	H	T	H
			G	A	Y		H	E	N		E	T	A	T
S	I	G	H		E	C	O		E	I	N			
O	N	O		S	O	L	V	E		N	I	C	E	R
P	R	O	K	O	F	I	E	V	S	F	I	R	S	T
H	E	N	N	A		O	N	E	T	O		A	T	E
		O	K	S		S	R	I		A	M	E	S	
B	L	O	W		E	L	S		R	O	T			
B	E	R	N	S	T	E	I	N	S	T	H	I	R	D
G	O	B		A	T	A	X	Y		T	E	N	O	R
U	N	I		G	E	S	T	E		E	N	A	T	E
N	E	T		S	E	T	H	S		R	A	T	E	D

59

O	S	A	K	A		S	O	A	K		S	T	A	Y
T	R	I	A	D		T	A	T	A		C	A	V	E
T	A	R	Z	A	N	O	F	T	H	E	A	P	E	S
		O	M	A	R		O	N	E	R				
O	H	I	O		S	E	A	R		R	E	E	V	E
R	A	N		H	Y	M	N	S		C	Z	A	R	
G	U	S	T	O		N	E	O	P	R	E	N	E	
	L	O	R	D	G	R	E	Y	S	T	O	K	E	
M	A	L	A	D	I	E	S		S	W	I	S	H	
A	G	E	D		S	C	I	O	N		E	S	E	
R	E	S	E	T		R	A	B	E		C	L	A	Y
			M	O	U	E		E	M	M	A			
M	E	T	A	R	Z	A	N	Y	O	U	J	A	N	E
A	V	E	R		I	N	R	E		L	U	N	A	R
P	E	E	K		S	T	A	R		E	N	T	E	R

60

H	A	G	S		K	A	F	K	A		B	O	S	S
A	L	O	E		O	B	O	E	S		O	K	L	A
I	T	O	R		D	U	R	A	N	D	U	R	A	N
R	E	D	M	E	A	T		T	E	E	N	A	G	E
			Y	O	R	K		N	O	R	A	D		
M	A	G	N	A		T	O	N		L	E	W	I	S
U	N	O	S		G	U	T		B	E	R	A	T	E
M	N	O		M	A	T	A	D	O	R		L	E	N
P	A	D	R	E	S		B	E	G		A	L	M	S
S	L	Y	E	R		R	L	S		E	R	A	S	E
			A	G	R	E	E		F	L	A	W		
A	P	O	G	E	E	S		G	U	M	B	A	L	L
S	U	G	A	R	S	U	G	A	R		I	L	I	E
T	M	E	N		E	M	E	E	R		A	L	D	A
A	P	E	S		T	E	L	L	Y		N	A	S	H

61

W	A	R	M		F	O	R	M	A		O	D	D	S
A	L	O	E		O	N	E	A	L		R	I	O	T
S	T	A	T	U	E	O	F	L	I	B	E	R	T	Y
H	O	N	O	R				C	L	O	T	H	E	
			O	G	R	E		C	I	A				
E	S	C		E	M	M	A	L	A	Z	A	R	U	S
S	H	A	M		S	O	M	E		E	R	A	S	E
S	I	R	E	N		T	E	A		D	O	Z	E	R
E	N	E	R	O		I	N	N	S		N	E	R	F
N	E	W	C	O	L	O	S	S	U	S		S	S	S
			D	E	N		E	M	I	T				
O	T	O	O	L	E				Z	O	W	I	E	
G	R	O	V	E	R	C	L	E	V	E	L	A	N	D
L	A	Z	E		E	P	O	X	Y		L	A	K	E
E	Y	E	R		D	A	N	T	E		S	C	A	N

62

A	H	A	B		M	A	S	T	S		C	A	M	S
L	E	E	R		A	S	C	A	P		A	L	O	E
L	A	R	A	S	T	H	E	M	E		M	I	D	I
S	T	O	V	E		N	E	E		E	B	O	N	
	S	O	P	H	I	E	S	C	H	O	I	C	E	
R	A	P		T	E	N		T	H	Y				
E	S	A	U		A	R	T		D	A	T	E	S	
V	I	C	T	O	R	I	A	S	S	E	C	R	E	T
S	N	E	E	R		P	U	N		T	I	L	E	
			S	L	A		P	A	W		A	S	P	
H	U	M	B	O	L	D	T	S	G	I	F	T		
A	S	E	A		A	D	O		L	A	H	R	S	
Y	A	M	S		M	U	R	P	H	Y	S	L	A	W
E	G	O	S		A	C	R	E	S		T	O	N	I
D	E	S	I		S	E	E	I	T		S	N	I	T

63

F	I	R	S	T		A	L	G	A		B	L	I	P
A	C	T	O	R		L	O	O	N		R	I	T	A
T	H	E	M	E		S	A	L	T		A	L	A	S
		B	A	D	O	F	F	I	C	I	A	L	S	
S	C	A	R	C	E				U	N	C	L	E	
A	R	E	E	L	E	C	T	E	D	B	Y			
B	A	R	R	Y		H	O	N	E	S		N	I	P
E	Z	I	O		M	A	N	L	Y		N	A	N	A
R	Y	E		D	O	R	I	A		M	E	D	A	L
		G	O	O	D	C	I	T	I	Z	E	N	S	
S	C	R	O	D					O	S	P	R	E	Y
W	H	O	D	O	N	O	T	V	O	T	E			
A	I	D	S		A	L	O	E		O	R	T	H	O
I	D	E	O		S	I	D	E		O	C	E	A	N
N	E	O	N		H	O	O	P		K	E	N	Y	A

64

I	C	A	L	L		L	O	S	T	A	S	T	E	P
M	E	D	E	A		A	T	L	I	B	E	R	T	Y
P	R	O	G	N	O	S	T	I	C	A	T	I	O	N
A	I	L		A	L	S	O	P		S	T	O	N	E
I	S	P	Y		D	O	M		B	E	E			
R	E	H	A	B		S	A	F	E		R	A	Z	Z
			R	I	B		N	O	R	M		P	O	E
C	L	I	N	T	O	N		E	L	E	C	T	E	D
A	U	R		S	A	R	A		E	R	R			
T	I	A	S		S	A	S	H		V	A	L	O	R
			A	I	T		P	A	S		B	A	R	A
A	W	A	R	D		E	E	R	I	E		M	A	P
M	I	S	T	E	R	P	R	E	S	I	D	E	N	T
O	S	T	R	A	C	I	S	M		R	I	N	G	O
S	H	O	E	L	A	C	E	S		E	N	T	E	R

65

S	C	O	W		I	L	S	A		C	H	I	T	S
A	R	L	O		L	O	A	D		R	I	C	H	E
W	E	E	W	I	L	L	I	E	W	I	N	K	I	E
N	E	G		G	I	L	D		A	T	T	E	N	D
			W	A	N	E		A	R	I		S	K	Y
V	E	N	I	V	I	D	I	V	I	C	I			
E	X	I	L	E			D	O	N		N	Y	E	T
T	A	L	L		T	H	I	N	G		F	O	T	O
S	M	E	E		O	O	O		M	A	G	O	O	
		M	A	K	E	M	I	N	E	M	I	N	K	
W	E	D		L	I	S		G	O	R	Y			
A	N	I	M	A	L		I	N	R	E		B	U	S
L	O	V	E	S	L	A	B	O	R	S	L	O	S	T
S	L	E	E	K		P	E	R	I		I	D	E	A
H	A	S	T	A		E	X	E	S		D	E	R	N

66

A	V	E	R		B	R	E	D			A	D	A	M
C	O	R	E		L	I	E	U		S	C	O	N	E
T	W	I	C	E	T	O	L	D		E	Q	U	A	L
A	S	C	O	T				S	C	R	U	B		
			R	A	T	I	O		A	V	I	L	A	
	O	D	D	L	O	T	S		B	I	R	E	M	E
D	A	I	S		R	A	T	S		L	E	T	O	N
E	X	T		V	I	L	L	A	G	E		A	L	Y
P	A	T	T	I		Y	E	L	L		F	L	E	A
S	C	O	R	N	S		R	E	E	B	O	K	S	
		A	M	A	T	I		S	M	E	A	R		
	A	N	N	E	S				J	A	U	N	T	
F	O	R	C	E		T	W	O	B	A	G	G	E	R
I	N	K	E	R		U	R	D	U		E	L	L	E
B	O	S	S		B	Y	E	S			S	I	L	K

67

P	A	P	A	■	L	E	A	S	H	■	I	S	N	T
I	L	L	S	■	A	L	B	E	E	■	S	T	I	R
C	L	A	S	S	C	L	O	W	N	■	L	U	N	A
T	E	N	E	T	■	A	M	E	N	■	A	D	A	M
S	N	O	R	E	D	■	B	R	A	W	N	Y	■	■
■	■	■	T	R	O	T	■	■	A	D	H	O	C	■
L	A	D	S	■	N	O	S	H	E	R	■	A	D	O
I	C	E	■	A	N	A	T	O	M	Y	■	L	I	T
A	L	A	■	N	A	T	U	R	E	■	K	L	E	E
R	U	N	O	N	■	■	A	N	D	A	■	■	■	■
■	■	S	C	A	R	F	S	■	D	E	R	A	I	L
L	O	L	A	■	I	O	U	S	■	L	A	S	S	O
A	V	I	S	■	G	Y	M	T	E	A	C	H	E	R
L	E	S	E	■	O	L	M	O	S	■	H	E	R	R
A	R	T	Y	■	R	E	A	P	S	■	I	S	E	E

68

A	B	E	T	■	T	A	M	P	A	■	O	L	L	A
L	A	V	A	■	E	M	I	L	Y	■	N	E	A	R
T	R	I	X	■	N	O	L	A	N	■	B	A	T	E
O	N	L	I	B	E	R	T	Y	■	O	R	R	I	N
■	■	■	■	E	T	A	■	M	A	D	O	N	N	A
S	P	O	O	N	■	■	L	U	A	N	D	A	■	■
H	O	R	N	E	T	■	S	T	A	■	D	R	A	B
A	L	L	Y	■	E	T	H	E	R	■	W	I	L	E
Y	O	Y	O	■	M	A	E	■	M	E	A	N	I	E
■	■	■	U	M	P	I	R	E	■	T	Y	K	E	S
Q	U	A	R	R	E	L	■	S	T	U	■	■	■	■
U	N	I	T	S	■	O	N	T	H	I	N	I	C	E
I	T	S	O	■	B	R	A	H	E	■	O	N	L	Y
T	I	L	E	■	R	E	N	E	S	■	S	T	A	R
O	L	E	S	■	A	D	O	R	E	■	H	O	P	E

69

H	A	S	H	■	B	L	O	T	■	S	H	R	E	W
A	G	H	A	■	L	O	A	N	■	T	O	O	T	H
P	R	I	N	C	E	O	F	T	H	E	C	I	T	Y
P	E	R	S	I	A	N	S	■	A	N	K	L	E	S
Y	E	T	■	C	R	Y	■	T	W	O	S	■	■	■
■	■	■	P	A	Y	■	B	E	A	S	■	C	A	B
S	T	E	E	D	■	A	L	A	I	■	S	O	S	O
A	S	T	R	A	N	G	E	R	I	N	T	O	W	N
L	A	N	K	■	E	E	N	Y	■	O	A	K	E	N
E	R	A	■	S	E	N	D	■	B	R	R	■	■	■
■	■	■	S	O	D	A	■	R	A	M	■	L	A	S
P	O	S	T	A	L	■	C	I	A	A	G	E	N	T
I	T	T	A	K	E	S	A	V	I	L	L	A	G	E
S	T	O	L	E	■	O	P	E	N	■	I	S	L	E
H	O	P	E	D	■	B	E	R	G	■	B	E	E	P

70

■	S	E	M	■	D	I	S	C	■	E	A	R	N	S
G	E	R	E	■	I	S	L	E	■	U	B	O	A	T
A	U	R	A	■	M	E	A	D	■	G	E	T	T	Y
F	R	A	N	K	I	E	V	A	L	E	T	■	■	■
F	A	N	T	A	N	■	■	R	A	N	■	U	G	H
E	T	D	■	P	I	C	T	■	D	E	B	B	I	E
■	■	■	P	U	S	H	E	S	■	R	E	L	Y	■
■	M	A	R	T	H	A	S	T	E	W	A	R	D	■
S	A	L	E	■	S	T	A	T	I	C	■	■	■	■
P	I	M	P	L	E	■	A	B	C	S	■	S	R	I
A	D	A	■	I	L	E	■	H	E	S	T	E	R	■
■	A	L	I	S	T	A	I	R	C	O	O	K	■	■
U	H	U	R	A	■	S	I	N	N	■	R	O	P	E
M	U	S	I	C	■	A	G	O	G	■	A	G	E	D
A	R	E	A	S	■	Y	E	N	S	■	P	E	N	■

71

T	O	R	E	■	A	R	B	O	R	■	S	A	N	S
A	P	E	S	■	D	I	A	N	A	■	C	L	A	P
B	E	S	T	W	I	S	H	E	S	■	A	L	M	A
O	R	E	■	O	D	E	S	■	C	A	L	M	E	R
O	A	T	B	R	A	N	■	C	A	G	E	Y	■	■
■	■	■	E	M	S	■	C	O	L	E	S	L	A	W
C	A	S	A	S	■	G	A	Y	L	E	■	O	L	E
A	R	I	D	■	C	O	N	E	Y	■	I	V	A	N
P	E	N	■	G	A	T	O	R	■	B	R	E	S	T
P	A	C	K	I	T	I	N	■	P	E	A	■	■	■
■	■	■	E	I	G	H	T	■	H	U	G	S	A	N	D
P	E	R	S	I	A	■	S	A	R	A	■	Z	O	O
A	L	E	S	■	Y	O	U	R	S	T	R	U	L	Y
R	I	L	E	■	A	D	I	E	U	■	O	R	A	L
K	E	Y	S	■	N	O	T	M	E	■	B	E	N	E

72

A	D	E	P	T	■	S	T	O	A	S	■	A	L	B
R	O	M	E	O	■	H	E	A	R	T	■	Z	O	O
C	L	I	N	T	W	A	L	K	E	R	■	T	U	X
H	E	R	N	I	A	■	L	E	N	A	■	E	S	E
■	■	■	I	N	D	I	A	N	A	P	A	C	E	R
S	T	E	■	G	E	M	■	S	P	A	■	■	■	■
H	U	E	S	■	D	A	N	A	■	E	R	R	O	L
I	N	L	A	W	■	G	A	L	■	D	O	O	N	E
P	A	S	H	A	■	E	G	O	S	■	N	O	T	E
■	■	■	I	T	S	■	■	F	I	R	■	F	O	R
G	L	O	B	E	T	R	O	T	T	E	R	■	■	■
L	A	X	■	R	E	E	L	■	A	T	E	A	S	E
A	M	I	■	B	L	A	D	E	R	U	N	N	E	R
Z	E	D	■	E	L	C	I	D	■	R	E	T	R	O
E	R	E	■	D	A	T	E	S	■	N	E	S	T	S

73

A	N	O	N		S	A	L	T			S	W	I	S	S
L	E	N	O		W	E	A	R			P	A	S	T	A
T	H	E	G	O	O	D	H	U	M	O	R	M	A	N	
O	R	O			D	O	E	R			A	I	D	E	R	S
S	U	N	L	E	S	S			P	Y	L	E			
			A	S	H			G	L	A	S	N	O	S	T
I	T	E	M	S			I	R	O	N			L	I	E
T	H	E	B	A	D	N	E	W	S	B	E	A	R	S	
C	O	L			R	A	G	S			A	B	Y	S	S
H	U	S	T	L	I	N	G			B	I	B			
			H	A	V	E			A	L	L	S	T	A	R
A	S	H	O	R	E			F	R	E	E			A	B	E
T	H	E	U	G	L	Y	A	M	E	R	I	C	A	N	
N	O	R	G	E			A	C	E	D			T	E	T	E
O	P	A	H	S			W	E	D	S			S	T	E	W

74

O	L	A	N	D		Q	E	D			B	A	J	E	R
B	O	R	E	R		U	S	A			E	N	E	M	Y
J	U	M	B	O	J	E	T	S			A	D	A	T	E
				G	A	E	A			S	T	E	N		
S	O	J	O	U	R	N			V	I	S	A	V	I	S
A	C	U	T	E	S			M	A	R	I	N	A	D	E
S	E	M	I	S			C	A	P	E	T			L	E	A
S	A	P	S			J	A	S	O	N			A	J	A	B
I	N	I			S	E	N	O	R			C	R	E	T	E
E	I	N	S	T	E	I	N			T	O	G	A	E	D
R	A	G	T	O	P	S			S	E	C	O	N	D	S
			J	U	G	S			P	E	N	H			
A	B	A	C	I			J	O	L	T	I	N	J	O	E
B	O	C	C	E			R	P	M			S	H	E	I	K
M	A	K	O	S			S	E	A			E	L	U	D	E

75

I	M	A	N		A	B	L	E			A	L	L	A	H
R	E	N	O		P	A	I	X			L	O	I	R	E
A	N	T	S		I	L	S	A			L	U	M	P	Y
Q	U	I	E	T	A	S	A	M	O	U	S	E		
			E	R	A			P	R	Y					
P	A	S	T	R	Y			R	A	T	E			N	O	W
A	F	T	E	R			M	A	G	I			T	O	P	O
C	O	O	L	A	S	A	C	U	C	U	M	B	E	R	
T	O	R	E			C	R	E	E			T	E	L	L	S
S	T	Y			C	H	E	R			F	I	N	E	S	T
			S	A	M			M	A	C					
		S	T	R	O	N	G	A	S	A	R	O	C	K	
A	L	L	O	T			A	U	N	T			O	P	I	E
S	E	I	N	E			S	A	S	E			M	A	A	M
P	I	P	E	R			A	M	E	R			P	L	O	P

76

A	F	R	O		S	T	A	R	R		A	B	B	A
S	L	E	D		L	E	V	E	E		L	A	I	R
H	E	A	D	T	O	H	E	A	D		M	C	L	I
E	E	L		A	P	E	R		E	V	O	K	E	D
			E	P	E	E		B	E	A	S	T		
A	L	F	R	E	D		S	E	M	I	T	O	N	E
M	E	A	N	S		H	O	V	E	L		B	I	N
I	N	C	A		S	A	N	E	R		T	A	C	T
S	T	E		R	I	V	A	L		C	A	C	H	E
H	O	T	C	I	D	E	R		H	A	N	K	E	R
		O	A	T	E	S		B	A	R	K			
R	I	F	L	E	S		G	A	L	L		T	A	E
S	L	A	M		H	A	N	D	T	O	H	A	N	D
V	I	C	E		O	S	A	G	E		O	B	O	E
P	E	E	R		W	A	T	E	R		G	U	N	N

77

L	E	A	P		A	T	T	I	C			B	A	B	A
I	T	E	R		C	H	I	N	O			E	M	I	R
A	C	R	E		H	E	L	L	O			A	I	R	E
R	H	O	D	E	I	S	L	A	N	D	R	E	D	S	
			A	L	E	E			S	O	U				
H	A	T	T	E	R			B	I	K	E	P	A	T	H
A	P	R	O	N			S	E	M	I			L	O	Y
F	L	O	R	I	D	A	S	U	N	S	H	I	N	E	
T	E	L			I	S	T	S			C	O	N	A	N
S	A	L	T	I	N	E	S			P	A	M	E	L	A
			U	N	O			R	O	L	E				
T	E	N	N	E	S	S	E	E	W	A	L	K	E	R	
R	Y	A	N			A	I	S	L	E			A	N	T	I
A	R	N	E			U	P	P	E	R			N	E	A	P
M	E	A	L			R	E	S	T	S			D	E	L	E

78

B	E	T	A		H	A	C	K			C	A	C	T	I
A	M	A	S		O	B	I	E			O	C	H	E	R
R	E	B	A		L	O	S	E			S	T	O	R	E
C	R	O	P	C	I	R	C	L	E	S			P	I	S
A	G	O			A	S	T	O			L	A	M	S	
R	E	S	O	R	T			A	L	C	O	H	O	L	
			N	A	I	L	E	D			K	R	O	N	E
P	A	C	T			C	U	T	I	N			A	P	E	D
E	L	L	A	S			V	E	N	O	M	S			
S	L	I	P	U	P	S			B	A	S	T	E	R	
			P	E	P	E			S	P	O	T			R	A	E
E	N	C			P	R	U	N	E	D	A	N	I	S	H
V	A	L	S	E			L	A	N	I			E	S	T	E
I	N	O	U	R			N	I	N	E			S	H	E	A
L	O	P	E	S			A	L	E	S			T	A	R	T

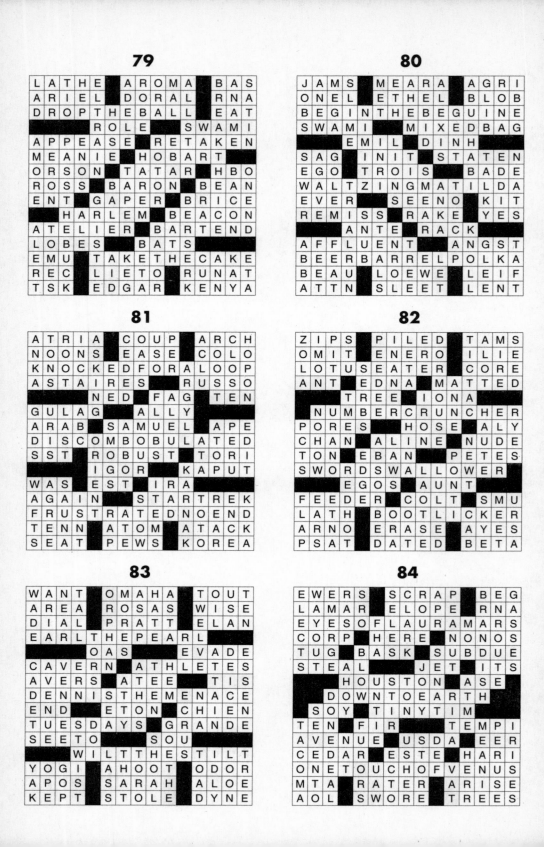

79

L	A	T	H	E	■	A	R	O	M	A	■	B	A	S
A	R	I	E	L	■	D	O	R	A	L	■	R	N	A
D	R	O	P	T	H	E	B	A	L	L	■	E	A	T
■	■	R	O	L	E	■	■	■	S	W	A	M	I	■
A	P	P	E	A	S	E	■	R	E	T	A	K	E	N
M	E	A	N	I	E	■	H	O	B	A	R	T	■	■
O	R	S	O	N	■	T	A	T	A	R	■	H	B	O
R	O	S	S	■	B	A	R	O	N	■	B	E	A	N
E	N	T	■	G	A	P	E	R	■	B	R	I	C	E
■	H	A	R	L	E	M	■	B	E	A	C	O	N	■
A	T	E	L	I	E	R	■	B	A	R	T	E	N	D
L	O	B	E	S	■	■	B	A	T	S	■	■	■	■
E	M	U	■	T	A	K	E	T	H	E	C	A	K	E
R	E	C	■	L	I	E	T	O	■	R	U	N	A	T
T	S	K	■	E	D	G	A	R	■	K	E	N	Y	A

80

J	A	M	S	■	M	E	A	R	A	■	A	G	R	I
O	N	E	L	■	E	T	H	E	L	■	B	L	O	B
B	E	G	I	N	T	H	E	B	E	G	U	I	N	E
S	W	A	M	I	■	■	M	I	X	E	D	B	A	G
■	■	E	M	I	L	■	D	I	N	H	■	■	■	■
S	A	G	■	I	N	I	T	■	S	T	A	T	E	N
E	G	O	■	T	R	O	I	S	■	B	A	D	E	■
W	A	L	T	Z	I	N	G	M	A	T	I	L	D	A
E	V	E	R	■	S	E	E	N	O	■	K	I	T	■
R	E	M	I	S	S	■	R	A	K	E	■	Y	E	S
■	■	A	N	T	E	■	R	A	C	K	■	■	■	■
A	F	F	L	U	E	N	T	■	A	N	G	S	T	■
B	E	E	R	B	A	R	R	E	L	P	O	L	K	A
B	E	A	U	■	L	O	E	W	E	■	L	E	I	F
A	T	T	N	■	S	L	E	E	T	■	L	E	N	T

81

A	T	R	I	A	■	C	O	U	P	■	A	R	C	H
N	O	O	N	S	■	E	A	S	E	■	C	O	L	O
K	N	O	C	K	E	D	F	O	R	A	L	O	O	P
A	S	T	A	I	R	E	S	■	R	U	S	S	O	■
■	■	■	N	E	D	■	F	A	G	■	T	E	N	■
G	U	L	A	G	■	A	L	L	Y	■	■	■	■	■
A	R	A	B	■	S	A	M	U	E	L	■	A	P	E
D	I	S	C	O	M	B	O	B	U	L	A	T	E	D
S	S	T	■	R	O	B	U	S	T	■	T	O	R	I
■	■	I	G	O	R	■	K	A	P	U	T	■	■	■
W	A	S	■	E	S	T	■	I	R	A	■	■	■	■
A	G	A	I	N	■	S	T	A	R	T	R	E	K	■
F	R	U	S	T	R	A	T	E	D	N	O	E	N	D
T	E	N	N	■	A	T	O	M	■	A	T	A	C	K
S	E	A	T	■	P	E	W	S	■	K	O	R	E	A

82

Z	I	P	S	■	P	I	L	E	D	■	T	A	M	S
O	M	I	T	■	E	N	E	R	O	■	I	L	I	E
L	O	T	U	S	E	A	T	E	R	■	C	O	R	E
A	N	T	■	E	D	N	A	■	M	A	T	T	E	D
■	■	T	R	E	E	■	I	O	N	A	■	■	■	■
■	N	U	M	B	E	R	C	R	U	N	C	H	E	R
P	O	R	E	S	■	H	O	S	E	■	A	L	Y	■
C	H	A	N	■	A	L	I	N	E	■	N	U	D	E
T	O	N	■	E	B	A	N	■	P	E	T	E	S	■
S	W	O	R	D	S	W	A	L	L	O	W	E	R	■
■	■	E	G	O	S	■	A	U	N	T	■	■	■	■
F	E	E	D	E	R	■	C	O	L	T	■	S	M	U
L	A	T	H	■	B	O	O	T	L	I	C	K	E	R
A	R	N	O	■	E	R	A	S	E	■	A	Y	E	S
P	S	A	T	■	D	A	T	E	D	■	B	E	T	A

83

W	A	N	T	■	O	M	A	H	A	■	T	O	U	T
A	R	E	A	■	R	O	S	A	S	■	W	I	S	E
D	I	A	L	■	P	R	A	T	T	■	E	L	A	N
E	A	R	L	T	H	E	P	E	A	R	L	■	■	■
■	■	O	A	S	■	■	E	V	A	D	E	■	■	■
C	A	V	E	R	N	■	A	T	H	L	E	T	E	S
A	V	E	R	S	■	A	T	E	E	■	T	I	S	■
D	E	N	N	I	S	T	H	E	M	E	N	A	C	E
E	N	D	■	E	T	O	N	■	C	H	I	E	N	■
T	U	E	S	D	A	Y	S	■	G	R	A	N	D	E
S	E	E	T	O	■	■	S	O	U	■	■	■	■	■
■	■	W	I	L	T	T	H	E	S	T	I	L	T	■
Y	O	G	I	■	A	H	O	O	T	■	O	D	O	R
A	P	O	S	■	S	A	R	A	H	■	A	L	O	E
K	E	P	T	■	S	T	O	L	E	■	D	Y	N	E

84

E	W	E	R	S	■	S	C	R	A	P	■	B	E	G
L	A	M	A	R	■	E	L	O	P	E	■	R	N	A
E	Y	E	S	O	F	L	A	U	R	A	M	A	R	S
C	O	R	P	■	H	E	R	E	■	N	O	N	O	S
T	U	G	■	B	A	S	K	■	S	U	B	D	U	E
S	T	E	A	L	■	■	J	E	T	■	I	T	S	■
■	■	H	O	U	S	T	O	N	■	A	S	E	■	■
■	D	O	W	N	T	O	E	A	R	T	H	■	■	■
S	O	Y	■	T	I	N	Y	T	I	M	■	■	■	■
T	E	N	■	F	I	R	■	■	T	E	M	P	I	■
A	V	E	N	U	E	■	U	S	D	A	■	E	E	R
C	E	D	A	R	■	E	S	T	E	■	H	A	R	I
O	N	E	T	O	U	C	H	O	F	V	E	N	U	S
M	T	A	■	R	A	T	E	R	■	A	R	I	S	E
A	O	L	■	S	W	O	R	E	■	T	R	E	E	S

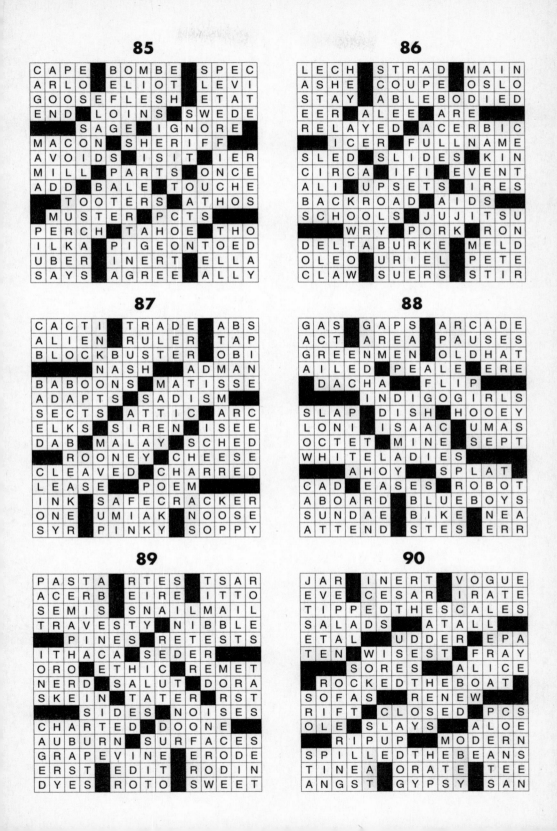

85

C	A	P	E		B	O	M	B	E	
A	R	L	O		E	L	I	O	T	
G	O	O	S	E	F	L	E	S	H	
E	N	D		L	O	I	N	S		

CAPE BOMBE SPEC
ARLO ELIOT LEVI
GOOSEFLESH ETAT
END LOINS SWEDE
SAGE IGNORE
MACON SHERIFF
AVOIDS ISIT IER
MILL PARTS ONCE
ADD BALE TOUCHE
TOOTERS ATHOS
MUSTER PCTS
PERCH TAHOE THO
ILKA PIGEONTOED
UBER INERT ELLA
SAYS AGREE ALLY

86

LECH STRAD MAIN
ASHE COUPE OSLO
STAY ABLEBODIED
EER ALEE ARE
RELAYED ACERBIC
ICER FULLNAME
SLED SLIDES KIN
CIRCA IFI EVENT
ALI UPSETS IRES
BACKROAD AIDS
SCHOOLS JUJITSU
WRY PORK RON
DELTABURKE MELD
OLEO URIEL PETE
CLAW SUERS STIR

87

CACTI TRADE ABS
ALIEN RULER TAP
BLOCKBUSTER OBI
NASH ADMAN
BABOONS MATISSE
ADAPTS SADISM
SECTS ATTIC ARC
ELKS SIREN ISEE
DAB MALAY SCHED
ROONEY CHEESE
CLEAVED CHARRED
LEASE POEM
INK SAFECRACKER
ONE UMIAK NOOSE
SYR PINKY SOPPY

88

GAS GAPS ARCADE
ACT AREA PAUSES
GREENMEN OLDHAT
AILED PEALE ERE
DACHA FLIP
INDIGOGIRLS
SLAP DISH HOOEY
LONI ISAAC UMAS
OCTET MINE SEPT
WHITELADIES
AHOY SPLAT
CAD EASES ROBOT
ABOARD BLUEBOYS
SUNDAE BIKE NEA
ATTEND STES ERR

89

PASTA RTES TSAR
ACERB EIRE ITTO
SEMIS SNAILMAIL
TRAVESTY NIBBLE
PINES RETESTS
ITHACA SEDER
ORO ETHIC REMET
NERD SALUT DORA
SKEIN TATER RST
SIDES NOISES
CHARTED DOONE
AUBURN SURFACES
GRAPEVINE ERODE
ERST EDIT RODIN
DYES ROTO SWEET

90

JAR INERT VOGUE
EVE CESAR IRATE
TIPPEDTHESCALES
SALADS ATALL
ETAL UDDER EPA
TEN WISEST FRAY
SORES ALICE
ROCKEDTHEBOAT
SOFAS RENEW
RIFT CLOSED PCS
OLE SLAYS ALOE
RIPUP MODERN
SPILLEDTHEBEANS
TINEA ORATE TEE
ANGST GYPSY SAN

91

```
F A C T   P A R A   S P A R K
A L O E   E V E R   H E M A N
I A N S   D O D O   A Z U R E
L I T T L E W O M E N   S E E
    R Y E S   A R G U E R S
J A I   S T E P   A H S
A L V A   A L A S   A I S L E
W E E W I L L I E W I N K I E
S E D A N   A R C H   G I R L
    I V E   S T O W   N A Y
T E X T I L E   D E A F
I M A   T I N Y B U B B L E S
P I X I E   R U I N   B I D E
S L I C E   O M N I   I N I T
Y E S E S   L A S T   E T T A
```

92

```
J A G S   B A S I S   C E D E
O G R E   E R I C A   A X E L
I R O N M A I D E N   S P A M
S E P T E T   E D I T I O N S
T E E   N I A   T A N S
    P U T T E R A R O U N D
A D D I S   T R U R O   R O Y
L I O N   D E R B Y   F E T E
P E W   M A N O R   R O S E S
S U N D A Y D R I V E R
    G O L D   C I A   E S C
S O R C E R E R   S C A M P I
T H A T   E L I J A H W O O D
U N D O   A L O N G   E T R E
B O E R   M E T R E   S E E R
```

93

```
D E L I   E L L A S   A F E W
E L O N   M E A D E   C O L A
J A C K S O N K E N T U C K Y
A N I S E T T E   A M I E S
        T I E   S A X E
M A D I S O N I L L I N O I S
I R O N O N   D O A   K O A
M O R A N   Z I P   A P I N G
I L S   M A O   A S O N I A
C L I N T O N M I C H I G A N
    O H M Y   L E I
A L O N E   N O T E P A D S
J E F F E R S O N O R E G O N
A N N A   P A G A N   A U R A
R O O T   M O O S E   L A M P
```

94

```
S A L A D   B A S K   N E S T
I M A G E   A N T I   O V E R
N A V A L   A G E S   M O V E
    P U L L U P S T A K E S
S E C E D E   S P E E D E R S
H M O   E T C   E R A
A C N E   G A S   C A F F E
H E A D F O R T H E H I L L S
S E N S E   Y E N   M O A T
    T S P   P I E   O R E
P R E A C H E D   A S I D E S
H I T T H E B R I C K S
O P A L   I B I S   I L I A D
T O G A   K L E E   M E N S A
O N E S   S E R E   O S C A R
```

95

```
F D I C   B A R D S   A S P S
L U N A   U B O A T   N E A L
E R I C   R O U S E   T R I O
D O T H E R I G H T T H I N G
    E C O L E   H E F T S
A L E P H     W H A M
D A D O O R O N R O N   A L P
A S I T   O N A I R   I D E A
M E T   M O U N T A I N D E W
    C O T S   B A S K S
S L O A N   A S P I C
P O S T A G E D U E S T A M P
O N C E   N A M E R   I C E R
R E A R   A V E R S   V I N E
E R R S   T E N S E   E D D Y
```

96

```
P I E S   T E M P E   C H E R
A N A T   E V E R Y   R A T E
S P R Y   R E N E E   I R A N
T U T   V E N U S D E M I L O
A T H E I S T   R A E
    A N N A   C R O S S S E A
M O N D E   E R U P T   A R C
E G G S   A R I E S   S T A R
A G E   A B I E S   M O U S E
L I L A B N E R   C A R R
    C O O   B A N A N A S
M E R C U R Y L Y N X   N R A
O L E O   M A I N E   D I E T
O M A R   A L T E R   A N N O
G O L D   L E E R S   D E A N
```

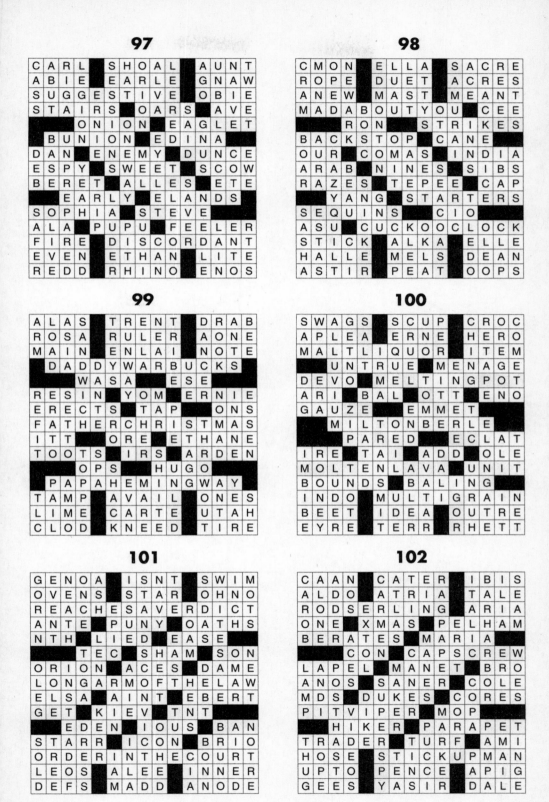

97

C	A	R	L		S	H	O	A	L		A	U	N	T
A	B	I	E		E	A	R	L	E		G	N	A	W
S	U	G	G	E	S	T	I	V	E		O	B	I	E
S	T	A	I	R	S		O	A	R	S		A	V	E
		O	N	I	O	N		E	A	G	L	E	T	
	B	U	N	I	O	N		E	D	I	N	A		
D	A	N		E	N	E	M	Y		D	U	N	C	E
E	S	P	Y		S	W	E	E	T		S	C	O	W
B	E	R	E	T		A	L	L	E	S		E	T	E
	E	A	R	L	Y		E	L	A	N	D	S		
S	O	P	H	I	A		S	T	E	V	E			
A	L	A		P	U	P	U		F	E	E	L	E	R
F	I	R	E		D	I	S	C	O	R	D	A	N	T
E	V	E	N		E	T	H	A	N		L	I	T	E
R	E	D	D		R	H	I	N	O		E	N	O	S

98

C	M	O	N		E	L	L	A		S	A	C	R	E
R	O	P	E		D	U	E	T		A	C	R	E	S
A	N	E	W		M	A	S	T		M	E	A	N	T
M	A	D	A	B	O	U	T	Y	O	U		C	E	E
			R	O	N			S	T	R	I	K	E	S
B	A	C	K	S	T	O	P		C	A	N	E		
O	U	R		C	O	M	A	S		I	N	D	I	A
A	R	A	B		N	I	N	E	S		S	I	B	S
R	A	Z	E	S		T	E	P	E	E		C	A	P
	Y	A	N	G		S	T	A	R	T	E	R	S	
S	E	Q	U	I	N	S		C	I	O				
A	S	U		C	U	C	K	O	O	C	L	O	C	K
S	T	I	C	K		A	L	K	A		E	L	L	E
H	A	L	L	E		M	E	L	S		D	E	A	N
A	S	T	I	R		P	E	A	T		O	O	P	S

99

A	L	A	S		T	R	E	N	T		D	R	A	B
R	O	S	A		R	U	L	E	R		A	O	N	E
M	A	I	N		E	N	L	A	I		N	O	T	E
	D	A	D	D	Y	W	A	R	B	U	C	K	S	
			W	A	S	A			E	S	E			
R	E	S	I	N		Y	O	M		E	R	N	I	E
E	R	E	C	T	S		T	A	P		O	N	S	
F	A	T	H	E	R	C	H	R	I	S	T	M	A	S
I	T	T			O	R	E		E	T	H	A	N	E
T	O	O	T	S		I	R	S		A	R	D	E	N
			O	P	S			H	U	G	O			
	P	A	P	A	H	E	M	I	N	G	W	A	Y	
T	A	M	P		A	V	A	I	L		O	N	E	S
L	I	M	E		C	A	R	T	E		U	T	A	H
C	L	O	D		K	N	E	E	D		T	I	R	E

100

S	W	A	G	S		S	C	U	P		C	R	O	C
A	P	L	E	A		E	R	N	E		H	E	R	O
M	A	L	T	L	I	Q	U	O	R		I	T	E	M
	U	N	T	R	U	E		M	E	N	A	G	E	
D	E	V	O		M	E	L	T	I	N	G	P	O	T
A	R	I		B	A	L		O	T	T		E	N	O
G	A	U	Z	E		E	M	M	E	T				
		M	I	L	T	O	N	B	E	R	L	E		
			P	A	R	E	D			E	C	L	A	T
I	R	E		T	A	I		A	D	D		O	L	E
M	O	L	T	E	N	L	A	V	A		U	N	I	T
B	O	U	N	D	S		B	A	L	I	N	G		
I	N	D	O		M	U	L	T	I	G	R	A	I	N
B	E	E	T		I	D	E	A		O	U	T	R	E
E	Y	R	E		T	E	R	R		R	H	E	T	T

101

G	E	N	O	A		I	S	N	T		S	W	I	M
O	V	E	N	S		S	T	A	R		O	H	N	O
R	E	A	C	H	E	S	A	V	E	R	D	I	C	T
A	N	T	E		P	U	N	Y		O	A	T	H	S
N	T	H		L	I	E	D		E	A	S	E		
			T	E	C		S	H	A	M		S	O	N
O	R	I	O	N		A	C	E	S		D	A	M	E
L	O	N	G	A	R	M	O	F	T	H	E	L	A	W
E	L	S	A		A	I	N	T		E	B	E	R	T
G	E	T		K	I	E	V		T	N	T			
			E	D	E	N		I	O	U	S		B	A	N
S	T	A	R	R		I	C	O	N		B	R	I	O
O	R	D	E	R	I	N	T	H	E	C	O	U	R	T
L	E	O	S		A	L	E	E		I	N	N	E	R
D	E	F	S		M	A	D	D		A	N	O	D	E

102

C	A	A	N		C	A	T	E	R		I	B	I	S
A	L	D	O		A	T	R	I	A		T	A	L	E
R	O	D	S	E	R	L	I	N	G		A	R	I	A
O	N	E		X	M	A	S		P	E	L	H	A	M
B	E	R	A	T	E	S		M	A	R	I	A		
			C	O	N		C	A	P	S	C	R	E	W
L	A	P	E	L		M	A	N	E	T		B	R	O
A	N	O	S		S	A	N	E	R		C	O	L	E
M	D	S		D	U	K	E	S		C	O	R	E	S
P	I	T	V	I	P	E	R		M	O	P			
			H	I	K	E	R		P	A	R	A	P	E	T
T	R	A	D	E	R		T	U	R	F		A	M	I
H	O	S	E		S	T	I	C	K	U	P	M	A	N
U	P	T	O		P	E	N	C	E		A	P	I	G
G	E	E	S		Y	A	S	I	R		D	A	L	E

103

```
F U S E . D A L I . . S I L O
O N T V . R U I N . L U C A S
O T O E . E N T R . O B E S E
D O W N I N T H E M O U T H .
. . . I O C . . . I S R . . .
U P I N T H E A I R . B A A S
T O N G A . L U T E . . D L I
T R U S S . I D A . S A L A D
E T S . P H I L . C L A R E
R E E L . O U T O N A L I M B
. . A N N . . . E M S . . . .
. B E S I D E T H E P O I N T
L E A S T . A R I D . U H O H
E E R I E . T I L L . L O V E
I S L E . S O L E . S P A N
```

104

```
C R A P S . C L A Y . B A R B
P I P I T . R O S A . O H I O
A G E N A . E R I N . N O D S
S A D A T . S N A K E E Y E S
. . . T U L S A . E L Y . . .
P L E A S E . R E G A L E D
R A D . S A B U . A R E N A
E I G H T T H E H A R D W A Y
S N E E R . M E R C . I T A
S E R R A T E . L E S S E N
. . . I I I . P L U S H . . .
L I T T L E J O E . T A P E S
O D E A . R U S E . A D U L T
B O N G . E N I D . T E S L A
E L S E . D O T S . E S S A Y
```

105

```
L O G E . A T L A S . F O R E
A V I D . P O I S E . A W O L
M A G I . P A S T E . L E E K
B L I T H E S P I R I T . . .
. . . O A T . . . R E H A B
R E C A L L . L I B E R A T E
E M A I L . B E S O . W O E
J O L L Y G R E E N G I A N T
E T O . A I D E . A R I E L
C E R A M I C S . A T T I R E
T R Y S T . . . S R O . . .
. H A P P Y W A R R I O R
S P E C . A R M O R . I D L E
M E G A . C O C O A . F E E D
U P O N . A D A P T . T A O S
```

106

```
E L S A . A J A R . R I L E D
D A L I . S A N E . E V O K E
I T E R . I N K S . L E V E E
T H E L M A A L O U I S E . .
S E P I A . D E R M A . S D S
. . . F R E E . T A N . T E A
T A F T . L A P . T H O N G
O B O E . K N E A D . O R S O
R H O D A . A D O . R Y E S
S O D . P I G . A M M O . .
O R C . A L A R M . A S S E T
. H E C K L E A J E C K L E
L O A T H . E L E A . O I L S
U N I T E . N A V Y . P E E L
G E N U S . A X E S . E D N A
```

107

```
S T O M P . L I M P . S A N S
P A L E O . U V E A . U H O H
O C E A N . L A M S . R O P E
I K I D Y O U N O T . E Y E D
L Y C E U M . . R A P T . . .
. . . P E R K Y . A H O L D
L I L Y . R A N . F R I D A Y
E R O O . T H E D A . N O D E
N E B U L A . L I L . G R A D
A D O B E . A T A L E . . .
. . . E A S T . A R A B I C
F A S T . A B S O L U T E L Y
E X E C . T A T A . P A N I C
T E C H . U T E S . T R I A L
A S T A . P S S T . S I N C E
```

108

```
S L A P . D E A F . A D M A N
I O L A . U G L I . P I A N O
G O I N G T O E X T R E M E S
H I C K E Y . E W E . A W E
S E E Y A . G A R I S H . .
. . . R E M U S . S E E D Y
O H M E . M A C . S K I D O O
G O I N G I N T O H I D I N G
R A N O U T . I D A . I T S A
E X I L E . L O D G E . . .
. . . A S I A N S . S W A T H
E G G . S I P . S T E R E O
G O N E W I T H T H E W I N D
A B A S H . O B I E . O S S A
D I T T O . P O N D . N E E D
```

109

M	A	R	C		W	O	R	D		E	S	T	E	E
A	S	E	A		A	R	I	A		C	H	E	A	T
I	T	E	M		F	A	C	T		L	A	S	S	O
L	I	F	E	O	F	T	H	E	P	A	R	T	Y	
		O	S	L	O		R	I	P					
C	A	T		T	E	R	R	I	E	R		A	S	H
A	G	A	T	E		E	L	L		U	L	N	A	
P	I	C	K	O	F	T	H	E	L	I	T	T	E	R
O	L	I	O		A	R	A		R	E	A	L	M	
N	E	T		T	R	I	B	U	N	E		R	L	S
		S	A	G		S	E	N	D					
	S	A	L	T	O	F	T	H	E	E	A	R	T	H
C	A	R	A	T		R	E	E	D		R	A	R	E
O	L	I	V	E		E	A	R	L		T	I	E	R
S	E	D	E	R		E	L	S	E		S	L	E	D

110

C	A	R	A		D	E	G	S		S	L	I	D	E
A	H	E	M		O	G	L	E		T	I	M	E	R
D	O	L	E		W	A	I	T		I	C	I	E	R
G	R	I	N	A	N	D	B	A	R	E	I	T		
E	S	E		C	B	S			E	S	T	A	T	E
D	E	F	A	C	E		R	U	B			B	E	D
		C	E	A	S	E	S		V	A	L	E	S	
	H	O	I	S	T	T	H	E	S	A	L	E	S	
W	A	R	D	S		E	A	S	E	U	P			
O	L	D		O	M	B		C	L	O	V	E	R	
E	L	E	C	T	S		T	U	T		E	V	E	
	R	A	Z	E	Y	O	U	R	S	I	T	E	S	
C	H	I	N	A		A	B	L	E		D	O	N	E
H	O	N	O	R		M	I	S	S		L	E	S	T
E	D	G	E	S		S	T	A	T		E	R	O	S

111

M	A	Z	E		O	F	F	S		S	T	A	T	S
A	M	E	S		R	A	R	E		T	O	L	E	T
M	I	S	T	E	R	B	I	G		O	P	I	N	E
A	S	T	E	R		I	S	O		O	B	E	S	E
		S	N	E	A	K		P	L	A	N	E	R	
S	A	G		I	N	N		P	A	I	N			
E	V	E	N	E	R		P	O	L	E	A	X	E	S
P	E	R	U		O	B	O	E	S		N	I	L	E
T	R	E	M	B	L	E	D		I	R	A	N	I	S
		E	E	L	Y		B	E	I		G	A	S	
S	P	A	R	E	S		B	A	D	G	E			
T	A	R	O	T		O	W	N		O	N	S	E	T
A	S	O	U	L		M	A	J	O	R	D	O	M	O
I	S	O	N	E		A	N	O	N		E	L	M	O
D	E	M	O	S		N	A	S	T		D	E	A	L

112

H	A	D	J		W	I	N	D		B	R	E	E	D
E	L	I	A		I	C	E	R		R	A	L	L	Y
M	I	S	C		L	I	L	Y	T	O	M	L	I	N
P	I	C	K	E	D		L	E	O	N		E	S	E
			P	E	R	E		R	A	Z	Z			
P	A	R	A	G	O	N	S		D	E	S	A	D	E
E	T	A	L		S	O	L	O		R	A	T	O	N
L	A	D	A		E	R	E	C	T		Z	O	N	E
F	L	I	N	G		M	E	T	E		S	L	U	R
S	L	I	C	E	S		P	A	L	O	A	L	T	O
			E	T	A	T		D	E	N	G			
A	B	A		A	R	I	A		G	E	A	R	U	P
G	E	N	E	W	I	L	D	E	R		B	O	N	E
U	L	T	R	A		E	Z	R	A		O	M	I	T
E	L	E	G	Y		S	E	A	M		R	A	T	E

113

A	F	A	R		A	R	D	O	R		M	A	T	S
N	O	R	A		P	I	E	C	E		A	Q	U	I
G	R	O	V	E	R	C	L	E	V	E	L	A	N	D
L	A	S	E	R		E	V	A		L	I	B	E	L
E	Y	E		A	B	S	E	N	C	E		A	R	E
			A	S	A		O	N	E					
	J	A	M	E	S	B	U	C	H	A	N	A	N	
C	O	P	S		T	O	R	R	E		S	P	O	T
A	R	P		P	E	R	S	O	N	A		T	O	O
M	E	L	L	O		N	A	P		D	R	E	S	S
P	L	E	A	S	E		A	Z	O	R	E	S		
		J	O	H	N	K	E	N	N	E	D	Y		
S	P	A	T		D	I	V	O	T		E	X	E	C
A	R	C	S		E	L	I	T	E		N	E	E	D
W	O	K	E		D	O	L	E	D		T	S	K	S

114

R	O	M	E		Q	U	A	D	S		S	C	A	M
A	L	E	X		U	N	D	I	D		P	E	T	E
M	I	N	I		A	B	A	C	I		O	L	E	S
S	O	U	T	H	F	O	R	K		C	O	L	A	S
			A	F	L		E	C	O	N	O	M	Y	
Y	E	A	S	T		T	Y	R	O	N	E			
A	L	L	I	E	S		E	E	R		R	A	D	S
M	A	L	L		P	R	A	D	O		I	N	R	I
S	L	A	V		A	E	R		T	A	S	T	E	S
			E	R	R	A	N	T		M	M	I	I	I
G	N	A	R	L	E	D		U	S	O				
L	O	E	W	S		J	A	C	K	K	N	I	F	E
O	L	G	A		T	U	L	S	A		A	D	I	N
V	O	I	R		A	S	P	O	T		D	O	J	O
E	S	S	E		S	T	O	N	E		A	L	I	S

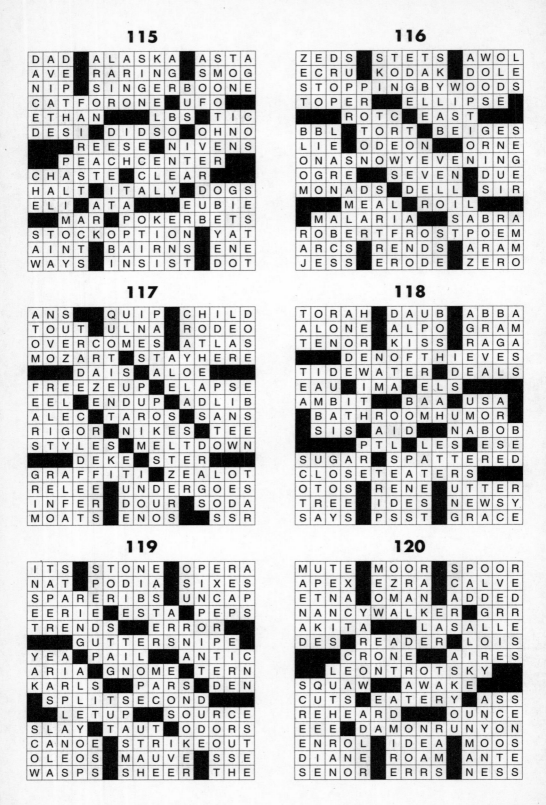

115

D	A	D		A	L	A	S	K	A		A	S	T	A
A	V	E		R	A	R	I	N	G		S	M	O	G
N	I	P		S	I	N	G	E	R	B	O	O	N	E
C	A	T	F	O	R	O	N	E		U	F	O		
E	T	H	A	N			L	B	S		T	I	C	
D	E	S	I		D	I	D	S	O		O	H	N	O
		R	E	E	S	E		N	I	V	E	N	S	
	P	E	A	C	H	C	E	N	T	E	R			
C	H	A	S	T	E		C	L	E	A	R			
H	A	L	T		I	T	A	L	Y		D	O	G	S
E	L	I		A	T	A		E	U	B	I	E		
	M	A	R		P	O	K	E	R	B	E	T	S	
S	T	O	C	K	O	P	T	I	O	N		Y	A	T
A	I	N	T		B	A	I	R	N	S		E	N	E
W	A	Y	S		I	N	S	I	S	T		D	O	T

116

Z	E	D	S		S	T	E	T	S		A	W	O	L
E	C	R	U		K	O	D	A	K		D	O	L	E
S	T	O	P	P	I	N	G	B	Y	W	O	O	D	S
T	O	P	E	R		E	L	L	I	P	S	E		
		R	O	T	C		E	A	S	T				
B	B	L		T	O	R	T		B	E	I	G	E	S
L	I	E		O	D	E	O	N		O	R	N	E	
O	N	A	S	N	O	W	Y	E	V	E	N	I	N	G
O	G	R	E		S	E	V	E	N		D	U	E	
M	O	N	A	D	S		D	E	L	L		S	I	R
		M	E	A	L		R	O	I	L				
	M	A	L	A	R	I	A		S	A	B	R	A	
R	O	B	E	R	T	F	R	O	S	T	P	O	E	M
A	R	C	S		R	E	N	D	S		A	R	A	M
J	E	S	S		E	R	O	D	E		Z	E	R	O

117

A	N	S		Q	U	I	P		C	H	I	L	D	
T	O	U	T		U	L	N	A		R	O	D	E	O
O	V	E	R	C	O	M	E	S		A	T	L	A	S
M	O	Z	A	R	T		S	T	A	Y	H	E	R	E
		D	A	I	S		A	L	O	E				
F	R	E	E	Z	E	U	P		E	L	A	P	S	E
E	E	L		E	N	D	U	P		A	D	L	I	B
A	L	E	C		T	A	R	O	S		S	A	N	S
R	I	G	O	R		N	I	K	E	S		T	E	E
S	T	Y	L	E	S		M	E	L	T	D	O	W	N
		D	E	K	E		S	T	E	R				
G	R	A	F	F	I	T	I		Z	E	A	L	O	T
R	E	L	E	E		U	N	D	E	R	G	O	E	S
I	N	F	E	R		D	O	U	R		S	O	D	A
M	O	A	T	S		E	N	O	S		S	S	R	

118

T	O	R	A	H		D	A	U	B		A	B	B	A
A	L	O	N	E		A	L	P	O		G	R	A	M
T	E	N	O	R		K	I	S	S		R	A	G	A
		D	E	N	O	F	T	H	I	E	V	E	S	
T	I	D	E	W	A	T	E	R		D	E	A	L	S
E	A	U		I	M	A		E	L	S				
A	M	B	I	T		B	A	A		U	S	A		
	B	A	T	H	R	O	O	M	H	U	M	O	R	
S	I	S		A	I	D		N	A	B	O	B		
	P	T	L		L	E	S		E	S	E			
S	U	G	A	R		S	P	A	T	T	E	R	E	D
C	L	O	S	E	T	E	A	T	E	R	S			
O	T	O	S		R	E	N	E		U	T	T	E	R
T	R	E	E		I	D	E	S		N	E	W	S	Y
S	A	Y	S		P	S	S	T		G	R	A	C	E

119

I	T	S		S	T	O	N	E		O	P	E	R	A
N	A	T		P	O	D	I	A		S	I	X	E	S
S	P	A	R	E	R	I	B	S		U	N	C	A	P
E	E	R	I	E		E	S	T	A		P	E	P	S
T	R	E	N	D	S		E	R	R	O	R			
		G	U	T	T	E	R	S	N	I	P	E		
Y	E	A		P	A	I	L		A	N	T	I	C	
A	R	I	A		G	N	O	M	E		T	E	R	N
K	A	R	L	S		P	A	R	S		D	E	N	
	S	P	L	I	T	S	E	C	O	N	D			
	L	E	T	U	P		S	O	U	R	C	E		
S	L	A	Y		T	A	U	T		O	D	O	R	S
C	A	N	O	E		S	T	R	I	K	E	O	U	T
O	L	E	O	S		M	A	U	V	E		S	S	E
W	A	S	P	S		S	H	E	E	R		T	H	E

120

M	U	T	E		M	O	O	R		S	P	O	O	R
A	P	E	X		E	Z	R	A		C	A	L	V	E
E	T	N	A		O	M	A	N		A	D	D	E	D
N	A	N	C	Y	W	A	L	K	E	R		G	R	R
A	K	I	T	A			L	A	S	A	L	L	E	
D	E	S		R	E	A	D	E	R		L	O	I	S
		C	R	O	N	E		A	I	R	E	S		
	L	E	O	N	T	R	O	T	S	K	Y			
S	Q	U	A	W		A	W	A	K	E				
C	U	T	S		E	A	T	E	R	Y		A	S	S
R	E	H	E	A	R	D		O	U	N	C	E		
E	E	E		D	A	M	O	N	R	U	N	Y	O	N
E	N	R	O	L		I	D	E	A		M	O	O	S
D	I	A	N	E		R	O	A	M		A	N	T	E
S	E	N	O	R		E	R	R	S		N	E	S	S

121

I	D	L	E		J	U	M	P	S		U	L	A	N
S	E	A	L		O	N	E	A	T		N	I	L	E
A	B	S	O	L	U	T	E	L	Y		D	E	A	R
A	R	E		E	R	I	K		L	E	O	N	I	D
C	A	R	B	I	N	E		P	E	R	U			
		U	S	A		D	A	T	A	B	A	S	E	
O	B	I	T		L	I	O	N		S	T	U	M	P
P	E	C	O	S		N	N	E		E	E	R	I	E
A	L	O	F	T		G	U	L	F		D	A	T	E
L	A	N	C	E	L	O	T		A	F	L			
		O	M	I	T		S	T	A	Y	P	U	T	
M	E	D	U	S	A		R	O	A	R		I	L	E
O	V	E	R		B	Y	A	L	L	M	E	A	N	S
P	I	N	S		L	O	C	A	L		A	N	A	T
E	L	S	E		E	M	E	R	Y		R	O	S	Y

122

M	A	M	E		D	E	G	A	S		O	W	L	S
A	L	E	X		A	B	A	S	E		O	R	E	O
C	A	S	T	I	R	O	N	S	T	O	M	A	C	H
S	W	A	R	M	I	N	G		S	A	P	P	H	O
		O	P	U	S		E	S	T	H				
G	R	A	V	E	S		B	A	A	S		S	H	A
E	A	T	E	N		T	O	R	I		S	P	A	N
S	W	O	R	D	S	W	A	L	L	O	W	I	N	G
T	E	N	T		C	I	T	Y		F	E	R	N	S
E	R	E		B	A	N	S		A	F	L	O	A	T
		W	A	V	E		W	R	I	T				
C	R	E	O	L	E		P	R	E	S	E	L	L	S
L	U	M	P	I	N	T	H	E	T	H	R	O	A	T
A	S	I	A		G	O	O	S	E		E	R	M	A
M	E	L	T		E	A	S	T	S		D	D	A	Y

123

E	N	T	E	R		P	O	P	E		M	A	M	E
L	O	R	R	E		A	C	E	S		I	M	A	M
B	E	I	N	G		W	H	A	T	A	D	U	M	P
A	L	S	O	R	A	N	S		E	L	I	C	I	T
			E	S	E		L	E	O		K	E	Y	
O	V	E	R	T	H	E	H	U	M	P				
T	E	X	A	S		O	R	E		I	P	S	A	
I	R	E	S		C	A	N	E	D		B	E	E	T
S	A	S	H		R	I	O		A	E	R	E	O	
			F	O	R	R	E	S	T	G	U	M	P	
B	U	S		E	S	S		L	A	T				
A	P	P	L	E	S		I	A	M	A	R	O	C	K
S	P	E	E	D	B	U	M	P		C	A	N	O	N
T	E	A	S		O	N	U	S		H	I	T	M	E
E	R	R	S		W	I	S	E		E	L	O	P	E

124

R	I	T	Z		S	T	O	P		A	O	R	T	A
I	D	E	A		L	I	V	E		P	R	I	O	R
F	L	A	G	P	O	L	E	S		T	I	N	G	E
F	E	M		A	G	E	N	T	S		E	G	O	S
			E	P	A		S	T	I	N	G			
T	U	P	P	E	N	C	E		A	C	T	U	A	L
O	N	A	I	R		O	L	D	I	E		A	D	O
W	I	G		C	A	L	L	I	N	S		R	A	P
E	T	E		L	I	T	E	R		H	E	D	G	E
D	E	T	A	I	L		S	T	R	E	S	S	E	D
			U	P	P	E	R		A	E	S			
C	A	R	R		D	E	C	E	N	T		H	O	T
R	U	N	O	N		H	A	I	L	S	T	O	N	E
A	R	E	N	A		A	R	N	O		A	L	E	X
M	A	R	S	H		B	L	E	W		B	E	S	T

125

I	N	G	E		A	M	I	S	H		S	O	N	G
C	E	L	A		C	A	N	T	O		H	A	I	L
B	R	A	V	E	H	E	A	R	T		O	K	L	A
M	O	D	E	L	T		N	A	B		V	E	E	R
			S	K	U	A		D	E	F	E	N	S	E
G	A	R	D	E	N	S	P	A	D	E				
E	V	E	R		G	E	E		S	E	W	N	O	N
L	E	D	O	N		C	A	W		S	H	A	V	E
T	R	O	P	I	C		R	A	F		I	T	E	R
			N	E	I	L	D	I	A	M	O	N	D	
W	E	S	T	E	R	N		I	N	I	S			
H	A	L	E		E	U	R		A	R	I	O	S	O
A	S	I	S		B	R	I	D	G	E	C	L	U	B
L	E	N	T		R	E	P	E	L		A	G	E	E
E	L	K	S		A	D	E	L	E		L	A	Z	Y

126

B	R	O	K	E		Z	A	P	P	A		F	D	A
M	A	R	I	S		S	N	E	R	T		A	E	R
W	H	E	N	T	H	A	T	E	E	L		M	A	I
			G	E	E	Z	E	R			M	I	R	E
G	A	S	S	E	R	S			P	S	A	L	M	S
O	N	I	T		B	A	T	S	A	N	E	Y	E	
P	E	S	O	S			O	H	N	O				
		W	I	N	K	R	I	G	H	T	B	A	C	K
				I	O	T	A			S	L	O	E	S
D	O	N	T	B	E	S	H	Y			C	O	D	E
G	R	O	U	S	E			I	M	P	A	S	S	E
L	I	L	T			W	A	S	H	U	P			
A	V	A		T	H	A	T	S	A	M	O	R	A	Y
D	E	L		O	A	K	I	E			A	N	O	D	E
E	R	A		W	H	E	T	S			S	E	W	O	N

127

```
ACTE  LIAR  MELTS
MAIL  URGE  IDEAL
ASTI  COON  LIEBY
STANDINGORDERS
SENORA   WIE
   RUNNINGWATER
BUD  BOAS  ASTHMA
ITEM  BIN   TEMP
DAMASK  NOAH  MAT
SHOOTINGSTAR
   ALA   TRAILS
 FLYINGSQUIRREL
ALIEN  STUN  IAGO
DANTE  ALEE  TNUT
ONAIR  TOSS  YIPS
```

128

```
PANAM  RAKE  SHAH
OMAHA  ASAP  CAME
SPEAKOFTHEDEVIL
    BEN  ONEONONE
SAP  TOW    RECON
MARDI  ABEAM
AROOM  DELI  ISNT
CONVERSEALLSTAR
KNEE  CURT  ELUDE
   LAPSE  AERIE
OSAKA    STP  MAD
LEWINSKY  UFO
STATEUNIVERSITY
ETRE   DOPE  OLDIE
NODS   STET  GOONS
```

129

```
LOLA  SLAB  ITALY
ICED  LENO  NOMAD
ATAD  AVER  FRAYS
REVOLVINGDOOR
STENO   DIOR  YAM
   SWAN  AAMILNE
ATT   RUE   ERLES
WHIRLINGDERVISH
ARGUE  OUT   STY
REENACT  BARS
EER  POET  ACHES
 SPINNINGWHEEL
QUEEN  ODOR  LALA
TRYST  RAGU  EVEN
SEETO  SLOB  PERT
```

130

```
SCAM  RATED  AFRO
NORM  EVOKE  PLEA
OKEEFFEMEABREAK
RIN  LURED  LOADS
TEABAGS    HON
   IKE  THOUSAND
ABAT   SHOOS  LAY
HALSOFMONTEZUMA
ACT  NOOSE   AMEN
SHORTAGE  WAN
   OIL  BRIEFED
SCRAM  BRAID  OVA
QUESEURATSEURAT
FEAT  RIGHT  SADE
TSPS  NOSES  EYED
```

131

```
EPSOM  GLEN  KANT
LAUDE  HERO  ALOE
SWEETHEART  NINA
ENTREAT  SADSACK
   RITE   OASES
HALF  LOAFERS
OCALA  SROS  ELL
STVALENTINESDAY
ESE  LANE  TRYME
   TOREROS  ASPS
AFOOT  NCAA
MINDSET  ENFORCE
ALIA  BILLETDOUX
SLOT  OLEO  ROUTE
SYNE  NEST  ARTES
```

132

```
BEGS  EWES  ELWES
ETRE  BERT  FERDE
REED  BENE  FEEDS
GREENSKEEPERS
ENCRE    PET  TSE
NEE  REEF  PEGLEG
   EVENED   LESE
WERNERKLEMPERER
ELEC  EDERLE
DESEED  SMEE  ETS
SEE  VET   BESET
  CREMEDEMENTHE
DETER  NEVE  THEE
EVENT  SLEW  REEL
CEDES  ELLS  ERSE
```

133

T	O	E	S		P	R	O	W		D	O	G	E	S
O	L	D	S		E	E	R	O		E	L	U	D	E
W	I	S	E	C	R	A	C	K		B	E	N	I	N
E	V	E		A	U	R	A		R	U	I	N	E	D
R	E	L	A	P	S	E		F	A	N	C	Y		
		F	E	E	D	B	A	C	K		S	O	P	
O	F	F	E	R		L	I	E	S		A	B	A	
D	R	A	W		T	H	I	R	D		S	C	O	T
D	E	S		A	R	O	N		S	A	K	E	S	
S	E	T		B	A	C	K	P	A	C	K			
	T	R	U	C	K		A	M	A	S	S	E	D	
P	A	R	I	T	Y		S	L	U	R		E	L	I
E	X	A	C	T		B	I	L	L	Y	J	A	C	K
N	I	C	H	E		A	L	O	E		A	T	I	E
A	S	K	E	D		T	O	R	T		G	O	D	S

134

S	H	E	A	R		T	A	T	I		B	A	B	A
L	E	N	T	O		O	P	U	S		A	P	E	R
A	R	O	O	M		N	A	T	O		S	O	F	T
G	O	S	P	E	L	T	R	U	T	H		G	O	I
			R	I	O			O	A	T	E	R	S	
G	E	C	K	O	S		R	A	P	S	H	E	E	T
A	L	A	I		A	B	I	L	E	N	E			
S	O	D	O	M		O	A	F		T	I	G	E	R
		S	U	R	I	N	A	M		S	O	R	E	
R	O	C	K	S	A	L	T		O	S	M	O	N	D
I	C	E	S	I	N		A	O	K					
V	E	L		C	O	U	N	T	R	Y	R	O	A	D
A	L	E	S		V	E	A	L		W	O	R	R	Y
L	O	R	E		E	L	I	A		A	L	E	T	A
S	T	Y	X		R	E	L	S		Y	E	M	E	N

135

A	U	R	A		O	P	R	A	H		S	H	A	D
C	R	O	C		M	A	I	N	E		T	I	L	E
H	I	T	T	H	E	R	O	A	D		A	G	E	E
E	S	S		A	L	I	T		G	A	T	H	E	R
			A	B	E	S		B	E	G	E	T		
R	A	B	B	I	T		M	A	R	I	N	A	T	E
A	D	U	L	T		S	E	T	O	N		I	R	S
M	I	R	E		T	H	R	E	W		F	L	A	T
P	E	N		U	R	A	L	S		S	L	I	D	E
S	U	R	I	N	A	M	E		S	T	A	T	E	S
		U	N	T	I	E		S	P	E	W			
G	I	B	S	O	N		S	H	O	E		A	S	U
R	O	B	E		M	A	K	E	T	R	A	C	K	S
E	W	E	R		A	L	E	R	T		B	R	I	E
W	A	R	T		N	E	E	D	Y		S	E	N	D

136

T	R	A	P		D	U	E	T	S		O	H	O	H
H	U	G	H		A	P	N	E	A		D	A	T	A
U	S	A	F		P	S	I	L	O	V	E	Y	O	U
S	T	R	A	P	P	E	D			A	S	S	E	T
			C	E	L	T		O	I	L	S			
C	A	S	T	L	E		P	T	B	O	A	T	S	
A	S	C	O	T		R	A	T	E	R		S	U	P
S	C	A	R		L	A	T	E	X		P	A	S	O
H	A	L		L	I	V	E	R		M	A	R	I	O
	P	D	J	A	M	E	S		G	A	S	S	E	R
		O	N	A	N		T	I	N	Y				
R	A	I	S	A		T	R	A	N	S	F	E	R	
P	G	T	H	I	R	T	E	E	N		T	A	L	E
M	U	T	E		A	I	M	A	T		E	R	S	E
S	A	Y	S		D	E	P	T	S		M	E	A	L

137

C	A	M	P	S		A	U	D	I		S	O	D	A
P	L	E	A	T		S	H	O	R		O	P	E	N
R	E	N	T	A		S	O	S	A		L	E	S	T
	C	U	T	T	O	T	H	E	Q	U	I	C	K	
			Y	U	P			D	I	N	T			
A	E	S		S	T	A	R		S	C	A	T	H	E
F	L	U	B		I	R	A	N		A	I	R	E	S
A	M	E	R	I	C	A	N	E	X	P	R	E	S	S
S	E	D	A	N		B	O	N	A		E	A	S	E
T	R	E	N	D	S		N	E	X	T		D	E	N
			D	I	E	S		I	O	N				
	J	O	N	A	T	H	A	N	S	W	I	F	T	
D	U	M	A		T	A	R	A		A	C	R	I	D
A	D	A	M		E	D	I	T		R	H	O	N	E
D	O	N	E		R	E	A	L		D	E	G	A	S

138

J	U	M	P		T	O	G	A		E	M	O	T	E
A	S	E	A		I	M	A	S		R	A	B	A	T
W	E	A	R		R	I	F	T		A	L	E	R	T
			I	F	A	T	F	I	R	S	T	Y	O	U
S	A	S	S	E	D		E	R	I	E				
H	U	P		E	E	E		C	R	I	T	I	C	
A	R	I	E	L		C	A	S	H		N	O	G	O
D	O	N	T	S	U	C	C	E	E	D	D	O	N	T
E	R	A	T		N	E	U	T		R	O	B	O	T
S	A	L	A	M	I		S	A	O		A	R	E	
			I	T	E	M		S	W	E	D	E	N	
T	R	Y	S	K	Y	D	I	V	I	N	G			
R	I	A	T	A		G	L	A	D		Y	A	L	E
A	S	K	E	D		E	L	I	E		P	R	A	Y
P	E	S	T	O		D	E	N	S		T	I	M	E

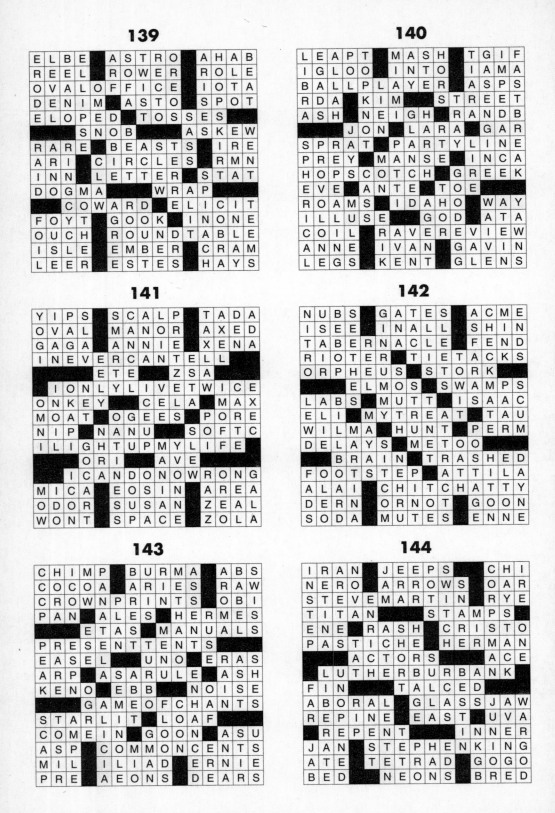

139

E	L	B	E		A	S	T	R	O		A	H	A	B
R	E	E	L		R	O	W	E	R		R	O	L	E
O	V	A	L	O	F	F	I	C	E		I	O	T	A
D	E	N	I	M		A	S	T	O		S	P	O	T
E	L	O	P	E	D		T	O	S	S	E	S		
		S	N	O	B				A	S	K	E	W	
R	A	R	E		B	E	A	S	T	S		I	R	E
A	R	I		C	I	R	C	L	E	S		R	M	N
I	N	N		L	E	T	T	E	R		S	T	A	T
D	O	G	M	A			W	R	A	P				
		C	O	W	A	R	D		E	L	I	C	I	T
F	O	Y	T		G	O	O	K		I	N	O	N	E
O	U	C	H		R	O	U	N	D	T	A	B	L	E
I	S	L	E		E	M	B	E	R		C	R	A	M
L	E	E	R		E	S	T	E	S		H	A	Y	S

140

L	E	A	P	T		M	A	S	H		T	G	I	F
I	G	L	O	O		I	N	T	O		I	A	M	A
B	A	L	L	P	L	A	Y	E	R		A	S	P	S
R	D	A		K	I	M			S	T	R	E	E	T
A	S	H		N	E	I	G	H		R	A	N	D	B
			J	O	N		L	A	R	A		G	A	R
S	P	R	A	T		P	A	R	T	Y	L	I	N	E
P	R	E	Y		M	A	N	S	E		I	N	C	A
H	O	P	S	C	O	T	C	H		G	R	E	E	K
E	V	E		A	N	T	E		T	O	E			
R	O	A	M	S		I	D	A	H	O		W	A	Y
I	L	L	U	S	E		G	O	D		A	T	A	
C	O	I	L		R	A	V	E	R	E	V	I	E	W
A	N	N	E		I	V	A	N		G	A	V	I	N
L	E	G	S		K	E	N	T		G	L	E	N	S

141

Y	I	P	S		S	C	A	L	P		T	A	D	A
O	V	A	L		M	A	N	O	R		A	X	E	D
G	A	G	A		A	N	N	I	E		X	E	N	A
I	N	E	V	E	R	C	A	N	T	E	L	L		
			E	T	E		Z	S	A					
	I	O	N	L	Y	L	I	V	E	T	W	I	C	E
O	N	K	E	Y		C	E	L	A		M	A	X	
M	O	A	T		O	G	E	E	S		P	O	R	E
N	I	P		N	A	N	U		S	O	F	T	C	
I	L	I	G	H	T	U	P	M	Y	L	I	F	E	
		O	R	I		A	V	E						
	I	C	A	N	D	O	N	O	W	R	O	N	G	
M	I	C	A		E	O	S	I	N		A	R	E	A
O	D	O	R		S	U	S	A	N		Z	E	A	L
W	O	N	T		S	P	A	C	E		Z	O	L	A

142

N	U	B	S		G	A	T	E	S		A	C	M	E
I	S	E	E		I	N	A	L	L		S	H	I	N
T	A	B	E	R	N	A	C	L	E		F	E	N	D
R	I	O	T	E	R		T	I	E	T	A	C	K	S
O	R	P	H	E	U	S		S	T	O	R	K		
		E	L	M	O	S		S	W	A	M	P	S	
L	A	B	S		M	U	T	T		I	S	A	A	C
E	L	I		M	Y	T	R	E	A	T		T	A	U
W	I	L	M	A		H	U	N	T		P	E	R	M
D	E	L	A	Y	S		M	E	T	O	O			
		B	R	A	I	N		T	R	A	S	H	E	D
F	O	O	T	S	T	E	P		A	T	T	I	L	A
A	L	A	I		C	H	I	T	C	H	A	T	T	Y
D	E	R	N		O	R	N	O	T		G	O	O	N
S	O	D	A		M	U	T	E	S		E	N	N	E

143

C	H	I	M	P		B	U	R	M	A		A	B	S
C	O	C	O	A		A	R	I	E	S		R	A	W
C	R	O	W	N	P	R	I	N	T	S		O	B	I
P	A	N		A	L	E	S		H	E	R	M	E	S
			E	T	A	S		M	A	N	U	A	L	S
P	R	E	S	E	N	T	T	E	N	T	S			
E	A	S	E	L			U	N	O		E	R	A	S
A	R	P		A	S	A	R	U	L	E		A	S	H
K	E	N	O		E	B	B		N	O	I	S	E	
		G	A	M	E	O	F	C	H	A	N	T	S	
S	T	A	R	L	I	T		L	O	A	F			
C	O	M	E	I	N		G	O	O	N		A	S	U
A	S	P		C	O	M	M	O	N	C	E	N	T	S
M	I	L		I	L	I	A	D		E	R	N	I	E
P	R	E		A	E	O	N	S		D	E	A	R	S

144

I	R	A	N		J	E	E	P	S			C	H	I
N	E	R	O		A	R	R	O	W	S		O	A	R
S	T	E	V	E	M	A	R	T	I	N		R	Y	E
T	I	T	A	N			S	T	A	M	P	S		
E	N	E		R	A	S	H		C	R	I	S	T	O
P	A	S	T	I	C	H	E		H	E	R	M	A	N
			A	C	T	O	R	S			A	C	E	
	L	U	T	H	E	R	B	U	R	B	A	N	K	
F	I	N			T	A	L	C	E	D				
A	B	O	R	A	L		G	L	A	S	S	J	A	W
R	E	P	I	N	E		E	A	S	T		U	V	A
	R	E	P	E	N	T			I	N	N	E	R	
J	A	N		S	T	E	P	H	E	N	K	I	N	G
A	T	E		T	E	T	R	A	D		G	O	G	O
B	E	D		N	E	O	N	S		B	R	E	D	

145

```
P I N G   S T O R M   A C T E
I D E A   M A R I O   S H E A
C L O S E E N C O U N T E R S
T E N   N A Y S   S E E F I T
      T A R A   T S A R
S M A R M Y   M E A T   W E S
A E R I E   S O A K   S E R A
F A T A L A T T R A C T I O N
E N I D   L E E S   H O R D E
R T E   D U E T   S A N D E R
      D A M P   P O S E
A G O U T I   E R I E   B O Z
L O V E A N D M A R R I A G E
A B E L   U N I T E   M A R T
S I N S   M A T T E   P L E A
```

146

```
A R C H   O W E S   A C U T E
S O L I   T A X I   W I S E R
A S I N   T R I M   A R E N A
P H O E B E   T O P I C
      S U R   N A T U R A L
F A S T S   D U E S   M E M E
I T T O   S I N G S   N E O N
S T A N   P A D R E   A L U G
C I T E   E M E E R   V E N T
A L E C   C O R E   W I D T H
L A N O L I N   D O G
      W E E D S   R E A C T S
A R U B A   M A L I   T H O R
M A S O N   I V A N   I O W A
S W A Y S   N E C K   O W N S
```

147

```
P R O W   G W E N   R A B B I
R O V E   L I D O   E L I O T
I D E A   O N E S   L I S L E
S E R V E S O N E R I G H T
M O T E L S   A N N O
      E Y E B A N K   P T A
A D D I N   R O T C   T R I G
L A Y S I T O N T H E L I N E
D I S H   O D E A   A C C T S
A S L   I N E R R O R
      E A S T   A T T I C S
  E X P L O R E S T H E N E T
S T I N E   O R M E   N U D E
T A C E T   B I E R   T R A P
E L S A S   S E E S   H E R S
```

148

```
D A B S   H I S   F R A P P E
E L E C   A S K   A E N E A S
C A B O O D L E   L A Y E R S
C R O W N J E W E L S   V E E
A M P L E   M I S T E R X
      M A R I N E R
A L A   C O V E R   R E U N E
T E M P L E O F A R T E M I S
M A C A O   C I T E S   P P S
      P U P A T E D
B R E A D E D   M A N T A
O E R   B R O W B E A T E R S
S T R E A K   H O W S T H A T
O R E L S E   E S E   A R C O
N O D D E D   N C R   R U E R
```

149

```
A R A B   I N S E T   B O B S
N O S E   F A C T O   A R L O
T O E R R I S H U M A N B U T
S T A G E   H O D   R I S E S
      M E R   L E A N S
I T T A K E S A   C O H O S T
B A R N   P O R T A L   C P A
E M U   A L A   O D D   T I P
A P E   G A R A G E   S E R E
M A D D E N   C O M P U T E R
      I N T R O   Y E N
S H A R D   A L I   E S T E S
T O R E A L L Y S C R E W U P
A L E C   O P T E D   T I R E
N E A T   S H E E R   S N O W
```

150

```
C A P O   A P I S H   M O A B
A P E X   C O R E R   O B I E
L O E B   E C O L E   T E D S
S P L O S T A C E   A S Y E T
      W H Y S   S A V E
C D S   A L E C   T E T R A D
L E T B Y   I N T O   I O L E
A B E L   S N O O P   O P A L
M A N O   A T T U   S N E R T
P R O L I X   E C R U   R M S
      O V E N   K E N T
S T E V E   E G E T S A R L Y
E R L E   A G R E E   R H E E
R E L O   P R E P S   P E A L
E X A M   E I G H T   S A H L
```

151

```
HORNS . ACT . LATTE
ABOUT . LOO . AMIES
HOWTOWINFRIENDS
AES . ORT . FORBADE
. ALIASES . ATEN
BOCA . NLWEST . URE
CARNEGIE . IGOR .
DREDD . AND . IONIA
. APEG . SELFHELP
FAM . NICOLE . ERLE
ALPE . JANITOR .
COUNTON . MUD . SAL
INFLUENCEPEOPLE
ASFAR . EPA . TWAIN
LOSIN . SAT . SETTO
```

152

```
ABOLISH . ALSORAN
TORONTO . DECLARE
EASYCOM . EEASYGO
ETO . LIEN . RECON
. CUING . PENH .
SACHS . GOURD . AMO
CLOUDS . SSE . DRAB
HERMANM . ELVILLE
MANS . ICU . LIVELY
OFF . STING . CASES
. ICES . TALES .
IHEAR . OOZE . GAP
SILVERM . EDALIST
ADDENDA . BOLIVIA
YESDEAR . ONENESS
```

153

```
SWALE . OSHA . ATL
SOMERS . AWES . RIA
WOMENLIKESILENT
. DORSET . ESSENCE
MTN . DEBT . FAUN
PRIMP . MAPS . TSPS
SITOUT . BEAST .
. MENTHEYASSUME
. ATOMS . STRONG
PARR . REAL . SNITS
ALEC . RTES . ERA
TOSHIBA . SONATA .
THEYRELISTENING
IAN . OLDS . SENECA
EST . NAST . DOSES
```

154

```
HAHAS . GABON . CAR
AROLE . OMEGA . ORE
JINGLEBELLS . MEG
JAIALAI . LET . EYE
INNESS . KOS . NOON
SEG . ERIC . DONUT
. RADON . MENTOS
. THEJUNGLEBOOK .
TOECAP . POLIS .
ARDOR . BIBI . GAD
NEON . GIN . SHARER
KIN . GAG . ASININE
ANI . MRBOJANGLES
RTS . ARENA . ELLIS
DOT . NYNEX . SEEDY
```

155

```
. DECAL . RELO . AWS
DELUDE . ATOM . DIM
OCELOT . SHOETREE
FLATBUSH . GEENA
FAN . EPA . SCANNER
EROS . PATH . DARE
DERATS . SEEP . LSD
. CHICKWEED .
DID . ERIE . PRESET
IFAT . ENDS . THRO
COMRADE . TAO . EOS
KRAIT . EELGRASS
EGGPLANT . FLUTIE
NEE . AREA . RESHOD
STS . SEWS . ESSEN
```

156

```
BEARCUB . PUPPIES
OSBORNE . UNALERT
SQUEEZE . SIBERIA
OUT . WITHHOLDING
MESH . PSI . NOG .
. UPS . GYM . ETCH
CAPRA . AHEAD . OHO
BRITISHHONDURAS
ELS . RESOW . ASIDE
ROAM . LOP . WYE
. OOF . ESE . SCOW
YOUTHHOSTEL . ADA
ANNOYER . IDOODIT
NOTREAL . FEBRILE
GROSSLY . FREEZER
```

157

```
THAT  GRINS  ELSE
HERA  EASED  SOME
ELMS  TISHA  TSAR
WEAKINTHEKNEES
AND  TOTEM  ORTHO
YEARS   IAN   IUD
  EMT  HADJ  MPS
 EASYONTHEEYES
PVC  TRIS  EWE
TIE  UNC   INFOR
ALTAR  OUSTS  RNA
 DOWNATTHEHEELS
BONA  RITES  CRIP
REEK  KNELT  RENE
ORSE  SERFS  USED
```

158

```
CUBA  ACHE  FALLS
ATEM  MOOG  APIAN
MAHAGONNY  LENYA
PHONO  TAPES  DEC
 LADYINTHEDARK
HOD  SEN   STR
ACES  LUAU  TASTE
THREEPENNYOPERA
ESSEX  SIDE  EROS
  ICE   EAN  ANT
SEPTEMBERSONG
AXE  LIANA  ROLFE
VIRAL  KURTWEILL
ELIDE  ERMA  LOAM
DELED  REST  SSTS
```

159

```
FALSE  ALOHA  SRS
ELECT  PATON  TIN
ISAACNEWTON  EGO
NORM  ORLOP  AVOW
  PAUSE  LITERS
BAAING  STAMEN
LTD  DAISY  MAJOR
EMANATE  PROMOTE
WOMAN  SNEER  BOA
 ASTUTE  TASSEL
CENTER  SWILL
LADY  SATAN  AMOS
ARE  WILLIAMTELL
MTV  ANDES  CELLO
SHE  YEAST  IDTAG
```

160

```
REED  SENSE  ABBA
AVER  CLOWN  SLUM
ZEROMOSTEL  PALE
ELOPER  HEADINGS
  PEPSI  RICK
LOCATION  GASSED
IRIS  ORGIES  TRA
TIPS   TIN   CARR
HEH  LIANAS  ARON
OLEFIN  CLIPPERS
 ROAN  OLLAS
OPTIMISM  ETUDES
HOES  NOMANSLAND
NEXT  GHOST  EDDA
OTTS  SONES  SASK
```

161

```
DORS  WRAP  PIZZA
EDIE  HALO  IDIOM
COLDMINER  TONNE
AULAIT  STAB  EEN
FLENSED  ANON
  CHILLYSAUCE
FEEL  ORE  SITON
URGE  TENDS  LAND
JIGGS  DAH  SHES
ICYITALLNOW
 TOGA  AVAILED
AKA  PEND  ENDIVE
DEBUG  COOLDESAC
DELTA  ELLE  ALDO
SLEEP  REED  LEER
```

162

```
PAPA  AMENS  POKE
ACES  RELET  OBIS
STOPPINGBYWOODS
TANCREDI  LAREDO
ASSAI  INRED
  SUN  OSSICLE
JAR  OFGAB  BOOR
ONASNOWYEVENING
ANNE  AEROS  LEO
NOTWELL  TWP
 CALIF  RINSE
STJOHN  GRAINIER
THEROADNOTTAKEN
LOSE  IRISH  NOTE
OUTS  SYSTS  ENOS
```

163

```
BASH  DING  IMAGE
ORCA  OREO  NOMAD
WEOWELOWE   CRAZE
ENO VON  SWEETEN
RAPPER  COHN
   ONETONESTONE
ABLE SON  TERROR
LOOTS  ATE  DEANS
SLUICE  ESS  ALOE
OLDCOLDSCOLD
   THAT  LESTER
CALLSIN  AVE  EVA
AXIOM  ISSISISIS
FENCE  SKIN  SLAP
ELTON  HANG  MANY
```

164

```
OSCAR   ELS  LITH
LEANON  LEI  ASEA
IMNOTYOUNG   ITLL
VIA  SEASON  CHET
ETRE   FIRST  AVE
SEDUCTIVE  ASTIR
   DOUSE  CLOSES
 ENOUGH  TOKNOW
STERNS  SERTA
CARAT  TUNAONRYE
RIV  STRAD  TEAM
ILIA  RAVENS  FRI
BEER  EVERYTHING
ERST  EEL  COOLER
SSTS  SLY  WILDE
```

165

```
BEEFY  DEBT  LAKE
ADELA  ARLO  OXEN
LILAC  REIN  OLDS
ITSWHENITTAKES
   ETS  HOPI
LARD  CAKE  INGLE
AMA  WORN  DETAIL
LONGERTORECOVER
AUGUST  LIFE  ETO
WRENS  SLOE  PLOY
   GOAT  CAR
 THANTOGETTIRED
JOAD  ALOT  BOOLA
ANTI  RIGA  ARMED
BEEN  IDOL  TYPEA
```

166

```
SETH  THIGH  SHAW
AQUA  HOWIE  KALE
CURRIERANDDIVES
KINDNESS  GETOUT
   CANE  DECOCTS
BOWANDDARROW
RAISE  INOR  LIZ
ITCH  TUROW  FIDO
TSK  HATE  AARON
 CAKESANDDALE
NATURES  CEDE
OMERTA  KIELBASA
HEAVENANDDEARTH
OBOE  AVAIL  CIAO
WARD  PERCE  KATY
```

167

```
PATES  POOL  CUT
EVENT  ALIKE  ASA
COTTONBALLS  RUB
KNEEWORN  ASTRAL
   REMATCH  HOLE
ALBEDO  ROBOT
WOOD  ANIMISTIC
ONT  OTTOMAN  ONO
LETSLOOSE  APSE
 ODEON  SAMSON
EMMA  LEETIDE
TALKER  ARMORERS
URI  LOTTOPRIZES
DIN  MORAN  EGRET
ESE  OMIT  ROADS
```

168

```
WAS  ADAM  EDNAS
EMT  URDU  YEASTS
DOR  DAHS  ELYSEE
SEEDAGE  ABU  IAM
 BEECOMPLEX  SRI
 ATEIN  ALAE  TAT
   DTS  RIM  COTE
SPRAY  TON  DUNES
ARAY  TEL  PIE
REM  SEVE  LETGO
ASS  KAYERATION
WAH  ABE  HISPEED
AGOUTI  TOTO  TRI
KERNEL  ODED  HUD
 SNARL  VERA  ENO
```

169

```
C R E W ■ I N S E T ■ B E C K
H E R O ■ T O R R E ■ E L I E
E N G R ■ S T A R T E V E R Y
Z O O M L E N S ■ ■ F E N C E
■ H I L O ■ S A L L I E S
D A Y O F F W I T H A ■ ■
E X I L E ■ M O O T ■ B O A
L O P E ■ R E P A Y ■ R O B B
E N S ■ A O N E ■ A E R I E
■ S M I L E A N D G E T
W E A R I E D ■ D R N O ■
R A P I D ■ N I C O L A U S
I T O V E R W I T H ■ E T N A
T I R E ■ H A N O I ■ N E I L
E N T R ■ O H A R E ■ T E S T
```

170

```
S A A B ■ P E R C E ■ A T R I
O K R A ■ E Q U A L ■ C H A N
N I G H T N U R S E ■ T E T E
■ M O N A C O ■ T A P ■ M I R
■ ■ L E I L A ■ I D I O T
G A M A L ■ D I N N E R S ■
A H E R O ■ G E E ■ A F T
G O N E W I T H T H E W I N D
■ Y I N ■ C A T ■ G E T T O
■ N A C E L L E ■ G E S S O
D O W S E ■ L Y M A N ■
R A H ■ E A U ■ E R O T I C
I T I S ■ C L A R K G A B L E
F E T A ■ C A R G O ■ M A X I
T R E Y ■ T H I E F ■ E R I N
```

171

```
B O B ■ O G L E ■ B E N U M B
A R I ■ R E A M ■ R E A P E R
B E L L Y R U B ■ E E Y O R E
A L L I ■ M E L B A ■ N I T
■ Y M A ■ R E I D ■ M A T T
T Y C O B B ■ M A C R O ■
I A L ■ U R I ■ F R I S B E E
C L U E S I N ■ R U S S E L L
S U B S E T S ■ A M E ■ A S K
■ T R I A D ■ B R A C E S
R E N E ■ S N U B ■ S H H
E L O ■ H E N R I ■ A C A T
H O T T I P ■ B U Z Z B O M B
A P E R C U ■ A T O E ■ M I A
B E D A U B ■ R E D D ■ B R R
```

172

```
B A J A ■ A R R A Y ■ W I S H
A L U G ■ S A U T E ■ O N T O
R O G E T S T H E S A U R U S
K E G ■ S U E R ■ S I L E N T
■ E V E R S ■ B I R D ■
S P R I T E ■ V A R Y ■ H A L
M A N E S ■ M A T E ■ M O D E
I S A W E S A U H E S A W M E
T H U S ■ T I L E ■ O R D E R
H A T ■ W A N T ■ O N I O N Y
■ K I T E ■ B R I N Y ■
O N F I R E ■ Z I N C ■ O A F
B O R D E L A I S E S A U C E
E G A D ■ A C T O R ■ I D E A
Y O Y O ■ W H I N Y ■ M O S T
```

173

```
H I V E D ■ M A C ■ A L L O W
A G O R A ■ O F A ■ L E E C H
D O U N I F O R M S I N T H E
J R S ■ R E D O A K ■ I T O N
■ X Y Z ■ R Y A N ■
S P E E ■ C L O D S ■ E B B
C A R N E G I E ■ I T A L I A
A R M O R E D D I V I S I O N
L E A N O N ■ O V E R C A M E
D D S ■ S T O N E ■ O N E S
■ C E L L ■ P A T ■
S I S I ■ E D U C E S ■ T A U
I N C L U D E T A N K T O P S
A D A I R ■ S A G ■ E R A S E
M O R A L ■ T H Y ■ D A T E D
```

174

```
A G E N T ■ O D D S ■ A R L O
D A N A E ■ L O U T ■ L A I R
D R D R E ■ D R A I N T I L E
O N E I N A M I L L I O N ■
N E A T ■ T A S S E L ■ C O W
S T R A I T S ■ S O O T H
■ M U T I S M ■ R A T A
T W O L A N E B L A C K T O P
H O N E ■ E R M I N E ■
R E P I N ■ C I N E M A S
U S A ■ O X T A I L ■ T O R A
■ T H R E E O N A M A T C H
S T R O M B E R G ■ A L O H A
P R O W ■ E T T U ■ A I R E R
Y E L L ■ C H A P ■ M A S S A
```

175

R	O	L	F	E			S	L	A	P			A	J	A	R
O	D	I	U	M			R	A	S	A			M	A	X	I
T	E	N	T	O			S	P	Y	S	G	I	R	L	S	
S	A	T	U	R	N			P	E	T	E			S	E	E
			R	Y	E	S			T	A	R					
C	A	F	E			P	O	I			A	W	A	K	E	
A	C	U	T			A	R	N	E			R	O	L	E	S
T	H	R	E	E	L	E	G	G	E	D	R	A	Y	S	
C	O	O	N	S			R	O	B	B			S	M	E	E
H	O	R	S	T				D	D	E			T	O	S	S
				A	T	E			F	R	E	Q				
E	L	F			T	A	X	I			T	R	U	I	S	M
S	E	I	Z	E	F	I	R	E			N	A	N	C	E	
S	A	V	E			F	L	A	N			S	I	L	A	S
E	K	E	D			Y	E	N	S			T	S	A	R	S

176

C	H	I	S			P	O	S	E	D			A	P	S	E
L	A	S	T			A	D	L	A	I			R	O	A	N
A	L	S	O			R	E	A	R	M			L	O	U	D
S	O	U	R	G	R	A	P	E	S			O	H	T	O	
S	E	E	Y	A					D	U	D			P	E	R
Y	D	S			B	E	A	M			M	A	J	O	R	S
			O	F	F	D	A	Y			N	O	O	N	E	
M	A	K	E	S	O	M	E	O	F	T	H	E				
A	R	I	L	S			S	A	L	V	O	S				
S	P	R	A	T	S			S	P	A	R			S	K	I
H	E	B			S	O	P				T	W	E	E	N	
C	A	R	S			B	E	S	T	W	H	I	N	E	S	
A	N	A	P			E	S	T	A	R			P	O	P	E
N	U	K	E			I	C	A	M	E			E	R	I	C
S	T	E	W			T	I	T	A	N			R	A	N	T

177

C	A	L			C	R	E	S	T	S			C	A	R	P
A	D	O			L	A	C	T	I	C			A	M	E	R
M	A	R	I	O	C	U	O	M	O			P	A	S	O	
E	M	E	R	G	E			R	E	U	P			P	U	P
R	A	T	E			P	E	R	R	Y	C	O	M	O		
A	N	T			R	O	A	D			R	O	L	E	S	
S	T	A	R	I	N	G			C	H	A	R	A	D	E	
			E	C	C	E			H	O	M	O				
P	E	R	C	H	E	D			I	M	I	T	A	T	E	
I	M	E	T	A			A	C	E	D			L	I	D	
M	A	J	O	R	D	O	M	O				B	A	R	I	
E	N	O			D	U	M	P			M	A	U	M	E	T
N	U	I	T			D	O	E	S	A	P	R	O	M	O	
T	E	C	H			E	R	R	A	T	A			D	E	R
O	L	E	O			S	E	E	D	E	R			E	N	S

178

B	A	C	H			D	E	A	F			S	N	A	P	S
E	L	L	A			I	N	C	A			Q	U	I	E	T
N	I	E	T	Z	S	C	H	E			U	L	T	R	A	
T	E	A	C	U	P			R	E	E	L	S	I	N		
			H	B	O			D	O	S	E					
N	E	A			I	S	P	I	E	T	Z	S	C	H	E	
O	R	D	I	N	A	L	S			E	T	H	A	N		
H	I	L	T			L	Y	C	R	A			L	I	L	T
O	C	A	L	A			A	P	P	R	O	V	E	R		
W	H	I	L	E	S	A	R	T	R	E			E	S	E	
			R	U	D	D			E	A	T					
A	R	T	F	O	R	M			S	T	O	A	T	S		
G	U	R	U	S			I	S	S	M	A	R	T	R	E	
A	L	A	M	O			T	O	T	O			S	T	E	W
R	E	P	E	L			S	O	L	I			O	N	E	S

179

S	H	E	L	F			A	L	T	A			O	T	I	S
L	A	M	A	R			L	A	I	D			S	A	S	E
O	V	I	N	E			U	V	E	A			I	K	O	N
P	E	G	G	E	D	M	A	R	G	A	R	E	T			
E	A	R			F	U	N			E	L	I	S	H	A	
S	T	E	P	A	S	I	D	E			A	S	T	E	R	
			A	L	T			A	L	S			E	R	A	
	B	I	L	L	E	D	W	I	L	L	I	A	M			
M	R	S			R	O	N			E	O	N				
M	A	N	N	A			A	S	S	I	S	T	I	N	G	
E	N	T	E	R	S			A	G	T			S	E	A	
	C	H	U	C	K	E	D	C	H	A	R	L	E	S	
T	H	O	R			U	T	A	H			R	E	A	D	S
H	E	M	O			N	O	D	E			T	I	T	L	E
E	D	E	N			K	N	O	T			S	N	E	E	R

180

C	A	E	N			P	A	S	O			P	R	O	S	
O	G	L	E			C	A	C	H	P	H	R	A	S	E	
Q	U	A	D	R	A	I	C	E	Q	U	A	I	O	N	
	A	L	B	I	N	O					H	E	L	L	O	
	E	P	A			R	O	B			R	A	E	R		
T	R	E	A			P	E	A	B	O	G	S				
S	O	F	T	C			N	A	T	E	R			A	R	M
P	O	L	Y	U	N	S	A	U	R	A	E	D	F	A	
S	K	A			G	O	U	T	S			E	X	U	D	E
			M	A	U	R	A	E	S			P	E	S	O	
M	O	T	A			N	E	S			E	T	A			
A	G	E	N	T				S	T	E	R	N	O			
G	R	E	A	E	X	P	E	C	T	A	I	O	N	S	
D	E	T	E	R	I	O	R	A	E			A	R	E	E	
A	S	H	E			S	W	A	S			E	I	L	A	

181

```
S O F I A ■ M O N A ■ S I C K
K H A K I ■ E L E M ■ T O R I
A I D E R ■ R O A N ■ A W O L
T O E ■ S T I F L E A Y A W N
■ S H O T ■ ■ S P E N D S
S T U P O R ■ S P I E D ■ ■
T H R O W A S P E A R ■ A N S
E A S T ■ A I T ■ D R A T
P T A ■ S I G N A T R E A T Y
■ A I M E E ■ R A M B L E
A L U M N A ■ E O N S ■
B I T I N G P E S T S ■ G I T
A V I D ■ I L E S ■ A L I N E
S E C S ■ N E N E ■ C O L T S
E R A T ■ E D Y S ■ K U D O S
```

182

```
E G G ■ T R I A D ■ M E S A
N I A ■ B R O N T E ■ O N E S
D J S A L I N G E R ■ P T A S
E A T S U P ■ A E S ■ A W E
A N O S E ■ F B S K I N N E R
R E N ■ L A R U E ■ R O G E T
■ S A N E R ■ O L D S
■ G P W O D E H O U S E
L I R A ■ T A B L E ■ ■
I C A N T ■ S T I E S ■ B E D
M E F O R S T E R ■ T I L D E
E F T ■ A H A ■ G E T O U T
A L I T ■ E T L A W R E N C E
D O N A ■ B E I G E S ■ D E C
E E G S ■ A D D O N ■ E S T
```

183

```
B O L O ■ V I A L ■ E K I N G
E M I L ■ I S N O ■ N O S E E
T O O M U C H O F ■ S W I N E
H O N E S T ■ S T R U T T E D
■ C H O R E ■ C R O
Q U E S E R A ■ M A E W E S T
U R N ■ R I N K Y ■ D E L T A
E I N E ■ A G O O D ■ D I O N
S A U N A ■ E P P I E ■ A O K
T H I N G I S ■ I S L A N D S
■ O N T ■ G A L A S ■
L A M B A S T E ■ O T T A W A
E X U L T ■ W O N D E R F U L
A L L E E ■ A D O G ■ O R S K
D E E D S ■ S E V E ■ S O S A
```

184

```
H A U L ■ H I D E ■ L I B R A
A N N O ■ A T O M ■ O B O E S
G O L D E N A G E ■ Y E L P S
G R A Z E D ■ G R E A T D A Y
L A C ■ N B A ■ G A L ■ F I R
E K E S ■ A L G E R ■ L A N I
■ O L L I E ■ D I C T A
■ Q U A L I T Y T I M E ■
B O U N D ■ I M H I P ■
E N I D ■ W I N C E ■ S L A G
L E X ■ B O D ■ A P T ■ E R E
G O O D Y E A R ■ I R O N O N
I N T E L ■ H A P P Y H O U R
U T I C A ■ O G R E ■ E R S E
M A C A W ■ S U E R ■ D E E S
```

185

```
W A D E ■ L L A M A ■ S C A T
O M E N ■ A L L E N ■ O H N O
L O S T A N D P R O F O U N D
F R I E N D ■ S T R I N G E D
■ R I F T ■ Z A G ■
J O B ■ L A W S ■ K A R A T E
A R E S ■ L E T S ■ R I V A L
C I R C U L A R P R O F I L E
K O R A N ■ K O L A ■ F A U N
S N A R L S ■ P I T H ■ N S A
■ A H A ■ T H U G ■
A R E A C O D E ■ B R U I S E
M I D T E R M P R O T E S T S
P O G O ■ T I E I N ■ S P A M
S T E M ■ S T E V E ■ T Y N E
```

186

```
H A S H ■ D E L V E ■ A P S E
O T T O ■ O N E I L ■ G R A F
T H E G L O V E S A R E O F F
T E E T E R ■ R I T A ■ T A U
U N L I N K S ■ T E T H E R S
B A S E ■ N A S ■ S T O G I E
■ B O N U S ■ A L E S
■ P A Y B A C K T I M E ■
■ R E N A ■ A R I E L ■
G U N G H O ■ E E L ■ C O R M
L I N E A G E ■ D E S I R E R
I N A ■ I R M A ■ V A N I S H
N O M O R E M R N I C E G U Y
D U E T ■ S E M I S ■ M I L D
A S S T ■ S T Y L E ■ A N T E
```

187

```
P E R T # P S H A W # J O L T
A X E R # A N I S E # A B O Y
T E N O R S A C K S # R S V P
O U T L O O K # F T S # T E E
I N A L L # E C O # O V A # #
S T L # F L O O R W H A C K S
# # # S E E I N # H O L L E R
D E M I # E L I D E # V E G A
E D I T O R # C E L I E # # #
L U X U R Y T A C K S # T B S
# E P A # A L I # L O R R E #
O D D # L A B # P L A T O O N
O R B S # T O T H E M A C K S
Z E A L # R O U E N # R H E E
E D G Y # A S T R O # Y E N S
```

188

```
P A U L # A L A W # P L E B E
A N N E # L A L A # R I V A L
S O C I A L D A R W I N I S M
T I L # S E I S M I C # L S T
E N O # E N D # U N E # D I R
L T G O V # A M P S # H O S E
# # # R E O # O T T # B E T E
# P A R T Y P O O P E R # #
S I L L # H E E # N R A # #
O P U S # E S S A # E M B E D
F A N # D L I # G A S # R I M
A N G # E L K H A R T # A L I
B E E I N O N E S B O N N E T
E M I R S # O R S O # O D E R
D A N S E # W E I R # T O N I
```

189

```
C L O G S # O L E S # J I F F
H O V E L # D E B T # E D I E
A G A N A # O V E R # D O N E
D E L I V E R Y R E V I L E D
# # # E E L # T A I # # #
C B S # S E M I # M O S T E L
H O P I # N O D E # L O R R E
E R O S S A W I W A S S O R E
S N O O P # N O E L # A T O Z
T E N N I S # T R I G # S R A
# # # R I A # E O S # # #
P A R T O N D I D N O T R A P
O M A R # K O B E # G R A V E
P A C E # E R I N # O A T E S
S T Y X # R E S T # O P A R T
```

190

```
F E A R # M A S H # M A N S E
A L P O # A G U E # I D E A L
R I O T # R E B A # M A U N A
# A P O L L O # P R O G R A M
# # O O F S # O S E # #
U P B O W # # I S A # R C A
# S H I P E A R T H # B A R I
M A Y A S # D E I # S O B E R
A G T S # W A T C H T H I S #
N E E # E A R # E A R N S #
# # A V A # C A L I # #
# T I M E C O N T I N U U M #
O I L E R # P O O P # K N I T
U P S E T # E T N A # E I R E
T S A R S # D E E D # S T Y X
```

191

```
A L A # L E S # F O E # M U M
D E S T I N E # I N S H A P E
S O S U E M E # S T A I N E R
# # G U E S T H O U S I N G #
S P A # S T O W # # S A D E
E I G H T H O U R D A Y # # #
A L L A N # # R A N T # M C I
T O E L O O P # P A Y L O A D
O T T # T R U E # O U T R E
# # D E E P T H O U G H T S
A G R I # T O O N # # S E T
G R A N D C E N T R A L # #
L I V E D I N # T A P I N T O
O P E R A N T # E M P T I E D
W E D # Y E S # A P T # L E D
```

192

```
B L U F F S # B A B B A G E
R E S O U N D # A B R A D E D
I N E R R O R # R O U N D E D
D A D D Y W A R B U C K S # #
A P T # # W A I T E # U F O
L E O # R A N G E # W I P E R
# # K I W I S # # S A N T E E
M O H I C A N # F L Y R O D S
A P A T H Y # M A I N E # #
D E L H I # F O R T E # S E T
E L F # E R R O L # # O N E
# S C R O O G E M C D U C K
B O O H I S S # F O R E S A W
I L L I C I T # T H E R E S A
B E E C H E S # S E N D E R
```

193

S	N	O	B		P	O	P	P	A		B	U	S	S
H	I	K	E		A	U	R	A	L		E	P	E	E
O	N	I	T		S	T	O	R	K		E	T	N	A
W	E	N	E	V	E	R	S	A	Y	I	T	I	S	
E	V	A		I	O	U		D	O	L	L	A	R	
R	E	W	A	X		N	O	R		S	E	T	T	O
S	H	A	D	E	S		S	A	C		S	E	E	
		O	N	L	Y	A	G	A	M	E				
H	U	G		Y	A	K		B	A	R	E	S	T	
I	N	U	R	E		P	A	D		Y	E	N	T	A
C	A	N	O	N	S		A	R	A		T	E	N	
	I	F	W	E	A	R	E	W	I	N	N	I	N	G
A	R	I	A		Y	A	R	D	S		O	T	T	O
B	E	R	N		S	T	I	L	E		A	L	O	E
O	D	E	S		O	A	K	E	N		H	E	R	D

194

R	O	W	E	D		R	A	S	P		Q	U	I	T
I	M	A	G	E		E	M	I	R		U	N	D	O
B	O	X	O	F	C	H	O	C	O	L	A	T	E	S
S	O	Y		E	R	A	S		C	A	R	O	M	S
			T	A	O	S		S	E	N	T			
H	E	A	R	T	S	H	A	P	E	D		N	A	B
A	R	G	U	E	S		M	A	D		H	O	M	E
Z	O	N	E	D		C	A	R		T	E	P	I	D
E	D	E	R		N	O	T		A	R	I	A	N	E
L	E	W		C	U	P	I	D	S	A	R	R	O	W
		J	U	R	Y		R	I	P	S				
O	S	I	E	R	S		S	O	A	P		E	B	B
S	T	V	A	L	E	N	T	I	N	E	S	D	A	Y
L	O	A	N		R	E	A	D		R	H	E	T	T
O	W	N	S		Y	E	N	S		S	E	N	S	E

195

T	O	M	B	S		O	P	E	D		M	A	R	S
O	B	E	A	H		P	O	R	E		A	L	O	U
D	O	W	J	O	N	E	S	A	V	E	R	A	G	E
D	E	L	A	W	A	R	E		E	N	V	I	E	D
			M	I	A		A	L	D	E	N	T	E	
N	O	R	M	A	L	S	C	H	O	O	L			
A	T	H	E	N	S		E	S	P	N		B	O	K
P	I	E	T		F	L	O		M	O	N	A		
A	S	A		T	E	A	L		S	M	O	O	T	H
		B	O	S	T	O	N	C	O	M	M	O	N	
A	C	C	E	P	T	S		E	A	R				
C	L	A	M	O	R		S	P	L	O	S	H	E	D
R	E	G	U	L	A	R	P	A	Y	C	H	E	C	K
E	R	E	S		D	E	A	L		C	A	R	O	N
S	K	Y	E		A	N	T	I		O	D	D	L	Y

196

J	U	L		M	P	S		R	A	N	A	T
O	N	O		O	A	H	U		S	O	N	O	M	A
B	E	W	A	R	Y	O	F		C	U	T	U	P	S
	A	N	Y	O	N	E	W	H	O	G	I	V	E	S
S	T	E	R	N	E		A	L	E		E	R	E	
R	E	C		P	I	N	A		G	A	E	L		
A	N	K	L	E		E	N	O	R	M	O	U	S	
		Y	O	U	A	D	V	I	C	E				
	C	R	O	S	S	T	I	E		D	R	I	E	D
R	O	A	N		U	B	E	R		N	Y	U		
O	C	T		O	R	O		A	B	A	S	E	D	
T	H	A	T	B	E	G	I	N	S	W	I	T	H	
A	L	T	A	I	R		B	E	W	A	R	Y	O	F
R	E	A	L	E	S		M	E	A	N		L	O	O
Y	A	T	E	S		D	N	A		E	K	E		

197

A	T	O	Z		S	E	L	E	S		P	R	O	D
M	A	X	I		A	T	I	L	T		R	E	N	O
A	D	E	N		F	A	T	H	A		O	L	E	O
	A	N	N	I	E	L	E	I	B	O	V	I	T	Z
		I	N	R	I		D	E	C	O	Y			
R	E	B	A	G		I	M	A	G	E	R			
O	C	A	S	E	Y		A	L	L	A	B	U	Z	Z
M	O	N		A	N	I	T	A		S	I	E		
A	L	C	A	T	R	A	Z		M	C	C	A	N	N
		V	E	N	T	E	D		O	R	F	E	O	
Q	U	E	E	N		A	R	N	E					
A	V	A	N	T	G	A	R	D	E	J	A	Z	Z	
T	U	T	U		A	C	I	D	S		K	I	E	V
A	L	A	E		T	A	N	Y	A		E	T	R	E
R	A	T	S		E	N	D	O	W		D	I	O	R

198

B	L	A	R	E		O	R	B	S		D	A	M	P
B	A	Y	E	D		R	E	E	K		E	S	A	U
C	I	N	C	I	N	N	A	T	I		S	T	I	R
			T	E	A	L		T	B	I	R	D	S	
A	L	S	O		A	T	I	T		A	R	O	S	E
P	E	E	R	P	R	E	S	S	U	R	E			
H	O	R	S	E		M	A	N	N		R	C	A	
I	N	F	O	R	C	E		R	O	O	T	O	U	T
D	E	S		S	Y	N	C		N	E	W	T	S	
	F	I	D	D	L	E	D	E	E	D	E	E		
F	A	I	R	S		O	O	N	A		M	Y	R	A
I	N	N	A	T	E		S	T	U	N				
E	D	A	M		B	E	E	R	B	A	R	R	E	L
L	I	N	E		B	R	I	E		P	A	U	L	A
D	E	E	D		S	A	N	E		A	N	T	I	C

199

```
EAST  SWAMP  STAB
RULE  LAKER  TAXI
EGAN  ARISE  ACID
CUTDOWNTOSIGHS
TRYON   ANSA
   NEVE    MANNA
LET  BATTHEBRIES
AQUA  SCROD  KNOT
PURPLEHAYES  ENO
PINTO    ANEW
    EDAM   GASPE
THEWIZARDOFAHS
JAIL  TUNER  EDIT
UCLA  CRONE  RILE
GOON  HEROD  SEER
```

200

```
LILAC   TOMB   OMEN
IRABU   OMAR   NOVO
BERET  WISEACRES
ENGLISHTEALEONI
LEE  ETE  RDA  STE
SSS  PIETA   REEFS
   BIN  ATT  GLUT
GREEKOLIVEOYL
PLED  OUI   STS
AIDES  TATER  JLO
IMF  HAS  BTU  OAT
SPANISHMOSSHART
ASCENSION  CONDE
NEED  ANNE  ASNER
ODDS  YEAS  NEARS
```

201

```
BESIEGER  EMMETT
OVERRATE  TOOTHY
WEWONDER  OUCHES
IRENE   OBIS  ITO
ETRE  HOWELSECAN
   DEAL  DEER
ALA  SLAP   ASTA
BIRDSOFAFEATHER
SEMI    LIMP  YET
   SURE  DIEM
FLOCKIFNOT  ONES
AOK  ASTO  STOVE
UPROSE  TOGETHER
NEARER  SHELLING
ASSESS  OMELETTE
```

202

```
LABS   DAHL   MEMOS
ELEC   AGEE   ALANA
TARO   RUIN   RECAP
SMARTCARD   IMAN
GOTNO    LEN   RDS
OSE  WHOS  RETOOL
   LEAKAGE   INFO
INTELLIGENTLIFE
NOUN  TEAROUT
STROVE  SEWN  SRA
TAN   ERS   IMPEL
   RITE  WISECRACK
MITER   IDES   BRAY
AZURE   SEAS   ITLL
TEPID   HALE   GALS
```

203

```
SAIL  PSHAW  CHAR
KITE  RAISE  HIRE
IRONOUTTHEKINKS
   SANITY  OLDIE
RIM  TERI   CLINT
USAGE   ENOCH
MAYORS  GOO  THAI
BABESINTHEWOODS
ACES  RAH  DISMAL
   JETER   THEME
ATSEA   LECH  SST
PRANK   PIGLET
PUTTERINGAROUND
LEER  MCKAY  AVON
EDDY  NOSES  DADA
```

204

```
SPARS  LAMB   GOBS
WOMAN  USER   RARE
ATONE  CITI   IKEA
THREEYEARS  DRAG
HETERO    ITS  IDA
ERS  AGOICOULDNT
    STAID  LEAGUE
CASE   LID   SETS
ALTAIR  OOMPH
SPELLAUTHOR  CAP
TAN  LIT   NOMORE
ICON  NOWIAREONE
RIPE  SPIN  ALLOW
ONAN  OINK  TOILE
NODE  NAGY  ANODE
```

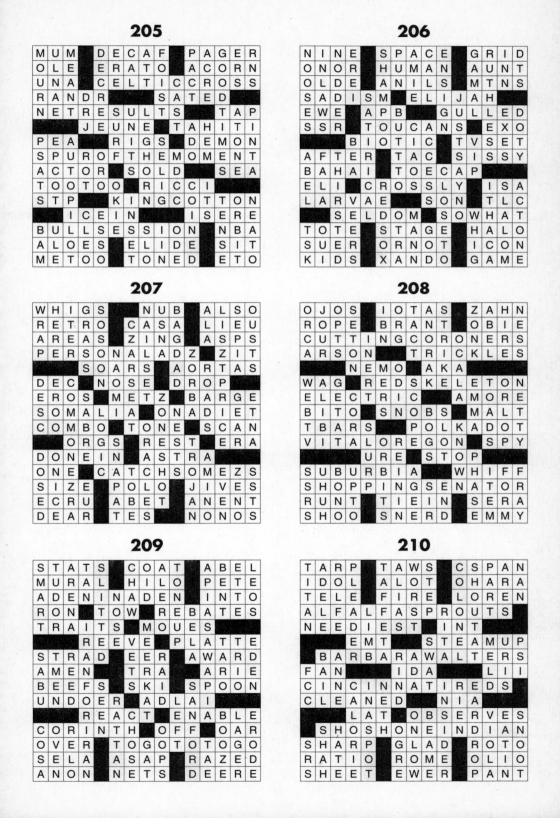

205

```
M U M   D E C A F   P A G E R
O L E   E R A T O   A C O R N
U N A   C E L T I C C R O S S
R A N D R     S A T E D
N E T R E S U L T S     T A P
    J E U N E   T A H I T I
P E A   R I G S   D E M O N
S P U R O F T H E M O M E N T
A C T O R   S O L D     S E A
T O O T O O   R I C C I
S T P   K I N G C O T T O N
  I C E I N       I S E R E
B U L L S E S S I O N   N B A
A L O E S   E L I D E   S I T
M E T O O   T O N E D   E T O
```

206

```
N I N E   S P A C E   G R I D
O N O R   H U M A N   A U N T
O L D E   A N I L S   M T N S
S A D I S M   E L I J A H
E W E   A P B     G U L L E D
S S R   T O U C A N S   E X O
    B I O T I C   T V S E T
A F T E R   T A C   S I S S Y
B A H A I   T O E C A P
E L I   C R O S S L Y   I S A
L A R V A E   S O N   T L C
    S E L D O M   S O W H A T
T O T E   S T A G E   H A L O
S U E R   O R N O T   I C O N
K I D S   X A N D O   G A M E
```

207

```
W H I G S   N U B   A L S O
R E T R O   C A S A   L I E U
A R E A S   Z I N G   A S P S
P E R S O N A L A D Z   Z I T
    S O A R S   A O R T A S
D E C   N O S E   D R O P
E R O S   M E T Z   B A R G E
S O M A L I A   O N A D I E T
C O M B O   T O N E   S C A N
  O R G S   R E S T   E R A
D O N E I N   A S T R A
O N E   C A T C H S O M E Z S
S I Z E   P O L O   J I V E S
E C R U   A B E T   A N E N T
D E A R   T E S   N O N O S
```

208

```
O J O S   I O T A S   Z A H N
R O P E   B R A N T   O B I E
C U T T I N G C O R O N E R S
A R S O N   T R I C K L E S
    N E M O   A K A
W A G   R E D S K E L E T O N
E L E C T R I C   A M O R E
B I T O   S N O B S   M A L T
T B A R S   P O L K A D O T
V I T A L O R E G O N   S P Y
    U R E   S T O P
S U B U R B I A   W H I F F
S H O P P I N G S E N A T O R
R U N T   T I E I N   S E R A
S H O O   S N E R D   E M M Y
```

209

```
S T A T S   C O A T   A B E L
M U R A L   H I L O   P E T E
A D E N I N A D E N   I N T O
R O N   T O W   R E B A T E S
T R A I T S   M O U E S
  R E E V E   P L A T T E
S T R A D   E E R   A W A R D
A M E N   T R A   A R I E
B E E F S   S K I   S P O O N
U N D O E R   A D L A I
  R E A C T   E N A B L E
C O R I N T H   O F F   O A R
O V E R   T O G O T O T O G O
S E L A   A S A P   R A Z E D
A N O N   N E T S   D E E R E
```

210

```
T A R P   T A W S   C S P A N
I D O L   A L O T   O H A R A
T E L E   F I R E   L O R E N
A L F A L F A S P R O U T S
N E E D I E S T   I N T
    E M T   S T E A M U P
  B A R B A R A W A L T E R S
F A N   I D A     L I I
C I N C I N N A T I R E D S
C L E A N E D   N I A
    L A T   O B S E R V E S
  S H O S H O N E I N D I A N
S H A R P   G L A D   R O T O
R A T I O   R O M E   O L I O
S H E E T   E W E R   P A N T
```

211

```
B K I T E   A P U     S H O E B
C O C O A   P E P     A M P L E
A L E U T   E A R E D S E A L
R A S P   B S C O R E   R I D
    E E L   O A R   W A N E
I R R E G U L A R   H A T E R
N E E   O N I T   M A L I
B O F F I C E   B A L L O T B
  L U S H   B I T S   N A E
B R E S T   P R O C E S S O R
R A C E   B O O   H Y P
E M T   M U S I C B   A L O T
A S I R E C A L L   P R I M O
D E V I L   D E E   E S S A Y
B S E A T   A R F   G E A R B
```

212

```
W A N N A   B A E Z   I C E S
A S I A N   L I N A   D A M P
R I G H T H A N D P R O P E R
N T H   S E N T   S A T I R E
  W T S   A C H E   N O T I E
S E C O N D H A N D G O A L
A R A B Y   E Y E D
P E P S U P       S C A M P I
      B R A C   O N E O N
  O F F H A N D R U N N I N G
S N A R E   A D O S   A N Y
O L D I E S   O W E S   H T S
F I E L D H A N D S T R E A M
A N I L   A N T E   A E R I E
S E N S   M O O D   B E R L E
```

213

```
S I L A S   A L F A   R I L E
K N E L T   R I A L   E D E N
I F Y O U W A N T L I F E T O
R U D E   A C E   C R A S S
T S E   G R A M E R C Y
S E N O R   R A R E   A S A
    B E G I N A T F O R T Y
A W E I G H     C A N C A N
D O N T G O E I G H T Y
D O E   S A G A   E X A M S
  P E T U N I A S   T A P
E T H E L     O T T   D O R A
W H E N Y O U R E T W E N T Y
E R I C   U S E R   H E C H E
S U R E   R O D S   O R E A D
```

214

```
W A S H   W O R E     P I T Y
E T T E   A S E A   C A C A O
T H E M I S S U S   U P E N N
N O W I N P A P E R B A C K
A M E N D   S U E   L A N
P E D   I D A   P O P C O R N
    S A U N A   C L A U D E
N O T I N T H E C A R D S
B O N I N G   S A U C E
C L E R K E D   T R E   U B I
D O T   O R A   B I S O N
  N O D I N A G R E E M E N T
A G O R A   P O I N T E D T O
L E N I N   E G G Y   A T O N
P R E P   S O S A   N O N E
```

215

```
A S T A   T A M E R   G O G O
G L I B   A M I L E   A R I D
R O T S   C A C H E   L E N D
I T H I N K H A I L T O
P H E N O L     A S T I R
  T H E C H I E F H A S A
T A C H   H A S N T   P A N
O P I E   C A R L O   M E A T
O R R   E L I D E   A R C S
N I C E R I N G T O I T
S L A N G     P O I S E D
  J O H N F K E N N E D Y
E C H O   A A R O N   E L A N
B U O Y   S T A K E   E M M E
B E E S   H O N O R   S A S S
```

216

```
S P A S   S C H W A   M A R T
P U T T   A H O O T   A R E A
A S H Y   T A B O O   C M D R
C H E X O U T O F R E H A B
E E N   M P S     L O G I N
D R A M A     L A T S   N R A
  A N O M A L Y   E A C H
K I X I T U P A N O T C H
M I N I   T R I S E C T
A L F   W O K S     T U L I P
E L E N A   A P E   O N E
  T R I X O F T H E T R A D E
J I N N   A L I E N   A T O P
A M A N   R O D A N   S H O E
R E L Y   S E E D Y   H E R D
```

217

E	L	G	A	R		M	A	G	N	A			T	B	A
L	E	A	S	E		A	P	R	I	L			I	O	N
F	I	R	S	T	S	T	R	I	K	E		G	L	O	
		I	R	E			T	E	E	T	H	E	R		
C	O	N	S	O	N	A	N	T	S		A	T	R	A	
U	N	I	T		I	S	A	Y		I	T	S	O	K	
B	I	G	S	H	O	T	S		L	A	I	C			
E	T	H		O	R	A	C	L	E	S		R	O	D	
		T	A	P	S		E	S	T	I	M	A	T	E	
P	A	S	S	E		A	N	A	S		E	P	I	C	
A	R	C	H		B	O	T	T	L	E	N	E	C	K	
S	C	H	E	M	E	R		I	T	O					
T	A	O		C	A	T	C	H	P	H	R	A	S	E	
O	N	O		I	D	A	H	O		O	A	S	I	S	
R	E	L		I	S	L	E	T		S	H	A	R	P	

218

S	O	R	E		A	T	D	A	W	N		T	S	P
E	R	A	S		B	E	R	T	H	A		O	Y	L
N	A	H	S		A	C	E	T	I	C		L	S	U
S	C	R	E	E	C	H	I	N	G	H	A	L	T	
O	L	A		L	I	I			S	O	R	R	E	L
R	E	H	A	B		E	M	O		S	L	O	M	O
		V	O	L		I	R	V		E	A	S	T	
	H	O	W	L	I	N	G	W	I	N	D			
I	M	A	C		D	O	C		S	H	E			
S	A	R	A	S		N	E	E		E	S	S	E	X
M	E	D	D	L	E		G	S	A		E	V	E	
	W	H	O	O	P	I	N	G	C	R	A	N	E	S
P	E	A		O	C	T	A	N	E		M	A	N	O
E	S	T		P	O	S	T	O	N		E	T	T	U
P	T	S		S	T	O	O	G	E		N	E	S	T

219

A	N	N	O		A	S	S	T		U	S	H	E	R
N	E	E	D		I	N	C	A		T	H	E	M	E
T	A	X	I		R	O	O	K		T	O	X	I	N
E	T	T	U	B	R	U	T	E		E	R	A	T	O
		M	O	A	T		T	O	R	T				
H	O	T		X	I	S	T	H	E		T	A	B	S
E	L	A	T	E	D		E	A	R		E	L	L	A
M	I	X	E	R		E	X	T		B	R	O	I	L
E	V	E	S		E	R	A		M	O	M	E	N	T
N	E	S	T		W	I	N	N	E	R		S	K	Y
		S	P	E	C		A	T	N	O				
D	E	C	C	A		I	N	T	H	E	W	A	S	H
D	R	O	O	P		D	O	T	O		E	X	P	O
A	G	O	R	A		L	I	E	D		N	L	E	R
Y	O	K	E	L		E	R	R	S		S	E	W	N

220

W	I	M	P	S		A	T	O	M		J	O	S	S
I	D	I	O	T		L	E	D	A		I	C	E	T
S	O	R	R	Y	I	A	X	E	D		G	A	V	E
P	L	O	P		L	I	T	R	E		G	L	E	E
		O	P	E	N	S		I	S	L	A	N	D	
A	C	T	I	O	N		E	R	I	E				
W	H	I	S	K	E	Y	F	L	A	X		B	B	C
A	I	M	E	E		A	A	H		L	E	R	O	I
G	A	S		M	U	L	T	I	T	A	X	I	N	G
		D	O	N	E		O	N	I	O	N	S		
Q	U	A	I	N	T		T	E	N	E	T			
U	R	G	E		A	B	O	V	O		P	A	D	S
A	S	I	S		M	A	X	O	F	Z	O	R	R	O
S	A	L	E		E	R	I	K		A	L	I	A	S
H	E	E	L		D	A	N	E		P	L	A	Y	A

221

B	E	T	A		M	A	I	N	E		A	R	A	B
O	N	E	R		A	R	D	O	R		D	E	M	O
S	Y	M	B	O	L	F	O	R	S	U	L	F	U	R
C	A	P	O	N			R	E	E	S	E			
		E	R	A		B	E	S	T	I	R	R	E	D
F	A	R	E	R		A	G	E	E					
E	R	A	T	O		H	O	T	N	U	M	B	E	R
A	C	T	U	P			N	E	E	D	Y			
T	H	E	M	E	S	O	N	G		S	T	A	I	N
		A	R	I	A		H	A	U	T	E			
R	E	F	A	S	T	E	N	S		O	P	T		
A	L	I	N	E			R	H	I	N	E			
C	O	N	T	R	A	C	T	I	O	N	O	F	I	S
E	P	E	E		H	O	A	R	D		R	U	N	S
S	E	S	S		A	G	R	E	E		S	L	O	E

222

O	C	U	L	I		H	A	R	P		A	D	D	S
W	A	T	E	R		A	G	H	A		N	O	O	K
L	L	A	N	O		V	E	E	R		T	O	N	Y
	C	H	A	N	G	E	S	A	T	T	I	R	E	
		B	A	N			T	A	C	K				
M	I	A	T	A	S		E	D	I	T		E	S	T
A	N	G	E	R		E	X	A	M		V	E	T	O
T	U	R	N	S	O	N	T	H	E	V	I	P	E	R
T	I	E	S		P	O	O	L		A	V	E	R	T
E	T	A		Y	E	L	L		B	L	A	R	E	S
		T	O	O	N		E	A	U					
	A	D	J	U	S	T	S	T	H	E	M	I	R	
A	R	E	A		L	A	T	H		D	O	R	I	S
S	L	A	Y		O	R	E	O		A	D	A	G	E
P	O	L	S		T	O	P	S		T	E	N	S	E

223

```
K I E V   · A S S N ·   M K T G
I N L E T   N E N E   · A E R O
A D O R E   T R E E   D Y E R
·   S L E E V E D   · E S S E
T A K E   K R A Z Y K A T ·
E R R S   E I N E · A B O U T
M R I   M O O T · O D E N S E
P A S T E U R · O N A T E A R
O N P O S T · A P E R · K B S
S T Y R O · S P E D · C O L E
·   K I N G K O N G · O P E R
O K R A · L I S T E N S
T E E M   O T T O · A S A M I
R E M O · V O L E · G E T I N
O N E S · E W E S · T E N K
```

224

```
P L U M P · S T E W · D I V A
G A T E S   T O D O   O L I N
A M I T Y · E R G O · Z I N G
·   B L A C K E Y E D P E A C E
·   H O P · S A N D E R
J E S T E R · S K Y E ·
E B A Y · A D I N · A M P E D
D O W N O N O N E S N I E C E
I N N E R · S U E T · L O O N
·   I C E S · E V E N L Y
S T E R N O · N A E ·
M Y D O G H A S F L E E C E
A L D O · E V I L · J I H A D
R E I N · R O T E · A R I S E
T R E E · E W E R · Y E N T L
```

225

```
S A W S · I P S O · M A S S E
A R I E · L O A M · A L T O S
N E N E · L O R E · N O I S E
C A N Y O U F I N D T E N ·
T W E A K S · S U R · K O S
U A R · A I D E · B A D B E T
M Y · S P O I L T · A U R A
·   T H I N G S W R O N G ·
L I E U · S E E I N G · P I
S W A T C H · S E N T · G U N
D O M · A A A · G O C A R T
·   W I T H T H I S P U Z L E
S H O D · A T A R I · P E O N
L O R E · H A L E D · I B I S
A N K A · A R O S E · D O N E
```

226

```
D W E E B · A J A R · C F O S
O H A R E · R E D O · S E N T
L A R G E B I R D O F P R E Y
E M S · G O O K · M E A N I E
·   E E L S · O M A N ·
T W O B E L O W P A R · T O M
I A M B S · E A T · W I F E
T R E E · E A G L E · H E F T
L E N D · G L O · B A U E R
E S S · F O O T B A L L P R O
·   F A M E · A G E E ·
S H E I L A · E N O S · N B A
T O P R A N K I N G S C O U T
U S E S · I O N E · E A R L E
B E E T · A P E D · D R A K E
```

227

```
R A P · S L A Y S · S T E I N
A C E · T O S E A · I G L O O
L T R · A C T A S · L I K U D
S U I T Y O U R S E L F ·
T A S K S · D O E R S · C N N
O T H O · R E F R Y · Z H O U
N E A · B E N T · B O A S T
·   B A R S T H E D O O R ·
A A L T O · E R I N · L A W
K I E V · S O M N I · P E L E
A R S · S O D O I · A I M E E
·   B U S I N E S S C A R D
A T A R I · S K E I N · G T O
D I G I N · T E L L A · N E U
Z E R O G · S Y S O P · E D T
```

228

```
M A K E · A L O O F · I H O P
A V I V · M E L B A · N U D E
G A R A G E S A L E · S M O G
M I O S I S · O R A T O R S
A L V I N · I G N I T E R ·
·   V O L T A G E S P I K E
A P S E · E L M · E S S A Y
A L P · M I L I T I A · T R E
R E E S E · E A T · S S T S
P A C K A G E S T O R E ·
·   T E N A N T S · A R I S E
A N A L Y S T · E Z I N E S
M I T T · M I D D L E A G E S
O T O E · E R R O L · L O D E
K E R R · N E S T S · S T Y X
```

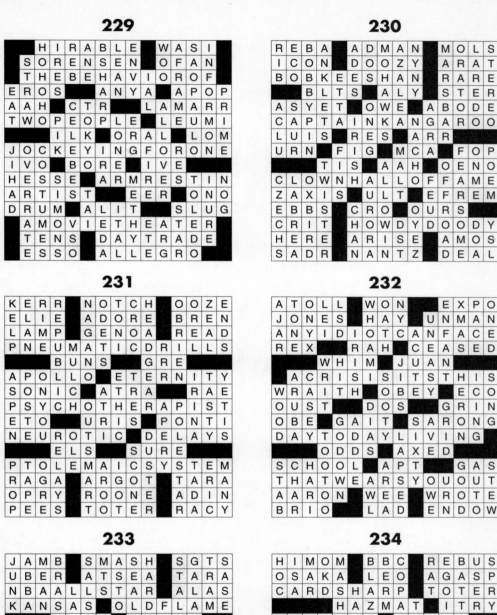

229

```
. H I R A B L E . W A S I .
. S O R E N S E N . O F A N .
. T H E B E H A V I O R O F .
E R O S . . A N Y A . A P O P
A A H . C T R . . L A M A R R
T W O P E O P L E . L E U M I
. . . I L K . O R A L . L O M
J O C K E Y I N G F O R O N E
I V O . B O R E . I V E . . .
H E S S E . A R M R E S T I N
A R T I S T . . E E R . O N O
D R U M . A L I T . . S L U G
. A M O V I E T H E A T E R .
. T E N S . D A Y T R A D E .
. E S S O . A L L E G R O .
```

230

```
R E B A . A D M A N . M O L S
I C O N . D O O Z Y . A R A T
B O B K E E S H A N . R A R E
. . B L T S . A L Y . S T E R
A S Y E T . O W E . A B O D E
C A P T A I N K A N G A R O O
L U I S . R E S . A R R . .
U R N . F I G . M C A . F O P
. . T I S . A A H . O E N O
C L O W N H A L L O F F A M E
Z A X I S . U L T . E F R E M
E B B S . C R O . O U R S .
C R I T . H O W D Y D O O D Y
H E R E . A R I S E . A M O S
S A D R . N A N T Z . D E A L
```

231

```
K E R R . N O T C H . O O Z E
E L I E . A D O R E . B R E N
L A M P . G E N O A . R E A D
P N E U M A T I C D R I L L S
. . . B U N S . . G R E .
A P O L L O . E T E R N I T Y
S O N I C . A T R A . R A E
P S Y C H O T H E R A P I S T
E T O . U R I S . P O N T I
N E U R O T I C . D E L A Y S
. . . E L S . S U R E . .
P T O L E M A I C S Y S T E M
R A G A . A R G O T . T A R A
O P R Y . R O O N E . A D I N
P E E S . T O T E R . R A C Y
```

232

```
A T O L L . W O N . E X P O
J O N E S . H A Y . U N M A N
A N Y I D I O T C A N F A C E
R E X . . R A H . C E A S E D
. . . W H I M . J U A N .
. A C R I S I S I T S T H I S
W R A I T H . O B E Y . E C O
O U S T . D O S . . G R I N
O B E . G A I T . S A R O N G
D A Y T O D A Y L I V I N G .
. . . O D D S . A X E D .
S C H O O L . A P T . G A S
T H A T W E A R S Y O U O U T
A A R O N . W E E . W R O T E
B R I O . L A D . E N D O W
```

233

```
J A M B . S M A S H . S G T S
U B E R . A T S E A . T A R A
N B A A L L S T A R . A L A S
K A N S A S . O L D F L A M E
. . . I T A L . S E R I A .
T A B L E S A W . N O N F A T
A L A I N . M O D E M . F D R
M I R A . J A R O D . S A D E
E B B . H U R T S . S T I L E
D I A D E M . H E C T A R E S
. . R U M B A . D A R N . .
B E A N P O L E . N O D I C E
I M A C . J A V A A P P L E T
D I N E . E M E N D . A S S N
S T N S . T O S C A . T A T A
```

234

```
H I M O M . B B C . R E B U S
O S A K A . L E O . A G A S P
C A R D S H A R P . T O T E R
. . . H A Z M A T . I T R Y
E B W H I T E . P O S S E .
T E H E E S . E L E C T R I C
C A I N . . A E R O . Y A Y
H T S . P O P T A R T . A M B
E E K . A R I A . . E C T O
S N E E R S A T . S E N I O R
. . Y U K O N . H A N G D O G
U S S R . N O V E L S . . .
S H O O T . B I T T E R E N D
C O U P E . A B U . A O L E R
G O R E D . R E P . L E F T Y
```

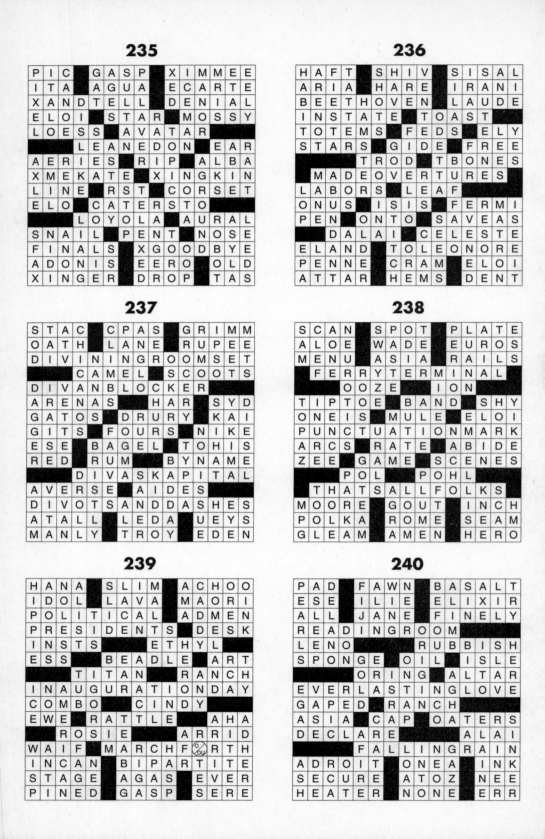

235

```
P I C . G A S P . X I M M E E
I T A . A G U A . E C A R T E
X A N D T E L L . D E N I A L
E L O I . S T A R . M O S S Y
L O E S S . A V A T A R . . .
. . . L E A N E D O N . E A R
A E R I E S . R I P . A L B A
X M E K A T E . X I N G K I N
L I N E . R S T . C O R S E T
E L O . C A T E R S T O . . .
. . L O Y O L A . A U R A L .
S N A I L . P E N T . N O S E
F I N A L S . X G O O D B Y E
A D O N I S . E E R O . O L D
X I N G E R . D R O P . T A S
```

236

```
H A F T . S H I V . S I S A L
A R I A . H A R E . I R A N I
B E E T H O V E N . L A U D E
I N S T A T E . T O A S T . .
T O T E M S . F E D S . E L Y
S T A R S . G I D E . F R E E
. . . . T R O D . T B O N E S
. M A D E O V E R T U R E S .
L A B O R S . L E A F . . . .
O N U S . I S I S . F E R M I
P E N . O N T O . S A V E A S
. . D A L A I . C E L E S T E
E L A N D . T O L E O N O R E
P E N N E . C R A M . E L O I
A T T A R . H E M S . D E N T
```

237

```
S T A C . C P A S . G R I M M
O A T H . L A N E . R U P E E
D I V I N I N G R O O M S E T
. . C A M E L . S C O O T S .
D I V A N B L O C K E R . . .
A R E N A S . H A R . S Y D .
G A T O S . D R U R Y . K A I
G I T S . F O U R S . N I K E
E S E . B A G E L . T O H I S
R E D . R U M . B Y N A M E .
. . D I V A S K A P I T A L .
A V E R S E . A I D E S . . .
D I V O T S A N D D A S H E S
A T A L L . L E D A . U E Y S
M A N L Y . T R O Y . E D E N
```

238

```
S C A N . S P O T . P L A T E
A L O E . W A D E . E U R O S
M E N U . A S I A . R A I L S
. F E R R Y T E R M I N A L .
. . . O O Z E . I O N . . . .
T I P T O E . B A N D . S H Y
O N E I S . M U L E . E L O I
P U N C T U A T I O N M A R K
A R C S . R A T E . A B I D E
Z E E . G A M E . S C E N E S
. . P O L . P O H L . . . .
. T H A T S A L L F O L K S .
M O O R E . G O U T . I N C H
P O L K A . R O M E . S E A M
G L E A M . A M E N . H E R O
```

239

```
H A N A . S L I M . A C H O O
I D O L . L A V A . M A O R I
P O L I T I C A L . A D M E N
P R E S I D E N T S . D E S K
I N S T S . E T H Y L . . .
E S S . B E A D L E . A R T
. . T I T A N . R A N C H
I N A U G U R A T I O N D A Y
C O M B O . C I N D Y . . .
E W E . R A T T L E . A H A
. R O S I E . A R R I D .
W A I F . M A R C H F [4/U] R T H
I N C A N . B I P A R T I T E
S T A G E . A G A S . E V E R
P I N E D . G A S P . S E R E
```

240

```
P A D . F A W N . B A S A L T
E S E . I L I E . E L I X I R
A L L . J A N E . F I N E L Y
R E A D I N G R O O M . . . .
L E N O . . R U B B I S H
S P O N G E . O I L . I S L E
. . . O R I N G . A L T A R
E V E R L A S T I N G L O V E
G A P E D . R A N C H . . .
A S I A . C A P . O A T E R S
D E C L A R E . A L A I .
. . . F A L L I N G R A I N
A D R O I T . O N E A . I N K
S E C U R E . A T O Z . N E E
H E A T E R . N O N E . E R R
```

241

```
A T E S T   S O H O   D C O N
C E N T S   E L A N   E I R E
S A V E A F T E R R E B A T E
      A R O O   T E R R
S L A M   R F K   D E I M O S
T I M E O F F E R   S E I N E
A M E R C E   E O E   F L E X
M I R   T I E P I N S   E F T
I T I S   T B S   C U R A R E
N E G E V   B U Y O N E G E T
A D O N I S   P A D   C E E S
      E V E N   W E A R
N O T S O L D I N S T O R E S
A S E C   E A V E   N O O N E
Y U L E   S K E D   O M E G A
```

242

```
S P A R S E   B N E G   P C P
T U R E E N   R E N O   L A H
O N O N E S G U A R D   I V Y
A D U E   T I T O   R O I L
T I S   I R O N O N D E C A L
S T E R N O         O T E R I
      I S S H O T   G E N E S
      O N T H E D O U B L E
R A N G E   P E N P A L
A G A S P         O N S A L E
D I V I S I O N O N E   L E X
I T I N   C R O W   F I F I
O A S   W O N O N P O I N T S
I T I   A M O N   I N D E B T
N E T   T E T E   G O O S E S
```

243

```
H B O   G A L A S   R E S I N
A R C   A B O R C   A R I S E
W I T   B O B B Y K N I G H T
S L A L O M   T O U C H
E L V I N B I S H O P   T O E
R O E G   S T E   S G T S
      H A S T E   S W E A T S
      S T E P H E N K I N G
C H E E S Y   P O I N T
B O A R   P L O   O R C A
S E T   E L L E R Y Q U E E N
      B O G I E   A U T U M N
I R E N E C A S T L E   S E A
M U L E S   S P A T S   E N L
P E T I T   E F L A T   D T S
```

244

```
A G O G   R A N I   A T O M
S O R E   U L A N   A V E R Y
T A B L E F O R T   L A R E S
A D S   C O U C H   F I R S T
      T H U D   E C O L I
P A T I O S   D A R N   B M W
R U B E   A C E S   L E E
A R I   T F O R T W O   E R A
H A T   R A R E   S T I R
A L S   A C I D   B O A S T S
      W A S T E   P A R D
S L O S H   N I E C E   M A L
T E R S E   T S C O M P A N Y
A N T E S   A L A N   S I N N
B A H T   L E N S   I M A X
```

245

```
N O V   B I O T A   S O A P Y
E R A   I D I O M   T O M E I
Z E N   B A L L O O N P A R K
  D C L   S E E N   D D E
O N E H I T   B U L B O U S
W A L L O O N P A P E R
S T L O   D E I   V I S A
  C A R T O O N W R I G H T
  H S I A   T O A   I A T E
    D R A G O O N S T R I P
S W E E P E R   D E T E C T
O H M   R U S H   N E W
L A M P O O N P O S T   I Q S
O M A H A   G A M E R   T O N
N O S I R   E N E M Y   H M O
```

246

```
A C T   S A S   S O W
R O W   G O U L A S H   C P A
T U E   I T S A L I E   R E N
S P L O T C H   S C H W I N N
A L F A S   I S A K   A P S E
L E T T   A B C S   W I P E S
E T H S   R A H   E A T S A T
      S C R U N C H
P O S S E S   L O T   P S I S
I N C A N   A T N O   O T R O
C A R L   I T Z A   C O R E S
K L A T S C H   S C H L E P P
S E T   P O E T I C A   T E A
O R C   A N N E A L S   C A D
N T H   A N N   H T S
```

247

```
Y E W S _ C L A W _ R E G A L
A C H E _ O A T H _ A L I N E
W H A T I S H O O _ M C R A E
N O T _ M I T Z I _ J I L T S
_ _ I R A N I _ S L E D _ _
A L S A C E _ C H A T _ W A S
P A W N S _ W O O D S _ H O T
H I E D _ S H O W S _ C A R E
I N N _ A W A K E _ G O T T A
D E N _ L A T E _ S A M I A M
_ _ Z I T I _ M A Z E S _ _
P I Z Z A _ S C A L E _ W E E
A B U T S _ W H O I S W A T T
C A N O E _ Y A R N _ A R O N
T R I P S _ E R I E _ X E N A
```

248

```
C U R D _ S H A R P _ J A Z Z
U L E E _ C A N E R _ O B O E
E T D S _ O D D F E L L O W S
B E R K E L E Y _ C A L L I T
A R I _ R D S _ D I L A T E S
L I B R A S _ L A N A _ _ _
L O B O _ F A N C L U B _ _
_ R O U L E T T E T A B L E _
_ N E E D L E S _ E A T A
_ N M E X _ B A R C A R
O P E N T O E _ S E N _ K I A
M I N I O N _ A C I D C E L L
E V E N S T E V E N _ A Y E S
G O R E _ O W I N G _ G E R E
A T O R _ N E S T S _ E S S A
```

249

```
S W A N _ E B A Y _ G E T U P
W A D E _ I R M A _ O P A R T
A L D A _ F A I R _ D O L L S
P E T R I F I E D R O C K _
_ S O B B E D _ E T H I C S
_ E E L _ W A H _ S N I T
S O R E R _ M Y N A S _ G T O
C L A R I F I E D B U T T E R
A L I _ A U N T Y _ B R O D Y
M I S S _ N T H _ S T A _
P E E P E D _ D E L P H I
_ C L A S S I F I E D A D S
C R A I G _ O W L S _ O R E O
O N I C E _ S I A M _ O P A L
S A N E R _ A N T S _ R O L E
```

250

```
J A D E _ T I E S _ S I F T S
A V O W _ I N C H _ O M A H A
G E N E _ T A R A _ A N T I S
_ T R E A S U R Y N O T E S
S A W _ N N E _ P E D _ E V E
D R A S T I C M E A S U R E S
A N I T R A _ E N R O N _
K O T O _ E L S _ C M O N
_ O R O N O _ M O L I N A
T H E D E F E N S E R E S T S
V E X _ T A R _ M L I _ O O H
S C O R I N G P O I N T S _
T U D O R _ I R K S _ A O N E
A B U S E _ Z E E S _ R U B E
R A S E D _ E Z R A _ O P A L
```

251

```
S A D A _ A N I L _ L O W L Y
T R I S _ Z E N O _ E L I T E
I A N S _ T O N Y A W A R D S
G R E A S E _ O V I N E _
M A R I A C A L L A S _ H A L
A T O L L _ M I A _ R A R E
_ U P O N _ E S K I M O
_ W E S T S I D E S T O R Y _
B A S K E T _ S R T A _
E L O I _ S A G _ L E R O I
G E T _ N E W Y O R K J E T S
_ E M O T E _ U S E N E T
C A R D S H A R K S _ C O L L
A R I S E _ T I E S _ T I L E
D I C E D _ Y O Y O _ S R O S
```

252

```
F A B _ T O B E G _ A M B L E
R R R _ A C E L A _ S O L A R
AUTOEXHAUST _ T W A N G
_ R N A _ S T E E L E _ I D O
G O T T A _ SAUERKRAUT
L O O _ R C A _ X E N A _
O N S E C O N D _ B O O P
BEAUJOLAISNOUVEAU
E Y R E _ Z O O M L E N S
_ C H A R _ B R A _ R O E
CHAUTAUQUA _ R A S P S
L A P _ G I M L E T _ N T H
A D A S H _ PAULGAUGUIN
S T I L T _ U G L I S _ F L Y
S O R R Y _ S H A F T _ F E E
```

253

```
P S I _ A C I D _ T H E L M A
O W N _ L A Z E _ H A V E A T
R E D _ S L O B _ U N E A S E
T R E E O F D I A M O N D S _
E V E R _ _ _ R B I _ P E A _
R E P A S T _ S R S _ M I N I
_ _ _ P E A L E _ C A P E R _
_ N O T A T R U S T R E E T _
N I K O N _ M E T O O _ _ _ _
O N L Y _ G A S _ T W I L L S
D E A _ S I N _ _ N O O N _ _
_ T H E T R I L L I S G O N E
M E O W E D _ E A S T _ P G A
R E M O V E _ N I L E _ E E K
S N A K E D _ D R E W _ D R Y
```

254

```
P S S T _ P A N A M _ A S A P
G O T O _ A N T R A _ L I N E
A M I S _ S T E E R C L E A R
_ B L E S S E S _ I R O N I C
B R E A K O U T I N A R A S H
R E T _ I S P _ B A G _ _ _ _
A R T O F _ F E R _ I M U S
G O O F F O N A T A N G E N T
A S S T _ P O X _ O N A I R
_ _ _ A P R _ G O P _ T V A
S L O W D O W N U P A H E A D
A E N E A S _ O N T R I A L _
S T E A M I R O N S _ V T E N
E B A N _ T E N E T _ E E N S
S E M S _ E N E R O _ S R T A
```

255

```
M E D A L _ U S E R _ P O C O
A D O R E _ R A V E _ O V A L
C U P I D C A K E S _ S E N D
A C E _ O O N A _ D E N S E _
W E S _ F L U I D S E A S O N
_ _ H A F T S _ E E L S _ _
O N E S _ _ A M A H _ P I A
F R E U D I A N S L I P I N S
F A T _ O R G Y _ _ I N C H
_ _ A R O O _ A P S E S _ _
S L I D I N G S H O T _ T V A
T U N I C _ A C N E _ R E L
E G A D _ H I G H D I V I D E
N A N A _ E R G O _ N I P A T
O R E S _ M A Y O _ S E E Y A
```

256

```
A G R O _ C L I P _ A C T U P
C L E V E L A N D _ P O R N O
C A L I C O C A T _ E M I R S
U D E _ O W E D _ A T M F E E
S I A M _ N U M B S _ I L S A
T O S I R _ P I A F _ S E T S
O L E S O N _ S L A T S _ _
M I S S M I S S I S S I P P I
_ _ T E M P I _ T O O H O T
B U S H _ B A B Y _ S N A P S
O N M E _ U R I E L _ S R T A
B R I B E S _ L O I S _ M A M
C O L O R _ T I M E S H A R E
A B E A M _ S T A G E A C T S
T E S T A _ P Y N E _ W Y S S
```

257

```
M A L L _ B L E S T _ O N K P
O V A L _ A O L E R _ N A L A
C O M B _ H O K E Y P O K E Y
S W E E T _ M E N S A _ E I N
_ _ _ A A A _ _ T R U D G E
C L I N K G L A S S E S _ _
A I T _ E I E I O _ _ E S M E
P E R S O N A L I Z E D P E N
N U Y S _ _ R E L O G _ A R G
_ _ G R A N D S L A M M E R
B U S T U P _ _ A D O _ _
I B M _ S L E E T _ S N A P E
J O I N T O W N E R _ I R O N
O L L A _ M E T R O _ C A R Y
U T E P _ B R O N C _ A T T A
```

258

```
M E S H _ T I C S _ T O S E A
A L I I _ E N C E _ A T I L T
L O N G S N O U T _ L E M M E
L I G H T S U P T H E R O O M
_ _ _ H O E R _ L E N I N _
A C C O R D _ P E R T _ E V E
S L O P E _ G I D E _ S W A N
C A M E R A E Q U I P M E N T
O R B S _ C O U P _ R E I N E
T A U _ L O G E _ C E L L A R
_ _ S T A R R _ O R E L _ _
A C T I O N A D V E N T U R E
S A I N T _ P L U S S E V E N
K N O T S _ H I L T _ S E N D
S E N S E _ Y V E S _ T A O S
```

259

```
A S A I R   A C L U   T W A S
G U I D O   R A I N   E A T A
F I R E S I G N T H E A T R E
A T F   S K U A   E A S E I N
  O K I E S   C A M E R A S
F A R I N A   D O T E L L
L A C T I   C A R E S   O W L
A R E S   O A R E D   S O I E
P E R   A P S I S   B O S S A
  E R R A T A   D U S T E R
A S S A I L S   S A M O A
T H E N C E   N E R D   T S U
E A R T H S H A T T E R I N G
I D V E   C O P T   A B O I L
N E E R   E S S O   L I N T Y
```

260

```
M A C H M E T E R   A B U Z Z
A T L E I S U R E   R E N E E
P O I N T O F N O R E T U R N
S P O R T   T O S A Y   M O O
      Y E A     W O E
B E R I N G S E A   U S A G E
I C U   E T A L   O A R E D
P O L K A D O T B I K I N I S
O L E I C   A M U R   E C O
D I R E R   S E M I C O L O N
    V I A     S I P
E M U   M I L N E   N E G R I
V I C T O R I A N P E R I O D
E L L E N   E S T I M A B L E
R E A D Y   S A R G A S S O S
```

261

```
G O N Z O J O U R N A L I S M
T H A I R E S T A U R A N T S
B E T T E R G E T M O V I N G
R D S   S R O   A B M   S S R
  A T Y O U   S A W
F O S T E R D A D   S H E D S
A C T I I I   R O I   O B E Y
T H E S A C K   O B O I S T S
W E E K   E O S   U N S E A T
A R L E S   P A W P R I N T S
  T E A   C A R E T
T D S   E L L   S O C   N R A
H O T E N O U G H F O R Y O U
I T A L I A N A M E R I C A N
S E C O N D A M E N D M E N T
```

262

```
O C T A N T S   S T E R E O S
P L A T O O N S E R G E A N T
P O R T R A I T P A I N T E R
O O Z E D   V A T   S T Y L I
S T A N   B E G I N   S O A P
E I N   T E L E C O M   U N E
R E T O O L E D   M I T R E D
  H H O U R   S I N G H
B O E I N G   A U N T I E E M
O R A   S A L I N E S   A R I
T I P I   S A R R E   S R A S
A N E R A   R I O   M A T S U
N O M O R E I L O V E Y O U S
I C A N T S A Y F O R S U R E
C O N S I S T   S W E A T E D
```

263

```
D A T E   A M B I   A H E M S
E V O C A T I O N   M O V I E
F E L L F O R I T   A R E S T
I N D I A N E L E P H A N T S
E G Y P T   R A S T E R
S E A S   B L A S S   I D A S
  E L L I O T T G O U L D
A S A   B A G L A D Y   P S I
C A L L S T H E T U N E
E L O I   A T R E E   N A S H
  T E N O N S   A T T H E
F I V E S T A R G E N E R A L
A N E A R   B U L L S N A K E
T E R R I   E M U L A T I O N
A S A B C   R P M S   E N S E
```

264

```
M M M M G O O D   O F F E D
A A A M E M B E R   P R O N E
T E L L S A L I E   T E R R A
T W A   T H A T S T O O B A D
H E R R   A D I O S   N A G S
A S I A N   I E R E   D E E
U T A H A N   S T T E R E S A
  A T O R   S S N S
E X P L O D E S   E N V I E D
X E R   I C E T   A P P L E
P R O B   C H E R I   S A A B
L O T U S E A T E R S   N I E
O X E Y E   L O V E S C E N E
R E G I S   L I O N T A M E R
E D E N S   T R E S P A S S
```

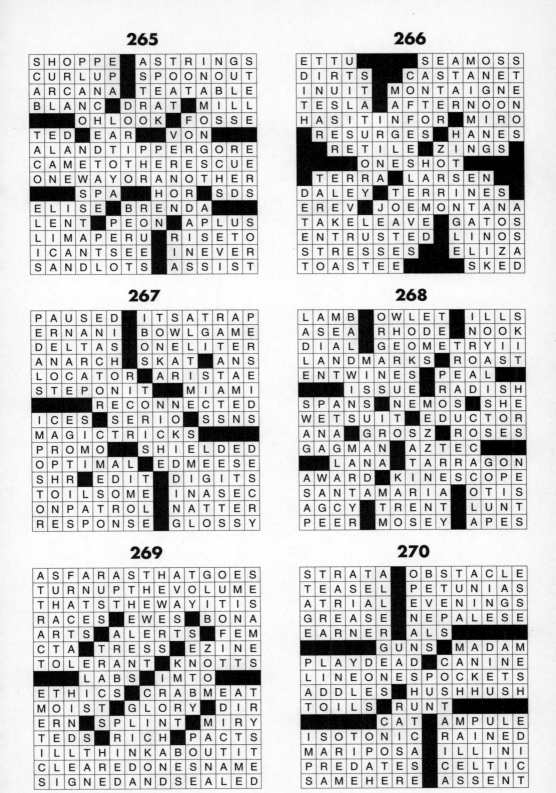

265

SHOPPE · ASTRINGS
CURLUP · SPOONOUT
ARCANA · TEATABLE
BLANC · DRAT · MILL
OHLOOK · FOSSE
TED · EAR · VON
ALANDTIPPERGORE
CAMETOTHERESCUE
ONEWAYORANOTHER
SPA · HOR · SDS
ELISE · BRENDA
LENT · PEON · APLUS
LIMAPERU · RISETO
ICANTSEE · INEVER
SANDLOTS · ASSIST

266

ETTU · SEAMOSS
DIRTS · CASTANET
INUIT · MONTAIGNE
TESLA · AFTERNOON
HASITINFOR · MIRO
RESURGES · HANES
RETILE · ZINGS
ONESHOT
TERRA · LARSEN
DALEY · TERRINES
EREV · JOEMONTANA
TAKELEAVE · GATOS
ENTRUSTED · LINOS
STRESSES · ELIZA
TOASTEE · SKED

267

PAUSED · ITSATRAP
ERNANI · BOWLGAME
DELTAS · ONELITER
ANARCH · SKAT · ANS
LOCATOR · ARISTAE
STEPONIT · MIAMI
RECONNECTED
ICES · SERIO · SSNS
MAGICTRICKS
PROMO · SHIELDED
OPTIMAL · EDMEESE
SHR · EDIT · DIGITS
TOILSOME · INASEC
ONPATROL · NATTER
RESPONSE · GLOSSY

268

LAMB · OWLET · ILLS
ASEA · RHODE · NOOK
DIAL · GEOMETRYII
LANDMARKS · ROAST
ENTWINES · PEAL
ISSUE · RADISH
SPANS · NEMOS · SHE
WETSUIT · EDUCTOR
ANA · GROSZ · ROSES
GAGMAN · AZTEC
LANA · TARRAGON
AWARD · KINESCOPE
SANTAMARIA · OTIS
AGCY · TRENT · LUNT
PEER · MOSEY · APES

269

ASFARASTHATGOES
TURNUPTHEVOLUME
THATSTHEWAYITIS
RACES · EWES · BONA
ARTS · ALERTS · FEM
CTA · TRESS · EZINE
TOLERANT · KNOTTS
LABS · IMTO
ETHICS · CRABMEAT
MOIST · GLORY · DIR
ERN · SPLINT · MIRY
TEDS · RICH · PACTS
ILLTHINKABOUTIT
CLEAREDONESNAME
SIGNEDANDSEALED

270

STRATA · OBSTACLE
TEASEL · PETUNIAS
ATRIAL · EVENINGS
GREASE · NEPALESE
EARNER · ALS
GUNS · MADAM
PLAYDEAD · CANINE
LINEONESPOCKETS
ADDLES · HUSHHUSH
TOILS · RUNT
CAT · AMPULE
ISOTONIC · RAINED
MARIPOSA · ILLINI
PREDATES · CELTIC
SAMEHERE · ASSENT

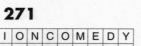

271

```
S I T U A T I O N C O M E D Y
T R A N S I S T O R R A D I O
O K L A H O M A S O O N E R S
  S I N E     Y E N     I N K
      I S E E     S E L F
S P A M   N A M   S I E S T A
E U R O   O R E O   P S H A W
T R O U B L E S H O O T I N G
T E N S E   D A Y O   D E K E
E R I C A S   S E Z   E R S E
    H U T T     S E T S
  C P O   R A M     A T T O
M A R I T I M E N A T I O N S
C R O C O D I L E D U N D E E
L O V E M E L O V E M Y D O G
```

272

```
A I R G U I T A R     C O C A
S N O O P D O G G   L A P A Z
T E S T A T O R S   A M E M O
A R I   T A T E     Z O N E
I R E S   G E E   A Y M A R A
R O T C S   D R O P S I N O N
E R H A R D   S H O U L D N T
    E R I E S   M O S E S
F I R E L A N E   R A T H E R
A N I T A L O O S   N E U R O
S A V A N T   L E A   A T M S
  H E C K   I N D S   C I I
C O T T A   I T S A P L A N E
O L E I N   T H E M A S S E S
M E R C   E S S A Y T E S T
```

273

```
C A S T L E G A T E S   W I T
A N T I O X I D A N T   E N O
L E O N P A N E T T A   B S A
  M O D E M S   E R A S E S
F I L E R S   D E R E L I C T
L A I R S   K I X   D I T T Y
U S E   S I N E W A V E S
    E N U M E R A T E
  M I L E P O S T S   S T N
R I G I D   N O S   C A M R Y
E D N O R T O N   S O B E I T
E D I T O R   D A M A T O
V A T   R U M M A G E S A L E
E Y E   E L A I N E B E N E S
S S S   M Y S T E R Y D A T E
```

274

```
  S T U D I O R E M A K E S
  J U N I O R P A R T N E R S
W A S T E N O T W A N T N O T
U N H   S T N S   S E N D A
R U I N   S O F A S   D E E R
S A B E R   N O S E S   L D S
T R A V I S   R E A P S
S Y R I A N S   A L L E G R O
  S T O O P   S A T E E N
A G S   A W R A P   T A N T E
S O A P   S T R O M   E D I E
S O C A L   O L E G   A R Y
A G R E E T O D I S A G R E E
Y O U S A I D I T N O T M E
S O M E P L A C E E L S E
```

275

```
S E I J I O Z A W A   M I S T
W A T E R C O L O R   O N C E
E S C R I T O I R E   N Y A H
E T H O S   M E N S S T O R E
    B E H I N D   H A U T E
A S N O   E N T O   A G R I
W H O A M I   O W N S   F S U
L E M M I N G   N O T P A S S
S E D   M E L O   C A U C U S
  R E P O   I N C H   B E E R
T A P A S   S E A E E L
U G L Y A S S I N   R I A T A
R O U E   K A R A T E C H O P
O N M E   I D O D E C L A R E
W Y E S   P E N A L T Y B O X
```

276

```
  S T A T I O N S   A M P S
I H A D A D R E A M   B O I L
N E V E R A G A I N   B O Z O
T R E   A H A   L O R E N Z
O P R Y   O N D O P E   W A S
W A N E   A Z U R   S T A P H
    M O N A D S   P O L I O
B E T E L S   B U N K E D
E L A N D   S T A I N S
R A D I I   H O S S   I S N T
T S P   S C A T H E   L A I R
  T O W H O M   A C T   M E A
M I L E   U P I N T H E S K Y
A C E S   P O S T E R I O R S
P S S T   O H I D U N N O
```

277

C	A	S	T	A	S	I	D	E	■	B	A	G	E	L
A	D	H	O	M	I	N	E	M	■	E	B	O	L	I
T	E	A	K	E	T	T	L	E	■	G	E	T	A	T
E	L	L	E	N	■	E	A	R	■	S	T	O	L	I
S	E	E	N	■	M	A	Y	A	S	■	S	W	A	G
■	■	■	P	A	R	S	L	E	Y	■	A	M	A	■
F	E	S	T	E	R	S	■	D	E	E	P	S	E	T
A	V	A	I	L	S	■	■	■	P	A	T	T	I	E
N	A	M	E	T	A	G	■	W	I	T	S	E	N	D
C	P	A	■	S	L	O	S	H	E	S	■	■	■	■
Y	O	R	E	■	A	F	T	E	R	■	N	A	R	C
T	R	I	N	A	■	O	R	E	■	H	O	M	E	R
H	A	T	E	D	■	R	I	D	E	A	L	O	N	E
A	T	A	R	I	■	I	D	L	E	H	A	N	D	S
T	E	N	O	N	■	T	E	E	N	A	N	G	S	T

278

I	N	C	A	H	O	O	T	S	■	R	A	M	P	S
A	I	R	W	O	R	T	H	Y	■	I	M	A	R	I
S	T	A	N	D	F	I	R	M	■	P	E	R	I	L
I	R	T	■	S	E	T	I	■	R	O	S	C	O	E
M	A	I	D	■	O	I	L	C	A	N	■	E	R	N
O	T	O	E	S	■	S	L	O	T	■	B	A	T	T
V	E	N	I	C	E	■	A	R	E	Y	O	U	O	K
■	■	■	C	A	R	D	I	N	D	E	X	■	■	■
B	L	U	E	M	O	O	N	■	R	A	C	I	S	M
B	A	K	R	■	D	I	M	S	■	N	A	R	C	O
Q	T	R	■	D	E	T	A	I	L	■	R	E	I	N
P	E	A	P	O	D	■	N	E	E	T	■	L	E	I
I	F	I	L	L	■	P	I	G	G	Y	B	A	N	K
T	E	N	E	T	■	C	L	E	A	R	A	N	C	E
S	E	E	D	S	■	T	A	L	L	O	R	D	E	R

279

J	O	B	L	E	S	S	■	H	O	L	Y	W	A	R
A	C	R	O	B	A	T	■	O	N	L	E	A	V	E
S	T	U	M	B	L	E	■	W	E	A	R	I	E	D
M	A	B	■	S	E	V	E	N	A	M	■	T	R	E
I	V	E	S	■	S	I	L	O	■	A	S	S	A	Y
N	E	C	K	■	W	E	A	V	E	■	L	O	G	E
E	S	K	I	M	O	■	L	E	G	B	O	N	E	S
■	■	■	J	A	M	B	■	L	O	E	W	■	■	■
N	O	N	U	S	E	R	S	■	C	L	I	M	E	S
I	M	A	M	■	N	O	L	T	E	■	S	A	X	E
T	I	P	P	I	■	K	A	H	N	■	H	D	T	V
P	C	T	■	T	H	E	P	I	T	S	■	I	R	E
I	R	I	S	H	E	R	■	G	R	E	A	S	E	R
C	O	M	P	A	R	E	■	H	I	T	H	O	M	E
K	N	E	A	D	E	D	■	S	C	A	N	N	E	D

280

Q	U	I	D	P	R	O	Q	U	O	■	G	E	T	A
U	L	T	R	A	S	O	U	N	D	■	O	X	E	N
I	T	S	I	N	T	H	E	R	E	■	O	P	E	N
V	I	A	■	L	S	A	T	■	D	O	T	O	■	■
E	M	T	S	■	M	A	T	T	S	■	A	S	H	Y
R	A	R	A	■	A	L	E	E	■	K	N	E	E	S
E	T	A	T	■	S	A	D	D	L	E	D	■	■	■
D	E	P	I	C	T	■	■	■	I	N	E	V	E	R
■	■	■	N	O	S	C	O	R	E	■	V	E	N	I
J	E	S	S	E	■	O	N	A	N	■	I	N	S	T
A	M	A	H	■	G	N	A	W	S	■	L	E	N	Z
C	O	T	E	■	A	C	T	H	■	R	A	I	■	■
O	T	O	E	■	S	E	E	I	F	I	C	A	R	E
B	E	R	T	■	E	R	A	D	I	C	A	T	E	S
I	S	I	S	■	S	T	R	E	S	S	T	E	S	T

281

S	P	E	E	D	D	A	T	I	N	G	■	O	R	T
L	A	T	E	A	R	R	I	V	A	L	■	N	E	H
E	L	E	C	T	R	I	C	E	Y	E	■	T	B	A
W	E	S	■	S	U	E	S	■	S	A	C	H	E	T
■	■	■	C	U	T	S	■	P	A	S	T	E	L	S
U	N	H	U	N	H	■	S	A	Y	O	N	A	R	A
S	E	A	R	S	■	L	I	N	E	N	■	L	E	M
A	S	I	S	■	V	O	T	E	R	■	N	E	B	O
I	S	R	■	M	A	R	E	S	■	R	A	R	E	R
R	E	P	A	I	R	E	D	■	G	E	N	T	L	E
F	L	I	T	S	I	N	■	G	A	M	S	■	■	■
O	R	E	L	S	E	■	D	A	Y	O	■	S	A	D
R	O	C	■	I	T	C	O	U	L	D	N	T	B	E
C	D	E	■	N	A	T	A	L	I	E	C	O	L	E
E	E	S	■	G	L	A	S	S	B	L	O	W	E	R

282

C	A	P	E	C	O	D	■	■	■	S	T	A	B	S
O	V	E	R	U	S	E	S	■	S	T	O	R	E	S
H	E	R	G	R	A	C	E	■	M	A	R	T	E	N
E	R	S	■	E	G	O	T	R	I	P	P	E	R	S
R	A	P	■	R	E	C	O	I	L	L	E	S	S	■
E	G	I	S	■	S	T	U	D	I	E	D	■	■	■
D	E	R	A	T	■	S	T	E	N	T	O	N	■	■
■	D	E	L	I	S	■	■	■	G	O	N	E	R	■
■	■	D	E	M	O	T	I	C	■	N	E	W	E	L
■	■	S	E	N	O	R	A	S	■	T	R	U	E	■
■	P	I	C	C	A	L	I	L	L	I	■	E	N	S
T	A	L	L	A	N	D	S	L	I	M	■	G	I	S
A	S	S	E	R	T	■	E	S	P	O	S	I	T	O
C	H	A	R	D	S	■	S	T	O	N	E	M	E	N
T	A	S	K	S	■	■	O	N	A	G	E	R	S	■

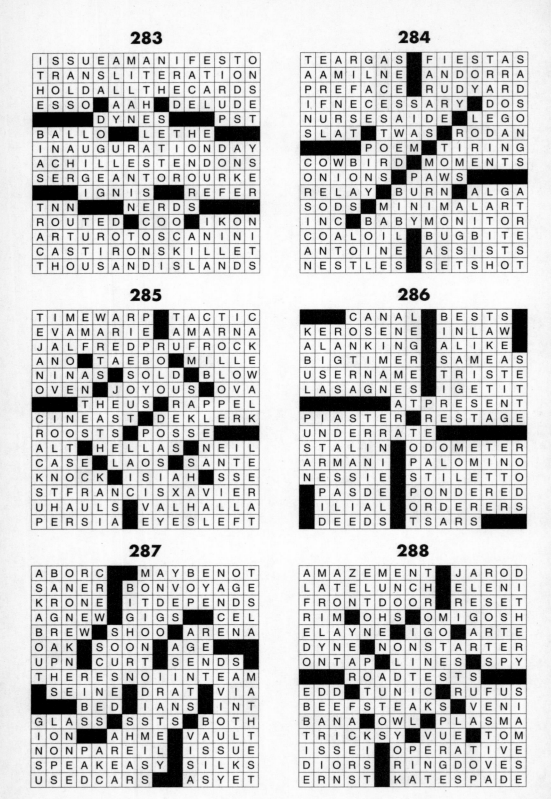

283

```
I S S U E A M A N I F E S T O
T R A N S L I T E R A T I O N
H O L D A L L T H E C A R D S
E S S O   A A H   D E L U D E
      D Y N E S     P S T
B A L L O     L E T H E
I N A U G U R A T I O N D A Y
A C H I L L E S T E N D O N S
S E R G E A N T O R O U R K E
      I G N I S     R E F E R
T N N     N E R D S
R O U T E D   C O O   I K O N
A R T U R O T O S C A N I N I
C A S T I R O N S K I L L E T
T H O U S A N D I S L A N D S
```

284

```
T E A R G A S   F I E S T A S
A A M I L N E   A N D O R R A
P R E F A C E   R U D Y A R D
I F N E C E S S A R Y   D O S
N U R S E S A I D E   L E G O
S L A T   T W A S   R O D A N
      P O E M   T I R I N G
C O W B I R D   M O M E N T S
O N I O N S   P A W S
R E L A Y   B U R N   A L G A
S O D S   M I N I M A L A R T
I N C   B A B Y M O N I T O R
C O A L O I L   B U G B I T E
A N T O I N E   A S S I S T S
N E S T L E S   S E T S H O T
```

285

```
T I M E W A R P   T A C T I C
E V A M A R I E   A M A R N A
J A L F R E D P R U F R O C K
A N O   T A E B O   M I L L E
N I N A S   S O L D   B L O W
O V E N   J O Y O U S   O V A
      T H E U S   R A P P E L
C I N E A S T   D E K L E R K
R O O S T S   P O S S E
A L T   H E L L A S   N E I L
C A S E   L A O S   S A N T E
K N O C K   I S I A H   S S E
S T F R A N C I S X A V I E R
U H A U L S   V A L H A L L A
P E R S I A   E Y E S L E F T
```

286

```
      C A N A L   B E S T S
K E R O S E N E   I N L A W
A L A N K I N G   A L I K E
B I G T I M E R   S A M E A S
U S E R N A M E   T R I S T E
L A S A G N E S   I G E T I T
      A T P R E S E N T
P I A S T E R   R E S T A G E
U N D E R R A T E
S T A L I N   O D O M E T E R
A R M A N I   P A L O M I N O
N E S S I E   S T I L E T T O
P A S D E   P O N D E R E D
I L I A L   O R D E R E R S
D E E D S   T S A R S
```

287

```
A B O R C   M A Y B E N O T
S A N E R   B O N V O Y A G E
K R O N E   I T D E P E N D S
A G N E W   G I G S   C E L
B R E W   S H O O   A R E N A
O A K   S O O N   A G E
U P N   C U R T   S E N D S
T H E R E S N O I I N T E A M
  S E I N E   D R A T   V I A
    B E D   I A N S   I N T
G L A S S   S S T S   B O T H
I O N   A H M E   V A U L T
N O N P A R E I L   I S S U E
S P E A K E A S Y   S I L K S
U S E D C A R S   A S Y E T
```

288

```
A M A Z E M E N T   J A R O D
L A T E L U N C H   E L E N I
F R O N T D O O R   R E S E T
R I M   O H S   O M I G O S H
E L A Y N E   I G O   A R T E
D Y N E   N O N S T A R T E R
O N T A P   L I N E S   S P Y
      R O A D T E S T S
E D D   T U N I C   R U F U S
B E E F S T E A K S   V E N I
B A N A   O W L   P L A S M A
T R I C K S Y   V U E   T O M
I S S E I   O P E R A T I V E
D I O R S   R I N G D O V E S
E R N S T   K A T E S P A D E
```

289

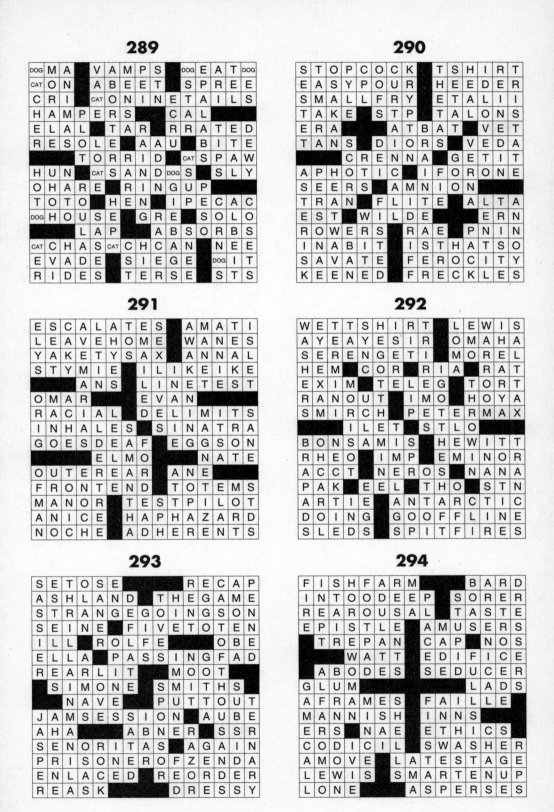

```
[DOG] MA ▓ V A M P S ▓ [DOG] E A T [DOG]
[CAT] O N   A B E E T ▓   S P R E E
 C R I  [CAT] O N I N E T A I L S
 H A M P E R S ▓ C A L
 E L A L ▓ T A R ▓ R R A T E D
 R E S O L E ▓ A A U ▓ B I T E
 ▓ T O R R I D ▓ [CAT] S P A W
 H U N [CAT] S A N D [DOG] S ▓ S L Y
 O H A R E ▓ R I N G U P
 T O T O ▓ H E N ▓ I P E C A C
[DOG] H O U S E ▓ G R E ▓ S O L O
 ▓ L A P ▓ A B S O R B S
[CAT] C H A S [CAT] C H C A N ▓ N E E
 E V A D E ▓ S I E G E [DOG] I T
 R I D E S ▓ T E R S E ▓ S T S
```

290

```
S T O P C O C K ▓ T S H I R T
E A S Y P O U R ▓ H E E D E R
S M A L L F R Y ▓ E T A L I I
T A K E ▓ S T P ▓ T A L O N S
E R A ▓ A T B A T ▓ V E T
T A N S ▓ D I O R S ▓ V E D A
▓ C R E N N A ▓ G E T I T
A P H O T I C ▓ I F O R O N E
S E E R S ▓ A M N I O N ▓
T R A N ▓ F L I T E ▓ A L T A
E S T ▓ W I L D E ▓ E R N
R O W E R S ▓ R A E ▓ P N I N
I N A B I T ▓ I S T H A T S O
S A V A T E ▓ F E R O C I T Y
K E E N E D ▓ F R E C K L E S
```

291

```
E S C A L A T E S ▓ A M A T I
L E A V E H O M E ▓ W A N E S
Y A K E T Y S A X ▓ A N N A L
S T Y M I E ▓ I L I K E I K E
▓ A N S ▓ L I N E T E S T
O M A R ▓ E V A N
R A C I A L ▓ D E L I M I T S
I N H A L E S ▓ S I N A T R A
G O E S D E A F ▓ E G G S O N
▓ E L M O ▓ N A T E
O U T E R E A R ▓ A N E
F R O N T E N D ▓ T O T E M S
M A N O R ▓ T E S T P I L O T
A N I C E ▓ H A P H A Z A R D
N O C H E ▓ A D H E R E N T S
```

292

```
W E T T S H I R T ▓ L E W I S
A Y E A Y E S I R ▓ O M A H A
S E R E N G E T I ▓ M O R E L
H E M ▓ C O R ▓ R I A ▓ R A T
E X I M ▓ T E L E G ▓ T O R T
R A N O U T ▓ I M O ▓ H O Y A
S M I R C H ▓ P E T E R M A X
▓ I L E T ▓ S T L O
B O N S A M I S ▓ H E W I T T
R H E O ▓ I M P ▓ E M I N O R
A C C T ▓ N E R O S ▓ N A N A
P A K ▓ E E L ▓ T H O ▓ S T N
A R T I E ▓ A N T A R C T I C
D O I N G ▓ G O O F F L I N E
S L E D S ▓ S P I T F I R E S
```

293

```
S E T O S E ▓ R E C A P
A S H L A N D ▓ T H E G A M E
S T R A N G E G O I N G S O N
S E I N E ▓ F I V E T O T E N
I L L ▓ R O L F E ▓ O B E
E L L A ▓ P A S S I N G F A D
R E A R L I T ▓ M O O T
▓ S I M O N E ▓ S M I T H S
▓ N A V E ▓ P U T T O U T
J A M S E S S I O N ▓ A U B E
A H A ▓ A B N E R ▓ S S R
S E N O R I T A S ▓ A G A I N
P R I S O N E R O F Z E N D A
E N L A C E D ▓ R E O R D E R
R E A S K ▓ D R E S S Y
```

294

```
F I S H F A R M ▓ B A R D
I N T O O D E E P ▓ S O R E R
R E A R O U S A L ▓ T A S T E
E P I S T L E ▓ A M U S E R S
▓ T R E P A N ▓ C A P ▓ N O S
▓ W A T T ▓ E D I F I C E
A B O D E S ▓ S E D U C E R
G L U M ▓ ▓ L A D S
A F R A M E S ▓ F A I L L E
M A N N I S H ▓ I N N S
E R S ▓ N A E ▓ E T H I C S
C O D I C I L ▓ S W A S H E R
A M O V E ▓ L A T E S T A G E
L E W I S ▓ S M A R T E N U P
L O N E ▓ A S P E R S E S
```

295

```
S P A M █ P O L K █ B L U R B
T E L E █ I R O N █ R E N E E
O N T H I N I C E █ O S C A R
W H A T T H E H E C K █ L I L
█ M A S O N █ S E E H E R E █
S F O █ A L T O █ R N A █ █ █
K I N G L E A R █ F E N D E R
A S T R O █ L A V █ N O R S E
T H E E N D █ L E G G I E S T
█ █ E G O █ S H E L █ W O E █
B E A T S M E █ E N I A C █ █
E X T █ T E X T M E S S A G E
E C O N O █ T E E S H I R T S
T I M O R █ R A N I █ G E O M
S A S S Y █ A R T S █ N Y S E
```

296

```
T A B L O I D T V █ A S P E R
I F Y O U D A R E █ S H O N E
R U R I T A N I A █ L O I N S
E S O S █ █ I A L S O █ S U E
D E N █ F E E L S U P T O I T
█ █ F U L L S C R E E N █ █ █
U R B A N A R E A █ █ S P U D
S H O R █ M A P L E █ L E N O
H O B O █ █ D A L L I A N C E
█ █ M U S I C R O L L S █ █ █
J A C K E T L A P E L █ S S E
E T A █ I S I T I █ █ S W A N
N O D O Z █ F I N A G L I N G
G L O B E █ F O I L P A P E R
A L O E S █ E N S L A V E R S
```

297

```
A C C O S T █ C A T █ O R E
S H O R T U █ O L I N █ S E X
F A L C O N C R E S T █ B A P
A S L █ L A I C A L █ T O D O
S T A B █ S N A R E D R U M S
T E R I █ A N S A █ E E R I E
█ █ G A L A █ N O C E N T S █
█ A B S C A M █ C N O T E S █
A V O C A D O █ E E R O █ █
H A T E R █ N E S S █ P A S S
B R A N D Y S N A P █ S M U T
L I N E █ O T E L L O █ A R E
I C I █ A D I M E A D O Z E N
S E S █ S E C Y █ C O M E T O
S S T █ E L K █ █ E R A S E S
```

298

```
X Z I B I T █ D E M O L I S H
M A K E M E █ E V A L U A T E
E N E R G Y █ C A R D I N A L
N E A T O █ D O N A S █ F T D
█ █ H O N E Y S U C K L E █
I N S █ D A L E █ D O R E M I
H O H O █ V I D A █ R U M E N
O R A N G E S █ T I E P I N S
P A R E E █ H I T S █ A N T E
S H E A R S █ N A P S █ G S T
█ J I M M O R R I S O N █ █
P O S █ A N I O N █ F E R M I
E N S E N A D A █ A T W O O D
R E U N I T E D █ R E T O O L
U S E D C A R S █ K N O T T Y
```

299

```
H S T █ S W I S S B A N K S
A O R B █ D I S P E R S I O N
S H U E █ I R R A T I O N A L
T I N G E █ E A S T O N █ █
Y O K E M A T E █ O N E A C T
█ █ N A T A L E █ █ L O U █
T H E T I P P I N G P O I N T
B E L L L A P █ G E O R G I E
S A L E S R E S I S T A N C E
P R E █ █ R E N T A L █ █ █
S T R A Y S █ N E S T E G G S
█ █ G E T F A R █ O X L I P
I N S I N U A T O R █ A O N E
F I R S T F L O O R █ M A Z E
S T A T E F A R M S █ T A D
```

300

```
S I M B A █ P U F F █ T B S P
O N A I R █ A T R O P H I E S
U S I N G █ N A I L F I L E S
S O N S O F T H E D E S E R T
E L F █ S A R A Z E N █ █ █
S E R B █ L I N E R N O T E S
█ █ A R I S E S █ I N A L L
R A M O N E S █ █ P A G E B O Y
O M E N S █ █ D O R S A L █ █
D I S C I P L I N E █ M E M O
█ █ S E A T I N G █ L A B █
S W E E T P O T A T O P I E S
M A D D O C T O R █ L Y N N E
U N I O N I Z E D █ F L E A S
T E E M █ D U D S █ S E N D S
```

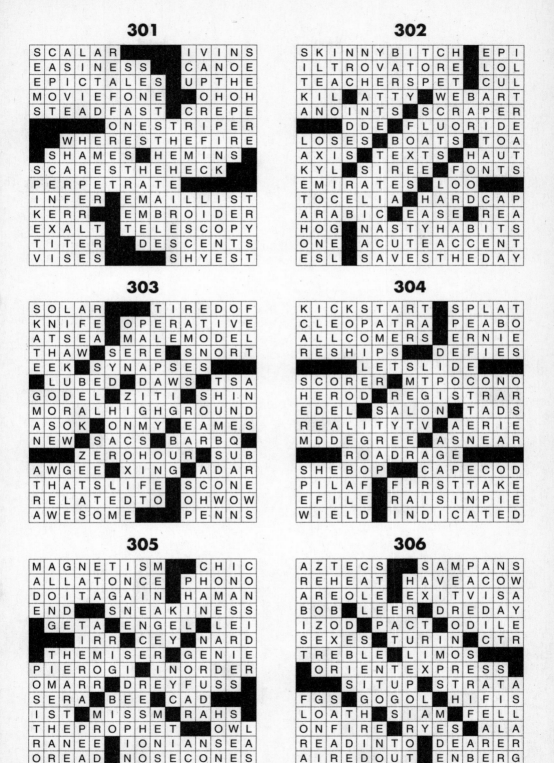

301

```
S C A L A R . . . I V I N S
E A S I N E S S . C A N O E
E P I C T A L E S . U P T H E
M O V I E F O N E . O H O H
S T E A D F A S T . C R E P E
. . . O N E S T R I P E R
. W H E R E S T H E F I R E
. S H A M E S . H E M I N S
S C A R E S T H E H E C K
P E R P E T R A T E
I N F E R . E M A I L L I S T
K E R R . E M B R O I D E R
E X A L T . T E L E S C O P Y
T I T E R . . D E S C E N T S
V I S E S . . . S H Y E S T
```

302

```
S K I N N Y B I T C H . E P I
I L T R O V A T O R E . L O L
T E A C H E R S P E T . C U L
K I L . A T T Y . W E B A R T
A N O I N T S . S C R A P E R
. . . D D E . F L U O R I D E
L O S E S . B O A T S . T O A
A X I S . T E X T S . H A U T
K Y L . S I R E E . F O N T S
E M I R A T E S . L O O
T O C E L I A . H A R D C A P
A R A B I C . E A S E . R E A
H O G . N A S T Y H A B I T S
O N E . A C U T E A C C E N T
E S L . S A V E S T H E D A Y
```

303

```
S O L A R . . T I R E D O F
K N I F E . O P E R A T I V E
A T S E A . M A L E M O D E L
T H A W . S E R E . S N O R T
E E K . S Y N A P S E S
. L U B E D . D A W S . T S A
G O D E L . Z I T I . S H I N
M O R A L H I G H G R O U N D
A S O K . O N M Y . E A M E S
N E W . S A C S . B A R B Q
. . Z E R O H O U R . S U B
A W G E E . X I N G . A D A R
T H A T S L I F E . S C O N E
R E L A T E D T O . O H W O W
A W E S O M E . . P E N N S
```

304

```
K I C K S T A R T . S P L A T
C L E O P A T R A . P E A B O
A L L C O M E R S . E R N I E
R E S H I P S . D E F I E S
. . . L E T S L I D E
S C O R E R . M T P O C O N O
H E R O D . R E G I S T R A R
E D E L . S A L O N . T A D S
R E A L I T Y T V . A E R I E
M D D E G R E E . A S N E A R
. . R O A D R A G E
S H E B O P . C A P E C O D
P I L A F . F I R S T T A K E
E F I L E . R A I S I N P I E
W I E L D . I N D I C A T E D
```

305

```
M A G N E T I S M . C H I C
A L L A T O N C E . P H O N O
D O I T A G A I N . H A M A N
E N D . S N E A K I N E S S
. G E T A . E N G E L . L E I
. . I R R . C E Y . N A R D
. T H E M I S E R . G E N I E
P I E R O G I . I N O R D E R
O M A R R . D R E Y F U S S
S E R A . B E E . C A D
I S T . M I S S M . R A H S
T H E P R O P H E T . O W L
R A N E E . I O N I A N S E A
O R E A D . N O S E C O N E S
N E D S . S T A R T W I T H
```

306

```
A Z T E C S . S A M P A N S
R E H E A T . H A V E A C O W
A R E O L E . E X I T V I S A
B O B . L E E R . D R E D A Y
I Z O D . P A C T . O D I L E
S E X E S . T U R I N . C T R
T R E B L E . L I M O S
. O R I E N T E X P R E S S
. . S I T U P . S T R A T A
F G S . G O G O L . H I F I S
L O A T H . S I A M . F E L L
O N F I R E . R Y E S . A L A
R E A D I N T O . D E A R E R
A I R E D O U T . E N B E R G
S N I D E S T . A T E A S E
```

307

```
S A D R C I T Y ■ B E I G E S
T R U E L O V E ■ E L N I N O
A T A L A N T A ■ E M A J O R
T I L ■ M I R R O R ■ R O T E
E C R U ■ C A N A ■ Q U E E N
S L O P E ■ Y E R O U T ■ ■
M E L O T T ■ D E S E ■ S K Y
A V E N U E C ■ D O N T L I E
N I S ■ D A R E ■ S C R I M S
■ ■ C E L I C A ■ H A D J I
S O N Y S ■ E S T D ■ P E O N
T E A R ■ I S E E I T ■ I N D
A S H A R P ■ G A S R A N G E
I T U N E S ■ A S C O T T I E
D E M O D E ■ R E I N H O L D
```

308

```
C O O K I E J A R ■ N O R M S
O P P O R T U N E ■ U B O A T
R E C O V E R E D ■ R I O J A
E R I K ■ S Y M S ■ S E T O N
S A T Y R ■ B I T T E ■ C R I
■ ■ E C O C A R ■ F A D S
J U N K F A X ■ R E T I N O L
E N U R E S ■ ■ P A J A M A
A D M I R A L ■ M A N I L O W
N E B S ■ B U S O N I ■ ■
G R E ■ B A R Q S ■ A B B A S
E R R O L ■ C U E S ■ L I Z A
N A O M I ■ H I L L S I D E S
E T N A S ■ E N L A R G E R S
T E E N S ■ S T E V I E R A Y
```

309

```
A S S U A G E ■ G R A P P L E
P O U R C O L D W A T E R O N
I M A G I N A R Y F R I E N D
E B B E D ■ P E N T A ■ N E Z
C E L S ■ A S S N S ■ P A S O
E R E ■ E L I S E ■ R A T O N
■ ■ C R O N Y ■ S E S A M E
W I S H I N G ■ G E N T L E S
A C T O N E ■ D I R T Y ■ ■
T E R M S ■ H O F F A ■ J E D
C H I P ■ R U N T S ■ M E M O
H O C ■ R E N E W ■ C I R C E
O U T R I G G E R C A N O E S
U S E D C A R S A L E S M E N
T E R S E L Y ■ P I N K E S T
```

310

```
A D E ■ R O L O ■ C O R N E R
D J S ■ E L O N ■ A R E O L A
Z I P P I E S T ■ J E S T E R
■ B R I N G T O J U S T I C E
P O E T S ■ O P E N ■ A M T S
R U S T ■ A N O N ■ N T E S T
O T S ■ R E F E R E E ■ ■
M I O ■ R E S T S O N ■ S T U
■ ■ P A S C H A L ■ T I S
A B R A M ■ O E I L ■ M A R E
D E A D ■ R O W S ■ F I R E D
V E N T R I L O Q U I S T S ■
I T C H E S ■ R U N F O R I T
S L O A N E ■ L O O T ■ E A R
E E R I E R ■ D I S H ■ K S U
```

311

```
M R I S ■ ■ E G O B O O S T S
A I N T ■ P A T E N T L A W
D P L U S ■ O Z O N E H O L E
L E E ■ T A X E S ■ N E W M E
I N A N E L Y ■ F I R E U P
B I G A P E ■ B L O G ■ R D S
S N U F F ■ H A I G H T ■ ■
■ G E T O N T H E S T I C K
■ ■ A R O M A S ■ S E A N S
P R O ■ D E L I ■ S T O P I T
R E N E W S ■ P L A N S T O
E L E M I ■ D E I O N ■ I T O
C A P E V E R D E ■ D A Z E D
I T I N E R A N T ■ J E R I
S E N D S A W A Y ■ A S S N
```

312

```
S A R C A S M ■ E M P O W E R
A Q U A R I A ■ T E A T I M E
N U L L I T Y ■ I N T E R I M
J A E ■ D U B U Q U E ■ E N E
O M O O ■ P E R U ■ R A M E N
S A U N A S ■ B E D S T A N D
E N T E R ■ S A T E ■ O N T
■ ■ G I G A N T I S M ■ ■
■ S T A ■ E L I E ■ K A F I R
S C H M A L T Z ■ C A N A D A
P R I E D ■ W E A R ■ T R E N
I O N ■ R O A D B E D ■ S A P
C O M F O R T ■ I W O J I M A
E G A L I T E ■ D E R I D E S
S E N A T O R ■ E L E M E N T
```

313

P	A	S	S	E	D	U	P	■	S	T	U	P	I	D
A	R	T	U	R	O	T	O	S	C	A	N	I	N	I
C	L	E	R	I	C	A	L	C	O	L	L	A	R	S
M	E	R	G	E	■	H	A	I	R	L	I	N	E	S
A	N	N	E	■	C	A	R	O	N	■	M	O	P	E
N	E	O	■	F	O	G	I	N	■	N	I	K	O	N
■	■	N	A	M	E	S	■	C	U	T	E	S	T	■
M	A	D	I	G	A	N	■	S	A	D	E	Y	E	S
C	L	O	N	E	S	■	D	O	M	E	D	■	■	■
E	G	G	O	N	■	L	O	C	U	S	■	M	U	D
N	E	W	T	■	H	U	L	K	S	■	T	I	L	E
T	R	A	C	T	A	B	L	E	■	P	U	N	T	S
I	N	T	H	E	N	E	A	R	F	U	T	U	R	E
R	O	C	K	A	N	D	R	O	L	L	S	T	A	R
E	N	H	A	L	O	■	S	O	U	P	I	E	S	T

314

G	E	T	S	M	A	D	■	C	E	R	E	A	L	S
A	C	E	T	O	N	E	■	U	T	E	N	S	I	L
B	U	R	E	T	T	E	■	C	H	A	T	T	E	R
F	A	R	T	H	E	R	■	H	Y	D	R	A	S	■
E	D	I	T	E	D	■	D	I	L	■	A	I	L	S
S	O	N	I	A	■	O	R	F	E	■	P	R	O	W
T	R	E	N	T	■	P	O	R	N	O	■	E	W	E
■	■	■	G	E	N	E	V	I	E	V	E	■	■	■
U	M	P	■	N	O	N	E	T	■	E	X	A	C	T
K	I	R	S	■	C	L	I	O	■	R	I	S	H	I
E	N	O	L	■	H	E	N	■	P	A	S	S	E	L
■	E	X	O	C	E	T	■	T	A	C	T	U	A	L
T	R	I	P	L	E	T	■	S	A	T	I	A	T	E
V	A	M	O	O	S	E	■	A	V	E	N	G	E	R
S	L	A	N	D	E	R	■	R	O	D	G	E	R	S

315

S	A	D	B	U	T	T	R	U	E	■	L	O	D	I
G	R	E	E	N	B	E	A	N	S	■	A	V	O	N
T	E	N	N	I	S	A	C	E	S	■	R	E	T	E
M	O	V	E	■	P	R	O	V	E	■	K	N	O	X
A	L	E	T	A	■	D	O	I	N	G	■	M	A	C
J	A	R	■	T	B	O	N	E	■	U	N	I	T	E
■	■	M	E	O	W	S	■	C	N	O	T	E	S	■
S	O	D	A	C	A	N	■	L	O	C	A	T	E	S
T	H	E	A	R	T	■	J	O	N	A	H	■	■	■
A	R	E	S	O	■	L	A	W	N	S	■	N	O	R
M	E	R	■	W	H	O	M	E	■	E	V	A	D	E
P	A	S	T	■	A	V	E	R	T	■	I	P	O	D
A	L	K	A	■	L	E	S	L	E	Y	G	O	R	E
C	L	I	P	■	A	L	V	I	N	A	I	L	E	Y
T	Y	N	E	■	S	L	I	P	N	S	L	I	D	E

316

F	A	T	B	A	C	K	■	N	E	T	F	L	I	X
A	R	E	A	M	A	P	■	A	N	A	L	O	G	Y
S	O	L	D	E	R	S	■	R	E	M	O	V	A	L
O	N	E	L	E	G	■	S	I	S	■	R	E	V	E
■	■	A	R	O	M	A	S	■	H	A	R	E	M	■
A	T	T	N	■	P	A	C	■	D	E	L	■	■	■
R	O	A	D	W	A	R	R	I	O	R	■	J	A	M
C	O	N	S	E	N	T	I	N	G	A	D	U	L	T
H	T	S	■	S	T	A	L	A	C	T	I	T	E	S
■	X	E	S	■	E	W	A	■	R	E	S	T	■	■
Q	A	T	A	R	■	I	G	E	T	I	T	■	■	■
U	L	A	N	■	P	R	E	■	C	A	R	T	E	L
A	V	I	A	T	O	R	■	S	H	M	O	O	Z	E
K	I	L	D	A	R	E	■	S	E	S	A	M	E	S
E	N	S	U	I	N	G	■	E	R	O	D	E	R	S

317

I	M	A	C	■	S	K	A	T	E	O	V	E	R
N	O	N	O	■	M	A	I	D	E	N	N	A	M	E
A	N	O	N	■	A	L	P	H	A	T	E	S	T	S
P	O	T	T	E	R	■	S	O	R	R	I	E	S	T
O	P	H	E	L	I	A	■	C	O	O	L	■	■	■
T	H	E	S	S	A	L	Y	■	S	P	L	A	T
H	O	R	S	E	■	G	O	R	E	Y	■	T	A	B
E	N	Y	A	■	C	A	K	E	S	■	M	A	K	E
R	I	O	■	B	L	E	E	P	■	V	A	L	E	T
■	C	U	R	I	E	■	L	E	M	O	N	L	A	W
■	A	F	A	R	■	L	E	T	I	T	B	E
B	E	D	C	O	V	E	R	■	R	E	T	I	R	E
I	C	E	I	C	E	B	A	B	Y	■	O	M	E	N
T	H	E	N	A	T	U	R	A	L	■	B	E	A	U
S	O	R	E	L	O	S	E	R	■	A	S	K	S

318

P	U	B	Q	U	I	Z	■	U	N	S	N	A	R	L
A	N	O	U	N	C	E	■	G	O	T	F	R	E	E
P	I	L	A	T	E	S	■	G	N	O	C	C	H	I
A	C	E	S	O	U	T	■	B	E	A	T	S	I	T
D	O	R	A	■	P	E	R	O	T	■	E	I	R	E
O	D	O	R	S	■	D	E	O	■	C	A	N	E	R
C	E	S	S	N	A	■	S	T	J	A	M	E	S	■
■	■	■	A	L	R	O	S	E	N	■	■	■	■	■
■	H	A	I	R	G	E	L	■	W	I	N	D	O	W
G	O	R	M	E	■	D	E	B	■	D	U	E	N	A
A	P	I	A	■	R	A	D	I	I	■	M	R	E	S
M	I	S	D	E	A	L	■	P	D	Q	B	A	C	H
E	N	T	E	N	T	E	■	E	S	T	E	L	L	E
S	T	A	I	N	E	R	■	D	A	Y	S	T	A	R
T	O	S	T	A	R	T	■	S	Y	S	T	E	M	S

319

```
  C L A I M T O F A M E
  T H E W O M A N I L O V E
J E A L O U S M I S T R E S S
A N N A L S   P O K E I N T O
M A N N S   B E N E   A B A B
I C E D   E A R S   C R E T E
E E L   S L U R   C U T T E R
    D I M M E M O R Y
N F L E R S   S I Z E   H E P
B L O T S   A I R Y   B O N O
C O C O   O R S O   B E T T E
T R A N S E C T   G A S L I T
V I T A L S T A T I S T I C S
  N O T A T A N Y P R I C E
    R E G E N T S P A R K
```

320

```
S P L A S H G U A R D   S R S
T O U J O U R S G A I   E E C
U N P A T R I O T I C   A S U
A G O   S T E P   L E G S I T
R E N     R E M B R A N D T
T E E D U P   N E A   G A U L
    A N A   S S R   S K E E
L I M N I N G   H O S T E S S
I L E T   C I A   N E E
E L L E   A V I   S E R B I A
A T T A C K E R S     E N G
B R O N Z E   B A E R   A G E
E E R   E D G A R B E R G E N
D A M   C A E S A R S A L A D
S T E   H Y M E N O P T E R A
```

321

```
S A L E S R E S I S T A N C E
T H E E L E V E N T H H O U R
A M E R I C A N D R E A M E R
Y E S   C O N T O U R   E D S
    H E N     M O B
L O P E R   G A S   B A S E D
A V E R S I O N T H E R A P Y
P I E R   M U N R O   R U I N
I N V I T E D A U D I E N C E
S E E N O   A N T   C L A S S
    G U T     W E S
A B S   G R E A S E D   J A I
W E A T H E R S T A T I O N S
A D L A I E S T E V E N S O N
R E A L E S T A T E A G E N T
```

322

```
S C H L I T Z   A B C N E W S
I H E A R Y A   M O R A V I A
K E Y W O R D   Y O U M I N D
H E M   N E O J A Z Z   L E D
I R R S   E R O D E   H E B E
S I D L E   A K A   M A Y A N
M O J A V E   E M P O W E R S
    N E L L   S A C K
C O A T R O O M   W H I L E D
A L L E Y   S E Q   A N O D E
M E L D   V E N U S   S W A M
E S T   N A H U A T L   T S P
O T H E L L O   C O U S I N S
F R A M E U P   K I K I D E E
F A T F R E E   S C E N E R Y
```

323

```
  T H E O N C E O V E R
  F O O T B A L L W I D O W
S A Y T H E M A G I C W O R D
A Z O R E S   M A N E A T E R
R O T O R   B O R G   R O T I
G O A D   P O R T   E D U C E
E L S   E A D S   S M I T H S
    A X I S   Q E I I
T I G G E R   S U E T   O L A
A N A I S   F L I P   D R I P
B A T T   B A E Z   L E D E R
A R E A C O D E   F I L E N E
C U L T U R E V U L T U R E S
  G E O R G I E P O R G I E
    G R E E N S C R E E N
```

324

```
A P O S T A T E   S E A W A R
P E C T O R A L   U M P I R E
P E T E R M E N   M I A S M A
A D A G E   B O O T T R E E S
L E N O   H O R N E   T U N S
L E T S B E   T E R A   P I U
    A L I N E S   B S T A R
M A G U I R E   E C O T O N E
A L E R T   P A T R I A
H A N   Z E A L   A L L P R O
I B E T   C L I N G   L E A N
M A R A C A I B O   B I R D S
A M I N O R   A M B R O S I A
H A C K I T   B A R O N I A L
I N S A N E   A D A M S A L E
```

325

```
S P R E E ■ P E A T ■ Y I N G
H O U R L Y R A T E ■ O M O O
O P E N S E A S O N ■ U P T O
P E R S I S T E N T ■ K U R D
■ ■ E W E S ■ H E N L E Y ■ ■
T A L E S E ■ B A S S O S ■ ■
W N E T ■ D A Y S ■ S W E D E
O K S H O O T ■ S H O W B I Z
D E S A C ■ K A T O ■ H U M E
■ I N T H A T ■ T R O Y E R
W A S H O E ■ T A M E ■ ■
A L M A ■ M R U N I V E R S E
S L O W ■ S I N G L E S B A R
P O R K ■ I C E S K A T I N G
S K E E ■ N E S T ■ L A S S O
```

326

```
S N A C K B A R S ■ P A S T A
F I L E N A M E S ■ E L T O N
U N L E A S H E S ■ Y E A R N
M E G ■ R I E L ■ O O C Y T E
A P O P ■ C R I S P ■ P O T
T I N A S ■ S N I P E H U N T
O N E S P O T ■ B O L O T I E
■ S I R ■ ■ S E T ■ ■
C R E A K E D ■ S E C T O R S
D I R T Y L O O K ■ T I B E T
R P I ■ S A T I N ■ P E L E
A T T L E E ■ I P O D ■ R I G
C O R A L ■ J O A N A L L E N
K R E M E ■ A S S E R T I V E
S N A P E ■ W E S T E R N E R
```

327

```
A L A B A M A ■ G R I S H A M
M O L O T O V ■ R E N A U L T
T H E A F R I C A N Q U E E N
O A R S ■ S A I D A ■ E Y E S
O N T ■ R E T A I L E R ■ ■
■ S E C E D E ■ S K I M P
A L O N S O ■ I N H O R R O R
W O R E ■ D I R T Y ■ A E R O
N A Z A R E N E ■ P A U S E D
S M O K E ■ A C C E N T ■ ■
■ T O P S T O R Y ■ F A O
A M A H ■ A N O U T ■ A A R P
M A G I C C A R P E T R I D E
F L E E C E R ■ E X A L T E D
M I S F I R E ■ S T J O H N S
```

328

```
J I F F Y P O P ■ R A C I S T
A R E A M A P S ■ A D O N A I
V O L T A G E S ■ D E S A D E
A N T E ■ E N T A I L ■ S S R
M A T ■ P R Y ■ L O A F P A N
A G I L E ■ O W L S ■ R I C E
N E P A L ■ U R G E ■ I N K Y
■ S E A R O U T E S ■
H I S S ■ N E T S ■ A C H E S
O D I E ■ N Y E S ■ R O A S T
W A N N A B E ■ I D S ■ I T A
A H A ■ U L S T E R ■ B R E T
R O T A R Y ■ A D O R A B L E
D A R N I T ■ T U N A R O L L
S N A T C H ■ S P E E D W A Y
```

329

```
M O T H ■ A D D I S A B A B A
I N R I ■ C R A N K C A S E S
A L O G ■ T E R R A C O T T A
S E T H L O W ■ A T T ■ R A J
M A T T D R U D G E ■ T I R O
A V E R S ■ P A S ■ K O D A K
S E R E ■ S O B ■ R I B E Y E
■ A V O N ■ D A T A ■
A V I S O S ■ J I F ■ C A R R
X E N O N ■ S A G ■ S C R E E
O N A N ■ W E R E D O O M E D
L T S ■ L E N ■ R I P S O N E
O U T S I D E M A N ■ H I T E
T R I P L I C A T E ■ O R E M
L A R R Y D A V I D ■ P E R S
```

330

```
P A S S T H E H A T ■ B R E R
O N T H E S T A G E ■ L A M E
K O O L A I D M A N ■ T I A S
E U R E K A ■ I V A ■ S N I T
S T E P S ■ S T E N S ■ M L S
■ A P U ■ T A M A L E
H A R D S H I P S ■ N O K I A
O N E U N I T ■ A N D R E S S
N A N C E ■ S T A G P A R T Y
E S T E E M ■ H B O ■
S T A ■ S A F E S ■ N A G A T
T A L K ■ D O W ■ S E S A M E
A S C I ■ A D A P T A T I O N
B I A S ■ M O V I E T I T L E
E A R S ■ E R E C T O R S E T
```

331

J	A	N	E	F	O	N	D	A		D	E	P	T	S
I	M	O	N	A	D	I	E	T		O	W	L	E	T
G	O	L	D	W	A	T	C	H		R	E	I	N	A
G	R	O	I	N			I	A	M	A	R	O	C	K
L	A	S	T		O	L	D	N	A	G		C	E	E
E	L	S		G	R	E	E	D	Y		K	E	N	O
		U	P	E	N	D			B	A	N	T	U	
H	A	N	S	O	L	O		L	E	A	N	E	S	T
I	D	E	E	S			S	I	L	K	S			
G	R	A	D		T	I	C	K	L	E		K	O	S
H	O	R		G	A	S	H	E	S		K	A	R	N
S	I	B	E	R	I	A	N			S	Y	R	I	A
P	T	E	R	O		Y	O	U	R	H	O	N	O	R
O	L	E	O	S		N	O	N	E	A	T	A	L	L
T	Y	R	O	S		O	K	E	Y	D	O	K	E	Y

332

S	A	M	E		S	M	A	R	T	D	R	U	G	S
E	B	O	N		P	E	N	T	H	O	U	S	E	S
X	E	N	A		L	A	T	E	D	I	N	N	E	R
O	R	T		R	I	T	Z			N	E	A	R	S
B	R	E	V	I	T	Y		M	U	G	S			
J	A	C	O	B	S		F	I	F	I		F	I	B
E	T	A	T	S		L	E	M	O	N	S	O	D	A
C	I	R	E		R	A	V	E	S		C	U	E	R
T	O	L	D	T	A	L	E	S		L	U	N	A	R
S	N	O		A	J	A	R		R	I	D	D	L	E
			S	L	A	W		S	E	T	S	A	I	L
F	R	A	N	K		C	E	D	E		T	S	R	
L	I	V	E	I	N	M	A	I	D		T	I	T	O
O	C	E	A	N	B	O	R	N	E		R	O	I	L
R	O	C	K	G	A	R	D	E	N		E	N	C	L

333

S	P	I	N	A	L	T	A	P		P	A	E	A	N
H	O	M	E	L	O	A	N	S		A	P	P	L	E
A	M	P	L	I	T	U	D	E		S	P	I	K	E
L	E	A	S	T			R	U	B	E		S	A	D
O	L	I	O		V	O	O	D	O	O	D	O	L	L
M	O	R	N		A	R	M	O	R		E	D	I	E
			I	S	E	E		G	L	E	N	S		
Z	I	E	G	F	E	L	D	F	O	L	L	I	E	S
I	D	L	E	S			A	L	D	O				
M	E	D	S		A	G	G	I	E		E	W	O	K
B	O	O	T	S	T	R	A	P	S		V	I	B	E
A	G	R		T	E	A	L			D	E	N	T	E
B	R	A	V	O		P	A	C	K	I	N	G	U	P
W	A	D	E	R		E	X	P	E	R	T	I	S	E
E	M	O	T	E		S	Y	L	V	E	S	T	E	R

334

E	G	G			O	R	F	F		N	O	M	S	G
T	O	R	T		L	E	O	I		I	R	E	N	E
A	R	E	A		I	L	O	V	E	P	A	R	I	S
L	E	A	K		O	U	T	E	R		L	E	T	T
	S	T	E	P		C	L	A	N					
	U	A	R		T	O	N		R	O	A	R		
M	A	N	T	O	M	A	N	D	E	F	E	N	S	E
O	N	C	O	M	I	N	G	T	R	A	F	F	I	C
R	O	L	L	O	N	T	H	E	G	R	O	U	N	D
A	X	E	L			D	O	N		A	C	R		
			C	R	T	S		D	U	L	Y			
O	A	T	H		H	A	D	T	O		S	O	U	P
P	L	E	A	S	E	G	O	O	N		E	U	R	O
E	M	A	I	L		O	G	R	E		S	G	T	S
D	A	L	L	Y		N	S	E	C			H	S	T

335

W	E	A	S	E	L	W	O	R	D	S		S	C	H
R	I	G	H	T	S	I	D	E	U	P		C	I	A
I	N	C	O	H	E	R	E	N	C	E		O	R	S
T	E	Y		I	V	E	S		K	L	A	T	C	H
			I	C	E	D		S	C	U	T	T	L	E
A	S	A	M	A	N		S	H	A	N	T	I	E	S
P	H	I	A	L		A	W	A	L	K		E	L	O
G	O	R	Y		T	C	E	L	L		C	D	I	V
A	R	C		R	A	R	E	E		R	O	O	N	E
R	E	A	R	E	X	I	T		S	I	N	G	E	R
S	C	R	I	B	E	D		S	H	O	E			
C	O	R	T	E	X		B	E	A	T		P	S	S
O	V	I		K	I	S	S	M	Y	G	R	I	T	S
R	E	E		A	L	U	M	I	N	U	M	C	A	N
E	R	R		H	E	A	T	S	E	N	S	O	R	S

336

R	A	Z	O	R		T	R	A	V	E	L	E	R	
A	Z	U	R	E	S		H	E	S	A	L	I	V	E
G	O	L	E	F	T		E	L	I	C	I	T	E	D
A	D	E		L	A	T	V	I	A			E	L	O
S	Y	M	M	E	T	R	I	C	M	A	T	R	I	X
		E	A	R	C	L	I	P		I	N	S	A	N	E
			S	T	E	M	S		N	A	P	L	E	S
E	S	C	H	E	R	S		W	O	K	S			
S	C	R	O	D		S	A	R	I		F	A	X	
C	H	E	W	I	N	G	O	N		N	I	E	C	E
A	R	P		M	O	O	N	E	D		S	E	E	R
P	O	E		A	P	E	S		R	E	A	D	T	O
A	D	P	A	G	E	S		J	U	R	Y	B	O	X
D	E	A	R	E	S	T		A	S	I	N	I	N	E
E	R	N	E	S	T	O		W	E	E	O	N	E	S

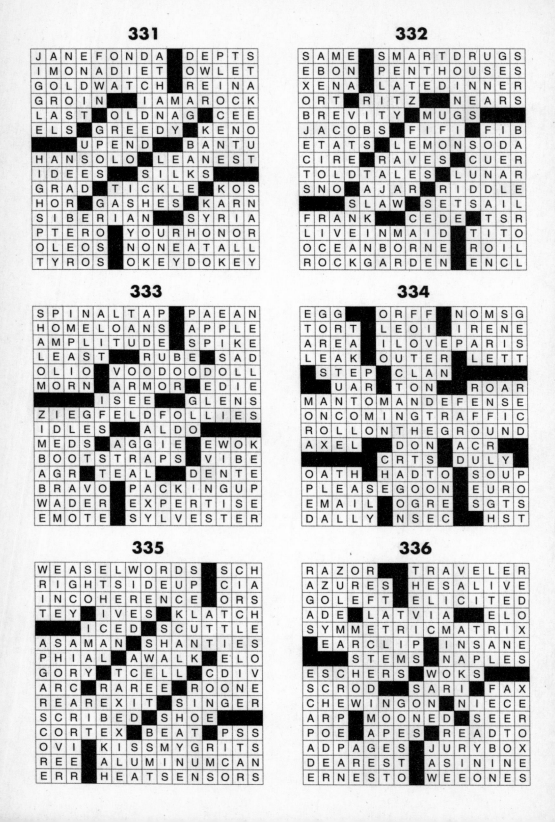

337

T	H	E	S	T	A	R	S	A	N	D	B	A	R	S
H	A	V	E	A	N	O	P	I	N	I	O	N	O	N
U	S	E	T	H	E	T	E	L	E	P	H	O	N	E
M	T	N	■	I	M	A	C	■	■	P	E	T	E	R
P	O	M	■	N	I	L	■	P	R	E	M	E	E	T
■	S	O	N	I	C	■	B	L	A	R	E	■	■	
A	T	N	O	S	■	C	O	U	P	S	■	W	A	D
M	O	E	T	■	W	A	R	M	S	■	P	E	R	U
S	P	Y	■	T	Y	P	E	B	■	N	O	N	C	E
■	■	G	R	E	E	D	■	R	A	I	T	T	■	
A	L	L	I	A	S	K	■	L	E	M	■	A	I	M
S	E	I	J	I	■	■	D	E	B	I	■	S	C	I
B	A	N	A	N	A	R	E	P	U	B	L	I	C	S
I	V	E	N	E	V	E	R	T	R	I	E	D	I	T
G	E	N	E	R	A	L	M	A	N	A	G	E	R	S

338

E	B	E	R	T	■	S	H	A	D	■	T	A	S	S
D	O	N	O	R	■	C	A	P	I	■	R	I	P	A
G	A	R	B	A	G	E	B	A	G	■	U	R	A	L
I	T	A	L	I	A	N	I	C	E	■	E	C	C	E
N	E	G	O	T	I	A	T	E	S	■	R	E	E	S
G	R	E	W	■	■	■	T	A	I	L	O	R		
■	■	E	L	E	C	T	R	I	C	B	L	U	E	
G	A	L	■	O	N	L	E	A	V	E	■	S	T	P
A	L	E	C	G	U	I	N	N	E	S	S	■	■	
S	L	A	L	O	M	■	■	E	S	S	A			
R	E	P	O	■	E	L	I	Z	A	B	E	T	H	I
A	Y	E	S	■	R	U	L	E	M	A	K	E	R	S
N	O	D	E	■	A	X	I	S	O	F	E	V	I	L
G	O	U	T	■	T	O	U	T	■	T	R	I	K	E
E	P	P	S	■	E	R	M	A	■	A	S	E	E	D

339

S	P	A	S	M	S	■	M	A	C	G	Y	V	E	R
T	I	L	T	A	T	■	O	N	L	O	A	N	T	O
A	S	T	A	G	E	■	N	E	E	D	H	E	L	P
S	T	A	R	E	■	V	I	T	A	L	■	C	A	Y
■	A	R	T	E	M	I	S	■	N	I	C	K	■	
A	C	R	O	■	A	A	M	I	L	N	E	■	■	
C	H	A	N	G	S	■	S	C	I	E	N	C	E	S
I	I	I	■	E	S	O	■	I	N	S	■	A	N	O
D	O	L	I	T	T	L	E	■	E	S	T	E	E	M
■	■	P	A	R	A	M	U	S	■	I	S	M	E	
■	H	O	R	A	■	B	A	S	E	P	A	Y		
E	T	E	■	A	N	D	R	E	■	N	O	R	M	A
D	O	A	S	I	S	A	Y	■	S	A	V	E	I	T
N	O	T	A	S	I	D	O	■	I	M	E	A	N	T
A	T	H	L	E	T	E	S	■	B	I	R	N	E	Y

340

M	O	R	T	A	R	A	N	D	P	E	S	T	L	E
A	V	E	N	G	E	R	■	O	R	D	E	R	I	N
C	O	S	T	I	N	G	■	S	I	G	N	I	N	G
H	I	P	■	O	D	O	R	I	Z	E	■	L	E	A
I	D	O	L	■	S	N	I	D	E	■	S	L	O	G
N	A	N	O	S	■	N	C	O	■	S	P	I	N	E
E	L	D	U	Q	U	E	■	S	T	E	I	N	E	M
W	■	R	U	N	■	■	I	A	N	■	■	E		
A	T	P	E	A	C	E	■	U	N	L	E	A	R	N
S	H	I	E	D	■	L	O	N	■	S	T	R	A	T
H	E	E	D	■	L	A	U	D	E	■	S	S	T	S
A	R	R	■	D	A	N	I	E	L	S	■	E	A	T
B	E	C	K	E	T	T	■	R	I	P	I	N	T	O
L	I	E	O	V	E	R	■	G	H	A	N	I	A	N
E	N	D	S	O	N	A	S	O	U	R	N	O	T	E

341

W	I	T	H	E	R	S	■	P	F	I	Z	E	R	
O	N	E	O	C	A	T	■	P	E	R	R	I	N	E
O	F	N	O	U	S	E	■	O	R	A	T	O	R	S
L	O	A	D	■	T	E	F	L	O	N	■	N	A	T
E	R	N	O	■	A	L	R	I	T	Z	■	I	G	O
N	I	C	O	L	■	M	I	T	■	M	S	E	C	
S	T	Y	■	A	D	A	G	I	O	■	O	M	S	K
■	R	O	U	G	H	C	A	S	T	■	■			
B	A	L	E	■	I	N	T	A	K	E	■	R	A	F
E	N	I	D	■	O	W	L	■	A	I	O	L	I	
E	G	O	■	F	I	L	I	A	L	■	M	M	I	X
F	U	N	■	E	M	I	G	R	E	■	P	U	M	A
A	L	I	B	A	B	A	■	E	P	A	U	L	E	T
L	A	Z	A	R	U	S	■	N	E	P	T	U	N	E
O	R	E	L	S	E	■	A	R	R	E	S	T	S	

342

R	A	I	S	A	■	P	E	T	T	I	S	H		
E	S	S	E	N	E	■	G	O	N	E	I	N	T	O
S	T	I	P	E	S	■	A	L	L	M	E	T	A	L
T	U	T	T	U	T	■	S	L	I	P	P	E	R	Y
A	T	T	I	R	E	■	B	U	S	L	I	N	E	
F	E	R	M	I	S	■	A	T	T	E	N	D	S	
F	L	U	E	S	■	O	G	E	E	■	■			
■	Y	E	S	M	A	N	■	R	E	E	F	E	R	
■	■	T	R	A	S	■	S	O	N	E	S			
■	I	M	P	E	T	U	S	■	T	O	O	T	L	E
■	N	O	R	M	A	N	S	■	Y	T	T	R	I	A
A	T	R	O	P	I	N	E	■	R	E	P	A	S	T
C	U	I	S	I	N	E	S	■	O	R	A	C	H	E
E	N	T	E	R	E	R	S	■	S	I	T	T	E	R
R	E	A	D	E	R	S	■	C	H	E	S	S		

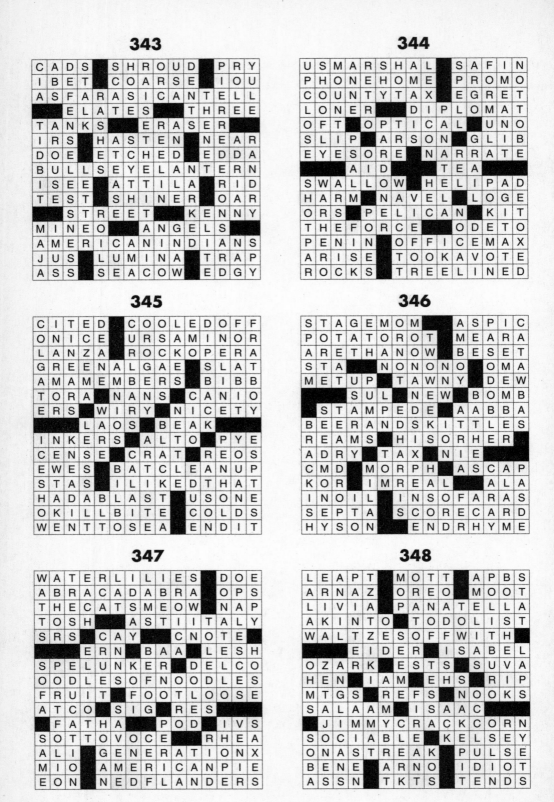

343

C	A	D	S	■	S	H	R	O	U	D	■	P	R	Y
I	B	E	T	■	C	O	A	R	S	E	■	I	O	U
A	S	F	A	R	A	S	I	C	A	N	T	E	L	L
■	■	E	L	A	T	E	S	■	■	T	H	R	E	E
T	A	N	K	S	■	■	E	R	A	S	E	R	■	■
I	R	S	■	H	A	S	T	E	N	■	N	E	A	R
D	O	E	■	E	T	C	H	E	D	■	E	D	D	A
B	U	L	L	S	E	Y	E	L	A	N	T	E	R	N
I	S	E	E	■	A	T	T	I	L	A	■	R	I	D
T	E	S	T	■	S	H	I	N	E	R	■	O	A	R
■	■	S	T	R	E	E	T	■	■	K	E	N	N	Y
M	I	N	E	O	■	■	A	N	G	E	L	S	■	■
A	M	E	R	I	C	A	N	I	N	D	I	A	N	S
J	U	S	■	L	U	M	I	N	A	■	T	R	A	P
A	S	S	■	S	E	A	C	O	W	■	E	D	G	Y

344

U	S	M	A	R	S	H	A	L	■	S	A	F	I	N
P	H	O	N	E	H	O	M	E	■	P	R	O	M	O
C	O	U	N	T	Y	T	A	X	■	E	G	R	E	T
L	O	N	E	R	■	D	I	P	L	O	M	A	T	■
O	F	T	■	O	P	T	I	C	A	L	■	U	N	O
S	L	I	P	■	A	R	S	O	N	■	G	L	I	B
E	Y	E	S	O	R	E	■	N	A	R	R	A	T	E
■	■	A	I	D	■	■	T	E	A	■	■	■
S	W	A	L	L	O	W	■	H	E	L	I	P	A	D
H	A	R	M	■	N	A	V	E	L	■	L	O	G	E
O	R	S	■	P	E	L	I	C	A	N	■	K	I	T
T	H	E	F	O	R	C	E	■	O	D	E	T	O	■
P	E	N	I	N	■	O	F	F	I	C	E	M	A	X
A	R	I	S	E	■	T	O	O	K	A	V	O	T	E
R	O	C	K	S	■	T	R	E	E	L	I	N	E	D

345

C	I	T	E	D	■	C	O	O	L	E	D	O	F	F
O	N	I	C	E	■	U	R	S	A	M	I	N	O	R
L	A	N	Z	A	■	R	O	C	K	O	P	E	R	A
G	R	E	E	N	A	L	G	A	E	■	S	L	A	T
A	M	A	M	E	M	B	E	R	S	■	B	I	B	B
T	O	R	A	■	N	A	N	S	■	C	A	N	I	O
E	R	S	■	W	I	R	Y	■	N	I	C	E	T	Y
■	■	L	A	O	S	■	B	E	A	K	■	■
I	N	K	E	R	S	■	A	L	T	O	■	P	Y	E
C	E	N	S	E	■	C	R	A	T	■	R	E	O	S
E	W	E	S	■	B	A	T	C	L	E	A	N	U	P
S	T	A	S	■	I	L	I	K	E	D	T	H	A	T
H	A	D	A	B	L	A	S	T	■	U	S	O	N	E
O	K	I	L	L	B	I	T	E	■	C	O	L	D	S
W	E	N	T	T	O	S	E	A	■	E	N	D	I	T

346

S	T	A	G	E	M	O	M	■	A	S	P	I	C
P	O	T	A	T	O	R	O	T	■	M	E	A	R	A
A	R	E	T	H	A	N	O	W	■	B	E	S	E	T
S	T	A	■	N	O	N	O	N	O	■	O	M	A
M	E	T	U	P	■	T	A	W	N	Y	■	D	E	W
■	■	S	U	L	■	N	E	W	■	B	O	M	B
■	S	T	A	M	P	E	D	E	■	A	A	B	B	A
B	E	E	R	A	N	D	S	K	I	T	T	L	E	S
R	E	A	M	S	■	H	I	S	O	R	H	E	R
A	D	R	Y	■	T	A	X	■	N	I	E
C	M	D	■	M	O	R	P	H	■	A	S	C	A	P
K	O	R	■	I	M	R	E	A	L	■	A	L	A
I	N	O	I	L	■	I	N	S	O	F	A	R	A	S
S	E	P	T	A	■	S	C	O	R	E	C	A	R	D
H	Y	S	O	N	■	E	N	D	R	H	Y	M	E

347

W	A	T	E	R	L	I	L	I	E	S	■	D	O	E
A	B	R	A	C	A	D	A	B	R	A	■	O	P	S
T	H	E	C	A	T	S	M	E	O	W	■	N	A	P
T	O	S	H	■	A	S	T	I	I	I	T	A	L	Y
S	R	S	■	C	A	Y	■	C	N	O	T	E	■
■	■	E	R	N	■	B	A	A	■	L	E	S	H
S	P	E	L	U	N	K	E	R	■	D	E	L	C	O
O	O	D	L	E	S	O	F	N	O	O	D	L	E	S
F	R	U	I	T	■	F	O	O	T	L	O	O	S	E
A	T	C	O	■	S	I	G	■	R	E	S	■
■	F	A	T	H	A	■	P	O	D	■	I	V	S
S	O	T	T	O	V	O	C	E	■	R	H	E	A
A	L	I	■	G	E	N	E	R	A	T	I	O	N	X
M	I	O	■	A	M	E	R	I	C	A	N	P	I	E
E	O	N	■	N	E	D	F	L	A	N	D	E	R	S

348

L	E	A	P	T	■	M	O	T	T	■	A	P	B	S
A	R	N	A	Z	■	O	R	E	O	■	M	O	O	T
L	I	V	I	A	■	P	A	N	A	T	E	L	L	A
A	K	I	N	T	O	■	T	O	D	O	L	I	S	T
W	A	L	T	Z	E	S	O	F	F	W	I	T	H	■
■	■	E	I	D	E	R	■	I	S	A	B	E	L
O	Z	A	R	K	■	E	S	T	S	■	S	U	V	A
H	E	N	■	I	A	M	■	E	H	S	■	R	I	P
M	T	G	S	■	R	E	F	S	■	N	O	O	K	S
S	A	L	A	A	M	■	I	S	A	A	C	■
■	J	I	M	M	Y	C	R	A	C	K	C	O	R	N
S	O	C	I	A	B	L	E	■	K	E	L	S	E	Y
O	N	A	S	T	R	E	A	K	■	P	U	L	S	E
B	E	N	E	■	A	R	N	O	■	I	D	I	O	T
A	S	S	N	■	T	K	T	S	■	T	E	N	D	S

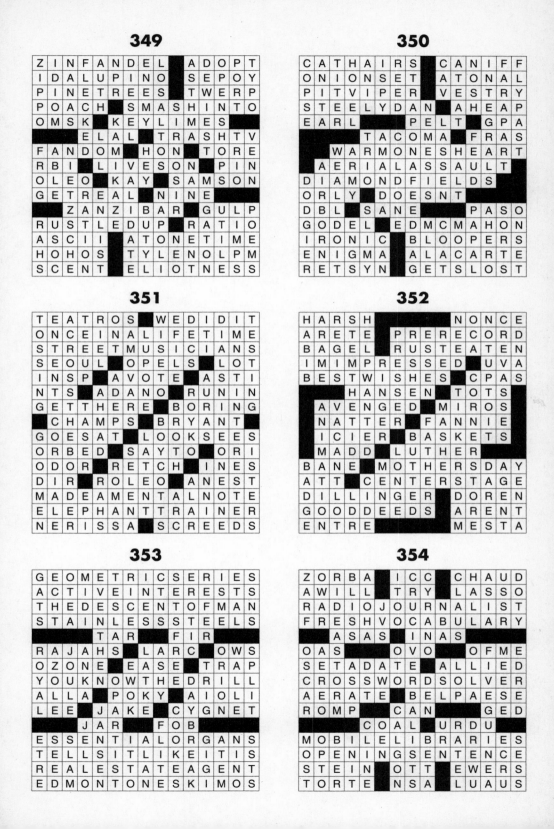

349

ZINFANDEL · ADOPT
IDALUPINO · SEPOY
PINETREES · TWERP
POACH · SMASHINTO
OMSK · KEYLIMES ·
· ELAL · TRASHTV
FANDOM · HON · TORE
RBI · LIVESON · PIN
OLEO · KAY · SAMSON
GETREAL · NINE ·
· ZANZIBAR · GULP
RUSTLEDUP · RATIO
ASCII · ATONETIME
HOHOS · TYLENOLPM
SCENT · ELIOTNESS

350

CATHAIRS · CANIFF
ONIONSET · ATONAL
PITVIPER · VESTRY
STEELYDAN · AHEAP
EARL · PELT · GPA
· TACOMA · FRAS
· WARMONESHEART
· AERIALASSAULT ·
DIAMONDFIELDS ·
ORLY · DOESNT ·
DBL · SANE · PASO
GODEL · EDMCMAHON
IRONIC · BLOOPERS
ENIGMA · ALACARTE
RETSYN · GETSLOST

351

TEATROS · WEDIDIT
ONCEINALIFETIME
STREETMUSICIANS
SEOUL · OPELS · LOT
INSP · AVOTE · ASTI
NTS · ADANO · RUNIN
GETTHERE · BORING
· CHAMPS · BRYANT ·
GOESAT · LOOKSEES
ORBED · SAYTO · ORI
ODOR · RETCH · INES
DIR · ROLEO · ANEST
MADEAMENTALNOTE
ELEPHANTTRAINER
NERISSA · SCREEDS

352

HARSH · NONCE
ARETE · PRERECORD
BAGEL · RUSTEATEN
IMIMPRESSED · UVA
BESTWISHES · CPAS
· HANSEN · TOTS ·
AVENGED · MIROS
NATTER · FANNIE
ICIER · BASKETS
MADD · LUTHER ·
BANE · MOTHERSDAY
ATT · CENTERSTAGE
DILLINGER · DOREN
GOODDEEDS · ARENT
ENTRE · MESTA

353

GEOMETRICSERIES
ACTIVEINTERESTS
THEDESCENTOFMAN
STAINLESSSTEELS
· TAR · FIR ·
RAJAHS · LARC · OWS
OZONE · EASE · TRAP
YOUKNOWTHEDRILL
ALLA · POKY · AIOLI
LEE · JAKE · CYGNET
· JAR · FOB ·
ESSENTIALORGANS
TELLSITLIKEITIS
REALESTATEAGENT
EDMONTONESKIMOS

354

ZORBA · ICC · CHAUD
AWILL · TRY · LASSO
RADIOJOURNALIST
FRESHVOCABULARY
· ASAS · INAS ·
OAS · OVO · OFME
SETADATE · ALLIED
CROSSWORDSOLVER
AERATE · BELPAESE
ROMP · CAN · GED
· COAL · URDU ·
MOBILELIBRARIES
OPENINGSENTENCE
STEIN · OTT · EWERS
TORTE · NSA · LUAUS

355

```
O F F I C E B O Y ■ T B A R S
H A R T C R A N E ■ E L I E L
B R O W N E Y E S ■ C A R G O
A M W A Y ■ S A N A ■ C R I S
B E N S ■ ■ O S H K O S H
Y R S ■ W A G S ■ S A L U T E
■ B A S T E ■ A G A T E S
J O E T H E P L U M B E R
R U P A U L ■ I S L A S
E D E S S A ■ A T T N ■ H M S
R I N S I N G ■ ■ F O A L
A C L U ■ D I C E ■ H I L D A
T I A R A ■ L A D I E S D A Y
E A T E N ■ D R I V E T I M E
S L E D S ■ S P E E D S T E R
```

356

```
B I G M A C ■ M I S S T E P
A D R A T E ■ P A R T T I M E
N E A R E R ■ O N E A R M E D
K A Z M A T S U I ■ C O B R A
E L I O T ■ K I L O ■ D A I L
R I O T ■ S O L A R C E L L S
S T S ■ F O A L ■ I O U
Y O U R F L Y I S O P E N
N E T ■ F R O S ■ P E I
R O A D T O R U I N ■ L I E N
A C M E ■ N E I N ■ G E L D S
S T A R A ■ U S A I N B O L T
H A N D G U N S ■ B O R G I A
E N D O R S E E ■ A M O U N T
S E A G O D S ■ R E N E G E
```

357

```
T H E W H O ■ S C H W A B
P E E L O U T ■ P H R A S E
S A N S K R I T ■ O R E L S E
C L O S E R S ■ C R I ■ K E G
H E R E S Y ■ C H E S H I R E
I T S ■ F O E ■ T A N T E
S T A G E M A N A G E R
M E X I C A N S T A N D O F F
B O Y M E E T S G I R L
C R I B S ■ A N D ■ L A U
H I S S Y F I T ■ H O O F I T
U P I ■ S I L ■ C A B R I D E
R O T A T E ■ C L U E L E S S
N U M B E R ■ H A N S O L O
S T E A M Y ■ I N T E N D
```

358

```
M A D P R O P S ■ P A T I N A
I V E H A D I T ■ O H S N A P
L A N D M I N E ■ L E A D U P
A L I ■ S U N R O O M ■ E T E
N O E S ■ M E N D S ■ M I A
O N D V D ■ D U O ■ T B A L L
■ E R A ■ M R P E A N U T
C A T L I K E ■ S O A N D S O
B R A T P A C K ■ I C K
A R I E S ■ L E S ■ H E S S E
T E L ■ P A T E N ■ R U I N
T S O ■ E A T C R O W ■ R E C
E T R A D E ■ H E R E W E G O
R E T I N A ■ U N S E A T E D
Y E O M A N ■ P E E P H O L E
```

359

```
B U I L D S ■ A L A R M S
E N T E R E D ■ G L A R E A T
G E S T A P O ■ R E D T A P E
F A D ■ W I N T E R S ■ C P R
O T O ■ A T E A T ■ S H I N
R E N T S ■ T A T ■ W H I N E
N E I L A R M S T R O N G
T I M E S A V E R
T R A N S A T L A N T I C
T H U N K ■ D E T ■ S A S H A
R E B S ■ W O R L D ■ R A D
I F A ■ H A N S A R P ■ A R E
S I D E A R M ■ K I S S E R S
T R U S T E E ■ E P A U L E T
E M B O S S ■ S T R I D E
```

360

```
I D E A M E N ■ L A S S I E S
B U F F A L O B I L L C O D Y
E N G A G E M E N T R I N G S
G E H R I G ■ L E O S ■ E E C
■ C A S T R O ■ O S S O
O D O M ■ N E W S N O W
T E X A S T E A ■ A G N A T E
I L E N E ■ P Y M ■ R I L E Y
C I N E M A ■ B E G E N T L E
■ T I L L A G E ■ G O L D
A L P S ■ L A N A T E
B I O ■ S H O D ■ I L L E S T
I N I T I A T I O N R I T E S
D E N A L I S T A T E P A R K
E N T I T L E ■ T O Y O T A S
```

361

```
SABU  . LIGHTSHOWS
EBAN ANOUKAIMEE
TORT ICONOCLAST
TREETRUNK KUNTA
LIBRE REEF MIST
EGO ASSYRIA
FINEST SENDHELP
ONETERM DIDOVER
RESCUERS TONITE
    PARAGON CBS
UBER MOLE TATAS
TODAY BANJOPICK
ISUZURODEO LOKI
LOCOMOTIVE UNIT
EXTRAMONEY SSNS
```

362

```
SISTINE SATHOME
CREASED IRAQWAR
RICKETY LAPSING
ESTERS DEBI EXO
WHINE HONING
SLOT RASTA RAID
INONIT INFERNO
ENOTES SLAMON
MENACES PEYTON
INES SIDEA PRES
  KLAXON SLEPT
ADA OBIT STADIA
RUNSFOR CHOICER
CENTAVO FURNACE
STOUTEN SEESRED
```

363

```
CRAZYTALK CUJO
XENIAOHIO ATONE
IMALLEARS DESEX
   LID ACHE EMO
ALFIE ION JON
MILO SCHULZ IRE
EBAN CLASSA MER
NETS LISZT BETA
DRS REMAKE UNIT
MAT ORATOR MEME
ELO SAX FAZED
NAM ALEG FAR
TRAWL SATIRIZED
ITCHY ALANADALE
 SHAN TAPEDECKS
```

364

```
SECONDCLASSMAIL
ONONESHIGHHORSE
ALITTLELEARNING
NINO INRI ZOO
DVD ADD TINE
SEE MARX FENS
ONASTREAK ROOM
SELA TAXIS CLAN
 DEVO MILKSHAKE
  RENT SOYA REG
  REOS SEX PAL
ICK LUCE PACE
NAUTICALALMANAC
GENERALINTEREST
ENGLANDANDWALES
```

365

```
RESTS PAWS DOIT
ESQUE ECOMMERCE
SPURT LIKEICARE
 NETTLED ANACIN
AZALEA BRIDLES
COLERIDGE SEEDY
ENOS DAMASKS
DEN WUPATKI GSA
  HAPPILY BOIL
SITON ELECTRODE
CLUSTER AMIDES
AORTAE ADMITIT
LINEDRIVE NIDRE
PLUSSIZES USEIT
SOPS EEOC SHAPE
```

366

```
SPOKESDUCK OHMS
TINALOUISE DUAL
EXOTICPETS IMNO
MINEO ESAS CBGB
SEESTO RLS LAB
   SALE EOCENE
CHAI FIXERUPPER
OEUFS AUF POISE
BADHAIRDAY SEED
BRIEFS EXES
SAT EES SACRED
ACOW CASA CHORE
LARA OVERTHETOP
ASIN NOLOVELOST
DEAD DRAWSTARES
```

367

```
M A S S M E D I A . I M A C S
A T T H E B E L L . C A R A T
S T E E L B E L T . A E T N A
H I R E E S . H O R N . L T R
E R O D E . H A N D . F O R T
R E L Y . S O V . S W I V E L
. . . I N F E R . A D E L E .
W O M A N O F T H E W O R L D
A B A C K . A H O R A . . . .
T E R E S A . E N E . A T O B
E D G Y . G L U E . S P I N E
R I A . L E O S . P L A T T E
L E R O I . A U D I O C L I P
O N E N D . M A I N T H E M E
O T T O S . S L A T H E R E D
```

368

```
S I M U L C A S T . C O P S E
C R A Z Y I D E A . O M A H A
R A D I O D I A L . M E D E S
I N O . N E E R . W E N T B Y
M I N D . R U S T Y . S H A W
P A N E L S . E M S . A N I .
S N A F U . V I T A L S I G N
. . . A N T I V E N O M . . .
C A S T A W A Y S . S A B O T
R I P . R E L . S H R I N E .
I R A Q . A S A H I . T E E M
S T R U C K . D A Z E . N A P
P A T I O . J A Z Z D A N C E
E X A C T . A G E L I M I T S
D I N K Y . W E R E T O A S T
```

369

```
S C H M I D T . R A M A D A N
W H O E V E R . A L A B A M A
E A R L O B E . V I C E R O Y
A I S . R I B T I C K L E R S
T R E S . T E A S E S . . . .
S C O T S . K O H . D U S T
H O P E T O . S E N T E N C E
O V E R U S E . S A I L S O N
P E R E N O E L . E L R O P O
S R A S . L I P . T I L E R
. . . A N G E R S . O V I S .
P O P U L A R V O T E . A T A
E R O T I C A . B A N D B O X
A N S W E R S . S K Y B L U E
K E T O N E S . T E A S E T S
```

370

```
A P L U S . A C M E . C N B C
H I T T H E R O A D . H O R A
E N D E A R M E N T . I N O N
M E S S . S A X E . B L O N D
. . . M E D I A F R E N Z Y
F L A M E . A S T I R . S E S
R A T E D R . T E X . V E S T
E S T R E E T . R U N I N T O
E T R E . F I B . P U L S A R
S M A . C E R E S . D E E R E
P I C T U R E S Q U E . . . .
I N T E R . S T U N . I H O P
R U I N . D O M A I N N A M E
I T O O . S M A T T E R I N G
T E N N . L E N S . A E G I S
```

371

```
C R I S P Y T A C O . A T M S
A I R C R E W M E N . C H O W
S P A R E R O O M S . T A D A
A U T O S . K E E P S T E P
S P E L L E D . N T H . S R S
. . . L E E R A T . D W A N
H O K E Y N E S S . S I L E X
E N I D . Y A C H T . T I R E
B E A U S . M O O R E H E A D
. S O P H . S T E A M S . . .
S E P . A T V . S P A T U L A
M A T H Q U I Z . N A P E S
A S I A . G L I S S A N D O S
C O M S . A L M O S T D O N E
K N A P . T E A D R E S S E S
```

372

```
S T E P H E N R E A . A I R S
S A L E S R O O M S . S T O W
G L I T T E R A T I . K A L E
T E E S . C A R . A D E L L E
. . . H A T H . O N A D I E T
G A T O R S . O R F F . A D E
E L O P E . D W E L T . N O N
T I E S . A E I O U . R A V E
I T T . F I N N S . J E T E R
N T H . A L I G . C A G E R S
S L E E V E S . S O Y A . . .
H E L P E R . M A N . T E D S
A B I E . O R A N G E T R E E
P I N E . N O M E A L A S K A
E T E S . S T A R S Y S T E M
```

373

```
Y O M A M A J O K E ■ M O N T
W H A T A L O S E R ■ A R C H
C O L O R A D O P L A T E A U
A H E M ■ M I S T E R T O A D
■ ■ ■ M O E ■ ■ R E C ■ ■ ■
C O S T A S ■ P O L A R O I D
A N T I C ■ P A N T Y H O S E
R E A M ■ C A S T S ■ O K L A
A T T E M P T T O ■ P R I E R
T O U L O U S E ■ N I N E T Y
■ ■ T I T ■ ■ S O X ■ ■ ■ ■
T H E M I S F I T S ■ A T O P
C A L I F O R N I A G I R L S
B R A T ■ W E L L L A D I D A
Y E W S ■ S T A T E T A X E S
```

374

```
G O A L P O S T ■ ■ S A M O A
H A V E A G O A T ■ I N A N E
A T A N Y R A T E ■ N A D E R
N E S T C E P A S ■ G R E C O
A R T O O ■ ■ L E E C H E S
■ ■ C A S P A R ■ H A L T
B A C K S P A C E ■ I S L A
T I N A ■ S O R O S ■ S T E T
A L A S ■ I R R I T A T E D ■
G A S H ■ S T Y L U S ■ ■ ■
A T T E S T S ■ ■ S O F A S
L E A S E ■ F A N T A S I S T
O R S O N ■ A M O U N T S T O
G A I U S ■ N E O N T E T R A
S L A T E ■ S N E E R S A T
```

375

```
O C E A N B O R N E ■ J A Z Z
H A D A B A D D A Y ■ A T O I
S I G N A L E A S E ■ M A N O
A R E D ■ E A S T O F E D E N
Y O R E ■ ■ P C S ■ ■ ■ ■
■ ■ S P A C E C A D E T
T H A I ■ P E C A N ■ G I V E
V E N T ■ I N U S E ■ E V E N
P R E F ■ C A T E R ■ E A R S
G O W I R E L E S S ■ ■ ■ ■
■ ■ G A G ■ ■ B A S S
N F L U N I F O R M ■ R E A L
A L A R ■ R E M E M B E R M E
V A N E ■ L E A V E S T I M E
E X E S ■ S T R E S S T E S T
```

376

```
M A S A L A ■ R A D I C A L
A N E M O N E ■ A V O C A D O
S T R I N G S ■ M O D E L E D
T H E D I E T O F W O R M S ■
■ ■ ■ L O U I S ■ ■
S L A V E A N T S ■ C H A P S
C A N A R S I E ■ R I G U P
A V I L A ■ A R C ■ A K I R A
M A T E S ■ M A G N E T I C
P L A T E ■ N O T R E D A M E
■ ■ P E S C I ■ ■
■ I T S F O R T H E B I R D S
R E A L I S E ■ E V A C U E E
C O L O S S I ■ R E J O I C E
S H E E T E D ■ D A N N O N
```

377

```
I T C O U P L E ■ A Z T E C S
H E A T S E A L ■ C O O P U P
E A R C A N D Y ■ U N T A P E
A R K ■ F A L S E R E T U R N
R O E S ■ L E I C A ■ E L I S
Y O Y O S ■ S U A ■ G R E T E
A M S T E L ■ M R M I S T E R
■ ■ E E L ■ D I M ■ ■
T H I N K B I G ■ A M T R A C
R E N O S ■ B U B ■ E R A T O
A N A T ■ O R N I S ■ A T T N
M R S M A L A P R O P ■ R I C
P E T A L S ■ O L D F L A M E
L I E N E E ■ R E D F A C E D
E D W Y N N ■ T R Y T H E S E
```

378

```
S A L E S A G R E E M E N T S
I D O N T F E E L L I K E I T
P I T C A I R N S I S L A N D
S A T E L L I T E S T A T E S
■ ■ I L E ■ ■ H E N ■
■ C A N I ■ W I Z A R D H A T
L E D T O ■ A V A ■ ■ E P H
O L D E N ■ N I X ■ E R A S E
E L I ■ D E I ■ X E R O X
W I N E G L A S S ■ C T N S
■ ■ D O E ■ ■ M E A ■
A F R I C A N A M E R I C A N
A L O T O N O N E S P L A T E
H A M I L T O N O N T A R I O
S T A N D O N O N E S T O E S
```

379

```
A R T C L A S S ■ ■ M A R I S
R A I L E D A T ■ S O L E N T
K N E E H O L E ■ T I B I A E
S I T A R ■ I N B A L A N C E
■ N O R ■ B E G E T S ■ F O P
■ ■ A S A R U L E ■ M O R N
H A M S T R I N G ■ B O R N E
A P E M E N ■ ■ M I N C E S
D P L U S ■ O D O M E T E R S
A L A D ■ O N E T E R M ■ ■
T E N ■ C R Y P T S ■ A G A
A P I A S A M O A ■ W R A T H
S I T S I N ■ S W E E T P E A
T E E I N G ■ E A T F R E S H
E S S A Y ■ ■ D N A T E S T S
```

380

```
S O Y U Z ■ C A N D I D A T E
A D O R E ■ O V E R T O N E S
S O U N D T H E R E T R E A T
H U D ■ ■ H E R D S ■ S A S E
■ L O W R E N T ■ S C A R E S
■ ■ H E S ■ ■ B F A ■ ■ ■
P O L I T I C A L A R E N A S
A L O T O N O N E S P L A T E
L I T E R A R Y S T U D I E S
O N I N T I M A T E T E R M S
■ ■ ■ E D S ■ ■ N E S ■ ■ ■
A R C A D E ■ A L E R T E D
V A I L ■ S A P O R ■ N E I
A N T I D E P R E S S A N T S
S C E N A R I O S ■ E X U R B
T H R E E T E N S ■ A L I E N
```

381

```
J I F F Y L U B E ■ S T A F F
U N R A V E L E D ■ C E L L O
M A Y B E B A B Y ■ E X L A X
P R E ■ S O N O ■ E N T I T Y
E E R ■ N O P E S T ■ A F L
R A S P S ■ V S O P ■ N E A
■ ■ A I D A ■ S O L A C E D
P A T I N A ■ S U R E T Y
A T I N G L E ■ B A L I ■ ■
L A M ■ T A L E ■ L E W I S
I L E ■ D O R A G S ■ I N K
N A T H A N ■ G O A T ■ G H I
I N R E M ■ W E R W H O W E R
S T A L E ■ M A R I O K A R T
M A X I S ■ D R A I N A G E S
```

382

```
R E S C U E D ■ C A T B O A T
E X T E N S I O N C O U R S E
D E A D A S A D O O R N A I L
T R Y A S ■ L E T O N ■ L A E
I C E R ■ B E T E L ■ S E T S
D I D ■ S E C T S ■ C C X I I
E S T I M A T E ■ S E R A C S
■ E H L E R S ■ B I R E M E ■
S M E L L S ■ W E N T W I L D
T A C I T ■ V A N E S ■ N E W
E C O N ■ D E S E X ■ C A P A
P H U ■ O U T O F ■ M O T H Y
D I R T Y P O L I T I C I A N
A N S W E R E D T O N O O N E
D E E P R E D ■ S O N A N T S
```

383

```
M U S L I M S ■ T E E N A G E
A N T O N I O B A N D E R A S
S P R I N K L E R S Y S T E M
■ L I N S E E D S ■ S T Y L E
S E P ■ ■ ■ ■ ■ ■ ■ ■ ■ ■
P A L I S H ■ A S O F ■ L I P
I S I N T O ■ T O R A B O R A
D A N G E R O U S C U R V E S
E N G E N D E R ■ A L I E N S
R T S ■ T E R N ■ S T E R E O
■ ■ ■ ■ ■ ■ ■ ■ ■ S A N
I N T W O ■ M A N I F O L D ■
D O M E S T I C A N I M A L S
E L E P H A N T T R A I N E R
D O N T A S K ■ L E T T E R S
```

384

```
C R E W M A T E S ■ D C U P S
P I X I E D U S T ■ R A N U P
L A P S E I N T O ■ E M O R Y
U T A H S T A R S ■ A E D E S
S A T I E ■ C A S T D O U B T
■ ■ ■ ■ B A Y E R ■ R E L O
■ B O L T O N ■ L I P I T O R
C O N O I D ■ ■ C O N R O Y
I D I O T I C ■ W E D G E D ■
G E O S ■ N O M A S ■ ■ ■
A G N E S G R E Y ■ M A S T S
R A S T A ■ N A C H O C H I P
A B O I L ■ I N O U R T I M E
S A U L T ■ S T O N E O V E N
H Y P E S ■ H O L D S F A S T
```

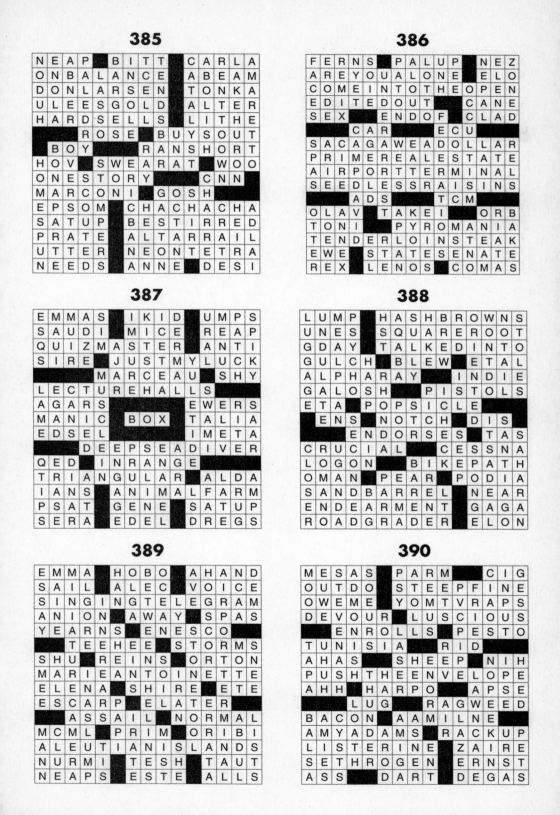

385

N	E	A	P		B	I	T	T		C	A	R	L	A
O	N	B	A	L	A	N	C	E		A	B	E	A	M
D	O	N	L	A	R	S	E	N		T	O	N	K	A
U	L	E	E	S	G	O	L	D		A	L	T	E	R
H	A	R	D	S	E	L	L	S		L	I	T	H	E
		R	O	S	E		B	U	Y	S	O	U	T	
	B	O	Y			R	A	N	S	H	O	R	T	
H	O	V		S	W	E	A	R	A	T		W	O	O
O	N	E	S	T	O	R	Y			C	N	N		
M	A	R	C	O	N	I		G	O	S	H			
E	P	S	O	M		C	H	A	C	H	A	C	H	A
S	A	T	U	P		B	E	S	T	I	R	R	E	D
P	R	A	T	E		A	L	T	A	R	R	A	I	L
U	T	T	E	R		N	E	O	N	T	E	T	R	A
N	E	E	D	S		A	N	N	E		D	E	S	I

386

F	E	R	N	S		P	A	L	U	P		N	E	Z
A	R	E	Y	O	U	A	L	O	N	E		E	L	O
C	O	M	E	I	N	T	O	T	H	E	O	P	E	N
E	D	I	T	E	D	O	U	T		C	A	N	E	
S	E	X		E	N	D	O	F		C	L	A	D	
			C	A	R		E	C	U					
S	A	C	A	G	A	W	E	A	D	O	L	L	A	R
P	R	I	M	E	R	E	A	L	E	S	T	A	T	E
A	I	R	P	O	R	T	T	E	R	M	I	N	A	L
S	E	E	D	L	E	S	S	R	A	I	S	I	N	S
		A	D	S			T	C	M					
O	L	A	V		T	A	K	E	I			O	R	B
T	O	N	I		P	Y	R	O	M	A	N	I	A	
T	E	N	D	E	R	L	O	I	N	S	T	E	A	K
E	W	E		S	T	A	T	E	S	E	N	A	T	E
R	E	X		L	E	N	O	S		C	O	M	A	S

387

E	M	M	A	S		I	K	I	D		U	M	P	S
S	A	U	D	I		M	I	C	E		R	E	A	P
Q	U	I	Z	M	A	S	T	E	R		A	N	T	I
S	I	R	E		J	U	S	T	M	Y	L	U	C	K
			M	A	R	C	E	A	U		S	H	Y	
L	E	C	T	U	R	E	H	A	L	L	S			
A	G	A	R	S					E	W	E	R	S	
M	A	N	I	C		B	O	X		T	A	L	I	A
E	D	S	E	L				I	M	E	T	A		
		D	E	E	P	S	E	A	D	I	V	E	R	
Q	E	D		I	N	R	A	N	G	E				
T	R	I	A	N	G	U	L	A	R		A	L	D	A
I	A	N	S		A	N	I	M	A	L	F	A	R	M
P	S	A	T		G	E	N	E		S	A	T	U	P
S	E	R	A		E	D	E	L		D	R	E	G	S

388

L	U	M	P		H	A	S	H	B	R	O	W	N	S
U	N	E	S		S	Q	U	A	R	E	R	O	O	T
G	D	A	Y		T	A	L	K	E	D	I	N	T	O
G	U	L	C	H		B	L	E	W		E	T	A	L
A	L	P	H	A	R	A	Y		I	N	D	I	E	
G	A	L	O	S	H		P	I	S	T	O	L	S	
E	T	A		P	O	P	S	I	C	L	E			
	E	N	S		N	O	T	C	H		D	I	S	
	E	N	D	O	R	S	E	S		T	A	S		
C	R	U	C	I	A	L		C	E	S	S	N	A	
L	O	G	O	N		B	I	K	E	P	A	T	H	
O	M	A	N		P	E	A	R		P	O	D	I	A
S	A	N	D	B	A	R	R	E	L		N	E	A	R
E	N	D	E	A	R	M	E	N	T		G	A	G	A
R	O	A	D	G	R	A	D	E	R		E	L	O	N

389

E	M	M	A		H	O	B	O		A	H	A	N	D
S	A	I	L		A	L	E	C		V	O	I	C	E
S	I	N	G	I	N	G	T	E	L	E	G	R	A	M
A	N	I	O	N		A	W	A	Y		S	P	A	S
Y	E	A	R	N	S		E	N	E	S	C	O		
		T	E	E	H	E	E		S	T	O	R	M	S
S	H	U		R	E	I	N	S		O	R	T	O	N
M	A	R	I	E	A	N	T	O	I	N	E	T	T	E
E	L	E	N	A		S	H	I	R	E		E	T	E
E	S	C	A	R	P		E	L	A	T	E	R		
		A	S	S	A	I	L		N	O	R	M	A	L
M	C	M	L		P	R	I	M		O	R	I	B	I
A	L	E	U	T	I	A	N	I	S	L	A	N	D	S
N	U	R	M	I		T	E	S	H		T	A	U	T
N	E	A	P	S		E	S	T	E		A	L	L	S

390

M	E	S	A	S		P	A	R	M		C	I	G
O	U	T	D	O		S	T	E	E	P	F	I	N	E
O	W	E	M	E		Y	O	M	T	V	R	A	P	S
D	E	V	O	U	R		L	U	S	C	I	O	U	S
		E	N	R	O	L	L	S		P	E	S	T	O
T	U	N	I	S	I	A		R	I	D				
A	H	A	S		S	H	E	E	P		N	I	H	
P	U	S	H	T	H	E	E	N	V	E	L	O	P	E
A	H	H		H	A	R	P	O		A	P	S	E	
		L	U	G		R	A	G	W	E	E	D		
B	A	C	O	N		A	A	M	I	L	N	E		
A	M	Y	A	D	A	M	S		R	A	C	K	U	P
L	I	S	T	E	R	I	N	E		Z	A	I	R	E
S	E	T	H	R	O	G	E	N		E	R	N	S	T
A	S	S		D	A	R	T		D	E	G	A	S	

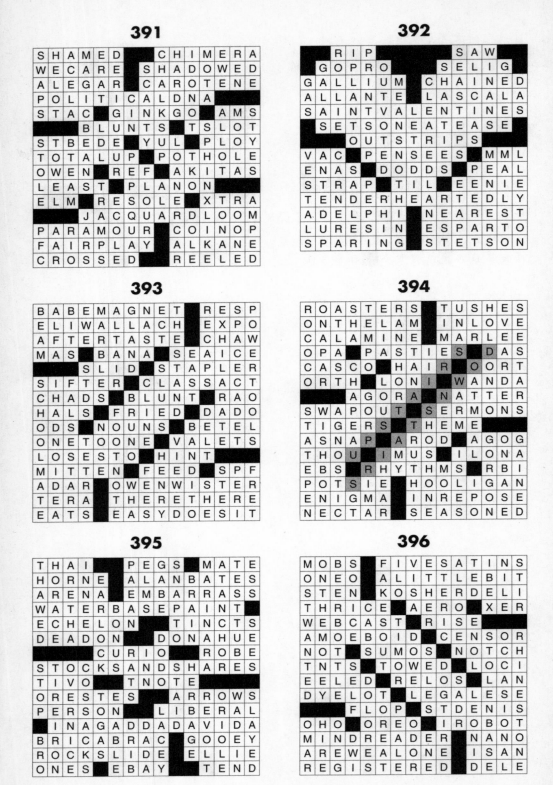

391

```
S H A M E D   C H I M E R A
W E C A R E   S H A D O W E D
A L E G A R   C A R O T E N E
P O L I T I C A L D N A
S T A C   G I N K G O   A M S
    B L U N T S   T S L O T
S T B E D E   Y U L   P L O Y
T O T A L U P   P O T H O L E
O W E N   R E F   A K I T A S
L E A S T   P L A N O N
E L M   R E S O L E   X T R A
    J A C Q U A R D L O O M
P A R A M O U R   C O I N O P
F A I R P L A Y   A L K A N E
C R O S S E D   R E E L E D
```

392

```
  R I P       S A W
  G O P R O     S E L I G
G A L L I U M   C H A I N E D
A L L A N T E   L A S C A L A
S A I N T V A L E N T I N E S
  S E T S O N E A T E A S E
    O U T S T R I P S
V A C   P E N S E E S   M M L
E N A S   D O D D S   P E A L
S T R A P   T I L   E E N I E
T E N D E R H E A R T E D L Y
A D E L P H I   N E A R E S T
L U R E S I N   E S P A R T O
S P A R I N G   S T E T S O N
```

393

```
B A B E M A G N E T   R E S P
E L I W A L L A C H   E X P O
A F T E R T A S T E   C H A W
M A S   B A N A   S E A I C E
    S L I D   S T A P L E R
S I F T E R   C L A S S A C T
C H A D S   B L U N T   R A O
H A L S   F R I E D   D A D O
O D S   N O U N S   B E T E L
O N E T O O N E   V A L E T S
L O S E S T O   H I N T
M I T T E N   F E E D   S P F
A D A R   O W E N W I S T E R
T E R A   T H E R E T H E R E
E A T S   E A S Y D O E S I T
```

394

```
R O A S T E R S   T U S H E S
O N T H E L A M   I N L O V E
C A L A M I N E   M A R L E E
O P A   P A S T I E S   D A S
C A S C O   H A I R   O O R T
O R T H   L O N I   W A N D A
    A G O R A   N A T T E R
S W A P O U T   S E R M O N S
T I G E R S   T H E M E
A S N A P   A R O D   A G O G
T H O U   I M U S   I L O N A
E B S   R H Y T H M S   R B I
P O T S I E   H O O L I G A N
E N I G M A   I N R E P O S E
N E C T A R   S E A S O N E D
```

395

```
T H A I   P E G S   M A T E
H O R N E   A L A N B A T E S
A R E N A   E M B A R R A S S
W A T E R B A S E P A I N T
E C H E L O N   T I N C T S
D E A D O N   D O N A H U E
    C U R I O   R O B E
S T O C K S A N D S H A R E S
T I V O   T N O T E
O R E S T E S   A R R O W S
P E R S O N   L I B E R A L
  I N A G A D D A D A V I D A
B R I C A B R A C   G O O E Y
R O C K S L I D E   E L L I E
O N E S   E B A Y   T E N D
```

396

```
M O B S   F I V E S A T I N S
O N E O   A L I T T L E B I T
S T E N   K O S H E R D E L I
T H R I C E   A E R O   X E R
W E B C A S T   R I S E
A M O E B O I D   C E N S O R
N O T   S U M O S   N O T C H
T N T S   T O W E D   L O C I
E E L E D   R E L O S   L A N
D Y E L O T   L E G A L E S E
    F L O P   S T D E N I S
O H O   O R E O   I R O B O T
M I N D R E A D E R   N A N O
A R E W E A L O N E   I S A N
R E G I S T E R E D   D E L E
```

397

```
K I M   S H A K E S   S T P
R A D I O T E L E S C O P E S
E T E R N A L O P T I M I S T
S I N A I   G H I A   A R T
T E T   N C A A   T H R A S H
  B I T E R   O R E O   L O O
S A F E   A L E E   Y E S N O
K R I S H N A   F E A S T E D
I T C H Y   O T I C   T A S S
T H A   P E S O   R E A I M
S E T S O N   P L U S   R E I
  D I Y   G A T E   P A C T S
M O O N L I G H T S O N A T A
N O N C O N T I G U O U S L Y
O R S   W E S S O N   T E E
```

398

```
A I R S I G N S   S L E A Z E
B R A I N R O T   P A S M A L
R O C K C A V E   I T S B I G
A N K H   M A A   T H E I R A
    O M S K   Z E S T E R
H A I R L A C Q U E R
A R M Y G R O U P S   O K A Y
L I A N A   T E T   A L E X A
F A C E   D I S O R D E R L Y
    S E A A N E M O N E S
R U B I E S   D O T S
A N O R A K   I G O   Y E L L
S C R A M S   L O U I S N Y E
P L A Q U E   L O C K E D O N
S E X I S T   A D H E R E N T
```

399

```
H O T S P E L L   S T I L T S
A C H I E V E S   H O H O H O
M E A T D I E T   O R A T E S
F A T C A T S   B E I T S O
I N S O L E   R A S A E
S L A M S   C A N T M I S S
T I N S   S A W T O O T H E D
E N O   G A N D E R S   O D O
D E N T A L C A R E   C R I P
  R O O T L E T S   T H E M E
    P H Y L A   V O I L E S
  L A S E R S   S A R G E N T
H E G I R A   R E L E G A T E
I C E D I N   I L L N E V E R
T H E E N D   M A I T R E D S
```

400

```
E B B A N D F L O W   W I T S
L E A V E A L O N E   W R A P
I N T E R L I N E D   I A G O
S T A N D I N G A G A I N S T
H O A G Y   T A L E S   G A P
A N N E   F I G S   T R A L A
    O R E O   G R A T E S
S H O C K E R   P R O W E S S
W A R N E D   D Y E S
I R E N E   A I R Y   G I B E
L P S   F A L D O   F I N E S
L E T T E R B O X F O R M A T
I D E A   G I V E O R T A K E
N O I R   O N E N I G H T E R
G N A T   S O R E L O S E R S
```

The New York Times

Crossword Puzzles

The #1 Name in Crosswords

Available at your local bookstore or online at nytimes.com/nytstore

St. Martin's Griffin